MW01041438

Entrepreneurship
Building a Business

Kathleen Allen Ph.D.

Earl C. Meyer Ph.D.

Mc Graw Hill Education

COVER: Vico Collective/Erik Palmer/Blend Images LLC

mheducation.com/prek-12

Send all inquiries to:
McGraw-Hill Education
8787 Orion Place
Columbus, OH 43240

ISBN: 978-0-02-137767-1
MHID: 0-02-137767-7

Printed in the United States of America.

4 5 6 7 8 9 QVS 22 21 20 19 18

Authors

Dr. Kathleen Allen is the author of more than 15 books in the field of entrepreneurship and technology commercialization. As a professor of entrepreneurship and the Director of the University of Southern California Marshall Center for Technology Commercialization, which she co-founded, Allen has worked with scientists and engineers to help them identify markets and applications for their technologies and to prepare them to seek funding. Her personal entrepreneurial endeavors include four successful companies including two in the real estate industry and two technology ventures. She is co-founder and CEO of N2TEC Institute, a non-profit organization focused on technology entrepreneurship and bringing the wealth creation process to rural America, and she serves as a consultant to the aerospace industry on commercial markets for aerospace technologies. She is also director of an NYSE company and serves on the boards of several private companies. Allen holds a Ph.D. with a focus in entrepreneurship from USC, an MBA, and an MA in Romance languages. She also has a degree in music.

Dr. Earl C. Meyer has extensive experience in both business and education. He is the former teacher educator for marketing and entrepreneurship education at Eastern Michigan University. Previously, he taught marketing and entrepreneurship as a high school teacher-coordinator. For 16 years prior to moving into education, he was involved in advertising sales, retail, and financial services management. He has also owned and operated his own golf enterprise and quick serve restaurant, as well as a business coaching and consulting company.

Meyer has been the project director and principal writer for curriculum guides that address three stages of entrepreneurship education. He has also authored articles, made state and national presentations, and held workshops on teaching entrepreneurship. In addition, he represented Michigan in the International Consortium for Entrepreneurship Education, for which he has served as president and as an executive board member. He was also the co-founding chair of the Entrepreneurship Professional Interest Category of the national Marketing Education Association.

Meyer holds a bachelor's degree in marketing education from the University of South Florida. He has an MA and a Ph.D. in vocational and career development (with an emphasis in marketing education) from Georgia State University.

Authors and Reviewers

Reviewers

Grace Brady
Marketing Teacher, DECA Advisor
Redmond High School
Redmond, WA

Claudia Dargento
Business Teacher
Fair Lawn High School
Fair Lawn, NJ

Brenda DeWire
Educator
Central Columbia High School
Bloomsburg, PA

Susan E. Hall, Ph. D.
Business Teacher Educator
State University College of New York
   at Buffalo
Buffalo, NY

Adam Reid
Founder, Instructor
Leadership & Entrepreneurship Public Charter
   High School
Portland, OR

Letitia Romas
Curriculum Leader, Business Department
Pittsford Mendon High School
Pittsford, NY

Michael Vialpando
Business/Marketing Department Chair
La Joya Community High School
Avondale, AZ

Entrepreneurship Galaxy Quest

Where do you find all of the chapter names?

Where would you look for math help?

How many chapters are in this book? How many units?

Where would you find a definition of limited liability?

Where would you look to find out about bundle pricing?

Where can you find a downloadable graphic organizer?

What is the name of the Chapter 7 Discovery Project?

Table of Contents

Table of Contents

Terry Vine/Blend Images LLC

Table of Contents

Table of Contents

Chris Ryan/OJO Images/age fotostock

Table of Contents

Radius Images/Alamy

Table of Contents

Table of Contents

BambooSIL/SuperStock

Table of Contents

Table of Contents

Table of Contents

Blend Images/Ariel Skelley/Getty Images

Going Into Business for Yourself

Connect the Photo

By the Hundreds Bobby Kim and Ben Shenassafar founded The Hundreds, an apparel and lifestyle company inspired by surf, skateboarding, punk, and hip-hop culture. Their online magazine attracts over one million unique visitors each month. *What is one possible reward of starting your business?*

Business Plan Project

Preview

Getting Started

Starting your own business can be exciting, rewarding, and challenging. You can do what you enjoy, flex your creative muscles, and be your own boss. But where should you begin? Who will be a part of your team? How can you decide what product or service you will sell?

The **Business Plan Project** will help you address and organize some of these concerns by focusing on these sections of the business plan:

▶ In the **Management Team Plan** section, you will present your management team's qualifications for making the venture a success.

▶ The **Company Description** outlines the company's basic background information, business concept, and goals and objectives.

▶ The **Product and Ser-vice Plan** describes the features and benefits of the business's products and services.

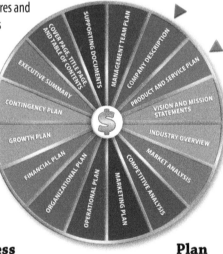

Prepare for the Business Plan Project

As you read this unit, use this checklist to prepare for the **Business Plan Project**:

- Make a list of the your personal characteristics, skills, and qualifications.
- Talk to local entrepreneurs about what it takes to succeed.
- Read articles about new trends, products, and services in newspapers, magazines, on the Internet, and in social media.

CHAPTER

1

What Is Entrepreneurship?

Chapter Objectives

SECTION 1.1
Entrepreneurship and the Economy

Define the role of small business and entrepreneurship in the economy.

Compare and contrast economic systems.

Explain how economics is about making choices.

Define the role of economic indicators and business cycles.

Describe what entrepreneurs contribute to the economy.

SECTION 1.2
The Entrepreneurial Process

Analyze entrepreneurship from a historical perspective.

Name the five components of the entrepreneurial start-up process.

Explain how to achieve business success.

Discovery Project

Entrepreneurship in Your Community

Key Question | *How does the entrepreneurial start-up process work in real life?*

Project Goal
Interview one or more local entrepreneurs about the process used to start up their businesses. Use the information gained during the interview to compare and contrast the entrepreneur's start-up process with the process described in this chapter.

Think About...
➤ *How will you choose a local entrepreneur?*
➤ *What questions will you ask about the start-up process the entrepreneur used?*
➤ *How will you determine whether the entrepreneur followed the start-up process described in the text?*

21ˢᵗ Century Skills
Analyze *Do you think the entrepreneur's start-up process was effective? Explain your answer.*

Evaluate
 Go to connectED.mcgraw-hill.com to download a rubric that you can use to evaluate your final project.

Ask AN EXPERT

Q: *I am saving money and paying off debts in order to start my own comic book store. What are some strategies for financial planning?*

A: A financial plan evaluates your current assets and debts, identifies your goals, and outlines a strategy for reaching your goals. It is a good idea to set short-term, mid-term, and long-term goals to track your progress. Proper planning can also help you beat inflation, minimize taxes, and plan for the unexpected.

©Moxie Productions/Blend Images LLC

Connect the Photo

We're Open! Entrepreneurs all over the world are opening their doors for new business. Whether it's a neighborhood floral shop or a software company that makes apps, starting a business is no easy feat. Understanding how the economy works and the entrepreneurial process are vital to running a successful start-up. *Why are start-up companies an integral part of the community?*

Entrepreneurship and the Economy

Reading Guide

● Before You Read ▪▪▪▪▪▪▪▪▪▪▪▪▪▪

Connect What are some economic choices you make every day?

The Main Idea

Entrepreneurship is the primary catalyst for economic growth. To be a successful entrepreneur requires an understanding of how the economy works.

Objectives

Define the role of small business and entrepreneurship in the economy.

Compare and contrast economic systems.

Explain how economics is about making choices.

Define the role of economic indicators and business cycles.

Describe what entrepreneurs contribute to the economy.

Content Vocabulary

◇ entrepreneur
◇ venture
◇ entrepreneurship
◇ economics
◇ free enterprise system
◇ profit
◇ market structure
◇ monopoly
◇ oligopoly
◇ goods
◇ services
◇ need
◇ want

◇ factors of production
◇ scarcity
◇ demand
◇ elastic demand
◇ inelastic demand
◇ diminishing marginal utility
◇ supply
◇ equilibrium
◇ Gross Domestic Product
◇ business cycle

Academic Vocabulary

You will see these words in your reading and on your tests. Use the academic vocabulary glossary to look up their meanings.

▪ enable   ▪ evaluate

Graphic Organizer

Before you read this section, draw a chart like the one shown. As you read, list the four questions economic systems attempt to answer.

 Go to connectED.mcgraw-hill.com to download this graphic organizer.

Four Economic Questions
1. What goods and services should be produced?
2. _____
3. _____
4. _____

Becoming an Entrepreneur

Have you ever considered going into business for yourself? If so, you may have thought about becoming an entrepreneur. An **entrepreneur** is an individual who undertakes the creation, organization, and ownership of an innovative business with potential for growth. The entrepreneur accepts the risks and responsibilities of business ownership to earn profits, create wealth, and achieve personal satisfaction.

Creating and running a business venture requires a variety of skills. A **venture** is a new business undertaking that involves risk. This book will help you understand what it takes to be a successful entrepreneur. Even if you do not become an entrepreneur, the lessons you learn will help you in any job you undertake and also make you a more informed consumer.

Small Business and Entrepreneurship

The terms *entrepreneurship* and *entrepreneurial* are used throughout this book. **Entrepreneurship** is the process of recognizing or creating an opportunity, testing it in the market, and gathering the resources necessary to go into business. Being entrepreneurial means acting like an entrepreneur or having an entrepreneurial mindset—a way of thinking.

You might know someone who is an entrepreneur. In about one in three households, someone is involved with a new venture or small business, often a family business. More than 90 percent of all businesses are small businesses with fewer than 100 employees. Sixty-two percent of those are home-based businesses.

Entrepreneurship Today

Owning and operating a business today is very different than it was in the past. The global marketplace, the Internet, and social media have brought new resources, opportunities, markets, competitors, and ideas. Computers, smart phones, and other kinds of information technology **enable** people to communicate instantly, collaborate from a distance, and keep records more efficiently.

As a result, customers now demand that business transactions and communication take place quickly. They expect innovative products to come out often. Therefore, businesses feel the pressure to provide better service and to make more options available.

To understand how entrepreneurs and customers interact in the economy, you need to start with economics and economic systems. **Economics** is the study of how people choose to allocate scarce resources to fulfill their unlimited wants. Economics has a profound influence on entrepreneurship.

The Green Economy

Every week brings news of another company "going green." The race to solve the world's energy and environmental problems may be creating the 21st century's greatest flow of new opportunities for entrepreneurs. These opportunities could involve either new, "green" products or services that solve old problems or established products and services that can be updated to make them "greener."

◈ **Critical Thinking**
Consider an environmental cause that you are passionate about. Write a paragraph identifying how you could translate that passion into a business.

 Reading Check Predict How is owning a business different than it was in the past?

Weathering an Economic Storm

Three tested ways to succeed when the economy turns down

Savvy entrepreneurs use long-term thinking to guide their businesses through economic ups and downs. Experts advise businesspeople to follow these strategies to thrive in bad times:

1. **Earn customer loyalty.** Current and repeat customers are the ones who pay your bills. Pay attention to their satisfaction even as you devote efforts to pursuing new customers.

2. **Spend efficiently.** Use funds wisely and cut unnecessary costs. Can you subcontract manufacturing instead of building a factory? Can you test a prototype (a low-cost model of a product) before going full steam ahead?

3. **Plan for lean times.** It is tempting to spend more when times are good. Instead of investing all your money into new ventures, however, it's important to put some aside for the next down cycle.

You have the ability to survive tough times. Remember that the economy will turn up, even if it is down now. Confidence in the future helps build the resiliency you need to weather the storms of business, and of life.

Active Learning

Think about businesses that have opened recently in your community—such as a restaurant, sporting-goods shop, clothing store, electronic store, or pet store. Which one do you think will best survive an economic downturn? Why? Choose one business, visit it, and write a 400-word blog post about what you observed. Describe the business and explain whether you believe this start-up will be able to weather tough economic times. Explain your reasoning.

Economic Systems

An economic system includes a set of laws, institutions, and activities that guide economic decision making. All economic systems attempt to answer these four fundamental questions:

- What goods and services should be produced?
- What quantity of goods and services should be produced?
- How should goods and services be produced?
- For whom should goods and services be produced?

History has seen several different types of economic systems. The traditional economic system relies on farming and simple barter trade. The pure market system is based on supply and demand with little government control. Command economic systems are run by a strong centralized government. They tend to focus more on industrial goods than on consumer goods. For example, the former Soviet Union had a command economy where nearly all agricultural and industrial enterprises were controlled by the government. Mixed economies combine the principles of market and command economies. The United States and the European Union both have mixed economies.

The Free Enterprise System

Most democratic nations have a free enterprise system. In a **free enterprise system**, people have an important right to make economic choices:

- People can choose what products to buy.
- People can choose to own private property.
- People can choose to start a business and compete with other businesses.

The free enterprise system is also called *capitalism* or a *market economy*. It is vital to the ability of entrepreneurship to exist.

● **As You Read** ▪▪▪▪▪▪▪
Identify What role does competition play in the economy?

The Profit Motive

Making a profit is a primary incentive of free enterprise. **Profit** is money that is kept after all expenses of running a business have been deducted from the income. It is one way of measuring success in a free enterprise system.

However, in the free enterprise system, there is also a risk of failure. That risk of failure serves a positive function in a free enterprise system because it encourages the production of quality products that truly meet the needs of consumers. Entrepreneurs also face market risks (lack of demand, changing customer needs), product risks (loss of customer interest, warranty problems), and financial risks (lack of funding, rising costs).

The Role of Competition

Competition among businesses is one of the basic characteristics of a free enterprise system. It is good for consumers because it provides choices, it forces companies to improve quality and become more efficient, and it leads to a surplus, which brings prices down.

Businesses compete on the basis of price and nonprice factors. In a mature industry such as electronics, for example, price is usually a factor because there are many competitors offering the same goods and services. The only differentiation is price. An established firm can usually offer lower prices than a new company because it benefits from lower costs. Lower costs come from producing in higher volume and from having a more experienced workforce. In contrast, a small firm setting up its first production line incurs much higher costs.

In younger industries, however, price is not as strong a factor. Other factors, such as quality, service, and reputation, are more important. Entrepreneurs typically avoid competing on price factors. Instead, they look for creative ways to create new value for customers through innovative products, quality, service, and reputation. In that way, they can better differentiate themselves from the competition.

Goods and Services Goods are tangible or physical products. Services are intangible or non-physical products. *Does an amusement park provide goods or services?*

Market Structures

The term **market structure** refers to the nature and degree of competition among businesses operating in the same industry. Market structure affects market price.

Economists group industries into four different market structures: perfect competition, monopolistic competition, monopoly, and oligopoly.

Perfect and Monopolistic Competition

Perfect competition is a market structure in which there are numerous buyers and sellers and many products that are very similar so they can be substitutes for consumers. Because there is no difference in quality, one seller's merchandise is just as good as another's. It is easy for new companies to enter the market, and prices are generally determined by supply and demand.

At the other extreme is monopolistic competition, a market structure in which many sellers produce similar but differentiated products. In this case, substitution is not always possible. Through differentiation, sellers have some power to control the price of their products. By making its product slightly different, the monopolistic competitor tries to dominate a small portion of the market.

Monopolies and Oligopolies

A **monopoly** is a market structure in which a particular commodity has only one seller who has control over supply and can exert nearly total control over prices. Monopolies are discouraged in free market economies. However, sometimes monopolies are in the public's best interest. For example, the government grants a temporary monopoly to inventors in the form of patents and copyrights to encourage innovation.

An **oligopoly** is a market structure in which there are just a few competing firms. For example, several large companies have dominated the automobile industry for decades. They can sell automobiles at a lower price than small manufacturers, so they have some influence over price. Under antitrust laws, most forms of monopoly and some forms of oligopoly are illegal.

 Reading Check **Differentiate** What is the difference between a monopoly and an oligopoly?

Basic Economic Concepts

To understand the entrepreneur's role in the economy, you need to know some basic economics. You may already be familiar with many economic concepts from your everyday role as a consumer.

Goods and Services

Goods and services are the products that our economic system produces to satisfy consumers' wants and needs. **Goods** are tangible (or physical) products. **Services** are intangible (or non-physical) products.

A **need** is a basic requirement for survival. Food, water, and shelter are all examples of basic needs. A **want** is something that you do not have to have for survival but would like to have. Consider a new smart phone. Even if you would like to have the new device, you do not necessarily need it for survival; therefore it is considered a want and not a need.

Factors of Production

Factors of production are the resources businesses use to produce the goods and services that people want. The factors of production include land, labor, capital, and entrepreneurship. These factors are explained in **Figure 1.1** on page 12.

Scarcity

Scarcity occurs when demand exceeds supply. According to the principle of scarcity, resources are in limited supply. Therefore, to have one thing may mean that you have to give up something else. A restaurant owner may forego a costly decor to have more money to put into kitchen equipment.

The 24-Hour Work Day
Business today takes place around the clock, thanks to technology and the global marketplace. For instance, products might be manufactured in an Asian country, meaning that any questions or problems would arise in the middle of the night for an American company doing business with them. This has led to changes in staffing and management strategies for many companies—as well as the increased stress that often comes from never truly being "off duty." *How does the Internet help make a 24-hour workday possible?*

● Figure 1.1   Factors of Production

Land	In economic terms, land is all of the resources upon and beneath the earth's surface. Land includes not only geographic territory but also air, wind, water, trees, minerals, and other natural resources.
Labor	The human effort used to produce goods and services is called labor. Labor is made up of full- and part-time workers as well as management.
Entrepreneurship	This factor consists of the opportunities and decisions of the business owner, or entrepreneur. He or she is the initiator, the one who brings together the other factors of production to create value in the economy.
Capital	Capital consists of the equipment, factory, tools, and other goods needed to produce a product. It also includes money used to pay all of the expenses.

● **Resources**   Resources are all of the things used in producing goods and services. The technical term for resources is *factors of production. If your school's student council decides to raise funds by selling smoothies at an upcoming basketball game, what specific factors of production would be involved?*

Supply and Demand Theory

In a free enterprise system, the price of a product is determined in the marketplace. Sellers want to sell at the highest possible price, and buyers want to buy at the lowest possible price. Customers decide what they are willing to pay for a product or service.

To understand how prices are determined, you have to look at both demand and supply. Supply and demand interact to determine the price customers are willing to pay for the number of products producers are willing to make.

These are the basic tenets of supply and demand theory:
- If something is in heavy demand but in short supply, prices will go up. The rise in price will reduce demand and expand supply.
- If something is in plentiful supply but demand is lacking, prices will go down. The decline in price will expand demand and contract supply.
- Prices tend to stabilize at the level where demand equals supply.

Demand

Demand is the quantity of goods or services that consumers are willing and able to buy. According to the law of demand, as price goes up, the quantity demanded goes down. Market prices ration goods and services among those who are willing to pay for them.

The demand curve in **Figure 1.2** shows the cost of the cost of gasoline that would be purchased at specific prices. Notice that more gallons would be bought at $3.50 than $4.50. This is because more people can afford the gas at the lower price.

The degree to which demand for a product is affected by its price is demand elasticity. Products have either elastic demand or inelastic demand. **Elastic demand** refers to situations in which a change in price creates a change in demand. For example, demand for butter tends to be elastic because there are lower-priced substitutes. **Inelastic demand** refers to situations in which a change in price has very little effect on demand for products. There is no acceptable substitute for milk, so demand for milk tends to be inelastic.

In general, demand tends to be inelastic in these circumstances:
- No acceptable substitutes are available, and customers need the product.
- The price change is small relative to buyer income, so if customers want the product, they will buy it.
- The product is a necessity; customers need it.

Even when a product's price is low, people will not keep buying it indefinitely. For example, they will not buy more than they can reasonably use. This effect is known as the law of **diminishing marginal utility**. The law of diminishing marginal utility establishes that price alone does not determine demand. Other factors (income, taste, and the amount of product already owned) play a role as well.

● Figure 1.2   **Demand Curve for Gasoline**

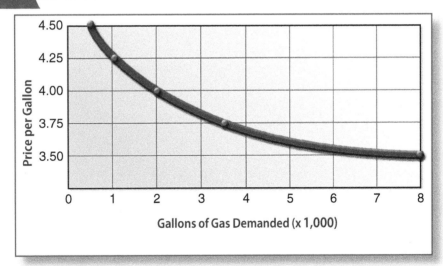

● **Price Affects Demand** This curve shows that fewer items will be purchased at higher prices than at lower prices. *Which price increment reduces demand the most?*

Supply

The amount of a good or service that producers are willing to provide is called **supply**. Producers are more willing to supply products in greater amounts when prices are high. In this way, market prices provide an incentive to produce goods and services. They are less willing to do so when prices are low. **Figure 1.3** depicts a supply curve for gasoline. Notice that as price goes up, the quantity supplied goes up, too.

Surplus, Shortage, and Equilibrium

Supply and demand are dynamic in the marketplace. That is, they are continually shifting. This change creates surpluses (more supplies than needed), shortages (fewer supplies than needed), and equilibrium. **Equilibrium** is the point at which consumers buy all of a product that is supplied. At the point of equilibrium, there is neither a surplus nor a shortage.

Consider the gasoline example again. During high traveling times (holidays, summer vacations), more people are buying gasoline. They purchase many gallons, and still ask for more. Without gasoline, the American economy would suffer significantly. Therefore, due to the high demand for gasoline, the prices for the supply increases.

However, after the busy season passes, the demand for gasoline decreases. Gasoline suppliers then lower the price of gasoline. The principals underling this situation are illustrated in **Figure 1.4**.

● **Figure 1.3**   Supply Curve for Gasoline

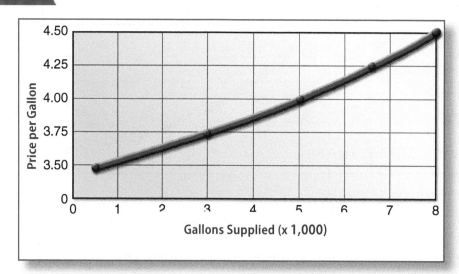

● **Price Affects Supply** This curve reveals a direct relationship between price and the number of items produced. *How does tripling the selling price from $3.50 to $4.00 affect supply?*

Figure 1.4 — Demand and Supply for Gasoline

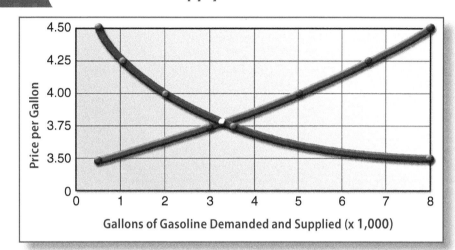

Point of Equilibrium Merging the supply and demand curves into a single graph allows you to locate the equilibrium point or price. *What is the equilibrium price for gasoline? At that price, approximately how many gallons will consumers demand?*

Market Research

Supply and demand graphs can be a bit misleading, though. They seem to suggest that where demand exists, supply just follows. Actually, it is not that simple.

For businesses to respond to consumer demand, they must know about it. Information about supply and demand influences entrepreneurial activities. For consumers to make purchases, they must be aware of what is available. How do businesses learn what consumers want? How do consumers find out what businesses have to offer? The answer in both cases is the same: market research. Market research is discussed in Chapter 6.

Business Cycles

The federal government publishes statistics that help entrepreneurs understand the state of the economy and predict possible changes. These statistics are called economic indicators.

Economic Indicators

Examples of economic indicators include the employment rate, consumer confidence, and the GDP, or Gross Domestic Product. **Gross Domestic Product** is the total market values of goods and services produced by a nation during a given period. It consists of the consumption of goods and services, investment, government expenditures, and net exports to other countries.

The Federal Reserve

The Federal Reserve (Fed) is a government agency that controls the economy and regulates the nation's money supply. The Fed controls the economy in several ways. It tells banks the percentage of their money they can lend. It controls interest rates, raising them to increase the cost of borrowing and reducing them to decrease the cost of borrowing. It also buys and sells government securities to increase or decrease the money supply.

The Federal Reserve constantly **evaluates** economic conditions. When necessary, the Fed makes adjustments to monetary policies to promote a healthy economy.

Expansion and Contraction

History shows that sometimes an economy grows, and at other times it slows down. This is called a business cycle. A **business cycle** is the periodic random pattern of expansion and contraction that the economy goes through. In terms of the national economy, business or economic cycles mean that a period of growth and prosperity (expansion) is usually followed by a contraction or slowdown in growth. If the contraction is severe, it is called a recession. When the GDP declines by more than 10 percent, it is called a depression, such as the Great Depression that the United States and the rest of the world experienced in the 1930s.

Inflation

The Fed reacts to different economic conditions (or stages of the business cycle) in different ways. If the economy is growing too rapidly, inflation may occur. Inflation is an unhealthy jump in prices that slows consumer and business spending. When spending decreases, companies reduce their production levels and lay off workers. The result is higher unemployment rates. All of these factors can lead to a recession.

Recession

If a recession occurs, the Fed will move to increase the supply of money. It does this by lowering interest rates to encourage people and businesses to borrow money and spend more. To avoid a recession when economic growth is too rapid, the Fed raises interest rates. An effective monetary policy balances the short-term goal of increasing output with the long-term goal of maintaining a low rate of inflation.

What Entrepreneurs Contribute

New companies are the driving force behind economic growth. Business start-ups are beneficial because they generate employment and increase the production of goods and services.

From what you have learned in this chapter, consider the role that entrepreneurs play in the U.S. economy:

- Entrepreneurs are the mechanism by which the economy turns demand into supply. They recognize consumer wants and see the economic opportunities in developing innovative products or services to satisfy them.
- Entrepreneurs create a market for venture capital. As part of the process of planning and setting up a new business, entrepreneurs gather resources. Money is one of the most important of these resources. Entrepreneurs usually start with their own funds and then seek contributions from private investors.
- Entrepreneurs provide jobs. To produce goods and services, they spend capital on setting up a place of business and hiring workers. In doing so, they provide for their own financial security and for the financial security of others.
- The most successful entrepreneurs change society. In 1976, Steve Jobs and Stephen Wozniak set out to create the Apple™, the first personal computer. In less than five years, they created an industry of hundreds of related businesses and thousands of new jobs. Today it is hard to imagine a workplace without computers, laptops, smart phones, and tablets.
- Entrepreneurs begin by responding to society's wants and end up changing society. As a result, they create even more wants to be satisfied. Entrepreneurs are the catalysts that make economic progress happen.

Changing the World Entrepreneurs like Steve Jobs have changed the way people live with products like personal computers and iPhones™. *How do entrepreneurs create jobs?*

Small Businesses and Entrepreneurial Ventures

This book makes a clear distinction between small businesses and entrepreneurial ventures. While most businesses do start small, not all businesses stay small. There are many reasons for this. However, the principal reasons are the intentions, motives, and goals of the founders of the business.

Small Businesses

Small business owners who start mom-and-pop or lifestyle businesses generally do so to create jobs for themselves. They want to create lifestyles that are satisfying and that meet their personal goals. A shoe repair shop in a shopping center near your home may be one such small business. An accountant or a lawyer may be another.

Entrepreneurial Ventures

Founders of entrepreneurial ventures have different motives for starting a business. Their principle goals are to innovate and grow the venture. Another goal is to create new value that can be harvested when they leave the business. The founder of an entrepreneurial venture should have a plan to expand to a regional, national, or global level.

SECTION 1.1   Review

After You Read ▪▪▪▪▪▪▪▪▪▪▪▪▪

Self-Check
1. **Describe** the roles profit motive and competition play in the free enterprise system.
2. **Explain** the impact of price and nonprice competition on business.
3. **Identify** the difference between wants and needs.

Think
4. **Evaluate** the relationship between cost and profit and supply and demand.

English Language Arts
5. **Comparing Retailers** Choose a product that you use frequently. Identify two or three different places where you can purchase this product. Create a box chart or Venn diagram to compare and contrast the price, availability, convenience, and customer service offered at each location. Then, use your chart to write a three-paragraph essay comparing and contrasting the stores. Explain which retailer does the best job at competing for your business and why.

Go to connectED.mcgraw-hill.com to check your answers.

The Entrepreneurial Process

Reading Guide

Before You Read ▪▪▪▪▪▪▪▪▪▪▪▪▪▪

Connect What are some resources you need to start up a business?

The Main Idea

The entrepreneurial start-up process includes the entrepreneur, the environment, the opportunity, start-up resources, and the new venture organization.

Objectives

Analyze entrepreneurship from a historical perspective.

Name the five components of the entrepreneurial start-up process.

Explain how to achieve business success.

Content Vocabulary

◇ enterprise zones
◇ opportunity
◇ start-up resources
◇ discontinuance
◇ new venture organization
◇ business failure

Academic Vocabulary

You will see these words in your reading and on your tests. Use the academic vocabulary glossary to look up their meanings.

▪ environment   ▪ technology

Graphic Organizer

Before you read this section, draw a chart like the one shown. As you read, fill in the chart with the five key components of the entrepreneurial start-up process.

 Go to connectED.mcgraw-hill.com to download this graphic organizer.

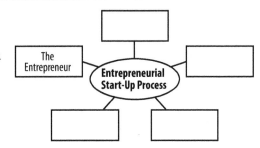

The Entrepreneur

Entrepreneurial Start-Up Process

The History of Entrepreneurship

Entrepreneurship has been a distinct feature of American culture since the American Revolution. Enterprising colonists found innovative ways to bring new products and services to what would later become the United States of America.

But it was not until the 1980s that entrepreneurship became a popular topic. **Figure 1.5** depicts the evolution of entrepreneurship in the United States by decade since the 1960s. It also describes the economic **environment** at that time.

In the early years of the U.S. economy, small businesses were the norm, and early entrepreneurs supplied basic needs. The Industrial Revolution brought about the growth of large companies in steel, railroads, and manufacturing.

By the 1960s, huge companies were common. With no international competition, U.S. companies were able to provide job security. This meant most workers spent their entire life with one company.

Figure 1.5 The Entrepreneurial Evolution

1960s	Large diversified companies were common. With no competition from Japan and Europe, job security was high.
1970s	A volatile economic climate with high interest rates, international competition, and the beginnings of the technology revolution.
1980s	More government regulation on business, large companies saw a drop in profits, and smaller entrepreneurial companies were emerging.
1990s	No job security and fewer benefits. Move to a service-based economy influenced heavily by the Internet and network technologies.
2000s	Markets are global; the Internet and other media technologies make it possible to do business anywhere and to serve customers anywhere in the world efficiently and at a relatively low cost.

Changes In Entrepreneurship Each decade showed changes in entrepreneurship. *In your opinion, what was the biggest change in entrepreneurship over the years?*

ETHICS and BUSINESS

Becoming an Entrepreneur

Situation You have worked for several financial institutions during your career and have learned the good and bad sides of the loan business. After thinking about it for a few years, you are now ready to open your own mortgage company with some investors.

Developing Your Company A number of the institutions you worked for have offered adjustable-rate mortgages (ARMs), which sometimes force homeowners into foreclosure when the rates change. Because ARMs will make money for the company, the investors are encouraging you to offer them as options to your clients.

English Language Arts/Writing

Borrower Beware As the owner of a business with investors, you have a responsibility to make money for your investors. What responsibility do you have toward your clients?

1. How could you offer ARMs and help your clients be financially responsible at the same time?
2. Write a one-page business plan to explain how you will market ARMs to clients.

The 1970s brought about huge changes. High levels of inflation produced high prices and higher-than-normal interest rates. As a result, borrowing and spending slowed. Companies were facing competition from countries with lower labor costs. Finally, the introduction of the microprocessor and the personal computer brought the world into the Information Age. Whole categories of products became obsolete. For example, adding machines and mechanical cash registers became outmoded.

Large companies were suffering by the early 1980s. New, smaller companies were responding to the changing market. They outsourced many of their activities to other companies. Service companies that handled those business needs began to emerge. As a result, many new jobs became available. The 1980s was known as the "Decade of Entrepreneurship."

The advent of the Internet in the mid-1990s changed the way most businesses operate. It also spurred many new entrepreneurial ventures. Most recently, the advent of new media **technologies** has made it possible for entrepreneurs to do business from anywhere and reach customers in cost-effective and efficient ways anywhere in the world.

The rapid evolution of technology continued through the 2000s and 2010s changing the way nearly all businesses function. It revolutionized longstanding business models and brought down companies that did not evolve rapidly along with it. It also brought about exciting new business opportunities across all industries. Modern technology has given rise to many new kinds of businesses and continues to provide great opportunities to entrepreneurs.

 Reading Check **Summarize** How did the creation of social media affect entrepreneurs?

The Entrepreneurial Start-Up Process

The entrepreneurial start-up process includes five key components. They are the entrepreneur, the environment, the opportunity, start-up resources, and the new venture organization. These five components work together to create a new business.

The Entrepreneur

The entrepreneur is the driving force of the start-up process. The entrepreneur recognizes opportunity and pulls together the resources to exploit that opportunity. He or she then creates a company to execute the opportunity in the marketplace. The entrepreneur brings to the process all life experiences and expertise. The entrepreneur is the calculated risk taker who has the passion and persistence to see the venture through from idea to market.

The Environment

A new business **environment** includes variables that affect the venture but are not controlled by the entrepreneur. In general, four categories of environmental variables affect a new venture's ability to start and grow:

1. The nature of the environment, whether it is uncertain, fast-changing, stable, or highly competitive.
2. The availability of resources, such as skilled labor, start-up capital, and sources of assistance.
3. Ways to realize value, such as favorable taxes, good markets, and supportive governmental policies.
4. Incentives to create new businesses. For example, **enterprise zones** are specially designated areas of a community that provide tax benefits to new businesses locating there and grants for new product development.

The Opportunity

A good opportunity can be turned into a business. An **opportunity** is an idea that has commercial potential. However, the opportunity has value only when customers are ready and willing to buy the product or service that the entrepreneur is offering. An idea plus a market equals an opportunity. New businesses are founded on recognized or created opportunities in the environment. Chapter 3 describes how to recognize opportunity and how to think creatively about opportunity.

Start-Up Resources

When an entrepreneur is ready to execute a concept for a new business, he or she must use his or her creative talent to pull together the necessary people and capital. The **start-up resources** include the capital, skilled labor, management expertise, legal and financial advice, facility, equipment, and customers needed to start a business.

The New Venture Organization

The fifth component of the entrepreneurial start-up process is the execution of the new business concept through a **new venture organization** or company. The company is the foundation that supports all of the products, processes, and services of the new business. Through it, the entrepreneur can create value to benefit the owners, the employees, the customers, and the economy.

 Reading Check **Explain** What is the driving force behind the start-up process?

New Business Success and Failure

There is a common myth that most new businesses fail. In fact, studies show that more businesses succeed than fail. Studies conducted by the Small Business Administration report that 66 percent of small businesses survive the first two years. That rate drops to about 40 percent by six years. Even when businesses close, about one-third of them do so successfully by selling, closing for retirement, or merging with another company.

 **Russia: An Emerging Market**

Russia is the largest country in the world. Russian is also spoken in the neighboring countries of Ukraine, Kazakhstan, and Belarus and is one of the six official languages of the United Nations. Nearly 300 million people speak the language.

Negotiating In Russia, compromise is generally seen as a sign of weakness, especially when done too early, meaning negotiations can be lengthy. Theatrics are also common, including emotional outbursts and threats to end the deal. This is just part of the negotiation.

Social Studies/Science Russia was part of the former Union of Soviet Socialist Republics, or USSR, which was dissolved in 1991. This has lead to Russia's transition from a socialist/communist republic to a capitalist republic. Research new Russian entrepreneurs and some of the businesses they have created. Summarize your findings in a one-page report.

Common Russian Words and Phrases		
Hello	Привет	privyet
Goodbye	до свидания	da svidanja
Yes/ No	Да / Нет	da/ njet
Please	Пожалуйста	pazjalste
Thank you	Спасибо	spasiba
You're Welcome	Не за что	ne za chto

The Facts about Business Failure

A **business failure** is a business that has stopped operating with a loss to creditors. Normally, an entrepreneur with a failed business files for bankruptcy. The business loses money for its lenders and investors and no longer appears on the tax rolls. However, some of these businesses may not be failures. Some are discontinuances. A **discontinuance** is a business that was purposely discontinued by an owner who wanted to start a new one; the business may also be operating under a new name. These are not failures; their closings were planned and caused no harm to creditors.

How Entrepreneurs Can Succeed

The chances of a new business succeeding are excellent with effective planning and management. The key to entrepreneurial success is recognizing a need in the market, testing that opportunity in the marketplace, and assembling a team with the necessary expertise to execute the business concept.

SECTION 1.2 | Review

After You Read ■■■■■■■■■■■■■■■

Self-Check
1. **List** the five components of the new venture creation process.
2. **Describe** how an enterprise zone encourages new businesses.
3. **Explain** why discontinuances should not be counted as business failures.

Think
4. **Describe** a good economic environment for a new venture.

Mathematics
5. **Success Rate** In the city of Bloomington, 187 new businesses opened in 2013. By 2014, 15 percent of these businesses were no longer in operation. How many were open in 2014? After another year 12 percent of the businesses operating in 2014 were considered discontinued. How many businesses were still open in 2015?

   Math Concept **Percent** Percent is a ratio that compares a number with 100.

   Step 1: Divide the percent by 100 to determine its decimal equivalent.

   Step 2: Multiply the number by the decimal to obtain the number of businesses.

   Step 3: Subtract the number of businesses that closed from the original amount.

   Go to connectED.mcgraw-hill.com to check your answers.

Entrepreneurs *in Action*

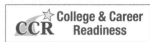

Alison Schuback
Creator
Invisibib

Q *What do you do?*

A I developed and now market my product, the Invisibib, a clear plastic bib that allows people with traumatic brain injury to eat with dignity. I am also the spokesperson for the Invisibib project with the Long Island Head Injury Association.

Q *What kind of training and education prepared you for this job?*

A I have a college degree with a few courses in advertising; however, I would say it was growing up with two entrepreneurial parents and my own experiences with business during college that prepared me for this opportunity.

Q *What do you enjoy most about your job?*

A I always enjoy creative activities where I get to design, so this is ideal for me. Also, I am thoroughly enjoying giving speeches. But the best part is the opportunity to watch something that I created being brought to the public where those who use it are enjoying and benefitting from it!

Q *How did you become interested in your field?*

A As a Traumatic Brain Injury survivor, I had a need, and I wanted to find a solution. I thought that if the Invisibib can be so wonderful for me, just think of all the people it can help and all the other uses to which it could be applied (arts & crafts, special occasions, and many more).

★ **CCR** College & Career Readiness

Write a Proposal Write a proposal to a possible client explaining how you can help his or her business.

1. Using a word processor, describe your services as well as the technology you offer.
2. On paper, or with an illustration program, depict possible promotional items that you can make for the client.
3. Using a spreadsheet program, create a table listing your services and their prices.

Career Facts

Real-World Skills	Academic Skills	Career Cluster
Problem Solving, Speaking, Listening	English Language Arts, Mathematics, Economics, Social Studies	Business, Management & Administration; Manufacturing

Alison Schuback

Review and Assessment

Visual Summary

Entrepreneurship and the Economy

Small Business and Entrepreneurship	• An entrepreneur is an individual who undertakes the creation, organization, and ownership of an innovative business. • Entrepreneurship includes the process of recognizing, creating, and acting upon an opportunity. • The global marketplace and new technologies have transformed the way businesses operate in today's economy.
Economic Systems	• An economic system refers to the ways in which goods and services are produced and consumed. • In a free enterprise system, individuals are able to choose what products to buy, individuals may own private property, and individuals may start a business and compete with other businesses.
Basic Economic Concepts	• Basic economic concepts include goods and services, needs and wants, scarcity, factors of production, and supply and demand.
Economic Indicators and Business Cycles	• The Gross Domestic Product is an example of an economic indicator and is used to understand the state of the economy. • A business cycle refers to the periodic expansion and contraction of the economy.
What Entrepreneurs Contribute	• Entrepreneurs turn economic demand into supply, contribute jobs, and provide a market for venture capital.
The History of Entrepreneurship	• American entrepreneurship has evolved along with the economy. • New technologies and the global markets are driving rapid changes in entrepreneurship.
Start-Up Process	• The five key components of the entrepreneurial start-up process include the entrepreneur, the environment, the opportunity, start-up resources, and the new venture organization.

Vocabulary

1. On a sheet of paper, use each of these terms and words in a written sentence.

Content Vocabulary

◇ entrepreneur
◇ venture
◇ entrepreneurship
◇ economics
◇ free enterprise system
◇ profit
◇ market structure
◇ monopoly

◇ oligopoly
◇ goods
◇ services
◇ need
◇ want
◇ factors of production
◇ scarcity
◇ demand
◇ elastic demand
◇ inelastic demand

◇ diminishing marginal utility
◇ supply
◇ equilibruim
◇ Gross Domestic Product
◇ business cycle
◇ enterprise zones
◇ opportunity
◇ start-up resources

◇ new venture organization
◇ business failure
◇ discontinuance

Academic Vocabulary

■ evaluate
■ enable
■ technology
■ environment

Key Concepts

2. **Define** the role of small business and entrepreneurship in the economy.
3. **Compare and Contrast** economic systems.
4. **Explain** how economics is about making choices.
5. **Define** the role of economic indicators and business cycles.
6. **Describe** what entrepreneurs contribute to the U.S. economy.
7. **Analyze** entrepreneurship from a historical perspective.
8. **Name** the five components of the entrepreneurial start-up process.
9. **Explain** how to achieve business success.

Academic Skills

Mathematics

10. **Calculate Profit** On Sunday, Dawson's flower shop sold 25 arrangements. The materials needed for 25 arrangements cost $250. If he sold each arrangement for $55, what was the net income?

    Math Concept **Net Income** To calculate net income, subtract overhead costs from gross income. In this case, overhead is $250 to purchase flowers. Gross profit is the total amount of money taken in by a business.
    Step 1: Multiply the number of arrangements sold by the retail cost of each arrangement to get the gross profit.
    Step 2: Subtract overhead from gross profit to calculate net income.

English Language Arts

11. **Write to Explain** In a letter to a classmate, describe the process of starting a small business. Explain factors of production, as well as the five components of the entrepreneurial start-up process.

Academic Skills *(continued)*

Social Studies

12. **Explaining Growth** Since the late 1970s, China's economy has blossomed, partly as a result of a major shift in economic philosophy. China moved from a centrally planned economy to a more decentralized one, with an emphasis on international trade. Research the Chinese economy and write a paragraph about how it has evolved over the last 25 years.

Science

13. **Think Like a Scientist** The scientific method involves collecting data, forming a hypothesis that explains the data and testing it, interpreting the results, and stating a conclusion. Create your own hypothesis about a familiar product. Brainstorm ways you would find data to test your hypothesis. Write a short summary of your proposed research project.

Real-World Skills

Financial Literacy

14. **Understanding Costs** Look at the monthly utility bills your family has received over the past year, including water, gas, and electricity. Write a short report comparing and contrasting your family's gas, water, or electricity usage from season to season and the rates you were charged by the utility companies.

21st Century Skills

Communication

15. **Listen Actively** Practice active listening during a conversation with a classmate, friend, or family member. Pay close attention to body language, tone of voice, speed, and volume, and try to understand the message. Respond to the speaker with comments or questions. After the conversation, write a paragraph describing the experience.

Connect to Your Community

16. **Analyze Factors of Production** Interview an entrepreneur or small business owner in your community. Ask what the factors of production are for that business. Then create a diagram illustrating the business's factors of production.

17. **Brainstorm Ideas** Working with a partner, brainstorm a list of ten businesses you and your partner might like to start. Consider the interests and skills of each partner to narrow down the list. Write a short description of one of the businesses. Include the product or service you will provide and the type of resources you need to begin.

Review and Assessment

CHAPTER

1

Competitive Events Prep

18. Situation You and two partners are planning a new business in your hometown. The downtown business district has many empty stores and is planning to create an enterprise zone to encourage new businesses to move in. Plans include favorable business tax rates and grants for building renovations. The town also plans to help attract customers by providing free parking and sponsoring a series of promotional campaigns. You feel that the enterprise zone can help your business.

Activity Prepare an outline of information describing enterprise zones and how this one could help your business be successful. You will then present the information to your partners.

Evaluation You will be evaluated on how well you meet the following performance indicators:

- Describe the relationship between government and business.
- Determine opportunities for venture creation.
- Use creativity in business activities/decisions.
- Enlist others in working toward a shared vision.
- Demonstrate initiative.

 Go to connectED.mcgraw-hill.com for more information about this activity and other competitive events.

Standardized Test Practice

 College & Career Readiness

Directions Choose the letter of the best answer. Write the letter for the answer on a separate piece of paper. For question #2, if the answer is False, rewrite the statement to make it true.

1. Which of the following is NOT an example of an economic system?
   A. pure market
   B. mixed
   C. equilibrium
   D. command

2. Goods and services are products created to satisfy consumers' wants and needs.
   T
   F

> **Test-Taking Tip**
> Exercising for a few days before the test can help reduce stress.

2

Your Potential as an Entrepreneur

Chapter Objectives

Discovery Project

The Impact of Entrepreneurship

Key Question *How do local entrepreneurs affect your community?*

Project Goal

Work with a partner to identify, research, and interview local entrepreneurs. Determine what kind of impact they have had on the community: Have they created more jobs? Do their businesses contribute to local charities?

Think About...

➤ *How will you identify your community's entrepreneurs?*

➤ *How will you determine what kind of effect they have had on your community?*

➤ *How have other local businesses been affected by the entrepreneurs?*

 21st Century Skills

Entrepreneurial Literacy *What do communities gain by supporting local entrepreneurs?*

Evaluate

Go to connectED.mcgraw-hill.com to download a rubric that you can use to evaluate your final project.

Ask
AN
EXPERT

Q: *I am saving money to start a company that makes all-natural skin care products for teens. What are the sources of capital used to get a business off the ground or to help a business grow?*

A: Sources of capital vary depending on the age and size of the company. Most of the start-up capital may be your own money. Venture capital firms specialize in investing large sums to help private companies develop and grow. Corporate financing often comes from multinational investment banks.

Juice Images/Glow Images

Connect the Photo

Got What It Takes? Want to explore a business idea you've been thinking about for years? There are many rewards, and risks, to owing your own business, and knowing about them is important. Perhaps even more important is knowing the characteristics and skills you need to have to be a successful entrepreneur. *What are the three most important characteristics entrepreneurs should possess to be successful? Why?*

Why Be an Entrepreneur?

Reading Guide

Before You Read ▪▪▪▪▪▪▪▪▪▪▪▪▪▪

Connect What do you think would be the most important personal reward of being an entrepreneur?

The Main Idea

When you consider going into business for yourself, an important first step is to analyze the advantages and disadvantages of entrepreneurship.

Objectives

Identify the rewards of going into business for yourself.

Recognize the risks of going into business for yourself.

Content Vocabulary

◇ competition
◇ investment
◇ capital

Academic Vocabulary

You will see these words in your reading and on your tests. Use the academic vocabulary glossary to look up their meanings.

▪ guarantee ▪ control

Graphic Organizer

Before you read this section, draw a chart like the one shown. As you read, list the risks and rewards of being an entrepreneur.

 Go to **connectED.mcgraw-hill.com** to download this graphic organizer.

Rewards	Risks
1. Being your own boss	1. Working long hours
2.	2.
3.	3.
4.	4.
5.	5.
6.	6.

Rewards of Entrepreneurship

What are the rewards of being an entrepreneur? You may think the rewards are owning a large house, driving a nice car, and leading a lavish lifestyle. However, having those things is not the primary motivation for most entrepreneurs. In fact, the greatest rewards are not material at all. For most entrepreneurs, the greatest rewards of owning a business are intangible. The rewards include such things as independence, personal satisfaction, and prestige.

Being Your Own Boss

Most entrepreneurs consider being their own boss as the biggest reward of owning a business. The reason is obvious—it gives them the freedom to make their own business decisions. They have the final word on all aspects of the operation. They can determine the hours of business, products offered, and direction for expansion.

Doing Something You Enjoy

Some business ventures start with an activity the entrepreneur enjoys. Someone who takes pleasure in cooking for others might start a catering business. Someone who likes to go surfing or skateboarding might give lessons and sell equipment. The new business owner derives special satisfaction from creating and developing the enterprise around a special interest.

Having the Opportunity to Be Creative

Most people who work for others merely follow procedures; entrepreneurs make them. In other words, entrepreneurs are able to shape a business in ways employees cannot. This is especially true with daring or creative ideas. When business owners have a creative idea, they have the power to act on it.

Having the Freedom to Set Your Own Schedule

Although entrepreneurs experience time demands, they have the flexibility to determine their own schedule. Also, they have the option of working at home, at the business, or at whatever location suits them.

Having Job Security

In today's world, employees are not **guaranteed** job security from their employers. Entrepreneurs, however, **control** their own destiny. As long as the business is successful, they are assured of a job.

Making More Money

People who work for others are paid wages or a salary. When they work hard or when the company does well, they may or may not get a raise. In contrast, a business owner's earnings are limited only by the potential of their business.

Tech Savvy

Gesture Technology

Some people are turned off by new electronic devices because it takes too long to learn how to use them. But devices like Apple®'s iPhone™ and Nintendo®'s motion-sensing Wii™ game console have made technology more user-friendly by allowing users to control them with gestures and touch. Entrepreneurs are scrambling to create and market more gadgets that can be controlled with gesture technology. Improved cameras can interpret movements accurately, but they are still expensive. *What other kinds of products could incorporate gesture technology?*

As You Read ■ ■ ■ ■ ■ ■ ■
Determine How can a business owner's income be both a reward and a risk?

Being Recognized Within the Community

Business ownership carries with it a certain amount of prestige. Entrepreneurs, after all, have taken on a responsibility that involves hard work, daring, and know-how. In the process, entrepreneurs make an economic contribution to the community through their investment in and creation of jobs.

 Reading Check Summarize Why do entrepreneurs have more freedom than their employees?

Risks of Entrepreneurship

If being an entrepreneur is so great, then how come everyone is not an entrepreneur? The rewards tell only one side of the story. There are also a considerable number of costs and risks associated with starting your own business.

Competition

Intense competition can make business ownership a difficult undertaking. **Competition** is the rivalry among businesses for consumer dollars. The prospective entrepreneur should consider the risks that occur because of this competitive environment. These include long hours, uncertain income, responsibility, and the potential loss of money.

Pillar of the Community Local business owners are often respected for what their business adds to the community. *How have entrepreneurs had an impact in your area?*

Young Entrepreneurs Are Changing the World

These teens didn't just wait for opportunity to knock—they went out and created it

Driving on the freeway one day, teens Daniel Rudyak and Curren Krasnoff got stuck behind slow-moving cement-mixing trucks. Where others saw only annoyance, Daniel and Curren saw a business opportunity. They developed a new kind of concrete that rolls out like carpet and hardens in less than 24 hours, making old-school cement mixers a thing of the past. Today their company, Cortex Composites, has more than $23 million in annual sales.

They aren't alone. Teens around the globe have started successful careers by finding opportunities everyone else overlooked. Moziah Bridges started creating custom bow ties at age nine because he couldn't find any he liked. Now he runs a company, Mo's Bows, and is on track to earn his first million by age 17.

For teen entrepreneurs, business success is about more than just money—it's also about creativity and innovation. Says Mo, "designing a colorful bow tie is just part of my vision to make the world a fun and happier place."

Active Learning

Search the Internet for a successful teen entrepreneur, and then answer the following questions in one to two sentences each: (1) What is the entrepreneur's name, the company's name (if applicable), and the type of product(s) or services offered? (2) How did the entrepreneur get started? (3) What success has the entrepreneur had? (4) What advice does the entrepreneur have for young people wanting to start a business?

Working Long Hours

It is not unusual for entrepreneurs to work long hours, especially during the start-up period. During start-up, the survival of the new business often depends on the entrepreneur's ability to make timely decisions. A lot of entrepreneurs cannot afford to pay others to help them. As a result, they devote a lot of time to the business, often working long hours, sometimes even working seven days a week. People who work for someone else do not usually have to do this. They have a set work schedule, which usually consists of a certain number of hours per day and days per week.

Having an Uncertain Income

Business owners can make more money than their employees make—but only when business is good. When business is bad, earnings can be low or nonexistent. Most businesses do not make a profit right away. Even when a business makes a profit, the owner often has to put the money back into the business. Business owners do not get a regular paycheck. In addition, they may not have benefits such as health insurance and time off for vacations.

Being Fully Responsible

The owner of a business is responsible for more than just decision making. For example, the small business owner must see that everything gets done—sweeping the floors, paying the bills, and taking care of repairs and maintenance. Ultimately, there is no one else who will make sure these tasks are completed.

While an employee is only responsible for assigned tasks, the business owner is ultimately responsible for all the work that needs to be done, no matter how small or tedious the task might be. The success or failure of the venture rests entirely on the owner. In other words, if you are an entrepreneur and want your new business to succeed, you need to be willing to take on a wide variety of tasks and see them through to completion.

Risking One's Investment

The biggest risk of being in business is the possibility of losing one's investment. **Investment** is the amount of money a person puts into their business as capital. **Capital** includes the buildings, equipment, tools, and other goods needed to produce a product or the money used to buy these things. Employees, however, do not risk losing money. Before an entrepreneur can count on earnings, the venture must be up and running.

SECTION 2.1 Review

After You Read

Self-Check

1. **Summarize** the risks and rewards of starting your own business.
2. **Explain** the difference between investment and capital.
3. **Describe** the various responsibilities you take on when you decide to start your own business.

Think

4. **Compare and Contrast** the advantages and disadvantages of owning a business to working for someone else.

English Language Arts

5. **Develop Communications Skills** Write, rehearse, and present a two-minute speech introducing yourself to potential investors. Describe your personal strengths to the audience by highlighting the skills, qualities, and characteristics that will make you a successful entrepreneur.

Go to connectED.mcgraw-hill.com to check your answers.

What Does It Take to Be an Entrepreneur?

Reading Guide

Before You Read ==============

Connect What characteristics or personality traits do entrepreneurs have in common?

The Main Idea

Before going into business, you should determine the characteristics and skills needed to reach your goal of being successful.

Objectives

Identify the background, characteristics, and skills of successful entrepreneurs.

Explain techniques that will improve your potential for becoming an entrepreneur.

Content Vocabulary

◇ role model
◇ foundation skills
◇ profile
◇ achiever

Academic Vocabulary

You will see these words in your reading and on your tests. Use the academic vocabulary glossary to look up their meanings.

■ determine
■ accurate

Graphic Organizer

Before you read this section, draw a chart like the one shown. As you read, fill in the chart with the 12 characteristics of successful entrepreneurs.

 Go to connectED.mcgraw-hill.com to download this graphic organizer.

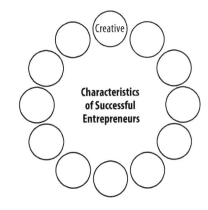

Characteristics of Successful Entrepreneurs

Creative

Web Savvy

Forums for Entrepreneurs

Going into business can be scary, and it helps to have a mentor. While many communities have local groups of retired entrepreneurs that provide counseling, support can also be found online. Type "entrepreneur forum" into your favorite search engine to find hundreds of Websites where you can connect with other start-ups, read success stories, and network with experienced professionals.

Besides online forums, where else can you look to find entrepreneurial mentors?

Who Are Entrepreneurs?

Entrepreneurs are important to the global economy. Even in popular culture, there is a great deal of interest in what makes them tick. They are featured in magazines, newspapers, and blogs. Bestsellers and movies are written about them. Some entrepreneurs have even become celebrities.

Research has been done to **determine** what, if any, traits, experiences, and skills entrepreneurs have in common. The object of these studies has been to learn whether entrepreneurs are born or made.

Background

A suprising variety of people become entrepreneurs. The research reveals a wide span of ages, educational backgrounds, and personal histories. It also reveals common life experiences and other factors that may lead people toward entrepreneurship.

- Forty-seven percent of entrepreneurs were under age 35 when they started their businesses; 16 percent were under age 25.
- Forty percent of entrepreneurs had a high school diploma or less.
- Twenty-seven percent of entrepreneurs had some college; 33 percent had completed a college degree.
- Many entrepreneurs were independent from an early age.
- Many entrepreneurs worked when they were young (paper routes, yard-care services, babysitting, etc.).
- Sixty-two percent of entrepreneurs had parents or close relatives who owned a business.
- Many entrepreneurs were influenced early in life by a **role model**, a person whose attitudes and achievements they tried to emulate.

Entrepreneurial Characteristics

Studies have also been done to pinpoint personal characteristics of successful entrepreneurs. These are distinctive traits and qualities needed to set up an owner-operated business and run it successfully. Successful competitors often show these same characteristics. Listings vary but usually include these 12 items.

1. **Persistent** Entrepreneurs are willing to work until a job is done, no matter how long it takes. They are tenacious in overcoming obstacles and pursuing their goals.
2. **Creative** Entrepreneurs look for new ways to solve old problems.
3. **Responsible** Entrepreneurs do not pass the buck. They take responsibility for their decisions and actions.

4. **Inquisitive** Entrepreneurs want to know as much as possible about whatever affects their venture. They conduct research and ask questions to solve problems.
5. **Goal-oriented** Entrepreneurs set and achieve goals.
6. **Independent** Entrepreneurs want to make their own decisions.
7. **Self-demanding** Entrepreneurs have high expectations for themselves.
8. **Self-confident** Entrepreneurs believe in themselves and trust their own ability to make decisions.
9. **Risk-taking** Entrepreneurs take calculated risks, but they are not reckless.
10. **Restless** Once entrepreneurs achieve their goals, they begin looking for new challenges.
11. **Action-oriented** Entrepreneurs are doers as opposed to spectators. They set goals, make decisions, and act on their decisions.
12. **Enthusiastic** Entrepreneurs are energetic and passionate about their pursuits.

● **As You Read** ▪▪▪▪▪▪▪
Explain How can improving your math skills help you succeed as an entrepreneur?

Foundation Skills

In addition to background, desire, and characteristics, the research identifies foundation skills needed to be a successful entrepreneur. **Foundation skills** are skills that entrepreneurs use regularly in setting up and running a business. These skills are essential to the process of creating a business. They include:

1. **Communication skills** Entrepreneurs need person-to-person, telephone, written, and electronic communication skills. They also need listening skills to build positive relationships and gather accurate information.
2. **Math skills** Are you prepared to maintain the business records required to run a business? Basic math skills are also needed to budget, make initial purchase decisions, calculate potential profit, and put together financial statements.
3. **Problem-solving skills** You need to be able to come up with ideas to solve problems. Some problems call for logical solutions. Others call for a great deal of creativity.
4. **Technical and computer skills** Technical skills are important in setting up the processes and technology of the business being created. Computer skills are essential in almost any business.
5. **Decision-making skills** To run your own business, you must be able to choose the best option from among many. Good decision makers know

Bright Ideas Vu Thai, founder of Efficient Lighting, came up with a creative solution to energy efficiency: compact fluorescent light bulbs that use 75 percent less energy than traditional light bulbs. *Besides creativity, what are some other characteristics of successful entrepreneurs?*

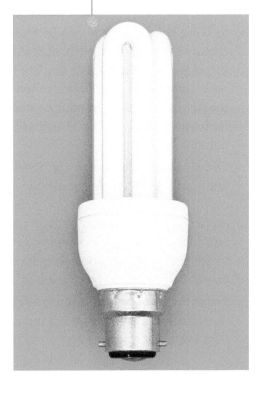

their values and are good at predicting the consequences of actions.

6. **Organizing and planning skills** Entrepreneurs must be expert organizers and planners, which require logical thinking and good time-management.

7. **Teamwork skills** Entrepreneurs have to coordinate and manage work teams. This involves respecting others, being flexible, and knowing when to exercise leadership.

8. **Social skills** You need good social skills to interact well with employees, customers, and vendors. This involves both verbal and nonverbal behavior.

9. **Adaptability skills** Because the business world is constantly changing, entrepreneurs need to be adaptable.

10. **Basic business skills** Entrepreneurs should have a basic understanding of how the economy works and an understanding of fundamental concepts of finance, marketing, and management to create a successful business.

> **Reading Check Connect** What kinds of communication skills do entrepreneurs need?

 GL BAL WORKPLACE

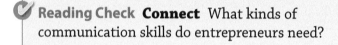 **Korean and Hangul: The Two Koreas**

Korean is the language of North and South Korea. Koreans once used Chinese characters to write their language but in the fifteenth century they created the alphabet used today, called Hangul. Hangul, like English, is a phonetic alphabet in which letters represent the sounds of language. Hangul can be written horizontally left to right or vertical columns right to left.

Social Structure Koreans emphasize age and social status in relationships. A person older than you automatically rates higher. The exchanging of business cards is customary, and allows you and your Korean counterparts to smoothly gauge where you stand in the business relationship by your job title.

Social Studies/English Language Arts Communication is a blend of verbal and nonverbal cues like body language and social dynamics, which differ by culture. Your potential as an

entrepreneur is often predicted by how well you communicate. Investigate ways in which Korean and American communication might differ and summarize your research in a one-page report.

Common Korean Words and Phrases		
Hello	안녕하세요	anyonghaseyo
Goodbye	안녕히가세요	anyonghegasayyo
Yes/No	네 / 아니오	nay/aneyo
Please	부탁합니다	butakhamnida
Thank ytou	감사합니다	kamsahamnida
You're welcome	천만에요	chunmaneyo

Build Your Potential as an Entrepreneur

As you have learned, the typical entrepreneur fits a certain profile. A **profile** is a set of characteristics or qualities that identifies a type or category of person.

What if you do not have a perfect match with the profile? That should not stop you from becoming an entrepreneur. What you really need is a can-do attitude and a genuine desire to go into business. There are many ways to build your potential as an entrepreneur.

Strengthen Your Entrepreneurial Characteristics

The personal characteristics described on page 38-39 are essential to people who want to set up and run their own business. The following steps can help you develop your entrepreneurial characteristics:

1. Determine the current strength of your entrepreneurial characteristics. You can use the Entrepreneurial Characteristics Assessment shown in **Figure 2.1** on page 42 to do a self-evaluation. This will help you to analyze the degree to which you possess the characteristics of an entrepreneur and help you identify the qualities you need to develop.
2. Think of entrepreneurial characteristics as habits you can improve. It is within your control to improve your entrepreneurial traits.
3. Develop your weak characteristics by practicing and acting as though you have the traits you want to develop. After a while, you will find that the traits become part of you.

Family Business Many entrepreneurs had parents or other role models who owned a business. *Which role models inspire you to be an entrepreneur?*

Think Like an Achiever

Another way to strengthen your entrepreneurial potential is to think and act like an achiever. An **achiever** is a person with a record of successes. Entrepreneurs are motivated by a need for achievement—an inner feeling of personal accomplishment. To attain this same kind of mindset, strive to think and act like an achiever on a daily basis.

- Set out to be the best at whatever you do.
- Write your goals down on paper.
- Pursue your goals with confidence and commitment.
- Set your sights on not only accomplishing your goals, but on accomplishing the extraordinary.
- View setbacks and other difficulties as opportunities to learn and grow.

Figure 2.1 — Entrepreneurial Characteristics Assessment

Each of the statements below represents a characteristic helpful to entrepreneurs. Read through the list, and on a separate sheet of paper, record your reactions. If you think a particular statement describes you very accurately, write a 5. If you think it does not describe you at all, write a 1. If you think it only partially describes you, place yourself between the two extremes by writing a number from 2 to 4.

1. You stay with a task despite difficulties. ❶ ❷ ❸ ❹ ❺
2. You are creative. ❶ ❷ ❸ ❹ ❺
3. You take responsibility for your actions. ❶ ❷ ❸ ❹ ❺
4. You want to know about things. ❶ ❷ ❸ ❹ ❺
5. You set goals for yourself and work toward them. ❶ ❷ ❸ ❹ ❺
6. You like to work at your own schedule. ❶ ❷ ❸ ❹ ❺
7. You set high standards for yourself. ❶ ❷ ❸ ❹ ❺
8. You believe in yourself and in what you are doing. ❶ ❷ ❸ ❹ ❺
9. You like a challenge, but you are not a gambler. ❶ ❷ ❸ ❹ ❺
10. Your successes bring a desire for more. ❶ ❷ ❸ ❹ ❺

Rating Your Characteristics By rating your entrepreneurial characteristics, you can assess your personal potential to become an entrepreneur. The circled numbers represent the strength of each characteristic. *If you had to use words instead of numbers to describe each level, what terms would you use?*

ETHICS and BUSINESS

Changing Companies

Situation While working for a software design company, you came up with many innovative uses for the software you helped to design. However, the president of the company would not market the innovations. When the economy became unstable, you lost your job at the company.

Gaining a Business After several interviews, you are offered a partnership at a competitor's software design company. After you begin working at the new company, the president asks you to share the innovations you came up with while working at your former job. He wants to use the ideas to gain a market advantage over your former employer.

 English Language Arts/Writing

Intellectual Property Rights Your thoughts belong to you. Or do they? Who owns the rights to the thoughts and ideas you generated while employed by a company?

1. Is it ethical to use the innovations you come up with while working for one company to help another company prosper?
2. Write a one-page research paper explaining your answer.

You can also strengthen your entrepreneurial characteristics by reading, writing, observing, and solving.

1. **Reading** Read articles and books about entrepreneurs and entrepreneurial activities.
2. **Writing** Write brief essays or stories about living or historical figures who overcame obstacles to achieve success.
3. **Observing** Watch films or videos about successful businesspeople, athletes, and other achievement-oriented individuals.
4. **Solving** Solve case problems that call for identification of goal-oriented behavior, creativity, and moderate risk taking.

Turning desirable traits and behaviors into habits takes time and practice, but these habits can become part of your makeup.

Develop Your Entrepreneurial Skills

To be a successful entrepreneur, it is essential that you develop the foundation skills discussed in this chapter. In order to start or run your business, it helps to have good communication skills, math skills, problem-solving skills, computer and technical skills, decision-making skills, organizing and planning skills, teamwork skills, social skills, adaptability skills, and basic business skills.

You do not have to be an expert in each of these areas. However, you must develop these skills in order to meet the various challenges that come with owning your own business.

Follow this three-step process to gain competency in the foundation skills for entrepreneurs:

1. Learn the techniques needed to use the skill.
2. Put the skill to work in real-world or simulated situations.
3. Ask yourself whether you got the results you want. If not, determine how you can improve and apply what you have learned.

Developing Technical and Business Skills

You can develop technical skills and basic business skills, including computer skills, in school, through work experience, and by reading. Practice using different computer software in your spare time at home. Use a search engine to find Websites that will help you develop new skills. When a proposed business's processes and technology are simple and straightforward, technical skills can be acquired quickly. In other instances, education and training are recommended for the prospective entrepreneur.

Obtaining employment in a similar or related business is a good way to develop technical skills. Another alternative is to take classes that pertain to the business. Still another option is to attend workshops. Workshops are often available through community colleges, economic development organizations, manufacturers, and suppliers.

SECTION 2.2 Review

After You Read

Self-Check

1. **Identify** what the research on entrepreneurs' backgrounds means to you personally.
2. **Name** the 12 characteristics of successful entrepreneurs.
3. **List** the six skills entrepreneurs need to organize their business.

Think

4. **Analyze** your class schedule to determine at least three ways that each course can strengthen your entrepreneurial characteristics or improve your entrepreneurial skills.

Mathematics

5. **Mental Math** Before Spencer and Kiyoni can open their sporting goods store, they need to research the investment required. In order to do this, they made the following table. Explain how you would use mental math to figure the approximate investment required.

Inventory	$110,250
Store Fixtures	$89,941
Computers and Systems	$9,680

Math Concept **Estimation** Some questions involving math can be answered by estimating instead of calculating an exact solution.

Step 1: Think about how to use rounding to estimate sums.

Step 2: Use words to explain your approach to estimating the answer.

 Go to connectED.mcgraw-hill.com to check your answers.

Entrepreneurs *in Action*

Ben Clark
Freelance Photographer

Q *What do you do?*

A I am a freelance photographer. Assignments or projects come from clients such as lifestyle magazines, clothing companies, skateboard gear manufacturers, event coordinators, and stock film agencies. I also shoot photos for artistic purposes.

Q *What kind of training and education prepared you for this job?*

A I started taking photos when I was in high school and concentrated on fine art photography when I attended college. After graduating, I had to go out, gain experience, and learn the business side of my work. I now run my own business and create my own jobs.

Q *What do you enjoy most about your job?*

A It isn't repetitive and I don't have to be sitting behind a desk from 9 to 5. Every assignment is different. When I arrive at a shoot, I have to figure out what kind of photos I can get out of my subject. I consider the person's appearance and mood, the environment, and the client's expectations. When I'm finished with a job, I move on to the next one.

Q *How did you become interested in your field?*

A I've always had an interest in cameras, and I really enjoy the process of photography. I appreciate the mechanical, analog style of shooting photos as well as the modern, digital process. Either way, I still feel excitement when I snap a picture and anticipate how the image will look. Then, using the technological advancements of digital photography, I can create the image that I need in postproduction.

CCR ☆ College & Career Readiness

Make a Brochure Write a description of photographic services offered. It can be portraiture, event photography, product shots, or other jobs.

1. Use word processing software to describe your services.
2. Use a spreadsheet program to create a table listing your services and their prices.
3. Combine the pieces to a make a brochure. It can be factual or artistic but should include information such as services, prices, and contact information.

Career Facts

Real-World Skills	Academic Skills	Career Cluster
Punctuality, Interpersonal Skills, Computer Skills	Mathematics, English Language Arts, Fine Arts	Arts, A/V Technology & Communications

CHAPTER 2

Review and Assessment

Visual Summary

Your Potential As an Entrepreneur

Look Before You Leap Before starting your own business, weigh the rewards and risks.

Rewards	Risks
• Be your own boss	• Work long hours
• Do something you enjoy	• Uncertain income
• Be creative	• Be fully responsible
• Set your own schedule	• Risk your own investment
• Job security	
• Earn more money	
• Community recognition	

Characteristics of Successful Entrepreneurs

- Persistent
- Creative
- Enthusiastic
- Responsible
- Action-oriented
- Inquisitive
- Restless
- Goal-oriented
- Risk-taking
- Independent
- Self-confident
- Self-demanding

Keys to Success Successful entrepreneurs have these traits and qualities.

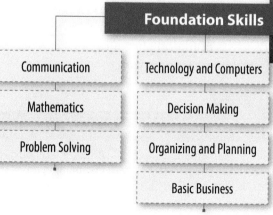

Skill Sets
Foundation skills are used when setting up and running a business.

Foundation Skills

Communication	Technology and Computers	Teamwork
Mathematics	Decision Making	Social Skills
Problem Solving	Organizing and Planning	Adaptability
	Basic Business	

Mike Kemp/RubberBall/Alamy

Review and Assessment

Vocabulary

1. On a sheet of paper, use each of these terms and words in a written sentence.

Content Vocabulary

◇ competition
◇ investment
◇ capital
◇ role model

◇ foundation skills
◇ profile
◇ achiever

Academic Vocabulary

■ guarantee
■ control
■ determine
■ accurate

Key Concepts

2. **Identify** the rewards of going into business for yourself.
3. **Recognize** the risks of going into business for yourself.
4. **Describe** the background, characteristics, and skills of successful entrepreneurs.
5. **Explain** techniques that will improve your potential for becoming an entrepreneur.
6. **Compare** owning a business to working for someone else.
7. **Explain** why some people become entrepreneurs and others do not.
8. **Name** some personality traits that could interfere with becoming a successful entrepreneur.
9. **Describe** why role models are important to entrepreneurial success.

Academic Skills

Mathematics

10. **Analyzing Data** A study showed that 47 percent of entrepreneurs were under age 35 when they started their businesses. The same study showed 16 percent were under the age of 25. If there were 1,855 total entrepreneurs, how many were under the age of 35 when they started their businesses? How many were younger than 25?

   Math Concept **Percents** Percents can be thought of as parts of the whole.
   Step 1: Divide the percent by 100 to determine its decimal equivalent.
   Step 2: Multiply the number by the decimal to obtain the number of businesses.

English Language Arts

11. **Personal Lists** Under separate headings, list the traits and skills you possess that are important to a successful business. Then list the traits and skills that you need but do not have today. Share your lists with classmates, and identify one or two others who have strengths that match your weaknesses. Discuss with them what kind of business you might like to start together and how you would share roles and responsibilities.

Academic Skills *(continued)*

Social Studies

12. Local Conservation Write a report about what businesses in your community are doing to recycle. Interview local entrepreneurs and draft a plan for a school-wide recycling program with their assistance.

Science

13. Task Efficiency Choose a task you and a classmate do on a regular basis and perform a "time and motion" study. To do this, keep a record of the steps you take to accomplish the task and the time it takes you to do each step. Compare your record with your classmates to see who accomplishes the task more efficiently.

 ## Real-World Skills

Communication Skills

14. Practice Persuasion Advertisments try to persuade you to buy a product. Pick a product that you feel strongly about. Write a short speech about your topic in which you try to persuade your classmates to agree with your point of view. After you present your speech, ask if anyone changed their opinion.

21st Century Skills

Information Literacy

15. Assess Your Potential Use a search engine to locate information about the characteristics, skills, aptitudes, abilities, and personality traits needed for entrepreneurial success. Then write a report that concludes whether you have the potential to be an entrepreneur based on your findings.

 ## Connect to Your Community

16. Analyze a Failed Business Select a local company that has recently gone out of business. List some of the reasons the business might have failed and how the owner might have prevented the business from closing.

17. Interview an Administrator Interview an administrator at your school. Share the characteristics of successful entrepreneurs that you learned about in this chapter and ask the administrator which traits he or she has. Ask him or her to compare being a school administrator to being an entrepreneur. Share your findings with the class.

Competitive Events Prep

18. **Situation** You are a student in a high school entrepreneurship class. You enrolled in this class because you want to open your own business some day. You have limited work experience and are not sure about the training and experience you should have to open a successful business.

Activity Your class has been assigned the task of evaluating individual potential as entrepreneurs. Use the list of essential skills of successful entrepreneurs provided in this chapter. Note to what degree you feel you possess each skill, and note ways that you can enhance each of the skills. Compile your self-evaluation in a written report.

Evaluation You will be evaluated on how well you meet these performance indicators:

- Describe desirable entrepreneurial personality traits.
- Evaluate personal capabilities.
- Conduct a self-assessment to determine entrepreneurial potential.
- Prepare simple written reports.

 Go to **connectED.mcgraw-hill.com** for more information about this activity and other competitive events.

Standardized Test Practice

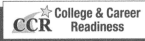
College & Career
Readiness

Directions Choose the letter of the best answer. Write the letter for the answer on a separate piece of paper. For question #2, if the answer is False, rewrite the statement to make it true.

1. Which of the following sets of skills is essential for an entrepreneur?
   A. Manufacturing skills
   B. Problem-solving skills
   C. Graphic design skills
   D. Engineering Skills

2. Nearly half of entrepreneurs were under age 35 when they started their business.
   T
   F

> **Test-Taking Tip**
> If each item on a test is worth the same number of points, do not spend too much time on questions that are confusing.

Recognizing Opportunity

Chapter Objectives

SECTION 3.1
Understanding Entrepreneurial Trends

Examine current trends that provide opportunities for entrepreneurs.

Identify ways to recognize opportunity.

Explain how to think creatively about opportunity.

Determine ways to find creative business ideas.

SECTION 3.2
Starting Versus Buying a Business

Identify the importance of personal values and goals in choosing an entrepreneurial pursuit.

Examine the challenges and rewards of entering a family business.

Determine the benefits and drawbacks of buying a business.

Describe how you can evaluate a business opportunity.

List the advantages and disadvantages of starting your own business.

Discovery Project

Creating Your Own Business

Key Question *What kind of business would you be interested in starting?*

Project Goal
Brainstorm a list of your interests that might be turned into a business. Prioritize your list according to criteria (such as your interest level, profitability, or ease of start-up), and select one idea or area of interest. Create a short plan that explains how you would start your business.

Think About…
➤ *What criteria will you use to prioritize your interests?*
➤ *How will you determine whether your idea for a business will be profitable?*
➤ *What will you need to do to get started?*

21st Century Skills
Innovation *What idea have you had for a new product that would simplify your life?*

Evaluate
 Go to connectED.mcgraw-hill.com to download a rubric that you can use to evaluate your final project.

Ask
AN
EXPERT

Q: *I do not have enough capital to get my Web-based business off the ground. What costs do I have to consider if I use my credit cards as a source of funding?*

A: The two major costs associated with credit cards are annual fees and finance charges. Annual fees are once-yearly charges for using the card. Finance charges are the cost of using credit, and amount is based on an annual percentage rate (APR). There are also over-limit fees, late-payment fees, and cash advance fees to keep in mind.

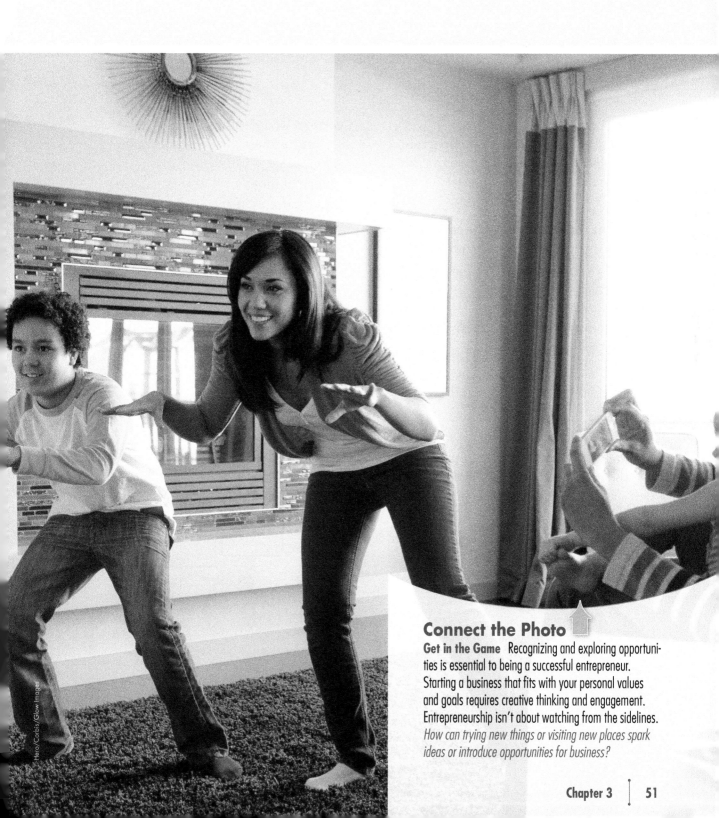

Hero/Corbis/Glow Images

Connect the Photo
Get in the Game Recognizing and exploring opportunities is essential to being a successful entrepreneur. Starting a business that fits with your personal values and goals requires creative thinking and engagement. Entrepreneurship isn't about watching from the sidelines. *How can trying new things or visiting new places spark ideas or introduce opportunities for business?*

Understanding Entrepreneurial Trends

Reading Guide

Before You Read ▪▪▪▪▪▪▪▪▪▪▪▪▪▪

Connect What entrepreneurial opportunities would make the most of your skills and talents?

The Main Idea

The ability to recognize new opportunities and think creatively is essential for success in today's global market.

Objectives

Examine current trends that provide opportunity for entrepreneurs.

Identify ways to recognize opportunity.

Explain how to think creatively about opportunity.

Determine ways to find creative business ideas.

Content Vocabulary

◇ online business
◇ services
◇ sustainability
◇ social entrepreneurs
◇ outsourcing
◇ strategic alliance
◇ corporate venture
◇ innovation
◇ niche
◇ brainstorm
◇ demographics
◇ trade magazine
◇ specialty magazine
◇ trade show

Academic Vocabulary

You will see these words in your reading and on your tests. Use the academic vocabulary glossary to look up their meanings.

■ conduct   ■ create

Graphic Organizer

Before you read this section, draw a chart like the one shown. As you read, fill in the chart with the eight entrepreneurial trends discussed in the section.

 Go to connectED.mcgraw-hill.com to download this graphic organizer.

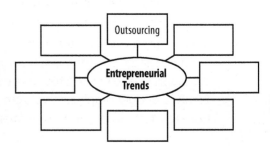

Current Entrepreneurial Trends

To begin the entrepreneurial process, you must take the steps to recognize an opportunity, develop a business concept, test it with potential customers, and create a business to execute that concept. The first step is to identify a business opportunity. One way to identify an opportunity is to study current trends. Trends that are sweeping the business world include Web-based businesses, service businesses, green businesses, social entrepreneurship, and outsourcing.

Internet Businesses

The Internet has transformed the way business is **conducted**. Many new types of Internet-based businesses have emerged, and most traditional companies have added online components. An **online business** is a business that conducts business by means of the Internet. Online businesses have the potential to attract a huge number of customers because anyone with an Internet connection can purchase from this type of business. Today there are millions of online businesses.

● **As You Read** --------

Describe What type of business interests you most? Why?

Business Case Study

Be a Data Detective

Charts, graphs, and studies may not be as scientific as they seem

To succeed in business, entrepreneurs need to understand economic trends. Economic numbers and reports are easy to find in the news, but you'll need a healthy dose of critical thinking to interpret them correctly.

Here are some common examples of misleading data:

Goofy graphs. Charts that compare and contrast should use the same units and start in the same place, which is usually zero. If a budget graph starts at zero and goes to $100 million, and a sales graph starts at $90 million and goes to $100 million, the data aren't comparable.

Trumped-up tests. Do the results of a study really prove what they seem to? If a company tests a product at room temperature but customers use it in freezing weather, for example, the test is not valid.

Survey spin. How you word a question affects the way people answer it. Guess which of these two questions is more likely to get a useful answer about whether gym users would pay for babysitting: "Do you want a health club that provides babysitting?" or, "What is most important in a health club: modern equipment, personal trainers, or free babysitting?"

The best test is common sense. If a headline sounds too good—or bad—to be true, look closer. It may not be correct.

Active Learning

Pick one of two activities: 1. Find a graph that presents economic information using different units and axes that do not start at zero. Share your graph with a small group of classmates and have them analyze what makes the graph misleading. 2. Write one biased and one non-biased question that asks consumers about a product or service. Ask your questions to a small group of classmates, then compare and contrast the answers to analyze the effects of the question wording.

Service Businesses

Service businesses dominate the modern American economy. Most small businesses are service businesses. Even if a company manufactures products, it also provides services to its customers.

Services are intangible things that businesses do for us that enhance our lives. Insurance, tourism, banking, and education are all considered services. So are accounting, printing, dry cleaning, personal training, childcare, and tax preparation.

Home-Based Businesses

The number of businesses that start in the home has been growing rapidly and now represents about 52 percent of all small businesses. Using readily available and inexpensive online tools, a home-based business can have an image that is just as professional as that of a large corporation.

Many people who lose their jobs due to cutbacks choose to work from home in the field where they were once employed. A few examples of home-based businesses include consultants, sales representatives, tradespeople, writers, graphic designers, and Web developers. Even companies that produce products can be operated from the entrepreneur's home if the manufacturing and distribution of products are outsourced to other companies.

In addition, many companies now choose homesourcing to fill human resource needs. *Homesourcing* refers to the transfer of service industry employment from offices to home-based employees. JetBlue® Airways, for example, homesources its customer support to employees who work from their homes in Utah. This arrangement provides the airline with significant savings.

ETHICS and BUSINESS

Outsourcing Clinical Trials

Situation You and your partner in a biotechnology company are ready to test a new drug on human subjects. Your partner wants to outsource the clinical trials to another country in order to save money and get the trials completed quickly.

Conducting Research You have learned that the government agencies in the target country do little to regulate clinical trials. You have also learned that many researchers believe a drug should be tested within the population for which it is being developed because of possible genetic differences that could affect outcomes.

English Language Arts/Writing

Ethics or Profit It is not illegal to conduct clinical trials in the country your partner has selected, but the results of the trials are sometimes questioned. Do you feel it would be worth the ethical risk involved in conducting trials there in order to make a bigger profit?

1. Would you go along with your partner's suggestion to outsource clinical trials for your company's new drug?

2. Write a one-page memo explaining to your partner why you would or would not agree to have the new drugs tested this way.

Green Businesses

Each week a different company announces that it is "going green." John Doerr, one of the most famous venture capitalists in the world, has said that green products and services could be the largest economic opportunity of the 21st century. What is a green business? Green businesses design their business practices so that they promote sustainability. **Sustainability** means that a venture seeks to achieve economic, environmental, and social goals without compromising the ability of future generations to meet their own needs. Issues related to sustainability include food quality, energy resources, pollution, and human rights. Companies as large as General Electric and Wal-Mart have adjusted their business practices to try to promote sustainability.

Social Entrepreneurship

Social entrepreneurs start their businesses to improve society. **Social entrepreneurs** identify social needs, such as finding employment for veterans, combating pollution, or providing shoes for children who cannot afford them, and recognize these needs as opportunities. Other social entrepreneurship ventures focus on the arts—a community theater company, for example—or on education. While other businesses measure success in terms of profit, social entrepreneurs measure their success by the positive impact they make on society. Therefore, some social entrepreneurs form nonprofit organizations, a type of business ownership discussed in Chapter 7. Many social entrepreneurs, however, start or work for businesses that try to make positive social changes *and* make a profit. Other social entrepreneurs work for government agencies.

Focus on Technology

An increased reliance on technology is the main trend that affects businesses today. Entrepreneurs who know how to use technology to improve their business processes **create** a strong competitive advantage and enjoy a greater chance of success. Whether technology is a company's product or it is used to increase productivity, it is a critical component of any business strategy.

Outsourcing

In today's economy, you can outsource just about any business activity. **Outsourcing** is contracting with other companies for services. The most common type of outsourcing is business-process outsourcing, such as accounting, benefits and finance functions. Running a small business is a complex task, and few entrepreneurs are experts at everything. Outsourcing allows a small business to focus on what it does best while tapping into outside expertise.

For example, suppose you have created a new video game. You can pay a software programmer to develop your game, contract with a packaging company to design the product packaging, and then contract with a distributor to find retail outlets for your game.

Superfruits and Sustainability

Zola™ was founded in 2001 with the goal of creating products that are "Great for You and Great for the Planet." They produce a range of smoothies made from açaí berries. The company is committed to social responsibility by empowering Brazilian communities through partnership and sustainability. Zola's sustainability practices help to protect the trees of the Amazon.

◈ **Critical Thinking**
Find businesses in your area that are dedicated to sustainability practices. Write a paragraph identifying at least three sustainability practices and the impact they have on the environment.

Outsourcing Benefits

These are some of the many benefits to outsourcing:

- Outsourcing allows greater efficiency, saving time and money.
- Outsourcing decreases overhead investment or debt.
- Outsourcing lowers regulatory compliance burdens.
- Outsourcing allows companies to start new projects quickly.
- Outsourcing makes companies more attractive to investors because it allows companies to direct more capital into money-making activities.

Strategic Alliances

One step beyond outsourcing is to form a partnership with another company. This kind of partnership is known as a **strategic alliance**. Your small company may form an alliance with a larger company to supply it with a product or service that is not part of the larger company's core competency.

For example, 3M®, the manufacturer of adhesive products such as Scotch® brand tape, looks to partner with small companies for complementary products such as tape dispensers. They form a strategic alliance in which the small company provides 3M with all the tape dispensers it needs to package with its adhesive tape.

Corporate Ventures

A **corporate venture** is a new venture started inside a large corporation. Large companies find that they must act like entrepreneurs to innovate and remain competitive. It is difficult for a large company to behave like a small, flexible company. A solution is to start a small company as a spin-off. The parent company supplies resources to the corporate venturers to help the new venture get started. Often the new corporate venture eventually becomes an independent company.

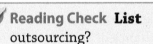 **Reading Check List** What are three benefits of outsourcing?

Learning to Recognize Opportunity

Entrepreneurial thinking is about generating ideas and recognizing opportunities. Entrepreneurial thinking involves training your mind to look at products and services in a different way and figuring out ways to improve upon them. To think like an entrepreneur, you also need to continuously learn about and evaluate other types of businesses. If you learn to think like an entrepreneur, you can position yourself to recognize opportunities as they develop.

Creativity and Innovation

You may wonder where ideas originate. How do people come up with great ideas? Is creativity something that comes naturally? Not necessarily. Can you learn to be creative? Absolutely!

In the Pipeline Scientific research often leads to innovations and new products. *What are some industries that rely heavily on scientific research?*

Creativity is the activity that results in **innovation**, which is finding new ways of doing things. Although everyone approaches creativity slightly differently, there are some definite patterns to the process. In general, all creativity leading to the invention of something new involves connection, discovery, invention, and application.

You make a connection when you bring together things that are not usually connected. For example, Leonardo da Vinci, the great inventor and painter, connected his observations about tree branches to the engineering of a canal system to carry water to the sea. A connection often leads to a discovery that is turned into an invention. In da Vinci's case, the invention was a hydraulic system to control water levels so that boats could cross under a bridge in his canal system. Application is going beyond the original invention to other uses in new areas. Da Vinci's application was the idea of mills powered by wind and water. Starting with a simple connection can produce a wealth of new and innovative ideas.

Idea or Opportunity

An idea is not the same thing as an opportunity. You generate ideas by thinking creatively. Opportunities are ideas that have commercial potential. Often an innovative opportunity can be turned into a business. Most good business opportunities result from the entrepreneur's alertness to unmet consumer needs and unfilled market niches. A **niche** is a small specialized market.

Understanding Industries

One way to identify opportunities is to understand industries. An industry is a grouping of businesses with a common purpose. In every industry, the landscape continuously changes. Changes in industries create profitable niches for new businesses to fill. The development of new products and services in any industry creates the need for complementary types of businesses.

If you know the inner workings of an industry and you examine and analyze industry trends, you can identify opportunities that exist as a result of those trends. You can also understand where the problems are that customers experience.

Strategies for Thinking Creatively

Creativity requires you to be aware of your surroundings. Use these strategies to activate your creativity and potentially develop new enterprise ideas:

- **Practice brainstorming.** When you **brainstorm**, you think freely to generate ideas. During brainstorming, ideas are not judged as good or bad. Even those that seem silly should be given a fair hearing initially.
- **Look at ordinary items in new ways.** Find a simple item, and figure out how many new products or uses you can find for it. With practice, you'll get better at seeing things in a different light.
- **Find creative solutions to common problems.** When you find yourself perplexed by a problem, think about how to find a solution. Have you ever used a flat-head screwdriver to pry something open? That's finding a creative solution to a problem.

Figure 3.1 — Removing the Roadblocks to Creativity

Believe in yourself.	Positive self-encouragement works.
Use nonlogical thinking.	Not everything has to make sense right away.
Free your mind!	Don't think of everything in practical terms.
Think positively.	View problems as challenges that offer opportunity to innovate.
Entertain all ideas.	There is no such thing as a frivolous idea.
Relax!	Relaxation is a key part of the creative process.
Have a playful attitude.	Don't worry about looking foolish.
Learn from experience.	Look at failure as a learning experience that will lead to success.
Model creative behavior.	Anyone can learn to think creatively.
Develop listening skills.	You can learn a lot by listening to other people talk about their wants and needs.

Enhance Your Creativity Entrepreneurs can stimulate and encourage creativity in many ways. *Can you think of any other techniques?*

- **Connect unrelated items.** Ask a friend to put together a tray of different items that have no relationship to each other. Then try to come up with a new product from the items. This forces you to look at things in new ways.

Challenges to Creativity

Being creative presents many different challenges. These challenges include time pressures, the influence of unsupportive people, a lack of confidence, and rigid thinking. The hardest challenges to overcome are the challenges you bring upon yourself. **Figure 3.1** outlines tips that will help you remove the roadblocks to creativity.

Creative Sources of Ideas

Good business ideas involve popular trends such as those described in **Figure 3.2**. Ideas can come to you from anywhere, and sometimes in the strangest moments. Research has found that some of the greatest ideas have come to people when they're brushing their teeth, driving, or sleeping. By incorporating some of the following activities into your life you can create an effective process for ongoing opportunity recognition.

● Figure 3.2	Business Opportunities from Popular Trends
Fitness and Health	Many people are concerned about improving their health and well-being.
Ethnic Products	Opportunities can be found with diverse groups that have particular tastes in food and other products and services.
Luxury Services	Leisure time, and the enjoyment of luxury products and services, has become popular.
Nostalgia	Technology has made many consumers look for products that remind them of the past, such as cupcakes, retro car designs, and oldies music.

● **Piece of Cake** You can find opportunities in traditional industries as well as new industries that did not exist five years ago. The secret to success is the ability to see these opportunities before anyone else does. *What are some other popular trends?*

Observe the World Around You

Start watching people. Find places in your community where you will be able to observe people. In a hotel lobby or a shopping mall, you can learn a lot about what people want and need. That is how Mary Naylor learned that people who work in office buildings wanted the same kind of concierge service offered in hotels. She was reading a mazagine on an airplane when the idea for the business came to her, and she later formed Capitol Concierge. Her business handles special services such as arranging for theater tickets, buying gifts, or making dinner reservations.

Watch for Demographic Changes

Demographics are personal characteristics that describe a population. These include age, gender, income, ethnic background, education, and occupation.

One demographic trend that affects entrepreneurship is the increasing diversity of the American people. Cultural diversity plays an important role in entrepreneurial ventures because it affects the kinds of products and services that entrepreneurs develop. Business owners who understand and appeal to the diversity of their customer base are more likely to succeed.

Be an Avid Reader

Most successful entrepreneurs stay on top of what is going on in business and in the world in general. You can do this by reading books, newspapers, magazines, and Websites every day. You should not read only in your own area of interest; sometimes reading about an unrelated field will spark an idea that you can apply to your field.

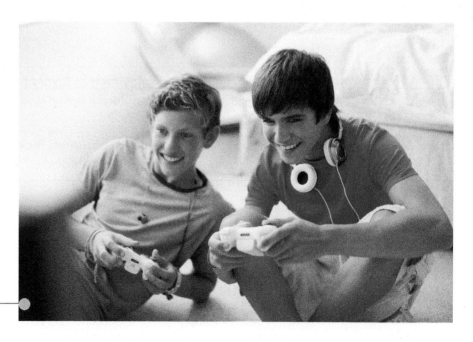

Avatars Web sites and games like *Second Life* ™ that allow players to create avatars, or characters, who represent them, need to be able to reflect their diverse customers. *What might happen if a site did not allow customers to create an avatar that reflects their diversity?*

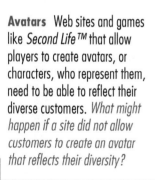

Paul Bradbury/OJO Images/age fotostock

Consider Your Own Experiences

Self-employment options within your own experiences are the easiest to identify and are excellent sources of opportunity. Look for opportunities in your interests, hobbies, and work.

Interests

Good business ideas often target problems observed in everyday life. Practice thinking about the problems you encounter each day as you pursue your interests. Then think about ways to solve the problems. Practicing these steps may help you think of great business ideas:

- List at least five of your interests.
- List at least one product or service you use while pursuing each of your interests.
- Identify one problem associated with each product or service.
- Describe ways you could improve each product or service.
- Evaluate whether any of your product or service improvements have business potential.

Hobbies

Many hobbies can be turned into successful ventures. Developing Websites, restoring cars, playing a sport, and making music are all pastimes that have potential. Try to evaluate your own favorite pastime in terms of its business potential. For example, suppose you play in a youth soccer league and you need a new type of protective gear that does not currently exist. You can use that experience as an idea source and turn that idea into an opportunity by designing and developing the gear you need.

Work

Your experiences in the world of work can be an excellent source of business ideas. When you work, you learn about the particular business you work in as well as the industry in which the business operates. You learn about the business's customers and suppliers and their wants and needs. You also learn about the technology used in the business and the industry and the government regulations that apply to the business and the industry.

These insights can help you to recognize opportunities. If you work after school, ask yourself:

- Is there room in the market for a similar business, possibly in a different niche?
- Are there any gaps in the company's network of suppliers? Is the company in need of services that are not being provided?
- Are the company's customers in need of products and services that are not provided?
- Has the evolution of technology altered business processes or created new business processes that provide new opportunities?

Tech Savvy

Green Chemistry

Method®, a company that produces cleaning supplies made with nontoxic, natural ingredients, is one of the fastest-growing companies in the United States. Founded in 2001, Method already has the whole consumer-packaged-goods industry following its lead. Method uses natural biological processes to create materials that are safe and high-performing. This approach is sometimes called green chemistry. Green chemistry examines not only a product's use, but where the product comes from and what happens when it is thrown away. Until recently, businesses were not looking into these issues. Increasingly, however, the market is pushing entrepreneurs to think small in order to go big. *Why do you think Method is growing so quickly?*

Consult Outside Sources

Look at people, places, and things in the business community for business ideas. Some outside sources to consult include trade magazines, specialty magazines, trade shows and exhibitions, newspapers, the Internet, and government agencies. As you explore these sources of information, routinely ask yourself, "What self-employment opportunities does this present to someone with my interests?"

Trade Magazines

A **trade magazine** is a periodical published for specific types of businesses or industries. Trade magazines often contain articles and advertisements about new products, services, or business concepts. They offer current, industry-specific news and access to the latest information on customers and market trends. Some also offer continuing education programs and networking opportunities. Many trade magazines are available on the Internet.

Specialty Magazines

A **specialty magazine** is a periodical that targets people with special interests in sports, camping, fashion, and a variety of other areas. A potential entrepreneur can use specialty magazines to identify the interests and needs of potential consumers. They can be a great source of ideas for new business ventures.

Trade Shows and Exhibitions

Nearly every field has national or regional trade shows. At a **trade show**, vendors and manufacturers introduce new items and promote established products and services. At a trade show, you can see exhibits and demonstrations of goods and services. These shows can be a source of spin-off ideas. Contact your local chamber of commerce or search the Internet for times and dates of shows and exhibitions.

Newspapers

Newspapers provide an ongoing source of ideas for businesses. Many have business sections that report on trends and innovations. Other sections of the paper, such as sports or lifestyle, can pinpoint problems people have that can be sources of opportunity for you. Most newspapers are on the Internet, which makes it easy to search for topics.

The Internet

The Internet can be a great source of opportunities and inspiration. Many sites offer ideas for entrepreneurs. You can explore successful businesses that currently exist. Social media can also introduce or encourage opportunities. Remember, however, that the best opportunities lie in the gaps where businesses have not yet gone. You want to find opportunities that serve unmet needs in the market.

Government Agencies

The federal government can be a source of new product ideas. The Bureau of Economic Analysis in the Department of Commerce, for example, publishes a survey of current business conditions.

The files of the U.S. Patent Office contain detailed descriptions of new products. Although the patents themselves are protected, they frequently include information that suggests other marketable product ideas. The U.S. Patent Office also publishes the *Official Gazette*, a weekly periodical that summarizes each patent granted and lists all patents available for license or sale.

New product ideas can also come in response to government regulations. For example, the Occupational Safety and Health Act included a government regulation that small businesses must keep a first aid kit on site. The legislation detailed the specific contents of the required kit. Entrepreneurs responded to the new regulation by manufacturing first aid kits with the required components and marketing them to small businesses that had to comply with the regulation.

SECTION 3.1 Review

After You Read ▪▪▪▪▪▪▪▪▪▪▪▪▪

Self-Check

1. **Identify** two current changes and trends that are a source for new enterprise ideas.
2. **Define** demographics and explain how they affect business.
3. **Explain** important ways that you can increase your chances of spotting an opportunity.

Think

4. **Describe** how brainstorming, creative thinking, and observations can be used to develop new enterprise ideas.

English Language Arts

5. **Research and Write** When scientists work to solve human problems—cure disease, create renewable sources of energy, slow climate change—they create new knowledge and invent new technologies. These advances in science and technology often spark the creation of new businesses. Cell phones and hybrid cars are examples of products invented by scientists and brought to the market by entrepreneurs. Choose a hi-tech product that you use frequently, and research the history of its development. Write a paragraph identifying the scientists and entrepreneurs who contributed to its success.

Go to connectED.mcgraw-hill.com to check your answers.

Starting Versus Buying a Business

Reading Guide

Before You Read ==============

Connect Why is it sometimes less risky to buy an existing business instead of starting one from scratch?

The Main Idea
Whether you start a business or buy an existing one, make sure it is compatible with your personal values and goals.

Objectives
Identify the importance of personal values and goals in choosing an entrepreneurial pursuit.
Examine the challenges and rewards of entering a family business.
Determine the benefits and drawbacks of buying a business.
Describe how you can evaluate a business opportunity.

List the advantages and disadvantages of starting your own business.

Content Vocabulary
◇ values
◇ goodwill
◇ franchise
◇ franchisee
◇ franchisor
◇ business broker

Academic Vocabulary
You will see these words in your reading and on your tests. Use the academic vocabulary glossary to look up their meanings.
■ objective
■ acquire

Graphic Organizer
Draw a Venn diagram like the one shown. As you read, write notes about franchisees and franchisors in the appropriate oval. Write notes that apply to both in the overlapping section,

⟨✈⟩ Go to connectED.mcgraw-hill.com to download this graphic organizer.

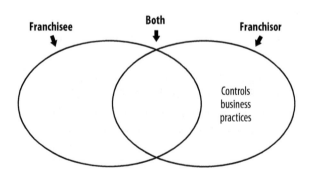

Franchisee Both Franchisor

Controls business practices

Personal Values and Goals

Owning a business is a huge responsibility and therefore a major decision to make. Deciding whether to buy or start a business can be easier if you consider your personal values and goals. Your core **values** are the beliefs and principles you choose to live by. Your values define who you are, shape your attitudes and your choices, and help you identify your priorities. Values are usually influenced by family, religious beliefs, teachers, friends, society, and personal experiences. Honesty, responsibility, courage, and hard work are examples of some of the values that are shared by many people despite their cultural differences.

Core values do not change in different situations, and they endure over time. Once you have identified your core values, you can use them to lay out goals for your future and guide your entrepreneurial pursuits. Goals are the **objectives** you are trying to achieve. Other factors that will affect your choice of business include your personality, abilities, lifestyle needs, background, hobbies, interests, experience, and financial resources.

● **As You Read** ▪ ▪ ▪ ▪ ▪ ▪ ▪
Describe What are some of the personal values that you might apply in your business?

Entering the Family Business

If your family owns a business, chances are you have had the opportunity to work there during the summers or after school. Perhaps you have even thought about taking over the business one day. Joining a family business is one way to experience entrepreneurship. Family businesses are an important part of the U.S. economy. Although they are typically smaller enterprises, some, such as Mattel™ Toys, Marriott™ Corporation, Comcast™, and Fidelity Investments™, have become large, successful companies.

The Rewards and Challenges of Family Businesses

Although family businesses have great potential for success, only about one-third of them survive to the second generation. The reason so many family businesses fail lies in the dynamics of the family itself. Some families work well together, and others do not.

The greatest advantage of a family business is the trust and togetherness that family members share. A family working as a team can often achieve more than its individual members can. At the same time, one of the greatest disadvantages of a family enterprise is that its owners can never get away from the business.

● ● ● ● ● **Web Savvy**

Embedded Videos
YouTube is the most popular video sharing Website in the world. YouTube also allows users to view its content on Webpages outside the site. Each YouTube video is accompanied by an HTML (Hypertext Markup Language) tag, which can be used to embed it, or link it permanently, on a page outside the YouTube Web site. Users often use these tags to embed YouTube videos on blogs or social networking sites. *Why would YouTube allow users to access its content on other sites?*

Therefore, they may have difficulty viewing the venture and its problems objectively. Another common source of conflict is parents who are unable to see their child as a business person capable of making wise decisions and taking responsibility.

To minimize family conflicts and prevent some of the problems that family businesses face, it is important to establish clear lines of responsibility, be objective about family members' qualifications, keep decisions unaffected by personal emotions, and respect individual family members' needs.

Questions to Ask Yourself

Before entering a family business, ask yourself these questions:
- Do I have the ability to work for a member of my family?
- Do I get along well with the family members who will be involved in the business?
- Do we share the same goals for the business?
- Do we share the same general goals for our personal lives?
- Can we be clear and specific about our expectations of each other?
- Can I leave business problems at work when I go home each night?
- Can we maintain a positive family relationship?

If you answered no to any one of these questions, you have identified a potential area of conflict. However, if the benefits to joining the family business outweigh the drawbacks, it will be worth your while to find a way to resolve the conflict.

> **Reading Check** **Summarize** What can you do to minimize conflict in a family business?

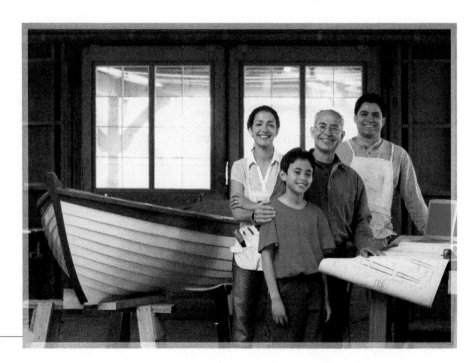

A Family Affair A family working as a team can often achieve more than its individual members can. *What is one potential problem that may occur in a family business?*

Buying an Existing Business

Another way to **acquire** a business is to buy an existing one. In many respects, buying a business is less risky than starting a new one because the employees are already hired and trained, the equipment is already in place, and the company already has customers. Customers are especially important. Their continued business after you take over increases your chances of success. Such loyalty, called **goodwill**, is an extremely valuable business asset.

Acquiring an existing business has other advantages. An existing business usually has established procedures in place. There may be substantial inventory on hand and trade credit to facilitate future purchases. The owner may even offer some expertise during the transition period.

Buying a Franchise

A franchise is another way to purchase a business opportunity. With a franchise, you can buy the right to set up a new business patterned on an existing model. A **franchise** is a legal agreement to begin a new business in the name of a recognized company. It gives the **franchisee** (buyer) the right to a product, process, or service; training and assistance in setting up the business; and ongoing marketing and quality support while the business is in operation. The most important advantage of buying a franchise is that the entrepreneur does not have to incur all of the risks associated with starting a new business.

The franchisee usually buys into a business that has an accepted name, product, or service. Chuck E. Cheese™, Chick-fil-A™, and McDonald's™ are all examples of franchises. The buyers of these franchises pay a fee and an annual royalty on sales, typically 3 to 8 percent.

The seller is the **franchisor**. The franchisee is buying a way of operating a business and a product with name recognition. The franchisor is selling its planning and management expertise.

If you buy a McDonald's franchise, you will be trained in methods of operation, learn how to prepare McDonald's products, and be supplied through McDonald's distribution channels. You will also have the benefit of the company's national advertising efforts. All of these things reduce the risk of failure.

Before buying a franchise, however, make sure you understand all of the costs and limitations involved. For one thing, the franchisor can restrict how you run the business. Also, investigate the market saturation. The best locations may already be taken, or another franchisee may have a location too close to yours, which will make it difficult to secure enough customers to succeed.

Evaluating a Business Opportunity

Whether you buy a regular business or a franchised business, it is important to evaluate whether the business is a good prospect. Many businesses are put up for sale because they are not successful.

GLOBAL WORKPLACE — A Multicultural Australia

Thanks to an open immigration policy, 24 percent of Australia's population comes from more than 200 countries. According to the government document "A New Agenda for Multicultural Australia," the nation's diversity is "a source of competitive advantage, cultural enrichment, and social stability."

Niche Markets Diverse populations offer many opportunities for entrepreneurs, who can target smaller market segments, called niche markets, and design products or services specifically for them. Big companies are often unable to serve niche markets profitably because they are too small.

Social Studies

Write a paragraph about ways in which businesses can make use of their employees' diverse backgrounds.

Australia at a Glance	
Population	22,507,617
Median Age	38 years
Life Expectancy	87.1 years
GDP	$998.3 billion
CO_2 Emissions	392 million tons
Literacy Rate	99%
Internet Users	15.81 million

Why is it for sale? It may be losing money or may have a poor reputation, which can be impossible to repair. Inventory may be dated, and equipment or facilities may need repairs. Employees may lack the skills needed to keep the business competitive. The owner may also simply be tired of running a business.

Every business has problems, but some problems are more critical than others. In order to prevent yourself from purchasing a business burdened with serious problems, you should investigate the company and the industry carefully. Do not rely only on what the seller tells you. Talk to customers, employees, and suppliers.

In addition, you can hire an accountant to verify the value of the business's inventory, accounts receivable, and assets. You can also hire an attorney to advise you and to investigate the business for any legal liabilities.

Where to Find a Business

People find businesses in many ways. The simplest way is to look in the newspaper. Businesses that are for sale are listed in local papers as well as national business publications such as the *Wall Street Journal*. The most effective way to locate a business is to network with people in the community. Accountants, attorneys, bankers, and local government administrators are good sources. Let them know what kind of business you are looking for. Then keep in touch with them.

You can also hire a business broker. A **business broker** is someone whose job is to bring buyers and sellers together. You can find business brokers in the telephone book or online.

Questions to Ask

Before you purchase a business, ask these questions:

- **Is the business interesting to me and to others?** Make sure that you really enjoy it and that there are plenty of existing customers who are interested in the business.
- **Why is the owner selling?** Owners sell for many reasons— retirement, lack of interest, illness, and need for cash. You will want to know if the owner is selling for these more personal reasons or because the business is not doing well or the industry is in decline. Check the firm's financial statements against information from suppliers and competitors.
- **What is the business's potential for growth?** Once businesses are born, they go through a life cycle of growth, maturity, and decline. Determine where the business is positioned in this life cycle. It is best to avoid a business or industry in the decline stage. Although it is possible to turn a declining enterprise to a growth stage, you cannot reverse an economic trend.

Starting Your Own Business

When you cannot find an existing business that meets your needs, you will need to start from scratch. Starting a business has many advantages. You can do things your own way, and you can build the company with fresh ideas and enthusiasm.

Questions to Ask

Before you start your own business, ask yourself these questions:

- Do I have the motivation to start a new business from nothing?
- Does the business align with my personality, abilities, values, and goals?
- Do I have sufficient knowledge of basic operations to undertake the business?
- Do I have the necessary managerial ability?
- Do I have the right partners to help me with the business?
- Do I have enough financial resources to start from scratch?
- Am I willing to accept the risk?

The answers to the preceding questions are deceptively simple, but the actual process of starting a new business is very complex. It requires extensive planning and resource gathering. As an entrepreneur, you will be responsible for gathering and processing all of this information. You will also need to think creatively about every aspect of the business.

What You Must Do

Some of the tasks involved in starting a business are listed below:
- Test the feasibility of your concept in the market to see if there are enough customers to make the effort worthwhile.
- Decide on a traditional business with a physical location or an online business or a combination of both.
- Prepare a business plan to seek capital, partners, and employees.
- Secure professional advisors—accountant, lawyer, etc.
- Hire employees and initiate relationships with suppliers.
- Purchase equipment and set up distribution channels.
- Create awareness for the business.

SECTION 3.2 Review

After You Read

Self-Check
1. **Identify** the role your goals play in the decision to buy or start a business.
2. **Explain** why you would start your own business instead of buying an existing one.
3. **List** three questions you should ask yourself before starting a business.

Think
4. **Describe** the relationship between franchising and other forms of business ownership.

Mathematics
5. **Number Relationships** Julia started a home-based business baking specialty cakes for parties. The table below shows the cost of ingredients for three different cakes and the price she charges for each. Write an equation that shows the relationship between the cost of ingredients (C) and the price charged (P).

Type of Cake	Cost of Ingredients	Price Charged
Birthday Cake	$3	$16
Sheet Cake	$13	$66
Wedding Cake	$25	$126

Math Concept **Patterns and Functions** The price charged for the cake is a function of the cost of its ingredients. Each pair of numbers is related in the same way.

Step 1 To find the pattern, look at the relationship between the cost and the price. How is it calculated?

Step 2 Write an equation using C to represent cost and P to represent the resulting price.

Go to connectED.mcgraw-hill.com to check your answers.

Entrepreneurs *in Action*

Mya Jacobson
Owner of Feed Your Soul

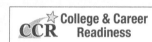

Q *What do you do?*

A I own Feed Your Soul, a gourmet cookie company.

Q *What kind of training and education led you to this job?*

A It's funny how life works. Prior to the conception of my company, I was a trader on the American Stock Exchange. I went to law school in the evenings and one day decided that it was time to do something more creative, more fulfilling—more "me." As for training and education, when I look back, I see it was my business knowledge, my legal background, and my life experiences that truly allowed me to follow my dreams. My advice is to always do what you love and be passionate about what you do, but make sure you plan strategically so that you can survive and prosper.

Q *What do you enjoy most about your job?*

A I love interacting with people and creating a product that so many people can enjoy.

Q *How did you become interested in your field?*

A I have always had a love for baking and for creating the perfect gift for the people in my life. I asked myself: What is it that I am passionate about? What makes me feel alive? What are the things in life that truly feed my soul? I combined my love for baking (oven-fresh, all-natural cookies), writing (each gift includes an inspirational message), and giving (a portion of the proceeds from every purchase is donated to the purchaser's charity choice), and created a culture in a brand based on a simple and timeless concept.

CCR ☆ **College & Career Readiness**

Make a Menu Write creative descriptions of menu items you would offer at a bakery.

1. Using word-processing software, describe five items you offer on your menu.
2. Using a photo editing or clip art program, select and edit images for each of your descriptions.
3. Combine the pieces to a make a menu. The menu can be factual or artistic but should include your descriptions, prices, and images.

Career Facts

Real-World Skills	Academic Skills	Career Cluster
Speaking, Listening, Problem Solving	Mathematics, English Language Arts	Agriculture, Food & Natural Resources

Review and Assessment

Visual Summary

Recognizing Opportunity

Before You Buy Owning a business is a huge reponsibility and a major decision to make.

Starting versus Buying

↓

identify your priorities

↓

evaluate the opportunity

↓

find the business

Opportunity The ability to recognize new opportunities and to think creatively are essential.

Business Trends

- strategic alliances
- internet
- nonprofit
- service
- socially responsible
- home-based
- green

Javier Larrea/Pixtal/age fotostock

Review and Assessment

Vocabulary

1. On a sheet of paper, use each of these terms and words in a written sentence.

Content Vocabulary

◇ online business
◇ services
◇ sustainability
◇ outsourcing
◇ social entrepreneurs
◇ strategic alliance
◇ corporate venture
◇ innovation

◇ niche
◇ brainstorm
◇ demographics
◇ trade magazine
◇ specialty magazine
◇ values
◇ goodwill
◇ franchise

◇ franchisee
◇ franchisor
◇ business broker
◇ trade show

Academic Vocabulary

■ create
■ conduct
■ acquire
■ objective

Key Concepts

2. **Examine** some current trends that provide opportunity for entrepreneurs.
3. **Identify** different ways to recognize opportunities.
4. **Explain** how to think creatively about opportunity.
5. **Determine** ways to find creative business ideas.
6. **Identify** the importance of personal values and goals in choosing an entrepreneurial pursuit.
7. **Examine** the challenges and rewards of entering a family business.
8. **Determine** the benefits and drawbacks of buying a business.
9. **List** the advantages and disadvantages of starting your own business.

Academic Skills

Mathematics

10. **Fruit Baskets** Ramsey is assembling fruit baskets to sell in his store during the holiday season. He has 36 apples, 24 bananas, and 18 kiwis. What is the greatest number of baskets he can make using the same number of each type of fruit in each basket? How many pieces of each type of fruit will go into each basket?

    Math Concept **Factoring** Factors are the numbers you multiply to get another number. To find the Greatest Common Factor (GCF) of a group of numbers, list all of their factors, and look for the greatest factor that they all share.
    Step 1 Determine the common factors of 36, 24, and 18. Look for the GCF.
    Step 2 Divide each number by the GCF to determine how many pieces of each type of fruit will go into each basket.

English Language Arts/Vocabulary

11. **Related Words** The words *franchise*, *franchisee*, and *franchisor* make a word family. Find and list other word triplets in which new words are built using the suffixes *-ee* and *-or* (or *-er*). Write a definition for the suffixes *-ee* and *-or* (or *-er*) as they are used in these word families.

Academic Skills *(continued)*

Social Studies

12. **Risk Management** Political risk is a big concern for entrepreneurs expanding businesses to other countries. The potential loss of an entire investment due to change in government policies can alter plans. Research what happened to Hong Kong's business community, both domestic and foreign, after its sovereignty reverted back to the People's Republic of China. Write a one-page report on your findings for the class.

Science

13. **Greener Products** Work with a partner to research the twelve principles of green chemistry. Develop an idea for a product that meets at least three of these principles. Create an advertisement for the product, highlighting its relation to the principles of green chemistry.

Real-World Skills

Financial Literacy

14. **Where Credit Is Due** Duke is starting a family business with his sister Margo. Duke and Margo do not have much start-up cash, so they want to use credit cards to purchase items for their business. Research interest rates, annual fees, and grace periods from three major credit card companies. Summarize your findings in a one-page report.

21st Century Skills

Life and Career Skills

15. **Social and Cross-Cultural Skills** Use a search engine to research the etiquette for exchanging business cards in two different countries. Working with a classmate, prepare a short presentation showing the proper way to exchange business cards in each country.

Connect to Your Community

16. **Cash in on Your Passion** Consider the hobbies and activities that interest you. What types of businesses in your community have made an entrepreneurial pursuit of these hobbies and activities? Prepare a list to present to the class.

17. **Locally Franchised** Working in teams, prepare a list of franchises in your town. Assign each team member a different franchise to research. Be sure to find out the cost of the franchise, the planning, training and management expertise offered, and the national advertising available. Each team member should present their findings to the class.

Competitive Events Prep

18. **Situation** You are the assistant manager of a business that is exceeding sales and growth projections. The owner is considering opening another business. However, she would like to open a different type of business rather than expand the current one. Since the owner knows that you have taken business classes, she wants your advice about outside sources of information for business ideas. She wants to discuss each source of information and have you explain the types of information each provides.

Activity Prepare an outline of the information you will present to the business owner.

Evaluation You will be evaluated on how well you meet these performance indicators:
- Describe external resources useful during concept development.
- Explain tools used by entrepreneurs for venture planning.
- Describe entrepreneurial planning considerations.
- Use external resources to supplement entrepreneur's expertise.
- Address people properly.

 Go to **connectED.mcgraw-hill.com** for more information about this activity and other competitive events.

Standardized Test Practice

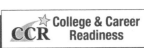
CCR ☆ **College & Career Readiness**

Directions Choose the letter of the best answer. Write the letter for the answer on a separate piece of paper. For question #2, if the answer is False, rewrite the statement to make it true.

1. A _____ is the buyer of a franchise who is given the right to its product, process, or service.
   A. corporate venture
   B. franchisee
   C. business broker
   D. franchisor

2. In the world of entrepreneurs, ideas and opportunities are basically the same thing.
   T
   F

Test-Taking Tip
Look for key words in test directions. For example, choose, describe, compare, and write a sentence are key words and phrases that tell you how to answer a question.

Global Opportunities

Chapter Objectives

Discovery Project
Understanding International Markets

Key Question *What do business owners need to know in order to succeed in other countries?*

Project Goal

Work with a small group to research the customs and culture of a different country. Determine how the customs and cultural differences might impact businesses. Analyze what a U.S. company would need to know to successfully conduct business in that country.

Think About...
➤ *What country will you research?*
➤ *How will you determine which customs will impact business collaborations?*
➤ *How will you present your research?*

21ˢᵗ Century Skills
Global Awareness *What do foreign business owners need to to know to succeed in your community?*

Evaluate

 Go to connectED.mcgraw-hill.com to download a rubric that you can use to evaluate your final project.

Ask AN EXPERT

Q: *I am considering investing in markets outside of the United States. What are financial risks I might face when investing overseas?*

A: *When you invest in international markets, your return is affected by how well your investments perform and by the fluctuating values of your domestic currency. For example, if the U.S. dollar gains in value against the currencies of the countries where you are invested, any earnings will be worth less than they would be had you invested using the currency in which the investment was priced.*

F1 online digitale Bildagentur GmbH/Alamy

Connect the Photo

Nín hǎo, Bonjour! Hello! From the rugged plateaus of China to the boutique cafés in Paris, countries around the world are linked in the global economy. Understanding the different cultures, traditions, and customs are necessary to conduct respectful business. Whether exploring business in person or via social media, the global business network presents various opportunities. Bon chance! *How has social media changed communication in the global economy?*

Global Entrepreneurship

Reading Guide

Before You Read ■■■■■■■■■■■■■■

Connect In what ways have you seen the effects of a global economy?

The Main Idea

The countries of the world are linked in a global economy made possible by free trade agreements and advances in communication technology.

Objectives

Describe the role of entrepreneurship in today's multicultural, global economy.

Explain why the global market is important.

List current trends that provide both domestic and global opportunities for entrepreneurs.

Content Vocabulary

◇ global economy   ◇ trade barrier
◇ exporting   ◇ tariff
◇ importing   ◇ gross domestic product (GDP)

Academic Vocabulary

You will see these words in your reading and on your tests. Use the academic vocabulary glossary to look up their meanings.

■ domestic   ■ region

Graphic Organizer

Before you read this section, draw a Venn diagram like the one shown. As you read, fill in the diagram with concepts that apply to importing, exporting, or both.

 Go to connectED.mcgraw-hill.com to download this graphic organizer.

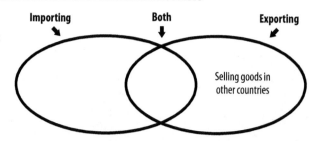

Importing   Both   Exporting

Selling goods in other countries

Global Entrepreneurship

Take a look at some of the things you own—your bike, your smart phone, even your favorite pair of jeans. They may have an American brand name or label. However, there is a good chance they were made in another country. Businesses sell and buy goods and services to and from other countries. In this section, you will learn about the global challenges and opportunities facing entrepreneurs today. You will also learn why international trade is so important to the U.S. economy.

The Global Economy

We live in a global economy. The **global economy** is the interconnected economies of the nations of the world. Entrepreneurship plays an important role in today's multicultural global society by engaging in the exporting and importing of goods. **Exporting** is the selling and shipping of goods to another country. **Importing** is buying or bringing in goods from other countries to sell.

When you purchase a laptop computer that was made in South Korea and is sold in the United States, South Korea benefits from a bigger market for the goods that it produces. The U.S. company that purchased the laptop computer from South Korea and sold it to you benefits from being able to offer a wider variety of products to its customers. You benefit by buying high-quality equipment at a competitive price.

©Terry Vine/Blend Images LLC

Off the Hook Call centers in India, where labor is less expensive, provide support to businesses in the international community with sales, technical support, and other services. *What are some of the key technologies that have made global business thrive?*

ETHICS and BUSINESS

Outsourcing for Increased Profitability

Situation You have been researching the pros and cons of outsourcing some of your company's workload to another country where the costs of labor are lower. You believe that the use of outsourcing will save your company as much as 20% in salaries and benefits.

Possible Drawbacks As you discuss your idea with your managers, one of them voices the concern that outsourcing work will lead to layoffs in the company. The layoffs will add to the already high unemployment rate in this country and will further weaken the economy.

English Language Arts/Writing

Comparing Costs Business owners must try to keep their costs low so they can compete with other businesses and make a profit. But what if cost cutting for a higher profit means laying off employees? Is this right?

1. How could you lower costs without laying off any employees?
2. Create a list of ideas for cutting costs.

If you are a small business owner today, you may purchase and sell goods or services to customers in other countries. You may also have goods manufactured in other countries or have competitors who are based in other countries. Two important factors that have brought about a global economy are a reduction in trade tariffs and advances in communications technology, particularly the Internet.

Trade Barriers Have Fallen

The World Trade Organization is a global coalition of governments that makes the rules that govern international trade. It works to eliminate or lessen trade barriers and promote free trade. A **trade barrier** is a restriction on goods entering or leaving a country. The lowering of trade barriers has increased the flow of goods among countries.

A **tariff** is a type of trade barrier. Tariffs are taxes imposed by a government on imported or exported goods, although primarily on imported goods. Governments often charge import tariffs to protect **domestic** industries.

Because of the North American Free Trade Agreement (NAFTA) between the United States, Mexico, and Canada, exporting and importing among these countries has become far more profitable. The European Union (EU) is Europe's trading bloc. The goal of the EU is to promote free trade and a shared currency among member nations.

Technology Has Made the World Smaller

In recent years, there have been major advances in technology. Developments in communication, information processing, and transportation technology have transformed the way business is done. The Internet has dramatically affected trade between countries by bringing world markets within reach of anyone. Today it is easier than ever to communicate with people in other countries by phone, with e-mail, and over the Internet and social media. Even small businesses can reach customers anywhere in the world.

 Reading Check **Recall** What effect have new technologies had on world markets?

Global Opportunities

The international market is several times the size of the U.S. market. It holds many opportunities for growing businesses. Cultural differences mean you have to study each country before attempting to do business there. Each year, the U.S. Department of Commerce lists the top countries and regions for exporting U.S. goods. You will find them listed in **Figure 4.1** on page 82. Today these countries and **regions** make up more than 25 percent of the world's gross domestic product. **Gross domestic product (GDP)** is the total value of all goods produced during the year.

Asia

Asia is an enormous and diverse continent that includes many unique and sophisticated markets, from India to Japan. Asia is also a growing source of products and services to the world. Many countries outsource their manufacturing to China and their information systems to India, where wages are low relative to countries like the United States.

China

In China, the government controls business, and laws and regulations are fairly strict. The Chinese government has, however, been making it easier for U.S. companies to do business in China. China is the fastest-growing economy in the world, and it is looking for new products and services from other countries that will help it grow.

Japan

In the past, marketers have called Japan a "closed" society. This meant it was hard to sell products that were not Japanese. Many Japanese people hold their culture in high regard. Some Japanese consumers prefer not to be influenced by other countries.

U.S. fast-food companies entered the Japanese market successfully by offering Japanese foods alongside the American favorites. Marketers came to realize that it was important to understand Japan's unique traditions, religion, and culture. Today, many Japanese consumers consider foreign or imported products, especially clothing and fashion accessories, to be highly desirable.

As You Read ━━━━━━
Explain How do U.S. consumers benefit from imported goods?

Figure 4.1 — Top Importers of U.S. Goods

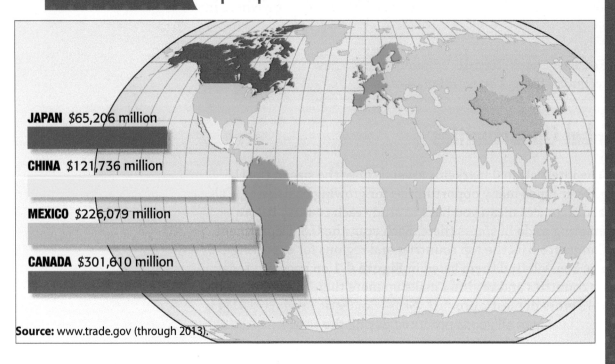

JAPAN $65,206 million

CHINA $121,736 million

MEXICO $226,079 million

CANADA $301,610 million

Source: www.trade.gov (through 2013).

Top Importers Finding out which countries and regions import American goods and services is a good start for your export business. *Which country imports the most American goods?*

Those companies that have found success in Japan have learned to provide advertising and products that make use of five fundamental beliefs: humor, fantasy, harmony, collective material success, and things uniquely Japanese.

Latin America

Like Asia, Latin America is a diverse community of nations with many cultural differences. Latin America includes very traditional cultures as well as modern cultures. Latin America consists of the countries of South America and portions of North America, including Central America and the islands of the Caribbean. People who live in Latin America speak Spanish, Portuguese, and French, among other languages.

Latin Americans tend to make buying decisions based on their family's needs rather than on one person's individual needs. Because of this, Latin Americans tend to choose products that will benefit the whole family.

Latin American consumers more often look at the merits of the products and do comparison shopping before they buy. In some countries, such as Mexico, consumers prefer U.S. goods. This presents a good opportunity for entrepreneurs.

Europe

In Europe, risk taking and business failure are not as accepted as they are in other parts of the world. However, that attitude is changing. More Europeans are becoming entrepreneurs. Englishman Richard Branson, for example, founded Virgin Atlantic Airways® and Virgin Records®.

Many Cultures

Europe is a difficult market to define because there is no common European culture. The conversion of European currency to the euro made commerce easier, but there are still considerable cultural differences. For example, Italy is very different from France. French people are more likely to eat in restaurants than Italians are. Italy's culture is very individualistic, whereas France's culture is more collectivist.

Marketing in Europe

Products that do well in one European country may not do well in another. Marketers attempt to seek out cultural information that will help them market across Europe. This information includes how people respond to uncertainty, the degree of individualism in the country, how individuals perceive power, the distribution of wealth, and masculinity. Marketers then use this information to create targeted campaigns. The same product may be promoted in one country with ads that display assertive, achievement-oriented behavior. In another country, the ads for the product might emphasize environmental consciousness and compassion.

Where cultural differences are small, marketing products across borders works well. Where cultural differences are great, products of one country may not sell well in the other. Marketers need to segment markets by cultural similarities rather than by national boundaries.

Tech Savvy

Thought-Controlled Robots

When it comes to robotics, Japan leads the world. More than half of all industrial robots used for manufacturing are found in Japan. Now Honda®, the Japanese carmaker, has developed a helmet that lets humans control robots by thought. The helmet reads patterns of electrical currents on a person's scalp and changes in blood flow in the brain. If the person wearing the helmet thinks about moving his or her hand, the helmet detects this and sends a wireless command to ASIMO™, a human-shaped robot developed by the company. After a few seconds, Asimo will move its own hand. *What kinds of opportunities could robots like Asimo provide to entrepreneurs?*

Need a Ride? New York City, New York, has one of the most efficient subway systems in the world. More than 4.3 million people ride the subway every day. *What kinds of products or services would be popular in New York City? what kinds would not?*

Lars A. Niki

Regions in Transition

Unstable or developing countries offer a risky form of opportunity for entrepreneurs. There are many barriers to starting up a business in such countries, including a lack of infrastructure, a shifting political landscape, and a lack of support once the business is in operation. Some examples of unstable or developing countries include certain African nations, members of the former Soviet Union, and parts of the Middle East. When doing business in unstable nations, research the culture and business practices carefully. Then consider partnering with a local company. Be sure you know your rights.

Entrepreneurship in the Global Marketplace

As the world shifts toward a truly integrated global economy, more and more businesses are getting involved in international business. Operating an international business is different from operating a domestic business for many reasons.

- Countries differ in their cultures, political systems, economic systems, legal systems, and levels of economic development.
- Cultural differences make the management of an international business more complicated than the management of a domestic business.
- Cross-border business transactions require an in-depth understanding of the rules of international trade.
- An international business must have policies for dealing with movements in exchange rates.

SECTION 4.1 | Review

After You Read ▪▪▪▪▪▪▪▪▪▪▪▪▪

Self-Check
1. **Discuss** two reasons for the current state of the global economy.
2. **Explain** what tariffs are and how they inhibit free trade.
3. **Define** gross domestic product.

Think
4. **Describe** the role you see technology playing in your ability to market products to other parts of the world.

English Language Arts
5. **Write to Explain** Explanatory paragraphs are often structured as a statement followed by examples. Imagine that you own and manage an import/export business. Write a paragraph explaining to your employees how to prepare for a first meeting with clients from another country.

Go to connectED.mcgraw-hill.com to check your answers.

Ways to Enter the Global Market

Reading Guide

Before You Read ▪▪▪▪▪▪▪▪▪▪▪▪▪▪▪

Connect Why do you need to understand the culture of the country in which you do business?

The Main Idea

To conduct international business successfully, you must understand foreign customs and cultures. Whether you choose to import or export products, the international market presents many profitable business opportunities.

Objectives

Identify the benefits and risks of international trade.
Explain how to find the best international markets.
Compare and contrast importing and exporting.

Content Vocabulary

◇ interpreter
◇ Standard Industrial Trade Classification (SITC) codes
◇ International Business Exchange (IBEX)
◇ trade missions
◇ "best prospect" list
◇ disposable income
◇ trade intermediary
◇ foreign joint venture
◇ export management company
◇ freight forwarder

Academic Vocabulary

You will see these words in your reading and on your tests. Use the academic vocabulary glossary to look up their meanings.
▪ contact   ▪ overseas

Graphic Organizer

Before you read this section, draw a chart like the one shown. As you read, write down five ways to show respect for foreign cultures.

 Go to connectED.mcgraw-hill.com to download this graphic organizer.

Respecting Foreign Cultures
1. Be punctual.
2.
3.
4.
5.

Understanding International Business

Understanding how other countries conduct business is important to your success as an entrepreneur. In this section, you will learn about differences in business customs. You will also learn how to modify business practices to facilitate interaction in the global marketplace.

The Importance of Culture

When you travel abroad for business, you should prepare by studying the customs in the country you are visiting. Failing to do so may keep you from closing an important business deal. For example, American business owners often travel to Japan in a hurry to close a transaction. They may allow themselves just a few days to negotiate an important business deal.

Japanese businesspeople, by contrast, do not feel this same time pressure to complete a deal. They want to get to know the person they are doing business with before they complete the transaction. Trust is very important to the Japanese and to people in many other countries. Because of this, they are willing to take the time to make sure that you are trustworthy.

Language and Culture Less than half a year after a Japanese version of Twitter was introduced, Japanese was the second-most-used language on Twitter. *What key factors are important to remember when doing business with another country?*

Tips for Showing Respect

It is important to show respect and understanding for the cultures of the people with whom you do business. Here are some tips.

- Dress conservatively.
- Do not correct the other person's use of English. Instead, make an effort to learn a few key words in the local language.
- Be prepared to remove your shoes in some situations. This shows respect.
- Respect different tastes in food.
- Do your homework before the first meeting. You should know something about the country and its culture.
- Build a relationship before you do business. The goal is to build trust with your potential business partner.
- If necessary, bring an **interpreter** to translate the other person's language into English.

Ken Seet/Corbis Images/SuperStock

Entering the Global Market

The world market is huge. There are count-less international opportunities for entrepreneurs who are willing to take the risk and go global. But how do you go about finding the best place to conduct business?

Sources for Locating the Best Market

Many sources can help you locate the best market for your product or service. Start by consulting the U.S. Census Bureau's Guide to Foreign Trade Statistics. It can be found online. There you will find help in locating sources for various trade statistics.

Using **Standard Industrial Trade Classification (SITC) codes**, you can learn what kinds of products are traded in specific countries. You can also find information about how well your product or service competes in different marketplaces.

Suppose you are planning to export a toy. You can find out how many toys are sold in different countries every year. You would look for a country that imports more toys than the average. The country should also have a history of importing goods from the United States. Generally, in order for a country to be considered a good export candidate, about 5 percent of its total imports should be American goods.

Other Sources of Help

You might want to **contact** the International Trade Administration office and the Department of Commerce in Washington, D.C. The U.S. Chamber of Commerce has an electronic commerce system called the **International Business Exchange (IBEX)**. It lets you sell products and services online anywhere in the world. It is a good way to find trading partners, too.

The U.S. government and private agencies offer small businesses the opportunity to go on trade missions. **Trade missions** let small business owners meet and talk with foreign agents, distributors, or potential business partners.

The participants make valuable contacts in other countries by traveling there. To participate in a trade mission, you need a product that is on the government's **"best prospect" list**. That means it is a product that other countries are looking to purchase.

You also need to have a good business plan. It should show how you plan to market your product in the country you have chosen. You will learn about business plans in Chapter 5.

● **As You Read** ▪▪▪▪▪▪▪▪
Select How should you go about selecting an international market?

Importing and Exporting

What is the difference between importing and exporting products? How do you decide on a product? What are some things you should consider before attempting to import or export? As an entrepreneur, you will need to know the answers to these questions.

Exporting means selling and shipping goods to another country. For example, you may decide to export snack foods to Brazil.

Importing means buying products from other countries to resell in your own country. You might import custom bicycles from France to sell in your community.

Deciding on a Product to Export

To be a successful exporter, you must sell products that other countries want. The best products for exporting are paper, electronics, chemicals, apparel, computers, and industrial and agricultural products.

If you are going to export consumer products, you need to find a country where people have enough **disposable income**. Disposable income is money people have to spend after paying for necessary expenses. It is important because the products you export may not be necessities.

Import Opportunities

The United States imports a lot of goods from other countries for two main reasons. One reason is that the low labor costs in other countries results in lower prices to U.S. consumers. The second reason is that some products are found only in other countries. Coffee is an example.

Where to Find Import Opportunities

To find opportunities in importing, attend trade shows. At these shows, representatives from other countries display their products and services. You can also read trade publications and catalogs that show products available for importing and give you an idea of what is available. However, these catalogs and trade shows will not tell you if people actually want the products. To answer that question, you must research the market. Talk to potential customers to find out what they are looking for and then determine if the products customers want can be found in international markets.

Export Opportunities

Exporting is a way to expand your business to a new market. Exporting is more complicated than importing because you need to understand in depth the countries with which you are doing business. It also takes longer to make a profit exporting because of the time necessary to build relationships in those countries.

Business Case Study

Global Opportunities Await Young Social Entrepreneurs

You can make money *and* help the world

The next generation of billionaires may be socially conscious young entrepreneurs. They will transform people's lives through innovative solutions to hunger, poverty, disease, and pollution.

How can new businesses help save the world? Imagine a stethoscope that automatically detects heart problems using a doctor's smartphone. Or an LED fixture that disinfects a room just through light. Or a round-the-neck air purifier that collects data about air pollution.

These are real products being created by young entrepreneurs supported by

the Kairos Society, an organization that works with emerging social entrepreneurs around the world to bring innovative products from idea to market.

Active Learning

Imagine you are a socially conscious college student who has an idea that a social-entrepreneurship fund like the Kairos Society might be interested to support. Write a letter that introduces yourself, explains your idea, and describes how it will help the world. Include information on why you think the product will also be profitable.

Where to Find Export Opportunities

Here are several ways to enter the global exporting market:

- Establish an e-commerce Web site.
- Use a trade intermediary. A **trade intermediary** is an agency that serves as a distributor in a foreign country.
- Establish a foreign joint venture. A **foreign joint venture** is an alliance between an American small business and a company in another nation.
- License foreign businesses to sell your business's products.
- Use an export management company. An **export management company** is a business that handles all the tasks related to exporting for a manufacturer in exchange for a commission.
- Hire a **freight forwarder**, a business that handles **overseas** shipments.

Opportunities can be found in every country in the world. You can be successful if you take time to learn about potential markets.

Government Regulations on International Trade

Over 100 federal agencies are involved in the import and export process. For example, the Food and Drug Administration regulates the import and export of food and drugs. The U.S. Customs Service is the primary federal agency with oversight over import requirements. General information on import requirements can be found at the U.S. Customs Service Website. General information on export requirements can be found at the U.S. Census Bureau's Website.

Export Assistance Programs

Exporting is a fairly complex process. A number of programs and forms of financial export assistance can help entrepreneurs export their goods. These types of programs are offered by U.S. government agencies and investment corporations.

The U.S. Department of Commerce International Trade Administration Trade Information Center (TIC) offers export assistance and export counseling programs. It employs trade specialists who guide businesses through the export process. You can find TIC's Export Programs Guide to Federal Export Assistance online.

The United States has more than 100 domestic Export Assistance Centers. These are operated in cooperation with the Small Business Administration and the Export-Import Bank of the United States. The centers provide marketing and trade finance support. Your local Export Assistance Center can direct you to your local District Export Council. These organizations are closely affiliated with the Export Assistance Centers. They offer advice and assistance to small- and medium-sized businesses that are interested in exporting.

> Reading Check **Apply** Which federal agency would be responsible for regulating the importation of rice?

GLOBAL WORKPLACE

China: Land of Opportunity

China has one of the world's oldest civilizations. Among the many contributions China has made to world culture are the "four great inventions": paper, the compass, gunpowder, and printing. In the 21st century, China has become a world center for business: It is a major source of goods and labor and is one of the world's most important markets.

Explosive Growth In the late 1990s, there were 2 million computer users and 10 million cell phone users in China. A decade later, there were over 300 million people on the Internet and 500 million people using cell phones! More and more U.S. firms are establishing operations in China to try to tap this fast-growing market.

Social Studies Mandarin Chinese is the official language that is spoken in the capital city of Beijing and is spoken by 70 percent of the population. However, there are several other Chinese languages spoken across the country. Research different Chinese dialects. Make a chart that lists Chinese dialects and where those dialects are spoken.

Common Mandarin Chinese Words and Phrases		
Hello	你好	ni hao
Goodbye	再见	zai jian
How are you?	你好吗	ni hao ma?
Thank you	谢谢	xie xie
You're welcome	歡迎您	bu ke qi

Things to Consider Before Going Global

When you think about going global, make sure you are ready for the challenge. Entrepreneurs who enter the international market are concerned with many of the same issues as domestic entrepreneurs. For example, they need to determine if there is a demand for the product or service they are offering. They also need to conduct market research to learn more about the market they are targeting.

However, entrepreneurs who seek to expand into international markets should also consider several other factors.

Offer Solutions

Anyone can supply a product or service. Ask yourself if you can solve a problem that people in a particular country are facing. To answer this question, you will need to study the country, its culture, and its people carefully.

Ideas do not have to be completely new. They can also be improvements on something that already exists. However, the improvement must have value for your customers and stand out from the crowd.

Conduct Market Research

Even if a product is extremely popular in the United States, this may not be the case in foreign markets. To determine if there is a market for your product or service, conduct market research. If you determine that there is a market for your offerings, the next step is to figure out whether you need to make any modifications in order to sell it in the foreign market.

Personal Traits and Contacts

How good are you at handling risk and frustration? Every country has different ways of doing business. Every group of customers has different needs and desires. You must be prepared to go through a process of trial and error.

You should also ask yourself if you have any good contacts in other countries. You need to develop a network of people who can help you. Contact your local chamber of commerce or Small Business Administration (SBA) office.

SECTION 4.2 Review

After You Read ━━━━━━━━━━━━━━

Self-Check

1. **Explain** why it is important to have your own interpreter with you when you do business in another country.
2. **Compare** and contrast importing and exporting.
3. **List** four issues you need to consider before going global.

Think

4. **Name** a product that you would like to export to another country. Which country you would choose to export this product to and why?

Mathematics

5. **Exchange Rates** Ernesto owns an importing firm in Mexico. Last year, Ernesto's Imports imported 137 million dollars worth of computers and transportation-related goods to Mexico from the United States. If these imports represent 0.1% of the total imports of U.S. goods to Mexico for the year, what is the value in dollars of all Mexican imports from the U.S. for that year?

Math Concept **Percents** Percents can be thought of as parts of the whole.

Step 1 Divide the percent by 100 to determine its decimal equivalent.

Step 2 Divide the amount Ernesto imported by the decimal equivalent to determine the total imports.

Go to connectED.mcgraw-hill.com to check your answers.

Entrepreneurs *in Action*

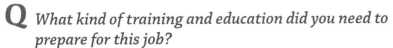

Ernie Wong
President
Playmaker Toys

Q *What do you do?*
A We manufacture and sell toys in China. Our offices are based in Hong Kong, but we have offices in Los Angeles as well.

Q *What kind of training and education did you need to prepare for this job?*
A The funny thing is that I have a bachelor's degree in Economics and a master's in Information Science. I didn't intend to work in in this industry, but there are things that you can learn from completely unrelated fields that you can apply toward anything. There isn't any formal training required to do what I do, but more on the job learning.

Q *What do you enjoy most about your job?*
A There are tons of things, but I think that the opportunities available to you as an entrepreneur are exciting. It's nice to know that you control your own destiny, and you get out what you put in. In other jobs, you are at the mercy of the company, like how many hours you work or how much you get paid. At least with my job, there are boundless opportunities. You just have to develop the knack for finding the right ones and maximizing that opportunity.

Q *How did you bceome interested in your field?*
A Before working here, I did an internship with the Department of Commerce, doing exports and international trade. I saw how much each country relies on the other for goods, and how the flow of information over the Internet would open up opportunities that were never there before.

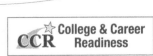

College & Career Readiness

Cross-Cultural Communication Even if a business does not enter the international market, there are many diverse communities here in the United States.

1. Identify a population in your city or state that speaks a language other than English.
2. Identify some common phrases that you think would be useful in communicating with this demographic.
3. Share these phrases with your class in a two-minute oral presentation.

Career Facts

Real-World Skills	Academic Skills	Career Cluster
Cross-Cultural Skills, Global Awareness, Communication	English Language Arts, Social Studies, Foreign Languages	Manufacturing

Ernie Wong

Visual Summary

Global Opportunities

● **The Global Market** The international market, which is more than four times the size of the U.S. market, holds opportunities for businesses.

The Global Marketplace	
Asia	• Enormous and diverse continent. • Many unique and sophisticated markets. • Growing source of products and services.
Latin America	• Includes traditional as well as modern cultures. • Tend to make buying decisions based on family vs. individual needs. • Some countries prefer U.S. goods.
Europe	• Entrepreneurship becoming more popular. • A common currency (the Euro), but no common culture. • Marketers need to segment markets by cultural similarities.
Developing Countries	• Risky form of opportunity. • Many barriers and little support for entrepreneurs. • Research culture and business practices carefully.

● **Showing Respect**
To succeed in international business, it is important to show respect and understanding for the cultures of the people with whom you do business.

Conducting International Business	
Speak in terms of the other person's currency.	Do research on the country and culture.
Try to learn a few words in the local language.	Bring an interpreter.
Be prepared to remove shoes.	Use formal greetings.
Respect different tastes in food.	Be on time.
	Do not set time limits.

Terry Vine/Blend Images LLC

Review and Assessment

Vocabulary

1. On a sheet of paper, use each of these terms and words in a written sentence.

Content Vocabulary

◇ global economy
◇ exporting
◇ importing
◇ trade barrier
◇ tariff
◇ gross domestic product (GDP)
◇ interpreter
◇ Standard Industrial Trade Classification (SITC) codes

◇ International Business Exchange (IBEX)
◇ trade missions
◇ "best prospect" list
◇ disposable income
◇ trade intermediary
◇ foreign joint venture
◇ export management company

◇ freight forwarder

Academic Vocabulary

■ domestic
■ region
■ contact
■ overseas

Key Concepts

2. **Describe** the role of small business and entrepreneurs in today's global multicultural economy.
3. **Explain** why the global market is important.
4. **List** current trends that provide both domestic and global opportunities for entrepreneurs.
5. **Identify** the benefits and risks of international trade.
6. **Explain** how to find the best international markets.
7. **Compare** and contrast importing and exporting.
8. **Name** some of the best products to export.
9. **Describe** some good ways to enter the global market.

Academic Skills

Mathematics

10. **Exchange Rates** Linh Lam works for a company that is opening a facility in England. She is being transferred later this year. At the time of her transfer, the exchange rate is expected to be 0.75. In other words, 1 U.S. dollar ($) will only buy 0.75 worth of English pounds (£). Linh earns $43,650 a year in the U.S. and will receive a 15% raise after her transfer. Write an explanation of how to determine the worth of Linh's salary in English pounds after the transfer.

    Math Concept **Currency Conversion** Exchange rates are used to convert one country's currency to another country's.
    Step 1 Determine Linh's salary after her raise.
    Step 2 Convert Linh's salary to English pounds.

English Language Arts/Writing

11. **Design an Advertisement** Choose a foreign country or culture that interests you. Design an advertisement for a product aimed at teenagers in that country. Write the ad copy (words) in English and incorporate color and visual images that will help communicate your message. Create a draft of your ad, and if possible, find people from your target culture to comment and suggest revisions.

Academic Skills *(continued)*

Social Studies

12. **British English** English words can have different meanings in different cultural settings. The word *dinner* refers to a midday Sunday meal in some parts of the U.S., but means the everyday evening meal in the U.K. Research what the following words mean to a British citizen: *yard, biscuit, bonnet, keen, caravan, public school*. Write a sentence or two explaining each word's British meaning.

Science

13. **Nuclear Waste** Write a short report on the dangers of nuclear waste and the problems involved with its disposal. Identify which countries use nuclear energy and the alternate ways different countries dispose of nuclear waste. Generate your own ideas about what to do with the waste.

Real-World Skills

Adaptability

14. **Prepare to Work Abroad** Interview someone who has worked in another country. Ask that person to compare experiences working in another country to experiences working in the United States. Ask for tips for preparing to work abroad. Summarize your findings in a short report.

21st Century Skills

Global Awareness

15. **Going Global** Research a major company that has not yet expanded into the global marketplace. Write a one-page letter to the president of that company. List the advantages and disadvantages of global expansion. Recommend two potential countries for expansion, and explain why they are good choices.

Connect to Your Community

16. **Identify Imported Goods** As a class, create a list of international products that are available in your community that students have enjoyed. Identify local businesses that either sell products made outside the United States or sell American products to international markets.

17. **Think Global, Ask Local** Locate a business in your community that imports or exports products. Interview the person involved with the buying and selling of goods. Ask about the preparation needed to enter the global market and the benefits of importing and exporting.

Competitive Events Prep

18. **Situation** The success of your business leads you to consider expanding into the international market. From your research, you learn that in some countries offering and taking bribes are acceptable ways of doing business.

Activity Team up with a classmate and present a role play. One can play the role of an American businessperson doing business in another country. The other can play the role of a foreign businessperson.

Evaluation You will be evaluated on how well you meet the following performance indicator:

- Explain whether offering or accepting a bribe while doing business in another country is ethical when it is an acceptable way of doing business in that country.

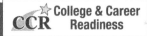 Go to connectED.mcgraw-hill.com for more information about this activity and other competitive events.

Standardized Test Practice

CCR ☆ **College & Career Readiness**

Directions Choose the letter of the best answer. Write the letter for the answer on a separate piece of paper. For question #2, if the answer is False, rewrite the statement to make it true.

1. _____ codes will help you learn what kinds of products are traded in specific countries.
   A. IBEX
   B. GDP
   C. NAFTA
   D. SITC

2. A tariff is a tax imposed by a government on imported or exported goods.
   T
   F

> **Test-Taking Tip**
> When taking a test, if you have time at the end, check your answers and solutions. Did you answer the questions asked? Did you answer each part of every question?

Business Plan Project

Getting Started

By describing your company and its management team, products, and services, you will lay the groundwork for your new business. *How will your products or services benefit your customers?*

Objectives

In this project, you will complete these three parts of your business plan:

- Create a chart that lists your management team and each team member's responsibilities.
- Write a company description that clearly identifies your business concept.
- Create a chart that describes the features and benefits your products will provide.

The Skills You'll Use

- **Academic Skills** Reading, Writing, Social Studies, Research Skills
- **Real World Skills** Observation, Communication, Critical Thinking
- **21st Century Skills** Leadership and Responsibility; Initiative and Self-Direction

▶ Management Team Plan

In the Management Team section of the business plan, you will present your management team's qualifications for making the venture a success.

Step 1 **Describe Yourself** Write a one-page biography that describes how your experience will help you run a business. For example, if you have played in a band or orchestra, you may have teamwork skills that can help you achieve success. Focus on what you can do to make your business work.

Step 2 **Think About the Skills You Have and the Skills You Need** Every business needs certain key skills and experiences. If you do not have these skills, you can bring in partners or hire employees with these skills or you can outsource the function. Create a chart like the one below and write down how each of these jobs will get done.

▶ Company Description

The Company Description section of the business plan outlines the company's basic background information, business concept, goals, and objectives.

Step 1 **Describe Your Company**
Describe your business. Include what makes your business unique. Clearly identify the business concept and why you are, or why you want to be, in business.

Step 2 **Outline Your Company's Goals** Create a chart like the one shown to document your company's goals, the steps you will take to reach the goals, and the resources needed to achieve the goals.

Skill	Job Title	How the Job Will Get Done
Leadership	Chief Executive Officer	
Oversight	Chief Operating Officer	
Human Resources	HR Manager	
Sales and Marketing	Sales and Marketing Director	
Finance	Chief Financial Officer	

▶ Product and Service Plan

The features and benefits of the business's products and services are described in the Product and Service Plan.

Step 1 **Think About Features and Benefits** To effectively sell products and services, you need to know how the product or service's features benefit the customer. Features are basic attributes and qualities. They differentiate competing brands, adding value to products. Benefits are the advantages or personal satisfaction a customer gets from a product or service. The more useful the feature, the more valuable the benefit is to the consumer.

Step 2 **Describe Your Product or Service** Create a chart to document the information needed to describe your company's product or service and its features and benefits.

Use the **Business Plan Project** Appendix on pages **572-583** to explore the content requirements of a business plan in more detail.

 Business Plan Project Template Go to connectED.mcgraw-hill.com for a business plan template that you can use to write your own business plan.

My Business Plan
When you have completed your Project, put your statements, charts, and other research in your Business Plan Portfolio.

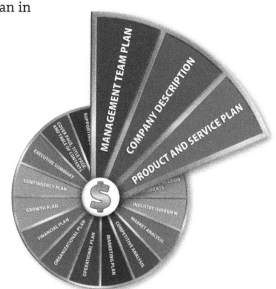

Connect the Photo

Setting Your Sites Entrepreneurs must consider many issues when planning a new business, including where to locate it. This spectacular office building was designed by Frank Gehry, who founded Gehry Partners, LLP, a celebrated architectural firm. *What are some of the advantages and disadvantages of starting a business in an office building?*

Business Plan Project

● *Preview*

Planning and Research

Will protecting the environment be one of your company's guiding principles? Are businesses in your industry using Twitter or Facebook? What kind of music do your customers like to download? These are just some of the issues an entrepreneur might consider when researching and planning a venture.

The **Business Plan Project** will help you address and organize some of these concerns by focusing on these sections of the business plan:

▶ The **Vision and Mission Statements** set forth the guiding principles by which a company functions.

▶ The **Industry Overview** addresses the basic trends and growth within those companies providing similar, complementary, or supplementary products and services.

▶ The **Market Analysis** presents your market research and features a customer demographic profile that defines the traits of the company's target market.

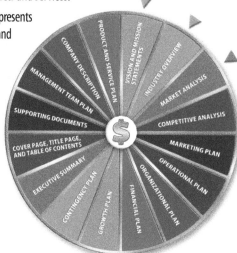

● Prepare for the Business Plan Project

As you read this unit, use this checklist to prepare for the **Business Plan Project**:

● Make a list of goals you would like your company to achieve.
● Think about what kinds of customers might make up your target market.
● Use a spreadsheet program to organize your research.

CHAPTER

5

Feasibility and Business Planning

Chapter Objectives

SECTION 5.1

Feasibility Analysis: Testing an Opportunity

Discuss the importance of defining a prospective business by writing a clear and concise business concept.

Describe how a feasibility study can be used to test a concept in the marketplace.

SECTION 5.2

The Business Plan

Explain the importance of business planning.

Identify and describe the components and formats of a business plan.

List two of the key mistakes that entrepreneurs make when writing a business plan.

Identify and analyze various sources of information for a business plan.

Describe how to professionally package and present a business plan.

Discovery Project

Your Business Concept

Key Question | *How do you plan a business?*

Project Goal

Think about a business you would like to start. Decide on a product or service your business would offer, then determine who your customers would be. Think about how your product or service would benefit your customers and explain how the benefit would be delivered.

Think About...

➤ *How will you determine whether your business will provide a product or a service?*
➤ *How will your product or service help your customers?*
➤ *What is a benefit?*

 21ˢᵗ Century Skills

Business Literacy *What types of products and services are provided in your community?*

Evaluate

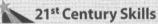 Go to **connectED.mcgraw-hill.com** to download a rubric that you can use to evaluate your final project.

Ask
AN
EXPERT

Q: *I am interested in starting a game development company. How can I find out whether the video game industry is growing?*

A: To find out whether the video game industry is growing, start with research on the Internet. Go to the lead video game companies and see what is in development from their websites. Also, be sure to check out any reputable Investment Surveys you find.

Connect the Photo

When Dreams Become Reality How does a business idea transform into something that is ready for the market? Entrepreneurs must plan and test business concepts thoroughly before sending the concept into the market. Determining that all business concepts and ideas are feasible is vital to a successful business venture. *How can you turn your talents into a feasible business concept?*

Feasibility Analysis: Testing an Opportunity

Reading Guide

● Before You Read ▪▪▪▪▪▪▪▪▪▪▪▪▪▪

Connect Why you would test a business concept before writing a business plan?

The Main Idea

Business concepts need to be tested in the market. Once a concept is judged feasible, a business plan will help the entrepreneur develop a strategy for executing the concept.

Objectives

Discuss the importance of defining a prospective business by writing a clear and concise business concept.

Describe how a feasibility study can be used to test a concept in the marketplace.

Content Vocabulary

◇ business concept
◇ beneficiaries
◇ feature
◇ benefit
◇ feasibility analysis
◇ industry

◇ target customers
◇ competitive matrix
◇ prototype
◇ business model
◇ value chain

Academic Vocabulary

You will see these words in your reading and on your tests. Use the academic vocabulary glossary to look up their meanings.

▪ potential   ▪ focus

Graphic Organizer

Draw a chart like the one shown. As you read, write down the seven categories of information you need to research when analyzing the feasibility of a new business venture.

 Go to connectED.mcgraw-hill.com to download this graphic organizer.

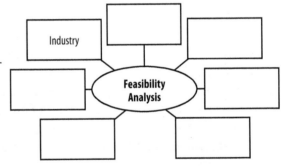

Industry

Feasibility Analysis

Language that Wins Customers

Appeal to target customers by following simple communication rules

Before they buy a product or service, customers want to know how it will make their lives easier. That's why understanding your target customers is so essential to planning an effective business. When speaking to customers, follow these communication tips:

Focus on benefits. Focus on how your product or service solves the specific problems your customers face. Convince through specifics.

Help, don't hype. Offer information that will help customers make buying decisions. Avoid exaggerated claims, which creates distrust.

Keep language simple. Use plain, clear language. Customers are busy; they look for honesty and brevity. Avoid long words and flowery "marketing-speak."

Be culturally sensitive. Know what languages your customers speak and the right way to reach them. You may need a good translator. You don't want to make Chevy's famous mistake of naming a car "Nova"—Spanish for "doesn't go"!

Active Learning

Create two advertisements, both for the same product. One ad should hype the product with lots of "marketing-speak." The other should be written in plain language that focuses on the specific benefits of the product to the customer. Show the ads to five different people and ask them which they find more convincing, and why. Tally your results.

Developing a Business Concept

Once you have an idea for a new business, you need to turn it into a business concept. A **business concept** is a clear and concise description of an opportunity. It contains four key elements: the product or service, the customer, the benefit, and the distribution. Its purpose is to **focus** your thinking.

For example, Karen Jashinsky wanted to develop a product or service that would help teens become more fit. She decided to open a fitness center geared toward teens. It was a good idea, but she needed to develop it further to find out if it would work. To build her business concept statement, Karen answered four questions.

Identify the Product or Service

What is the product or service being offered? This is the solution to the problem the customer is having. Karen wanted to offer a wide variety of group fitness programs to teenagers. She also wanted to offer them a selection of nutrition classes.

Identify the Customer

Who is the customer? The customer is the person who pays for the product or service. Karen's customers are the parents of the teens for whom she is providing the services, or if they have their own source of income, the teens themselves.

Benefits and Features

What is the benefit that is being provided? A **benefit** is something that promotes or enhances the value of the product or service to the customer. In this case, the benefit the teens will receive is convenience and better health. Their parents, the customers, will have peace of mind that their children are spending after-school time in a safe place. A **feature**, by contrast, is a distinctive aspect, quality, or characteristic of a product or service. For example, Karen will offer a neighborhood location.

Delivery

How will the benefit be delivered to the customer? Businesses have many ways to distribute the benefits of their products and services. Some of the choices are through a retail store, wholesalers, mail order, the Internet or social media, or door-to-door delivery. Karen chose to deliver the service to the customer via a retail outlet.

Writing a Concept Statement

After answering the four questions, Karen could write the following concept statement:

High End Grocery Shopping Whole Foods® sells only natural and organic food and produce not found in most grocery stores. *What are some advantages and disadvantages of this business approach?*

O2 Max Fitness is the first fitness club designed exclusively for teens, providing a convenient neighorhood location where teens can achieve their health and fitness goals. Parents will enjoy peace of mind knowing that their child is spending after-school time in a safe place.

Once you have a clear and concise concept statement, ask yourself, "What is the compelling reason for this business to exist?" In Karen's case, she was trying to address the increasing rates of obesity in 13- to 18-year-olds, which causes them to experience serious health problems such as diabetes.

Testing the Concept in the Market

The process used to determine the initial feasibility of an idea is called **feasibility analysis**. Feasibility analysis helps the entrepreneur decide whether a new business concept has **potential**.

A feasibility analysis can also help you to determine if there is enough demand for your business's products or services and whether business conditions are appropriate for you to go forward with the launch. Additionally, it can help you understand what must be in place for your business to be successful.

A feasibility analysis includes questions related to the industry and value chain, customers, the competition, product and service requirements, the founding team, and start-up resource needs. **Figure 5.1** on page 108 lists factors to consider in a feasibility analysis.

Testing the Industry

The broadest level of analysis looks at the industry in which the business will operate. An **industry** is a group of businesses with a common interest, such as financial services, computers, retail, or groceries. In the analysis, you look at factors such as the demographics of the industry, the health of the industry, trends and patterns of change, and major players.

Talking to Customers — The Market

Understanding the target market and testing the customer may be the most important part of the analysis. You should talk with potential customers to measure the interest in your product and to better define the features and benefits. For Karen Jashinsky's business, parents are the **target customers**, those most likely to buy her products and services. Teens are the **beneficiaries** or end-users of the service. Karen will want to learn as much as she can about both of their needs.

Testing Product or Service Requirements

In this part of the analysis, you consider what it will take to develop your product or service into a **prototype**. A prototype is a working model of the new product.

Tech Savvy

Radiating Good Ideas

Does getting into the right business at the right time spell *success*? The failure rate of new businesses suggests that many ideas never make it off the ground floor. Though radiant floors have been around for years—Koreans have used *ondol* floors for centuries—the technology has only begun to penetrate the American marketplace. Radiant flooring, or underfloor heating, works through direct heat transfer from hot air or water pipes, running below floorboards or embedded in concrete, to the air. Radiant floor businesses may not be feasible in tropical climates, but they have made inroads in cold-climate regions where customers appreciate the warm floors and potential energy savings afforded by radiant heating. *Why would a radiant floor installation business be more feasible in a cold-climate state?*

Blueprints and Layout Planning

Even businesses that do not manufacture products need to design prototypes. These kinds of prototypes are not physical. They are designs, blueprints, story boards, or flowcharts that map out the business and the processes that will take place at the business.

For example, if you plan to open a sports-themed restaurant, you will create a blueprint of the layout of the restaurant, including the placement of kitchen equipment, tables, reception area, and the flow of customers and employees through the workspace. Chapter 9 discusses layout planning.

Intellectual Property

When you develop a new product or service, you create an asset that must be protected. Your feasibility analysis must consider how you will protect your product or service. You can protect your intellectual property through patents, trademarks, copyrights, and trade secrets. Chapter 8 discusses intellectual property laws.

Figure 5.1   Feasibility Analysis Consideration

| Industry | Market/Consumer | Founding Team | Product/Services | Finance | Value Chain Analysis |

Industry
- Demographics
- Trends
- Life cycle stage
- Barriers to entry
- Status of technology and R&D
- Typical profit margins

Market/Consumer
- Target market demographics
- Customer profile
- Plan for speaking to customers and competitors

Founding Team
- Knowledge and skills
- Gaps and how to fill them

Product/Services
- Features and benefits
- Product development tasks
- Intellectual property rights
- Product or service differentiation

Finance
- Business model
- Start-up capital requirements
- Positive cash flow
- Break-even point

Value Chain Analysis
- Value chain description
- Distribution channel alternatives and innovations

Testing the Concept The process used to test a business concept is called feasibility analysis. *How does feasibility analysis help an entrepreneur decide whether a new business concept has potential?*

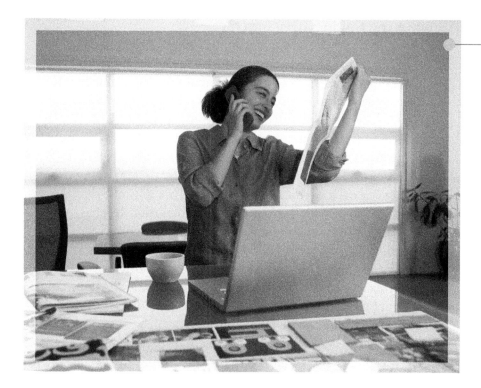

Is the Customer Right?
When starting a new business, customer feedback is an important part of product feasibility. *What information can you obtain from target customers?*

Evaluating the Founding Team

Because the business world has become more complex, many successful businesses today are founded by teams—two or more people working together to launch a new venture. Teams bring together the knowledge, experience, resources, and skills of the people involved. This is important because a founding team must gather together all of the necessary resources to begin development of the business.

An effective founding team can get a new business launched, which is important to investors. In general, investors look at the team first and the market second. That is why it is important to have a team with a variety of knowledge and experience.

Studying the Competition

One way to study the competition after you have done your research is to create a matrix. A **competitive matrix** is a tool for organizing important information about the competition. You can secure this information by reading about your competitors, talking to them, visiting their businesses and Websites, buying their products, and talking to their customers and suppliers.

The Competitive Matrix

Create a five-column competitive matrix. If you want, you can add additional columns for marketing and research and development. You can also add another row to fill in information about your own proposed business. This will help you to compare your proposed business to your competitors' businesses and more clearly identify your business's competitive advantage. Fill in your matrix as shown in **Figure 5.2** on page 110.

As You Read
Contrast What is the difference between direct and indirect competitors?

Filling In the Competitive Matrix

1. *Competitor.* In the first column, list your direct and indirect competitors. Direct competitors are in the same or nearly the same business as you and compete for the same customers. Indirect competitors include other ways your customers receive the same benefits. (For Karen Jashinsky, another fitness center in the neighborhood would be a direct competitor. Her indirect competitor might be a series of fitness DVDs.)

2. *Customer.* In the second column, list the primary target customer for each of your competitors. This list may overlap.

3. *Benefits.* In the third column, list the benefits that customers receive from each of the competitors. Be sure to describe benefits, not features, of the product or service. Benefits are always described from the customer's point of view.

4. *Distribution.* In the fourth column, list the way the company delivers the benefit to the customer and tell whether it is direct or through an intermediary.

5. *Strengths/Weaknesses.* In the fifth column, list your opinion on the strengths and weaknesses of your competitors.

● Figure 5.2   Competitive Matrix

Competitor	Customer	Benefits	Distribution	Strengths/Weaknesses
Large Gyms	Individuals seeking to improve their fitness	Get fit, convenience	Direct through retail gym	S – Resources to enter O2 Max's niche W – Not currently focused on programming for teens
DVD Fitness Programs	Individuals seeking to exercise at home	Get fit, convenience, save money	Online and offline Retail outlets	S – easy to use and inexpensive W – no on-site guidance and easy to stop doing
O2 Max Fitness	Parents	Peace of mind	Direct through retail center	S – teens more likely to stay involved in a social environment W – Costly in terms of building and equipment

● **Organize Your Research** Making a competitive matrix can help you organize and understand the research on your competitors. *Where can you find the information to fill in your matrix?*

Looking at Start-Up Resource Needs

Feasibility analysis will help you determine the potential profitability of an idea. Jeffrey Bezos knew when he started Amazon.com that the company would not turn a profit for some time. However, he was able to raise money because he could show strong projections and a strong business model. A **business model** describes how you intend to create and capture value with your business concept.

To perform a feasibility analysis, you need to calculate how much money is needed to purchase or lease equipment, furnishings, and a facility. You also need to calculate the cost of starting inventory and supplies, wages and salaries, and product development. Finally, you will also need to be able to carry the company's expenses until your sales generate a positive cash flow.

Analyzing the Value Chain

The **value chain** is the distribution channel through which your product or service flows from the producer to the customer. The value chain includes manufacturers, distributors, and retailers. Your goal is to deliver maximum value for the least possible total cost. You can create a competitive advantage by looking at ways to make the value chain more efficient and by bringing products and services to customers in new ways. For example, the Internet made it possible for entrepreneurs to sell directly to customers easily and at a lower cost.

SECTION 5.1 Review

After You Read ▪▪▪▪▪▪▪▪▪▪▪▪

Self-Check
1. **Explain** the purpose of a business concept.
2. **List** the four components of an effective business concept.
3. **Identify** two things a feasibility analysis accomplishes.

Think
4. **Develop** a clear and concise business concept statement for an idea you have for a new business.

English Language Arts/Writing
5. **Write to Persuade** A business plan tries to persuade its readers to invest in your business idea. Write a paragraph designed to persuade someone to support one of your business ideas. State your position clearly in a topic sentence and provide two or three reasons why the reader should support your business.

Go to connectED.mcgraw-hill.com to check your answers.

The Business Plan

Reading Guide

Before You Read ▪▪▪▪▪▪▪▪▪▪▪▪▪▪

Connect What are some instances when you might want to start a business before you write a business plan?

The Main Idea

A business plan presents a strategy for turning a feasible business concept into a successful business.

Objectives

Explain the importance of business planning.

Identify and describe the components of a business plan.

List two of the key mistakes that entrepreneurs make when writing a business plan.

Identify and analyze various sources of information for a business plan.

Describe how to professionally package and present a business plan.

Content Vocabulary

◇ business plan
◇ executive summary
◇ vision statement
◇ mission statement
◇ distribution channel
◇ direct channel
◇ indirect channel
◇ Small Business Administration (SBA)
◇ trade association

Academic Vocabulary

You will see these words in your reading and on your tests. Use the academic vocabulary glossary to look up their meanings.

▪ analyze
▪ source

Graphic Organizer

Draw the reading organizer like the one shown. As you read this section, write the 18 components of a business plan.

 Go to connectED.mcgraw-hill.com to download this graphic organizer.

Business Plan Components	
• Executive Summary	•
•	•
•	•

The Business Plan: Your Road Map to Entrepreneurial Success

Once you have a feasible business concept, the next step is to develop a business plan. A **business plan** is a document that presents a complete and detailed picture of the new business and the strategy to launch that business.

The Importance of Planning

Planning is important to the success of any business. Entrepreneurs write business plans to help them achieve their goals. Preparing a business plan helps you organize and **analyze** critical data. Researching costs and developing strategies about operations and markets may reveal problems that you had not seen previously. For many of these problems, it is important that you work through them and come up with possible solutions before actually going into business. A formal business plan helps ensure that you prepare for all aspects of a business's operations.

Exceptions to the Rule

For some types of businesses, you may want to start the business before you write the business plan. Internet businesses, service businesses, and businesses that do not involve complex operations can often be launched based on a positive feasibility analysis. The reason for doing this is to start small, gather real market feedback, and begin to bring in some sales. Then you can write a more realistic business plan for growing the company.

ETHICS and BUSINESS

Promoting Your Business

Situation The newspaper in the town where you just opened your new business would like to interview you for their local business feature. Since you just moved to town, it would be a good way for people to get to know you and your business.

Marketing Yourself Your friend sees the interview as an opportunity for you to market yourself as having a strong business background and an education from a major business college. You have had a number of different jobs and you did receive a two-year degree from a business school. You are considering whether you should take your friend's advice.

English Language Arts/Writing

Self Promotion Business owners need to promote themselves and their businesses to help build the business. If no one is hurt, is it all right for an owner to fictionalize his business background to help build the business?

1. What might happen if you lied and told half-truths about your business and personal background?
2. Create a list of outcomes that could occur if people found out you had not been totally honest.

As You Read ▪▪▪
Connect Why is it important to include an executive summary in the business plan?

Who Will Read the Business Plan?

Many people will be interested in your business plan. These people include investors, bankers, potential management, and strategic partners. Each of them looks for different things in a business plan. For example, investors are interested in the track record of the founding team and the ability of the business to grow into larger markets. This is because their primary goal is to recover their initial investment plus a substantial return. By contrast, bankers are interested in the company's ability to repay its loans. They want to see the business generate a positive cash flow. Potential management will be interested in the company's ability to provide a stable work environment and opportunities for advancing in the company.

The Parts of the Business Plan

There is no right or wrong format for a business plan. However, you need to include the sections that investors, bankers, and others expect to see. Your aim is to emphasize the key points that will persuade the reader of the value of your business concept.

Formulating a business plan involves a lot of research in many different areas of the business. Therefore, it makes sense to divide the business plan into parts. A thorough business plan includes these sections: executive summary, company description, mission and vision statements, management team plan, product and service plan, industry overview, market analysis, competitive analysis, marketing plan, operational plan, organizational plan, financial plan, growth plan, and contingency plan. A business plan should also include a cover page, title page, table of contents, and supporting documents.

The components of the business plan are described here and covered in greater detail in later chapters. You can learn more about business plans by completing the Business Plan Unit Projects, the Business Plan Project Appendix, and the Business Plan Project Workbook.

Executive Summary

The **executive summary** is a brief explanation of the key points contained in a business plan. Its purpose is to give the reader a convincing reason to read the full plan. Investors and lenders read many business plans every day. To save time, they rely on the executive summary to help them decide whether the concept interests them and is worth pursuing. Therefore, the executive summary should be no more than two pages and include the most important information from each section of the plan. It should open with a compelling story of the problem the business is addressing to persuade the reader that the business is going to be a success. Then it should support that statement by providing the evidence that was gathered through market research.

Company Description

The company description outlines the company's background information and basic business concept. It helps investors understand the size, scope, and type of business. It describes the entrepreneurial opportunity and explains why you think the venture will succeed. It also provides a brief history of the development of the business with development milestones that have been completed to date.

Vision and Mission Statements

The vision and mission statements section of the business plan states the guiding principles by which a company functions. A **vision statement** establishes the scope and purpose of a company and reflects its values and beliefs. Walt Disney's vision for his company was "to bring happiness to millions." As you think about your company's vision, try to keep the vision broad so it will stand the test of time. Continuing with the example from Section 5.1, Karen Jashinsky's vision statement might be "to make sure every teen is healthy and fit." This broad vision lets you take your business in many directions as it grows.

A **mission statement** expresses the specific aspirations of a company, the major goal for which it will strive. Think about a mission statement to go along with Karen's vision statement for her teen fitness center. It might be "To get 100 teens at their best weight and fitness level by the end of the year."

Management Team Plan

This section presents your qualifications and those of any partners. You must describe why your team has the capabilities to execute your business concept. Because you may be missing some expertise, you should discuss how you will fill the gaps. Sometimes these gaps can be filled through partnerships or advisory board members.

Product and Service Plan

In this section of the business plan, you present the product or service you are offering. The nature of your business should be understandable to the reader. Understanding can be accomplished by writing a clear and compelling concept statement. You should also note the unique features and benefits of the product/service and possible spin-offs. Spin-offs are additional products or services that you might do later when the business is more established. Spin-offs alert the reader to the fact that this venture has growth possibilities.

Web Savvy

Planning for a Net Presence
When a business plans to have an Internet presence, it needs to establish its online brand, or the face that it puts forward to this new audience. This ranges from simple things like colors and fonts, to bigger-picture ideas like how it comes across emotionally (whimsical, serious, etc.). Ideally, that brand would be consistent with how the business behaves elsewhere. A shopper who is comfortable with a retailer's in-store brand should also be comfortable with its online brand. *What are some companies that have an online brand that is consistent with their real-world brand?*

GLOBAL WORKPLACE

Biotechnology in Sweden

Sweden, the home of the Nobel Prize, is part of the European Union, although it uses its own currency, called the krona. Swedish is the primary language, but most people speak English. Even though Sweden is a small country with a population of nine million, it has 220 biotech companies, ranking it ninth worldwide. The Oeresund region, which connects Sweden to Denmark, has the nickname "Medicon Valley."

In the Pipeline Sweden has one of the most liberal attitudes in the world toward science. There are no intense debates about genetic research like there are in the United States. Many Swedish biotech companies focus their research on new medical applications. There are more than one hundred products in clinical trials, many of them for treatments related to cancer.

Science According to the Convention on Biological Diversity, biotechnology uses biological systems to "make or modify products or processes for specific use." Biotech entrepreneurs need to know these terms: *pipeline, clinical trials, gene therapy,* and *genetic testing*. Look up their definitions and write a sentence using each word.

Common Swedish Words and Phrases	
Hello	hej
Goodbye	hej då
Yes/ No	ja/nej
Please	snälla
Thank you	tack
You're welcome	du är välkommen

Industry Overview

This section of the business plan presents your research into the industry. Think of your industry as those companies providing similar, complementary, or supplementary products and services. Every business operates within an industry. Your business plan must address the trends and patterns of change within the industry. It must also address changes in demographics and in the product or service's stage in the life cycle.

Market Analysis

Why is market analysis important? The more you understand your customers, the better your chances of success. This section presents your primary and secondary research that led to a customer profile. The results of your research help you determine your overall marketing and sales strategies, which are detailed in the marketing plan. In addition, this section analyzes your customers and the competition you might face. The market analysis should also contain geographic, economic, and demographic data about the site for your business if the business is offline.

Competitive Analysis

The competitive analysis section should demonstrate that the proposed business has an advantage over its competitors. You can gather information about your competitors from many **sources**. One way is to search for and explore their Web sites. Another way is to talk to their customers, vendors, suppliers, and employees.

You can also attend trade shows or find out more about your competitors. Alternatively, you could look for information in newspaper and magazine databases.

Marketing Plan

A marketing plan discusses how a company makes its customers aware of its products or services. It includes such features as the market niche, pricing, company image, marketing tactics, a media plan, and a marketing budget.

Operational Plan

The operational plan includes all of the processes in the business that result in production and delivery of the product or service. If you are manufacturing a product, you will want to discuss the status of product development. You will also want to explain the distribution of your product or service. A **distribution channel** is the means by which you deliver the product or service to the customer. If you are building Websites that provide a service, you will probably have a **direct channel**. That is, you will be delivering the service directly to the customer. On the other hand, if you are manufacturing a computer game, you may have an **indirect channel**. This means you will sell your game to a wholesaler. The wholesaler then finds retail stores and other types of outlets to carry your product.

Organizational Plan

The organizational plan looks at the people aspects and the legal form of the business. It discusses the management philosophy and whether the company will be a partnership, corporation, or limited liability company. The organizational plan also discusses the role and compensation of key management personnel and important employment policies.

Financial Plan

The financial plan presents forecasts for the future of the business. It explains the assumptions made when the forecast figures were calculated. The assumptions form the basis for the financial figures that appear in the financial statements. This part of the business plan is designed to show that all claims about the product, sales, marketing strategy, and operational strategy can create a financially successful business.

Go Green

Environmental Solutions

Whole Foods Market is not your average grocery store. The company's motto is "Whole Foods, Whole People, Whole Planet." The company puts action behind their motto. One day a year, all stores worldwide contribute 5 percent of their sales to the Animal Compassion Foundation. Whole Foods Market is also committed to recycling programs, reducing and reusing packaging, and water and energy conservation. The commitment to find solutions is paying off. Whole Foods Market is the world's leading natural and organic food supermarket.

◈ **Critical Thinking**
In its Mission Statement, Whole Foods aims "to support the health, well-being, and healing… of…the planet." Write a paragraph describing why you would or would not include a similar statement in your own Vision and Mission Statement.

Growth Plan

The growth plan looks at how the business will expand in the future. Investors like to know that a business has plans to grow and that it will deal with growth with appropriate systems and controls.

Contingency Plan

The contingency plan looks at the probable risks for the business, such as changing economic conditions and lower-than-expected sales. It then suggests ways to minimize the risk.

Cover Page and Finishing Touches

Every business plan should have a cover page that includes the company name, address, phone number, Website address, e-mail address, social media icons, and company logo. The page following the cover page is the title page. It includes the company name; the names, titles, and addresses of the owners; the date the business plan was issued; and the name of the person who prepared the business plan.

The table of contents details the components of the business plan and the page numbers where these components can be found. The supporting documents section of the business plan includes resumes, exhibits, and documentation relevant to the business.

Creating a Business Plan
There are several steps involved in creating a business plan. *Which of these steps do you think is most important in creating an effective business plan?*

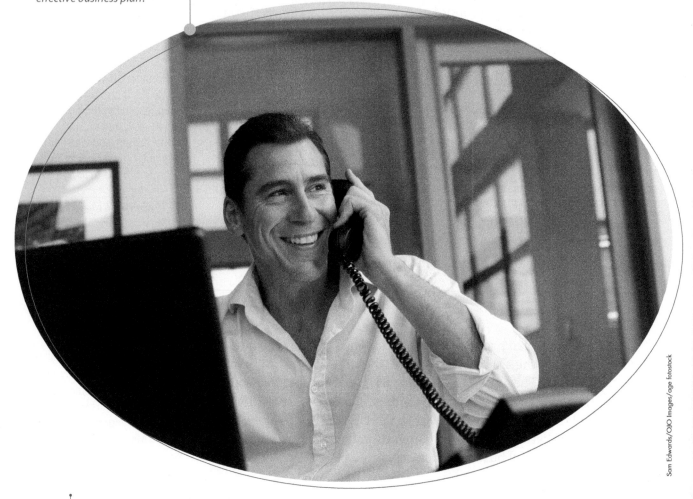

Sam Edwards/OJO Images/age fotostock

Developing a Business Plan

Plan and Research	Begin with the questions that need to be answered. Identify the type of data that will answer those questions and perform the research.
Organize Your Data	As you conduct research, record your findings in a business plan notebook. The notebook should have a separate section and at least one folder for each part of the business plan.
Write a Draft	After you have finished your research, you are ready to compile a first draft of your business plan. Set up a document with the headers you need, or use the business plan template document that can be found at connectED.mcgraw-hill.com.

● **Planning for Success** *What is the purpose of the business plan?*

Common Mistakes in Preparing Business Plans

There are many steps between learning what goes into a business plan and actually assembling one. Some of these steps are illustrated in **Figure 5.3**.

Unfortunately, when entrepreneurs sit down to write their business plans, they often make incorrect assumptions about what potential investors are looking for. Before preparing your business plan, consider these common mistakes.

Projecting Exaggerated Growth Levels

Entrepreneurs often believe that investors will be impressed with big sales figures. In fact, quite the opposite is true. Investors may think that the founding team cannot manage and control such rapid growth. Use conservative figures in your business plan, with the goal of exceeding your projections.

Trying to Do Everything

Many entrepreneurs are proud of their ability to multitask. They may even claim to have expertise in all areas of the new venture. In fact, they may have a general knowledge of all aspects of the business and real expertise in only one area. For this reason, investors prefer a team to a solo entrepreneur.

Claiming Performance that Exceeds Industry Averages

A new venture does not usually outperform industry averages. Therefore, your business plan should project performance slightly below average. However, you should discuss how you plan to exceed industry averages at some time in the future.

Underestimating the Need for Capital

Your business plan should project enough capital to grow the company until there is sufficient internal cash flow. The business will then need additional capital to prepare itself for growth. If you underestimate the amount of money you need, investors may think you do not understand the business, so when estimating capital needs, allow extra for the unexpected.

 Reading Check **Recognize** Why do investors generally prefer a team to a solo entrepreneur?

Sources of Business Plan Information

Where should you gather information for a business plan? There are local, state, and national organizations that offer resources to help entrepreneurs develop business plans. There are also government agencies that can provide you with more assistance. The following organizations are great sources of information.

Small Business Administration (SBA)

To encourage entrepreneurship in our free enterprise system, the government runs the Small Business Administration. The **Small Business Administration (SBA)** is a federal agency that provides services to small businesses and new entrepreneurs. The agency offers helpful publications for a minimal charge. In addition, the SBA provides special assistance to women, minorities, and the physically challenged in order to encourage them to become entrepreneurs. The SBA provides both financial and informational resources.

Service Corps of Retired Executives (SCORE)

SCORE is dedicated to providing free, confidential face-to-face and e-mail business counseling to small businesses. SCORE has hundreds of satellite offices throughout the United States. You can find templates and guides for business planning on its Website.

Small Business Development Centers (SBDCs)

The SBDC program is administered by the SBA. It provides management assistance to current and prospective small business owners. Its nearly 1,000 service centers offer a wide variety of information and guidance.

Business Plan Information
The Small Business Administration provides assistance and resources to entrepreneurs in areas of starting, managing, and financing a business. *How can use use organizations like this one to develop your business plan?*

Chambers of Commerce

Local chamber offices provide information about the local economy, business trends, and business needs. In many cities, chambers of commerce operate small business development and assistance programs. In addition, the U.S. Chamber of Commerce provides many resources and acts as an advocate for entrepreneurs at the national level.

Trade Associations

A **trade association** offers technical and general assistance to entrepreneurs in a specific profession or industry. Many trade associations also publish publications such as newsletters and magazines. Trade associations often supply information such as average start-up and operating costs and trend analysis. An association can also provide market research, technology news, and supplier contacts. You can find the representative trade association for any industry on the Internet.

Packaging and Presenting Your Plan

Once you have completed your business plan, you must make it presentable. The appearance of a business plan is as important as its contents. The business plan's physical appearance is the first step in getting potential investors and lenders to read it. It must look professional without being distracting. To package your business plan effectively so that it appears professional, pay attention to both how it is packaged and to how it is formatted.

Packaging

Bind your completed business plan so that it lies flat. A spiral binding works well. Use index tabs to separate the components of the business plan to make it easier to find each section.

Formatting

Use an easily readable 12-point type font, such as Times New Roman. Use bold subheadings and bullets to improve readability. If you have a business logo, include it at the top of every page.

Number each copy of the business plan and include a Statement of Confidentiality that the reader should sign. Keep track of who has a copy of the plan. Place a statement on the cover page prohibiting copying of the plan.

SECTION 5.2   Review

After You Read

Self-Check

1. **Explain** why you should develop a business plan after you know you have a feasible concept.
2. **Identify** the difference between the market analysis and the marketing plan.
3. **Name** two resources you can use to prepare your business plan.

Think

4. **Describe** the importance of a vision/mission statement in identifying direction and objectives of a business.

Mathematics

5. **Opening Costs** Darla wants to open a retail T-shirt business. She has determined that her start up cost will be $235,000. This amount includes $39,500 for the first year's rent on the store, $22,750 for the equipment, $41,800 for the initial inventory, $18,500 for insurance, and $28,950 for heating and electricity. The rest of the cost would be for employee salaries. Write an equation that would allow you to calculate the cost of employees' salaries. Solve the equation.

   Math Concept **Using Symbols** Letters and other symbols can be used to stand for unknown quantities.

   Step 1 Think of a symbol to stand for the unknown quantity, the cost of the employee's salaries.

   Step 2 Write and solve an equation substituting the symbol for the unknown.

   Go to connectED.mcgraw-hill.com to check your answers.

Entrepreneurs *in Action*

Wesley Mitchell III
CEO
Elite Business Network

Q *What do you do?*

A We produce a TV show called "Hip Hop in the Ville," as well as a magazine and radio show. The TV show is an outlet for rap artists in the Southeast. The magazine is a spinoff of this, as well as the radio show, where we play unsigned artists on 98.9 FM (Radio Free Nashville).

Q *What kind of training and education did you need to get this job?*

A In my case, I guess it's being hungry, because I didn't study business in college. I always knew that I wanted to have my own company. I used to be in advertising, and I guess I had a hunger to stay in it, so I started my own magazine. Then, a friend told me I should start my own TV show. He showed me what I needed to do and I ran with it. The radio show came the same way. I studied, I started meeting people who were involved in radio and I learned from them.

Q *What do you enjoy most about your job?*

A I definitely enjoy meeting different people. I also enjoy hearing people's testimonies because I love hearing what it takes for them to get to where they're going or where they're trying to go to and where they're already at. Just that alone makes me happy.

Q *How did you become interested in your field?*

A I got interested in it initially because I used to work for the Yellow Pages and what I do now, when it comes down to it, is advertising. And I enjoy that.

The Pace of Innovation
Today you can watch television on mobile phones and other handheld electronic devices. You can even record video and broadcast on the Internet to viewers all over the world.

1. Use the library or Internet to research the early days of television. How was television different from the way it is today?
2. Think of ways that television has changed in your lifetime. Have television programs changed?
3. Write a few paragraphs explaining how television may change in 20 years. Use the correct tense when talking about the future.

Career Facts

Real-World Skills	Academic Skills	Career Cluster
Problem Solving, Speaking, Listening	English Language Arts, Social Studies	Marketing, Sales and Service

Wesley Mitchell

Visual Summary

Feasibility and Business Planning

Idea to Product Once you have a new idea for a business, you need to develop a business concept and test it in the market. When you have a feasible concept, you need to develop a business plan.

1. Develop a Business Concept

2. Conduct a Feasibility Analysis

3. Develop a Business Plan

John Lund/Marc Romanelli/Blend Images LLC

Vocabulary

1. On a sheet of paper, use each of these terms and words in a written sentence.

Content Vocabulary

◇ business concept
◇ feature
◇ benefit
◇ feasibility analysis
◇ industry
◇ target customers
◇ beneficiaries

◇ prototype
◇ competitive matrix
◇ business model
◇ value chain
◇ business plan
◇ executive summary
◇ vision statement

◇ mission statement
◇ distribution channel
◇ direct channel
◇ indirect channel
◇ Small Business Administration (SBA)
◇ trade association

Academic Vocabulary

■ potential ■ analyze ■ focus ■ source

Key Concepts

2. **Discuss** the importance of writing a clear and concise business concept.
3. **Describe** how a feasibility study can be used to test a concept in the marketplace.
4. **Explain** the importance of business planning.
5. **Identify** and describe the components and formats of a business plan.
6. **List** two of the key mistakes that entrepreneurs make when writing a business plan.
7. **Identify** and analyze various sources of information for a business plan.
8. **Describe** how to professionally package and present a business plan.
9. **Explain** where to find help in preparing a business plan.

Academic Skills

Mathematics

10. **Hosting Services** Debbie wants to create a Website. The hosting service she contacted charges $9.99 to register a domain name for a year and offers 10 GB of space for $57 a year. Another service will register a domain name for $7.50 a year and offers 10 GB of space for $5.75 each month. Which hosting service is a better value over a 3-year period?

Math Concept **Estimating** Before solving the problem, use estimation to predict the better value.

Step 1 Round the numbers and use mental math to compute the cost of each service for one year. Compare to predict the better value.

Step 2 Write equations to determine the exact cost of each option.

Step 3 Subtract to find the difference.

Social Studies

11. **Research Your Community** Ken wants to start a catering company out of his garage. In your neighborhood, would it be legal to run such a business at home? Research your community's guidelines for home businesses. Write a two-paragraph summary of your findings.

Academic Skills *(continued)*

English Language Arts\Writing

12. **Write a Bibliography** A bibliography is a list of resources about a certain topic. Research the standard format for bibliographies and create one that lists recent books containing instructions that a beginner might use to create a business plan. Include at least five titles.

Science

13. **The Scientific Method** The scientific method is a way to ask and answer scientific questions by making observations and doing experiments. The steps in the scientific method are: Ask a Question; Do Background Research; Construct a Hypothesis; Test Your Hypothesis by Doing an Experiment; Analyze Your Data and Draw a Conclusion; Communicate Your Results. Write a paragraph explaining the similarities and differences between business planning and the scientific method.

Real-World Skills

Public Speaking Skills

14. **Self-Management** Michael is in the middle of a presentation to investors. Suddenly, he feels very stressed and nervous and begins to stumble on his words. Write a paragraph describing how you would keep yourself on track in a presentation and what you would do to feel calmer and finish the presentation successfully.

21st Century Skills

Social and Cross-Cultural Skills

15. **Punctuality** People in different cultures have different ways of understanding and using time. This can be a challenge for businesses in the global workplace. Research cultural perceptions of time management and productivity in a country other than the United States. Summarize your findings in a one-page report.

Connect to Your Community

16. **Solve a Problem** Identify a problem in your community that might be solved through a business you create. Develop a business concept statement for a product or service to solve the problem. Include the product or service, the customer, the benefit you are providing, and the delivery method.

17. **Community Support** Select one of the sources of assistance when starting a business, such as SBDC, SBA, chambers of commerce, or SCORE, and research the agency. Find out what kinds of assistance are available to entrepreneurs and request brochures publications and other materials. Report your findings to the class in a short presentation.

Review and Assessment

Competitive Events Prep

18. Situation You are the owner of a successful business in your community. You are chatting with a long-time friend who has been working as the assistant manager of a local restaurant for the past three years. Your friend has decided to purchase and operate a coffee shop. Your friend has several questions about completing a business plan for the coffee shop venture and about the ongoing value of a business plan.

Activity Explain to your friend the importance of each of the sections of a business plan and how a business plan can be effectively used once a business has begun operating.

Evaluation You will be evaluated on how well you meet the following performance indicators:
- Develop a business plan.
- Develop company goals/objectives.
- Explain the concept of financial management.
- Describe considerations in selecting capital resources.
- Track performance of business plan.

 Go to **connectED.mcgraw-hill.com** for more information about this activity and other competitive events.

Standardized Test Practice

 College & Career Readiness

Directions Choose the letter of the best answer. Write the letter for the answer on a separate piece of paper. For question #2, if the answer is False, rewrite the statement to make it true.

1. Which of the following is not a part of a business plan?
   A. Executive Summary
   B. Vision Statement
   C. Financial Summary
   D. Product and Service Plan

2. A business concept contains three elements.
   T
   F

> **Test-Taking Tip**
> In a multiple choice test, the answers should be specific and precise. Read the question first, then read all the answer choices before you choose. Eliminate answers that you know are incorrect.

CHAPTER

6

Market Analysis

Chapter Objectives

SECTION 6.1

Doing Market Research

Define areas of analysis for industry and market research.

Describe how to conduct effective market research.

SECTION 6.2

Industry and Market Analysis

Explain how to research an industry.

Create a customer profile and customer needs analysis.

Discovery Project

Researching Your Business

Key Question

What do you need to know about the industry and market before starting your business?

Project Goal

Work with a small group to research what you need to know about the industry and market before starting a new business. Prepare a short report that focuses on who your customer will be, what will be the source of your supplies, and how you can best market your business.

Think About...

➤ *What business will you choose to research?*
➤ *Where will you find information about the industry?*
➤ *How will you divide the responsibilities among your group?*

21st Century Skills

Collaboration How might collaborating with another business help grow your business?

Evaluate

 Go to connectED.mcgraw-hill.com to download a rubric that you can use to evaluate your final project.

Q: *I have been researching potential investments with my business partner. She suggested that we put some money into a certificate of deposit (CD). What should I know about CDs before investing?*

A: When you put money into a bank CD, you are expecting to get it back at a specific time, plus the interest earned. In return for that security, you agree to leave your money on deposit for a set period of time, generally six months to five years. The minimum deposit is usually $500 and there is rarely an upper limit. CDs are popular because they are considered a safe investment.

Connect the Photo

Riding the Market Ensuring a successful business starts with understanding the market and industry. Entrepreneurs devote time and effort analyzing and researching the market, developing a customer profile, and estimating the demand long before they open their doors. *What trends do you see in the cycling world?*

MoxieProductions/Blend Images LLC

Doing Market Research

Reading Guide

Before You Read ▪▪▪▪▪▪▪▪▪▪▪▪▪▪
Connect Why is it important to study the market you have targeted?

The Main Idea
To ensure success, entrepreneurs need to understand the industry and the market. They should define areas of analysis and conduct effective industry and market research.

Objectives
Define areas of analysis for industry and market research.
Describe how to conduct effective market research.

Content Vocabulary
◇ industry
◇ value chains
◇ carrying capacity
◇ complexity
◇ market
◇ target market
◇ market segmentation
◇ market segments
◇ geographics

◇ psychographics
◇ industrial markets
◇ market research
◇ exploratory research
◇ focus group
◇ descriptive research
◇ historical research
◇ secondary data
◇ primary data

Academic Vocabulary
You will see these words in your reading and on your tests. Use the academic vocabulary glossary to look up their meanings.
■ assess   ■ income

Graphic Organizer
Before you read this section, draw a chart like the one shown. As you read, fill in the chart with the five steps of the marketing research process.

 connectED.mcgraw-hill.com to download this graphic organizer.

Step 1	_____
Step 2	_____
Step 3	_____
Step 4	_____
Step 5	Analyze the data

Defining Areas of Analysis

To succeed and make a profit, a business must satisfy the needs of its customers. However, you cannot satisfy current customers or attract new customers if you do not know who they are and what they want. To find out, you must conduct market analysis.

Market Analysis

Markets for products and services are found within and across industries. An **industry** is a collection of businesses that are categorized by a specific business activity, such as transportation, electronics or food services. Within the industry are **value chains** that support a common line of products or services that satisfy market demands. A value chain includes raw material producers, manufacturers, suppliers, distributors, retailers, and anyone else who deals with other businesses in the industry.

A market is defined by the customers for a particular product or service. Thorough market analysis requires that you examine your market from two different perspectives. You need to identify prospective customers and determine their buying habits. You also need to analyze your industry and **assess** your chances for success within it. This section will focus on how to conduct market research. The next section will discuss what to study about your market.

Industry

Your industry represents the environment in which your business will operate. Therefore, you want to learn what the industry's current status is and where it is going. Ideas for new ventures frequently come from understanding and having experience with an industry. Knowledge of an industry can also help you find strategic partners and identify competitors.

Four broad factors are useful in understanding the nature of an industry. These are carrying capacity, uncertainty, complexity, and stage of life cycle.

Carrying Capacity

Carrying capacity is a way to understand the industry's ability to support new growth. You want to find an industry that can support expansion, thereby allowing your new venture to grow and prosper. Is there room for new businesses like yours?

Uncertainty

Uncertainty is the degree of stability or instability in an industry. An industry that is fast-changing presents a high degree of uncertainty and therefore more risk. Because of this, the rewards are typically greater, but you need to be prepared for a chaotic environment. Many high-tech ventures are found in industries with uncertain climates.

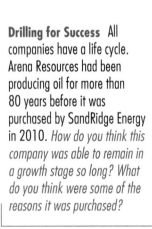

● **As You Read** ▪▪▪

List What are some things you would want to know about your target market?

Complexity

Complexity is the number and diversity of contacts with which you must deal to do business. Firms that operate in complex industries usually have more suppliers, customers, and competitors than firms in other industries. Highly complex industries, which are often global in nature, are very competitive and are costly to enter.

Stage Of Life Cycle

Like people, industries move through a life cycle. The stages of the life cycle include birth, growth, maturity, and then decline if research and development do not produce innovations that spur more growth. If you know the life cycle stage your industry is in, you can design a business strategy that is compatible with that life cycle.

Target Market and Customer

A **market** is a group of people or companies who have a demand for a product or service and are willing and able to buy it. The particular group of customers of interest to you is the **target market**. The target market will be the focus of your company's efforts. You want to know as much as you can about this market in as much detail as possible.

Market Segmentation

Market segmentation is the process of grouping a market into smaller subgroups defined by specific characteristics. When you study the characteristics of the total market, you will be able to identify **market segments**, or subgroups of buyers who have similar characteristics. Once market segments are clearly identified, a business can customize its product offerings and marketing strategies to specific groups of potential customers.

Drilling for Success All companies have a life cycle. Arena Resources had been producing oil for more than 80 years before it was purchased by SandRidge Energy in 2010. *How do you think this company was able to remain in a growth stage so long? What do you think were some of the reasons it was purchased?*

Oleg Kozlov/Alamy

ETHICS and BUSINESS

Marketing Ethics

Situation Your company makes baked goods for hotels, restaurants, and other service industries. Your products include cakes, cookies, pies, breads, and assorted sweet rolls. Business has dropped off lately and you are looking for other markets for your products.

Advertising Your Business You have the opportunity to buy television commercial time at a local cable station. You can choose to air your commercials during the Saturday morning children's segment or during the evening news segment. The station has more viewers during the Saturday morning segment.

English Language Arts/Writing

Marketing to Children Children under 12 have a big influence on what products their families purchase. Because of this, many people believe it is unethical to market unhealthful foods that are high in sugar and fat to children. Do you agree?

1. Would you choose to market foods high in sugar and fat content to children?
2. Write a television news story to explain your reasoning.

Consumer markets (customers who buy goods for personal use) are usually segmented in these ways:

- **Geographics** is the study of the market based on where customers live. This includes region, state, county, city, and/or area.
- Demographics are the personal characteristics of a population. This includes age, gender, family size, family life cycle, **income**, occupation, education, religion, race, nationality, and/or social class. Many of these demographics also apply to business customers, such as size, number of employees, growth rate, and so forth.
- **Psychographics** is the study of consumers based on social and psychological characteristics. These include personality, values, opinions, beliefs, motivations, attitudes, and lifestyle elements, including activities and interests.
- Buying characteristics include knowledge of and personal experiences with the actual goods or services. How customers buy a product and how often they buy it are two examples.

Customers who buy goods or services for business use make up **industrial markets**. Industrial goods are goods or components produced for sale to manufacturers and used in the production of other goods. These markets are segmented differently. Variables include type of business, size, goods or services sold, geographic location, and products needed. Businesses that cater to industrial markets must consider customers' individual situations. When you divide or segment the total market, you create profiles of the customers you are considering. **Figure 6.1** on page 134 shows an example of a market segment profile. Notice that only variables relevant to the business are included.

Market Segment Profile

Situation: Music Store
Specializes in pop and classical sheet music and musical instruments. Located in a large suburban area with several high schools and colleges.

Profile Of One Market Segment
Male or female music students, 15 to 18 year olds. Reside nearby areas. Part-time annual income of $1,200–$2,000. Rarely buy very expensive musical instruments. Dependent on parents for large purchases. Active in band, orchestra, or chorus. Many take private lessons. Aware of current trends and popular songs, and their attitude toward where to buy is influenced by peers.

● **Market Segmentation** Segmenting your market can make your customers' needs more clear. *What type of market is this company targeting?*

Target Marketing

After identifying all of the market segments, you are ready to select your target market. This is the specific market segment on which you will concentrate your efforts. Within this segment, you will find your first customer. This person has a problem that you can solve or recognizes an opportunity that you are offering.

Here are some guidelines to use when segmenting the target market:

- The market segment should be measurable. You need to know how many potential buyers are in the market. Otherwise, how do you know if your venture is worth pursuing?
- The segment should be large enough to be potentially profitable. The segment you select must be big enough to enable you to recover your costs and make a profit.
- The segment should be reachable. First, you must be able to get information about your product and its availability to interested buyers. Second, you must be able to reach potential customers physically. You must be able to deliver your product to their homes or businesses or to the places where they shop.
- The market segment should be responsive. You should have some indication from your research that people in the segment are, in fact, interested in your product and willing to buy it.

A business owner can select and serve multiple market segments, but that does not usually happen in the start-up stage. If you have identified more than one target market, you need to decide which market will be easiest to enter first. In which market will you find it easiest to make sales? Typically, the easiest first market is one where customers have a problem that you can solve. Those easy sales will give you the foundation needed to explore other markets as your company grows.

 Reading Check **Recall** How does targeted marketing help businesses focus their marketing strategies?

Conducting Market Research

Once you know the areas of the market you need to analyze, you can begin investigating them. **Market research** is the collection and analysis of information aimed at understanding the behavior of consumers in a certain market. The marketing research process can be used to identify potential markets, analyze demand, forecast sales, and make other decisions. The market research process is the same whether you are doing research for an existing business or a new venture.

Identify the Focus of the Research

To begin market research, you need to focus your research so you do not waste time gathering useless information. For example, assume area high school students have never been able to buy healthy snacks from their campus vending machines. This situation may give you an opportunity to satisfy a need. To begin, you want to understand how the vending machine industry works, because this will tell you where to get your supplies, acquire the equipment you need, and determine the schedule for refilling the machines, among many other things. You also need to know whether the market can support a healthy snack vending machine business. This information comes from assessing customer demand and willingness to pay.

Select the Type of Market Research

Once you have a research question, you can select a research approach. Ways to structure research are called research designs. The information you require will determine the design you use.

Exploratory and Descriptive Research

Exploratory research is used when you know very little about a subject. It forms the foundation for later research when you are more focused. A good place to start exploratory research is government or industry publications. You can also talk to people who are knowledgeable about your field. You can organize a focus group. A **focus group** is a group of people whose opinions are studied to estimate the types of opinions that can be expected from a larger population.

Descriptive research is done when you want to determine status. For example, you may want to develop a customer profile. To do so, you need to learn the age, gender, occupation, income, and buying habits of potential customers. Such information can be collected through questionnaires, interviews, or observation.

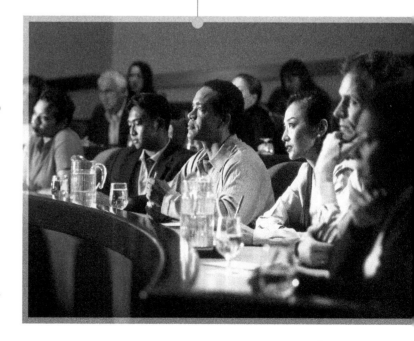

Stay Focused A focus group can help you learn which features and benefits are important to customers. *What would you do to make a focus group a success?*

©Comstock/Corbis

Historical Research

Historical research involves studying the past. Patterns from the past can then be used to explain present circumstances and predict future trends. Trade associations and trade publications are two sources of useful historical data. Owners in similar businesses can also provide you with historical information. You can use these findings to help predict your business's potential.

Start the Research Process

To successfully research your industry and market, you need a plan. An effective plan includes the following five steps:

Step 1: Identify Your Information Needs

Before you begin to collect data on your market, you should identify the kinds of information you need. For example, before launching an Internet business that focuses on people who like to cycle, you would want to know what customers might want to be able to do on a biking Website. You would also gather information about other Websites that focus on the same kind of customer. Do you satisfy a need that your competitors cannot meet? Your competitors' weaknesses are your opportunities.

GLOBAL WORKPLACE — Turkey: A Nation in Flux

When Turkey became a republic in 1923, an important transformation took place. After centuries of cultural restrictions, women were emancipated. Later, polygamy was abolished, women were allowed to vote, and in 1966, equal wages for both sexes were ratified.

New Currency, Old Problems In 2005, Turkey introduced a new currency, the New Turkish Lira, which was later renamed the Turkish Lira. Its introduction was intended to stabilize the economy. This seemed to succeed, as both inflation and the unemployment rate fell. Unfortunately, Turkey was not immune to the global recession, as unemployment hit record highs in 2009.

Social Studies

Turkey's economy, which was once dependent on agriculture and focused on the rural areas, has become much more reliant on its larger cities. The service, electronics, and automotive industries are now much larger than the agricultural industry. Use the Internet to find government or industry publications on one of Turkey's growing industries, and write one page of exploratory research.

Common Turkish Words and Phrases	
Hello/Hi	Merhaba
Goodbye	Güle Güle
Yes/No	Evet/Hayir
Please	Lütfen
Thank you	Tesekkür derim
You're welcome	Buyrun

Step 2: Obtain Secondary Resources

Information that has already been collected by someone else is called **secondary data**. It is easily obtained and inexpensive. A good place to begin your search is the Internet. However, pay attention to the sources you find. Just because information appears on a Web page does not mean it is true.

Government and community organizations are excellent sources of secondary data. The U.S. Census Bureau's Website provides information that is helpful in defining your market by a number of demographics. Your local chamber of commerce keeps statistics on local population trends and other economic issues. You can also consult trade associations, trade publications, and commercial research agencies.

Keep these questions in mind when collecting secondary data:
- What are the demographics of the customer?
- What are the psychographics of the customer?
- How large is the market?
- Is the market growing?
- Is the market affected by geography?
- How can you reach your market?
- How do your competitors reach the market?
- What market strategies have been successful with these customers?

Step 3: Collect Primary Data

Primary data is information you collect yourself. It is important because it is current and relates directly to your objectives.

The most common methods of gathering primary data about customers are observation, interviews, and surveys. For your Internet business, you might go to a competitor's site and observe the kinds of content and activity on the site. If the site has a way for you to make comments or interact with other users, you will gain a lot of information about their likes and dislikes.

In surveys, individuals answer questions in person, by telephone, through the mail, or online. In-person surveys will achieve the highest level of success. In-person interviews produce an even higher response rate than other methods. Focus groups, which are more efficient than one-on-one interviews, can also be used. There are also several Websites that can help you develop an online survey. Whichever type of data you collect, use several reputable sources. Keep these questions in mind when collecting primary data:
- What are the demographics of your customer?
- Would potential customers purchase your product or service? Why or why not?
- How much would customers purchase?
- When would customers purchase?
- How would customers like to find the product or service?
- What is it that customers like about your competitors' products and services?

Step 4: Organize the Data

Categorize data based on the research question it answers. Working on each question, note how many of your sources supported a particular conclusion and how many did not.

Next, create charts and graphs to depict your findings. You may also record your results in report form. The results will help you assess your venture's feasibility. As you continue the entrepreneurial process, you can refer to this information or add to it as needed. This data will help you refine your market analysis and can eventually serve as the basis for a marketing plan.

Step 5: Analyze the Data

Now that your information has been organized, ask yourself some basic questions.

- Is there a market for the product or service?
- How big is the market?
- Will the industry support such a business?
- What do substitute products/services reveal about demand for the product/service?
- What do customers, end users, and intermediaries predict the demand will be?

The answers to these questions will help you judge your chances of having a successful business.

SECTION 6.1 | Review

After You Read ■■■■■■■■■■■■■

Self-Check

1. **Explain** why it is important to study your industry before developing a business concept.
2. **Describe** the role of market research.
3. **List** the different types of market research and the steps in the market research process.

Think

4. **Explain** how you will analyze the industry and the target market for your own business ideas.

English Language Arts/Writing

5. **Analyze Language** Choose a type of product that you can purchase under various brand names in a grocery store such as shampoo, pet food, or pasta sauce. Go to a grocery store and look at the language used on the packaging. List the descriptive words and phrases different brands use. Write a paragraph that explains how each brand uses language to differentiate itself from the competition.

Go to **connectED.mcgraw-hill.com** to check your answers.

Industry and Market Analysis

Reading Guide

Connect Why should you research the industry?

The Main Idea
Studying a company's industry and market helps an entrepreneur create a product or service that people want. It also helps the entrepreneur develop a customer profile, estimate demand, and increase the chances for success.

Objectives
Explain how to research an industry.
Identify a customer profile and customer needs analysis.

Content Vocabulary
◇ barriers to entry
◇ economies of scale
◇ brand loyalty
◇ market share
◇ niche
◇ market positioning
◇ competitive advantage
◇ customer profile
◇ customer needs analysis

Academic Vocabulary
You will see these words in your reading and on your tests. Use the academic vocabulary glossary to look up their meanings.
■ trend
■ project

Graphic Organizer
Before you read this section, draw a chart like the one shown. As you read, write the four questions to ask when creating a customer profile.

 Go to connectED.mcgraw-hill.com to download this graphic organizer.

Customer Profile Questions
1. Who are my customers?
2.
3.
4.

Researching the Industry

In this section, you will look at industry **trends** and demographics and the competition. With this information, you can develop a profile of your first customer.

Trends and Patterns of Change

You can find opportunity in an industry by looking at trends and patterns of change. For example, is it becoming more difficult for new companies to enter the industry? Has the rate of sales growth slowed? How volatile is the industry? (Volatility refers to how quickly things change in the industry.)

Industry Forces that Affect Your Business

A number of forces will affect your ability to do business. They will also influence your business strategy. Understanding these competitive forces can help you plan a strategy to succeed.

Barriers to Entry

In established industries, the dominant businesses have advantages called barriers to entry. **Barriers to entry** are conditions or circumstances that make it difficult or costly for outside firms to enter a market to compete with the established firm or firms. Established businesses have achieved economies of scale in production, marketing, and distribution. These are barriers to entry for entrepreneurs. **Economies of scale** are situations where the cost of producing one unit of a good or service decreases as the volume of production increases. This means that production costs decline relative to the price of goods and services.

Brand loyalty is loyalty to or the tendency to buy a particular brand of a product. Customers who are brand loyal do not easily switch to a new company that enters the industry.

Existing businesses may prevent new companies from entering certain distribution channels and may cooperate with other businesses to keep out new players. The government regulates many industries and this results in higher costs. If you want to start a business that is subject to many government regulations, you may want to partner with an existing business in your industry that knows how to deal with the regulations to gain access to customers and distribution channels.

Threats From Substitute Products

If the industry that you have selected is extremely competitive, you will be competing with companies that produce products and services that are similar to yours. In addition, your

Web Savvy

Must Love Blogs
Until recently, most blogs (Web logs) were created by individuals, either to explore a hobby or to keep an online journal. But businesses now see blogs as a possible way to get closer to their customers and create loyalty. In fact, more than 60 percent of businesses have a blog of some type. Blogs are interactive: readers can leave comments, thereby starting a conversation with the company. When managed properly, this feature assures customers that the company cares about what its users think. Some companies even use blogs to announce new features and products. *How do major companies use blogs, and what kinds of comments do they generate?*

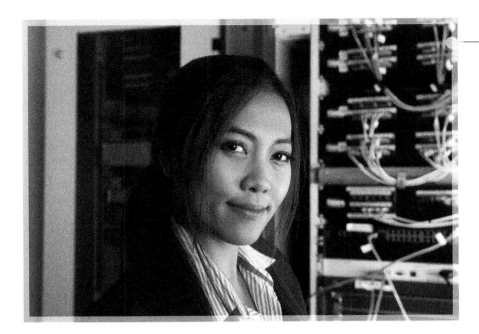

Barriers to Entry Certain conditions or circumstances can make it difficult for outside firms to enter a market to compete with established firms. *How might technology be a barrier to entry?*

business will also be competing with companies that produce substitute products, those that offer an alternative to customers.

For example, suppose you are planning to open a restaurant serving low-carbohydrate meals. You will be competing with other restaurants in your area, with grocery stores, and with specialty food stores. Most products have substitutes.

Sources of Supply

Your suppliers will have an impact on sales. You must have access to affordable sources of inventory, raw materials, and goods. Otherwise, you will not be able to offer your product or service at prices that generate sales. You should also consider where your suppliers are located, the trade discounts they offer, and the availability of alternate sources. These can affect your costs, pricing, and sales.

Buyers' Ability to Bargain

In industries where buyers have bargaining power, a new business may have difficulty gaining a foothold. Large discount buyers, such as Wal-Mart™, Costco™, and Home Depot™, have enormous bargaining power. This enables them to purchase their inventories at deep discounts. Small businesses do not generally have that power and must look for other ways to compete. Generally, they do this by offering personalized service and customized products.

Technology

Technology enables companies to improve their business processes. Companies that use technology to operate effectively and efficiently are more likely to remain competitive.

Industry Demographics

Each industry has basic characteristics, or demographics. These include the number of companies, annual revenues, and average size of the companies by number of employees. These facts reveal whether the industry is growing, shrinking, or remaining stable.

● **As You Read** ▪▪▪▪▪▪▪
Recognize What are some trends you see in industries that interest you?

darren wise/Getty Images

The Competition

Outstanding sales potential for a product does not guarantee success. Usually, competing products are already established in the market. To succeed, you must be able to capture market share by differentiating your business. **Market share** is a portion of the total sales generated by all competing companies in a given market.

Many entrepreneurial companies succeed by studying the competition to define an unserved niche in the market. A **niche** is a small, specialized segment of the market based on customer needs discovered in market research. **Market positioning** is the act of identifying a specific market niche for a product or service.

To succeed in the face of competition, you must do a thorough analysis of the competition. First, create a competitive matrix (see Chapter 5). Use the information in the matrix to identify what is unique about your business and define your competitive advantage. A **competitive advantage** is a feature that makes a product more desirable than its competitors' products.

> **Reading Check Interpret** What does brand loyalty mean? Are you loyal to any brands?

Researching the Target Customer

No matter how large the target market, you must know your customer and have a market penetration strategy. A market penetration strategy is a plan to reach initial customers and grow. You must establish relationships with customers and target your marketing efforts toward them.

Creating a Customer Profile

A **customer profile** is a complete picture of a business's prospective customers. It includes geographic, demographic, and psychographic data, such as age, income level, education, buying habits (when, where, and how much), places customers typically shop, and method of purchase. In the case of a business customer, you will want to know the size of the business in terms of number of employees and sales levels, purchasing patterns, and where they typically purchase. This customer profile helps you make decisions about your product or service. It also assists you in developing a marketing concept—a strategy for how you will reach the customer.

When you are creating your customer profile, ask yourself:
1. Who are my customers?
2. What do they generally buy, and how do they hear about the products and services they buy?
3. How often do they buy?
4. How can my products or services meet their needs, or what value can I provide?

Evaluating Customers' Needs

A **customer needs analysis** pinpoints the features and benefits of your goods or services that customers value. Suppose you are proposing to sell a new type of breakfast energy bar. You learn that more students like bars that are firm and crunchy better than bars that are soft and chewy. Because students are hungry before school starts, they want food that is easily accessible. Firmness and crunchiness are features of the product, while convenience and portability are benefits. You must provide the features and benefits that your target customers want. If you do, there is a greater chance that they will choose your product or service over the competition's.

Forecasting Demand

Even if you know that your target customers prefer your product over the competition's, you still need to know how much of a product or service they will buy and how often they will buy it. It is difficult to determine demand with any degree of certainty. Several methods can be used to forecast a demand figure.

Business Case Study

Young Entrepreneurs Can Be Big Winners

Students in low-income communities reap success by exercising their business smarts

Could you sell a product in 60 seconds? Students in the Elevator Pitch Challenge, sponsored by the Network for Teaching Entrepreneurs (NFTE), compete ever year to do just that. Winners receive $2,500 toward their education and their business.

Participants in an even bigger competition—the NFTE's National Youth Entrepreneurship Challenge—present business plans to a board of judges for a chance to win $25,000 and meet the President in the Oval Office.

The NFTE aims to assist middle school and high school students in low-income communities. It provides year-round programs to encourage students to stay in school and help them plan for successful careers as entrepreneurs. NFTE has taught entrepreneurial skills to more than 500,000 young people both in the United States and around the world.

> **Active Learning**
>
> Make a spreadsheet or chart. Across the top, list 10 reasons to be an entrepreneur. Put a check beneath each reason that appeals to you. Choose the three reasons that appeal to you most. Write a short paragraph about each reason, explaining why it appeals to you and how it harmonizes with your goals, skills, aptitudes, and personality. Share your ideas with the class.

One way to forecast a demand figure is to use analogous products. You may be able to **project** the demand for your product or service based on demand for another one. The demand for Blu-ray discs, for example, was a result of the historical demand for DVDs and videotapes. You also may be able to forecast demand by considering demand for a similar product.

A second way to forecast demand is to interview prospective customers and intermediaries. No one knows the market better than the people who work in it. Talking with customers, distributors, wholesalers, and retailers can give you a good estimate of demand.

A third way to forecast demand is to go into limited production to test the market. The only way to test the reaction of potential customers may be to produce a small number of products. Then you can put them in the hands of people to test. Using a kiosk is a relatively inexpensive way to gauge demand for a product. A kiosk is an independent stand from which merchandise is sold, often placed in the common area of a shopping center. If you are starting an Internet business, putting up an inexpensive version of your site to gauge interest is one way to prove your concept.

SECTION 6.2 | Review

After You Read ▪▪▪▪▪▪▪▪▪▪▪▪▪▪▪

Self-Check

1. **Explain** the importance of defining a target market and a market niche.
2. **Describe** the role of competition in marketing.
3. **List** the four key questions you should ask about your target customer.

Think

4. **Examine** the trends and patterns that affect an industry that interests you. In a one-page report, predict where the industry will be in ten years.

Mathematics

5. **Calculating Price Increases** Sara Twoomey runs a market research firm in Indiana. Last year she was paying $1,465 a month for utilities. She received a notice that her costs will increase 4.5% next year. Describe two different ways you could determine the new price. What will she pay for utilities next year?

   Math Concept **Computing Fluently** Multiplying the original cost by a percent increase, then adding that amount to the original cost, is the same as multiplying the original cost by 100% plus the percent increase.

   Step 1 Write an equation using the percent increase.

   Step 2 Write a different equation using 100% plus the percent increase.

✈ Go to connectED.mcgraw-hill.com to check your answers.

Entrepreneurs *in Action*

Rahim Fazal
CEO and Co-Founder
Involver

Q *What do you do?*

A I am the CEO of Involver, a brand marketing platform for social networks. We work with some of the largest brands in the world, including Nissan, Puma, and Pepsi, and help them distribute and track their multimedia content (like videos and photos) to targeted audiences—and their friends!

Q *What kind of training and education did you need to get this job?*

A The nice part about running a start-up is that there are no prerequisite qualifications. You do learn a lot from your mistakes, and in the start-up world, the more mistakes you make early on in your career, the better. After starting a successful company, and failing at another, I decided to head to business school and graduated with my MBA before starting Involver. The rigorous academic training and problem-solving have been helpful in making quicker—and higher quality—decisions this time around.

Q *What do you enjoy most about your job?*

A Working with some of the smartest people in the world.

Q *How did you become interested in your field?*

A I started programming when I was 6 years old. By the time the Internet became mainstream, my best friend and I already had several online businesses running. Since they all made money from online advertising, figuring out how brands sell to their customers became one of the most interesting and profitable opportunities to pursue.

CCR ☆ College & Career Readiness

Collecting Information
Research a business in your community to find out how it collects demographic information about its customers.

1. Select a company in your state or city.
2. Identify the ways the company collects and uses a customer's name, address, phone number, occupation, age, spending patterns, and other information.
3. Summarize your findings in a one-page report.

Career Facts

Real-World Skills	Academic Skills	Career Cluster
Problem Solving, Teamwork, Presentation Skills	English Language Arts, Computer Science, Marketing	Marketing; Information Technology

Visual Summary

Your Potential as an Entrepreneur

Subgroups Market segmentation is the process of grouping a market into smaller subgroups defined by specific characteristics.

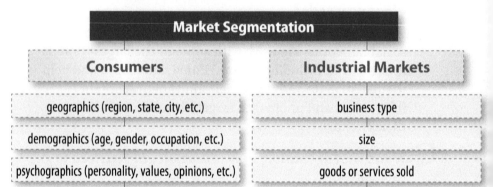

Market Segmentation

Consumers	Industrial Markets
geographics (region, state, city, etc.)	business type
demographics (age, gender, occupation, etc.)	size
psychographics (personality, values, opinions, etc.)	goods or services sold
buying characteristics	geographic location
	products needed

Research Market research aims to understand the behavior of consumers in a certain market.

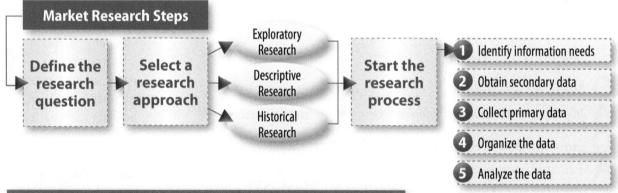

Market Research Steps

Define the research question → Select a research approach → Exploratory Research / Descriptive Research / Historical Research → Start the research process →

1 Identify information needs
2 Obtain secondary data
3 Collect primary data
4 Organize the data
5 Analyze the data

Industry Research	
Barriers to Entry	Keep new business from either entering or succeeding in an industry.
Competition	Determine your own competitive advantage and your ability to capture market share from other companies in the field.
Customer Profile	Gives the entrepreneur critical information that can be used to refine the product or service and select the correct distribution channel.

Trends Look at patterns and trends of change within an industry.

Vocabulary

1. On a sheet of paper, use each of these terms and words in a written sentence.

Content Vocabulary

◇ industry
◇ value chains
◇ carrying capacity
◇ complexity
◇ market
◇ target market
◇ market segmentation
◇ market segments
◇ geographics
◇ psychographics

◇ industrial markets
◇ market research
◇ exploratory research
◇ focus group
◇ descriptive research
◇ historical research
◇ secondary data
◇ primary data
◇ barriers to entry

◇ economies of scale
◇ brand loyalty
◇ market share
◇ niche
◇ market positioning
◇ competitive advantage
◇ customer profile
◇ customer needs analysis

Academic Vocabulary

■ assess   ■ income   ■ trend   ■ project

Key Concepts

2. **Define** some areas of analysis for industry and market research.
3. **Describe** how to conduct market research effectively.
4. **Explain** how to research an industry.
5. **Develop** a customer profile and customer needs analysis.
6. **Define** market segmentation.
7. **Compare** the three types of research.
8. **Determine** the value of studying an industry.
9. **List** the key steps in market research.

Academic Skills

Social Studies

10. **Product Survey** Select a product that is available at a variety of prices. List several brands of the product in order from least expensive to most expensive. Ask as many people as you can to identify which they would choose. Describe the results to the class.

Science

11. **Renewable Energy** Nonrenewable sources of energy such as coal, oil, and uranium cannot be replaced once they are gone. Identify a company that is using renewable resources. Find out why the company is using them and who their target market is. Present your findings to the class.

Academic Skills (continued)
Mathematics

12. **Market Share** Emi owns a paper store. In the store's first year, its market share was 8%. The following year it was 11.5%. The market share over the next three years was 15%, 18.5%, and 22%, respectively. What will it be the following year if the pattern continues? If the market share grows at the same rate, how long will it take for it to reach 36%?

Math Concept **Patterns** A pattern is a sequence of numbers that changes in a consistent way. Patterns can be determined by analyzing how each number is different from the one that comes before and after.

Step 1 Write the market share for each year in order. Compare the numbers to determine the pattern.

Step 2 Extend the pattern until the amount is greater than or equal to 36%.

English Language Arts

13. **Expand Your Vocabulary** Synonyms are words or phrases that mean the same or almost the same thing. Identify a word or phrase for each of the following words that means the same or almost the same thing: *prospect, revenue, niche, barrier, trend, data.*

Real-World Skills

Research Skills
14. **Market Analysis** Pick your dream location to open a new shop in your city. Research the area, who shops there, and what types of products they buy. With detailed facts and figures, explain why a store in that location would or would not be profitable.

21st Century Skills

Information Literacy
15. **Industry Research** Locate the U.S. Census Bureau's Website and the County Business Patterns Economic Profile for your county. Use this profile to identify the industry that employs the most people. Summarize your findings in one or two paragraphs.

Connect to Your Community

16. **Identify the Competition** Select a business concept and identify potential real-world competitors. Create a chart that lists the competitor companies by name and location and determines the market share percentage for each company.

17. **Interview a Specialist** Invite a marketing specialist from a local company to speak to your class about the company's target market. Find out how market research is conducted. Ask about the demographics of its target customers.

Review and Assessment

Competitive Events Prep

18. **Situation** You own a company that conducts market research for small businesses. You have recently hired a high school student as a summer intern. The intern will assist you with your work and in turn, you are to provide market research training. Today you are going to explain the sources of marketing data, particularly secondary data.

Activity Explain to the intern the importance of secondary data and sources of that data.

Evaluation You will be evaluated on how well you meet the following performance indicators:
- Identify information monitored for marketing decision making.
- Describe sources of secondary data.
- Conduct an environmental scan to obtain marketing information.
- Monitor internal records for marketing information.
- Collect marketing information from others.

 Go to **connected.mcgraw-hill.com** for more information about this activity and other competitive events.

Standardized Test Practice

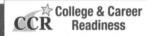

Directions Choose the letter of the best answer. Write the letter for the answer on a separate piece of paper. For question #2, if the answer is False, rewrite the statement to make it true.

1. If you know very little about a subject, the best kind of market research to conduct is _____ research.
   A. exploratory
   B. descriptive
   C. historical
   D. geographics
2. Economies of scale are situations where the cost of producing one unit of a good or service increases as the volume of the production increases.
   T
   F

Types of Business Ownership

Chapter Objectives

SECTION 7.1
Sole Proprietorships and Partnerships

Discuss the sole proprietorship legal form.

Identify the partnership legal form.

SECTION 7.2
Corporations

Explain how the corporate form gives owners more protection from liability.

List the advantages and disadvantages of a C-corporation.

Describe the purpose of a Subchapter S corporation.

Compare nonprofit corporations to C-corporations.

Define the limited liability company.

Discuss how to decide which legal form is best.

Discovery Project

Ownership in Your Community

Key Question? *What types of business ownership can you find in your community?*

Project Goal
Work with a partner to research different businesses in your community and identify the types of ownership. For each business, prepare a short profile that describes its type of ownership (i.e., sole proprietorship, partnership, LLC) and tells why that type was chosen.

Think About...
➤ *How will you find local businesses?*
➤ *How will you determine what type of ownership each business has?*
➤ *How will you organize your research?*

21st Century Skills
Critical Thinking *What qualities or characteristics help businesses thrive in your community?*

Evaluate
 Go to connectED.mcgraw-hill.com to download a rubric that you can use to evaluate your final project.

©DreamPictures/Blend Images/Corbis

Ask
AN
EXPERT

Q: *I want to start up my own software company. If my company does well, where do I find enough money to expand?*

A: Banks offer favorable lending rates to successful businesses that appear poised to grow. The U.S. Small Business Administration also offers loans through its Certified Lenders Program. You can also raise equity capital. This means that you seek out individuals who are looking for an investment opportunity with a potential for a high return. The investors take a financial risk by contributing money to help you expand your business. You agree to give them a share of future profits.

Connect the Photo

Solo or Partners? Understanding the advantages and disadvantages of the different business types helps entrepreneurs determine how best to run their business. Whether you decide a partnership will help you achieve your dreams, or whether a corporation is the way to go, finding the solution that meets your needs and values is key. *How can partnerships give you a competitive advantage?*

Sole Proprietorships and Partnerships

Reading Guide

Before You Read ■■■■■■■■■■■■■■

Connect What are some good qualities to look for in a business partner?

The Main Idea

Entrepreneurs need to understand the advantages and disadvantages of various types of businesses so that they can choose the one that best suits their needs.

Objectives

Discuss the sole proprietorship legal form.
Identify the partnership legal form.

Content Vocabulary

◇ sole proprietorship   ◇ partnership
◇ liability protection   ◇ general partner
◇ unlimited liability   ◇ limited partner

Academic Vocabulary

You will see these words in your reading and on your tests. Use the academic vocabulary glossary to look up their meanings.
■ authority
■ technical

Graphic Organizer

Before you read this section, draw a chart like the one shown. As you read, list facts about sole proprietorships and partnerships.

 Go to connectED.mcgraw-hill.com to download this graphic organizer.

Sole Proprietorships	Partnerships
• one owner	• two or more owners
•	•
•	•

Sole Proprietorship

The easiest and most popular form of business to create is the sole proprietorship. A **sole proprietorship** is a business that is owned and operated by one person. Nearly 76 percent of all businesses in the United States are sole proprietorships.

What Is a Sole Proprietorship?

The owner of a sole proprietorship receives the profits, incurs any losses, and is liable for the debts of the business. Most businesses begin as sole proprietorships because they are easy to create. However, entrepreneurs often switch to a form that provides more personal financial protection as the business grows.

Choosing a Sole Proprietorship

To decide whether a sole proprietorship is right for you, ask yourself the following questions:

1. How much **liability protection**, or insurance, do you need?
2. Do you need to seek investment capital?
3. What effect will the business have on your tax status?

Consider these questions as you take a look at the advantages and disadvantages of the sole proprietorship.

Advantages

The sole proprietorship is easy and inexpensive to create. It gives the owner complete **authority** over all business activities. It also allows the owner to receive all of the profits. It is the least regulated form of ownership. In addition, the business itself pays no taxes because it is not separate from the owner. Instead, the income from the business is taxed at the personal rate of the owner. The personal tax rate often is lower than the corporate tax rate.

Disadvantages

The biggest disadvantage of a sole proprietorship is financial. To start, the owner has **unlimited liability**, or full responsibility for all debts and actions of the business. That means the owner is personally responsible for any and all debts of the business. The debts may have to be paid from the owner's personal assets. Thus, the owner's home, car, and bank account may be at risk. In addition, raising capital may be more difficult. The owner may not have enough assets to qualify for a loan or to satisfy investor requirements.

Other disadvantages center on the owner as a person. A sole proprietorship may be limited by its total reliance on the abilities and skills of the owner. These may not be sufficient. Finally, the death of the owner automatically dissolves the business unless there is a will to the contrary.

● **As You Read**.........
Compare What is the difference between a general partner and a limited partner?

Go Green

Small Business Equals Big Green

Large corporations tend to dominate the focus of attention when it comes to environmental practices. Small businesses, which make up 98 percent of all companies in the U.S., can play a key role as well. The Business Alliance for Local Living Economies (BALLE) is a network that brings small businesses together to share ideas, experiences, and tools about green business across 22 states, Washington, D.C., and Canada.

❖ **Critical Thinking**
Research a small business in your area that is using new and innovative environmental practices. Write a paragraph identifying these practices and their environmental impact.

Business | Case Study

When Business Partners Disagree

Mediation and arbitration are alternatives to a court battle

People in a business partnership disagree from time to time. How and when partners resolve conflicts can determine whether the business thrives or fails.

Disagreement can actually be good for a business. Your partner may have spotted a pitfall you overlooked. You may see an opportunity your partner hasn't. In fact, research shows that disagreement helps teams make better decisions. If your difference of opinion is hurting the business, however, the best remedy may be mediation or arbitration.

In mediation, an outsider with no stake in the outcome of the dispute looks at the issues and makes a recommendation. If the problem is more complex, you may

need arbitration. Arbitration is like mediation but it is a legal process, so you and your partner must abide by the decision.

You and your partner may need to part ways. If you want to work it out, mediation or arbitration can help you proceed with fairness and good will.

> **Active Learning**
>
> Create a list of issues that you think might cause disagreements in a business partnership. Pick one item from the list. Write three paragraphs: the first presenting one view of the issue, the second presenting the opposing view, and the third presenting the solution from a mediator's point of view.

How to Set Up a Sole Proprietorship

Operating as a sole proprietor is as simple as deciding on the company name. When using a name other than your own, you must apply for a Certificate of Doing Business Under an Assumed Name. This is often called a DBA ("doing business as") or a fictitious business name statement. You can get a DBA from the government offices in your target location. Filing a DBA ensures that the name you have chosen for your business is the only one in the area.

If you are going to hire employees, you need an Employer Identification Number (EIN). This number, which comes from the Internal Revenue Service, is used for tax purposes to track federal income tax withheld and federal income tax returns.

You need a sales tax identification number if you are a vendor or retailer. This number is assigned by a state's Department of Revenue. It is used for sales tax record keeping. The retailer acts as an agent for the state by collecting and remitting the required amount. You can apply for this number on the Internet.

 Reading Check Recall What is a sole proprietorship?

Partnerships

A **partnership** is an unincorporated business with two or more owners. A partnership is the most common business organization involving more than one owner. Two or more people own a business and share the decisions, assets, liabilities, and profits. As a legal form of ownership, the partnership compensates for some of the shortcomings of a sole proprietorship. The partnership can draw on the skills, knowledge, and financial resources of more than one person. This is an advantage when seeking loans. A partnership requires a DBA ("Doing Business As") when the last names of the partners are not used in naming the business. Professionals such as lawyers, and accountants are frequently set up as partnerships.

General versus Limited Partners

A partnership may be set up so all of the partners are general partners. A **general partner** is a participant in a partnership who has unlimited personal liability and takes full responsibility for managing the business. Anyone entering into a general partnership must remember that each general partner is liable for all the debts of the partnership. Furthermore, any partner alone can bind the partnership on contracts. The law requires that all partnerships have at least one general partner.

Partners do not have to share a business equally. They can assign the interest in the partnership according to the amount contributed at start-up. How the partnership interests are divided is spelled out in the partnership agreement. Sometimes businesses have limited partners.

Tech Savvy

Clean Tech

Entrepreneurs see a golden opportunity in clean tech, or new technologies that are friendly to the environment. Coskata, Inc. has partnered with General Motors to develop technology that can convert old tires, plastic containers, and other kinds of garbage into 99.7 percent pure fuel-grade ethanol. Coskata uses a high-temperature oxygen-empowered process to convert carbon-based material into a synthesis gas called syngas. Proprietary microorganisms then eat and digest the syngas, producing ethanol as their waste. If successful, this technology could turn landfills into gold mines, while at the same time cleaning up the environment. *What kinds of clean technology can you find in your community?*

Shared Liability If you form a partnership, you should choose your partner carefully. *Why should you clearly define your partner's role?*

ETHICS and BUSINESS

Starting Your Own Business

You have been the assistant manager of a coffee shop for the past four years and have made friends with many of the regular customers. Recently, you have been thinking about opening up a coffee shop of your own.

Going out on your own An ideal space is available in a busy shopping center around the corner from your current place of work. Your instincts tell you that many of the customers that you have befriended would follow you to your new business.

English Language Arts/Writing

Fair Competition Business owners must deal with competition, but they might not think it is fair for a former employee to compete with them directly. Do you think it is fair?

1. How could you open your own business but stay on good terms with your current employer?
2. Write a one-page report explaining your reasoning.

A **limited partner** is a partner whose liability is limited to his or her investment. If a limited partner invests $10,000 in a business, the most he or she can lose is $10,000. Limited partners cannot be actively involved in managing the business. If they become involved, they lose their limited liability status.

Advantages

The advantages of a partnership are similar to those of a sole proprietorship. This form of business is inexpensive to create, and the general partners have complete control. Partnerships have other benefits. They can share ideas and secure investment capital more easily and in greater amounts.

Disadvantages

Despite the advantages, a partnership may not be the preferred form of ownership. It is difficult to dissolve one partner's interest in the business without dissolving the partnership. In other words, if one partner wants out or dies, the partnership ends. The business is likely to survive only when specific provisions have been placed in the partnership agreement.

Personality Conflicts

Personality conflicts among partners are why most partnerships end. Problems often start as disagreements over authority. Therefore, partners' roles must be clearly defined.

Technical Disadvantages

There are **technical** disadvantages, too. Partners are bound by the laws of agency. This means partners can be held liable for each other's actions. If one partner signs a contract with a supplier, the other partner is bound by the terms of the contract. Otherwise, the business may be sued for breach of contract.

Planning for a Successful Partnership

Partnerships start with the best of intentions. However, disagreements are bound to occur. Partners must consider each other's needs before committing to the partnership. Even more important is that they plan for disagreements.

Making a Partnership Work

In general, a partnership has the greatest chance of surviving when partners:
- Share business responsibilities.
- Put things in writing.
- Be honest about how the business is doing.

It is also important for partners to establish a partnership agreement before the business is started.

The Legal Side

The law does not require a partnership to be based on a written agreement. However, a partnership should still have one. Partnership agreements are usually drawn up by attorneys and are based on the Uniform Partnership Act.

Agreements answer many questions, including how profits will be shared among partners and how the responsibilities of the business will be divided. They also spell out what happens if one partner dies or quits. A well-constructed partnership agreement can solve many problems.

SECTION 7.1 | Review

After You Read ━━━━━━━━━━━

Self-Check
1. **Describe** a sole proprietorship.
2. **Explain** the purpose of a partnership agreement.
3. **Differentiate** between general and limited partners.

Think
4. **Explain** the procedure for registering a sole proprietorship and obtaining a sales tax identification number.

English Language Arts
5. **Design a Flyer** You recently purchased a neighborhood restaurant. The restaurant has been in the neighborhood for a long time and has been losing customers for years. The restaurant has been closed for two months while you remodeled the building and revamped the menu. Design a one-page flyer that will let people know the restaurant will be reopening soon.

Go to connectED.mcgraw-hill.com to check your answers.

SECTION 7.2

Corporations

Before You Read ■■■■■■■■■■■■■■■

Preview What are some corporations with which you are familiar?

The Main Idea
In a corporation, the owners of the business are protected from liability for the actions of the company.

Objectives
Explain how the corporate form gives owners more protection from liability.
List the advantages and disadvantages of a C-corporation.
Describe the purpose of a Subchapter S corporation.

Compare nonprofit corporations to C-corporations.
Define the limited liability company.
Discuss how to decide which legal form is best.

Content Vocabulary
◇ corporation
◇ C-corporation
◇ shareholders
◇ limited liability
◇ Subchapter S corporation
◇ nonprofit corporation
◇ limited liability company (LLC)

Academic Vocabulary
You will see these words in your reading and on your tests. Use the academic vocabulary glossary to look up their meanings.
■ register   ■ generate

Graphic Organizer
Before you read this section, draw a chart like the one shown. As you read, list six key advantages of corporations

 Go to **connectED.mcgraw-hill.com** to download this graphic organizer.

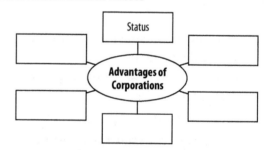

What Is a Corporation?

A **corporation** is a business that is **registered** by a state and operates apart from its owners. A corporation lives on after the owners have sold their interests or passed away. Ownership or equity in a corporation is represented by shares of stock. Corporations can purchase goods, sue and be sued, and conduct any type of business transaction.

Three major types of corporations are the C-corporation, Subchapter S corporation, and nonprofit corporation. **Figure 7.1** on page 160 compares the types of business forms and identifies factors that influence the choice of ownership type.

C-Corporation

A **C-corporation** is an entity that pays taxes on earnings. Its shareholders pay taxes as well. It is the most common corporate form. It can protect the entrepreneur from being sued for the actions and debts of the corporation.

An attorney should guide the entrepreneur through the process of forming a corporation. This includes the filing of a Certificate of Incorporation with the state and the issuing of stock. **Shareholders** are the owners of the corporation. In smaller private corporations, the founders generally hold the majority of the stock. Therefore, they make the policy decisions. A corporation is also required to have a board of directors that makes decisions and selects officers to run the company.

Advantages

There are many benefits and advantages to incorporation. These include status, limited liability, the ability to raise investment money, perpetual existence, employee benefits, and tax advantages.

An officially incorporated business has a more professional appearance. Corporate status can help a business get loans. Corporations must hold certain types of meetings and appoint certain kinds of officers, which can help a business run more efficiently.

● As You Read ....
Connect How can you decide which legal form of business is right for you?

Lock, Stock, and Barrel At stock exchanges, traders buy and sell stock, which represents ownership or equity in a corporation. *What is the advantage of holding the majority of a company's stock?*

Legal Forms of Ownership—A Comparison

Issues	Sole Proprietorship	Partnership	Limited Liability Company	C-Corporation	Subchapter S Corporation
Number of Owners	One	No limit	No limit; most states require minimum of two	No limit on share-holders	75 shareholders or fewer
Start-up Costs	Filing fees for DBA and business license	Attorney fees for partnership agreement; filing fees for DBA	Attorney fees for organization, documents, filing fees	Attorney fees for incorporation documents; filing fees	Attorney fees for incorporation documents; filing fees
Liability	Owner liable for all claims against business; can overcome liability with insurance	General partners liable for all claims; limited partners liable only for amount of investment	Members liable as in partnerships	Shareholders liable to amount invested; officers may be person-ally liable	Shareholders liable to amount invested
Taxation	Pass-through taxation; the profits or losses of the business pass-through to the owner to be taxed at his or her individual tax rate	Pass-through taxation; the profits or losses of the business pass-through to the partners to be taxed at their indi-vidual tax rates	Pass-through taxa-tion; the profits or losses of the busi-ness pass-through to the members to be taxed at their individual tax rates	Tax-paying entity; taxed on corpo-rate income	Pass-through taxation; the profits or losses of the business pass through to the shareholders to be taxed at their indi-vidual tax rates
Continuity of Life of Business	Dissolution upon death of owner	Dissolution upon death or separa-tion of partner unless otherwise specified in the agreement; not so in the case of limited partners	Most states allow perpetual life; unless otherwise stated in Articles of Organization, existence termi-nates upon death or withdrawal of member	Perpetual life; the entity may live forever without interruption by death of share-holders, directors or officers	Perpetual life: the entity may live forever without interruption by death of share-holders, directors or officers
Transferability of Interest	Owner is free to sell; with valid will, assets trans-ferred to estate upon death of owner	General partner requires consent of other generals to sell interest; limited partners' ability to transfer subject to agree-ment	Permission of majority of mem-bers to transfer interest	Shareholders free to sell unless restricted by agreement	Shareholders free to sell unless restricted by agreement
Distribution of Profits	Profits go to owner	Profits shared based on part-nership agree-ment	Profits shared based on mem-ber agreement/ articles of organi-zation	Paid to sharehold-ers as dividends according to agreement and shareholder status	Paid to share-holders accord-ing to percentage of ownership
Management Control	Owner has full control	Partners have equal voting rights unless there is an agreement	Management committee	Board of directors appointed by shareholders	Board of directors appointed by shareholders

● **Advantages and Disadvantages** Each form of ownership has benefits and drawbacks. *Which kinds of businessess are suited for a C-Corporation?*

Limited Liability

Corporate shareholders have **limited liability**; they are liable only up to the amount of their individual investment. However, some banks require corporate officers to personally guarantee the debts. The corporation can raise money by issuing stock.

Corporations have perpetual existence. They have a continuous life regardless of changes in ownership. Corporations can accommodate employee benefits. Corporate owners can create pension and retirement funds and offer profit sharing plans. Corporations have tax advantages. They can deduct certain expenses from their reportable income, including salaries and contributions to benefit plans.

Disadvantages

The corporate form is expensive to set up. It can cost between $500 and $2,500 to create a corporation. A corporation's income is more heavily taxed. The corporation is subject to double taxation on its earnings. The corporation pays taxes on profits; then stockholders pay taxes on dividends they receive from those earnings.

 Reading Check **Recall** What are the advantages of the corporate form?

GLOBAL WORKPLACE — Portuguese: Brazil and Beyond

Portuguese is the official language of Brazil, the largest country in South America. It is also an official language of several other countries around the world, including Portugal, Mozambique, Angola, Macao, and East Timor. The Portuguese spoken in Brazil differs from the Portuguese spoken in Portugal, just as North American English differs from English in the United Kingdom.

Time Standards In Brazil, punctuality is flexible. Meetings rarely start on time, and it is not considered rude to be late for an appointment, except when meeting at a restaurant. However, it is important to bear in mind that your clients can keep you waiting, but you cannot do the same.

Social Studies/Science The majority of the Amazon Rainforest is in Brazil. Scientists and entrepreneurs are exploring the Amazon's biological diversity for new ideas in medicine and biotechnology. Research the entrepreneurial opportunities being developed in the rainforest and summarize your findings in a one-page report.

Common Brazilian Portuguese Words and Phrases	
Hello, hi	alo, oi
Bye (informal)	tchau
Yes/ No	sim/ não
Please	por favor
Thank you	obrigado/ obrigada
You're welcome	de nada

Subchapter S Corporation

An entrepreneur can avoid the double taxation of a C-corporation by setting up a Subchapter S corporation. The **Subchapter S corporation** is a corporation that is taxed like a partnership.

Advantages

Profits are taxed only once at the shareholder's personal tax rate. Therefore, unlike the corporation, the Subchapter S corporation is not a taxpaying entity.

Disadvantages

In general, Subchapter S corporations can have no more than 75 stockholders who must be U.S. citizens. Subchapter S corporations can have only one class of stock.

Cash businesses, such as restaurants, are often Subchapter S corporations. If the business produces enough cash, the form works. If the business shows a large taxable profit but has not **generated** enough cash to cover the taxes, the owners must pay the taxes out of their personal earnings.

Nonprofit Corporation

Many entrepreneurs run businesses that benefit a certain cause in the community. A **nonprofit corporation** is a legal entity that makes money for reasons other than the owners' profit. The types of nonprofit corporations are shown in **Figure 7.2**. Nonprofit businesses can make a profit. However, the profit must remain within the company and not be distributed to shareholders.

Limited Liability Company

A **limited liability company (LLC)** is a company whose owners and managers enjoy limited liability and some tax benefits, but it avoids some restrictions associated with Subchapter S corporations. An LLC is similar in some aspects to a corporation and in other aspects to a limited partnership. There are many benefits to forming an LLC, including:

- An LLC is simpler to set up than a corporation.
- An LLC allows for the flexibility of a partnership structure.
- The LLC protects its owners with the limited liability of a corporation. Its members are not liable for the company's debts.

- An LLC is not subject to double taxation. The LLC provides the pass-through tax advantages of a partnership. Profits are taxed personally, and shareholders are taxed only once.
- Unlike a Subchapter S corporation, there are no limitations on the number of members or their status.

Many law and medical firms form LLCs to protect their partners. LLCs are also popular with foreign investors and family owners. Check with your state for its requirements on forming LLCs.

 Reading Check **Contrast** What are some of the differences between a corporation and a limited liability company?

Making the Decision

It is very important that the entrepreneur carefully evaluate the pros and cons of the various legal forms before organizing a new venture. Consider your skills, access to capital, and expenses. Also consider your willingness to assume liability and the degree of control you would like to have over your business. The length of time you expect to own the business should also be taken into account.

 **Figure 7.2** Nonprofit Corporations

Charity — Charitable causes include feeding the poor and providing job training for the unemployed.

Public Benefit — Many nonprofit foundations are created to advance science, education, and the arts.

Mutual Benefit — Trade associations, amateur sports leagues, and political groups are formed to benefit a specific group.

Not for Profit Nonprofit corporations must fall within one of four categories: religion, charity, public benefit, and mutual benefit. *How would you categorize an after-school program designed to help elementary school children learn about building a business?*

Questions to Ask

With a good understanding of legal forms, you can make a wise decision about which form is best for you. Ask yourself these questions before making the final choice.

- Do you and your team have all of the skills needed?
- Do you have the capital needed to start the business alone, or must you raise it through cash or credit?
- Will you be able to run the business and cover living expenses for the first year?
- Are you willing and able to assume personal liability for any claims against the business?
- Do you want complete control over the operation of the business?
- Do you expect to have initial losses, or will the business be profitable from the beginning?
- Do you expect to sell the business some day?

SECTION 7.2 | Review

After You Read ....

Self-Check

1. **List** three reasons people choose the corporate form.
2. **Explain** the difference between a C-corporation and a Subchapter S corporation.
3. **Describe** a limited liability company.

Think

4. **Describe** how a nonprofit business can benefit both the owner and the community.

Mathematics

5. **GDP** Robert Gomez was considering starting his own business consulting firm. He knew that the economy was in recession, and starting a new business during a downturn was risky. He read that the change from the previous quarter's GDP was −0.3%. Write an explanation of how to calculate this quarter's GDP using paper and pencil.

   Math Concept **Rational Numbers** 0.3% is a rational number. Any rational number can be expressed as a fraction, a decimal, or as a percent. Multiplying by the decimal equivalent of a percent is a convenient way to calculate the result of change.

   Step 1: Think about how to express the percent as its decimal equivalent.

   Step 2: Describe the operations you would use to calculate the resulting GDP.

   Go to **connectED.mcgraw-hill.com** to check your answers.

Entrepreneurs *in Action*

Una Kim
Owner and CEO
Keep

Q *What do you do?*

A I am the CEO of a women's footwear and apparel company called Keep. I oversee the operations of the business and creatively direct our products and our marketing.

Q *What kind of training and education did you need to get this job?*

A I have a bachelor's degree in Economics and a master's degree in Business Administration. School provides a really important backbone, but getting out there and working on projects is the best preparation. This can mean working at other jobs that will give you relevant skills, but it can also mean your own projects. I worked in marketing, but I also organized music festivals, played in bands, and contributed to zines! Keeping up with the latest technology is also really important.

Q *What do you enjoy most about your job?*

A I love working with people I respect and who inspire me every day. It's also really great to be involved in all the little details of the company. I feel proud when I see my shoes and clothing come into being.

Q *How did you become interested in your field?*

A I've always loved bridging creativity with business. The whole process of taking an idea and bringing it to life is a really fulfilling and challenging journey. Business is just an avenue to bring cool ideas into the world to share with other people.

Career Facts

Real-World Skills	Academic Skills	Career Cluster
Speaking, Listening, Problem Solving	Mathematics, English Language Arts, Industrial Design, Marketing	Business, Management & Administration; Marketing, Sales & Service

Una Kim

Visual Summary

Types of Business Ownership

		Advantage	Disadvantage
Sole Proprietorship	• Owned and operated by one person. • Easy and inexpensive to create.	Taxed at personal rate of owner.	Unlimited liability.
Partnerships	• Unincorporated business of two or more owners. General partners are responsible for all liability and management; limited partners' liability is limited to his or her investment.	General partners have complete control.	If one person wants out, the partnership ends.
C-Corporation	• An entity that pays taxes on earnings. • The most common corporate form.	Protects entrepreneurs from being sued for the corporation's actions.	Share-holders pay taxes as well.
Subchapter S Corporation	• Must have 75 shareholders or fewer. • Often chosen for cash businesses, such as restaurants.	Taxed like a partnership.	Owners might end up paying taxes out of their personal earnings.
Limited Liability Corporation	• Avoids some restrictions associated with Subchapter S corporations. • No limitations on the number of members or their status.	Some tax benefits and flexibility.	Members liable as in partnerships.
Nonprofit Corporation	• Makes money for reasons other than the owner's profits. • Four categories of nonprofits: religion, charity, public benefit, and mutual benefit.	Eligible for public and private grants.	Finances are open to public inspection.

Vocabulary

1. On a sheet of paper, use each of these terms and words in a written sentence.

Content Vocabulary

◇ sole proprietorship
◇ liability protection
◇ unlimited liability
◇ partnership
◇ general partner

◇ limited partner
◇ corporation
◇ C-corporation
◇ shareholders
◇ limited liability

◇ Subchapter S corporation
◇ nonprofit corporation
◇ limited liability company (LLC)

Academic Vocabulary

■ authority
■ technical

■ register
■ generate

Key Concepts

2. **Discuss** the sole proprietorship legal form.
3. **Explain** the partnership legal form.
4. **Explain** how the corporate form gives owners more protection from liability.
5. **Discuss** the advantages and disadvantages of a C-corporation.
6. **Explain** the purpose of a Subchapter S corporation.
7. **Compare** nonprofit corporations to C-corporations.
8. **Explain** the limited liability company.
9. **Discuss** how to decide which legal form is best.

Academic Skills

Mathematics

10. **Landscaping** James and Julia formed a partnership to start a landscaping business. Their first job is to lay sod for the front and back lawns of a new home. The front yard measures 22 feet by 48 feet and the backyard measures 20 feet by 54 feet. How many square feet of sod will they need? If sod costs $.12 per square foot, how much it cost for this job?

    Math Concept **Calculating Area** Area equals length times width. Area is always measured in square units. Calculate the area of each yard by multiplying the two lengths by their respective widths. Add the two areas together to get the total area. Remember to label with square units. Calculate the total cost by multiplying the total area of the yard by the cost per square foot.

English Language Arts

11. **Speaking and Listening** Team up with a classmate. Choose a type of business ownership and explain it to your classmate. When you are finished, ask your classmate to summarize your explanation. Discuss any discrepancies in what you said and what your classmate heard.

Academic Skills *(continued)*

Social Studies

12. **The British East India Company** One of the longest-running and most profitable ventures in history, the British East India Company, began as a corporation of merchants in the early 1600s. It grew from a small trading company chartered by the Crown and eventually achieved the position of pseudo-ruler of India and other British colonies. Research and write a one-page report on the history of this company.

Science

13. **Patents** Research the U.S. Patent Office and how it determines if an invention is patentable. Write a one-page paper giving examples of how these standards are applied to an invention, and how scientists and entrepreneurs use these inventions to start-up new ventures.

Real-World Skills

Problem-Solving Skills

14. **Give Good Customer Service** Kano is the sole proprietor of a coffee shop. During the morning rush, the customers become upset when waited on out of order or the service is too slow. Kano is worried about losing loyal customers, but cannot afford to pay another employee. What else can she do to keep her customers coming back?

21st Century Skills

Information Literacy

15. **Identifying Resources** You have decided to start your own auto shop. You need money for tools, materials, rent, and a business license. Identify ways to finance your start-up. For example, you could enter in to an equipment leasing agreement for tools. Explain the details of your research in a one-page report.

Connect to Your Community

16. **Volunteer at a Nonprofit** Volunteer to work or job-shadow in a nonprofit organization. Learn about the nonprofit's structure. As a class, share your experiences and compare your findings.

17. **Host a Panel Discussion** Invite local businesspersons representing different types of business ownership to serve on a panel discussion in your class. Have a list of questions ready before the panel members arrive. Ask them what qualities they believe are important for succeeding in their type of business ownership.

Competitive Events Prep

18. **Situation** You are the sole proprietor of a bicycle shop. You sell a variety of bikes, accessories, clothing, and parts. Because you are a sole proprietor, you work seven days a week. A friend has approached you and has asked to become your partner.

Activity Team up with a classmate and research the advantages and disadvantages of sole proprietorships and partnerships. Then role-play a discussion between the business owner and the potential partner about forms of business ownership.

Evaluation You will be evaluated on how well you meet the following performance indicators:
- Identify factors that influence choice of ownership type.
- Compare and contrast these two types of business ownership.
- Select the most appropriate form of ownership for the business.

 Go to connectED.mcgraw-hill.com for more information about this activity and other competitive events.

Standardized Test Practice

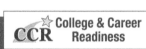
CCR ☆ College & Career Readiness

Directions Choose the letter of the best answer. Write the letter for the answer on a separate piece of paper. For question #2, if the answer is False, rewrite the statement to make it true.

1. Which of the following is not an advantage of a sole proprietorship?
   A. inexpensive to create
   B. gives owner complete authority
   C. unlimited liability
   D. least regulated form of ownership
2. Subchapter S corporations and C-corporations are taxed in the same way.
   T
   F

> **Test-Taking Tip**
> Before you turn in your test, review the test questions and your answers to them. Make any changes you feel are important, but do not change an answer unless you have a good reason.

CHAPTER
8

The Legal Environment

Chapter Objectives

SECTION 8.1

Legal Issues Facing Start-Ups

Explain how to protect your intellectual property.

Discuss the laws affecting the start-up of a business.

SECTION 8.2

Handling Government Regulations

Explain the laws that affect employees.

Identify the laws that regulate trade.

Discuss the tax laws that apply to a new venture.

Discovery Project
Regulating Businesses

Key Question ? | *What laws and regulations apply to different types of businesses?*

Project Goal

Research two different types of businesses—one that provides goods such as a retail clothing store, and one that provides services such as a child care center. Record the federal, state, and local laws that the two different businesses would have to follow.

Think About...

➤ *How will you decide which businesses to research?*
➤ *Where will you find the applicable laws?*
➤ *How will you present your results?*

★ 21st Century Skills

Civic Literacy *What agencies regulate the laws businesses must follow?*

Evaluate

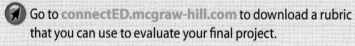 Go to connectED.mcgraw-hill.com to download a rubric that you can use to evaluate your final project.

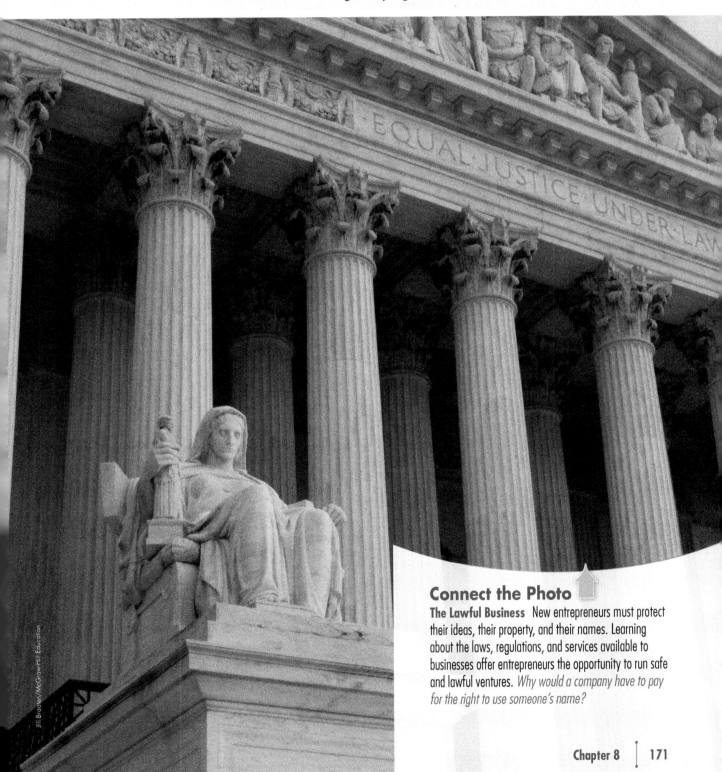

Ask
AN
EXPERT

Q: *I want to raise money by investing in capital markets to start an educational Website for children. I am concerned that I will not have access to the same opportunities as experienced traders. Is there any type of legal regulation that protects me?*

A: The U.S. capital markets are regulated by a system that keeps trading fair and efficient by setting and enforcing standards and rules, settling disputes among market participants, mandating changes, and initiating improvements. Given the scope and complexity of this job, no single regulator can supervise all aspects of capital markets. There are two major groups of regulators: government regulators at both the federal and state level, and self-regulatory organizations (SROs).

Connect the Photo

The Lawful Business New entrepreneurs must protect their ideas, their property, and their names. Learning about the laws, regulations, and services available to businesses offer entrepreneurs the opportunity to run safe and lawful ventures. *Why would a company have to pay for the right to use someone's name?*

Jill Braaten/McGraw-Hill Education

Legal Issues Facing Start-Ups

Reading Guide

Before You Read ■■■■■■■■■■■■■■

Connect What types of things does your business own that you would you want to protect?

The Main Idea

A new product or service must be protected through patents, copyrights, trademarks, or trade secrets. Other aspects of a business are protected by law as well.

Objectives

Explain how to protect your intellectual property.

Discuss the laws affecting the start-up of a business.

Content Vocabulary

◇ intellectual property law
◇ Uniform Trade Secrets Act
◇ patent
◇ public domain
◇ patent pending
◇ copyright
◇ trademark
◇ service mark
◇ permit
◇ license
◇ contract
◇ consideration
◇ capacity

Academic Vocabulary

You will see these words in your reading and on your tests. Use the academic vocabulary glossary to look up their meanings.

■ legal
■ vary

Graphic Organizer

Before you read this section, draw a chart like the one shown. As you read, write down the three categories of laws that affect the start-up of a business.

Go to **connectED.mcgraw-hill.com** to download this graphic organizer.

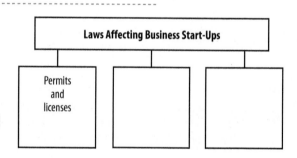

Laws Affecting Business Start-Ups

Permits and licenses

Protecting Ideas: Intellectual Property Law

When you develop a new product or service, you create an asset that must be protected. **Intellectual property law** is the group of laws that regulates the ownership and use of creative works. Protecting an invention falls under patent law. Protecting a logo for a business is a trademark issue. Writing music, software, or books involves copyright law. Trade secrets include anything not covered under patents, trademarks, or copyrights. **Figure 8.1** explains how intellectual property laws protect the inventions and new ideas of businesses.

Trade Secrets

The basis of all intellectual property is trade secrets, which are covered under the **Uniform Trade Secrets Act** (UTSA). According to the UTSA, trade secrets may consist of a formula, device, idea, process, pattern, or compilation of information that is not general knowledge to or accessible by other people. You cannot hold as a trade secret anything that is commonly known. For example, you cannot hold a Web page design that is available on the Internet as a trade secret. It can, however, be copyrighted, which is discussed later in the chapter.

Companies often ask employees and others to sign confidentiality agreements that detail what is considered a trade secret. They also do not give all the components of a trade secret to any one individual, and all trade secrets are market "confidential" or "classified."

● **As You Read** ▪▪▪▪▪▪▪▪
Connect How can you protect items that are not covered by patents, copyrights, and trademarks?

● **Figure 8.1** Protecting Your Ideas

Patents
A patent grants an inventor the right to exclude others from making, using, or selling an invention during the term of the patent. The iPhone®'s touch screen is protected by patent law.

Trademarks
A trademark is a word, symbol, design, or color that a business uses to identify itself or something it sells. The electronics store chain Best Buy® uses this trademark.

Copyrights
A copyright is a legal device that protects original works of authors. These works include books, movies, software, and music.

● **Protecting Ideas** Intellectual property laws protect the inventions and new ideas of businesses. *What kind of intellectual property law protects an invention?*

(t)Laurens Smak/Alamy; (c)Andrew Resek/McGraw-Hill Education

Prevent Legal Headaches Before They Begin

Smart entrepreneurs learn where to get help—before there's a problem

Entrepreneurs need to understand the laws and regulations that apply to their business. They also need to understand where to go when they have questions and need legal advice. As a business owner, you will need to know:

- What licenses and permits are needed for your business.
- How to read a contract (a legally binding agreement).
- How to find and hire a lawyer.
- How much legal assistance costs, and how lawyers bill.
- What arbitration is and how it works.
- Where to find reliable legal information online.
- What to do if someone brings a lawsuit against you or your business.

Being armed with this basic knowledge before starting a business will help you take swift action when a legal problem does occur.

Active Learning

Break into teams or pairs. Research the answer to one of the questions listed above and share your answer with the class. Compile the answers into a one-page legal "cheat sheet."

Patents

A **patent** is a document that grants an inventor the right to exclude others from making, using, or selling an invention during the term of the patent. This means the inventor can defend the patent against anyone who attempts to manufacture and sell the invention. A non-provisional patent lasts for a period of 20 years from the date of application. Inventors can gain one more year of patent life by filing a provisional patent first. This form of the patent was devised to help inventors protect their inventions while they talk to manufacturers and investors.

Public Domain

Once the patent life has expired, the patent is placed in public domain. The **public domain** comprises all intellectual property whose protection has expired; people can use any aspect of the device in their own invention free of charge.

Qualifying for a Patent

To qualify for a patent, the invention must meet these four rules of the United States Patent and Trademark Office (USPTO):

1. **The invention must not contain prior art.** It should not be based on anything publicly available before its invention.
2. **The invention must fit into one of five classes.** It must be a machine (e.g., a rocket, a fax), a process (e.g., chemical reactions), articles of manufacture (e.g., furniture), a composition (e.g., gasoline), or a new use for one of the four categories.
3. **The invention must be "unobvious."** It should be new and unexpected, even to someone skilled in the field.
4. **The invention must have utility.** This means it must be useful, not just whimsical or silly.

Many companies choose not to patent a new device; instead, they hold it as a trade secret. They know that once the patent is issued, anyone can view it and may try to find a way around the patent.

Patent Application

To protect an invention at its earliest stages, you should file a disclosure document with the USPTO. In the application, confirm that you are the inventor of the product and describe it in detail.

Your first patent application may be for a provisional patent. The provisional patent lasts for 12 months. During this time period, you must file a non-provisional patent application. How you word your claim can determine whether or not you receive the patent. Therefore, you should use a qualified patent attorney when writing a patent application.

The Patent Search

After you apply for a patent, the USPTO does a patent search. During this time, the patent is pending. **Patent pending** is the status of an invention between the time a patent application has been filed and when it is issued or rejected. If the USPTO decides your claims are valid, it will issue you a patent. It may also decide that some or all of your claims are not valid, in which case you should revise and resubmit your application. Once the USPTO declares that your claims are accepted, it will issue the patent. At that point, the public may view it.

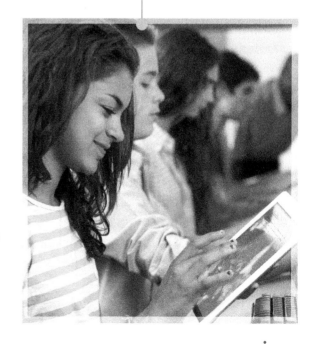

Tablet Craze Although Apple's iPad hit the market in 2010, it wasn't the first attempt at the tablet computer. Entrepreneurs have been prototyping tablets since the 1960s. *What kind of intellectual property laws protect technology and software?*

Patent Infringement

Patent infringement occurs when someone makes and sells a product that contains all elements of a patent claim. A patent is a powerful document. It gives the holder the right to enforce the patent in federal court. If the holder wins, the court will issue an injunction preventing the infringer from further use. The court will also award the patent holder monetary damages.

Stockbroker/age fotostock

Copyrights

A **copyright** is a **legal** device that protects original works of authors. These works include, among other things, books, movies, musical compositions, and computer software. A copyright lasts for the life of the author plus 70 years. After that, the work goes into the public domain. A copyright protects only the form in which the idea is presented. It does not protect the idea itself.

If you plan to publish (or make public) your work, copyright law recommends doing two things. First, place a notice of copyright in a prominent location on the work. This notice must include the symbol © or the word *copyright,* the year of first publication, and the name of the copyright holder. Second, register the work with the Copyright Office, a branch of the Library of Congress.

Trademarks

A **trademark** is a word, symbol, design, or color that a business uses to identify itself with something it sells. Trademarks are followed by the symbol ™ before it is registered and the symbol ® after it is registered. For example, the image of an apple with a bite taken out of it is the trademark of Apple®. A logo, or a company's emblem, such as McDonald's double arches can be trademarked. Even container shapes, such as Coca-Cola's classic glass beverage bottle, can be trademarked. A word, symbol, design, or color that describes a service business is called a **service mark**.

GLOBAL WORKPLACE — Guatemala: ¡Mucho gusto!

Guatemala is the most populous country in Central America. Nearly half the population is *ladino*, people of mixed European and native Mayan ancestry. The Mayan culture is known for its rich textiles and ancestral ruins. Though the official language is Spanish, you can hear 21 distinct indigenous languages spoken.

Courtesies In Guatemala, it is customary to address a person by title, such as *Abogado* (lawyer) or *Ingeniero* (engineer). Handshakes are commonplace, as are greetings of *"¡Mucho gusto!"* or "Nice to meet you!"

Social Studies/Science With a history of political unrest, Guatemala is only just emerging as a global economy. Research the government regulations for setting up a new business in Guatemala and describe your findings in a one-page essay.

Common Spanish Words and Phrases	
Hello, hi	Hola
Bye	Adiós
Yes/ No	Sí/No
Please	Por favor
Thank you	Gracias
You're welcome	De nada

Like a patent or a copyright, a trademark provides legal protection. If a business registers its trademark with the USPTO, a competitor cannot use the trademark. However, a trademark cannot be registered until it is actually in use. The business must also prove that the design is original and distinctive.

Unlike a patent, a trademark can be held indefinitely unless it becomes common usage in the English language. Words such as aspirin, yo-yo, and thermos were once registered trademarks. Today they are no longer used exclusively by the businesses that created them. They have become generic terms.

 Reading Check **Explain** What does it mean for a patent to be in pending status?

Laws that Affect Start-Up of a Business

Certain legal requirements are fundamental to your ability to do business. If you do not meet the requirements, you cannot start a company. You need to be aware of three categories of laws: permits and licenses, contracts, and zoning and building codes.

Permits and Licenses

Before you can officially open the doors of your business, you must get a business permit or license. A **permit or license** is a legal document giving official permission to run a business. You can obtain this from the office that issues business licenses in your city. You will probably have to renew it annually. In addition, you will be required to pay periodic fees over the life of the business. The amount is usually based on how much the business earns.

Certain professions may also require you to get a license. In this case, the license is a certificate that shows you have the necessary education and training to do a job. For example, doctors, nurses, barbers, accountants, real estate brokers, and counselors all need special licenses. Such licenses protect consumers from unskilled or unqualified business operators. Licensing requirements **vary** from one state or locality to another. Therefore, you should check with the appropriate government agency for more information.

Contracts

A **contract** is a binding legal agreement between two or more persons or parties. As an entrepreneur, you will sign contracts to start and run your business. It is helpful to distinguish among various types of contracts. An oral contract is an unwritten contract that does not last for more than one year. A void contract is one that never existed in the first place because the parties did not have the capacity to enter into the contract. A valid contract is most common for businesses because it meets several important criteria. To be valid and legally inferable, a contract must meet certain conditions.

Agreement

An agreement occurs when one party to a contract makes an offer or promises to do or refrain from doing something, and the other party accepts. Suppose a vendor offers to sell your business a scanner. There is no agreement until you send the vendor a purchase order or a check. Doing so signifies that you accept the offer.

Consideration

A **consideration** is what is exchanged for the promise. The money you pay the vendor for the fax machine is valuable consideration. It causes the contract to be binding. Money is not the only form of consideration. Being prevented from doing something by the terms of the contract is also consideration.

Capacity

Capacity is the legal ability to enter into a binding agreement. By law, minors, intoxicated persons, and people who are legally insane cannot enter into valid contracts. If they do sign such a contract, the agreement can be considered void.

Legality

The final contract element is legality. For a contract to be valid, it must be legal. That is, it cannot have any provisions that are illegal or that would result in illegal activities. If one of the parties fails to meet his or her obligations, the other party may be entitled to monetary damages. The right to these damages is usually determined in court. To avoid misunderstanding, the parties need to draw up a legally binding contract. The contract should clearly state the intentions of all parties.

Location

The law also affects where you locate the business; only certain types of real property are available to business owners. These types are designated by zoning laws and building codes.

Zoning Laws and Building Codes

If you build a new facility or locate your business in an existing building, you must conform to local zoning laws. Cities typically designate particular areas, or zones, for certain uses. Zones are usually specified as residential, commercial, industrial, or public. You cannot locate a tire manufacturing plant in a residential neighborhood.

Zoning laws also address environmental issues. They may restrict disposal of waste, noise and air pollution, and unsuitable building styles. A residential neighborhood might permit office buildings but only those that fit in with the established architecture. Zoning laws may also define the type and style of signs that businesses can use and the appearance of buildings.

It is also important to check the laws that relate to the actual construction of your facility. These are called building codes. Building codes set standards for construction or modification of buildings. These standards include such things as strength of concrete, amount of insulation, and other structural requirements.

Local governments employ inspectors to verify that building code requirements are met at each stage of construction. Licensed building contractors or architects should be familiar with local building codes. You can assure your facility is built to code by hiring such a person to supervise your project.

Leasing

Most entrepreneurs start with few resources and little money. Therefore, prudent entrepreneurs usually lease buildings and equipment rather than buy them. A lease is a contract to use a facility or equipment for a specified period of time. The lessee (the person who is leasing the building or equipment) has no ownership rights. Those belong to the lessor (the person who owns the building or equipment).

Leasing usually does not require spending a large amount of money up front. The money saved can be used for purchasing inventory and supplies and hiring employees. This can be a definite advantage for a new business. Another advantage is that some lease expenses are tax-deductible. This can reduce the tax liability of the company.

Nevertheless, leasing may bring its own set of troubles. For example, the lease contract is a very complex document. It states the terms, length of the lease, monthly rent, penalty for failing to pay, and procedure for termination. Because a lease is a long-term contract, an entrepreneur should consult an attorney before signing.

SECTION 8.1   Review

After You Read ■■■■■■■■■■■■■■

Self-Check
1. **Explain** What is the first document you should file in the patent process? Why?
2. **Describe** how you can protect the use of your business logo.
3. **Identify** the role of consideration in a contract.

Think
4. **Define** license, permit, contract, patent, copyright, and logo. Then identify the issuing agency for each.

English Language Arts
5. **Changing Copyright Laws** Use your local library or search networks and databases on the Internet to research current and future copyright laws related to music, film, television, or other types of media that can be found on the Internet. Find out if there are any exceptions to these laws. Summarize your findings in a one-page report.

Go to connectED.mcgraw-hill.com to check your answers.

Handling Government Regulations

Before You Read ●●●●●●●●●●●●●●●

Preview What are the six main areas of business that the government regulates?

The Main Idea
Laws and regulations are designed to protect employees, other businesses, customers, and the general public from unfair, unsafe, or unhealthy business practices.

Objectives
Explain the laws that affect employees.
Identify the laws that regulate trade.
Discuss the tax laws that apply to a new venture.

Content Vocabulary
◇ Equal Employment Opportunity Commission (EEOC)
◇ wrongful termination
◇ price discrimination
◇ Uniform Commercial Code
◇ warranty of merchantability
◇ bait-and-switch advertising
◇ FICA

Academic Vocabulary
You will see these words in your reading and on your tests. Use the academic vocabulary glossary to look up their meanings.
■ regulate
■ purpose

Graphic Organizer
Before you read this section, draw a chart like the one shown. As you read, write down four types of taxes for which business owners are responsible.

 Go to connectED.mcgraw-hill.com to download this graphic organizer.

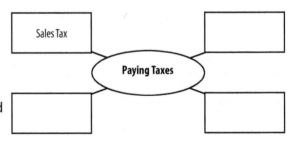

Laws that Affect Employees

Large and small businesses are affected daily by the laws of federal, state, and local governments. This section will touch on some of the more important laws that affect business. You will gain a better understanding of what you need to know to start a business. **Figure 8.2** provides an overview of the areas covered.

When you start a business, you usually hire employees. Many laws affect the hiring, firing, and paying of employees. They are designed to protect employees in the workplace.

Laws Against Discrimination in Hiring

The **Equal Employment Opportunity Commission (EEOC)** is the government agency charged with protecting the rights of employees. It ensures that employers do not discriminate against employees because of age, race, color, national origin, religion, gender, or physical challenge.

An employer cannot refuse to hire, promote, or give pay increases to an employee based on any of these characteristics. A company may give tests or use screening devices when hiring. However, the U.S. Department of Labor states that these tests or devices must be related directly to the job.

● Figure 8.2 — Laws Affecting a New Business

PRODUCT IDEA
Patents
Copyrights
Trademarks

START-UP
Permits
Licenses
Contracts

LOCATION
Zoning laws
Building codes
Leases
Contracts for purchase of real estate

EMPLOYEES
Equal opportunity
Child labor
Wrongful termination
Sexual harassment
Americans with Disabilities Act
Family medical leave
Equal pay for equal work
Fair labor standards
Workplace health and safety

TRADE ISSUES
Price discrimination
Consumer protection
Uniform commercial code
Truth in lending
Truth in advertising

TAXES
Sales tax
Payroll taxes
Federal unemployment tax
Business income tax

Legal Requirements Every business is affected by government regulations and requirements. *How might these laws protect a new business?*

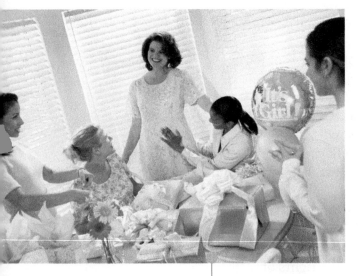

Child Labor Law

Federal child labor laws protect young workers. Employment cannot interfere with their education or be harmful to their health or well-being. Persons under the age of 18 cannot work in jobs the government considers hazardous. The hours that persons younger than 16 are allowed to work are restricted. Youths under 14 may only work in certain jobs. These jobs include delivering newspapers to consumers; performing in theatrical, motion picture, or broadcast productions; and working in a business owned by their parents, except in manufacturing or hazardous occupations.

Leave of Absence The Family Medical Leave Act (FMLA) provides employees with time off for family and medical issues, such as the birth of a child. *How long a leave of absence can employees take under FMLA?*

Laws Against Wrongful Termination

Wrongful termination is the right of an employee to sue his or her employer for damages in the event that he or she is terminated for an unacceptable reason. As a business owner, you should carefully document important events related to each employee. Keep records of all employee evaluations, disciplinary actions, and warnings. Notify in writing those employees who violate the rules. Then get a receipt from the employee, proving he or she was notified of the violation. Keeping good records helps if you are ever faced with a lawsuit for wrongful termination.

Sexual Harassment

Sexual harassment is any unwelcome sexual conduct on the job. It creates an intimidating, hostile, or offensive working environment. At the federal level, Title VII of the Civil Rights Act forbids harassment. In addition, most states have their own fair employment practices laws that prohibit sexual harassment.

Americans with Disabilities Act

The Americans with Disabilities Act requires employers to provide reasonable accommodation in the workplace so that qualified employees can do the basic functions of their jobs. The act also restricts the questions business owners can ask job applicants about their disabilities before they make a job offer. Business owners can ask about people's abilities, but they can not ask about people's disabilities. Owners can ask how applicants plan to do the job, not what prevents them from doing the job.

Family Medical Leave Act

The Family Medical Leave Act (FMLA) impacts employers with 50 or more employees. The act provides employees with the right to an unpaid leave of absence for up to 12 weeks. The time off can be used to address family and medical issues. These issues include serious health conditions of the employee or his or her child, parent, or spouse. The time off can also be for the birth, adoption, or foster care placement of the employee's child. In most cases, the employer must reinstate the employee when he or she returns from leave.

Laws Requiring Equal Pay for Equal Work

The Equal Pay Act of 1963 says that all employers must pay men and women the same wage for the same work. Same work involves similar skills, responsibility, and effort. The Lily Ledbetter Fair Pay Act of 2009 expands workers' rights to sue in cases of unequal pay.

Laws Requiring Fair Labor Standards

The Fair Labor Standards Act was passed in 1938. This law established a minimum wage and maximum working hours. It also ensured that children under the age of 16 could not be employed full-time except by their parents.

Laws Requiring Workplace Safety and Health

The Occupational Safety and Health Act of 1970 was passed to ensure safe, healthful working conditions for employees. You have probably heard of the agency created by this Act—OSHA, the Occupational Safety and Health Administration.

OSHA requires employers to look for hazardous areas in their workplace. Employers must maintain health and safety records and provide safety training. They must also stay up-to-date on new OSHA standards and take care of violations promptly. The agency charges heavy fines on companies that do not follow its rules.

 Reading Check **Explain** What is the purpose of the Occupational Safety and Health Administration?

Laws that Regulate Trade

In general, the American government allows businesses to compete in the marketplace with relative freedom. However, since the early 1800s, many laws have been enacted that **regulate** and restrict business practices. These key trade laws were created to preserve competition and fairness in the marketplace.

Price Discrimination Laws

The Clayton Act of 1914 and the Robinson-Patman Act of 1936 are aimed at prohibiting price discrimination. **Price discrimination** is the charging of different prices for the same product or service in different markets or to different customers. Businesses must justify giving one customer a lower price than they gave another. They must show that the favored customer bought more, bought lower-quality goods, or benefited from the cost savings. This means entrepreneurs must be fair to all customers when setting prices.

Environmental Enforcement

The Environmental Protection Agency was established in 1970 to create and implement environmental protection standards. Among the EPA's duties are the monitoring of industrial pollutants and the enforcement of environmental regulations by business. The number and scope of EPA regulations can be mind-boggling, which is why the EPA has created a number of programs and information sources to assist the small business owner.

◈ **Critical Thinking** Industry is one of the world's chief polluters. List at least five ways in which EPA policies have compelled American industry to clean up its act.

Consumer Protection Laws

If you are manufacturing products for the public, you must become familiar with consumer protection laws. That way, you can avoid possible recalls of your product and potential lawsuits.

Most laws pertaining to trade are designed to protect the consumer. These laws protect against unscrupulous sellers, unreasonable credit terms, unsafe products, and mislabeling of products.

The Food and Drug Administration (FDA)

One of the largest federal regulatory agencies that monitors product safety is the FDA. It researches and tests new products and inspects the operations of food and drug manufacturers. If your new product idea is a cosmetic, drug, or food item (or even suntan lotion), you need FDA approval to market it.

The Consumer Product Safety Commission (CPSC)

Th CPSC serves as a watchdog for consumers over products that may be hazardous. It also creates safety standards for products such as toys for children under the age of five.

The Fair Packaging and Labeling Act

The act requires that manufacturers create labels that truthfully list all ingredients and raw materials used in production. Labels must include the name and place of business of the manufacturer, packer, or distributor. The act also requires that the size, weight, and contents of a product be on the label.

Consumer Protection
Businesses are not allowed to market new drugs (or food items) without FDA approval. *What other products must meet FDA approval?*

INGREDIENTS: ROASTED PEANUTS, SUGAR, PARTIALLY HYDROGENATED VEGETABLE OILS (RAPESEED, COTTONSEED AND SOYBEAN) TO PREVENT SEPARATION, SALT.

MANUFACTURED AND UNCONDITIONALLY GUARANTEED BY ©UNILEVER BESTFOODS ENGLEWOOD CLIFFS, NJ 07632-9976

Comments and questions call 1-866-4SKIPPY.

Good source of Vitamin E

The Uniform Commercial Code

The **Uniform Commercial Code (UCC)** is a group of laws that regulates commercial business transactions. The UCC has been adopted by all fifty states. It applies to sales transactions among merchants. Because of this, and because you will be dealing with different types of vendors, there is a good chance that its provisions will affect you

Formation of Contracts

When entering into an agreement to sell a product, you create a valid contract. This means you must abide by contract laws. However, as a merchant, you must also abide by the requirements of the UCC. In some cases, the two are not the same.

In a valid contract, all terms of price, place, delivery date, and quantity should be present. Suppose you are a manufacturer, for example. You have ordered parts from a supplier, but you have not asked the price. When the parts arrive, you find they cost more than you expected. Do you have a contract despite the confusion over price?

The UCC says yes, but assigns a price that is reasonable at the time of delivery. The code assumes the parties intended to form a contract and knew the consequences of any ambiguity. Why? Because both are merchants—professionals who understand the business. Different rules, the UCC rules, apply to merchants than nonmerchants.

Warranties

The law looks after the safety and economic interests of buyers. It also regulates sales warranties. Many of these laws and legal principles have been made part of the UCC.

Just about everything that you buy comes with an implied warranty of merchantability. A **warranty of merchantability** is a guarantee about the quality of goods or services purchased that is not written down or explicitly spoken. It is an assurance that a new item will work for its specified **purpose**. The item does not have to work wonderfully. In addition, if you use it for something it was not designed for, say trimming shrubs with an electric carving knife, the warranty does not apply.

Product Liability

You have probably seen or heard news stories about product liability. This is the legal theory that manufacturers are responsible for injuries caused by their products. For example, automobiles can be recalled because of defects. Manufacturers can also be sued if their products cause injuries.

Increased Cost

The costs of product liability have boosted insurance costs for manufacturers. This raises prices for consumers. For example, about 25 percent of the cost of a football helmet pays for insurance.

If you are manufacturing a product to sell to consumers, you must be very careful. You must include clear instructions for the product's use. You must also give clear warnings of potential dangers involved. This protects you and your consumer.

Truth in Lending

Those involved in retail businesses must familiarize themselves with the Consumer Credit Protection Act. This act requires those who give credit to reveal all terms and conditions of their credit agreements. As a result, it is called the Truth in Lending Act. Like price discrimination laws, it is enforced by the Federal Trade Commission.

Web Savvy

Facing the Music

For years, the music industry has been in decline, partly due to peer-to-peer networks, which allow users to swap music files easily—and illegally—over the Internet. Entrepreneurs have seized on this opportunity to create online services like Pandora® and Last.fm™. Licensing their content from major music companies, these services allow users to listen to streaming music on their computers or mobile devices. However, instead of driving fans to buy more music, the services have become a substitute for downloads or CDs.

How do online music services like Pandora and Last.fm generate revenue?

Truth in Advertising

The Federal Trade Commission is also concerned with protecting customers from false and misleading advertising. The laws that address this trade issue are sometimes called *truth-in-advertising laws*. When you advertise, be aware of the following rules:

- **Misleading ads** Your advertising should not claim that the product can do something it can not.
- **Sale prices** You can not offer a reduced price on your product unless it has been offered to the public at the regular price for a period of time.
- **Price comparisons** When advertising that your prices are lower than your competitors', you must have proof.
- **Bait and switch** Bait-and-switch advertising involves advertising at a very low price to attract customers who are then persuaded to switch to a more expensive product.

Tax Laws

All for-profit business owners are responsible for certain taxes, including sales, payroll, unemployment, and income tax.

Sales Tax

Sales tax is a percentage of the price of an item that goes to a state or local government. The percentage varies from state to state. Retailers collect sales tax from their customers and send it to the appropriate government agency. Usually, this is the State Board of Equalization. Most retailers make payments every three months.

Payroll Tax

When you hire employees, you need to deduct certain payroll taxes from their earnings. One such payroll tax is the **FICA**, or Social Security tax. (FICA stands for Federal Insurance Contributions Act.) The tax is figured as a percentage of an employee's income. You are required to contribute an amount equal to the amount deducted from each employee's paycheck. If you deducted $20.27 from an employee's paycheck for FICA, you would have to match that amount. You would send a total of $40.54 to the Internal Revenue Service. There is a ceiling on the amount of wages subject to the FICA tax. Wages above that ceiling are not taxed.

Withholding these taxes can be complex. You must be aware of changes in the FICA tax rate and in the amount of wages subject to it. You can obtain information on the current FICA tax rate and ceiling from the Social Security Administration.

You are also required to withhold certain income taxes from an employee's paycheck. These include federal and, usually, state income tax. These taxes are based on a percentage of gross pay. Contact your local and state governments and the Internal Revenue Service for information about these deductions.

Federal Unemployment Tax

As an employer, you are required to make contributions under the Federal Unemployment Tax Act (FUTA). The act was designed to help workers who are temporarily unemployed. You may also be responsible for state unemployment taxes. However, they are usually credited against the federal taxes paid.

Business Income Taxes

Your business is also responsible for paying federal and possibly state and local taxes on the income it earns. As a sole proprietor or a partner, the income your business earns is considered your personal income. As a result, the business income is taxed at your personal tax rate.

Imagine you are the sole owner of a catering business. Based on your income statement, your business's net income before taxes is $32,500. You use that amount as your personal income when paying taxes to your state and the Internal Revenue Service. As a self-employed business owner, you also pay a FICA tax. It is double what an employee pays because you are considered both employer and employee. The ceiling on the amount taxed is the same.

Corporate Taxes

If your business is a corporation, the income tax situation is different. The business must pay a corporate income tax. You pay personal income tax based on the salary you earn and other income derived from the business.

In addition, the shareholders pay personal income tax on dividends. There are severe penalties for failure to file and pay income taxes. Because of this, you should consult an accountant to help you plan for taxes.

ETHICS and BUSINESS

Truth in Advertising

Situation You own a small retail store that sells popular electronics. You have been successfully growing your electronics business for several years, but you want to gain market share from the larger retailers in your area.

Advertising Tactics You decide to advertise a television as a weekend special in limited quantities. Your store quickly sells out of the television. As customers arrive looking for the out-of-stock item, the salespeople attempt to sell them other, more expensive televisions.

English Language Arts/Writing

Business Profitability Often businesses will attempt to drive customers to their stores using advertised specials, but in many cases businesses do not profit as much from selling these items. Is it ethical for a store to keep limited stock of an advertised item in order to sell more expensive, profitable items?

1. Can customers claim bait-and-switch tactics because the store ran out of the advertised item and is offering other, more expensive products in its place?
2. Write a letter to a customer who is upset over the circumstances explaining the situation and how you will address it in the future.

Getting Legal Advice

Since all businesses are regulated by the law, you need to be aware of any regulations that may affect your new venture. At different stages of the start-up, you will need legal advice. A good working relationship with a lawyer will give you confidence and ease some of the risk of starting a new business.

Many sources provide information for finding an attorney or getting up-to-date information on your legal obligations. They include the American Bar Association, the National Resource Center for Consumers of Legal Services, and the Commissioner of Patents and Trademarks. The Internal Revenue Service often holds workshops and seminars to make business owners aware of their tax obligations.

If your business is involved in areas regulated by the government, you should consult the appropriate agencies or consult an attorney who specializes in regulatory matters.

SECTION 8.2 Review

After You Read ∎∎∎∎∎∎∎∎∎∎∎∎∎

Self-Check
1. **Identify** the four primary types of taxes that businesses pay.
2. **Explain** the purpose of the Truth-in-Lending Act.
3. **Contrast** What is the difference between general business contracts and contracts that fall under the Uniform Commercial Code?

Think
4. **Research** the current taxes and tax rates that business owners must pay at the federal, state, and local levels on the income they produce. Create a chart to present your findings.

Mathematics
5. **Calculating Cost** Janik Industries is planning to build a new office building. Local zoning laws state that the maximum square footage of a new building should not exceed 35,000 square feet. For a larger building, the builder has to pay a $1,525 fee for each square foot over that amount. The building Janik Industries wants to build is in the shape of a rectangle. The length will measure 75 yards, the width will measure 50 yards, and it will be only one story tall. Will Janik Industries be charged a fee for extra square feet? If yes, how much will the company be charged?

   Math Concept **Equivalents** Measurements can be expressed in many different ways depending on the units you use. For example, length can be expressed in inches, feet, yards, or miles. Three feet and one yard are equivalent.

   Step 1 Convert the measurement from yards to feet.
   Step 2 Determine the square footage.

   ✈ Go to connectED.mcgraw-hill.com to check your answers.

Entrepreneurs *in Action*

Frank Brown
President and Founder
Defense Contract Services, Inc.

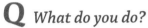

Q *What do you do?*

A We are a contractor that provides a variety of services for the United States Air Force, Army and Coast Guard, promoting the principles of integrity, excellence and quality services.

Q *What kind of training and education helped to prepare you for this job?*

A I attended college and graduated with an associate's degree in Occupational Science degree after entering the U.S. Marine Corps. Upon completion of my tour, I opened up several small restaurants in the Florida area where I learned the importance of providing quality services, controlling my operational costs and overhead, and listening to my customers' suggestions.

Q *What do you enjoy most about your job?*

A I enjoy the challenge of doing something different every day. It can be traveling to attend a site visit on a military installation or developing price and technical proposal strategies. There's the thrill of being awarded a contract along with the nervous anxieties in getting each contract started up on time. And there's the honor of receiving outstanding performance evaluations from inspection teams and personnel.

Q *How did you become interested in your field?*

A The Marine Corps provided me with dedication and commitment. I was proud to serve and wanted to continue to support and contribute to our great country, but in a civilian capacity. Knowing that DCSI provides services to men and women that directly support the mission of our military and of our country is my greatest inspiration.

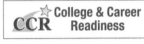

Government Regulations Even the smallest businesses must comply with government regulations. One of these regulations is the Americans with Disabilities Act.

1. Research the Americans with Disabilities Act.
2. How does it define a disability? How does it protect those who have disabilities? What does it require businesses to do?
3. Focus on those parts of the Act that you think are most relevant to small business. Convey your findings in a one-page report.

Career Facts

Real-World Skills	Academic Skills	Career Cluster
Leadership, Research, Punctuality	English Language Arts, Mathematics, Civics and Government	Government & Public Administration

Frank Brown

Visual Summary

The Legal Environment

Protecting Ideas When a new product or service is developed, it must be safeguarded through intellectual property protections.

Ways to Protect an Asset	
Patents	Gives the inventor the right to exclude others from making, using, or selling the invention.
Copyrights	Protects the original works of authors, including books, movies, musical compositions, and software.
Trademarks	Forbids competitors from using the word, symbol, design, or color used to identify your business.
Trade Secrets	Protects intellectual property that gives a competitive advantage by asking employees not to share it with the public.

Protecting Employees It is important to identify regulations that protect employees.

Laws that Affect Employees	
Civil Rights Act, Title VII (Sexual Harrassment)	Fair Labor Standards Act
Americans with Disabilities Act	Occupational Safety and Health Act
Family Medical Leave Act	Equal Employment Opportunity Commission
Equal Pay Act	Federal Child Labor Laws
	Wrongful Termination

Review and Assessment

Vocabulary

1. On a sheet of paper, use each of these terms and words in a written sentence.

Content Vocabulary

◇ intellectual property law
◇ Uniform Trade Secrets Act
◇ patent
◇ public domain
◇ patent pending
◇ copyright
◇ trademark
◇ service mark
◇ permit
◇ license

◇ contract
◇ consideration
◇ capacity
◇ Equal Opportunity Employment Commission (EEOC)
◇ wrongful termination
◇ price discrimination
◇ Uniform Commercial Code (UCC)

◇ warranty of merchantability
◇ bait-and-switch advertising
◇ FICA

Academic Vocabulary

■ legal
■ vary
■ regulate
■ purpose

Key Concepts

2. **Explain** how to protect your intellectual property.
3. **Discuss** the laws affecting the start-up of a business.
4. **Explain** the laws that affect employees.
5. **Identify** the laws that regulate trade.
6. **Discuss** the tax laws that apply to a new venture.
7. **Identify** government agencies that protect consumers.
8. **Explain** why the government oversees workplace safety.
9. **List** the group of laws that regulates commercial business transactions.

Academic Skills

Mathematics

10. **Car Payments** Burnett just signed a contract at a dealership to buy a new car. The list price is $29,000. He made a down payment of $1,500. The monthly payments are $602.15 for 48 months. What is the total amount Burnett will pay for the car?

   Math Concept **Problem Solving** Solving some problems involves more than one step and more than one operation.
   Step 1 Determine the total amount paid in monthly payments.
   Step 2 Add this to the down payment to determine the total amount paid.

English Language Arts

11. **Acronyms** Many government agencies and laws are commonly referred to by acronyms, or abbreviations formed by the initial letters of their names, such as OSHA or FMLA. Create a spreadsheet of terms used in this chapter that lists both their full name and their acronym.

Academic Skills *(continued)*

Social Studies

12. Government and Business There are many state and federal laws that influence business practices. Write an explanation of the role of government in the business activities of an entrepreneur and in dealing with customers and employees.

Science

13. Advances in Science and Technology Advances in science and technology lead to inventions that make an important impact on our society. Choose an information or communication device you use frequently, such as a smart phone or laptop computer, and research its history. Create a time line showing key dates, people, events, and patents in the history of the device you have selected.

Real-World Skills

Media Literacy

14. License and Registration Many types of businesses require that you be licensed or certified. Examples may include hair stylists, doctors, or truck drivers. Find three types of businesses that must be certified or licensed. In a short report, explain what it takes to get these legal credentials.

21st Century Skills

Civic Literacy

15. Break-Room Reading Businesses are required by law to post various legal notices—such as the state minimum wage—that can help their employees. Visit a local business, list all the legal notices you see, and research how each can help employees. Present your findings as a list with short explanations.

Connect to Your Community

16. Local Start-Up Choose a business you would like to launch. As part of the start-up process, research and determine the necessary permits and fees, required licenses, and laws and regulations that affect the business. Summarize your findings in a business report.

17. Zoning In Interview a member of the local zoning board or commission in your community. Ask about residential, commercial, industrial, and public zones in your town. Note these areas on a map. Find out about any restrictions regarding environmental issues. Report your findings to the class.

Review and Assessment

CHAPTER

8

Competitive Events Prep

18. **Situation** You own an advertising agency and participate in community activities whenever possible. You have agreed to help with a new mentoring program for new entrepreneurs, which consists of weekly discussions led by local entrepreneurs who have run successful businesses. Your discussion topic is truth in advertising.

Activity Prepare an outline for your discussion. Your outline should explain the main laws and rules relating to truth in advertising.

Evaluation You will be evaluated on how well you meet these performance indicators:
- Explain legal issues affecting businesses.
- Explain ethical considerations in providing information.
- Describe the need for and impact of ethical business practices.
- Prepare simple written reports.
- Demonstrate creativity.

 Go to **connectED.mcgraw-hill.com** for more information about this activity and other competitive events.

Standardized Test Practice

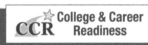

Directions Choose the letter of the best answer. Write the letter for the answer on a separate piece of paper. For question #2, if the answer is False, rewrite the statement to make it true.

1. The pricing technique in which items in a certain category are priced the same is called
   A. price lining.
   B. promotional pricing.
   C. psychological pricing.
   D. bundle pricing.

2. The break-even point is the point at which the gain from an economic activity equals the cost incurred in pursuing it.
   T
   F

> **Test-Taking Tip**
> Re-read all questions that include negative words, such as *not* or *least*. Look out for double negatives used in a question.

Site Selection and Layout Planning

Chapter Objectives

SECTION 9.1
Community and Site Selection

List the factors involved in deciding on a community in which to locate a business.

Identify the factors to consider when selecting a business site.

Describe the resources that can be used in finding potential business sites.

Explain the steps involved in analyzing potential sites for a business and choosing between those sites.

Describe the advantages of starting a business at home or in an incubator.

SECTION 9.2
Layout Planning

List the steps in layout planning that are common to all businesses.

Describe the layout needs for each type of business.

Summarize the final details of layout planning.

Discovery Project
Planning the Physical Layout

Key Question *What physical layouts are used by businesses in your community?*

Project Goal
Visit at least three different types of businesses in your community (for example, a restaurant, a convenience store, and a theater) and draw the floor plan for each business. Compare and contrast the layouts and explain why you think they differ.

Think About...
➤ *How will you gain permission to draw the floor plan of the businesses?*
➤ *How will you analyze the floor plans?*
➤ *What features will you compare and contrast?*

21st Century Skills
Productivity *Of the businesses you visited, which do you feel has the most efficient floor plan? Explain your answer.*

Evaluate
 Go to connectED.mcgraw-hill.com to download a rubric that you can use to evaluate your final project.

Ask
AN
EXPERT

Q: *A local yogurt shop is interested in buying some chairs that I designed. How much should I charge in order to make a profit?*

A: To make a profit, you need to first figure out how much it costs to make the chairs. Next, research the selling prices of similar items. You need to charge a reasonable, competitive price and earn a profit. The difference between the cost to make the chairs and the sale price is your net profit. For example, if your net profit rate is 20%, that means you sell $120 worth of chairs for every $100 in expenses.

Connect the Photo

Best Laid Plans Have you ever felt overwhelmed by the disorganization of aisles in a clothing store? Or perhaps you felt quite relaxed at the restaurant with the low lighting and soothing music? Entrepreneurs consider many factors when choosing the best location and interior layout of their businesses. Determining what will best serve the needs of the customers lies in site selection and layout planning. *What are some factors you would consider when choosing your business's location and layout?*

Community and Site Selection

Reading Guide

Before You Read ━━━━━━━━━━━━━━

Predict What are some key considerations in selecting a community for your business?

The Main Idea

Selecting a community and a specific location in which to establish a business each involve a systematic process.

Objectives

List the factors involved in deciding on a community in which to locate a business.

Identify the factors to consider when selecting a business site.

Describe the resources that can be used in finding potential business sites.

Explain the steps involved in analyzing potential sites for a business and choosing between those sites.

Describe the advantages of starting a business at home or in an incubator.

Content Vocabulary

◇ economic base   ◇ trade area
◇ incentive   ◇ industrial park
◇ census tract   ◇ incubator

Academic Vocabulary

You will see these words in your reading and on your tests. Use the academic vocabulary glossary to look up their meanings.

■ automatic
■ establish

Graphic Organizer

Before you read this section, draw a chart like the one shown. As you read, fill in the chart with the major factors or steps to consider at each level.

 Go to connectED.mcgraw-hill.com to download this graphic organizer.

Community Selection	Site Selection
labor supply	accessibility

Factors in Community Selection

Where should you locate your new business? This is one of the important decisions an entrepreneur must make. A location can make or break certain kinds of ventures. It can also determine who sees your business, how easily they can get to it, and if they will give it a try. In addition, your choice of location may become permanent. Once you invest in land, a building, fixtures, and equipment, it may be difficult, if not impossible, to move.

When selecting a location for your business, you must first select a community in which to do business. Second, you must select a specific site within the community. Community selection will be addressed in this section. Site selection will be discussed in the following section.

Your first thought may be to consider your own community as the place to start your business. That decision should not be **automatic**. Neighboring or even distant communities may offer more suitable markets for your business. In addition, they may present a more favorable climate. Potential localities for your business should be evaluated in terms of the following questions.

Is the Economic Base Favorable?

First, you should determine the community's **economic base**, or its major source of income. Usually the economic base is characterized as "primarily industrial," "primarily service-oriented," or by another category that indicates the main source of income. What should concern you the most, however, is whether that economic base is growing or whether it is shrinking.

If more money is coming into the community than leaving it, the economic base is growing. A growing economic base is a favorable environment for a new business. A strong economy ensures more growth. Additional money creates additional demand, which translates into new business opportunities. Additional money also provides the investment capital that entrepreneurs can use to take advantage of those opportunities. Local government agencies regularly conduct economic analyses of the community. You can contact local agencies for up-to-date information.

Snow Business It is probably easier to sell snowboarding gear in a region with mountains and snow. *What kinds of businesses might be suited to a dry, arid climate with little snow or rain?*

Purestock/SuperStock

Are There Financial Incentives?

Many communities try to attract new businesses by offering special incentives. An **incentive** is a reward or advantage that helps businesses. Incentives include lower taxes, cheaper land, and employee training programs. At a community's request, states sometimes **establish** enterprise zones in distressed areas, which give tax-favored status to new businesses. Local economic development offices can tell you whether such programs are available in your community.

What Is the Makeup of the Population?

Is the community's population aging as young people move away? Is it getting younger as families with children settle into the area? Such trends can affect a business. These trends determine who will spend. They also determine how much and on what types of products or services people will spend. Contact your local economic development office or chamber of commerce for information on population trends.

Every ten years, the Census Bureau conducts a survey to track changes in population size and demographics. Demographics include characteristics such as general age, education, gender, race, religion, and income. This information can tell you if a location matches your target market.

Look at the Census Bureau's Website for demographics that interest you. Follow the links from the home page until you reach the *Detailed Tables* page, where you can narrow your search to census tracts. A **census tract** is a small geographic area into which a state or county is divided for the purpose of gathering and reporting census data. In the United States, the average tract contains 4,000 to 5,000 residents or approximately 1,200 households. Census tract outline maps are also available from the U.S. Census Bureau. Several standard demographic tables are available for all census tracts. You can also access estimated population changes for each year since the last census was taken.

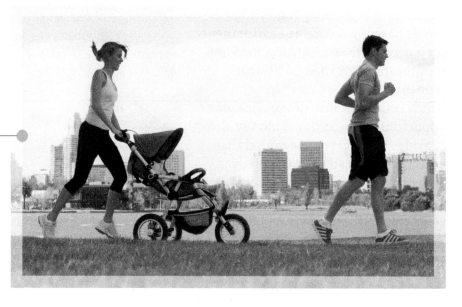

Population Trends If younger families with children are settling into your area, products or services that cater to children or babies will probably do well. *What kinds of products or services would do well in an area with many senior citizens?*

Does the Labor Supply Match Your Needs?

When considering a community, you must consider your labor needs. You also need to determine how well the local labor pool meets those needs. Ask yourself these questions: How many employees do I need? Are there enough potential employees to meet my needs? Does the available pool have the appropriate skills to help my business?

 Reading Check **Describe** What are some examples of businesses incentives?

Criteria for Site Selection

Once you determine that a community is suitable for your business, you can begin looking for sites. The factors to consider and the criteria used to judge sites vary with the type of business.

Retail Business Considerations

If you start a retail business, you will be selling directly to consumers. Therefore, you need to be accessible to your target market. You need to determine your **trade area**, the region or section of the community from which you expect to draw customers.

The type and size of your business determine the size of your trade area. If you offer a specialized line of merchandise, you may draw customers from a great distance. The only store in town that sells phonograph needles will attract record collectors from far away. A convenience store that offers general merchandise will draw from a much smaller trade area.

Once you select the area of the community you want to serve, you can begin locating potential sites. A city map is especially helpful. You can mark critical data on it as you investigate each site.

Number and Size of Competing Businesses

You should mark all potential competitors. Then you can calculate the number, size, and location of stores that will compete directly or indirectly with you. This gives you a sense of where customers shop. It also tells you how large your trade area is. Look for clusters of stores and low vacancy rates. Vacancy rate can be determined by a simple walk-through, count, and calculation (vacancy rate = amount of vacant space/total space available).

Nature of the Competition

What if your business is similar in size and merchandise to the competition? You may want to locate near them to encourage comparison shopping. That is why you often see an entire block of furniture shops, clothing stores, and auto dealers. However, your operation may be significantly larger and offer a greater variety of products. You may be able to generate your own drawing power, allowing you to locate away from your competitors.

Character of the Area

Look carefully at the character of the area. Is it attractive and inviting? Does it have the appearance of success? In general, consumers like to shop in attractive, safe, and thriving environments. Individual businesses or blocks that do not give this impression are potential problems. You should mark them on your map.

Accessibility and Traffic

Mark your map with the routes customers will use to reach your business. Identify the highways, streets, and public transportation routes that lead to the site. Make sure that the site is convenient and accessible. It should be easy to find.

Foot and car traffic are both important to a retail business. Entrepreneurs often stand at a potential site and count the cars and pedestrians passing by. If you use this technique, make sure you note variations in time of day and day of the week. Compare your results with data from different sites to help you make a more informed choice. Finally, make sure your site has adequate parking. Customers appreciate convenient, safe, and free parking.

Desirability Atmosphere, character, convenience, and personal preferences all play a part in site selection. *What kinds of customers might prefer this kind of atmosphere?*

Service/Wholesale Business Considerations

In many ways, service and wholesale businesses have similar needs to those of retail businesses. This is especially true when the customers actually come to their location. If this describes your business, all the factors relevant to a retail site apply.

Customer Traffic

Many types of service businesses must accommodate customer traffic. Hair and nail salons, dry cleaners, and tax preparation services are all good examples. In addition, wholesale outlets that sell to the public also need to take into account customer traffic.

In contrast, many service and wholesale businesses do not have customers or clients coming to their business site. For example, exterminators and plumbers go to their customers' homes.

Distributors

Distributors are in a similar position and do not have to take into account customer traffic. Their clients are manufacturers and retailers. Because distributors serve these clients primarily through sales representatives and purchase orders, they do not need to invest in expensive, high-profile locations. Many do business exclusively through catalogs or the Internet.

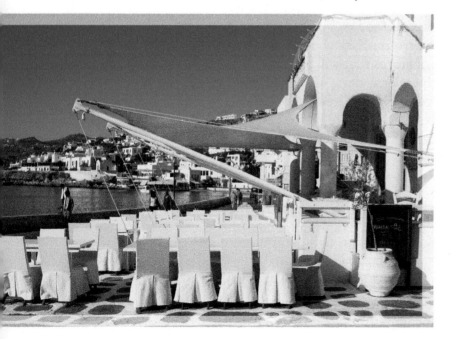

Glow Images

Manufacturing/Extraction Business Considerations

If you start a manufacturing or extraction business, your location will be largely determined by the nature of your business. An extraction business must be near the product it is extracting or taking away—ore, fish, or trees, for example.

A manufacturing firm can be located only where local zoning laws allow. Most communities set aside certain areas for industrial uses, sometimes called **industrial parks**.

Manufacturers and extractors are not concerned about access for pedestrians. Rather, they need access to sources of supply and major transportation routes. Being close to sources of supply can cut transportation costs and shipping times. Being close to major transportation networks makes it possible to get products to buyers quicker and at a lower cost.

E-Commerce Business Considerations

Electronic commerce sites are unique in that they can be located almost anywhere. In that respect, they are similar to service and wholesale businesses that do not have customer traffic. The difference is that these businesses reach their customers through the Internet. In other respects, they are similar to retail operations.

Smaller E-Commerce Businesses

The biggest factor in site selection for e-commerce is the size of the operation. For example, a Website design service does not require a large facility. Work is done on a personal computer, and jobs can be sent or sampled via the Internet. A small e-commerce company that sells a service or uses distributors to ship products does not need much space; one room may suffice.

Larger E-Commerce Businesses

A larger operation needs more space for equipment. It also needs more space for personnel. A retailer that stores and ships its own inventory may need an even larger facility. To get products out quickly, this type of operation must be located near a post office or near shipping facilities.

Locating Potential Sites

Knowing what to look for is one thing. Finding it is another. A number of practical resources are available to you. When property owners want to rent or sell space, they often advertise in the classified section of newspapers. Realtors who specialize in business properties display ads on the Internet and in social media. You can conduct visual surveys by driving through the community in which you plan to locate. This allows you to identify vacant facilities and get a sense of how suitable the property and the surroundings are. Personal or business contacts may have firsthand knowledge of available facilities.

Go Green

Take the LEED

Developed on an abandoned site on Chicago's West Side, Christy Webber Landscapes is an award-winning example of green construction. The building meets LEED (Leadership in Energy and Environmental Design) certification standards and generates some of its own energy with a wind-powered turbine and solar water heater. Rooftop maple trees and juniper bushes insulate the building and also help manage storm water. A central area collects rain and pumps it to company trucks, which use the water for landscaping.

◈ **Critical Thinking**
Research the LEED certification standards for schools. Find out which parts of the standards, if any, your school meets. Summarize your findings in a short report.

Site Analysis and Decision Making

Once you identify possible sites for your business, you must consider the surrounding area, the building, and the costs of buying, building, or leasing. The criteria outlined earlier in this section addressed site area considerations. Each of the potential sites you identify should be evaluated on the basis of those criteria.

Building Evaluation

The building on your site must be big enough to take care of present needs and to allow for expansion. Most businesses need space for customers, storage, inventory, offices, work areas, and restrooms. It costs much less to pay for more room at the outset than to pay for a move later.

Exterior

Begin your evaluation by considering the building's construction. You may want to hire a professional building inspector to examine it for structural soundness. Then judge the building's appearance. Remember, customers get their first impression from the front of the building. Check any signage. Most communities have regulations that limit the number, type, and size of signs you can have. Make sure your signs are easy to read, attractive, and correct. Finally, evaluate the parking accommodations. Your community may have requirements on the number of parking spaces.

The UAE: Boom and Bust

The United Arab Emirates, a federation of seven states bordering Oman and Saudi Arabia, enjoys rich deposits of oil and natural gas. The official language is Arabic.

Business Cycles Dubai, the UAE's most populous city, enjoyed a boom in the early 2000s, with huge real estate developments such as Burj Dubai, the world's tallest skyscraper. Dubai, however, was hit hard by the global recession, including its property values.

Social Studies/Science Though oil is crucial to the UAE, the federation is attempting to diversify. Abu Dhabi built Masdar City, the world's first "sustainable city." When completed, Masdar City will rely solely on renewable energy. Research the plans for Masdar City and summarize your findings in a one-page report.

Common Arabic Words and Phrases		
Hello	سلام	salam
Goodbye	مع السلامة	maasalaamah
Yes/No	نعم / لا	naam/la
Thank You	شكرًا	shukran
You're Welcome	عفوًا	aafwaan

Interior

Next, check the building's interior. Look at the walls, floors, and ceilings to see how they meet the needs of your business. Are they functional, attractive, and easy to maintain? Are there sufficient lighting fixtures and outlets? Is there access to enough power to run all of the necessary equipment? How efficient are the heating and cooling units?

Lease, Buy, or Build?

Another factor you must consider in your site analysis is whether to lease, buy, or build your facility. In most instances, for a new business, the advantages of leasing outweigh other options. Specifically:

- **A large cash outlay is avoided.** The money saved by leasing can be used for inventory, supplies, and other expenses.
- **Risk is reduced.** You can get an idea of how successful the business is going to be before you invest in buying or building.
- **Lease expenses are tax deductible.** A reduction in your tax liability can increase profits.

If you decide to lease, obtain information about the terms for each property under consideration. Terms include monthly rent, length of the lease, and provisions for termination. Common area maintainance (CAM) could also be an expense if you share the property with other businesses. Determine who is responsible for insuring against various risks, remodeling costs, and repairs. If you decide to buy or build, gather similar information. Buying and building usually require more time and effort. For example, you must apply for financing.

Whether you lease, buy, or build, study any lease or contract before signing. Have an attorney review the document. Remember that these types of agreements are negotiable. Before completing the deal, discuss the terms and agree to those that are best for you.

Making Your Decision

When your location analysis is complete, examine and compare the possible sites. For each, consider the three variables listed below. Then make your decision.

- **Cost comparison** What is the initial outlay for each site? What is the monthly expense? What are the other expenses, such as utilities, water, and sewage?
- **Advantages and disadvantages** What are the comparative advantages and disadvantages of each option? Consider the physical environment, the exterior, and the interior.
- **Desirability** Besides the factual considerations, intangibles are often an issue. Atmosphere, character, convenience, and personal preferences all factor into the final decision.

Alternative Sites

Two sites that do not fit the traditional mold are home-based businesses and incubators. Both can be attractive choices for new entrepreneurs.

Tech Savvy

The Dynamic Tower

Designed by architect David Fisher, the Dynamic Tower, an 80-floor skyscraper under construction in Dubai, operates like a wind chime: each floor rotates independently, reacting to the air flow and constantly shifting at different speeds. Wind turbines and solar cells harness so much energy that the tower is able to provide surplus power to buildings that surround it. The Dynamic Tower is one of the world's first prefabricated skyscraper, with 90% of the tower being built in modules at Fisher's factory in Italy. The tower hosts offices, luxury hotel rooms, apartments, and villas. How does the Dynamic Tower unique qualities affect its offices, hotels, and other businesses?

Home Business Option

The main advantage of working from home is financial. You do not have to pay rent, and you may be able to save on your taxes. This option can work well for businesses that require little personal contact with customers.

Whether you decide to start your business at home depends on the type of business, space, and equipment you have; the effect on those with whom you live; and the laws of your community.

Incubator Option

An **incubator** is a facility that is set up to provide flexible and affordable leases, office space, equipment, management assistance, mentoring assistance, and access to financing for start-up businesses. Business incubators are set up by economic development agencies, nonprofit groups, and increasingly by venture capitalists, especially for new technology businesses.

Like home-based businesses, there are major financial advantages. Rent is less, and shared administrative services mean reduced expenses. Other savings can come from on-site legal and accounting resources as well as group purchasing power. A second major benefit is the availability of business development services. These services may include financing, marketing, and management assistance.

SECTION 9.1 Review

After You Read

Self-Check

1. **Name** three incentives a community might use to attract entrepreneurs.
2. **Explain** how information can be obtained to calculate a vacancy rate.
3. **List** three services that incubators typically provide to tenants.

List

4. **Explain** why surrounding area analysis is equally important for all types of businesses.

English Language Arts

5. **Collaborate and Listen** Visit a retail store that you frequent often with one of your classmates. Analyze the type of layout the store uses and look for ways the layout could be improved. If possible, contact the store's owner or manager and discuss the advantages and disadvantages of the layout. Create a diagram of the store. Incorporate your findings into a five-minute talk and present it to your class.

Go to connectED.mcgraw-hill.com to check your answers.

SECTION 9.2

Layout Planning

Reading Guide

Before You Read ■■■■■■■■■■■■■

Connect What kinds of layouts have you seen in businesses in your community?

The Main Idea

The steps in layout planning apply to all types of businesses. In contrast, development of a facility layout is based on the operational needs of the business.

Objectives

List the steps in layout planning that are common to all businesses.

Describe the layout needs for each type of business.

Summarize the final details of layout planning.

Content Vocabulary

◇ layout
◇ workstation
◇ façade
◇ appointments

Academic Vocabulary

You will see these words in your reading and on your tests. Use the academic vocabulary glossary to look up their meanings.

■ sequence
■ function

Graphic Organizer

Before you read this section, draw a chart like the one shown. In the middle column, list the key considerations for each type of business. In the third column, list the workable layouts.

 Go to connectED.mcgraw-hill.com to download this graphic organizer.

Type	Considerations	Layouts
Manufacturing	production sequence	efficient placement of machinery
Retail		
Wholesale		
Service		
Extraction		

Physical Layout

Once you have a site in mind for your enterprise, you are ready to plan the layout. A **layout** is a floor plan or map that shows the arrangement of a business. It shows how you intend to use the space in your site to conduct business. An interior layout might include display cases, lighting fixtures, and the traffic pattern for customers or production processes. An exterior layout might show landscaping, parking spaces, and the traffic pattern for pedestrians and vehicles.

Like site selection, proper layout planning is important to the success of a business. A well-planned layout can mean a more efficient operation, a more appealing sales floor, and greater customer convenience. A poorly planned layout can mean just the opposite.

The basic steps in layout planning are the same for all types of businesses. There are six steps:

1. Define the objectives of the facility.
2. Identify the primary and supporting activities that will take place in the facility.
3. Determine the interrelationships between the activities.
4. Determine the space requirements for all activities.
5. Design alternative layouts for the facility.
6. Evaluate the various layouts and choose one.

Layout Needs and Possibilities

Although the steps in layout planning are the same for all businesses, the considerations and options and are not. Different types of businesses have different operational needs. A manufacturing business, for example, must be laid out differently than a retail operation.

In addition, business owners must follow regulations when planning a layout. All cities have standards that relate to safety and zoning, for example. The Americans with Disabilities Act requires certain businesses to provide access for people with physical, hearing, or visual impairments.

This section will describe layout factors and plans needed for all types of businesses. As you read, focus on those considerations and layout options relevant to your type of business.

Manufacturing Businesses

If your proposed business involves manufacturing goods, your key layout concern will be the placement of machinery. You want an arrangement that maximizes the efficiency of your operation.

What To Consider

The following groups of questions will help you formulate your specific layout needs:

- **Production processes** What kinds of manufacturing processes will you use? Will you break down raw materials into products? Will you assemble products from parts? Will you convert raw materials into products?
- **Production sequence** Will your operation call for mass-producing standardized goods in assembly-line sequence? Will you manufacture your products one at a time or in batches? Will you use a combination of these two approaches?
- **Materials flow** What is the most efficient flow of materials in your operation? **Figure 9.2** shows your options. Will materials come in one end of the building and finished goods leave the other? (That is an I Flow.) Will materials enter and finished products leave from the same end? (That is a U Flow.) What will you do when space is limited? (That is when you use an S Flow.) What will you do if there is a side entrance/exit? (That is an L Flow.)
- **Control** What is the best arrangement for managing your operation? What is best for inventory control?
- **Environmental needs** Will you need to provide for chemical, water treatment, or other special processes? Are temperatures, noise, or fumes likely to be problems?
- **Space requirements** How much space will you need for the placement and moving of equipment? What are your specific needs for machine maintenance, plant service, and storage? What is your anticipated production capacity?

● **As You Read** ▪▪▪▪▪▪▪
Predict What would be your primary site and layout considerations for a frozen yogurt business?

● **Figure 9.2** Patterns for Production Materials

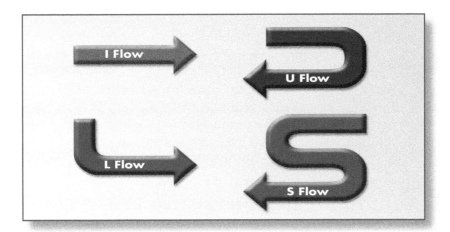

● **Go with The Flow** In most business operations, the flow of production materials is determined by the placement of entrances and exits and the total amount of space available. *By this standard, when would you use an L Flow?*

ETHICS and BUSINESS

Caring About Customers

Situation The town where you have your business has been hit by a tornado. There were no injuries and the damage is minor, but some areas of the town are without electricity and water for the next several days. People are flooding into your hardware store to purchase batteries.

Supply and Demand Because demand is high and supplies are low, your competitors have raised their prices on batteries, water, and other essential items needed by the towns-people. Your business partner is suggesting that you, too, raise your prices.

English Language Arts/Writing

Price Gouging Business owners have a right to make a profit on their products and services. But is it fair to take advantage of people in their time of need?

1. How could you make a profit selling bat-teries, and at the same time show the townspeople that you are concerned about their well-being?
2. Write a letter to the editor of a local news-paper discussing the issue.

Types of Layouts

The layout of a manufacturing business is influenced by the production process. There are three basic layouts that can be modi-fied to suit a particular operation's needs or used in combination.

- **Product layout** In this layout, all machines and supporting activities are arranged along a product flow line. As products come down the line, something is done to them at each workstation. A **workstation** is an area with equipment for a single worker. This layout is often used in an assembly-line **sequence**. It is useful for producing large quantities of a product.
- **Fixed-product layout** This layout is used when the product is too heavy or bulky to be moved around the plant. An air-plane is a good example. In fixed-product arrangements, parts are brought to the job and workers come to the product.
- **Process layout** This type of layout involves the grouping of machines and equipment by function. For example, machines that perform welding functions are placed in one area and machines that do sanding are placed in another area. Prod-ucts are then moved from one area to another, with a specific **function** being performed at each location. This setup is par-ticularly efficient for producing small quantities of goods.

Secondary areas to map out include areas for shipping, receiving, storage, warehousing, maintenance services, and office space. Outside, they include storage yards, repair areas, loading docks, and parking.

Retail Businesses

The arrangement of a retail store has a major impact on sales and, hence, profits. The most important design consideration is the flow of customers through the operation. Merchandise and aisles should be laid out to "pull" customers through the store.

What to Consider

To plan for customer flow, decide on an appropriate layout. Some options are described in **Figure 9.3**. Also, be sure to select the most effective merchandise placement. Placement considerations include:

- **Products to be sold** Does the merchandise require special care, such as refrigeration or extra security? Can the merchandise be shelved, or must it have standing space?
- **Projected clientele** Will customers be concerned with the atmosphere (including space and comfort)? Will they be concerned with getting in and out quickly?
- **Sales per square foot of selling space** Is the store arranged efficiently? Is the opportunity for self-service maximized? Is the space for individual items of on-floor stock minimized?
- **Sales value of area within store** Are the most salable goods placed in the area with the highest potential for sales (the middle and right)? Are staples in the low-sales-value area (the rear)? Are impulse and convenience items spread throughout?
- **Product coordination** Is related merchandise placed in the same area to facilitate customer shopping? Are groups of complementary products (such as shorts and tops) placed together to encourage multiple sales?
- **Aisle exposure** Does merchandise get maximum exposure? Do customers have ample time and space to examine it? Are there barriers to customer movement?

Figure 9.3 Types of Layouts

Right-Angle Grid	Right-angle grids provide a highly structured system that helps the flow of traffic. They are often found in supermarkets.
Open Layout	Open layouts feature open sales space bounded by outside walls. This enhances the visibility of merchandise, sales coverage, and security.
Enclosed Layout	Many department stores place walls between types of merchandise to create separate shopping environments.
Landscaped Layout	The landscaped layout combines elements of the open and enclosed layouts, improving customer and sales staff interaction.

Retail Layouts This fruit juice shop features an open layout. Most store layouts fall into one of four categories, producing different selling effects. *How important is layout to a particular retail establishment?*

Wholesale Businesses

Wholesale operations can take a variety of forms. One common form used by wholesalers who take possession of goods is warehousing facilities. Two primary goals in planning a warehouse layout are to provide cost-effective storage and allow efficient movement of products in and out of the facility.

What to Consider

When planning the layout of a wholesale business, your most important considerations are storage and space utilization. When planning for storage, follow these guidelines:

- Store popular items near shipping points to minimize in-house travel distances.
- Store together those items that were received together and that will be shipped together.
- Provide for a variety of sizes of storage space.
- Assign storage space on the basis of ease of handling and on popularity of items.
- Plan entrances, exits, and aisles so products can be easily reached.

Business Case Study

Find the Right Site for Your Business

A little research goes a long way toward picking the right location

Whether you are opening a restaurant or launching a tech start-up, few things are as important as finding the right physical location for your business. Fortunately, there are resources that help you understand your options and weigh their pros and cons.

The Small Business Administration. The SBA and its offshoot, the Small Business Development Centers, provide counselors and mentors who know your local area.

Real Estate Professionals. Realtors understand the needs of entrepreneurs. They also know what properties are available and how much they cost.

Lawyers. The complexities of a commercial lease often require the expertise of a lawyer.

Other Entrepreneurs. Experienced business owners and managers are often happy to share their experiences and offer advice.

Online Tools. City and state zoning requirements and tax-incentive programs are listed online. Browse local laws and regulations to see which areas would be a good fit.

Active Learning

Make a list of the top five factors you would seek in a location for a sporting goods store or hair salon. (For example, heavy foot traffic, fashionable area of town, lots of parking, affordable rent.) For each factor, list one professional or organization that could help you in evaluating the specifics of a site. Write a letter to one of the professionals or organizations asking all the questions you can think of about this specific factor.

Types of Layouts

Most modern wholesale operations are housed in single-story buildings. This makes controlling and moving stock easy.

Receiving, storage, order assembly, and shipping areas should be arranged so goods can be moved through them quickly and easily. This means working with and around certain key features. These include exterior access points (such as rail or truck sidings) and fixed interior obstacles (such as columns).

Interior layout plans should include office space and, if necessary, showroom areas. Exterior plans might show loading docks and vehicle storage areas.

Service Businesses

The physical layout of a service business depends largely on the specific service it provides. Consequently, there is no prescribed set of guidelines or layout patterns for these enterprises. However, service businesses can be categorized into general types.

Extraction Businesses

Like service businesses, extraction firms have unique layouts. This is because they must adapt to the particular environment in which the extraction operation takes place. However, extraction businesses do share a few features in common. These businesses include an office area, storage areas for equipment and supplies, and the extraction site itself.

The exterior physical operation of an extraction business may be spread out over a wide area. Consider a farm, for example. The operation may also be geographically separated from the business. Some mining ventures are headquartered in large cities far removed from the actual mining site. The business and extraction operations can also be combined (as in a small fishing operation). All of these variations demand a different combination of layout plans.

E-Commerce Businesses

E-commerce companies require one or two areas. Layout of the operations area depends on how computers, phones, equipment, and storage are adapted to the workspace. If the business carries and ships products, a storage area is required. Wholesale storage principles apply to the layout of this area.

Final Countdown Before you open your doors to the public, plan interior design features and alterations or improvements to the face of the building. *What finishing touches would you want to include in your location?*

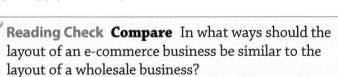

✔ **Reading Check Compare** In what ways should the layout of an e-commerce business be similar to the layout of a wholesale business?

Finishing Touches

Once you settle on a particular layout, you can begin filling in the final details. This includes planning interior design features and alterations or improvements to the **façade**, or face of the building.

Every business owner needs space to take care of paperwork and administrative tasks. In some cases, desk space in a back room is sufficient. In businesses where the office is the hub of activity, virtually all of the workspace is devoted to the office space function.

If cost, space, employee supervision, or access to files and equipment are important, an open office layout may be best. This arrangement often uses partitions to divide workspace into cubicles. On the other hand, if privacy and noise reduction are primary concerns, a closed office layout is a better option.

If your operation requires multiple offices, you can connect them with corridors or aisles. You can also use appointments to define the traffic patterns. **Appointments** are furniture, equipment, and accessories, such as planters and fish tanks. You also need to plan for the placement of other components, including equipment, furnishings, supplies, and inventory. Your decisions should be based on your business's operational needs.

SECTION 9.2 | Review

After You Read

Self-Check

1. **Summarize** the six steps in layout planning.
2. **Identify** the different layout needs of retail and wholesale businesses.
3. **Describe** the advantages of a closed office layout.

Think

4. **Analyze** the components used to design a business's physical layout.

Mathematics

5. **Vacant Space** A mall in Indianapolis has store space at several different sizes. There are eight 300 square foot stores, one 800 square foot store, and one 900 square foot store. Two of the 300 square foot stores are vacant; the others are occupied. What is the ratio of vacant space to occupied space? What percent of the space is occupied?

   Math Concept **Ratios** A ratio compares two related numbers. Ratios are often expressed as fractions.

   Step 1 Compute the total space of the strip mall.

   Step 2 Compute the amount of vacant space and compare the two totals.

   Go to connectED.mcgraw-hill.com to check your answers.

Entrepreneurs *in Action*

Sean King
President
SMK Construction Inc.

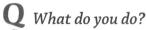

Q *What do you do?*

A I'm a sustainable builder. I go to the job site each morning, go over the plans, order the materials, and tell the guys what to do. I have a home office, but my clients never really go there. Everything is usually on site or at the architect's office.

Q *What kind of training and education did you need for this job?*

A I went to UCLA, then worked for my stepdad, who was a carpenter. After that, I got my contractor's license. I recently did a seminar for Green Point Rating and became a Green Buildng Professional. I also took a nine-month Sustainable Building Advisor program. Right now, green construction is the hottest thing. I did a house in Venice last year, and got a LEED Platinum rating. It's the first Platinum in all of Southern California. It was written up in DWELL Magazine and was on the Venice Architectural Walk.

Q *What do you enjoy most about your job?*

A I enjoy the building process. I enjoy creating, being involved in the design, seeing the finished project, and having a happy client. I like being able to step back and look at it.

Q *How did you become interested in your field?*

A It was when my stepdad said, "Hey, why don't you come and work with me?" Our first job was a redwood deck. When I saw how easy it was to build, and saw the finished product, it got me really excited about it. The trick is to visualize something before it's built, to build it in your head.

College & Career Readiness

Work It Out Plan the location of a construction firm by writing one or two paragraphs to answer each question.

1. Describe the type of community and location where you would locate your firm.
2. What size site will you need for your business? Will the site need to have special features? If so, what kind?
3. What type of layout will be best for a construction firm and why?

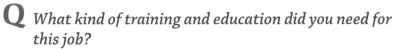

Career Facts

Real-World Skills	Academic Skills	Career Cluster
Visualization, Creativity, Communication	Mathematics, Science, English Language Arts	Architecture & Construction

Sean King

Visual Summary

Site Selection and Layout Planning

Line of Site When selecting a community in which to start a business, consider the following.

Community and Site Selection

Retail Consider the competing businesses, the character of the area, and the site's accessibility to customers.

Wholesale and Service Consider whether or not customers will be coming to your place of business.

Manufacturing and Extraction Look for sites with easy access to transportation, suppliers, and raw materials.

E-commerce Consider the size and nature of your operations.

A building should be chosen based on its suitability for its intended use, whether you will buy or lease, and costs.

Plan Ahead Layout planning is necessary to make a site effective and efficient.

Specific Steps in Layout Planning

1	**Name** facility objectives.
2	**Define** primary and supporting activities.
3	**Determine** activity interrelationships.
4	**Identify** space requirements.
5	**Design** alternative layouts.
6	**Select** the final layout.

Layout considerations are different for each type of business. Once a particular layout has been selected, consider the following details: minimum office space needed; space for equipment, furnishings, and supplies; and interior design features and alterations to the façade.

Rick Gomez/Alamy

Vocabulary

1. On a sheet of paper, use each of these terms and words in a written sentence.

Content Vocabulary

◇ economic base
◇ incentive
◇ census tract
◇ trade area

◇ industrial park
◇ incubator
◇ layout

◇ workstation
◇ façade
◇ appointments

Academic Vocabulary

■ automatic
■ establish

■ sequence
■ function

Key Concepts

2. **List** the factors involved in deciding on a community in which to locate a business.
3. **Identify** the factors to consider when selecting a business site.
4. **Describe** how to find potential business sites.
5. **Explain** the steps involved in selecting potential sites for a business.
6. **Describe** the advantages of starting a business at home and in an incubator.
7. **List** the steps in layout planning that are common to all businesses.
8. **Identify** the layout needs for each type of business.
9. **Summarize** the final details of layout planning.

Academic Skills

Mathematics

10. **Heating Costs** Jai is having a small warehouse built for his business. The warehouse measures 125 feet wide and 200 feet long. The height of the ceiling is 25 feet. Heating the building will cost $1.13 for every 1,500 cubic feet per day. What will it cost to heat the warehouse for the year?

   Math Concept **Multi-Step Problems** Multi-step problems require more than one calculation to be performed.

   Step 1 Determine the volume of the warehouse.

   Step 2 Calculate the cost to heat the volume of the warehouse for a year.

English Language Arts

11. **Analyze Text Organization** Explanatory paragraphs usually include a main idea, or topic, sentence. They also include sentences that introduce, conclude, or elaborate on the main idea with facts and details. The topic sentence can occur as the first sentence in the paragraph, or it can occur elsewhere in the paragraph. Skim this chapter and find at least one paragraph whose topic sentence is the first sentence, and one paragraph where the topic sentence occurs later.

Review and Assessment

Academic Skills *(continued)*

Social Studies

12. **Green Construction** Imagine that you and a group of friends have decided to promote the idea of green buildings in your community. Research green building methods and prepare a brief talk to explain what advantages, if any, they may offer. Identify the government officials, boards, and commissions in your community that you would have to lobby in order to turn your policy ideas into laws and regulations.

Science

13. **Sustainable Materials** More and more construction companies are considering environmental impact when choosing construction materials. Use a search engine to find out more about green construction materials, and why they are less harmful to the environment. Write a few paragraphs about the pros and cons of using them.

 ## Real-World Skills

Investigative Skills

14. **Site Selection** Think of a place where you, a friend, or relative has worked. What type of business is it? What kind of community is it? Explain why the community and business are or are not a good match in a two-paragraph essay.

21st Century Skills

Critical Thinking & Problem Solving

15. **Love to Shop?** Give a short presentation on your favorite retail store and tell why it is your favorite. Explain what features, such as the store's merchandise, layout, interior design, or location, make you like the store. Determine whether location and layout are as important as what is sold.

 ## Connect to Your Community

16. **Pros and Cons** Interview two entrepreneurs about how they selected their sites. Find out what skills helped them in the process. Have them explain the pros and cons of the sites they considered. Report your findings to the class.

17. **Compare Sites** Choose two potential sites for your business. Visit each site, noting potential competitors and available buildings in the area. On a map, mark trade areas, potential competitors, and transportation routes for your sites. Compare your site possibilities. Summarize your findings in written or table form and make a final choice.

Review and Assessment

Competitive Events Prep

18. **Situation** You have recently purchased a nursery and garden center. The outdoor plant area is in excellent condition, but the building housing the retail and office areas is in need of major renovations. Although, the building is sound, the interior space is inefficient and dated. You plan to gut the interior of the building and create new selling and office areas. Today you are concentrating on the layout of the selling space.

Activity Prepare an outline of the different types of store layouts and the advantages and disadvantages of each as they apply to your business. Discuss your ideas with your assistant manager.

Evaluation You will be evaluated on how well you meet the following performance indicators:
- Plan business layout
- Determine equipment needs
- Build brand/image
- Determine issues and trends in business
- Demonstrate creativity

 Go to **connectED.mcgraw-hill.com** for more information about this activity and other competitive events.

Standardized Test Practice

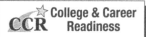
College & Career Readiness

Directions Choose the letter of the best answer. Write the letter for the answer on a separate piece of paper. For question #2, if the answer is False, rewrite the statement to make it true.

1. Which type of manufacturing layout is used when the product cannot be moved around the plant because of its weight?
   A. Process layout
   B. Fixed-product layout
   C. Enclosed layout
   D. Product layout

2. An economic base is the region or section of the community from which you expect to draw customers.
   T
   F

Test-Taking Tip
When studying in small groups, make sure your study group includes only students who are serious about studying. Some should be at your level of ability or better.

Business Plan Project

Planning and Research

Identifying your mission, industry, and market will help you address and organize your company's concerns. *What does your company stand for, and who are your customers?*

Objectives

In this project, you will complete these three parts of your business plan:

- Write a vision and mission statement for your company.
- Create a chart describing your industry and its past, current, and future trends.
- Create a chart that organizes information about your target market.

The Skills You'll Use

- **Academic Skills** Reading, Writing, Social Studies, Research Skills
- **Real World Skills** Observation, Communication, Critical Thinking Skills
- **21st Century Skills** Social and Cross-Cultural Skills; Entrepreneurial Literacy

▶ Vision and Mission Statements

The vision and mission statements set forth the guiding principles by which a company functions. They communicate what the business stands for, what its founders believe in, and what the company intends to achieve.

Step 1 **Describe Your Company's Vision** Write answers to the questions below. These issues need to be answered in your company's vision statement.
1. What is your company's scope and purpose?
2. How does your company's scope and purpose reflect the company's core values and beliefs?

Step 2 **Define Your Company's Mission** Write answers to the questions below. These issues need to be answered in your company's mission statement.
1. What are the specific aspirations of your company?
2. Are these aspirations measurable and achievable? Explain your answer.

▶ Industry Overview

Your business plan must describe the industry and address the basic trends and growth within the industry. Think of your industry as those companies providing similar, complementary, or supplementary products and services.

Step 1 Describe the Industry Write a description of your proposed business's industry, including size by both revenue and number of firms. Describe the industry's distribution system, barriers of entry, failure rate, and typical profitability.

Step 2 Define Industry and Economic Trends Use industry publications and online resources to conduct research on trends. Create a chart like the one shown to describe past, current, and future trends and the impacts of those trends on your business and the industry.

Area of Analysis	Trends	Impact of Trends
Government Regulations		
Industry Demographics		
Industry Growth or Decline		
Industry Standards		
Distribution Systems		
Regional Unemployment		
Regional Wages		

▶ Market Analysis

The Market Analysis section of the business plan presents your market research and features a target market demographic profile.

Step 1 Describe Consumer Markets Create a chart to research and organize information about your target market.

Step 2 Define B2B Markets If your product or service is marketed to businesses, research and organize information about your target market in terms of industry, product and/or service, geographic location, years in business, revenue, number of employees, and buying motivations. Create a chart to organize your research.

Use the **Business Plan Project Appendix** on pages **572–583** to explore the content requirements of a business plan in more detail.

 Business Plan Project Template Go to connectED.mcgraw-hill.com for a business plan template that you can use to write your own business plan.

My Business Plan
When you have completed your Project, put your statements, charts, and other research in your Business Plan Portfolio.

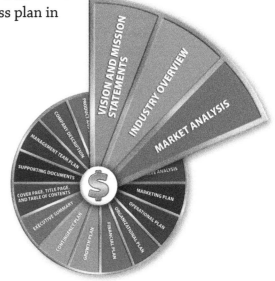

Managing Market Strategies

Connect the Photo ⬆

Bringing Products to Market Jimmy Williams owns Hayground Organic Gardening. As part of his marketing strategy, Williams personally sells his produce at the Santa Monica Farmer's Market. *How have some of your favorite products or services been marketed to you?*

Business Plan Project

Preview

The Marketing Mix

Marketing will determine whether or not your product or service sells. What advantage will you have over the competition? Will you advertise on digital billboards? Will customers pay a monthly fee to play your online game? Will they self-scan and bag their purchases, or will you have cashiers and a sales staff?

The **Business Plan Project** will help you address and organize some of these concerns by focusing on these sections of the business plan:

▶ The **Competitive Analysis** section of the business plan should focus on demonstrating that the proposed business has an advantage over its competitors.

▶ The **Marketing Plan** describes a company's marketing mix strategies or how it plans to market, promote, and sell its products or services.

Prepare for the Business Plan Project

As you read this unit, use this checklist to prepare for the **Business Plan Project:**

- Keep a journal of the advertisements you see on the Internet in social media, on TV, in print, and outdoors.
- Browse a local store and compare prices for different brands of the same type of product.
- Conduct an interview with a store manager about how to manage a sales force.

CHAPTER 10

The Marketing Plan

Chapter Objectives

SECTION 10.1
Developing a Marketing Plan

Identify the purpose of the marketing plan.

Name the five marketing strategies that make up the marketing mix.

Describe the part marketing tactics play in the marketing plan.

SECTION 10.2
Updating the Marketing Plan

State the importance of ongoing market research.

List the factors to consider for each strategy when reviewing the marketing mix.

Describe how to update the marketing mix and marketing plan.

Discovery Project
Marketing Your Product

Key Question *How would you develop a marketing plan for your business?*

Project Goal
Work with a partner to create a marketing plan for your business, which sells clothing for skateboarders. Determine who your target market will be and how you will reach that market with information about your product. Use that information to design your marketing plan.

Think About...
➤ How will you identify your market?
➤ How will you locate information about potential target markets?
➤ How will you organize your plan?

21st Century Skills
Creativity *What methods would you use to reach a target audience of 11–18 year olds?*

Evaluate
 Go to connectED.mcgraw-hill.com to download a rubric that you can use to evaluate your final project.

Ask AN EXPERT

Q: *I plan to run my own marketing firm someday. What are some disadvantages and advantages of having a tax preparer file my company's tax return instead of doing it myself?*

A: A tax preparer can cost several hundred dollars to hire. However, if you do your own taxes, you may spend many hours going through paperwork, filling out forms, and studying tax laws. Tax preparers ensure your tax return is accurate and can save you money by pointing out deductions to which you are entitled. They can also save time and trouble.

Connect the Photo

Appealing to the Customer Target market, customer demands, and competition changes over time. Developing an ideal marketing mix considering these factors may take time, but it is necessary for a successful business. *How are display windows part of a marketing plan?*

Developing a Marketing Plan

Reading Guide

Before You Read ---------------

Connect What kinds of market research are needed as the starting point for the marketing plan?

The Main Idea

To succeed and grow, a business must have a marketing plan with realistic objectives, the proper mix of the five Ps, and an action plan for implementation.

Objectives

Identify the purpose of the marketing plan.
Name the five marketing strategies that make up the marketing mix.
Describe the part that marketing tactics play in the marketing plan.

Content Vocabulary

◇ marketing plan
◇ marketing objectives
◇ marketing mix
◇ brand
◇ package
◇ label
◇ product positioning
◇ product mix
◇ channel of distribution
◇ intermediaries
◇ intensive distribution
◇ selective distribution
◇ exclusive distribution
◇ marketing tactics

Academic Vocabulary

You will see these words in your reading and on your tests. Use the academic vocabulary glossary to look up their meanings.

■ concept
■ target

Graphic Organizer

Before you read this section, draw a chart like the one shown. As you read, fill in the chart with the five strategies of a marketing mix.

 Go to connectED.mcgraw-hill.com to download this graphic organizer.

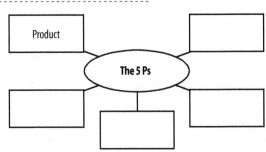

Product

The 5 Ps

Marketing and Market Planning

Marketing is important to every business because the success of a business is determined in the marketplace. Marketing involves the process of developing, promoting, and distributing products to satisfy the objectives of customers and businesses. It also brings the marketing **concept**—and its supporting concepts of customer orientation and customer satisfaction—to life.

Marketing Plans

A **marketing plan** is a blueprint used by a business to guide its marketing activities to a desired conclusion. The plan is built on information obtained through market research and on your intentions for the company. The plan includes a profile of the **target** market, marketing objectives, the mix of marketing strategies, marketing tactics, and a marketing budget. The plan also includes a rationale for your decisions in each area. When a business has multiple target markets, it needs to create variations of the plan to address differences in those markets.

Forming Marketing Objectives

Marketing objectives are goals a business wants to accomplish through its marketing efforts. In a start-up marketing plan, the objectives should include such things as:

- Creating awareness of your business
- Educating the target market about the features and benefits of your products
- Understanding of the current and future needs of your target market
- Reaching specific sales projections
- Obtaining projected market share
- Building a repeat customer and/or referral base

The objectives should be consistent with the overall goals of the business. They should be reasonable and consistent with the marketing situation. They should be based on the resources that are available to you.

It is important to write objectives in clear and simple language. The objectives must be measurable. Finally, in order to ensure that they can be monitored and controlled, it is best to limit the number of objectives.

Buzz One objective of marketing is to create awareness of your business. *How do marketers create awareness on the Internet or social media?*

Developing the Marketing Mix

Forming marketing objectives enables you to specify what you want to accomplish through your marketing initiatives. Developing the marketing mix enables you to map out how you are going to do it.

The **marketing mix** is made up of five marketing strategies you will use to reach your market. Historically, businesspeople have worked with four strategies. These strategies, commonly referred to as the four Ps, are product, place, price, and promotion. In recent years, a fifth P (the people strategy) has emerged and gained widespread acceptance.

The strategies of a marketing mix must be used together to ensure success. One strategy alone will not work. The strategies must be coordinated to influence the target market. They must be synchronized to result in company profits. The right combination used in the marketing mix will produce good results. The wrong combination will produce less than satisfactory results.

The following sections will discuss the product, place, and people strategies. Price and promotion will be discussed in separate chapters.

Business Case Study

Make Your Marketing Social

To build relationships with customers, entrepreneurs turn to social media

Social media is a powerful tool to dialogue with customers, build trust in your company, and show your human (and humorous!) side.

In a recent study, 84 percent of respondents said they expect a business to have a presence on Facebook. Sixty-four percent said they expect to see a company on Twitter as well. Coming in third, over Google+, Instagram, and Pinterest, was YouTube. Respondents also expected businesses to reply quickly to questions and complaints shared on social—in two hours or less.

Effective social media for business relies on solid strategy and consistent execution. Top tips:

- Adopt a different strategy for each platform. What works on Facebook, for example, may not work on Twitter.

- Give people a good reason to follow you. Are your posts entertaining, informative, interesting? Always ask, "Why would someone find value in this?"

- Follow the 80/20 rule: 80 percent of your content should be about your followers' interests. Only 20 percent should be about your brand.

Active Learning

Conduct a short interview with a marketing representative from a local newspaper, television or radio station, or business that is active on social media. Ask the person how social media is used to promote the organization. Ask about their goals, what metrics (numbers) they track, how much time they spend, and how they evaluate success. Write a short report about their social media strategy and what you would do similarly or differently for your brand.

The Product Strategy

The product strategy deals with the goods or services your business will provide. The scope of products and services will vary based on the type of business. Product decisions are crucial to the success of your business. Products that do not match up with customer needs or expectations will not sell. When you did your market analysis, you gathered product information and made preliminary decisions. This section will help you mold those efforts into a product strategy.

Product Features and Benefits

A product is made up of all of the features and benefits it offers to consumers. When considering your product, you must think of a package of features and benefits your customers find desirable.

Branding, Packaging, and Labeling

Your product will be identified by its branding, packaging, and labeling. A **brand** is the name, symbol, or design used to identify a product. A **package** is the physical container or wrapper that holds the product. The **label** is the part of the package used to present information. All three, especially branding, serve as strategies for maintaining customer loyalty. For example, wearers of Puma® footwear may buy this brand repeatedly. They expect a certain quality of athletic shoe in a specific type of box with a clearly marked label.

Product Selection

What products and/or services will your business offer? The answer depends on whether you are manufacturing or reselling your products.

Developing and manufacturing new products to sell adds value. You change raw materials into a form that satisfies customer needs. Manufacturing a product also involves several steps:

1. First, you generate product ideas and sort out the good from the bad.
2. Next, you study the potential costs and revenues of product you have selected.
3. You develop the product and test-market it.
4. Finally, if everything looks promising, you introduce the product.

In contrast, choosing products for resale is largely a matter of gathering information. First, you study consumer demand and product availability. Then you make decisions to bring the two together. A second related concern is how well your new product fits in with other items you sell.

A Book By Its Cover A product's package, the physical container or wrapper that holds it, can serve as a strategy for creating customer interest and loyalty. *Based on this product's package, who do you think is the target market?*

As You Read ·········

Explain What part of a package is used to present information?

Product Positioning

Product positioning refers to how consumers see your product compared to the competition's product. Do you want consumers to see your product as prestigious? Do you want them to see it as a good bargain? Do you want them to see it as equal in quality to other products? How you position your product relative to the competition depends on your marketing objectives.

Positioning can be achieved through quality, availability, pricing, and uses. Branding, packaging, and labeling can also have a bearing on your product's image and, thus, on its positioning.

Product Mix

The last part of the product strategy that you need to consider is your **product mix**, or all of the products a company makes or sells. If you plan to offer multiple products, you should think about how they relate to one another. That depends on the image you want to project and the market you are targeting. If you want to reach a single market, you may include only products that complement one another. If you are trying to reach multiple markets, you may decide on a more diversified mix.

Questions to Ask About Product Decisions

The following questions will help you develop a product strategy for your marketing plan. As you develop a strategy, keep your target market in mind.

- What products should I manufacture or sell?
- How will my products meet the needs of my target market?
- What level of quality should my goods or services have?
- How much inventory should I maintain?
- How will my products be different from or better than my competitors'?
- How will I position my products?
- What will my customer service policy be?
- Will my products be environmentally friendly?

Impact of Technology on the Product Strategy

With the Internet, businesses can let customers participate in the design of products they are purchasing. Clothing, furniture, and automobiles are examples.

Technology has greatly affected the manufacture of products. Products function better, are more precise, and include more unique features. Production costs are cheaper. Packaging and labeling also benefit from technology.

Advances in technology have resulted in the emergence of new products and services. Examples include smart phones high-definition (HD) or smart televisions, portable GPS navigators, and iPods. Other goods and services may spin off from new products. Some new products make existing products obsolete. For example, Blu-ray discs replaced DVDs. These situations open windows of opportunity for manufacturing or reselling new products.

The Place Strategy

The place strategy involves how you will deliver your goods and services to customers. It involves making sure your product is ready and available for sale, when and where your customers want it. Having your product available when and where customers want it adds to its value. Because place strategies involve movement of your product, this part of the marketing mix is also known as the distribution strategy.

You have probably already begun to plan some portions of this strategy. When you did your market analysis, you learned how your competitors operate. Do you want to copy them or go your own way? Likewise, when you investigated potential sites, you identified the options available to you. Examining the following areas will help you finalize your strategy.

Channels of Distribution

To formulate your place strategy, you need to understand the possible channels of distribution. A **channel of distribution** is the path a product takes from producer (or manufacturer) to final user (or consumer). As shown in **Figure 10.1** and **Figure 10.2** on pages 230 and 231, consumer and industrial markets have different channel members. However, there are only two basic types of channels—direct and indirect.

Direct and Indirect Channels

A direct channel moves a product from producer to customer with no one in between. Service businesses are typical examples. When you give a tax preparer your financial records, he or she returns your finished taxes. No one else is involved.

In contrast, an indirect channel employs **intermediaries**. These are people or businesses that move products between producers and final users. They include wholesalers and retailers, who sell in the consumer market. They also include distributors, who sell in the industrial market, and agents, who arrange sales. For example, a clothing designer might use an agent to contact wholesalers and retailers. The designer can then reach a large market without worrying about maintaining a sales staff or store. This allows the designer to concentrate on designing.

Selecting a Channel of Distribution

The type of business you have determines where you fit in your channel of distribution. If you are a producer, you send products through a channel. If you are a retailer, you receive them. If you are a wholesaler, you do both.

The channel of distribution you choose affects your product. It can raise or lower your product's cost. It can affect the potential for risk, such as the loss of or damage to your product while it is in transit. Most importantly, it can determine how quickly your product reaches customers. If you can find a highly efficient channel, you can gain a competitive edge.

Go Green

Green Marketing

Consumer demand for environmentally-friendly products continues to grow. With companies as far-ranging as Target, McDonald's, and Toyota developing green products or launching green initiatives, entrepreneurs are finding out that if they fail to respond to these trends, they risk having their brands pushed aside by more green-savvy competitors. Managing products is now more complicated. Entrepreneurs must keep tabs on technological changes, consumer attitudes, and even the scarcity of natural resources that might someday threaten their brand. The greener brand will make more green!

◈ **Critical Thinking**
Look for a product that claims to be environmentally friendly and examine it more closely. If it is recycled, see what percentage of the material is recycled from post-consumer waste. Write a short report summarizing your findings.

Channels of Distribution—Consumer Market

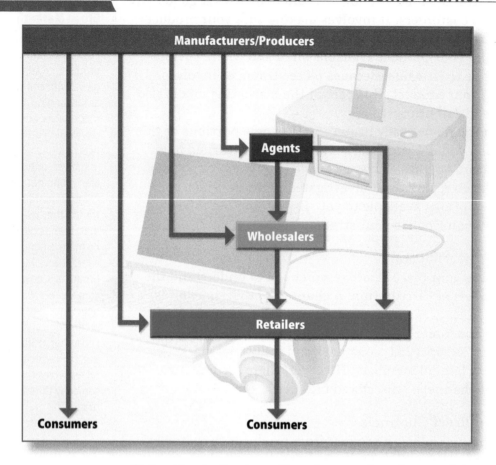

● **Reaching the Consumer** The path your product takes to reach the consumer can be either direct or indirect. *How many of the channels of distribution shown here are indirect?*

Intensity of Distribution

How broadly will you distribute your product? You have three choices:

- **Intensive distribution** When you want to find a best-selling paperback, you can find it at a bookstore, supermarket, or magazine stand. These products have been been distributed intensively. **Intensive distribution** involves placement of a product in all suitable sales outlets.
- **Selective distribution** Textbooks might only be found near schools or online. This is selective distribution. **Selective distribution** limits the number of sales outlets in a given area.
- **Exclusive distribution** **Exclusive distribution** limits the number of outlets to one per area. For example, a museum might sell a special book for an exhibit.

Transportation

The physical movement of goods is part of your place decisions. How will your product be shipped? Your choices include by truck, train, airplane, ship, or pipeline. If you deal with information, you might be able to send your product via the Internet. The method of transportation you select affects how fast your product reaches consumers. It also determines your shipping costs. Generally, air transportation is most expensive, and waterway is least expensive.

Location, Layout, and Availability

As you learned earlier, location, or site considerations, are also important to your place strategy. They are especially important to retail and service businesses that depend on customers to come to them. You can increase customer access and encourage sales by selecting a location near transportation routes. You might also lay out your site to have entries from the street and parking lot. You might favor evening over morning hours of operation. What do these options have in common? They are designed to match the needs and opportunities of potential customers. In other words, they are designed to make it easy for people to do business with you.

● **Figure 10.2**   Channels of Distribution — Industrial Market

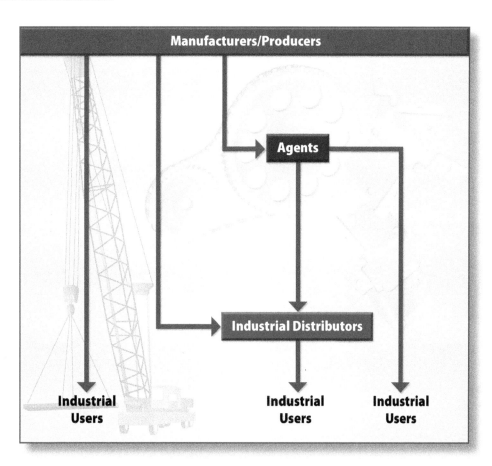

● **Reaching the Industrial User**   Channels of distribution for industrial products differ from those for consumer products. *How do they differ?*

Questions to Ask About Place Decisions

When you make your place decisions, keep your target market in mind. Ask yourself the following questions:

- How will my product be sold and distributed?
- Will my product go directly from producer to user, or will it go through an intermediary?
- Can I use more efficient channels of distribution?
- What channel members will I use to obtain my products?
- What channel members will I use to distribute my products?
- How intensively will I distribute my products?
- Is my location appropriate for my target market(s)?
- Will the physical layout of my business encourage or discourage sales?
- Do my hours of operation match the times my target market prefers to do business?

Impact of Technology on the Place Strategy

In the place strategy, the Internet has had the biggest impact on channels of distribution. In particular, distributors have seen an increase in productivity. Their customers have benefited as a result.

Use of the Internet by distributors has eliminated expensive guesswork related to customer needs, as shown in **Figure 10.3**. Suppliers can deliver what customers want in a timely manner and at lower costs. By doing so, suppliers can cut back on inventory. In addition, geography is no longer a problem. Distributors can connect easily with customers. Finally, the Internet can reduce the time customers spend searching for information. Many distributors have Websites that provide prices, specifications, and third-party ratings of products. The Internet does not reduce the need for personal customer service. However, it does reduce the cost of that service.

The Internet and other technologies have affected suppliers and other channel members, too. For example, virtually all businesses

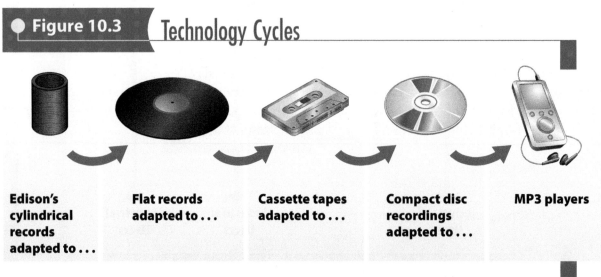

● **Figure 10.3**   Technology Cycles

Edison's cylindrical records adapted to . . .

Flat records adapted to . . .

Cassette tapes adapted to . . .

Compact disc recordings adapted to . . .

MP3 players

● **Changing Tunes** Advances in technology have resulted in the emergence of new products and services. *How have advances in technology changed the distribution of movies?*

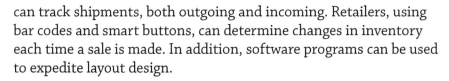

ETHICS and BUSINESS

Collecting Customer Information

Situation Your company is holding a drawing to give away an MP3 player. As customers come into your store, you suggest that they fill out an entry form and drop it into the box. You will use the contact information provided on the entry blanks to market your products.

Marketing Issues A neighboring business owner has asked if you will share with him the list of names and contact information you collected from the entry-blanks so that he can use the information to market his products. When you refuse, he offers to buy the information.

English Language Arts/Writing

Protecting Customers' Rights Customers have a right to expect that their information will be kept private when they provide it to a business unless notified otherwise. Is it fair for a business owner to profit from information his customers have freely provided?

1. How would you justify your decision to sell or not to sell your customers' information?
2. Write a half-page report explaining your reasoning.

can track shipments, both outgoing and incoming. Retailers, using bar codes and smart buttons, can determine changes in inventory each time a sale is made. In addition, software programs can be used to expedite layout design.

The People Strategy

The people strategy means assembling, preparing, and maintaining the people who will help you achieve success. The actions, attitudes, and individual decisions of employees will impact your business on a daily basis. Good employees are a key ingredient in your marketing mix. They make all of your other marketing mix strategies work.

Chapters 17 and 18 describe specific techniques for hiring and motivating employees. The focus in this chapter is on the broader aspects of people strategy planning and decision making.

Basic Hiring Criteria

Hiring the right people will help you to reach your objectives more quickly. Qualifications for hiring are dictated by the needs of your business. If your business does not require unique skills, a good attitude and the ability to learn may be sufficient. If you need people with special skills, these special skills are an important part of the qualifications. You need employees who can help you reach your marketing objectives immediately.

Developing Employees

Employee development consists of two parts. The first is orientation. Orientation includes your vision for the company, plans to carry it out, and expectations of high performance. The second is providing training for the skills and knowledge employees need now and in the future. This process allows them to contribute to the performance and financial goals of the company.

Establishing a Productive Environment

A productive environment is one with a healthy atmosphere. Employees are treated with respect and trust. They are empowered to do the right thing. In a productive environment, employees consider themselves members of a winning team. Team membership brings pride, cooperation, and team spirit. These factors set the stage for positive results.

Rewarding Your People

Recognize and reward employee contributions and achievements. If possible, share the financial rewards of the business. Investing in people is just as important as investing in other strategies. When people know their efforts are appreciated, they are more likely to stay for the long term. Committed, long-term employees will be more effective at implementing your marketing mix strategies.

Questions to Ask About People Decisions

As you consider your people strategy, ask yourself the following questions:
- What specific qualifications must my employees have?
- What training do I need to provide?
- Can I provide the training, or do I need to outsource it?
- What rewards will provide the greatest motivation?

The Price Strategy

The price strategy impacts business in two ways. First, it is a financial decision that ensures costs are covered and a profit is made. More important, however, price is a marketing strategy that affects the customer's motivation to buy. Set your prices too high and you may turn away customers. Set them too low and customers may be led to believe your product lacks quality. Chapter 11 examines other factors that can affect your pricing strategy.

The Price and Promotion Strategy

The promotion strategy is designed to tell potential customers about your products and their characteristics, benefits, and availability. It should also be used to enhance your company's image.

The promotion strategy of a business coordinates all aspects of a product. It involves planning, determining the right mix, and selecting specific activities. The different aspects of the promotion strategy is addressed in detail in Chapters 12 and 13.

Reading Check **List** What are the five Ps of the marketing mix?

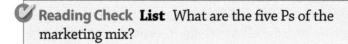

Marketing Tactics

To apply marketing strategies, you must develop an action plan to put the components of the mix into operation. The action plan consists of the **marketing tactics**, or activities that need to be taken to carry out the marketing plan. The action plan also includes a schedule. The primary activities in the action plan are the day-to-day marketing actions, also called marketing functions. They include financing, risk management, selling, promotion, pricing, purchasing, marketing-information management, product/service planning, and distribution. The scheduling and assignments are management functions.

Implementing the strategies also involves costs. When developing your action plan, you estimate and budget for costs. These costs will be used when preparing your financial plan.

In addition, you need to know how you will evaluate your marketing plan. The evaluation plan should include how you will (1) judge your business's performance, (2) evaluate the effectiveness of your marketing plan, and (3) identify and solve problems. The information you obtain will help you make adjustments to your strategies and mix.

SECTION 10.1 — Review

After You Read

Self-Check
1. **List** the components of the marketing plan.
2. **Decscribe** why the five marketing strategies must be synchronized.
3. **Explain** the importance of the product and place strategies.

Think
4. **Develop** preliminary drafts of the product, place, and people strategies for a proposed business.

Mathematics
5. Scott manages a packaging plant. The plant makes packaging for three different types of toys. The packaging for Product A costs $2.00 more than twice the cost of Product C's packaging to make. The packaging for Product B costs 1.7 times the cost of Product C's. Write equations that would allow you to determine the cost to produce A's and B's packaging if C's costs $0.39. Write another equation to find the total cost of producing 1000 of each type of package.

Math Concept **Logical Reasoning** Real-life problems involving math require logical step-by-step reasoning.
Step 1 Determine what unknowns are and choose appropriate symbols to substitute for the unknowns.
Step 2 Write the equations by thinking logically about the information given in the problem.

 Go to connectED.mcgraw-hill.com to check your answers.

Updating the Marketing Plan

Reading Guide

Before You Read ■■■■■■■■■■■■■■

Preview How would you organize the marketing information you have collected?

The Main Idea

The target markets, customer demands, and competition of a business change over time. For a business to succeed, you must make timely adjustments in your marketing plan.

Objectives

State the importance of ongoing market research.

List the factors to consider for each strategy when reviewing the marketing mix.

Describe how to update the marketing mix and marketing plan.

Content Vocabulary

◇ private brand
◇ guarantee
◇ diversification

Academic Vocabulary

You will see these words in your reading and on your tests. Use the academic vocabulary glossary to look up their meanings.

■ constant   ■ predict

Graphic Organizer

Before you read this section, draw a chart like the one shown. As you read, fill in the second column with possible changes for each strategy.

 Go to connectED.mcgraw-hill.com to download this graphic organizer.

The 5 Ps	Possible Changes
Product	
Price	
Place	
Promotion	
People	

Why Is Ongoing Market Research Important?

Do not assume that target markets, customer demands, and competitors identified at start-up will remain the same. In business, change is **constant**. Technology makes some products obsolete, sometimes quickly. Clothing styles evolve from year to year. A social activity that is popular now will be replaced over time. You must stay on top of any changes. If you do not, you may lose customers and miss promising opportunities.

Ongoing Market Research

How can you measure the ongoing changes in business? How can you **predict** changes and prepare for them? You need up-to-date information to stay profitable. You must keep up with what is going on. To do that, you must continue your market research.

Ongoing market research will be similar, in some ways, to your start-up research. However, there will also be some important differences. Specifically, you will have large amounts of data to deal with over time. You will also have in-house information as a major resource.

Marketing Information

An effective way to address these changes is to put a marketing-information management system in place. That is, a set of procedures for the regular collection of accurate, timely information that you can systematically store. Then you can easily access, analyze, and use the data when making adjustments to the marketing plan.

Primary Sources of Information

For ongoing market research, you will have another source of primary information—your customers and former customers. You can use that source to conduct surveys by mail, on the phone, over the Internet or social media, in personal interviews, and through focus groups.

Secondary Sources of Information

Your operations records will provide secondary information—accounting records and sales receipts indicate your expenses. They also show which products are moving and which are not.

You can also collect and keep a chronological file of information that is pertinent to your business and industry. Newspapers, magazines, the Internet or social media, and trade publications can all yield valuable articles.

Along with the opportunity to use in-house information, cited above, comes responsibility. That is the responsibility of observing ethical practices in storing and using customers' information. Protecting the customer's privacy is a critical part of effectively managing the information.

As You Read ...

Compare How do product strategy decisions differ for start-ups and ongoing business?

Reviewing Your Marketing Plan and Mix

There are many benefits to ongoing market research. It provides information you need to make adjustments to your marketing plan. By being aware of what is happening in your market, you can revise your objectives and rework your marketing mix strategies to make them more effective.

Changes to the Product Strategy

Concerns about product strategy are the same for both start-up and ongoing businesses. The only difference is that you will be making decisions about existing products rather than projected ones. What goods or services should you offer? How will your products be different from your competitors'? What can you do to make sure customers identify your products?

A change in any one of your products may affect other products. Changes may stimulate sales through increased traffic. However, changes could possibly cause a loss of sales if there is a negative reaction from customers.

When Toyota® introduced the Scion® line of vehicles targeted at younger consumers, the increase in showroom traffic benefited all Toyota models. In contrast, if a car model gets a bad reputation, the entire image of a manufacturer may suffer.

GLOBAL WORKPLACE — Iceland: Hot and Cold

Despite its name, Iceland has a lot of heat to share. Located south of the Arctic Circle, Iceland is a volcanically active island. Volcanoes dot the landscape and occasionally spew lava. Renewable energy, produced in geothermal and hydroelectric plants, provides over 90 percent of Iceland's energy needs.

Patronymics Few Icelanders have distinct last names. Many take their fathers' names and add –son or –dóttir (daughter) to the end. First names are generally preferred, although Mr. and Ms. may be used among foreigners.

Social Studies/Science Research geothermal energy and how entrepreneurs around the world are using it to develop new products and services. Identify locations in the U.S. that may be able to harness geothermal energy and sum-marize your findings in a one-page report.

Common Icelandic Words and Phrases	
Hello/Hi	hallo
Goodbye	sjáumst síðar
Yes/No	já/nei
Please	gætirðu
Thank you	takk kærlega
You're welcome	það var ekkert

Adding Products

Before adding products to your line or adding lines, ask yourself if there is sufficient demand to add the new product. You should also determine if the product is consistent with your current business. Will the new product compete with your current products? It may sell very well, but if it hurts current sales, what is the point?

Finally, ask yourself if adding the product is the best use of your economic resources. Can money, labor, and facilities be put to better use? Can they be put to better use in another part of your marketing mix?

Eliminating Products

One reason to eliminate a product is poor sales. Sometimes businesspeople are slow to take such action, thinking they can make the item sell. Not cutting a product can lead to a buildup of inventory and financial losses. By not cutting a poor seller, you may be using sales and/or production efforts unwisely.

Another reason for eliminating products is to simplify your line of goods or services. This allows you to focus on the things you do well. However, you should consider whether a broad range of products is necessary for you to compete.

New Tricks Identifying new uses for your product can expand its market or extend its life. Corn is now being used to make ethanol, a kind of fuel that can power automobiles. *Can you think of other products that have found new uses?*

Changing Products

Changing the style or design of your product can give you a competitive edge. Your changes must be consistent with customer demand. For example, you may decide to make changes to keep in step with current fashions. You may also improve your products by taking advantage of the latest technology. However, changing your product may affect your prices and distribution. Timing, too, must be considered. You want your offerings to be up-to-date, but you do not want to be ahead of the market.

Identifying New Uses for Products

Identifying new uses for your product can expand its market or extend its life. One way to find new uses is to monitor how customers use the product. For example, Straight Arrow Products found that customers were buying their Mane and Tail horse shampoo for personal use. As a result, they repackaged the product for the human market. Another way to find new uses is to conduct research. For example, soybeans are now being used to make biodiesel fuel and printer ink. The maker of Tums®, an antacid, increased sales by marketing the product as a calcium supplement.

Shades of Green More and more business people are asking themselves if their products are friendly to the environment. *How can environmentally friendly packaging help sales?*

Changing Brands

If you manufacture products under different brand names, you may want to consolidate them all under one brand. This could help build brand loyalty among customers. You may choose to sell your own private brand. A **private brand** is a brand that is owned and initiated by a wholesaler or retailer. Large supermarkets often offer a variety of products on their own label.

Changing Packaging or Labels

You may also want to try changing your packaging and labels to enhance the attractiveness and salability of your product. Many entrepreneurs are now changing their product packaging for environmental reasons. Consumers are becoming increasingly concerned about the effect that certain kinds of plastics and other materials might have on people or the environment. Because of these concerns, packaging changes could make the product more appealing.

Revising Guarantees and Service Policies

To build customer confidence and increase sales, a business can improve or add guarantees and service policies. A **guarantee** is an assurance of the quality of a product. Guarantees and policies can make all the difference in a sale. Of course, you must be able to provide the additional guaranteed services.

Making Changes to the Place Strategy

You are most likely to make changes in your ongoing place strategy with regard to location, layout, and availability. To some extent, you may also make changes in your channels of distribution.

Improving Location

As your business grows, you may look for ways to improve your location. You may extend it by using kiosks, or stands, on street corners or in malls. With some businesses, you may decide to "take your location to the customer" through mobile units.

You may also want to consider more permanent and substantial changes. You might add outlets or branch operations. You might change your base location to be more accessible to customers. Because these are more permanent steps, they must be coordinated with your plans for growth.

Rearranging Layout

You may also want to rearrange the physical layout of your operation. For retail and some service businesses, this change can enhance sales. Adding or expanding parking or access to your business can do the same. If you are a manufacturer, a wholesaler, or an extractor, you might reorganize your distribution. This could increase your ability to serve customers and, thus, increase sales.

Thinkstock/Superstock

Increasing Availability

Availability is generally the easiest adjustment to make in your place strategy. It can also be the most effective because it allows customers to do business with you.

If you have a tutoring service, you might change your hours to increase your availability and business by staying open evenings and Saturdays. If you have a business that supplies food to restaurants, you might change your delivery schedule to better meet the restaurants' needs. Both examples are ways to increase availability.

Changing Channels of Distribution

The type of business you have and where you are in the channel determine your choices. If you are in a manufacturing business, you have some control over channel decisions. You can look for ways to improve your channel choices.

Businesses at other points in the channel have more limited options. If you are a retailer or wholesaler, you can look for different product sources. You may look for those sources that deliver more effectively and efficiently. You may also seek alternatives where you do have some control—channels between you and your customers. Before you make any change in channels, you should look at the new channel and try to determine what effect it will have on sales volume, stability, gross profit, and operating costs.

Making Changes to the People Strategy

Major changes in the people strategy may be necessary. Changes may be needed because of shifts in demand, changes in the nature of the business, or growth. If the demand for your goods or services goes down, you may need fewer people. If demand goes up, you may need more people. Your business may go from a people-intensive to a mechanized business. In this case, the size of your workforce will decrease. Qualifications of your workforce will change as well.

As your business grows, human resources responsibilities become more formalized and expand. Team-building responsibilities may shift to others in your organization. In addition, as times change, you must revisit your system of rewards.

Making Changes to the Price and Promotion Strategies

Chapter 11 discusses price strategies. Price revision considerations include profit, reacting to market prices, and revising terms of sale.

Promotion strategy and promotion strategy revisions are discussed in Chapters 12 and 13. Promotion revision considerations include making the most of your advertising dollars, stimulating sales, and planning for the long term.

Keeping it Fresh Changing the style or design of your product can give you a competitive edge. *What are some products you use that have undergone changes?*

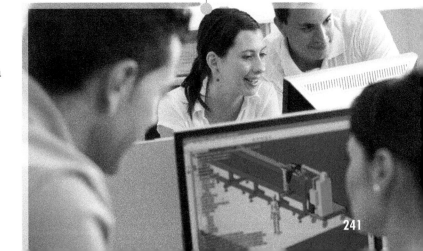

Revising Your Marketing Plan and Mix

As you adjust each of your marketing strategies, you may need to change other strategies to get the right mix. Here is an example:

- **Situation** You are the owner of a no-frills golf driving range.
- **Change in Product Strategy** You decide to upgrade your facility by covering the tee areas.
- **Change in Price Strategy** You adjust your prices to pay for the improvements.
- **Change in Promotion Strategy** You advertise more to let the golfing public know about your new facilities.
- **Change in Place Strategy** The increase in business allows you to keep your business open all winter.
- **Change in People Strategy** The increase in business requires that you hire more employees.

You should schedule an annual review of your marketing objectives and marketing plan. Once your business is under way, the result of this review may be expansion and revision. You may decide to add **diversification**. This is the process of investing in products or businesses with which you are not currently involved.

SECTION 10.2 Review

After You Read

Self-Check

1. **Describe** how ongoing market research is different from start-up market research.
2. **Identify** the questions should you consider before making changes on your channels of distribution.
3. **Explain** why it is important to review and revise your marketing mix on a regular basis.

Think

4. **Create** a separate review checklist for the product, place, and people strategies for your business.

English Language Arts

5. **Order Words by Degree** The words *exclusive, selective,* and *intense* are used in this chapter to describe different types of distribution. Intense distribution is the most extreme followed in degree by selective and then exclusive. Put the following groups of three words in order from most extreme to least extreme. Be prepared to explain your choices: *widely, completely, usually; pricey, expensive, costly; thorough, exhaustive, sketchy.*

Go to connectED.mcgraw-hill.com to check your answers.

Entrepreneurs *in Action*

Gabriela Lopez de Dennis
Owner and Creative Director
Soap Design Co.

Q *What do you do?*

A I am the owner and creative director/graphic designer at Soap Design Co., a commercial art and graphic design company, working primarily in the entertainment and art industry. I've created marketing pieces for a lot of interesting artists, including album covers.

Q *What kind of training and education do you have for this job?*

A I have a bachelor's of Fine Arts from Otis College of Art and Design, along with some additional business and accounting classes right after college.

Q *What do you enjoy most about your job?*

A I enjoy the industry I'm in very much. I also enjoy working with each and every client I've had, the type of work my job allows me to create, the people I meet, and the flexibility I have in running my own business.

Q *How did you become interested in your field?*

A I was born into an artistic family that always supported my interest in the arts when I was young. As I got older and explored and learned about the different types of work one can do in the arts, graphic design and the type of designing I do seemed like the perfect match for my skills and passions.

CCR ☆ College & Career Readiness

Plan to Succeed
Research a small business in your community to find out how it uses marketing plans.
1. Contact a company by phone or e-mail.
2. Explain that you are a student researching entrepreneurship.
3. Ask how the company uses marketing plans. Summarize your findings in a one-page report.

Career Facts

Real-World Skills	Academic Skills	Career Cluster
Interpersonal Communication, Speaking, Listening	Fine Arts, Marketing, English Language Arts	Marketing

Gabriella Lopez

Visual Summary

The Marketing Plan

The Marketing Mix The five Ps make up the marketing mix.

The Five Ps
1   **Product**   Goods or services and how they match customer needs and wants.
2   **Price**   The financial decision that ensures costs are covered and profit is made and is motivating customers to buy.
3   **Place**   How goods or services are delivered to customers.
4   **Promotion**   Tells customers about a product's characteristics, benefits, and availability.
5   **People**   Assembling, preparing, and maintaining the people who will help achieve success.

Making Changes A marketing plan must change along with the business environment.

Changes to the Place Strategy

- Improving location
- Rearranging layout
- Increasing availability
- Changing channels of distribution

Changes to Product Strategy

- Adding products
- Eliminating products
- Changing products
- Identifying new uses for products
- Changing brands, packaging, or labels

Lars A. Niki

Vocabulary

1. On a sheet of paper, use each of these terms and words in a written sentence.

Content Vocabulary

◇ marketing plan
◇ marketing objectives
◇ marketing mix
◇ brand
◇ package
◇ label
◇ product positioning
◇ product mix
◇ channel of distribution

◇ intermediaries
◇ intensive distribution
◇ selective distribution
◇ exclusive distribution
◇ marketing tactics
◇ private brand
◇ guarantee
◇ diversification

Academic Vocabulary

■ concept
■ target
■ constant
■ predict

Key Concepts

2. **Identify** the purpose of the marketing plan.
3. **Name** the five marketing strategies that make up the marketing mix.
4. **Describe** the part marketing tactics play in the marketing plan.
5. **State** the importance of ongoing market research.
6. **List** the factors to consider for each strategy when reviewing your marketing mix.
7. **Describe** how to update the marketing mix and marketing plan.
8. **Explain** the fundamental marketing concepts used by small businesses.
9. **Define** the nine marketing functions.

Academic Skills

Mathematics

10. **Cost and Discount** Lu is the shipping manager for a chemical company. The shipping company she uses offered a discounted rate this year in order to keep her business. This year, if the company ships the same amount as last year, the discounted shipping cost will be $101,200. The total cost for the previous year was $132,100. What is the percent of the discount?

    Math Concept **Percents** A percentage is a ratio between two numbers, such as those representing a part and a whole. It uses a percent sign (%).
    Step 1 Divide the new cost by the original cost to determine the ratio in decimal form. Multiply by 100 to find the percentage.
    Step 2 Subtract the percent from 100 to determine the discount.

English Language Arts/Writing

11. **Edit and Revise** Reviewing and revising are steps in the writing process. These steps are important in a marketing plan and in your own work. Choose a brief essay you have written as an assignment for this or another class. Ask three different people to read and comment on it. Rewrite the paper incorporating changes that you think are appropriate.

Academic Skills *(continued)*

Social Studies

12. Ecotourism You are creating an ecotourism business for a developing country. Your goal is to attract vacationers from developed nations to experience the country's natural beauty. Choose a developing country and research the natural resources (for example, beaches, mountains, or wildlife) that might make it a great tourist destination. Write a paragraph that explains the benefits the country offers the ecotourist.

Science

13. Sonic Boom Lee operates a training program for pilots. He told his students that the speed of sound in air is about 761 miles per hour, or Mach 1. Mach is the ratio of an object's speed to the speed of sound. Calculate the speed of a pilot flying at Mach 3.

Real-World Skills

Problem-Solving Skills

14. The Right Level of Competition Amanda has started a company to sell iPhone apps. If she creates apps that are too different from existing, popular apps, no one may want them. If she creates apps that are similar to existing apps, there may be too much competition. What should she do?

21st Century Skills

Leadership and Responsibility

15. A Tastier Future You run a successful restaurant with a staff of 30 people. Inspire your employees by writing a paragraph that describes your vision of how the business will grow and improve in the next year. Be sure to explain how these improvements will benefit them.

Connect to Your Community

16. Local Distribution Interview a retail business owner, a wholesale business owner, and a service business owner. Ask about the products and services they offer and the distribution methods appropriate for the particular business. Prepare a report that identifies how the scope of products and services varied based upon business type.

17. Product Research Conduct market research on a product or service sold at school to determine whether possible product changes are needed. Create and conduct the survey, compile your results, and make recommendations in writing to the principal on your findings.

Competitive Events Prep

18. **Situation** You and a partner are owners of a small hardware store. Your store is located in a suburban area that is experiencing moderate but steady population growth. The store's sales have been steady, but not growing at the rate they should in light of the area's population growth. Both you and your partner are concerned about the lack of sales growth. You are to discuss with your partner some ideas about how the use of a marketing plan could help remedy this situation.

Activity You are to suggest some ways to determine the solution to the lack of sales growth and discuss them with your partner.

Evaluation You will be evaluated on how well you meet these performance indicators:
- Describe the nature of marketing planning.
- Conduct marketing analysis.
- Develop marketing plan.
- Conduct an environmental scan to obtain marketing information.
- Monitor and evaluate performance of marketing plan.

 Go to **connectED.mcgraw-hill.com** for more information about this activity and other competitive events.

Standardized Test Practice

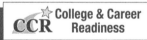
College & Career Readiness

Directions Choose the letter of the best answer. Write the letter for the answer on a separate piece of paper. For question #2, if the answer is False, rewrite the statement to make it true.

1. Products are not identified by which of the following?
   A. costing
   B. branding
   C. packaging
   D. labeling

2. You can not develop marketing mix before choosing a target market.
   T
   F

Test-Taking Tip
To reduce anxiety that can be caused by a test, write down important formulas, facts, definitions and/or key words in the margin first so you will not worry about forgetting them.

Chapter Objectives

The Price Strategy

Discovery Project
Pricing Merchandise

Key Question *How do business owners determine the best prices?*

Project Goal
Contact a local business owner to discuss the factors considered when determining prices for products. Prepare a list of questions to ask the owner before your discussion. Compare and contrast the information you have gathered with your classmates.

Think About...
➤ Which local business owner will you contact?
➤ What questions will you ask about how prices are set?
➤ How will you present the information you gather?

21st Century Skills
Economic Literacy *Use your own pricing strategy to set prices for two products of your invention.*

Evaluate
 Go to connectED.mcgraw-hill.com to download a rubric that you can use to evaluate your final project.

Ask
AN
EXPERT

Q: *I have been running my own Internet cafe for two years and want to expand to a second store. Developers are building a new shopping center on the other side of town. Where can I find enough money to open a second shop?*

A: Many business owners use loans to grow their business. Banks offer favorable lending rates to businesses that appear poised for growth. The U.S. Small Business Administration offers loans through its Certified Lenders Program. You can also attempt to raise equity capital. This means you look for people who are looking to invest with a potential for a high return. The investors take a financial risk and you agree to share your future profits.

Connect the Photo
BOGO (Buy One, Get One) Developing and keeping your prices aligned to the market are both part of an effective pricing strategy. Ensuring the prices are consistent with your objectives and expectations requires ongoing attention and revisions. *What are the advantages of bundle pricing?*

Price Strategy Considerations

Reading Guide

Before You Read ■■■■■■■■■■■■■■■

Connect What do want you to accomplish through pricing?

The Main Idea

Developing an effective price strategy is an important part of a marketing plan. It enables you to keep prices consistent with your objectives and appropriate for your target market.

Objectives

Identify factors that affect price strategy.
Summarize the marketing objectives related to pricing.
Describe the components that go into making price strategy decisions.

Content Vocabulary

◇ fixed
◇ variable
◇ price gouging
◇ price fixing
◇ resale price maintenance
◇ unit pricing
◇ return on investment
◇ price skimming
◇ penetration pricing
◇ psychological pricing
◇ prestige pricing
◇ odd/even pricing
◇ price lining
◇ promotional pricing
◇ multiple-unit pricing
◇ bundle pricing
◇ discount pricing

Academic Vocabulary

You will see these words in your reading and on your tests. Use the academic vocabulary glossary to look up their meanings.
■ goal
■ ensure

Graphic Organizer

Before you read this section, draw a chart like the one shown. As you read, fill in the price strategy considerations.

 Go to connectED.mcgraw-hill.com to download this graphic organizer.

Factors Affecting Price

Setting a price for a good, a service, or an idea is not easy. You must consider costs, expenses, supply and demand, consumer perceptions, the competition, government regulations, and technological trends. Each of these factors can affect the market price.

Costs and Expenses

To stay in business, you must make a profit. That means your prices have to exceed your costs and expenses. Costs and expenses can be fixed or variable. **Fixed** costs such as rent, utilities, and insurance premiums do not vary with the number of units sold. **Variable** costs do change depending on the number of units sold. Examples of variable costs are cost of goods sold, sales commissions, and delivery expenses.

The cost of products are also affected by the pricing structure in the channel of distribution. Each channel member has to make a profit to make handling the goods worthwhile. If you sell magazines, both the publisher and the distributor need to make money. Otherwise, you will not have magazines to sell. Their cost and profit together is your cost.

If you are selling services (pool cleaning, landscaping, financing) or ideas (self-improvement courses, weight-loss programs, counseling), your channel and thus your pricing structure are much simpler. Chapter 10 discusses how these channels go directly from the producer—the service or idea provider—to the customer. In these cases, the cost is that of the resources that go into providing the service or idea.

Products that include a combination of goods, services, and/or ideas have the same price structure as goods. Products made up of goods and services have the same channel price structure. The price structure of such combinations should reflect the total cost of the goods, services, and ideas that are included in the product.

Supply and Demand

The law of supply and demand also affects price. When the demand for your product is high and supply is low, you can command a high price. When the reverse is true (low demand and high supply), you must set lower prices.

Prices are not always affected by supply and demand. That is because prices reflect the sensitivity of market demand. When customers buy a product regardless of price (gasoline or milk, for example), the demand is inelastic. In contrast, when prices are especially sensitive to demand (gourmet foods or other luxury items), the demand is elastic. Chapter 1 discusses elastic and inelastic demand.

As You Read

Compare If you run a pool cleaning service, will your pricing structure be simple or complex?

Web Savvy

Subscription-Based Pricing
Subscription-based pricing models, which are popular with certain kinds of software companies, online games, and services like Netflix™, were popularized by magazines and newspapers. Customers have to pay a subscription price, usually once a month, to have access to the product or service. Massively multiple online roleplaying games (MMORPGs) like *Everquest™*, *Eve Online*, and *World of Warcraft* have had huge success with subscription-based pricing. Players pay a monthly fee for the ability to create and maintain online characters that interact with thousands of other characters around the world. *Other online games allow users to play for free. How do they generate revenue?*

Consumer Perceptions

The price of your products helps create your image in the minds of customers. Prices set too low can lead customers to believe that your product lacks quality. Prices set too high may turn away customers. Prices set at the high end of a competitive range, however, convey quality and status. Consider the perceptions of your target market in particular. Different target markets have different perceptions and opinions about prices.

Competition

Competition also affects price. When the target market is price conscious, competitors' pricing may determine your pricing. Sometimes businesses choose to charge more than their competitors for a similar product. Businesses can charge higher prices by offering services that add value. Customers usually pay more for personal attention, credit, and warranties.

Government Regulations

Your price strategy may be affected by federal and state laws. The Clayton Act and the Robinson-Patman Act are two federal laws that impact pricing. Both make it illegal for businesses to sell the same product to different customers at different prices. For example, an auto dealer cannot charge a lower price to men than to women. Businesses that do must be able to show that certain conditions exist. For example, one customer may buy a higher volume or lesser quality of products.

To avoid problems, you should always be fair to customers. Familiarize yourself with federal and state laws that address pricing. You should also be mindful of laws involving price gouging, price fixing, resale price maintenance, unit pricing, and bait-and-switch advertising.

Price gouging is the practice of pricing above the market when no alternative retailer is available. **Price fixing** is an illegal practice in which competing companies agree, formally or informally, to restrict prices within a specified range.

Resale price maintenance is price fixing imposed by a manufacturer on wholesale or retail resellers of its products to deter price-based competition. **Unit pricing** is the required pricing of goods on the basis of cost per unit of measure, such as pound or ounce, in addition to the price per item.

Chapter 8 discusses bait-and-switch advertising, an illegal practice in which sellers attract customers with sale-priced items, then persuade them to purchase a higher-priced item.

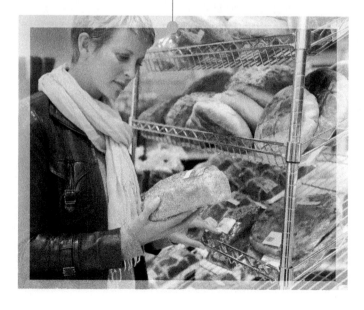

Expensive Taste Prices set at the high end of a competitive range convey quality and status. *Do you think certain kinds of food items are high quality? If so, which kinds and why?*

Onoky/SuperStock

The Psychology of Price

Boost sales with pricing, special offers, BOGOs, and other incentives

Why do so many prices end in 99? It's simple. English speakers read left to right, so the first number—the one before the .99—is the one people notice and remember. For example, if your product is $7.99, the customer sees the price as $7.00.

Premium products often drop the .99. Athletic shoes may be $39.99 at a discount store, but at premium sporting goods store they may cost $40—or $150!

Another good strategy is to offer three versions: a bare-bones starter item, a mid-priced version, and a professional-quality option. Most people opt for the item right in the middle.

Remember the appeal of the word "free." Most of us love getting something for nothing, even if it's only free shipping.

Free samples can boost sales, too. Coupons are always hot, too: they draw shoppers into a store, where they buy additional products.

Beware of using sweepstakes and contests. If you do, be sure to follow both your state and federal laws.

Active Learning

Choose a consumer product—a food product, a toy, or an electronic or software item—and prepare an advertisement for it. The ad can be online, point-of-purchase, or some other type. Use one of the pricing strategies detailed above. Then write a paragraph explaining why you chose the particular pricing strategy. Find another student and compare your ads and strategies.

Technological Trends

Technology trends affect price strategy. Big bookstores such as Barnes & Noble or Borders were competing with each other in the mid-1990s. At that same time, Amazon.com began changing the way people bought books. Through the Internet, Amazon provides customers with easy access to prices, product information, and services. Also, the company saves overhead by not running a chain of brick-and-mortar stores. These savings are passed on to the customer in the form of discount prices. Part or all of many traditional businesses have since become Web-based. Consumers today compare prices on products and services ranging from flowers and fashion designs to digital music files, cars, and even homes.

Adapting to technological changes can give you a competitive edge. Not adapting can cause some businesses to become obsolete.

Reading Check **Describe** What is the best way to avoid legal problems regarding pricing?

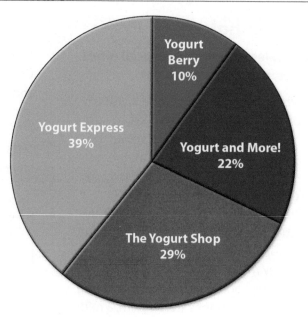

● **A Piece of the Pie Chart** The Yogurt Express shop has the largest market share of sales for the yogurt shops in one community. *What kinds of business tactics could other shops employ to increase their market share?*

Pricing Objectives

Before setting prices, you must decide what you want to accomplish through pricing. For new companies, obtaining a return on investment and obtaining market share are the most important **goals.**

Obtaining a Return on Investment

A **return on investment** (ROI) is the amount earned as a result of that investment. Targeting a ROI is the practice of setting a price to achieve a specified return.

Say that you invest $20,000 in productive assets and you want a 20 percent return. The product should be priced to earn an expected profit of $4,000 ($20,000 x 0.20).

Obtaining Market Share

Market share is a business's portion of the total sales generated by all competing companies in a given market. **Figure 11.1** shows that Yogurt Express has a 39 percent market share of local yogurt shops. If your objective is to attract a percentage of customers who are doing business with competitors, you must set your prices accordingly. If your products are price-sensitive, offering lower prices may work, but remember customer perception. Lower prices may not be necessary or even desirable You may be better off setting prices higher. You also may be able to gain market share through nonprice competition. Nonprice strategies include product quality, customer service, promotion, and packaging.

Other Objectives

Additional pricing objectives can include social and ethical considerations. They can also include meeting the competition's prices and establishing an image. During difficult economic times, they might include survival.

Pricing Strategy Decisions

To determine a pricing strategy, take these steps:
1. Select a basic approach to pricing (cost-based, demand-based, or competition-based).
2. Determine your pricing policy (flexible-price or one-price).
3. Set a price based on the stage of the product life cycle (introduction, growth, maturity, or decline) using an effective pricing technique (psychological pricing or discount pricing).

Setting a Basic Price

When setting a basic price for your product, you can use cost-based, demand-based, or competition-based pricing strategies. In practice, you may employ a combination of the three. If you have a range of products, you may use all of them. Regardless, the strategy or strategies you choose must be compatible with your target market and consistent with your pricing objectives.

Cost-Based Pricing

With a cost-based strategy, you must consider your business costs and your profit objectives. To calculate price using this strategy, figure your cost to make or buy your product. Then figure the related cost of doing business. Finally, add your projected profit margin to arrive at a price. The amount added to your cost to cover expenses and **ensure** a profit is called your *markup*.

Demand-Based Pricing

This strategy requires you to find out what customers are willing to pay for your product. You then set the price accordingly. Demand-based pricing is useful only when certain conditions exist. One is when demand for your product is inelastic. Another is when customers believe your product is different from or has greater value than the competition's.

Competition-Based Pricing

To determine prices using this strategy, you need to find out what your competitors charge. Then decide whether it is to your advantage to price below, in line with, or above the competition. This strategy does not involve cost or demand. It is only concerned with being competitive.

It's Up To You The rock band Radiohead released its album, *In Rainbows*, as a digital download on its own Website, and allowed customers to pay any price they wanted, including nothing. *Why would Radiohead do this?*

Pricing Policies

Establishing a pricing policy frees you from making the same pricing decisions over and over again. It also lets employees and customers know what to expect. There are two types of pricing policies: flexible-price policy and one-price policy.

Flexible-Price Policy

Flexible pricing—allowing customers to bargain for price—has several advantages. If you allow your customers to haggle with you over price, you may make sales you would otherwise lose. It can also bring customers to your business. Finally, it takes into account market conditions, such as increased or decreased demand, and competitors' prices, allowing you to react to these factors through your prices. Most car dealerships employ a flexible-price policy.

One-Price Policy

A one-price policy is one in which all customers are charged the same price. With flexible pricing, a customer who did not negotiate may be upset to discover that the price was flexible. Also, the customer can never be sure they got the best deal. A one-price policy, however, tells customers they are treated equally. One-price policies are strongly recommended for service businesses. If customers are allowed to haggle over the value of a service, the price will invariably go down. Most of the retail stores that you are familiar with employ a one-price policy.

Product Life Cycle Pricing

All products move through a four-stage life cycle: introduction, growth, maturity, and decline. To maximize profit, these stages need to be considered when setting prices. The life cycle applies to a brand or to a category of product. Some products move through the stages quickly. Others spend many years in one stage. The automobile has been in the maturity stage for more than 30 years.

ETHICS and BUSINESS

Fair Pricing

Situation The airline you run has been losing money lately because of higher fuel costs and fewer people being able to afford the high cost of flying. You and your partner are looking for ways to make your company profitable.

Checking the Competition You decide to check out your competition, and you learn that they use Yield Management (YM) to help increase their profits. Using YM the airline sets their prices low for people who book early. The closer the date of the flight comes, the higher the price goes.

English Language Arts/Writing

Yield Management How would you feel if you sat next to a passenger on a plane who paid half what you paid for the same flight because they bought their ticket earlier than you?

1. Would you consider using Yield Management in your business?
2. Write an e-mail to your partner explaining your feelings about Yield Management.

Stage 1: Introduction

In the introduction stage, sales volume is relatively low, marketing costs are high, and profits are low or even negative. Two methods are commonly used when introducing a product—price skimming or penetration pricing. **Price skimming** involves charging a high price to recover costs and maximize profit as quickly as possible. Then the price is dropped when the product is no longer unique. **Penetration pricing** builds sales by charging a low initial price to keep unit costs to customers as low as possible. This approach may discourage competition.

Stage 2: Growth

In the growth stage, sales climb rapidly, unit costs are decreasing, the product begins to show a profit, and competitors come into the market. If you use price skimming during the introduction stage, you would lower prices to appeal to price-conscious customers in the growth stage. If you use penetration pricing during the introduction stage, you would make only minor price changes during the growth stage. Other promotions would be used to keep sales high.

Stage 3: Maturity

The principal goal of the maturity stage is to stretch the life cycle of the product. In this stage, sales begin to slow and profits peak, but profits fall off as competition increases. In order to maintain steady prices, businesses must identify new markets or make product improvements. If the effort is successful, the product will have an extended maturity stage. If not, the product will move into the decline stage.

Product Life Cycles With the introduction of Blu-ray disc players and other High-Definition formats, DVD players moved closer to the end of the maturity stage of their life cycle. *What are some products that are still in their growth phase?*

Stage 4: Decline

In the decline stage, sales and profits continue to fall. At this stage, businesses should cut prices to generate sales or clear inventory. It is also helpful to try to reduce manufacturing and promotional costs during the decline stage. Once a product is no longer profitable, it is phased out.

Pricing Techniques

The final pricing decision is to select specific techniques for pricing your product. You are already familiar with penetration and skimming techniques for new products. Once your product is established, you have to decide on methods for arriving at a more permanent price. The goal is to adjust your prices so that they are the most attractive prices to buyers.

These techniques fall into two broad categories: *psychological pricing* and *discount pricing*.

Psychological Pricing

Psychological pricing refers to pricing techniques that are based on the belief that customers' perceptions of a product are strongly influenced by price. These techniques are most often used by retail businesses.

Prestige pricing is a pricing technique in which higher-than-average prices are used to suggest status and prestige to the customer. Many customers associate higher prices with higher quality and are willing to pay more for certain goods and services. For example, a shirt that costs $100 suggests exclusiveness, status, and quality.

Odd/even pricing is a pricing technique in which odd numbers, such as $19.99, are employed to suggest bargains. The psychological principle on which the technique is based is that odd numbers convey a bargain image, and even prices, such as $20, suggest higher quality.

Price lining is a pricing technique in which items in a certain category are priced the same. For example, a store may price all of its jeans at $25, $50, and $75. When deciding on price lines, entrepreneurs must be careful to make the price differences great enough to represent low, middle, and high prices for the category of goods being offered for sale.

Promotional pricing is a pricing technique in which lower prices are offered for a limited period of time to stimulate sales. The main characteristic of promotional pricing is that it is temporary—after the promotion ends, prices go back to normal. A fast-food restaurant may promote its new "super-burger" for 99 cents "for a limited time only."

Multiple-unit pricing is a pricing technique in which items are priced in multiples, such as 3 items for 99 cents. Pricing items in multiples suggests a bargain. This pricing technique can increase sales volume.

Bundle pricing is a pricing technique in which several complementary products are sold at a single price. The price is lower than it would be if the customer purchased each item separately. Computer companies use bundle pricing when they include software in the sale of a computer. Bundle pricing helps businesses sell items they may not have sold otherwise, which increases their sales and revenue.

Discount Pricing

Discount pricing offers customers reductions from the regular price. These reductions may encourage customers to buy. Discounts are used by all types of businesses. In some instances, they are basic percentage-off price discounts. In other situations, they are specialized discounts, some of which are listed below.

Cash discounts are given to customers for prompt payment. For example, you might see 2/10, n/30 on an invoice. This means the buyer can reduce the bill by 2 percent by paying within 10 days of the invoice. If the bill is not paid within 10 days, the full amount (net) is due within 30 days.

Quantity discounts encourage buyers to order larger quantities than they would ordinarily buy. The buyer gets a reduction in price. The seller reduces selling expenses and may shift part of the storing, shipping, and financing responsibilities to the buyer. Quantity discounts can be cumulative. For example, a buyer of more than $50,000 of materials during a year might be given a 10 percent discount.

GLOBAL WORKPLACE — Israel: High-Tech Land

The modern state of Israel was founded in 1948. Israel is home to several languages, including Hebrew, Arabic, Russian, and English. Recognized as a technology hotbed, the country boasts the largest percentage of engineers per capita in the world, and has pioneered such technological innovations as drip irrigation in agriculture.

Cultural Mix Israel is a potpourri of East and West, religious identities, and ethnic groups. Jewish and Muslim groups differ culturally from mainstream society, but it is not uncommon to find non-religious Israelis following Jewish Kosher laws when eating, such as never serving meat and dairy dishes together.

Social Studies/Science Israeli engineers are experts in solar technology. More than 9 out of 10 homes in the country use solar energy for hot water, the highest per person usage in the world. Identify two Israeli companies that provide solar energy and write a paragraph about the pricing strategies they might use.

Common Hebrew Words and Phrases		
Hello/Goodbye	שלום	Shalom
Yes/No	כן / לא	ken/lo
Please	בבקשה	bevakasha
Thank you	תודה	todah
You're welcome	על לא דבר	al lo davar

Trade and Promotional Discounts

Trade discounts are given to distribution-channel members who provide marketing functions for the manufacturer. These discounts are based on the manufacturer's suggested retail price (MSRP) and specify wholesaler and retailer discounts. As an example, a manufacturer might designate a discount relationship of 30–15 percent. This means the retailer takes 30 percent of the manufacturer's list price. The wholesaler keeps 15 percent for handling, storing, and delivering merchandise to the retailer.

Promotional discounts are used when manufacturers want to pay wholesalers or retailers for carrying out promotional activities. The discounts may be given in the price paid for promotional goods or made by a direct cash payment. They may even be in the form of promotional materials supplied by the manufacturer.

Seasonal Discounts

Seasonal discounts are used for products that have a high seasonal demand. For example, heavy coats are usually not in demand in the middle of summer. Likewise, short-sleeve shirts are not in demand in the dead of winter.

Manufacturers give seasonal discounts to customers who buy them in the off-season. This enables manufacturers to keep operations going throughout the year. It also enables them to shift storage costs to other points in the channel of distribution.

SECTION 11.1   Review

After You Read ·················

Self-Check
1. **Compare** elastic demand to inelastic demand.
2. **Define** market share.
3. **List** two factors must be considered in cost-based pricing.

Think
4. **Describe** the pricing method would you use to introduce a new product to the market and why you would use it.

English Language Arts
5. **Write Explanations and Directions** Calculating a discounted price involves working with rational numbers. First, explain what a rational number is, and provide examples. Then, describe the process of calculating a discount price in your own words. Remember, when writing directions, it is important to be concise and present the steps in a sequence in a clear order.

Go to connectED.mcgraw-hill.com to check your answers.

Calculating and Changing Prices

Reading Guide

Before You Read ■■■■■■■■■■■■■■
Preview When is a break-even point reached?

The Main Idea
Implementation of the price strategy requires an understanding of pricing formulas. Keeping your price strategy in tune with your market requires ongoing review and revision.

Objectives
Explain how to carry out a break-even analysis.
Calculate markup and markup percentages.
Use markdown formulas to determine sale price.

Explain how to employ formulas used to calculate discounts.
List considerations for updating the price strategy.

Content Vocabulary
◇ break-even point   ◇ markup
◇ selling price   ◇ markdown

Academic Vocabulary
You will see these words in your reading and on your tests. Use the academic vocabulary glossary to look up their meanings.
■ formula
■ percent

Graphic Organizer
Before you read this section, draw a chart like the one shown. As you read, complete the possible price strategy change.

 Go to connectED.mcgraw-hill.com to download this graphic organizer.

Possible Price Strategy Changes

Adjusting	_____
Reaching	_____
Revising	_____

As You Read •••

Integrate Why is it important for small business owners to have good math skills?

Calculating Prices

The **break-even point** is the point at which the gain from an economic activity equals the costs incurred in pursuing it. It is reached when sales equal the costs and expenses of making or distributing a product. Break-even analysis does not tell you what price you should charge for a product. It does, however, give you an idea of the number of units you must sell at various prices to make a profit.

To calculate the break-even point, divide fixed costs by the selling price minus your variable costs. Fixed costs, such as rent and insurance, do not change with the number of units produced or sold. Variable costs, such as the cost of goods or services and advertising, do change with the number of units sold. **Selling price** is the actual or projected price per unit.

$$\frac{\text{FIXED COST}}{\text{UNIT SELLING PRICE}} - \text{VARIABLE COSTS} = \text{BREAK-EVEN POINT (UNITS)}$$

For example, a developer wants to sell a new Web-based game for $10 per unit. The cost per unit will be $6.50. To produce the game, the developer must purchase $7,000 of new equipment. How many units must be sold at $10 for the developers to break even?

$$\frac{\$7,000}{\$10.00} - \$6.50 = \text{2,000 UNITS}$$

The developer is also considering entering the market with a selling price of $12. They believe this would enable them to recover their costs quickly. How many units would have to be sold at $12 to break even? (Note: If your calculation includes a partial unit, round up to arrive at the break-even point.)

Break-even analysis has other applications. You can determine how many units it will take to break even and reach a profit target. You can determine how many dollars in sales it will take to break even. You can also use break-even analysis when planning your business or when dealing with banks and investors by calculating how many units it will take to break even on an investment.

Revved Up Prices tend to be high when a product is first introduced. Elon Musk, (left) the CEO of Tesla Motors, debuted his company's all-electric sports car, the Roadster, at $100,000. *What can break-even analysis tell you about your prices?*

Bill Stafford/NASA/JSC

Markup

Businesses that purchase or manufacture goods for resale use markup pricing based on the cost of the item. **Markup** is the amount added to the cost of an item to cover expenses and ensure a profit. Businesses selling services or ideas use cost-plus pricing. Here markup consists of the costs and related expenses of the job plus a planned profit. In each case, the floor for estimating profit is the total of the costs and expenses. The ceiling is the highest price customers will pay. The business owner must decide what price point is best for his or her circumstances and target market. The difference between that point and the floor is the projected profit.

Calculating Markup

To illustrate a manufacturer's markup, suppose it costs $5 to make a fancy ballpoint pen ($3 for the casing and $2 for the ink refill). The manufacturer must charge more than $5 to make a profit. If the manufacturer marks up the cost by $2, the cost and markup are added to make a price of $7. The total of the cost and markup is the selling price.

$$\text{COST} + \text{MARKUP} = \text{PRICE}$$
$$\$5 + \$2 = \$7$$

Once you understand the relationship among these items, you can compute any one figure if you know the other two. For example, if you know the price and the markup, you can figure the cost:

$$\text{PRICE} - \text{MARKUP} = \text{COST}$$
$$\$7 - \$2 = \$5$$

If you know the price and the cost, you can determine markup:

$$\text{PRICE} - \text{COST} = \text{MARKUP}$$
$$\$7 - \$5 = \$2$$

To convert that figure to a percentage, use this **formula**.

$$\frac{\text{MARKUP}}{\text{COST}} = \text{PERCENTAGE MARKUP ON COST}$$

$$\frac{\$2}{\$5} = 0.40 \text{ OR } 40 \text{ PERCENT}$$

The $2 markup represents a 40 **percent** markup on cost.

You can also calculate markups as a percentage of selling price. This is the approach used most frequently by retailers. The formula is the same except selling price is substituted for cost. The following example shows that the dollar markup on the pen is the same, but the percentage is different.

$$\frac{\text{MARKUP}}{\text{SELLING PRICE}} = \text{PERCENTAGE MARKUP ON SELLING PRICE}$$

$$\frac{\$2}{\$7} = 0.285 \text{ OR } 0.29 \text{ PERCENT}$$

Standard Markup

As a rule, business owners do not figure markup on an item-by-item basis. Instead, they decide on a standard markup or percentage of markup. One way they do this is to use the average markup for their industry. Another way is to match their competitors' markup. They can also do individual calculations and apply them to all of their products.

Service businesses that provide products (for example, a restaurant) may also use a standard markup. Other businesses that provide the same service repeatedly can assume stable costs and a preset profit. However, businesses that offer contracted services or ideas do not have a standard cost and profit that applies to all situations. These companies often obtain their customers through competitive bids, estimates, or proposals. Consequently, they must stay abreast of changes in industry costs and rates.

Markdown

To reduce inventory, businesses sometimes mark down their merchandise. By lowering their prices a certain percentage, they tempt shoppers to buy. In other words, they have a sale.

Suppose the manager of an electronics store decides to encourage sales of $105 cell phones by giving them a 30 percent markdown. First, they determine the **markdown**, the amount of money taken from the original price:

PRICE	×	MARKDOWN PERCENTAGE	=	$MARKDOWN
$105	×	0.30	=	$31.50

The manager then computes the sale price:

PRICE	−	MARKDOWN	=	SALE PRICE
$105	−	$31.50	=	$73.50

Discounts

A discount is a reduction in price to the customer. First, figure the dollar amount of the discount by multiplying the price by the discount percentage. Then, subtract the discount from the price to get the amount the customer actually pays.

Say a golf pro shop is overstocked on starter sets of clubs. To move the $200 sets, a 20 percent discount is implemented. The discount price is calculated by applying the following steps:

1. PRICE × DISCOUNT PERCENTAGE = DISCOUNT DOLLARS
   $200 × 0.20 = $40

2. PRICE − DISCOUNT DOLLARS = DISCOUNTED PRICE
   $200 − $40 = $160

Although the calculation is the same, some discounts involve additional steps. Cash discounts, discussed on page 259, are stated in terms. In the example 2/10, n/30, the only discount calculation is the first number (2 percent). The other numbers identify when payment is due—with and without the discount. Trade discounts are often quoted in a series. In the example on page 260, the discount was 30 percent for retailers and 15 percent for wholesalers. These series of discounts are calculated in sequence. Thus, if the manufacturer's list price is $100, in the example, the calculation is as follows:

RETAILER'S DISCOUNT	$100	×	0.30	=	$30
COST TO RETAILER	$100	−	$30	=	$70
WHOLESALER'S DISCOUNT	$70	×	0.15	=	$10.50
COST TO WHOLESALER	$70	−	$10.50	=	$59.50

Note that in a series discount, the wholesaler's discount is based on the retailer's discount, not the list price.

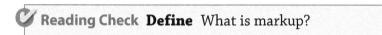
Reading Check **Define** What is markup?

Making Changes to the Pricing Strategy

Once a strategy has been established, it is difficult to change prices without affecting it. Nonetheless, changes in the business environment may require an immediate response. To protect and increase your market share, you can to attend to this strategy continually.

Adjusting Prices to Maximize Profit

Profit or loss is determined by the difference between your selling price and your costs. This fact may cause you to try to increase profits by increasing prices or by lowering prices to increase sales volume. Before you do either, ask yourself two questions:

1. **Are your products' prices elastic or inelastic?** If the price is elastic, a small change in price may cause a significant change in demand. If the price is inelastic, changing the price will have little or no effect on demand.
2. **What are your competitors' prices?** Whether you raise or lower the price, it should relate to the competition's price in a way that benefits you.

Reacting to Market Prices

As part of ongoing market research, keep an eye on current market prices. If you are in a competitive market and prices fall, you can lose customers quickly if you do not lower prices. If prices are on the rise, raising prices is equally important to your success.

Occasionally, special market circumstances call for a temporary price increase. National conventions bring tourists who spend money. Natural disasters and other emergencies also increase demand for goods and services. These cases require a balance between good business and social responsibility.

Altering Terms of Sale

Another way to change your pricing strategy is to revamp the terms of sale. You can change your credit policies or introduce trade, quantity, or cash discounts. You might offer leasing or arrange financing for customers with an outside lender. Whether any of these options is useful to you depends on the nature of your business.

Revising the Price Strategy

Review your pricing objectives and strategies regularly. Focus on basic price strategies, pricing policies, possible shifts in your product's life cycle, and pricing techniques. The overall effectiveness of the price strategy should also be considered. Where necessary, objectives should be revised, added, or deleted. Adjustments to price strategies should reflect the changes in objectives. Changing your price strategy may affect your other marketing strategies. If you do make changes, you may also have to make adjustments your marketing plan.

SECTION 11.2 Review

After You Read ▪▪▪▪▪▪▪▪▪▪▪▪▪

Self-Check
1. **Explain** the formula for calculating the break-even point.
2. **Describe** the two step formula for determining discounted prices for final consumers.
3. **List** three ways you could change your pricing strategy by revising terms of sale.

Think
4. **Describe** the focus of each of the steps when reviewing and revising pricing objectives and price strategy.

Mathematics
5. **ROI** Steve expects to make an initial investment of $100,000 in his new start-up and to make a salary of $28,000. Create a graph to calculate Steve's earnings. How long will it take to make a return on investment?

   Math Concept **Cartesian Coordinates** The x-axis extends to the right and left of the origin, and the y-axis extends above and below the origin. The origin is the point (0, 0) at which the two axis intersect.

   Step 1: The first point on the graph should be (-$100,000, 0). Steve did not take an initial salary.

   Step 2: At the end of the first year he kept $28,000, reducing his loss to $72,000 (1, -$72,000 on the y-axis).

   Step 3: Continue to plot points until Steve has made a return on his investment.

🛱 Go to connectED.mcgraw-hill.com to check your answers.

Entrepreneurs *in Action*

Max Drucker
Former Managing Partner
Steel Card

Q *What do you do?*

A I co-founded Steel Card, an enterprise software company that made web-based software for property and casualty insurers. Steel Card was acquired by ChoicePoint in 2006.

Q *What kind of training and education did you need to get this job?*

A My degree was in international political economies at Colorado College. I got my core experience working for Apple's web group right out of school. Later, I was recruited along with my business partner, Michael DeGusta, to be the technology arm of a Web-based company called eCoverage, an e-insurance company that sold auto insurance directly to customers online.

Q *What do you enjoy most about your job?*

A We were creating software for companies that they couldn't get anywhere else and the functionality that we delivered was truly unique to the marketplace. That made it satisfying and also very lucrative. I also had a great team and loved working with my employees. As a small company, we had a lot of flexibility, so we could do a lot of fun trips together.

Q *How did you become interested in your field?*

A I grew up with an Apple II in my household. My parents were very supportive of computers and my older brother was a real computer geek growing up. I looked to him and all the work that he did, and it was always an interest, so when I had the opportunity to work at Apple, I jumped on it, and I've been in the industry ever since.

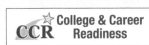

College & Career Readiness

Price Check in Court
National and local governments often regulate the prices of certain products or services.

1. Identify a product whose price is regulated by your local, state, or national government.
2. Explain how the government regulates prices, and why it does so.
3. Summarize your findings in a one-page report.

Career Facts

Real-World Skills	Academic Skills	Career Cluster
Collaboration, Networking, Innovation	Mathematics, English Language Arts	Information Technology

Max Drucker

Visual Summary

The Price Strategy

The Price Is Right To develop an effective price strategy, you must consider costs, expenses, and many other factors..

Price Strategy Considerations
To develop an effective price strategy...   • Consider costs and expenses as well as external forces that affect your strategy.   • Determine pricing objectives that are appropriate for your business.   • Make price strategy decisions regarding your base price strategy, pricing policy, product life cycle stage, and your pricing techniques.
Carry out the pricing function   • Break-even analysis: **FIXED COST/UNIT SELLING PRICE − VARIABLE COSTS = BREAK-EVEN POINT (UNITS)**   **COST + MARKUP = PRICE**   • Markdown: **PRICE − MARKDOWN = SALE PRICE**   • Discounts: **1. PRICE × DISCOUNT PERCENTAGE = DISCOUNT DOLLARS**   **2. PRICE − DISCOUNT DOLLARS = DISCOUNTED PRICE**

Bill Stafford/NASA/JSC

Vocabulary

1. On a sheet of paper, use each of these terms and words in a written sentence.

Content Vocabulary

◇ fixed
◇ variable
◇ price gouging
◇ price fixing
◇ resale price maintenance
◇ unit pricing
◇ return on investment

◇ price skimming
◇ penetration pricing
◇ psychological pricing
◇ prestige pricing
◇ odd/even pricing
◇ price lining
◇ promotional pricing

◇ multiple-unit pricing
◇ bundle pricing
◇ discount pricing
◇ break-even point
◇ selling price
◇ markup
◇ markdown

Academic Vocabulary

■ goal
■ ensure

■ formula
■ percent

Key Concepts

2. **Identify** factors that affect price strategy.
3. **Summarize** the marketing objectives related to pricing.
4. **Describe** the components that go into making price strategy decisions.
5. **Explain** how to carry out a break-even analysis.
6. **Explain** how to calculate markup and markup percentages.
7. **Show** how to use markdown formulas to determine sale price.
8. **Explain** how to employ formulas used to calculate discounts.
9. **List** considerations for updating the price strategy.

Academic Skills

Mathematics

10. **Hat Trick** Vidmar Industries produces top hats. The cost-per-unit of one hat is $5.75. The selling price is $9.95. The company must buy a new piece of equipment for $7,500. How many hats must be sold at $9.95 to break even? Round your answer to nearest whole number.

    Math Concept **Rounding** To round to the nearest whole number, look at the digit in the tenths place. If it is 5 or greater, add one to the digit in the ones place.

    Step 1 Remember the formula for calculating the break-even point.

    Step 2 Substitute the values given for the unknowns in the equation.

English Language Arts

11. **Opposites Attract?** Words that are similar in meaning are synonyms; words that are opposite in meaning are antonyms. Classify each pair of words as synonyms or antonyms: *elastic/inelastic; discount/reduction; supply/demand; costs/expenses; markup/markdown.*

Academic Skills *(continued)*

Social Studies

12. Made in America Clothing is often marked up by more than 100 percent. Choose a piece of clothing that you or your family recently purchased at a store. Examine the labels to identify the country where the piece of clothing was made. Using the Internet, try to estimate average wages made by a worker at a textile factory in that country. Write a paragraph explaining what this means in terms of the price you paid.

Science

13. High Tech, Low Price Items such as computers, smart phones, and hybrid cars have improved over time because of scientific and technological advances. As they have improved, demand for them has gone up and prices have come down. Research the prices charged for some common technological tools we use in our daily lives. Create a graph showing how prices have changed over time.

 Real-World Skills

Graphing Skills

14. Demand Curve Choose a product that is familiar to you and your classmates and estimate its price. Ask six students if they would buy the product at that price or at prices 50% above and below. Graph the results to create a demand curve.

21ˢᵗ Century Skills

Financial Literacy

15. Develop a Pricing Strategy Choose a product or service you would like to sell. Develop a pricing strategy and include your basic strategy, the type of price policy, the pricing techniques you will employ, and the cost and break-even point. Explain your decision-making process.

 Connect to Your Community

16. Pricing Objectives Find the receipt for your most recent purchase. How much did it cost? What do you think the pricing objective is of the company that sold you the product? Explain your answer in one paragraph.

17. Local Pricing Strategies If you are employed, choose a product sold by your company and determine the company's pricing strategy, the product's stage in the life cycle, and any recent price changes and the reasons they were made. If you are not employed, interview a local businessperson to obtain the same information for a selected product.

Review and Assessment

Competitive Events Prep

18. **Situation** You are the owner of a costume jewelry store. You are ordering a shipment of earrings in five popular styles from your major supplier. The cost price of the earrings is $1.50 per pair. You are in the process of determining a retail-selling price for the earrings and know that if you set the price too low, the earrings will not sell well. Your lead salesperson has asked you about pricing strategies for the earrings and how you will determine the price of each style. Among the decisions you must make is whether to price all the styles at one price point or to price the different styles at separate price points.

Activity Discuss your pricing strategy with your lead salesperson.
Evaluation You will be evaluated on how well you meet these performance indicators:
- Describe the concept of price.
- Explain factors affecting pricing decisions.
- Assess factors affecting a business's profit.
- Set prices and adjust prices to maximize profitability.

 Go to **connectED.mcgraw-hill.com** for more information about this activity and other competitive events.

Standardized Test Practice

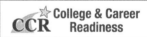

Directions Choose the letter of the best answer. Write the letter for the answer on a separate piece of paper. For question #2, if the answer is False, rewrite the statement to make it true.

1. The pricing technique in which items in a certain category are priced the same is called
   A. price lining.
   B. promotional pricing.
   C. psychological pricing.
   D. bundle pricing.
2. The break-even point is the point at which the gain from an economic activity equals the cost incurred in pursuing it.
   T
   F

> **Test-Taking Tip**
> Re-read all questions that include negative wording, such as *not* or *least*. Look out for double negatives used in a question.

The Promotion Strategy

Chapter Objectives

SECTION 12.1

Developing a Promotion Strategy

Explain the role of the promotion strategy.

Explain how to formulate promotional plans.

Identify considerations for putting together a promotional mix.

Describe the elements of a promotional mix.

SECTION 12.2

Budgeting and Implementing Promotional Plans

Determine promotional costs for a start-up business.

Describe ways to implement your promotion strategy.

Examine options for short-term changes in your promotion strategy.

Identify considerations for updating the promotion strategy.

Discovery Project

Creating a Profitable Company

Key Question *What promotional strategy will help your company reach profitability?*

Project Goal

Work with a partner to research promotional strategies used by different businesses in your community. Evaluate the effectiveness of the strategies you research. Analyze the strategies to determine which you think will work best for the company you would like to start.

Think About...

➤ *What promotional strategies will you evaluate?*
➤ *What criteria will you use to evaluate the potential effectiveness of these strategies?*
➤ *How will you determine which strategy is the best fit for your company?*

⭐ 21st Century Skills

Media Literacy *What impact has the Internet had on promotion strategies in your community?*

Evaluate

 Go to connectED.mcgraw-hill.com to download a rubric that you can use to evaluate your final project.

Ask
AN
EXPERT

Q: *I want to start my own magazine, and I have been researching the equipment I will need to start the business. What do I need to consider when making large equipment purchases?*

A: When buying business equipment, business owners have to consider depreciation. Depreciation is the decrease in the value of an item because of its age or condition. A product that is known for high quality loses its value at a lower rate than a cheaply made product. The lower the depreciation rate an item has, the better the investment. Cheaper equipment may cost less up front, but could cost more due to maintenance and repair costs.

Connect the Photo

It's Showtime! Convincing customers to purchase your product can be the result of successful promotional planning. Whether it's advertising, direct mail, or using social media, entrepreneurs need to determine the best mix that matches their goals, and their budgets. *What are some ways to promote a new movie?*

Developing a Promotion Strategy

Reading Guide

Before You Read ■■■■■■■■■■■■■■■

Connect What are some ways you have seen new products or services promoted?

The Main Idea

The promotion strategy is the most visible marketing strategy, designed to get the attention of prospective customers to convince them to buy from you. Promotional activities must be in the right mix.

Objectives

Explain the role of the promotion strategy.

Explain how to formulate promotional plans.

Identify considerations for putting together a promotional mix.

Describe the elements of a promotional mix.

Content Vocabulary

◇ image
◇ preselling
◇ campaign
◇ promotional mix
◇ advertising
◇ specialty item
◇ publicity
◇ news release
◇ public relations
◇ premium
◇ rebate
◇ sweepstakes

Academic Vocabulary

You will see these words in your reading and on your tests. Use the academic vocabulary glossary to look up their meanings.

■ maintain
■ interactive

Graphic Organizer

Before you read this section, draw a chart like the one shown. As you read, fill in the four promotional elements.

 Go to **connectED.mcgraw-hill.com** to download this graphic organizer.

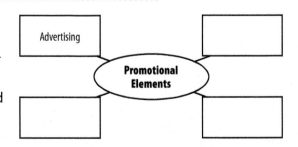

The Promotion Strategy

Promotion is communication intended to persuade, inform, or remind a target market about a business or its products. Businesses use product promotion to urge potential customers to buy from them instead of competitors. Businesses use institutional promotion to **maintain** positive relationships between themselves and various groups—including consumer and environmental groups.

The promotion strategy of a business coordinates all aspects of a product and institutional promotion. It involves planning, determining the right mix, and selecting specific activities.

Promotional Plans

A new business needs two kinds of promotional plans. To start, you need a plan to lay the groundwork for your opening. You need a second plan to support your operation once it is under way.

Preopening Plan

You need to ensure that money is coming in as soon as you open your doors. To do that, you must promote your business beforehand. This is called a *preopening plan*. Preopening plans usually include these objectives:

- **Establish a positive image.** Your company's **image** is the impression people have of your company. It is, in effect, your company's personality. As such, it sets the tone for the implementation of your other objectives and your promotional plan.
- **Let customers know you are opening for business.** Timing is an important factor in your preopening plan. A good rule is to begin your promotion at least six weeks prior to opening. Promotional efforts should intensify as you near your opening date.
- **Bring in customers or have them contact you.** In some types of businesses, preopening efforts should be capped off with a grand opening. In others, a party or reception for prospective customers is more appropriate.
- **Interest customers in your new company and your products or services.** Make the most of your preopening strategies to make doing business with you an appealing option to potential customers.

The U.S. Air Force sponsored the The NASCAR Nextel Cup Series. *What is the U.S. Air Force's target market?*

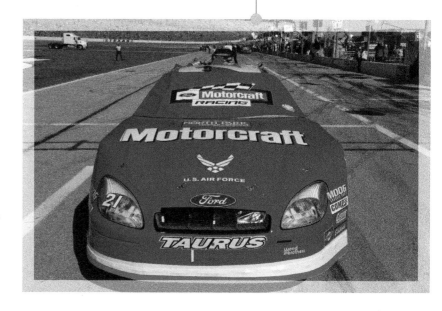

Ongoing Plan

Once your business has opened, what is the next step? You need an ongoing promotional plan to help you maintain and build sales. Some objectives for this plan parallel your preopening objectives. For example, you must maintain the positive image you have established. Other objectives, however, are new. They are added to help you presell your goods or services.

Preselling is influencing potential customers to buy before contact is actually made. Objectives for ongoing promotional plans usually include:

- Explaining major features and benefits of your products
- Communicating information about sales
- Clearing up customers' questions and concerns
- Introducing new goods or services

The length of your ongoing plan depends on your business. Promotional plans may be seasonal (every six months), quarterly, monthly, or weekly. When shorter plans (weekly or monthly) are used, they are usually based on quarterly or seasonal plans. Once the planning cycle is established, you should continually update promotional plans on that same basis.

For your new business, start with quarterly or seasonal plans. Then rough out monthly plans to estimate your promotional costs.

Promotional Plan Format

You can use the same format for your preopening and ongoing plans. Both can be organized around independent activities or a campaign, or a combination of the two. A **campaign** is a series of related promotional activities with a similar theme. For each activity in your promotional plans, you should provide certain information, including a brief description, specific media placement, submission dates, scheduled date of run or release, number of runs, copies, or items, costs, and rationale.

Selecting a Promotional Mix

A **promotional mix** is the combination of different promotional elements that a company uses to reach and influence potential customers. The exact mix varies considerably from business to business. This is partly due to the fact that different types of businesses have different promotional needs.

For example, a manufacturer of exercise equipment might use a television infomercial along with a call center. A produce store might use local newspapers to advertise specials and lighted signs to attract customers. A lawn service might use flyers and word of mouth to promote its work.

Even in the same type of business, promotional mixes vary greatly. Consider the cosmetics field. Revlon® concentrates heavily on advertising, while Avon® focuses on personal selling.

● **As You Read ▪▪▪**

Hypothesize
How would you decide what products to buy without advertising or promotion to help you make a decision?

You do not need to use all of the major elements—advertising, sales promotion, publicity, Internet marketing, and personal selling—in your promotional mix. You should, however, coordinate the promotional elements that you do use.

Without coordination, your efforts at communicating to your target market may not be effective or efficient. When customers do not receive your message, they cannot respond. When promoted items are not available or salespeople not informed, sales are lost and customers are dissatisfied. In addition, misused promotional dollars are lost.

The following considerations provide general guidelines for allocating promotional efforts.

The only books you'll need.

Target Marketing Promotional plans must be aimed at a target market. *Who is the intended target of this product's advertising?*

- **Target market** You must match your promotional option to your target market. For example, a manufacturer sells heavy equipment to the construction market. Its promotional mix must emphasize personal selling. Pull-up diapers, sold to parents, depend more on effective advertising.
- **Product value** Most companies that sell low-value products, such as soap, soft drinks, and candy, cannot afford to emphasize personal selling. Instead, they use advertising and sales promotion. High-ticket items such as real estate and automobiles rely heavily on personal selling.
- **Promotional channels** Products have established lines of communication the same way they have established channels of distribution. For example, when people want to know what is playing at the movie theater, where do they look? Probably on the Internet or in a newspaper. Finding new promotional channels for your products might provide an edge. However, remember that traditional channels exist because they are effective in reaching the intended market.
- **Time frame** Advertising is often needed in advance of new products, upcoming seasons, and sales. It can create a receptiveness to personal selling assistance as well as completion of unassisted transactions.
- **Cost** You need to decide what combination of promotional activities will give you the best results for your money. For most, but not all, businesses, you determine the advertising or personal selling budget first. After that decision is made, you determine the level of sales promotion and publicity efforts.

Another area that should be addressed as you finalize your promotional mix is ethical considerations. Components of the mix should be examined to ensure that you are not deliberately making promises that are not true or using deceptive statements.

Reading Check **Explain** Why is it important to coordinate the elements of your promotional mix?

Andrew Resek/McGraw-Hill Education

The Elements of the Promotional Mix

This section describes the elements of the promotional mix. It also describes the activities within each element and identifies their advantages and disadvantages. The breakdown will help you make decisions about how to put together your promotional mix.

Advertising

Advertising is the paid nonpersonal presentation of ideas, goods, or services. It is directed toward a mass audience by an identified sponsor. There are two types of traditional advertising media—print and broadcast. Print media include newspapers, magazines, direct mail, outdoor advertising, directories, and transit advertising. Television, radio, Internet, and social media are examples of broadcast media. Internet and social media advertising are the feast-growing media.

Newspapers

Newspaper advertising can be tailored to the local community and can reach many people in a target area. Ads can be placed on short notice. They generate immediate sales and cost relatively little.

Newspaper ads also have disadvantages. Not everyone who sees an ad is interested in the product. Newspaper ads also have a short life span. In addition, newspaper readership is declining, partly because of changes in technology.

Magazines

By advertising in general-interest magazines such as *People* and *Time*, a business can reach a large national audience. For a new business, this can be very costly. Specialty magazines, such as *Vogue*, *PC World*, and *Sports Illustrated*, can supply information that describes their readers. This simplifies your task of targeting a specific market. Trade magazines provide a similar opportunity for business-to-business advertisers.

ETHICS and BUSINESS

Honesty in Advertising

Situation You have been surfing an online message board about high tech products because you want to buy a new smart phone. One product in particular has been getting a lot of positive reviews.

Taking the Bait You like what users on the site have been saying about the phone and are thinking about purchasing it. However, you notice that many of the posts use identical phrases to describe the product. A friend suggests that the reviews are fake.

English Language Arts/Writing

Fair Advertising With a little research, you discover that the people who had been writing positive reviews on the message board were hired by the smart phone company. Their reviews were part of the company's promotional strategy.

1. Do you think that this type of advertising is ethical?
2. Write a one-page letter to the smart phone company explaining your feelings.

Direct Mail

Direct mail advertisements are sent directly to the homes and businesses of potential customers. Direct mail includes announcements of grocery store specials, letters offering credit cards, and mail-order catalogs.

This promotional method allows you to cover a wide geographic territory and direct your mailings to a specific target market. A restaurant may send coupons to residents within a five-mile radius. A mail-order sports collectibles store may send catalogs to basketball fans across the country. You can purchase mailing lists of people with specific interests or backgrounds.

Disadvantages include the cost of printing and postage and the risk that the ads will not be read.

Eye Catching Some communities restrict the use of outdoor displays such as these, citing them as distractions or even traffic hazards. *Why might these displays pose a traffic hazard?*

Outdoor Advertising

The advantage of outdoor displays is that they expose their message to large numbers of people. This category includes billboards, painted signs, digital displays, and neon displays. It also includes small movable signs. On the sidewalk outside its entrance, a café may put up a sign listing its daily specials. Unfortunately, after the first few viewings, people often ignore outdoor displays. In addition, some communities restrict their use.

The yellow pages of the telephone directory are a relatively inexpensive form of advertising. Telephone books are also long-lasting because potential customers refer to them for a full year. The downside is that you can not update or make changes to your ad until the next printing.

Transit Advertising

Advertising placed in public transportation has an obvious and unique advantage. It reaches a captive audience. Reading advertisements may be the only way for riders on a bus, subway, or train to pass time. Advertisements placed on the outside of buses serve as billboards that travel the streets of a city. Naturally, these forms of advertising are limited to areas that have public transportation.

Other Print Media

A **specialty item** is a giveaway such as a pen, cap, or T-shirt printed with a business name or logo. Such items serve as a reminder of your business. Suppose your business hands out message pads that feature your company name, address, and phone number. If someone has a message pad, he or she can easily contact you about a possible job.

There is no guarantee, however, that your specialty items will fall into the hands of potential customers. Also, you probably will not be able to distribute the items to a wide area.

TongRo Image Stock/Alamy

Television

Television, a form of broadcast media, is the leader in national advertising. Its main advantage is that people can see your product as well as hear your message. It can also be used to reach audiences of various sizes. These include selected major market areas as well as national audiences. It can even be used to reach small local markets through cable channels.

Cost is the biggest obstacle to the use of television advertising. Large businesses may spend millions of dollars on major ad campaigns. Buying a spot of airtime can also be expensive. The prime-time hours of 7 P.M. to 11 P.M. are the most costly.

Radio

Radio is an effective and economical way to reach a lot of customers. It allows advertisers to target a geographic area and an audience using listener demographics.

Rates for radio advertising vary according to the time of day. Prime-time hours are usually during the early morning and the late afternoon when people are driving to and from work.

There are disadvantages to radio advertising. Radio advertisements have a short life-span. Also, the lack of visual involvement causes some listeners to become distracted and miss some or all of the message.

Online Advertising

Online advertising can be very flexible, dynamic, and interactive. Advantages include that it allows for very specific targeting and the effectiveness of online promotions can be tracked through the data collected. Disadvantages are that some forms of online advertising can be blocked by software designed to seek out and shut down ads. Social media have revolutionized how businesses reach their customers. Companies can identify trends, get customer input, and promote products through social media. Some businesses advertise explicitly through social media, while others seek to engage people in conversations about the brand.

Publicity

Publicity is placement in the media of newsworthy items about a company or product. Taking advantage of publicity means you must do more than just hope your efforts are noticed.

Here are some ways to call attention to your enterprise.

- **Write news releases.** A **news release**, also called a press release, is a brief newsworthy story that is sent to the media.
- **Write feature articles.** Write articles on your area of business expertise. Submit articles to newspapers, magazines, blogs or newsletters that reach your target market.
- **Submit captioned photos.** Send photos and brief explanations of your company's new products, facilities, or employees to the media.

- **Call a press conference.** Make major announcements about your company to the media.
- **Seek interviews.** You might hold interviews with the media to discuss some newsworthy aspect of your business. You might also conduct interviews to offer your expert opinion as background for a story.

Unsolicited publicity can also come from public relations. **Public relations** are activities designed to create goodwill toward a business. Such activities are often reported by the media. It can also control any damage done by negative publicity. News about an accident or unsafe product claim can hurt a company's image. Such incidents require a quick response with an apology, if warranted, and a pledge to monitor and/or correct any problems.

One advantage of publicity is that it is free. Also, because publicity is not company-sponsored, people often think it is more credible than advertising. There is a downside to publicity. You have no control over it. You do not know when, where, how, or even if it will be printed or aired.

Sales Promotion

Sales promotion involves the use of incentives or interest-building activities to stimulate traffic or sales. Examples of the most visible forms of sales promotion are described below.

Displays

Window, showroom, point-of-purchase, and exterior displays all increase buyer awareness. While many displays are designed in-house, others are put together by manufacturers and wholesalers.

Premiums

A **premium** is anything of value that a customer receives in addition to the good or service purchased. Premiums include coupons and gifts. Premiums can be used to attract new customers or build loyalty among existing customers.

Rebates

Many companies give **rebates** (a return of part of the purchase price) as an incentive for customers to purchase their products. Rebates are available for software, computers, and many other types of goods.

Samples

Free trial-size and travel-size packages are particularly useful in introducing new products. Such samples can be distributed by mail, given out door to door, or handed out in retail stores.

Sweepstakes and Contests

Sweepstakes and contests are games used by businesses to get customers thinking and talking about what the company has to offer. **Sweepstakes** are simple games of chance. Contests require the customer to do something to win.

Visual Merchandising

A specialized form of sales promotion is visual merchandising. This is the coordination of a business's physical elements to create an inviting image and encourage purchases. It includes a business's front, layout, interior, and displays.

Trade Shows and Conventions

Exhibits at trade shows and conventions are also a form of sales promotion. They are excellent for introducing products, since they draw customers who have a specific interest.

Internet Marketing

Internet marketing is the marketing of products and services over the Internet. It is the newest and fastest growing element of the promotional mix. Since its inception, Internet marketing has had a major impact on several industries. In the music industry, for example, increasing numbers of consumers have been purchasing and downloading music for several years. Virtually all banks now offer online banking services. Online advertising has grown to billions of dollars annually and is expected to increase for the rest of the 21st century.

Benefits of Internet Marketing

Businesses can realize a variety of benefits from engaging in Internet marketing. One is expanded markets. Goods and services can be sold to customers regardless of geographic location. Another is cost savings. Ace Hardware, for example, estimated reduced inventory costs of approximately 20 percent by selling online. Still another is an increase in on-time delivery to customers. Online retailers as well as many manufacturers can provide a quick turnaround of products because of reduced ordering and processing time.

Website Goals

To capitalize on the opportunities presented by this promotional vehicle, you have to maximize the use of your Website. It is the focal point of Internet marketing.

A well-designed Website is important. However, having a good Website is not enough. For potential customers to come in contact with it, they have to be made aware that it exists and know where to find it. In turn, you want to be able to determine if customers check it out and are using it. That means you should have two goals for your Website:

1. **Attract visitors.** Use different strategies to drive traffic to your site.
2. **Convert visitors.** Convert the traffic into visitors who take steps toward making or solidifying a purchase.

A Thousand Words To get publicity, you could send captioned photos of your company's product to the news media. *What is the disadvantage of using publicity to promote your products?*

teekid/iStockphoto.com

Attracting Visitors

The most effective tool for attracting visitors to your site is *search engine optimization* (SEO). SEO is the process of driving traffic to a Website through the results of search engines. It is estimated that 78 percent of Web users initially find sites through search engines such as Google and Bing.

Search engines create their listings by crawling across the Web to gather information from existing pages based on keywords. A listing near the top will bring more visitors to your site.

Keeping a position near the top is an ongoing process. There are some techniques that can help. One is to list with search engines when you launch your site. Another is to use *meta tags*—special lines of code or keywords that identify what your site is about. You can also put keywords in titles. In addition, you can add pages on a regular basis that are focused on single keyword phrases. Another tactic is to get people who have their own site to put a link to your site on one of their pages.

Business Case Study

Use Color to Promote Your Brand

Color conveys emotion, and emotion drives sales

Research shows that up to 90 percent of impulse buying can be based on the color of a product or its packaging. The right color can make customers take out their wallets and spend.

Color plays a large role in the image of a brand. When you think of McDonald's, you think of golden arches. When you think of Coca Cola, you think of red and white. Apple Computer's brand is high-tech and elegant, so they use white and silver. Outdoor sporting goods shops convey nature and ruggedness with greens and browns.

Different colors evoke different emotions and values:

- Gold equates with wealth.
- White is pure innocence.
- Pink is linked to femininity.
- Green says nature.
- Brown shows ruggedness.
- Red expresses danger or risk.
- Blue conveys trust, but baby blue implies weakness.
- Orange implies cheerfulness, but be careful; orange is one of Americans' least favorite colors.

Color perception varies with culture, personal experiences, and gender, so when planning your product, make sure you test in your target market.

Active Learning

Choose an ad on the Web or in a magazine and analyze the colors used. With another classmate, discuss the following for each of your chosen ads: What is the ad trying to promote? How is color used? What do the color choices communicate? What does it say about the target audience? Do the colors add to or detract from the product or service? How?

Online, Lifeline An effective online presence can increase the performance of traditional brick-and-mortar operations. *How can entrepreneurs use Websites to drive customers to brick-and-mortar businesses?*

Other Ways to Promote Your Site

To attract visitors to your site, you can also use banner ads on related or social media sites, e-mail, pop ups (an ad that opens in a new browser window), pay-per-click advertising (online advertising in which payment is based solely on qualifying click-throughs), and affiliate programs (selling your program through someone else's site).

Of course, any offline promotional medium can also be used to increase awareness of your Website. This includes traditional sales promotion items such as business cards, brochures, and stationary.

Although there are many tools you might use to attract visitors, your focus should be on the quality of the traffic. That is, it should be on targeting visitors that are likely to convert to buyers, rather than on the quantity of visitors. If your site attracts large numbers of visitors that do not convert, you have not been successful.

What Visitors Want

Once visitors find your site, they will expect some basic components to be present. These include:

- **The Website delivers what it promises.** If a Web user types "interior decorator" into a search engine and Island Furniture comes up, the user will expect that Island Furniture offers interior decorating services. If it does not, the user will be annoyed about visiting a site that does not offer what they are looking for.

- **It loads quickly.** Companies frequently make the mistake of including large images, sound, animation, or video clips on their sites. Compared to text, graphics and sound take a long time to load. Users who must wait several minutes for a Web page are likely to move on to other sites.
- **Contact information is easy to find.** Users want to know where companies are located. List your address as well as phone and fax numbers. This reassures the visitor that the site belongs to an actual company. It is also helpful to those who still prefer to call a company or mail an order.
- **The site is frequently updated.** Keeping the site fresh is important if you expect visitors to return. Users will quickly go somewhere more exciting if your site rarely changes.
- **It provides interactive experiences.** A big advantage of Web sites is that they allow immediate interaction. Users can always send e-mail, enter a contest, request information, or give other kinds of feedback. This immediate response is part of the excitement of browsing the Web.

Converting Visitors

Converting visitors into customers takes place in stages. If a visitor buys one of your products or services, that is a conversion. If a visitor furnishes contact information, they have converted from a visitor to a prospect. If a visitor spends twice as much time on your Website as the typical visitor, that is a small conversion. Customer support, such as answering questions about products or services or solving a customer's problem, also qualifies. In these instances, you are either moving the customers toward additional purchases or eliminating concerns about their purchases.

Advantages and Disadvantages

Some benefits of Internet marketing were listed earlier. Another advantage is that companies can reach a wider audience for a fraction of traditional promotional budgets. Results can also be measured easily and inexpensively. Through the use of Web analytics, Internet marketers can provide advertisers with a greater sense of accountability. There is also evidence that an effective online presence increases the performance of traditional brick-and-mortar operations.

Internet marketing also has certain limitations. Some buyers want the opportunity to touch, taste, or try products before they make a decision to purchase. Security concerns are another issue. Many consumers are reluctant to make an online purchase for fear that their personal information will be misused. Others are concerned that they will not receive their order. To address these issues, many businesses put in place liberal return policies, guarantees, rating systems, and buyer protection programs. These measures should reduce the problems and increase buyer confidence.

Go Green

Environmentally Friendly Ads

Promoting a company and its products takes time, money, and a lot of paper. Companies do not have to forget their green philosophy when it comes to printing. Promotional literature—brochures, direct mail, news releases, ads—can be printed on recycled paper with earth-friendly soy ink. Using recycled paper reduces a company's carbon footprint and preserves natural resources by recycling pre- and post-consumer paper waste.

❖ **Critical Thinking**
In a one-page paper, explain how a company might promote its green practices to upgrade its image with green consumers and, hopefully, increase sales. If possible, submit this assignment electronically or on recycled paper.

Personal Selling

The intent of personal selling is to make a sale. It consists of oral presentations given to one or more potential buyers. Personal selling is often designed to close a sale after advertising, publicity, or sales promotions have attracted the customer.

Personal selling is the most adaptable of all of the promotional elements because the message can be modified to suit the individual buyer. However, personal selling is also the most expensive.

To incorporate personal selling into your mix, you can hire and train your own sales force. You can also contract with marketing intermediaries such as sales agents or manufacturers' agents. They can represent you and your products on a commission basis.

One variation of personal selling is telemarketing—selling over the telephone. This technique is less expensive than using salespeople, but it may not be well received by prospects. Another variation is network, or multilevel, marketing. This is sometimes called direct marketing. It involves the salesperson calling on his or her network of family and friends to sell products and to recruit them to sell. Distributors are paid commissions on the sales they generate as well as the sales generated by distributors they recruit into the business.

SECTION 12.1 | Review

After You Read ■■■■■■■■■■■■■

Self-Check

1. **Describe** what objectives can be accomplished through preopening promotional plans amd ongoing plans.
2. **Explain** when should preopening promotion begin.
3. **List** the five options that can be used in a promotional mix.

Think

4. **Develop** a preopening promotional plan for your proposed business. Then develop a promotional plan for your first six months of operation.

English Language Arts

5. **Write a Press Release** Imagine that you are about to open a new gym for teenagers. To generate publicity, you want to send the media a press release. Use a search engine to find out the standard format for a press release. For example, press releases begin with a headline that is often followed by a subhead. Write a four paragraph news release announcing the grand opening of your store. Make sure your press release answers these key questions: Who? What? Where? When? Why?

 Go to connectED.mcgraw-hill.com to check your answers..

Budgeting and Implementing Promotional Plans

Reading Guide

Before You Read ■■■■■■■■■■■■■■■

Connect How should you carry out promotional plans if you are on a tight budget?

The Main Idea
Thorough planning and information gathering can help you arrive at a realistic promotional budget. That budget will have a direct effect on how you implement your promotional plans.

Objectives
Determine promotional costs for a start-up business.

Describe ways to implement your promotion strategy.

Examine options for short-term changes in your promotion strategy.

Identify considerations for updating the promotion strategy.

Content Vocabulary
◇ industry average
◇ cooperative advertising
◇ advertising agency
◇ consumer pretest

Academic Vocabulary
You will see these words in your reading and on your tests. Use the academic vocabulary glossary to look up their meanings.
■ estimate
■ unique

Graphic Organizer
Before you read this section, draw a chart like the one shown. As you read, write the three most common adjustments to promotion strategies.

 Go to connectED.mcgraw-hill.com to download this graphic organizer.

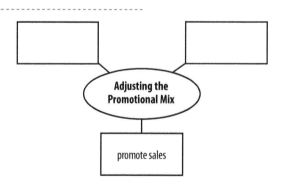

Adjusting the Promotional Mix

promote sales

Web Savvy

Promoting with Facebook

Social media sites like Facebook and Twitter are not just ways to entertain yourself and your friends—they are also solid platforms for new product launches. Companies that have a presence on Facebook, for instance, can build a page within the site for their product, complete with photos and descriptions, and invite people to view it and like the product. Companies using Twitter can easily "tweet" their products' features to an ever-growing audience of followers, who will (hopefully) tell their friends about it. *What are some products or services that are well-suited to marketing on social media sites?*

Budgeting for Promotion

In an established business, you have previous plans and sales figures to help you develop your promotional budget. With a new venture, you must gather information and **estimate** your expenditures.

Cost Out Promotional Activities

You can obtain advertising rates directly from radio stations, newspapers, and other media sources. Their sales representatives will quote you prices and supply you with rate charts. Another source is the Standard Rate and Data Service. It publishes rate cards for most major media.

Sales promotion items are **unique**. They have to be prepared specifically for the promotion. To determine their cost, you must contact whoever is going to produce the promotional pieces.

Publicity your business gets from community or other events does not cost you anything. However, the event itself will. Grand openings, sneak previews, and press conferences can be expensive. If you are planning to use any of these options, include their costs.

Finally, you may hire an agency or a consultant to handle all or part of your promotion. In that case, you need to budget for those fees. Personal selling staff and sales training are not included in your promotional budget. These costs are part of your operating expenses.

Compare Industry Averages

After you know prices for all of the parts of your proposed mix, you can calculate the cost. Your next step, then, is to contact trade associations, business publications, the SBA, or business owners in the field. From them, you can find out the **industry average** (the standard used to compare costs) for promotional expenses. The figure is usually expressed as a percentage of sales.

Make Final Adjustments

The industry figures help you measure your estimate. If the difference between the two figures is large, you might want to reexamine and adjust your plan. If the difference is small, you probably have a realistic budget.

> **Reading Check** **Compare and Contrast** How is creating a promotional budget for an established business different from creating one for a new venture?

Carrying Out Your Plans

● **As You Read** ━ ━ ━ ━ ━
Identify Where would you look for help when putting together your promotional activities?

Now it is time to put your promotional plans into action. You or someone you hire must prepare and place ads, generate publicity, create sales promotion pieces, and set up your Website. If personal selling is part of your mix, you may need sales training.

Doing It Yourself

If your budget is limited, you may have to design the ads and other components of your promotional plan yourself. This does not mean your promotional efforts will be ineffective or unprofessional. Many of the ads you see and hear everyday are created by small business owners. Likewise, many business owners have built their own Web sites.

If you do design your own ads, use basic media formats as a starting point. For example:

- **Print** Print advertisements should include a headline, copy, illustrations, and a signature. The headline should gets the readers' attention. The copy is the selling message and can be a few words or several paragraphs. The illustration can be a photograph or drawing. The signature identifies the business and should include contact information.
- **Radio** Radio spots require essentially the same elements as print ads. Radio ads may also include music and/or sound effects. Scripts lay out the sequence and provide the wording and direction.
- **Television** Television has the same elements, too, but it is more complex. It requires casting, set design, sound, and filming. A script spells out the sequence for both audio (words, music, sound effects) and video (settings and action). A storyboard (miniature sketches of scenes) is used to help visualize the sequence.
- **Internet** It is possible to successfully build and manage your own Website without being a computer expert or making a large investment. There are software programs available that have point-and-click interfaces designed for non-programmers. Using one of these, you could have your site up and running quickly. The advantage is that you can maintain control and make changes with minimal cost. The disadvantage of a do-it-yourself Website is that it may lack professionalism and functionality.

Getting Help

You can also hire professional help for some or all of your promotional activities. The cost can vary. It may be a no-fee arrangement or a sizable percentage of your promotional budget. The range depends on the services you receive. Professional help can come from the media, manufacturers and suppliers, advertising agencies, and Web designers.

Media

All of the major advertising media—television, radio, newspapers, magazines, and Websites—have advertising departments. To encourage sales, they often help you prepare the ads or commercials that you run with them. In some instances, they even create the ads or commercials themselves.

Manufacturers and Suppliers

You may be able to get suppliers or manufacturers of goods you sell to share your advertising costs. **Cooperative advertising** is an arrangement in which advertising costs are divided between two or more parties. Usually, manufacturers offer such programs to their wholesalers or retailers as a means of encouraging those parties to advertise the product.

Agencies

An **advertising agency** is a company that acts as an intermediary between a business and the media to communicate a message to the target market. Advertising agencies can handle all phases of your advertising. They write the copy, create the artwork, choose the media, and produce the ad or commercial. Nearly all television and national magazine ads are produced by professional agencies.

Promoting on Twitter Kogi, a taco truck that combines Korean BBQ with tacos, uses Twitter updates to let people know where they will be selling tacos next. *What are some advantages and disadvantages of creating a Web-only promotional mix?*

Shutterstock/Gaudilab

For their services, advertising agencies charge a substantial fee. Agencies typically charge a 15 percent fee. For example, if an agency creates and places a $200,000 ad, the agency bills the client for the full amount and retains $30,000 of the total as its fee. Because of such high costs, advertising agencies tend to be used by large companies.

Web Designers

Instead of building your own Website, you could hire a Web designer or developer. The cost will depend on the complexity of your site. Basic sites usually involve few pages and little high tech work. Intermediate and complex sites cost more because they may require programmers and software engineers. The more expensive sites have sophisticated e-commerce features. Most Web designers charge a flat fee for setting up your site. Usually, that fee is roughly double their hourly labor costs.

Web designers can also assist you with obtaining and registering a domain name. Registration provides other computers on the Internet with the information needed to find your Website or send you an e-mail. If your company's name is not available as a domain name, choose something close to it. Also, choose an e-mail name that is consistent with your domain name.

When you register your domain name, you will have a contract that specifies the terms for owning your domain name. The length of the contract and the cost of the contract will vary with the registrar. In addition, your Website designer can assist you with finding a hosting company. They could host it themselves or suggest a third party. The host company will charge a monthly or yearly fee for its services.

Whatever you choose, there are certain problems you want to avoid. They are:

- **Going live too early** It pays to test your site before publicizing it.
- **Clarity issues** Your home page should let the visitor know clearly what you do. Every other element of the site should promote that basic purpose.
- **Difficult navigation** Be sure each page has a navigation bar so visitors can move around the site easily. Also, contact information should be displayed prominently.
- **Slow response time** Check e-mail and comment boards regularly and respond as quickly as possible.
- **Poor marketing** Ongoing efforts to make your Website visible to prospective visitors should be a priority.

If you use Web analytic tools to help you evaluate the results you get from your Website, you can deliver continuously improving return on investment (ROI).

 Reading Check **Describe** How can you carry out promotional plans on a tight budget?

Optimization About 78 percent of Web users find sites through search engines such as Ask.com, Google, and Bing. A listing near the top of a search will bring more visitors to your site. *What are some problems you want to avoid when setting up your Web site?*

Making Possible Promotion Changes

You may need to make changes in the promotion strategy if you are not getting the desired results. The three most common adjustments are described below.

Adjust Your Advertising

Advertising is expensive. When a campaign is not working, you should change it as quickly as possible. Most advertising problems result from using the wrong media or having bad timing. One way to head off problems is to do a consumer pretest. A **consumer pretest** is a procedure in which a panel of consumers evaluate an ad before it runs, giving their reactions.

After the ad has run, specific factors should be addressed in a postevaluation. These factors include:

- **Market** How well did the ad succeed in reaching its target market?
- **Source** Was the source the most effective one available?
- **Motives** What motivated the customer to buy?
- **Messages** How appropriate was the message?
- **Media** Did the selected media succeed in reaching the target market with the message?
- **Results** How well did the ad accomplish its objectives?
- **Budget** Was the budget acceptable?

You can use several techniques for getting information to measure. You can obtain feedback from customers and monitor sales to determine the direct effects of ads. You can conduct market research and hire professional advertising researchers. You can use the results of your information gathering and evaluation to make immediate and long-range changes.

Generate Publicity

As part of your promotional mix, plan activities that will result in favorable publicity. In addition, you can monitor community events that might generate positive exposure. This may take the form of sponsorships, leadership roles, or service roles.

Promote Sales

No matter how well you plan, sales may not move as quickly as you would like. To get sales rolling, you can use additional promotions, such as displays, premiums, sweepstakes, contests, rebates, and samples. These are often used to enhance other promotional tools and can be put in place quickly.

In other instances, adding salespeople or increasing productivity of the existing sales force may get results. Personal selling helps ensure that customers' needs are met. Chapter 13 will provide guidelines for recruiting, training, and overseeing your sales force, an essential part of the promotion strategy.

GLOBAL WORKPLACE — Rwanda: Tradition in Transition

Music and dance are very important in Rwandan culture, to help pass along stories from one generation to the next. Included in that tradition are Intore dancers, who perform the dance of heroes, one done by returning warriors to tell of their victory following a battle. This dance was once performed in front of the royal court and features blood-curdling battle cries.

Farming In Rwanda, most of the people who work are farmers, with agriculture comprising nearly 40% of the gross domestic product as of 2006. Exported crops that bring in the most money are coffee and tea. Many times, the production of food is not able to keep with the growth in population, so the republic must import food to feed its residents and visitors.

Social Studies/Science In 2000, Rwanda's government decided to transform its economy from relying on agriculture to becoming more knowledge-based. Part of this transformation has occurred with increased Internet access,

as fiber-optic cables bring high-speed broadband across the republic. Research the entrepreneurial opportunities being developed because of Internet availability and summarize your findings in a one-page report.

Common Kinyarwanda Words and Phrases	
Hello	muraho
Goodbye	murabeho
Yes/ No	yego/ oya
Thank you	murakoze
You're welcome	murakorewe

Revising the Promotion Strategy

You should review your promotion strategy on a regular basis, perhaps quarterly or semiannually. Apply evaluation strategies to determine the effectiveness of your campaign.

Begin with your sales forecast for the upcoming period. You can then arrive at a promotional budget necessary to support that level of sales. Next, formulate a revised promotional mix. Like your original mix, you want the best combination of elements for reaching your target market, which may have shifted. You now have your previous research, plans, and decisions to draw on, as well as experiences that give you an idea of what does and does not work.

Once you have determined your mix, you can prepare a new promotional plan. Any revisions in the promotional plan should be consistent with other marketing objectives and strategies. Any changes you make in the promotion strategy should become part of your new marketing plan.

SECTION 12.2 Review

After You Read

Self-Check
1. **List** the advantages and disadvantages of hiring an advertising agency.
2. **Compare** the advantages and disadvantages of setting up your own Website.
3. **Describe** two techniques for determining whether or not your advertising is effective.

Think
4. **Develop** a list of guidelines for reviewing and revising the promotional plan for your proposed business.

Mathematics
5. **Print Ads** Kofi Burbridge wants to advertise his delivery service in his city's newspaper. A full-page color advertisement will cost $1,050, and measures 9½×7¼. A ¼ page ad will cost $295 and measures 2¼×7¼. In terms of cost per square inch what is the difference in price?

   Math Concept **Area** Figuring out the cost per unit of area is a good way to compare the price of print advertisements as well houses or apartments.

   Step 1 Convert fractions to decimals. Determine the area of each advertisement.

   Step 2 Calculate the cost per square inch by dividing the cost by the area.

   Go to connectED.mcgraw-hill.com to check your answers.

Entrepreneurs *in Action*

Georgina Lightning
Co-Founder
Tribal Alliance Productions

Q *What do you do?*

A I am promoting the film *Older Than America*, which I also directed and starred in. I've had 38 screenings and attended every one of them to do the promotion. I book gigs, send out promotional information, and compile all the data about the screens and the audiences, figuring out who our market is based on the audience and participation. We've been to 20 film festivals and won 18 awards so far.

Q *What kind of training and education did you need to prepare for this job?*

A I have an acting background. I went to the University of Alberta, then was invited to attend the American Academy of Dramatic Arts in Los Angeles. There were 370 of us the first year; 67 got invited back the second. By the third year, there were only 15. Later, I became an acting coach and worked on set. I paid attention to everything that was going on, and pretty soon I thought, "I can do this!"

Q *What do you enjoy most about your job?*

A I enjoy being an artist. Surround yourself with top notch people and they will pull you along. The business part can be challenging, but I have to do it in order to get to be creative.

Q *How did you become interested in your field?*

A When I got into film, I decided that we needed to start our own company and create our own jobs for Native Americans. With Tribal Alliance, we've employed more Native Americans in one movie than the TV networks have employed in ten years.

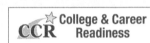

College & Career Readiness

What's in It for Me?
Even with a great product, effective marketing should identify the compelling benefit of the product to the people who will buy it.

1. Choose one of your favorite films. List all the things you like about it.

2. If you were the marketing director for this film, what benefits or features would you emphasize to customers and why?

3. Briefly explain the difference between a benefit and feature.

Career Facts

Real-World Skills	Academic Skills	Career Cluster
Teamwork, Communication, Media Literacy	English, Arts, Social Studies	Arts, A/V Technology, & Communications

Georgina Lightning

Visual Summary

The Promotion Strategy

The Promotional Mix When allocating for promotional efforts, consider the following factors.

- Target Market
- Type of Business
- Product Value
- **Selecting a Promotional Mix**
- Cost
- Promotional Channels
- Time Frame

Different Strategies A promotional mix is the combination of different elements used to reach and influence potential customers.

The Elements of the Promotional Mix

Advertising
Includes television, radio, outdoor ads, print ads, transit ads, and direct mail.

Publicity
Includes news releases, press conferences, feature articles, interviews, and other forms of public relations.

Sales Promotion
Includes window displays, premiums, rebate offers, samples, sweepstakes, contests, and trade shows.

Internet Marketing
Includes building a Website, optimizing search engine results, use of interactive Web 2.0 tools, banner ads, and pop-up windows.

Personal Selling
Includes hiring and training your own sales force, contracting with sales agents, and telemarketing.

Vocabulary

1. On a sheet of paper, use each of these terms and words in a written sentence.

Content Vocabulary

◇ image
◇ preselling
◇ campaign
◇ promotional mix
◇ advertising
◇ specialty item
◇ publicity
◇ news release

◇ public relations
◇ premium
◇ rebate
◇ sweepstakes
◇ industry average
◇ cooperative advertising
◇ advertising agency
◇ consumer pretest

Academic Vocabulary

■ maintain
■ interactive
■ estimate
■ unique

Key Concepts

2. **Describe** the purpose of the promotion strategy.
3. **Explain** the components of the promotional mix.
4. **List** considerations for putting together a promotional mix.
5. **Summarize** the process of formulating a promotional plan.
6. **Describe** how to determine promotional costs for a start-up business.
7. **List** four sources of help when implementing your promotion strategy.
8. **Discuss** options for short-term changes in your promotion strategy.
9. **Identify** considerations for updating the promotion strategy.

Academic Skills

Mathematics

10. **Budgeting for Promotion** Yao Chai works in the promotional department of a large corporation. Yao is trying to determine what percent of the company's monthly sales should be used for promotion. The industry average for the company's field is 18%. Using the industry average for his calculations, Yao determines $5,760 should be used for promotion. What were the corporation's monthly sales?

Math Concept **Operations with Percents** Percents can also be expressed as fractions or decimals, which are easier to work with when performing calculations.
Step 1: Convert the percent to the decimal equivalent.
Step 2: Divide the amount used for promotions by the percent.

English Language Arts

11. **Tutor a Classmate** Imagine that you are tutoring a classmate who is new to this country and for whom English is a new language. Write a sentence or two explaining what the following terms mean: *advertising, sales promotion, publicity, public relations*. If possible, have your sentences translated into an English language learner's first language.

Academic Skills (continued)

Social Studies

12. **Endorsements** Celebrities and sports figures are often hired by companies to promote products at events and in media advertisements. These companies are careful to choose people who have received good publicity for doing positive things for their community. Compile a list of ten celebrities or sports figures. Survey your classmates to find out which person on the list they would most trust as a spokesperson for a major product. Report your findings to the class.

Science

13. **Follow Your Nose** Marketing and branding experts say touch and smell are the future when it comes to creating a brand identity. Chemists can develop special scents, and aestheticians can design sound and tactile (touch) elements. These create a deeper emotional connection to the brand. Use a search engine to research the patented smell created by Singapore Airlines. Write a short report describing how the scent is used to differentiate the airline.

Real-World Skills

Creative Skills

14. **Shoestring Budget** You have invented a great sports drink, but your annual marketing budget is just $1,000. Brainstorm a list of ideas that will cheaply and effectively create awareness of your product.

21st Century Skills

Information Literacy

15. **Stick Around** Marketing is about attracting customers—and keeping them! Imagine you sell custom bikes online. In a short essay, identify the information you should record about each customer and how to use that information to encourage more buying.

Connect to Your Community

16. **Promotional Goals** Contact the person who handles a local business's advertising. Conduct an interview to determine the company's promotional objectives, promotional planning cycle, and promotional mix.

17. **Rates and Services** Contact at least three media outlets that you plan to use to advertise your proposed business. Obtain information about rates and services they provide. Write a summary of your results and compare your findings with those of your class.

Review and Assessment

Competitive Events Prep

18. **Situation** You own a local convenience store that is right next to a busy commuter route. You are also an enthusiastic fan of the local professional football team who normally has winning seasons. You want to show your support for the team; therefore, you have decided to celebrate the team's victories by offering customers a free regular sized coffee on Monday mornings following a victory by the football team.

Activity Prepare a report with a promotional plan that includes the free coffee. The report should include a budget estimate.

Evaluation You will be evaluated on how well you meet these performance indicators:
- Describe elements of the promotional mix
- Develop promotional plan for a business
- Select sales-promotion options
- Prepare a promotional budget
- Prepare simple written reports

 Go to **connected.mcgraw-hill.com** for more information about this activity and other competitive events.

Standardized Test Practice

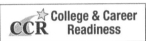

Directions Choose the letter of the best answer. Write the letter for the answer on a separate piece of paper. For question #2, if the answer is False, rewrite the statement to make it true.

1. All of the following are elements of a print advertisment, *except*
   A. headline.
   B. illustrations.
   C. script.
   D. signature.

2. *Publicity* is the paid nonpersonal presentation of ideas, goods, or services.
   T
   F

> **Test-Taking Tip**
> Just before taking a test, try to avoid talking about it with other students. Test anxiety can be contagious.

The Promotion Strategy: Developing and Managing Sales

Chapter Objectives

SECTION 13.1
Organizing and Preparing a Sales Force

Explain the role of personal selling in businesses.

Define the two types of selling situations.

Describe the kinds of training needed by salespeople.

SECTION 13.2
Planning, Directing, and Evaluating Sales

Identify the components of sales planning.

List the elements that are involved in directing sales.

Discuss the procedures used in evaluating sales performance.

Discovery Project

Hiring the Right People

Key Question *How would you go about hiring the right people to staff your sales force?*

Project Goal
To ensure that you employ the best people possible, it is necessary to develop hiring procedures for sales positions in your company. Create an advertisement for the position, a job description, and an outline of the process from application to interview.

Think About...
➤ *What model will you use to write your advertisement?*
➤ *How will you determine what to include in the job description?*
➤ *How will you present your procedures?*

21ˢᵗ Century Skills
Critical Thinking *How would you present yourself to a potential employer at a job interview?*

Evaluate
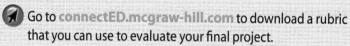 Go to connectED.mcgraw-hill.com to download a rubric that you can use to evaluate your final project.

Ask
AN
EXPERT

Q: *I want to take out a loan to expand my mobile application business. My bank said I qualified for a loan at two percent above the prime rate. What is the prime rate?*

A: The prime rate is a benchmark for interest rates on business and consumer loans. A bank may charge you the prime rate plus two percentage points on a car loan. The prime rate is determined by the federal funds rate, which is the rate banks charge each other to borrow money overnight. If banks must pay more to borrow, they raise the prime rate. If their cost drops, they drop the prime rate.

Digital Vision/SuperStock

Connect the Photo

How Can I Help You Today? Finding the right people to promote and sell for your business is only the first step in developing and managing sales. Entrepreneurs must continue to train, direct, develop salespeople in order to maximize their talents and make a successful business. *What kind of knowledge do you think an appliance salesperson should have?*

Organizing and Preparing a Sales Force

Reading Guide

Before You Read ■■■■■■■■■■■■■■■■

Connect What qualities would you want in your salespeople?

The Main Idea

By thoroughly preparing the salespeople you hire, you can maximize their effectiveness. This is true no matter what background and experience they bring to the job.

Objectives

Explain the role of personal selling in businesses.

Define the two types of selling situations.

Describe the kinds of training needed by salespeople.

Content Vocabulary

◇ personal selling
◇ prospect
◇ sales force
◇ order getting
◇ order taking
◇ rational buying motive
◇ emotional buying motive

◇ customer benefits
◇ buying process
◇ prospecting
◇ preapproach
◇ approach
◇ objections
◇ suggestion selling
◇ sales check

Academic Vocabulary

You will see these words in your reading and on your tests. Use the academic vocabulary glossary to look up their meanings.

■ crucial   ■ series

Graphic Organizer

Before you read this section, draw a chart like the one shown. As you read, write the major areas of sales training.

 Go to connectED.mcgraw-hill.com to download this graphic organizer.

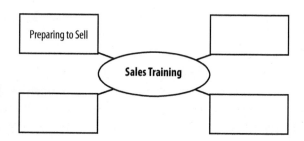

Preparing to Sell

Sales Training

Personal Selling

Personal selling is a direct person-to-person presentation to help a prospect make a buying decision. A **prospect** is a potential customer. For many companies, personal selling is a key ingredient in their marketing mix. It is important because it involves the human aspect of promotion.

Personal selling is particularly important to new entrepreneurial ventures and established small businesses that rely on direct contact to sell to their customers. Personal selling is also **crucial** to companies whose customers need detailed information. For example, most people need assistance when buying large appliances, high-tech items, and real estate.

Staffing the Sales Force

Your **sales force** is the group of employees involved in the selling process. To put together your sales force, you must determine what kind of salesperson you need. The types of sales jobs and the necessary requirements vary with the nature of the business. A salesperson who calls on a group of retail stores has one kind of job. A manufacturer's rep who calls on wholesalers has another. Both are different from a salesclerk's job in a retail or service business. You should define a position before you fill it.

Order Getting

Sales are classified into two groups: order getting and order taking. **Order getting** is seeking out buyers and giving them a well-organized presentation. It is sometimes called "creative selling." Order getting is necessary when customers may not be aware of their need for a product. Many people will go to a vacation resort or add home improvements after they discover what is available. Selling highly technical products and complex services also requires order getting.

Many order-getting positions involve calling on customers. Other positions can be found in retail stores where customers require a high level of sales assistance. For example, a family buying their first computer may seek help. They want to select the computer with the functions and features that are right for them.

Order Taking

In contrast, **order taking** is the completion of a sale to a customer who has sought out a product. Retail clerks who stand behind counters are an example of order-taking salespeople. Sales reps who call on retail stores are also typically order takers. They do little creative selling. Delivery people also take orders, but their primary function is to deliver products. Their selling responsibility is secondary.

Traits of Successful Sales People

Besides determining the type of selling your people will do, you need to determine what traits you want in them. Some desirable sales traits identified by professional buyers include the following:

- Knowledge
- Organization
- Follow-through
- Punctuality
- Energy
- Empathy
- Promptness
- Ability to solve problems
- Willingness to work hard
- Honesty

Although these traits were identified by buyers who work with order getters, they are equally desirable for order takers.

 Reading Check **Differentiate** What is the difference between order taking and order getting?

Providing Sales Training

Whether you hire new or experienced salespeople, you must provide training. Your program must prepare them to sell your products. You must also teach the principles of selling—the buying and selling processes. Training may also include the mechanics of selling.

Preparing to Sell

Before a salesperson is ready to sell your products, he or she must have the necessary knowledge base. Specifically, a salesperson must have company, product, and customer knowledge. In addition, a salesperson needs training in the foundational skills of selling.

Company Knowledge

Sales trainees should understand the company's background, goals, organization, policy, and procedures. They also should understand operating systems and values. With this knowledge, they will feel they are part of the company. The knowledge will also ensure that they represent your company's interests in their sales efforts.

Product Knowledge

Your salespeople should be knowledgeable about their products on three levels. First, they should know the benefits to the customer. Just knowing a product's features is not enough. Feature/benefit selling requires being able to describe the features as benefits to the customer. **Customer benefits** are the advantages of personal satisfaction that a customer will get from the product. People buy products for their benefits.

They must be familiar with the goods or services they are selling. The more complex the product, the more training they will need. Third, they must also be familiar with the competition. They should be able to tell customers the advantages of their products over the competition.

Customer Knowledge

Salespeople need an awareness of customer buying motives. They should be familiar with the company's customers and know how to handle different kinds of customers.

Customers have either rational or emotional motives for making a purchase. A **rational buying motive** is a conscious, logical reason to make a purchase. Reasons may include:

- Product dependability
- Time or money savings
- Convenience
- Comfort
- Health or safety issues
- Recreational value
- Service
- Quality

Information is Power Product knowledge is essential for success in selling. *Why is it important for salespeople to know the competition?*

An **emotional buying motive** is a feeling a buyer associates with a product. Feelings may include the following:

- Social approval
- Recognition
- Power
- Affection
- Prestige

Salespeople should be trained to read a customer's motivation in a selling situation. With that knowledge, they can match the product to the customer's motivation.

Readiness and Disposition

Regardless of their motivation, customers can be at various stages of buying readiness when a salesperson makes contact. They may be decided customers—they know what they want. They may also be casual lookers or information gatherers who do not intend to buy now.

Customers may also exhibit different dispositions during the sales contact. They may be talkative or silent. They may be impulsive or procrastinating. In other cases, they may be disagreeable, opinionated, suspicious, shrewd, decisive, or timid. Salespeople must be trained to recognize a customer's buying stage and mood. They must also be trained to handle a customer according to the situation and select appropriate methods to respond to customer concerns.

Foundational Skills for Selling

Sales training must include several foundational skills. Time management is an important skill, especially for sales representatives on the road. Legal knowledge is also important, especially for issues of product liability and false promotion. Depending on your business situation, salespeople may need to develop additional foundational skills.

Sales training might also include Internet skills for selling. In many companies, the sales staff can obtain information through their office and home computers. Additionally, many companies now equip their salespeople with laptops.

Laptops enable salespeople to access customer databases, prospect lists, and other essential information from the field. In addition, sales staff can input orders, update databases, post to social media, and exchange e-mail messages with clients. They can also draft proposals and access information. Salespeople can use these tools to research prospective clients before making a sales call.

The Buying Process

In preparation for selling, the sales trainee also must understand the buying process. The **buying process** is a **series** of steps a customer goes through when making a purchase. All promotional activities, including selling, should be designed to take the customer through that process.

These steps are often referred to as the stages of selling, or the AIDA formula:

- **Attention** Getting the prospective buyer's attention.
- **Interest** Developing an interest in the product.
- **Desire** Creating a desire to have the product.
- **Action** Getting the customer to take action to buy.

The Selling Process

Salespeople can be much more effective when they are well-acquainted with steps of the selling process. In today's market, there are two approaches to selling that are widely in use. One is the traditional selling process. The other is the relationship, or consultative, selling process.

Traditional Selling

Traditional selling is a ten step process that is focused on the product. In order getting, the salesperson usually carries out all of the steps. In order taking, many of the steps have been completed before the customer and salesperson come together. Even so, order takers will be more effective if they know all of the steps of the traditional selling process.

1. **Prospecting** **Prospecting** is a systematic approach to developing new sales leads or customers. Prospects can be identified through referrals, public records, or surveys. They can also be found through *cold canvassing*, that is, making contacts without leads.

2. **Preapproach** The **preapproach** is research that precedes a salesperson's approach to a prospective customer. It should include information about the prospect's needs and wants. For example: What products are they currently using? Are they satisfied? Why or why not?

3. **Approach** The **approach** is the salesperson's first contact with the customer. The salesperson should establish a friendly and professional relationship. Then, the salesperson should foster open communication and build credibility. These steps must be planned to get the customer's attention and interest.

4. **Determining needs** The salesperson must listen carefully and ask questions to determine the customer's wants and needs.

5. **Presentation** In demonstration or presentation of the product to the customer, the salesperson explains the benefits of the product to the prospective customer. If possible, the customer should become involved with or try out the product. This will enable them to get a feeling of ownership.

6. **Overcoming objections** Customers may voice objections during the presentation. **Objections** are concerns, hesitations, doubts, and other reasons a customer has for not making a purchase. A good salesperson selects appropriate methods to respond to customer concerns. The salesperson anticipates objections and uses them to provide clarification and additional information. Salespeople can often overcome objections by encouraging customers to talk about their concerns.

7. **Closing the sale** The salesperson must ask for the sale to complete the process. Often, it is necessary to attempt a number of trial closes to get the sale. Questions such as "Will this be cash or charge?" or " When would you want delivery?" are examples of closing techniques.

8. **Suggestion selling** **Suggestion selling** is selling additional goods or services to the customer. The salesperson should suggest items that go with the products customers buy. For example, if a customer is buying a dress shirt, the retail salesperson may suggest a tie.

9. **Closing mechanics** The mechanics of closing vary with the situation. They may involve writing up the order in an order-getting situation. In an order-taking situation, closing mechanics may involve wrapping the merchandise and ringing up the sale.

10. **Follow-up** The sale is not over until the salesperson is sure the customer is satisfied with the purchase. Follow-up might involve making sure that delivery and installation were carried out effectively. It might also include contacting the customer to make sure the customer is happy with the purchase. Follow-up contacts can lead to additional sales. They can also lead to a long-term relationship with a customer.

Suggestion Selling As part of the sales process, the salesperson suggests items that go with the products the customer is already buying. *What additional items might a server suggest to a customer who is ordering dinner?*

Business Case Study

Training Is for Everyone

Learning boosts productivity and engagement for workers young and old

All employees—whether just starting out or with years of experience—need training to be effective in their jobs. And training doesn't stop once someone knows the ropes of a specific job. All workers need to learn throughout their careers. Policies and products change. Technology changes. Workers themselves change.

Company training is necessary to help employees be more informed at their jobs. Suppose you want to introduce a new electric drill to your product mix. Take the time to show salespeople the advantages of the drill, and let them practice using it. Then they'll have the information they need to answer customers' questions about the drill's features.

Training can also go beyond specific skills or facts. Thoughtful feedback on an employee's work, coaching on interpersonal skills, and career mentoring are other valuable types of training known as employee development. This kind of training helps employees grow in their jobs and feel like they are a valued part of the business.

Active Learning

Practice your training skills. Work with two other students to select a common task such as wrapping a present or fixing a printer paper jam. Take turns, with each student instructing the other two in how to complete the task. After each student has the opportunity to be the trainer, discuss the challenges of giving clear explanations, and how the instruction could be improved.

Relationship Selling

Relationship selling is frequently used in business-to-business and other order-getting situations. It requires more time in the early stages because of the emphasis on building the relationship and identifying needs.

Relationship selling relies heavily on the use of questions to lead prospects through the following stages.

1. **Build Rapport and Set Agenda.** The initial interaction should put the prospect at ease. Both parties establish an agenda, and the salesperson requests permission to ask questions and take the lead.
2. **Background.** Questions are asked to determine background details to help put the prospect's situation into perspective.
3. **Uncover Problems.** Questions are asked to uncover problems which the salesperson's products or services might address. For example: What brought you here today? What are your biggest concerns?

4. **Implications.** Questions are asked to get the prospect to see and feel the inconvenience caused by the problem. By discussing the implications, they are likely to be open to the solutions the salesperson has to offer.

5. **Need Resolution.** With careful questioning, the salesperson may be able to get the prospect to ask for the product without ever having seen it. Such questions might include: If you could overcome these obstacles, how would you feel?

6. **Providing a Solution.** The salesperson advises the prospect that they have a product that they believe can help with their situation and asks: Would you like to hear about it?

7. **Presenting the Product.** If the prospect is ready, the salesperson presents the product that is the best match for the prospect's needs. As noted earlier, any needed modifications should be approached in terms of solving the problem.

8. **Customer Relations.** Follow-up is replaced by continuing to build an ongoing relationship with the customer.

Order Forms and Proposals

Manual operations are sometimes necessary near the end of a sale. Outside sales representatives closing orders in the field must complete order forms, which show the quantity ordered, a product description, and costs. Outside sales reps, making a bid on a job, write up proposals. A proposal describes the job, the responsibilities of the company (materials and labor), and the proposed price.

Cash Register Operations

Most salespeople in retail and service operations use electronic cash registers to complete their sales transactions. These machines total purchases, figure sales tax, subtract refunds and returns, and calculate change due to customers.

The most common way to enter information in is by using the register keys. Some businesses, such as department stores, use electronic wands to scan data from sales tags. Many supermarkets use optical scanners. Businesses such as Fresh & Easy™ and The Home Depot® allow customers to check out their own merchandise with electronic self-checkout machines.

Opening Cash Funds

At the start of each day, the owner or a designated employee must supply the cash register with currency and coins. This is called an *opening cash fund.* The cashier should count it and write down the amount of each denomination. In addition, the overall total should be verified against the total planned for the register.

Sales Force To put together your sales force, you have to determine what kind of salespeople you need. *What are some traits of successful salespeople?*

Juice Images/Glow Images

GLOBAL WORKPLACE

Traditional + Futuristic = Japan

After World War II, rapid economic growth meant environmental concerns were overlooked in Japan, with pollution increasing in the 1950s and 1960s. Now, Japan is one of the world's environmental leaders. The country has developed many environmentally friendly technologies and served as conference host for the 1997 Kyoto Protocol, a treaty concerning climate change.

Economic Efficiency Between 70 to 80 percent of Japan is not suitable for agricultural, industrial or residential use. In addition, Japan is more than 45 times smaller than Russia in total land area. Despite all of this, Japan is an economic power. As of 2013, it trailed the United States and China in nominal gross domestic product, which is the market value of all goods and services produced within the country.

Social Studies Attempting to sell a product or service in Japan is a very formal exercise, due to the importance of business etiquette.

For instance, there are some rules about the presentation and receipt of a Japanese business card, known as *meishi*, and each person's status plays an important role in how he or she is treated. Research how entrepreneurial opportunities can be affected by business etiquette in Japan and summarize your findings in a one-page report.

Common Japanese Words and Phrases		
Hello	今日は	konnichiwa
Goodbye	さようなら	sayonara
Yes/ No	はい ・ いいえ	hai/iie
Please	お願いします	onegai shimasu
Thank you	ありがとうございます	arigato gozaimasu
You're welcome	どういたしまして	dou itashimashite

Making Change

When a cash sale is made, the salesperson should make change while announcing key amounts and counting aloud. This way, the customer can follow each step of the transaction. The salesperson begins with a statement of the purchase total, proceeds with the receipt of cash, and ends by making change, counting upward from the purchase total.

Credit and Debit Card Sales

Credit and debit card sales are rung up like cash sales. For credit sales, the salesperson accepts the card, checks the card user's identity, processes the card, and asks for the customer's signature. Once the signature is obtained, the salesperson places the signed credit slip in the cash drawer and gives a copy to the customer.

Debit sales are handled in the same way, but they do not require a signature. They may, however, require the customer to enter a personal identification (PIN) number. Most computerized cash registers secure authorization and print out the credit/debit slips.

Balancing the Cash Register

At the end of each business day, the designated employee should balance the cash register. Computerized cash registers keep a running tally of the day's sales. To balance, the employee simply compares the sales tape with the contents of the cash drawer. Any discrepancies need to be accounted for.

Sales Checks and Sales Tax

A **sales check** is a written record of a sales transaction. It provides the customer with an itemized receipt. It also provides valuable information to the business. To complete a sales check form, the salesperson enters the date, the items purchased, and the purchase price. Many businesses use electronic cash registers that provide the same information.

Computerized cash registers also calculate sales tax. However, there are many instances where sales tax must be calculated by salespeople in the field. There are also instances when cash registers malfunction or need maintenance.

To calculate sales tax, you must begin with the local rate. Sales tax varies from state to state, and sometimes county and city taxes are added. The sales tax is calculated on the total price of the items purchased. If, for example, you sell a CD for $20 and the tax rate is 7 percent, you would compute the tax as follows:

PURCHASE TOTAL	$\times$	TAX RATE	=	SALES TAX
$20.00	$\times$	0.07	=	$1.40

SECTION 13.1 Review

After You Read ▪▪▪▪▪▪▪▪▪▪▪▪▪

Self-Check
1. **Determine** what type of salesperson would be best for a bakery.
2. **Describe** the knowledge and skills needed by salespeople.
3. **List** the steps in the buying and traditional selling processes.

Think
4. **Explain** why the sales staff needs a training plan and schedule.

English Language Arts/Writing
5. **Writing with Tact** One of your sales reps has exceeded expectations recently. However, she has also not followed up properly with a few key customers who are unhappy with her service. You are afraid that if you reprimand her, her morale will suffer. Write your sales rep a letter that compliments her on her recent performance, but also makes it clear that her customer service needs to improve.

Go to connectED.mcgraw-hill.com to check your answers.

Planning, Directing, and Evaluating Sales

Reading Guide

Before You Read ▪▪▪▪▪▪▪▪▪▪▪▪▪▪

Connect Besides money, what kinds of rewards could you offer to your staff to motivate them?

The Main Idea

Effective sales operations are developed through careful planning, directing, and controlling.

Objectives

Identify the components of sales planning.

List the elements that are involved in directing sales.

Discuss the procedures used in evaluating sales performance.

Content Vocabulary

◇ sales planning
◇ sales forecast
◇ sales territory
◇ sales quota
◇ salary
◇ commission
◇ sales call reports
◇ SWOT analysis
◇ morale

Academic Vocabulary

You will see these words in your reading and on your tests. Use the academic vocabulary glossary to look up their meanings.

▪ period   ▪ technique

Graphic Organizer

Before you read this section, draw a chart like the one shown. As you read, write the three key functions of managing sales.

 Go to connectED.mcgraw-hill.com to download this graphic organizer.

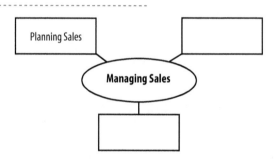

Planning Sales

Managing Sales

Planning Sales

Sales operations differ with the type of business and size of operation. As the number of people involved in your sales operation grows, the nature of your sales operation may change, too.

However, before you put your new sales force to work, you must complete your sales planning. Sales planning is tied to a company's marketing plan. **Sales planning** involves determining the goals, timing, and budgets of sales efforts. It involves making forecasts, determining sales budgets, establishing territories where necessary, and setting sales quotas.

Forecasting Sales

A **sales forecast** is an estimate of sales for a given **period**, such as the next quarter. When creating a marketing plan, an entrepreneur creates a market analysis. This market analysis includes an estimate of the market share the entrepreneur thinks the business could obtain. The entrepreneur's sales forecast would be based on that estimate.

Forecasting Methods

When you start a new business, you must rely on your market analysis and industry information for forecasting. Once your company is up and running, however, there are other methods you will be able to use in order to obtain a forecast range. These methods include surveys, data analysis, and operational analysis.

- **Surveys** You can use surveys of executives, customers, and sales staff to arrive at a forecast. These surveys are based on the opinions of both groups and individuals.
- **Data Analysis** You can apply mathematical methods to company records or historical data to obtain a forecast. These methods may use sales for the last period or an average of sales in recent periods. They may also use projections based on sales trends as their base.
- **Operational Analysis** The operation of the company is analyzed. One method of forecasting is based on sales volume needed to accomplish certain company goals. Another is based on capacity. If a company can sell everything it makes, its capacity is its sales forecast. Still another method is based on test market results.

Web Savvy

Webinars

With budgets getting tighter and tighter, more companies are cutting back on business-related travel—and this is making web-based seminars, or webinars, more popular than ever. Companies hosting these online events pick a day, time, and topic, and then invite people to register. "Attendees" sign up and are then given a special URL, which they visit at the time of the event. Most webinars feature graphics, text, and audio; attending one is much like watching a corporate presentation, but without all of the participants in the same room. *What are some possible business uses for webinars?*

Budgeting Sales

Three basic budgets are needed for your sales activities. In order of development, they are:

- **Sales budget** The sales budget begins with the sales forecast. From that calculation, a detailed sales budget is developed.
- **Selling expense budget** This budget projects expenditures related to personal selling activities.
- **Administrative sales costs budget** Administrative costs of managing the sales operation are budgeted separately.

When completed, these budgets, along with the sales forecast, give you criteria for judging performance. If sales are below budget, you can determine the cause and take steps to increase them. If costs are above budget, you can look for ways to control them.

Establishing Territories

A **sales territory** is a geographical area in which existing and potential customers are grouped. Sales territories are not needed if you conduct only inside sales. Even with outside sales, territories may not be needed. Having just a few salespeople selling in a local market does not require sales territories. However, if your market covers a wide geographic area, setting territories ensures market coverage, reduces selling costs, and improves customer relations. See **Figure 13.1.**

Establishing territories involves a three-step process. First, determine the probable areas—cities, counties, states, or other divisions. Next, determine the sales potential or time needed to cover the proposed territories. Third, make adjustments and

---

● **Figure 13.1** Sales Territories

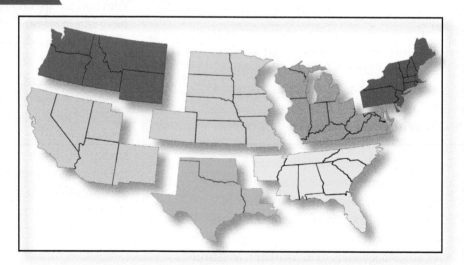

● **Sales Regions** Sales territories are beneficial when you have a wide geographic area to cover. *What are some common ways to divide markets into territories?*

decide on the boundaries. Once territories are established, you can assign salespeople.

Setting Sales Quotas

A **sales quota** is a performance goal assigned to a salesperson for a specific period. These goals serve several purposes. They give you an indication of strong and weak areas in your sales operation. They provide incentives for your workforce, improve the effectiveness of your compensation plans, and control selling expenses.

There are three general approaches to setting quotas for a new business. One approach is to set quotas based on territorial sales potential. For example, some territories may have a higher population that better fits the target market profile. A second approach is to set quotas in relation to your company's total sales forecast. For example, each of four sales reps should make about one-quarter of the total sales. The third is to base quotas simply on your judgment. Using this approach, you must be able to provide a reason for giving different quotas to different salespeople.

After your business is in operation, there is a fourth approach. That approach is to use past sales as a guide.

There are disadvantages to sales quotas as well. Salespeople may view quotas as a threat to their well-being. Thus, quotas may have a negative effect on their morale. Also, quotas set too high can cause salespeople to put too much pressure on customers. You need to set sales quotas that are realistic, objective, fair, and attainable. They must also be easy to understand and to implement. As a first step, conduct a thorough overview of sales quotas and consider their advantages and design.

Directing Sales Operations

Once your sales staff and plans are in place, you must direct your sales activities. Doing so ensures that you reach your goals. You must provide motivation and leadership to your salespeople. This enables them to do their job and reach their objectives.

Motivating Your Salespeople

Motivated salespeople are more effective at their job than unmotivated salespeople. Your responsibility is to determine the right combination of motivators.

Some motivational **techniques** are particularly useful when working with salespeople. For example, financial incentives such as bonuses are important. Salespeople are achievement-oriented. Therefore, reaching a goal to get a bonus is as important as the bonus itself. Nonfinancial rewards such as plaques, pins, trophies, and certificates are also important. Motivational sales meetings, contests, and congratulatory communications can likewise be effective techniques.

Compensating Your Sales Staff

Your pay plan must be designed to attract and keep good salespeople. It should provide the opportunity for steady income and incentives. The pay plan should also be competitive with what similar companies are paying. Like sales quotas, it must be fair and easy to understand and implement.

The right pay plan for your sales staff depends on your type of operation and your sales needs. The following options are often used as methods of payment for salespeople:

1. **Straight salary** A **salary** is regular wages an employee receives from an employer. When a salesperson receives a salary, they are paid a specified amount. This amount is for a certain period of time, no matter how many sales the salesperson makes. This plan ensures a regular and stable income. Because of this, it often results in a low turnover rate. Straight salary plans also allow management to direct salespeople into other sales-related activities. However, this option does not provide an incentive and is a fixed cost to the company.

2. **Straight commission** A **commission** is a fee for services rendered based on a percentage of an amount sold. In this case, payment is based on sales alone. Because income opportunities are usually unlimited, commission provides a strong incentive. It is a variable expense to the company—the expense occurs only when a sale is made. However, it is difficult to direct commission salespeople. They may tend to concentrate on easy-to-sell items; company interests are not their primary goal.

Expense Accounts Sales reps are usually reimbursed for food, lodging, and travel expenses. *What are some costs incurred when doing business out of the office?*

3. **A combination of salary and commission** With this option, a salary is paid, and sales are rewarded. This plan makes use of the advantages of straight salary and straight commission and overcomes their weaknesses. Most pay plans fall into this category.

Handling Expenses and Transportation

Typically, outside sales reps are reimbursed for their food, lodging, and travel expenses. They may also be reimbursed for personal expenses as a result of their travels.

Expense Plans

A good expense plan is fair, easy to understand, and easy to administer. To keep track of their expenditures, salespeople must keep receipts for business meals, hotel rooms, and airfare. They must also itemize (explain on paper) their expenses. This shows that the costs are reasonable. As expenses increase, more plans include limits on certain expenditures.

Reducing Travel Expenses

If travel expenses are high, you may want to consider alternatives. For example, leasing company cars may be less expensive than paying for mileage. Inside sales calls may be less expensive and just as effective as making outside contacts. These decisions depend on the size and nature of your operation.

Supervising Your Sales Force

The primary goal of sales force supervision is to increase sales while reducing costs. Reaching that goal requires training the sales staff, setting sales policies, and monitoring the activities of the sales force. Several techniques are useful in supervising a sales staff.

- **Personal contact** Personal visits with inside and outside salespeople serve several purposes. They provide an opportunity to assist with sales problems and training. They also show support for the sales staff.
- **Sales reports** A **sales call report** is an account of sales activities. It provides a way to monitor and evaluate outside sales activities. These reports include numbers of calls made, orders obtained, and miles traveled. They also include days worked, new prospects contacted, and new accounts sold. Salespeople who know they must account for their activities focus their efforts on those items.
- **Electronic communications** Another way to maintain contact with salespeople is through electronic communications. The telephone, fax, voice mail, and e-mail provide those opportunities.
- **Meetings** Motivational sales meetings can be used for training, providing information, and solving problems.

ETHICS and BUSINESS

Meeting Sales Goals

Situation You work at an electronics store that sells state-of-the-art televisions. It is nearing the end of the month and you have not met your sales goal. Your manager has been on your back about making more sales.

Doing the Right Thing A customer comes in to purchase a television that will put you over your sales goal for the month. But the customer needs the television in two days and you know it will take four days for it to be delivered. You cannot risk losing this sale.

English Language Arts/Writing

Ethical Sales Your manager tells you to say that the television can be delivered in two days and then make up an excuse when it does not happen. What should you do?

1. How could you make the sale and be honest with the customer?
2. Write a conversation you might have with the customer.

Adjusting to Sales Environment Changes

You can stay on top of changes in the internal and external sales environment by conducting a periodic analysis. One such technique to use is a SWOT analysis. A **SWOT analysis** is a strategic planning technique that analyzes a company's internal strengths and weaknesses, and studies opportunities and threats in the external sales environment.

Using SWOT analysis, you can assess your current situation on factors that influence selling. It also lets you identify strategies, thereby increasing strengths and opportunities and reducing weaknesses and threats

Internal Factors

Internal factors that may cause a difference in the performance of salespeople include variations in:

- Spending on other parts of the company's marketing and promotional mix
- What is happening in different territories or markets
- Sales management practices
- Number of salespeople supervised by one person

External Factors

External factors that may vary from one territory or market to another include:

- Intensity of competition
- Total market potential
- Concentration of potential high-volume buyers
- Geographic distribution of customers

SWOT analysis can be used to plan beyond short-range adjustments. It can be used to assess the sales operation, then to revise promotional and marketing plans.

Maintaining Morale

A high level of morale is an important factor in a sales staff's success. **Morale** is a state of individual psychological well-being based upon a sense of confidence, usefulness, and purpose. To maintain high morale, foster a positive work climate and job satisfaction. Encourage productive interaction among members of the sales force.

 Reading Check **Question** What does the acronym SWOT represent?

Evaluating Sales Performance

The final step in managing your sales operation is to evaluate sales performance. Sales performance evaluation involves evaluating company-wide sales and the sales of individual salespeople.

Evaluating the Company's Sales Performance

Evaluating the entire company's performance enables you to consider the effectiveness of your marketing plan and your operations. Two types of analyses are useful in this evaluation.

Sales Volume Analysis

Sales volume analysis is a comparison of your company's actual sales volume to its budgeted sales goals. In addition to total sales, sales territory, products, customer groups, order size, and individual salespeople should also be examined. Comparing these categories with industry figures indicates how your sales results stack up against the competition.

Marketing Cost Analysis

The second way to evaluate a company's performance is to perform a study of marketing expenses to determine the profitability of the company's various marketing units. This is called a *marketing cost analysis*. Although the company's overall picture is positive, some units may be costly, but getting few results. This analysis helps you identify misdirected marketing efforts and unprofitable segments.

Evaluating Individual Sales Performance

Formally evaluating individual sales performance can benefit the company and the salesperson. Salespeople often welcome the opportunity to improve their performance.

Before evaluating individual sales performance, you should explain the process to your salespeople. When employees know what to expect, they understand they are being evaluated objectively and often welcome the opportunity to improve their performance.

Black Gold

Supermarkets produce tons of food waste. Often, supermarkets pay landfills to dispose of old produce. But a few ingenious chains have begun sending food waste to farmers, who call the nitrogen-rich compost "black gold" and use it for soil enhancement. In return, supermarkets save money on landfill fees. To help the program along, supermarkets have trained employees to separate non-meat and non-dairy waste for composting.

◈ **Critical Thinking**
School cafeterias also produce food waste. Suppose your school began a food composting program. In a one-page report, analyze the ways the program would affect the lives of students, teachers, your family, and your community.

Evaluation Steps

Sales staff evaluations include five steps:

1. **Establish guidelines.** Guidelines should include who will do the ratings, when and how often they will be done, the criteria for ratings, and how the results will be used.
2. **Identify factors to be measured.** Include quantitative factors (calls per day, sales volume, etc.) and qualitative factors (product knowledge, customer relations, etc.).
3. **Set standards for performance.** Standards, or benchmarks, must be equitable and reasonable, tied to company goals, and based on records and on analysis of sales jobs.
4. **Compare performance to standards.** Each salesperson's performance is compared to the standards.
5. **Discuss results with salespeople.** Individual conferences should be held to discuss achievements and possible areas for for improvement.

SECTION 13.2 Review

After You Read ·············

Self-Check

1. **Summarize** the sales planning process.
2. **Name** three methods frequently used for the payment of salespeople.
3. **List** the steps in establishing a procedure for evaluating salespeople.

Think

4. **Design** an evaluation form for salespeople, including benchmarks.

Mathematics

5. **Budgeting** Bautista Coffee has seven salespeople who are each paid a $60,000 salary, with sales-based bonuses. Last year, six salespeople worked the full year; one worked for one month. They earned $5,000, $79,550, $60,000, $60,000, $92,125, $80,752, and $90,900. What is the mean, median, and mode of the salaries? Which number is an outlier? Which is the best to use when projecting salaries for next year's budget?

Math Concept **Outliers** Given a set of numbers in a sequence, the mean is the average, the median is the number in the middle of the sequence, and the mode is the most frequently occurring value. An outlier is a value at the extreme end of the set that skews the average.

Step 1 List the numbers from least to greatest.

Step 2 Calculate the mean (average) and identify the median, mode, and outlier.

Go to connectED.mcgraw-hill.com to check your answers.

Entrepreneurs *in Action*

Lisa Nicholson
Owner and CEO,
Lisa's Salsa Company

Q *What do you do?*

A Lisa's Salsa Company is a small company, which means, as the owner, I wear a lot of hats. We make salsa—and we do everything from start to finish here—core the tomatoes, peel the onions. It's a handcrafted item. I oversee the making of the salsa. I handle the marketing and sales. But my big job is to keep the company moving forward and to manage the product branding.

Q *What kind of training and education helped you to this career path?*

A I received a Bachelor's degree in Business and then went to law school for Business Law. Even though the business started small—just me and my pickup truck—the degrees gave me confidence as the business grew.

Q *What do you enjoy most about your job?*

A I get a deep satisfaction from our product, which I believe is the best salsa on the market. It's fresh, not something you buy off a shelf. Being a good employer is also important. I enjoy working with our crew, mostly women who've worked here for eight or nine years. We have a nice family feel.

Q *How did you become interested in your field?*

A In law school one summer, I grew a lot of tomatoes. So I started experimenting with recipes and created a salsa, which got a lot of enthusiastic feedback. Pretty soon I was designing a label and selling the salsa at the farmer's market.

CCR ☆ College & Career Readiness

Juice It Up You are starting a company that produces and sells all-natural fruit juices. To be successful, what type of sales people should you hire? What is the best way to compensate your sales force?

1. Review the basic ways sales people are compensated.
2. Evaluate this information and determine what kinds of sales people you should hire and how you think they should be compensated.
3. Explain your reasoning in a short report.

Career Facts

Real-World Skills	Academic Skills	Career Cluster
Planning, Multitasking, Interpersonal Skills	Economics, Science, Mathematics	Agriculture, Food & Natural Resources

Lisa Nicholson

Visual Summary

The Promotion Strategy: Developing and Managing Sales

Making a Sale Traditional selling is a ten-step process that is focused on the product.

The Sales Process
1   Prospecting
2   Preapproach
3   Approach
4   Determining Needs
5   Presentation
6   Overcoming Objections
7   Closing the Sale
8   Suggestion Selling
9   Closing Mechanics
10   Follow-up

Vocabulary

1. On a sheet of paper, use each of these terms and words in a written sentence.

Content Vocabulary

◇ personal selling
◇ prospect
◇ sales force
◇ order getting
◇ order taking
◇ customer benefits
◇ rational buying motive
◇ emotional buying motive

◇ buying process
◇ prospecting
◇ preapproach
◇ approach
◇ objections
◇ suggestion selling
◇ sales check
◇ sales planning

◇ sales forecast
◇ sales territory
◇ sales quota
◇ salary
◇ commission
◇ sales call report
◇ SWOT analysis
◇ morale

Academic Vocabulary

■ crucial   ■ series   ■ period   ■ technique

Key Concepts

2. **Define** the role of personal selling.
3. **Discuss** the difference between the two types of selling situations.
4. **Describe** the kinds of training needed to prepare salespeople to sell.
5. **Explain** the steps in the buying process.
6. **Identify** the differences between the traditional selling process and relationship selling.
7. **Explain** the basic budgets needed for sales activity.
8. **List** the key areas for maintaining a high level of morale in a sales staff.
9. **Discuss** the procedures used in evaluating a company's sales performance.

Academic Skills

Mathematics

10. **Percentages** Zuleyka sells advertising time for a television network. She receives a bonus if her sales exceed her quota by 12%. Her quota is $750,000. She sold $870,000 worth of advertising last year. Did she receive a bonus? How much more, or less, than her quota did she sell?

    Math Concept **Whole Plus Part** To exceed a number by 12% is the same as achieving 112% of that number.
    Step 1 Determine Zuleyka's quota. Find 112% of $750,000.
    Step 2 Determine the difference between Zuleyka's sales and her quota.

English Language Arts

11. **Effective Want Ads** Look at help wanted ads for sales positions in newspapers and on the Internet. Identify an ad that best describes the qualities a good salesperson should have. Prepare a one-minute explanation of your ad to present in class.

Academic Skills *(continued)*

Social Studies

12. Job Shadowing Ask permission from a retail store manager to spend several hours in the store. Observe how different salespeople interact with different customers. Give an oral report to your class on your findings.

Science

13. Selling Science Scientists and their work are supported in large part with funds that come from government sources. In order to secure funding for their research projects and experiments, scientists have to be good salespeople. Find out more about how the National Science Foundation (NSF) funds the work of scientists. Review this chapter and create a list of tips and ideas that could help a scientist be a better salesperson when applying for funding.

Real-World Skills

Interview Skills

14. From the Horse's Mouth Interview a salesperson you or your friends or family know. Find out what the person sells, how they are compensated, and how they are evaluated. Describe what you learn in a short report.

21st Century Skills

Critical Thinking

15. Hiring Decision You run a company that sells business software. Your two leading candidates for a sales job are a candidate with far superior technical knowledge and another candidate with much better people skills. How would you decide between the two candidates and why? Write one or two paragraphs explaining your answer.

Connect to Your Community

16. Select a Product Choose a product you would like to sell. Prepare and present a sales presentation to your class that includes the benefits of the product, how the product will meet prospective customers' needs, potential objections that might be raised about the product, and follow-up activities you can use to ensure that your customers are satisfied.

17. Interview a Salesperson Interview the owner of a sales-oriented business (for example, a real estate agent, insurance agent, or automobile dealer). Determine the internal and external environmental factors that affect sales. Ask how he or she would adjust sales plans as those factors changed.

Review and Assessment

CHAPTER
13

Competitive Events Prep

18. **Situation** You are the owner of a kitchen supply store. Your store carries cooking-related small appliances, cookbooks, gadgets, and cookware. The store offers outstanding customer service and a knowledgeable staff. You personally spend time with each new employee during training. You use this time to stress the importance of customer service and of personal selling. Later today, you will review the selling process and its importance with a new employee.

Activity Prepare your presentation to give to the new employee. Include each of the steps of the selling process and an explanation of each.

Evaluation You will be evaluated on how well you meet these performance indicators:

- Explain the selling process.
- Establish relationship with customer.
- Train staff to support sales efforts.
- Orient new employees.
- Foster positive working relationships.

 Go to connectED.mcgraw-hill.com for more information about this activity and other competitive events.

Standardized Test Practice

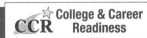 **College & Career Readiness**

Directions Choose the letter of the best answer. Write the letter for the answer on a separate piece of paper. For question #2, if the answer is False, rewrite the statement to make it true.

1. _____ is selling additional goods or services to the customer.
   A. Closing the sale
   B. Overcoming objections
   C. Prospecting
   D. Suggestion selling

2. A salary is a fee for services rendered based on a percentage of an amount sold.
   T
   F

> **Test-Taking Tip**
> Study for tests over a few days or weeks, and continually review class material. Do not wait until the night before to try to learn everything.

Business Plan Project

The Marketing Mix

To succeed with your marketing efforts, you need to study the competition. You also need to plan each of your marketing mix strategies. *How will you reach your customers?*

Objectives

In this project, you will complete these three parts of your business plan:

- Determine your company's competitive advantage.
- Write a description of your marketing objectives.
- Plan and organize your marketing mix strategies.

The Skills You'll Use

- **Academic Skills** Mathematics, English Language Arts, Social Studies
- **Real World Skills** Research, Organization, Critical Thinking
- **21st Century Skills** Media Literacy, Global Awareness

▶ Competitive Analysis

The competitive analysis section of the business plan should focus on demonstrating that the proposed business has an advantage over its competitors.

Step 1 **Gather Information About Your Competitors** Conduct research on the top direct and indirect competitors of your proposed business. Prepare a competitive matrix (see Chapter 5, page 110) to present highlights from your research.

Step 2 **Determine Your Company's Competitive Advantage** Use the information from your competitive matrix to answer the following questions and determine your competitive advantage: How are your products or services different from the competition's? How are they better? What key assets do you have that your competitors do not have? How will your strategies attract and defend market share? Create a Competative Advantage chart like the one on page 327 to organize your research.

▶ Marketing Plan

A marketing plan describes a company's marketing mix strategies or how it plans to market, promote, and sell its products or services.

Step 1 Describe Your Marketing Objectives Write a description of your proposed business's marketing objectives. Explain your plan for finding the best market. Describe the message your marketing mix strategies are meant to convey, and explain how the marketing mix strategies will be implemented and evaluated for effectiveness.

Step 2 Plan Your Marketing Mix
Create a chart like the one to the right to organize information about the product, price, place, promotion, and people strategies your company will use to reach its target market. Evaluate the impact of each of the strategies on the other marketing mix strategies.

Strategies	Description	Impact on Other Strategies
Product Strategy		
Price Strategy		
Place Strategy		
Promotion Strategy		
People Strategy		

Use the **Business Plan Project Appendix** on pages **572-583** to explore the content requirements of a business plan in more detail.

Competitive Advantage	
Question	**Answer**
How are your company's products and services different from your competitors' products and services?	
How are your company's products and services better than your competitors' products and services?	
What key assets does your business have that your competitors do not have?	
How will your business strategies and marketing mix strategies help your business to attract and defend market share?	

Business Plan Project Template Go to connectED.mcgraw-hill.com for a business plan template that you can use to write your own business plan.

My Business Plan
When you have completed your Project, put your statements, charts, and other research in your Business Plan Portfolio.

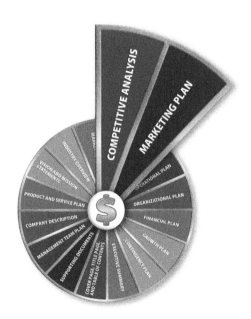

Connect the Photo

Brain Power The One Laptop Per Child project recruited top talents like Dr. Mary Lou Jepsen to develop innovative, low-cost technologies for children in developing countries. Dr. Jepsen later founded Pixel Qi, which is revolutionizing the design of computer screens. *How do you think you might use technology in your business plan?*

(bkgd)Dragon Images/Shutterstock.com; (inset)Courtesy of Mary Lou Jepsen

Business Plan Project

Preview

Getting Organized

To execute all your plans, you will need business management skills. You will need to organize, plan, and control resources. Will you need computers and copy machines? Will you use hybrid cars to transport your products? What kind of benefits will you offer to your employees? Will they be able to work from home?

The **Business Plan Project** will help you address and organize some of these concerns by focusing on these sections of the business plan

▶ The **Operational Plan** section of the business plan includes information about all the processes that take place in the business.

▶ The **Organizational Plan** offers information about the business's legal structure, methods of and responsibilities for record keeping, human resources, and legal and insurance issues.

Prepare for the Business Plan Project

As you read this unit, use this checklist to prepare for the **Business Plan Project:**

- Ask teachers, local businesspeople, or family members what kinds of benefits are available to them through their employees.
- Visit a business similar to the one you would like to start. Make a list of the equipment and machinery used.
- Compare and contrast different job descriptions by looking through job postings on the Internet or in a newspaper.

Preparing and Planning to Manage

Chapter Objectives

SECTION 14.1
Entrepreneur or Manager?

Describe the difference between the entrepreneurial role and the management role of a new business owner.

Identify the management functions.

List the key elements in a positive business climate.

SECTION 14.2
Management Styles and Skills

Name the three basic management styles.

List the skills needed for managing.

Explain the principles of management excellence.

Discovery Project
Leadership Skills

Key Question *How do managers motivate people?*

Project Goal
Ask teachers, administrators, coaches, and the managers of local businesses for permission to observe them at work. Pay attention to how they interact with others, especially the ways they encourage employees or students to do their best work.

Think About...
➤ *How will you select different teachers and managers to observe?*
➤ *How will you observe different classes or workplaces without disrupting them?*
➤ *What will you do with the information you have collected?*

21st Century Skills
Leadership and Responsibility *What skills do you need to develop in order to be a good manager?*

Evaluate
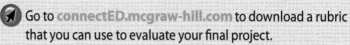 Go to connectED.mcgraw-hill.com to download a rubric that you can use to evaluate your final project.

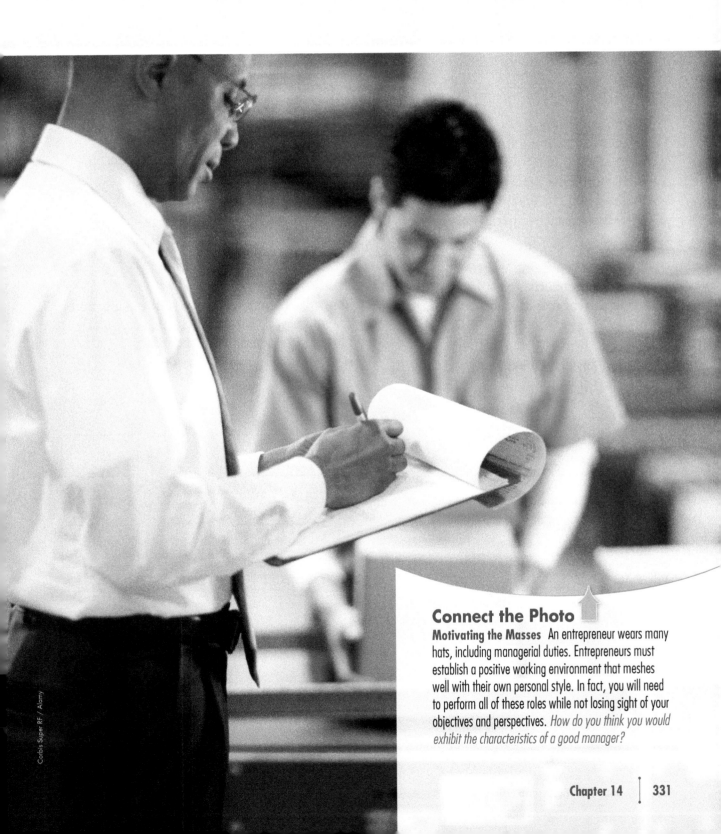

Ask
AN
EXPERT

Q: *I am creating a social media site and looking for investors. The investors I have talked with have asked for a projected cash flow. How do I calculate cash flow?*

A: Investors do consider cash flow when they evaluate a company, since without money to pay its bills, it will have a hard time staying in business. If a car dealership sells $100,000 worth of cars in a month and spends $35,000 on expenses, it has a positive cash flow of $65,000. But if it only takes in $35,000 and has $100,000 in expenses, it has a negative cash flow of $65,000.

Connect the Photo

Motivating the Masses An entrepreneur wears many hats, including managerial duties. Entrepreneurs must establish a positive working environment that meshes well with their own personal style. In fact, you will need to perform all of these roles while not losing sight of your objectives and perspectives. *How do you think you would exhibit the characteristics of a good manager?*

Entrepreneur or Manager?

Reading Guide

Before You Read ■■■■■■■■■■■■■

Connect How can managers create a positive climate?

The Main Idea

To be successful in a new business, an entrepreneur must perform management functions, establish a positive working climate, and maintain an entrepreneurial perspective.

Objectives

Describe the difference between the entrepreneurial role and the management role of a new business owner.

Identify the management functions.

List the key elements in a positive business climate.

Content Vocabulary

◇ manager
◇ planning
◇ strategic plans
◇ tactical plans
◇ operational plans
◇ organizing
◇ directing
◇ controlling
◇ quality control program
◇ climate
◇ image
◇ team building
◇ communication

Academic Vocabulary

You will see these words in your reading and on your tests. Use the academic vocabulary glossary to look up their meanings.

■ community   ■ compare

Graphic Organizer

Draw a chart like the one shown. As you read, list the four management functions.

 Go to connectED.mcgraw-hill.com to download this graphic organizer.

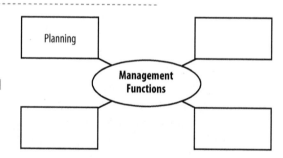

Planning

Management Functions

Managers, Leadership, and Teamwork

As a business owner, you must look to others for assistance. The saying "There's no *I* in *TEAM*" means that everyone in your organization is a valuable resource. Everyone works together toward a common goal. Graphic designers rely on salespeople to tell them that customers like letter-pressed invitations. Salespeople rely on garment workers to create cutting-edge fashions. Without an accountant, no one in the organization can be sure if the company is losing money or making a profit.

This section will discuss how entrepreneurs organize their human resources and structure their businesses. You will also learn what it takes to be a responsible leader, an effective manager, and a team builder.

Entrepreneur and Manager

Once you open the doors of your business, you take on a second role. You continue to bear the responsibilities of an entrepreneur, but your focus shifts from starting your own business to growing and expanding it. Your second role is that of a manager.

A **manager** is a person who coordinates the people, processes, and other resources of a business. As the manager of your own operation, you will carry out those duties on a daily basis.

You juggle those responsibilities to achieve your principal objectives—to survive and to make a profit. Even if you hire someone else to manage your business, you still must oversee the operation. For this reason, and because your operation is likely to start out small, you will probably do your own managing.

Your Management Role

As a manager, you must deal with many situations, often at the same time. On any given day, you might send out orders, review sales, and attend a meeting with members of the **community**. You might also handle an employee dispute, interview a job applicant, and deal with a dissatisfied customer. You might spend an entire day negotiating a contract or revising short-term plans. To run a business effectively and provide good service, you must perform management functions and establish a positive climate.

How is it possible to manage so many situations and still provide your customers with competitive products or services? This is where management skills come in. Managers must plan, organize, direct, and control their operations. Decisions to make range from purchasing and production to operations and staffing. Acquiring and improving your management skills will allow you to run your business smoothly and profitably.

> **Reading Check** **Recall** How does an entrepreneur's focus shift once the business has been opened?

Performing Management Functions

When managers are managing, they use a series of activities called management functions to achieve their objectives. These functions include the following:

1. Planning
2. Organizing
3. Directing
4. Controlling

The four functions occur in that order. When managers are working, the sequence may not be apparent. That is because they often deal with multiple objectives—each at a different stage—in the same time frame.

Planning

The first step in managing is planning. **Planning** is the act of setting goals, developing strategies, and outlining tasks and timelines to meet those goals. When you plan, you determine your business's objectives or specific desired results. You also determine how you are going to reach those objectives. Plans are on three levels—from the long range to the present.

Strategic Plans

Strategic plans are long-range objectives based on long-term goals. They map out where you want your business to be in three to five years. Usually, they do not include a specific target date. For example, you may want your baby clothing manufacturing company to grow into the largest in the industry.

Tactical Plans

Tactical plans are midrange objectives that focus on a period of one to three years. They are built on specific objectives with target dates. Tactical objectives and plans help ensure that you accomplish strategic goals and plans. A major objective of your marketing plan for the year may be to increase market share.

Operational Plans

Operational plans are short-term objectives that help achieve tactical plans. They bring the tactical plans to life. These plans also include policies, rules and regulations, and budgets for the day-to-day operation of the business—and the immediate steps you want to accomplish. Your operational plan may, in part, call for an ad campaign to roll out new baby clothes.

Web Savvy

Skype is the Limit

Skype, a service that lets users make "calls" over the Internet, provides managers with an inexpensive alternative to long-distance telephone charges. Using a computer, a headset microphone, or a special Skype-enabled phone, callers dial the person they want to reach. Instead of the signal going through the traditional telephone lines, it is converted to digital data and sent over the Internet. Skype originally could handle only conversations between two people using the service, but now it allows people to use Skype to call people on their normal phones. *What are the pros and cons of using Skype in the business environment?*

Strategic, Tactical, and Operational Plans

STRATEGIC PLANS
- Double pet toy production capacity within four years.

TACTICAL PLANS
- Complete new factory with increased output.
- Travel to trade shows to see the latest technology in manufacturing equipment.

OPERATIONAL PLANS
- Purchase equipment for new plant.
- Have equipment installed.
- Schedule and promote open house for chain and wholesale buyers.

● **Planning** Strategic, tactical, and operational plans are great ways to zero in on your goals. *How might you use these plans to assist you with your studies?*

Suppose a part of your strategic plan is to double your baby clothing production capacity within the next four years. One tactical plan might be to complete a new baby clothes factory by next March, increasing output 25 percent. Operational plans may include a request for bids to be sent to contractors for the proposed plant. **Figure 14.1** provides another example of how the three types of planning work together.

Reviewing Plans

Planning is an ongoing process. Strategic and tactical plans must be reviewed at least once a year. Operational plans are done for much shorter periods. They can be reviewed on a monthly, weekly, or even on a daily basis.

Reasons why you may have to review your plans include policy changes, technological advances, and the economy. For example, a new law requiring expensive safety gear may dampen your company's expansion plans. Likewise, a weak economy may restrict your advertising campaign.

Organizing

To carry out your company's plans, you must organize people, equipment, materials, and other resources. **Organizing** is the grouping of resources in combinations that will help you reach your objectives. This means deciding what jobs need to be done. You must set up an organizational chart that includes the jobs. You must then hire and train new employees to fill the positions. You also need to give your new hires authority and responsibility.

● **As You Read** ▪▪▪▪▪▪▪
Interpret Is a manager ever finished with planning?

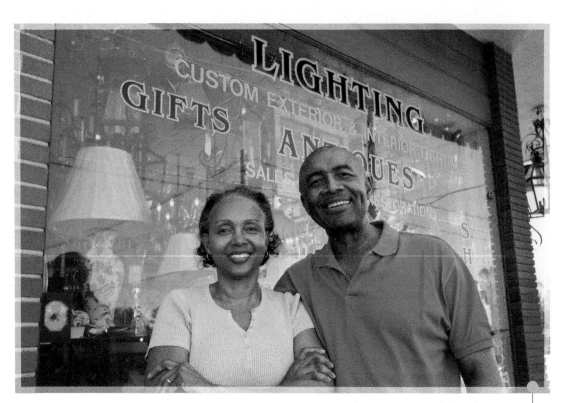

Multitasking Once you open your business, you must balance being an entrepreneur and a manager. *How is the entrepreneurial role different from the management role?*

Directing

Employees require guidance and supervision. After organizing your people and resources, you need to direct your employees' efforts to accomplish your planned objectives. **Directing** is the process of guiding and supervising employees, often one-on-one, while they work.

Directing is carried out by communicating policies, rules, tasks, assignments, and instructions to your employees. Effective directing often requires handling equipment, materials, and other resources. It also includes motivating employees to perform at their best and providing effective leadership.

Controlling

The final step in managing is controlling. **Controlling** is the process of comparing your expected results (your objectives) with actual performance. What can you do if there are significant differences between what you plan and what actually happens? If things are not working out as planned, you need to take corrective action.

How do you **compare** your plans with what is actually happening? There are several ways to assess performance. First, you can use your budget to compare budgeted costs with actual costs. Second, you can use personal observations to try and determine if there are any discrepancies. Finally, you can also develop a quality control program for your business.

Ariel Skelley/Blend Images LLC

Quality Control

A **quality control program** is a set of measures built into the production process to make sure that products or services meet certain standards and performance requirements. A company that makes canned soup, for example, has to keep the machinery and the food very clean. The product has to taste good and be nutritious. Such companies also have strict government regulations they must follow regarding content, safety, and portion size.

Making Changes

If you find significant differences between what you planned and what actually happened, you must take steps to correct the problem. You may decide to replace people resources, or processes. You may put preventive measures in place to keep things from going wrong in the future. You may also decide to revise your objectives.

 Reading Check Compare and Contrast What is the difference between strategic plans and operational plans?

GL○BAL W○RKPLACE — Land of 7,000 Islands

Residents of the Philippines, a nation of 7,107 islands in Southeast Asia with more than 90 million people, have quickly taken to cell phone texting. In 2007 alone, Filipinos sent an average of 1 billion text messages a day. In 2001, text messaging was said to have played a major role in bringing residents together for the "people power" revolt, which removed President Joseph Estrada.

Economic Growth The current president of the Philippines aims to have the country reach the goal of being "developed" by 2020. As part of that goal, she has established five economic "super regions" within the country, each of which would concentrate on their economic strengths to help grow the economy. The development themes include agribusiness, tourism, and information technology.

Social Studies Management styles in the Philippines tend to be paternalistic, but great care is also taken not to embarrass others publicly. Being criticized in front of others is the greatest insult that can be given. Managers must be able to treat subordinates respectfully while maintaining their status as a leader. Research how differing managerial styles may affect entrepreneurial opportunities in the Philippines and summarize your findings in a one-page report.

Common Tagalog Words and Phrases

Hello/How are you?	kumusta
Goodbye	paalam
Yes/ No	oo/ hindi
Please	paki
Thank you	salamat po
You're welcome	walang anuman

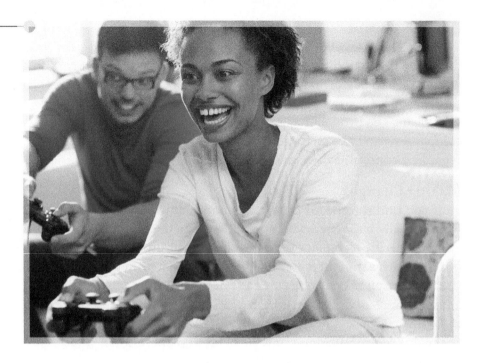

Life in the Googleplex In order to create, Google's management believes people need a creative environment. Employees are encouraged to set aside 20% of their time for individual projects. *What are some advantages and disadvantages of giving employees so much creative freedom?*

Establishing a Positive Climate

The climate that exists in a new business is linked to the tone the manager sets. **Climate** is a prevailing atmosphere or attitude. As the manager, you want to create a climate that provides for growth of employees as well as the business; creativity, innovation, and change; problem solving, goal development, and goal achievement; and effective communication within the business. Three key elements in positive business climates include image, team building, and communication.

Image

To develop a positive business climate, strengthen your company's image with customers and the community. A business's **image** is the mental picture and feelings people have when thinking about the business. Employees want to be associated with a winner, and your company's image becomes part of their self-image.

Establish a program for improving company image by changing customer policies and improving customer service. Use a public relations approach to build your company's image. Identify a company spokesperson to handle media contacts. Put together a fact sheet that includes information about accomplishments. Finally, share your successes whenever they occur.

Team Building

Team building involves activities designed to encourage teamwork. Team building contributes to a positive climate in several ways. Most importantly, employees buy into common goals. As a result, work gets done. Team building also results in the development of respect, trust, cooperation, camaraderie, and communication

Caia Images/Glow Images

among employees. These positive benefits spread throughout the entire business.

As the entrepreneurial leader in the team approach, you can take an active role in guiding the team by facilitating social interaction; encouraging participation; clarifying team roles, norms, and values; and facilitating task accomplishment.

Communication

Communication is the process of exchanging information. Effective staff communication is communication that takes place in an atmosphere of respect and trust. The traditional channels of communication among management and staff are interpersonal, departmental, interdepartmental, and company-wide. Interpersonal communication is communication with another person. Departmental communication is communication among members of a department. Interdepartmental communication is communication among members of two or more departments. Company-wide communication is communication among all members of a company.

Another effective channel can be the grapevine—the informal flow of information within an organization. Recognizing it as a part—though an unofficial part—of company communication can provide you with useful information and help head off misinformation. And, it is not difficult in a small venture where, at least in the beginning, most of your information flow is informal.

SECTION 14.1 Review

After You Read ▪▪▪▪▪▪▪▪▪▪▪▪▪

Self-Check
1. **Describe** the tasks a manager must coordinate on a daily basis.
2. **Determine** what action should be taken if there are small differences between what you planned and what actually happened.
3. **Identify** the formal and informal channels of communication in a business.

Think
4. **Explain** why is it important to link the goals of the individual to the goals of the team.

English Language Arts/Writing
5. **Understanding Suffixes** The terms *strategic, tactical,* and *operational* have slightly different, but related, suffixes. They all lend a similar meaning to the root word. Identify the suffixes in the three words and explain what they mean. Then identify the part of speech of the words and list some other words that use the same suffixes.

Go to connectED.mcgraw-hill.com to check your answers.

SECTION 14.2

Management Styles and Skills

Reading Guide

Before You Read ■■■■■■■■■■■■■■■■

Connect What management skills would be most important in your planned business?

The Main Idea

To manage successfully and excel in leadership situations, you must establish a management style and draw on a specific set of skills.

Objectives

Name the three basic management styles.

List the skills needed for managing.

Explain the principles of management excellence.

Content Vocabulary

◇ situational management
◇ human relations
◇ nonverbal communication
◇ networking
◇ time management
◇ conceptual skills

Academic Vocabulary

You will see these words in your reading and on your tests. Use the academic vocabulary glossary to look up their meanings.
■ approach   ■ principles

Graphic Organizer

Draw a chart like the one shown. As you read, list the three different leadership styles.

 Go to connectED.mcgraw-hill.com to download this graphic organizer.

Management Styles
1. power-oriented
2.
3.

Adopting a Management Style

Now that you know the functions of management, you need to think about the different styles you might employ in order to be an effective manager. Your management style is the manner in which you approach your management responsibilities. It is a major factor in the directing function.

Certain personal characteristics are needed in management situations. These include self-assuredness, decisiveness, and a desire to be the best. However, there are many differences in how managers with different styles go about managing. The question you must answer is which style is best for managing your particular type of business.

Power-Oriented Style

Managers who use a power-oriented style try to maintain total control over their whole operation. This style works in large organizations and situations where employees are untrained, inexperienced, or involved in a crisis. For example, a newly hired employee might accidentally place an order for a part that is not only the incorrect part, but also extremely expensive. In this situation, the manager might have to step in and take control of the order.

Routine-Oriented Style

Routine-oriented managers are concerned with keeping the operation running smoothly rather than accomplishing other goals. This style is most appropriate in middle management in large corporations and organizations.

Achievement-Oriented Style

Managers who are achievement-oriented are open to new ideas and seek out ways to empower employees to be creative, innovative, and to make suggestions. Achievement-oriented management is most effective where a manager is dealing directly with employees who are turning out work.

Situational Management

Generally, an achievement-oriented **approach** is most appropriate for small businesses. However, at times, you may have to adopt one of the other approaches, at least temporarily. You may have to take a power-oriented approach if you are at risk of losing a major customer because an order will not get out on time. You may have to become routine-oriented to stabilize a part of your operation, like daily office procedures.

Good managers are able to use whatever approach their circumstances dictate. This is called **situational management**. Making the adjustment from one style to another is not difficult. This is particularly true when you regard situational management as a supplement to your basic approach.

Tech Savvy

Employee Monitoring Software

Years ago, business courses heralded "management by walking around," an approach to employee management that encouraged managers to walk around and chat with employees as a way of getting to know them. These days, you might very well experience another style: management by monitoring. NetVisor's Network Monitoring Software, Keystroke Software, and Spector Spy Software allow managers to monitor employees' computer usage, read their e-mail, record their keystrokes, and even control their workstations from a remote location. Some may call stealth monitoring software unethical, but others, searching for new methods to rein in Internet-surfing employees, call it good business. *Why would managers want to monitor employee computer usage?*

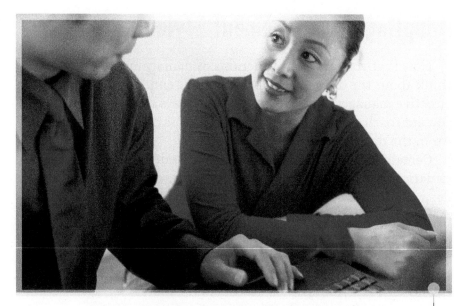

Empathy It is important for managers to be able to listen to and understand the concerns of their employees. *What kinds of body language show someone that you are listening attentively?*

Developing Management Skills

Whether a business is new or well-established, managers must draw on a specific set of skills in order to manage it successfully. These skills can be gained through education and training. They can also be improved with practice and experience.

Human Relations

Human relations skills are considered the most important management skills. **Human relations** is the study of how people relate to each other. Human relations skills help managers interact with employees, customers, suppliers, and vendors.

Human relations skills are interpersonal skills. They are tied closely to communication skills. Managers with good human relations skills are considerate, fair, and attentive when dealing with others.

These skills are also a key ingredient in a manager's ability to lead and motivate employees. You will rely heavily on human relations skills no matter how large your operation becomes.

Communication

Communication is essential to your effectiveness whether you are planning, organizing, directing, or controlling. Communication skills include speaking, listening, writing, and negotiating.

Nonverbal communication is communication not involving words. It is transmitted through actions and behaviors and includes facial expressions, gestures, posture, eye contact, personal space, and even clothing choices.

PhotoAlto/SuperStock

Networking

Networking is the process of building and maintaining relationships with people whose acquaintance could bring business opportunities. Business networking organizations provide a formal structure for owners and managers to meet, establish relationships, and exchange referrals. You can also develop informal business networking sources to discuss mutual opportunities, solve problems, and share or maximize resources. Increasingly, managers are using LinkedIn®, Facebook, or other social media to make and establish contacts and to find new business opportunities.

Networking can also help with recruiting and screening. Most business owners or managers welcome applications from friends of their employees because they trust the opinions of current employees. Valued company employees make good recommendations because they understand the skills, values, and mission of their company.

Math

The ability to perform math computations is another foundation skill that managers need. Math is necessary for managing daily operations, evaluating business performance, and making long-range projections.

Problem Solving and Decision Making

Managers use problem-solving and decision-making skills frequently. Sometimes they are used for planning, sometimes they are used to carry out planned actions. At other times, they are used to handle situations that must be dealt with immediately. Many of these problems call for logical solutions, while others require creative solutions.

ETHICS and BUSINESS

Serving the Customer

Situation You are the manager of the kitchen supply department at a high-end department store. You are training a new hire who has excellent product knowledge and an ability to put customers at ease. The new hire has already made a number of big sales.

Meeting the Customer's Needs A customer needs to set up a kitchen but is not sure exactly what she needs. The new hire sees an opportunity to sell her the best and most expensive equipment in the store, but you realize that less-expensive models will work well for her needs. What will you do?

English Language Arts/Writing

Lead by Example Your department will look good if you make the big sale, but the customer might become angry if she realizes you have sold her more than she needs.

1. What should you advise the new hire to do in order to look after the best interests of both the store and the customer?
2. Write a short report that explains the reasoning behind your decision.

Technical Skills

Technical skills involve the use of tools, equipment, procedures, and techniques that are critical to the business. These skills usually come from prior education and training. As your business grows, you may turn over management of technical aspects to supervisors you hire. However, in the early stages, you will need to know how things work.

Time Management

At any given time, managers may have several objectives to accomplish. The skill of time management can have a big impact on successful management. **Time management** is the process of allocating time effectively. Here are some useful time management techniques:

- Set and prioritize your goals.
- Delegate work to others whenever possible.
- Plan to spend blocks of time on specific activities that help you achieve your goals.
- Schedule your activities on a planning calendar.
- Schedule your most important work for times (mornings, evenings, etc.) when you do your best work.
- Group your activities for the most efficient use of time.
- Handle or eliminate interruptions so they take up as little time as possible.

Remote Access Meetings Many companies are taking advantages of the technological advancements that allow teams to communicate via the Internet. *Why would companies encourage communication this way?*

Ariel Skelley/Blend Images LLC

To Be a Good Manager, Learn How to Lead

Effective managers do more than give orders—they inspire by example

Managers are responsible for getting results. They plan work, provide feedback, and advocate for their teams. The best managers, however, are also leaders.

Leaders influence and inspire. They offer people a sense of purpose. They motivate workers and help them reach their potential. They lead by setting an example, not by giving orders.

The biggest pitfall new managers face is believing that because they are the boss, they can do whatever they want. Good managers value the opinions of others, including employees, suppliers, and customers. In fact, many of the best managers do more listening than talking.

Don't just give an order and expect it to be carried out. Instead, consult with your employees, listen to their input, and make them a part of the decision. This is not just good management—it's good leadership.

Active Learning

In small groups, have each member role-play a manager. Stage a meeting to discuss a company decision such as an expansion, handling shoplifting, or writing a policy on personal use of company computers. Evaluate one another on the manager's ability to listen and interact with the rest of the team. Was respect shown? Were all ideas taken into consideration and discussed? Provide feedback on the manager's strong points and where improvement is needed.

Conceptual Skills

Conceptual skills are skills that enable a person to understand concepts, ideas, and **principles**. They involve thinking, reasoning, and logic. In a managerial context, conceptual skills allow you to see and understand the relationship between the details and "the big picture."

As a small business owner/manager, your conceptual skills enable you to appreciate how day-to-day decisions affect your business's future. Conceptual skills also help you make big decisions, such as when and how to expand your business.

✔ **Reading Check** **Summarize** What is networking?

Principles of Management Excellence

In the book *In Search of Excellence*, managerial researchers Thomas Peters and Robert Waterman list eight keys to management excellence. According to Peters and Waterman, good managers:

1. Take action rather than overanalyze plans.
2. Listen to customers and put themselves in customers' shoes.
3. Encourage employees to act independently, be innovative, and treat the business as if it were their own.
4. Emphasize respect for the individual.
5. Instill commitment to values and objectives by staying in touch with all employees.
6. Keep the business focused on what it does best.
7. Keep the organization simple, flexible, and efficient; they do not overstaff.
8. Keep operations under control and keep an eye on detail.

SECTION 14.2 · Review

After You Read

Self-Check
1. **Select** the management style that works best in a new small business.
2. **List** two key management skills.
3. **Describe** two of the principles of management excellence.

Think
4. **Explain** how the principles of management excellence help a business meet its goals.

Mathematics
5. **Time Management** Jessica realized that she was wasting some of her time at work. She determined she could cut the amount of time she wasted in half by doing certain tasks during lunch. She could eliminate another third by making other scheduling changes. If she was left with 4 minutes of wasteful time, what was the total amount of time Jessica realized that she had been wasting?

   Math Concept **Algebra** Some problems can be made easier if you write an equation. An equation is a mathematical sentence that explains what you are trying to solve for.

   Step 1 Write an equation, use x to represent the unknown. In this case the unknown is the total amount of time wasted.

   Step 2 Solve the equation for x to determine how much time was being wasted.

 Go to connectED.mcgraw-hill.com to check your answers.

Entrepreneurs *in Action*

C.H. Greenblatt
Creator and Executive Producer
Chowder

Q *What do you do?*

A I am the creator and executive producer of "Chowder," an animated children's show.

Q *What kind of training and education helped you get this job?*

A Most of my cartooning training was self-taught. I studied advertising in college but switched to animation after four years of working as an art director for an advertising agency. Most of what I've learned has been on the job, in both fields. In this case, my experience and creativity, along with my college experience, led me to this career.

Q *What do you enjoy most about your job?*

A The best part about my job is the variety of things I get to do. Some days I spend working on writing stories, other days I spend going over drawings and paintings, and some days I oversee music and post-production. It's also great to make up crazy things in my head and see them come to life.

Q *How did you become interested in your field?*

A I've always loved animation and cartoons. Around the sixth grade, I began drawing comic strips to bring into school everyday to show my friends. During college, I drew a daily comic strip for the school paper. And when I was out of school, I continued drawing comic strips until I realized that I was more interested in telling stories through animation rather than newspapers.

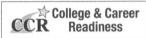

College & Career Readiness

Entrepreneur or Manager? Steve Jobs, Oprah Winfrey, and Michael Dell have all acted as both entrepreneurs and managers. After founding their respective companies, they had to make day-to-day management decisions.

1. Use the Internet to research one of these famous personalities.
2. Think about the definitions of entrepreneur and manager in this chapter. Decide if this person is a better entrepreneur or manager.

Career Facts

Real-World Skills	Academic Skills	Career Cluster
Creativity, Technology Skills, Collaboration	English Language Arts, Fine Arts	Arts, A/V Technology & Communications

Review and Assessment

Visual Summary

Preparing and Planning to Manage

Being a Manager
When entrepreneurs open their business, they take on a second role—that of a manager.

Management Functions
Plan
Organize
Direct
Control

Management Styles
Power-oriented
Routine-oriented
Achievement-oriented

Planning A plan determines the objectives or desired results of a business.

Types of Plans		
Strategic Plans	**Tactical Plans**	**Operational Plans**
Long-range. Usually do not include a target date.	Mid-range. Built on specific objectives with target dates.	Short-term objectives. They help achieve tactical plans.

Skill Sets To manage a business successfully requires different skills.

Math

Human Relations

Technical

Skills of Successful Managers

Conceptual

Time Management

Communication

Ariel Skelley/Blend Images LLC

Vocabulary

1. On a sheet of paper, use each of these terms and words in a written sentence.

Content Vocabulary

◇ manager
◇ planning
◇ strategic plans
◇ tactical plans
◇ operational plans
◇ organizing
◇ directing

◇ controlling
◇ quality control program
◇ climate
◇ image
◇ team building
◇ communication

◇ situational management
◇ human relations
◇ nonverbal communication
◇ networking
◇ time management
◇ conceptual skills

Academic Vocabulary

■ community
■ compare

■ approach
■ principles

Key Concepts

2. **Explain** the difference between entrepreneurs and managers.
3. **List** the management functions in their order of occurrence.
4. **Explain** why it is difficult to observe the management functions in sequence.
5. **List** and explain the key elements in a positive business climate.
6. **Describe** the achievement-oriented management style and explain where it is most effective.
7. **Describe** the power-oriented management style and explain where it is most effective.
8. **List** the skills needed for managing.
9. **Identify** the principles of management excellence.

Academic Skills

Mathematics

10. **Strategic Plans** At the yearly meeting to discuss Tanner Dance Studios's strategic plan, the company decides to aim for a 24% increase in sales over the next four years. The current year's sales totaled $15,450. If the company increases the sales by equal amounts each year over the next four years, what will the total sales be after the first three years?

   Math Concept **Percents** Percents can be thought of as parts of the whole.
   Step 1 Divide the percent by 100 to determine its decimal equivalent.
   Step 2 Multiply the current year's sales by the decimal.
   Step 3 Divide this target amount by the number of years to determine the annual increase.

English Language Arts

11. **Character Sketch** Locate and read an article about the manager of a company. Prepare a two-minute presentation about the person for the class. Discuss the person's leadership style and management techniques.

Academic Skills *(continued)*

Social Studies

12. Leadership and Group Dynamics Think about your own experiences with adults who have managed or influenced some aspect of your life. Consider the leadership style used by these adults: family members, teachers, employers, or club leaders who are familiar to you. In a small group, share examples of each of the three leadership styles discussed in this chapter. Discuss the types of situations in which each style is most effective.

Science

13. Accidental Inventions The history of science is filled with examples of inventions that brought about tremendous change. Some of these innovations resulted from accidental discoveries. Rubber, superglue, microwave ovens, sticky notes, penicillin, and non-stick coating for cookware are some examples. Research one of these accidental inventions and write a paragraph about how it changed our world.

Real-World Skills

Career Skills

14. Job Hunting You are applying for a job as the manager of a record label. Write a cover letter that explains your management style and why it will be effective for running the record label.

21st Century Skills

Leadership and Responsibility

15. Peacemaker You run a small advertising agency where, unfortunately, your ad writer and your ad designer are not getting along. Because they must work together closely, the quality of their work is suffering. What can you as their manager do to improve the situation?

Connect to Your Community

16. Observe a Manager If you are employed, observe the activities of your manager for a one-week period. If you are not employed, observe the activities of a particular teacher for one week. Record what he or she does at the end of each day. At the end of the week, make a chart categorizing each activity as planning, organizing, directing, or controlling.

17. Time Management Interview the manager of a business in your community and ask how he or she implements time management principles. Ask how he or she prioritizes his or her tasks. Summarize the interview in a short presentation to your class.

Competitive Events Prep

18. **Situation** You are a managing partner for a regional chain of electronics stores. The business is opening two new stores and seeks qualified individuals for management positions. These positions include store manager, assistant store manager, and department manager. You will be making a presentation to a group of potential management trainees.

Activity Prepare information about some of the traits your company seeks in the individuals it hires as managers, assistant managers, and department managers. Organize your information in outline form.

Evaluation You will be evaluated on how well you meet these performance indicators:

- Explain the concept of management.
- Describe the role of management in the achievement of quality.
- Explain the nature of managerial ethics.
- Recruit new employees.
- Prepare simple written reports.

 Go to connectED.mcgraw-hill.com for more information about this activity and other competitive events.

Standardized Test Practice

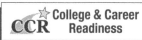
College & Career
Readiness

Directions Choose the letter of the best answer. Write the letter for the answer on a separate piece of paper. For question #2, if the answer is False, rewrite the statement to make it true.

1. _____ skills are considered the most important management skills.
   A. Networking
   B. Human relations
   C. Math
   D. Conceptual

2. Strategic plans are short-term objectives that help achieve tactical plans.
   T
   F

> **Test-Taking Tip**
> When you first receive your test, do a quick review of the entire test so that you know how to budget your time.

Managing Purchasing and Inventory

Chapter Objectives

SECTION 15.1

Purchasing Management

Describe the importance of planning purchases.

Identify factors that affect purchasing.

SECTION 15.2

Inventory Management

Examine inventory procedures used by small businesses.

Explain the importance and types of inventory control.

Discovery Project

Managing Business Purchases

Key Question *How do business owners buy the products or materials that they need?*

Project Goal

Think of a product you would like to manufacture and sell. Make a list of the materials and equipment you would need to make the product. Determine how and from whom you would obtain them. Ask local business owners for advice on who to contact and how to get the best price. Select the best supplier or suppliers for your business.

Think About...

➤ How will you locate vendors and suppliers?

➤ How will your choice of materials affect the product and your business as a whole?

➤ What criteria can you use to select the best vendor?

21st Century Skills

Productivity and Accountability *Why would business owners want to have more than one supplier for the same type of inventory?*

Evaluate

 Go to connectED.mcgraw-hill.com to download a rubric that you can use to evaluate your final project.

Ask
AN
EXPERT

Q: *My export business has grown over the last few years and I need to expand to a larger facility to make room for new inventory. How can I get a copy of my credit report to check my credit score before I apply for a loan?*

A: There are three major credit-reporting agencies: Experian, Equifax, and Transunion. As a provision of the Fair and Accurate Credit Transaction Act (FACT Act), you are entitled to a free copy of your credit report each year from each of the credit-reporting agencies. You can call or write to request a copy of your credit report.

Connect the Photo

In Stock Making smart purchasing and inventory decisions can result in more profits for entrepreneurs. Purchasing the best products at the best possible prices and keeping a close watch over these valuable assets are a top priority for business owners. *How can business owners make sure their inventory matches the market's need?*

Purchasing Management

Reading Guide

Before You Read ==============
Connect How can purchasing decisions make the difference between success and failure for an entrepreneur?

The Main Idea
Businesses need to get the best possible products or materials for the price. Making smart spending decisions can result in better values for customers and larger profits for the business.

Objectives
Describe the importance of planning purchases.
Identify factors that affect purchasing.

Content Vocabulary
◇ purchasing
◇ model inventory
◇ vendors
◇ trade discount
◇ quantity discount
◇ cash discount
◇ secured funds
◇ invoice

Academic Vocabulary
You will see these words in your reading and on your tests. Use the academic vocabulary glossary to look up their meanings.
■ minimum
■ relationship

Graphic Organizer
Draw a chart like the one shown. As you read, write the six key factors that enter into purchasing decisions.

 Go to connectED.mcgraw-hill.com to download this graphic organizer.

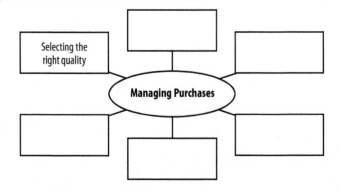

Selecting the right quality

Managing Purchases

Planning Purchases

Planning your purchases means you can buy items at a low price and sell them at a profit. Planning involves reviewing your sales objectives, then making purchasing decisions. What will you buy? From whom will you buy? How will you get the best price? How much inventory should you stock? These questions are answered as you plan your purchases.

Buy Inventory

Purchasing, also known as *procurement*, is the buying of all the materials needed by the organization. In this chapter, purchasing refers to buying inventory. Inventory includes products for resale and the materials to create such products. Chapter 9 discusses the selection of goods and services for a business's operational needs.

Develop a Model Inventory

A **model inventory** is a target inventory of what you think you will need to keep in stock. As a beginning entrepreneur, you should have already identified your inventory needs, researched competitors, and received input from suppliers as well as trade associations. This information will help you make your best estimate to arrive at a start-up inventory.

Make Changes

Once your business is under way, you can use sales records to guide your inventory decisions. In addition, you may be doing ongoing market research. By being in the business, you become aware of inventory trends and cycles. You also can rely on regular input from **vendors**, the businesses that sell you inventory.

 Reading Check **Recognize** What is another name for purchasing?

Managing Purchases

Purchasing management is a primary concern to retail, wholesale, and manufacturing businesses. It may also be a concern to service businesses. For example, a copier repair business needs to purchase copier parts. Only extraction businesses, such as mining and farming, have little concern with purchasing management.

Purchasing decisions may mean the difference between success and failure for an entrepreneur. If that seems extreme, consider how much money is invested in purchasing. Manufacturers spend up to 50 percent of every dollar they make on inventory. Retailers spend up to 70 percent, while wholesalers spend up to 85 percent. Several key factors affect purchasing.

Recycled Chic

Forward-thinking green entrepreneurs have turned to fashion. Some have sought out sustainable fibers like bamboo, which grows quickly and provides a luxurious fabric. Others have found inspiration in the recycle bin. Plastic soda bottles have discovered a second life as polar fleece, hats, gloves, and T-shirts. Recycled plastic costs less than cotton or wool, and by reusing it, manufacturers help keep plastics out of landfills.

◈ **Critical Thinking**
In Europe and Japan, there are few sites left that can be used for landfills. Most of the waste in these countries is plastic. Write a one-page report on how this might affect attitudes toward recycling and the opportunities that might exist for entrepreneurs.

Select the Right Quality

To determine the quality of inventory to purchase, buy the products or materials that match your needs. For example, if you manufacture shelving, you should buy durable materials. If you are a retailer dealing in moderately priced footwear, stick to moderately priced products. If you buy high-priced products or budget footwear, your customers may go elsewhere to find what they want.

Buy the Right Quantity

How much inventory should you buy? You should purchase enough to maintain your chosen inventory levels. The act of deciding on inventory levels is called inventory management. This topic is discussed in Section 15.2.

Time Your Purchases

Time your purchases so your money and storage space are not tied up any longer than necessary. Also, take advantage of economic conditions. If prices are beginning to rise, stock up before they go even higher. If the economy is in a recession, keep purchases to a **minimum**. Making such timely buying decisions requires that you stay in touch with news.

Choose the Right Vendors

Locating vendors is not a difficult process. However, in order to select the right vendors, you will need to make a number of thoughtful decisions. Consider the following factors when choosing a vendor.

Reliability

Is the vendor able to deliver enough products or materials? Does the vendor deliver them on time? If deliveries are late or inadequate, you can lose sales and customers.

Movies by Mail Netflix, has changed the way people rent movies with a subscription-based service that allows people to rent movies by mail or watch them instantly online. *How would this shift in rental delivery affect purchase planning?*

Pamela Carley

ETHICS and BUSINESS

Planning Your Business Purchases

Situation You have been successfully building your bicycle sales business for several years and have three full-time employees. You take care to make wise purchases so that you can pass savings on to your customers and still be profitable.

Purchasing Power You have an opportunity to purchase professional racing bikes at a very good price if you purchase a minimum quantity. If you sell the bikes, you will make a big profit. If you cannot sell all of the bikes, you run the risk of not being able to meet payroll.

English Language Arts/Writing

Risky Business This deal could provide very good deals for customers and make a good profit for the business. Should you make the purchase and risk the employees' salaries?

1. How could you take advantage of the good deal on bikes and not risk your employees' salaries?
2. Create a plan for making this deal work to everyone's advantage.

Distance

What is the location of the vendor under consideration? The cost of transporting products or materials can be expensive. Local vendors often provide better service. In addition, coordination problems are easier to handle when the vendor is nearby.

Service

Before you select a vendor, you should inquire carefully about what services are offered. Ask the following questions about the vendor's services:

- Do sales representatives call on a regular basis?
- Do they know the product line?
- Can they assist you with planning layouts, setting up displays, and solving production problems?
- If there is equipment involved, can they repair it?
- Do they make unscheduled deliveries in an emergency?
- What is the return policy?
- What other appropriate assistance can they provide?

Number of Vendors

Should you buy from one vendor or from several? When you buy from just one vendor, you may be able to get special treatment. For example, a vendor may reward you for making an exclusive agreement by offering quantity discounts.

However, if you use only one vendor and something goes wrong with the working relationship, you will be vulnerable. The same holds true if the vendor goes out of business.

To lessen your risk, work with more than one vendor. If the **relationship** with one vendor goes amiss, you will have other established vendors with whom you can do business. For a good combination, consider using one vendor for 70 to 80 percent of your purchases. Divide the rest among several vendors.

Getting the Right Price

Contact several vendors to find the best price. When orders are large, prices may be negotiable. However, the lowest price is not always the right price. You should factor quality and service into your decision. If quality is poor or delivery is undependable, you may lose more than you gain. The average dissatisfied customer tells ten people about poor products or services he or she received.

Purchase discounts can also affect prices. You may be able to take advantage of trade, quantity, or cash discounts. This depends on where you are in the channel of distribution.

Discounts

A **trade discount** is a discount from the list price of an item allowed by a manufacturer to wholesalers and merchants. For example, a manufacturer might give discounts of 50 percent to wholesalers and 40 percent to retailers to reward channel members for their role in getting the products to consumers. A **quantity discount** is a discount that a vendor gives to a buyer who places large orders. A **cash discount** is an amount deducted from the selling price for payment within a specified time period, such as 10 days. Cash discounts accelerate payments and improve cash flow for a business.

Dating Terms

In addition to discounts, dating terms affect price. They specify when you must pay a bill and what discount you can take for paying early. Ordinary dating terms, such as 2/10, net 30, are based on the date of the invoice. In this case, the percent of discount for paying early is 2 percent. The number of days within which the discount can be taken is 10. The number of days in which you must pay in full is 30. Other dating terms are as follows:

- **Advance dating** This occurs when manufacturers give a date other than the invoice date for the terms to take effect. For example, the invoice may be dated June 15 and read 2/10, net 30—as of August 1. August 1 is the date the billing terms go into effect.
- **Extra dating** This gives additional days before the terms take effect. For example, the invoice terms may read 2/10, net 30, 60 extra. The 2/10, net 30 applies after the 60 days have passed. These terms can also be read as 2/70, net 90.
- **End-of-month (EOM) dating** These terms change the date from which the terms take effect to the end of the month. For example, an invoice is dated June 15 with terms of 2/10, net 30, EOM. You can take the discount up to 10 days after June 30. The last day to pay the bill is July 30.
- **Receipt-of-goods (ROG) dating** These terms begin when you receive the goods. Assume you receive an invoice dated June 15 with terms of 2/10, net 30, ROG. The goods are received on June 20. The last day for taking the discount is June 30. The last day for payment is July 20.

GL🌀BAL WORKPLACE

Mobile Phones, *por favor*

Greater Mexico City is the second largest metropolitan area in the world, with more than 19 million people. The city itself produces a significant amount of the country's gross domestic product. It is the only city in Latin America to have hosted an Olympic games (the 1968 Summer Olympics) and is home to the second oldest university in the Americas, the National Autonomous University of Mexico, which started in 1551.

Telecom Titan In a country where a large percentage of the population lives below the poverty level, Carlos Slim Helu stands out. As of 2013, he is the second richest person in the world, worth approximately $74.2 billion. He bought Telefonos de Mexico (Telmex) in 1990 and now controls 90% of the country's telephone landlines.

Social Studies/Science In the past decade, Mexico has become much more involved in producing electronics, and is now among the top five countries in the world producing mobile phones and consumer electronics.

Be-cause Mexico is one of the top five countries exporting goods to the United States, a number of Mexican firms act as vendors for American companies. Research American companies that have purchasing relationships with Mexican companies and summarize your findings in a one-page report.

Common Spanish Words and Phrases	
Hello/Hi	hola
Goodbye	adios
Yes/No	si/no
Please	por favor
Thank you	gracias
You're welcome	de nada

Purchase Orders

The price, discounts, and terms have been agreed upon. Now you usually prepare and submit a purchase order to the vendor. The purchase order includes the quantity, style, and number. It also includes the unit price of each item purchased along with extensions.

Extensions are the result of multiplying the number of units by the cost per unit. Suppose you had several items on the same purchase order. You would total all of the extensions and enter them at the bottom of the Total column. Other entries on the purchase order might include shipping and delivery instructions.

Payment Methods

Until you establish a good working relationship, your new vendor may request secured funds. **Secured funds** are a form of guaranteed payment. These include a credit card, a cashier's check, a wire transfer, or cash. As you establish credit, a vendor may be willing to accept a single-party check. It is important to pay your vendors on time. Then if you ever need to stretch your credit, they will allow you to do so.

Receiving and Following Up on Purchases

Purchasing management does not stop with placing your order. You or an employee must verify and record its arrival. If customers are unsatisfied with your goods or services, you should review quality issues with your vendors.

Retailers and wholesalers must mark size, cost, selling price, and other information on each unit. Manufacturing and service businesses may need to mark the grade or source of materials.

Effective managers follow up on how their purchased inventory performs. Retailers and wholesalers follow up on complaints and returns. Manufacturers and service businesses follow up on the performance of materials they use.

Checking Invoices

When you receive a shipment from a vendor, it should be accompanied by an invoice. An **invoice** is an itemized statement of money owed for goods shipped or services rendered. The invoice is based on and contains much of the same information as your purchase order. At the time of arrival, you should check the shipment against the invoice. This allows you to verify the correctness, quality, and condition of the order. You should match the invoice against the purchase order and check the accuracy of entries and extensions. If you find something wrong with the shipment or on the invoice, report it to the vendor immediately. Keeping a close eye on incoming shipments protects you from paying for somebody else's mistakes.

SECTION 15.1 Review

After You Read ••••••••••••••

Self-Check
1. **Name** the factors you should consider when timing your purchases.
2. **List** three types of discounts that apply to purchasing.
3. **Decide** what you should do if you find something wrong with a shipment or an invoice.

Think
4. **Explain** why manufacturers and service providers spend different percentages of their income on inventories.

English Language Arts
5. **Vocabulary Review** Write a letter to a new employee that explains how to conduct purchase planning. In your letter, define each of the following terms in your own words: *invoice, vendor, durable material,* and *extraction business*.

Go to connectED.mcgraw-hill.com to check your answers.

SECTION 15.2

Inventory Management

Reading Guide

Before You Read ▪▪▪▪▪▪▪▪▪▪▪▪▪▪

Connect Is it possible to have too much inventory? Why or why not?

The Main Idea
An entrepreneur's main profit stems from the sale of inventory. He or she needs to keep careful control over this valuable asset.

Objectives
Examine inventory procedures used by small businesses.
Explain the importance and types of inventory control.

Content Vocabulary
◇ financing cost
◇ opportunity cost
◇ storage cost
◇ insurance cost
◇ shrinkage cost
◇ obsolescence costs
◇ warehousing
◇ lead time
◇ usage rate
◇ safety stock

Academic Vocabulary
You will see these words in your reading and on your tests. Use the academic vocabulary glossary to look up their meanings.
▪ purchase
▪ method

Graphic Organizer
Draw a chart like the one shown. As you read, compare the advantages and disadvantages between too much and too little inventory.

 Go to connectED.mcgraw-hill.com to download this graphic organizer.

Too Little Inventory	Too Much Inventory
lost sales	

Inventory Management

Inventory management is used to find and maintain inventory levels that are neither too small nor too large. Too little inventory may result in lost sales. It can mean losing customers or having your operations interrupted. Too little inventory also leads to frequent reordering. Time and energy on your part are required to place these additional orders.

However, too much inventory can add as much as 25 percent to the cost of inventory. Added costs may include the cost of financing, seizing new opportunities, storage, insurance, shrinkage, and the obsolescence of products or materials.

- **Financing cost**: the cost of the interest you pay to borrow money to **purchase** inventory.
- **Opportunity cost**: the cost associated with giving up the use of money tied up in inventory.
- **Storage cost**: the cost associated with renting or buying the space needed to store the inventory.
- **Insurance cost**: the cost associated with insuring the inventory.
- **Shrinkage cost**: the cost associated with the loss of inventory items that are broken, damaged, spoiled, or stolen.
- **Obsolescence cost**: the cost associated with products or materials that become obsolete while in inventory.

Unfortunately, it is difficult to determine and maintain an ideal inventory level. Inventories constantly change, and the "right" amount of inventory shifts with changes in demand and season. However, by adopting sound inventory procedures, you can strike a profitable balance between too much and too little. Careful planning enables you to establish realistic inventory levels. Once you settle on these levels, you need to implement additional procedures to maintain them.

These procedures should be designed to help you do three things:

1. They help you keep track of inventory.
2. They result in cost-effective storage.
3. They allow you to reorder the right amounts, keeping the levels where you want them.

Planning Inventory

Planning inventories to achieve a balance between too much and too little requires that you answer two questions:

- How many months' supply should be on hand?
- How much of an investment would that represent?

Web Savvy

Fulfillment Services

Before you can sell a product online, you must decide where that product will be warehoused and who will ship it. Many online retailers use a fulfillment service, a company that stocks all the products and ships them every time an order is placed. As a result, the e-tailer does not have to maintain its own warehouse full of products, and can focus its money and efforts on marketing and growing the business.

What are the some potential benefits and drawbacks of using a fulfillment service?

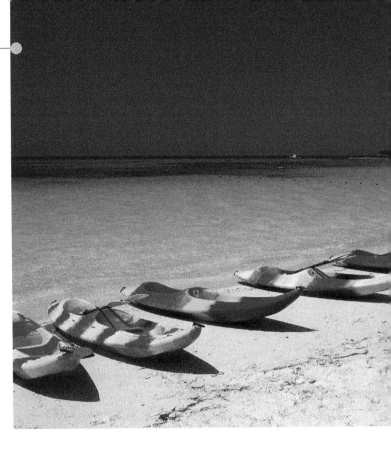

Lightly Seasoned Certain businesses are seasonal or sell seasonal items. *How can a business adjust its purchasing strategy for the off-season?*

Calculating the Supply You Need

Determining the amount of inventory you need is a two-step process. First, you must determine the inventory, or stock, turnover rate for your business.

This is the average number of times the inventory is sold out during a time period such as a year. Once you know the turnover rate, you can find the number of months' supply to keep.

You can calculate inventory turnover rate for your business in several different ways. The one you decide to use depends on the information you have available and your type of business. Stores that keep records of the retail dollar value of their stock use this **method**.

$$\frac{\text{NET SALES (IN RETAIL DOLLARS)}}{\text{AVERAGE INVENTORY ON HAND (IN RETAIL DOLLARS)}}$$

Average inventory on hand is the total of the inventory amounts for each month divided by the time period. Net sales are retail sales minus returns and allowances.

For example, if the total inventory for a 12-month period was valued at $870,000, the average inventory would be $72,500. If the net sales during that time period were $344,000, the inventory turnover rate would be 4.74.

$$\frac{\$870,000}{12} = 72,500 \qquad \frac{\$344,000}{\$72,500} = 4.74$$

This calculation shows that, on average, the inventory was sold and replaced 4.74 times in a 12-month period.

You can use a second calculation to determine inventory turnover rate when you have only cost information. The formula for that method is as follows:

$$\frac{\text{COST OF GOODS SOLD}}{\text{AVERAGE INVENTORY ON HAND (AT COST)}}$$

You can calculate average inventory on hand (at cost or retail) even if you do not have monthly inventory figures. Simply add the beginning and ending inventories for the period and divide by two.

● **As You Read** ▪▪▪▪▪▪▪

Calculate How can you calculate inventory on hand if you do not have monthly inventory figures?

Purestock/Superstock

Using Industry Averages

Another option is to use the industry average turnover rate for your type of business. For example, men's clothing stores have an average inventory turnover rate of 3, whereas restaurants have an average inventory turnover rate 22. Some chemical manufacturers' rates are as high as 100. To identify the average turnover rate for your type of business, contact trade associations in your field.

In some situations, you may want to calculate unit inventory turnover rather than dollar inventory turnover. To do this, use this formula:

$$\frac{\textbf{NUMBER OF UNITS SOLD}}{\textbf{AVERAGE INVENTORY ON HAND IN UNITS}}$$

Once you know your inventory turnover rate, you can determine how many months' supply you should have on hand. To do this, simply divide the number of months in a year by your average turnover rate.

If, for example, your average inventory turnover rate was 4, the calculation would be:

$$\frac{12}{4} = \textbf{3 MONTHS' SUPPLY}$$

Apply the calculation to the retail example with an average of 4.74. The retailer would need 2.53 (about 2½) month's supply. Applied to the restaurant average of 22, restaurants would need 0.54 (about ½) month's supply. Obviously, businesses that depend on a constant supply of fresh inventory must reorder frequently.

Calculating Your Inventory Investment

You know how to estimate the amount of inventory to keep on hand. Now you need to figure out how much it will cost you. To do this, divide the cost of goods sold for your forecasted annual sales by your average inventory turnover rate.

For example, suppose you forecast sales for the coming year to be $100,000. Your cost of goods sold is 75 percent of sales. If you have an average inventory turnover rate of 4, you can determine your inventory investment as follows:

$$\$100,000 \times \frac{0.75}{4} = \frac{\$75,000}{4} = \$18,750$$

For this situation, you should keep three months of inventory on hand at a cost of $18,750.

This example suggests that one set of calculations applies to the entire inventory. In many businesses, you must make calculations for different product lines or types of materials. Socks, for example, have a higher turnover rate than raincoats. Each type of product or material may require separate calculations.

Comparing with Industry Averages

The average inventory turnover rate for your industry can help you gauge your inventory management. Compare the number of turnovers you have in a year to the industry average. Of course, you want to try to turn your inventory over quickly. However, if you are far ahead of the industry average, your prices may be too low. It may also mean you are not able to meet customer needs because you run out of inventory. A lower-than-industry average may indicate that your inventory is tied up in slow-moving merchandise or material.

> ✔ **Reading Check** **Recall** What is an inventory turnover rate?

Inventory Control

Keeping tabs on how much inventory you have in stock is the first step in controlling inventory levels. With a young business, you may be able to track inventory by looking at what you have. As your business grows, however, you will probably have to switch to one of the more structured inventory control systems. As a cross-check against any of those systems, you will also need to do a physical inventory count. Four of the structured systems used to keep track of inventories are described below.

1. **Visual Inventory System** A small produce store might use this simple and quick visual inspection system: You look at how much inventory you have in stock and compare it to what you want to have on hand. This system usually works best where sales are steady, inventory is handled personally, and items can be obtained quickly.

2. **Perpetual Inventory System** As inventory is sold, it is subtracted from the inventory list. As new inventory arrives, it is added. Computerized cash registers allow retail businesses to use this accurate and instantaneous system, which is also popular with warehouses and storage facilities.

3. **Partial Inventory System** The partial inventory control system is a combination of systems. In this system, a perpetual inventory is maintained for only those items that account for a large share of the company's sales.

4. **Just-in-time (JIT) Inventory System** The JIT system shifts most of the inventory chores to the vendor. By having suppliers deliver inventory just before it is used, stocks are kept at a minimum. For many manufacturers, this provides a very effective control.

Knit One, Purl Two A small yarn shop might use color coding system to track inventory. *Which inventory system might you use in your business?*

Physical Inventory Count

No matter which inventory control system you use, you should conduct periodic physical inventory counts. Errors can occur when making visual estimates or when recording changes in inventory. Items can be removed from stock and not recorded. Merchandise or materials can be lost, be stolen, or go bad. Taking physical inventory gets your books in line with what you actually have in stock.

Taking a physical count also helps you evaluate your inventory control system. If, for example, your physical count is very different from your perpetual count, your perpetual system is not very accurate.

Physical inventory counts usually involve two employees. One counts and calls out the item and number. The other records the count on a tally sheet.

Frequency

Physical counts can be done often (for example, when a JIT system is used) or as infrequently as once a year. If you plan to take a physical inventory count every year, you can keep your counting costs down by getting your inventories as low as possible before the inventory count. In retail, this is often done through special year-end sales.

Warehousing

Warehousing is the act of holding and handling goods in a warehouse. The warehouse is where purchasing and inventory planning are put into effect. The warehouse can be an actual structure or an assigned space. When you plan your warehouse operations, plan the following areas:

- **Receiving and shipping docks** Vendors and transportation companies need easy access to and within your facility. To make sure things are running smoothly, you should keep their physical paths to you as clear as possible.
- **Bulk storage areas** These are places where goods remain in their original crates, waiting to be broken down into more usable quantities.
- **Staging areas** This is free space where inbound or outbound materials are sorted, organized, or temporarily stored. A staging area can help to organize your entire warehouse.
- **Picking rows** These are rows of small and large inventoried goods that may be placed in bins or on pallets. Here they can be gathered as needed for assembly and packing.
- **Assembly areas** Here, goods are assembled individually or as kits.
- **Packing areas** Boxing takes place in packing areas. Also, individual products ready for the consumer may need to be repacked in bulk units for shipping.
- **Management office and lockers** Your employees need space to work and to keep their personal belongings.

Too Much Stuff? Move It Out!

Don't let excessive inventory drag your business down. Get creative and sell

You've got a bulging warehouse with too much inventory. How can you turn this negative into a positive?

First, count the inventory so you know how much product you have. Second, be realistic about the product's market value. Third, turn that overstuffed warehouse into cash. Here's how:

- Reposition your product with new photographs and advertising copy to give your buyers a fresh look and add to your sales.
- Update keywords and phrases when selling on the Web. Use search tools to find the keywords your customers use when looking for your type of product.
- Hold a promotional event. Cut the price of your product and time it with a calendar event—like a sweater sale or back-to-school backpack special in fall.
- Put your product on sale for a specific time such as a week or a day. Make sure you let your customer base know about the sale.

Experts recommend turning inventory every 90 to 120 days. To keep cash flowing in, businesses have to keep products moving out.

Active Learning

With a classmate, create a promotional sale to clear out an overstuffed warehouse. Decide what is in your warehouse, then create a promotion timed to a calendar event, such as the New Year or the beginning of summer. Make a list of tactics to promote the product and then create one of the following: a print ad, a social media campaign, or an email blast. Share your project with the class.

Reordering

To maintain proper inventory levels, you need to decide when and how much to reorder. The type of inventory you keep determines which reordering system is best for you.

Periodic Reordering

Products or raw materials that are inexpensive should be reordered periodically. You should also periodically reorder any products or raw materials that are used often or are easy to get. They should be automatically reordered to keep inventory at the proper level.

For example, a manufacturer who uses nuts and bolts might restock such hardware every 60 days. A restaurateur that specializes in French bread and other pastries might restock baked goods daily.

Nonperiodic Reordering

Inventory that is not suited to periodic reordering must be reordered in another way. Three key questions must be considered:

1. What is the lead time? **Lead time** is the gap in time between placing an order and receiving delivery.
2. What is the usage rate? **Usage rate** is how quickly the inventory will be used in a given period of time.
3. How much safety stock will be needed? **Safety stock** is a cushion of products or materials. It keeps you from running out of inventory while you are waiting for an order.

Reordering Procedures

No matter what method of reordering is used, an entrepreneur should approach the matter systematically. Inventory should be planned, ordered, and reordered in accordance with the plan. Entrepreneurs should also check to see how well the plan has worked and make any necessary adjustments.

SECTION 15.2 | Review

After You Read ▪▪▪▪▪▪▪▪▪▪▪▪▪

Self-Check

1. **Explain** how you can calculate the average inventory on hand if you do not have monthly inventory figures.
2. **Determine** which inventory system would work best for you if you were to run a small mailbox rental business.
3. **Generate** some plans you could put in place to keep your inventory from shrinking.

Think

4. **Produce** a warehouse floor plan for a business that sells hair care products by mail order and write an explanation of how it meets the business's needs.

Mathematics

5. **Turnover Rates** The industry where you work has a turnover rate of 9. The company you work for is forecasting sales of $85,000 next year. If the annual cost of goods sold is 55% of sales, what is the cost for inventory and how many months' supply should be kept on hand?

(**Math Concept**) **Number and Operations** Writing an equation can help you keep track of what operations to use when solving a multi-step problem.

Step 1 Write an equation to determine the number of months of inventory that should be kept on hand.

Step 2 Divide the cost of goods sold by the average inventory turnover rate to determine the cost of keeping the inventory.

(➤) Go to connectED.mcgraw-hill.com to check your answers.

Entrepreneurs *in Action*

Todd Brown
Founder and CEO
180 Medical

Q *What do you do?*

A I am the owner and CEO of 180 Medical, a medical supply distributor. Our primary business is catheter supplies. We're one of the largest urology suppliers in the country. We also distribute power and high-end wheelchairs. We distribute supplies directly to patients' homes, so they don't have to go to the pharmacy.

Q *What kind of training and education prepared you for this job?*

A I have a bachelor's degree in Business Management and a minor in Finance. I owned my first business—some sandwich shops—when I was in college.

Q *What do you enjoy most about your job?*

A I like being my own boss, the freedom and flexibility that come with that. I also like hiring highly-qualified people and giving them the freedom and flexibility to do their jobs well. I tell people to do something you're passionate about. You've found the right job when you don't consider it a job.

Q *How did you become interested in your field?*

A I suffered a spinal cord injury in 1994 and have been in a wheelchair since then. My first wheelchair didn't fit through my front door. So, basically, the medical supply business started because I saw a need for myself. Then doctors started using me as a referral. Other patients were having similar problems and it helped to speak to someone who was an end user and knew the supplies.

CCR ☆ **College & Career Readiness**

On the List A grocery list is an everyday form of purchase planning.

1. Think about grocery lists you or your relatives have made.
2. Recall how you or your relatives selected items for your grocery list.
3. How can you use the purchase-planning methods from this chapter to write a better grocery list? Write your answer in a one-page report.

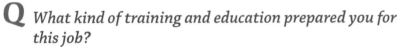

Career Facts

Real-World Skills	Academic Skills	Career Cluster
Networking, Customer Service, Motivation Skills	English Language Arts, Health, Mathematics	Health Science; Transportation, Distribution & Logistics

Todd Brown

Review and Assessment

Visual Summary

Managing Purchasing and Inventory

Purchasing Goals Planning purchases requires answering critical questions about inventory needs before committing financial resources.

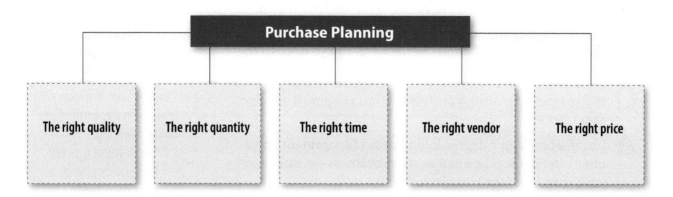

Purchase Planning				
The right quality	The right quantity	The right time	The right vendor	The right price

Inventory Systems Maintain manageable inventory levels.

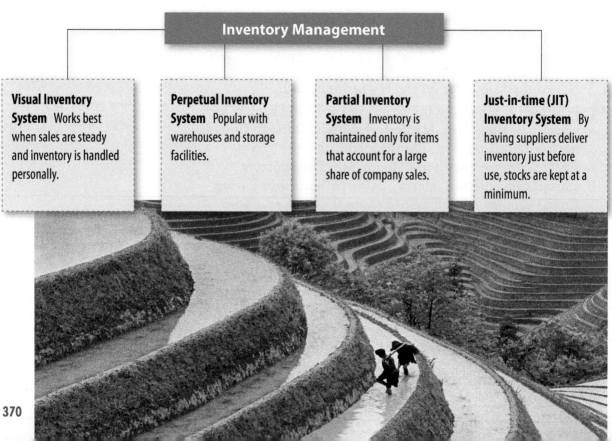

Inventory Management			
Visual Inventory System Works best when sales are steady and inventory is handled personally.	**Perpetual Inventory System** Popular with warehouses and storage facilities.	**Partial Inventory System** Inventory is maintained only for items that account for a large share of company sales.	**Just-in-time (JIT) Inventory System** By having suppliers deliver inventory just before use, stocks are kept at a minimum.

BambooSIL/SuperStock

Review and Assessment

Vocabulary

1. On a sheet of paper, use each of these terms and words in a written sentence.

Content Vocabulary

◇ purchasing
◇ model inventory
◇ vendors
◇ trade discount
◇ quantity discount
◇ cash discount
◇ secured funds
◇ invoice

◇ financing cost
◇ opportunity cost
◇ storage cost
◇ insurance cost
◇ shrinkage cost
◇ obsolescence cost
◇ warehousing
◇ lead time

◇ usage rate
◇ safety stock

Academic Vocabulary

■ minimum
■ relationship
■ purchase
■ method

Key Concepts

2. **Describe** the importance of planning purchases.
3. **Define** inventory.
4. **Examine** inventory procedures used by small businesses.
5. **Explain** the importance and types of inventory control.
6. **Compare** the advantages and disadvantages of buying from just one vendor.
7. **Identify** factors that can increase the cost of carrying too much inventory.
8. **List** the types of inventory control systems available for keeping track of your inventory.
9. **Define** warehousing.

Academic Skills

Mathematics

10. **Inventory Pricing** Meredith Pierce is in charge of purchasing for Fortner Sporting Goods. Last year's inventory cost the store $75,500. The list price of the inventory was $94,375. What was the discount that Meredith received?

    Math Concept **Percents** To convert a decimal to a percent, multiply the decimal by 100.
    Step 1 Divide the cost of the inventory by the list price to determine the percentage, or part, of the list price that the inventory cost.
    Step 2 Subtract the percent from 1.00 to determine the discount received.

English Language Arts

11. **Write a Memo** You and a friend work as shipping and receiving clerks in a warehouse. You have noticed that there are no procedures for receiving inventory when it arrives. Discuss with a partner the procedures you think should be in place. Together, write a memo to the warehouse manager recommending a set of procedures for managing inventory when it is received.

Academic Skills (continued)

Social Studies

12. Transportation History Today, small packages are often shipped by the U.S. Postal Service or FedEx on one day and are delivered the next. In the mid-nineteenth century, such swift service was not possible. Research the history of the U. S. Postal Service and the Pony Express. Write a paragraph explaining how a small package was shipped to the west coast of North America at that time.

Science

13. Just-in-Time Just-in-Time (JIT) inventory is an important technological innovation that has revolutionized how factories work. It has made businesses more efficient and brought down the cost of manufacturing goods. Research the history of JIT inventory and Lean Manufacturing. Write a paragraph or two about how and when it was developed and the effect it has had.

Real-World Skills

Forecasting Skills

14. A Jump in Inventory You run an e-commerce site that only sells one product: what you call the world's best pogo stick! In a one-page report, explain the criteria you should use to determine how many pogo sticks you should have in your inventory.

21st Century Skills

Negotiation Skills

15. Request for Proposal You're opening a high-end coffee shop and you need to find a supplier to provide and install a top-of-the-line espresso machine. You will get the best price by soliciting competitive bids. Write a request for proposal (RFP) to prospective suppliers.

Connect to Your Community

16. Select a Vendor Investigate the possibility of choosing a product line to sell in a business. Talk with at least three local vendors. Evaluate them based on reliability, distance, and service. Ask them about payment methods and discounts. Based on the information you obtain, select the vendor or vendors for your business. Explain your decision.

17. Purchasing and Inventory Interview a manager of a local business regarding purchasing and inventory procedures. Ask about the handling or prevention of common purchasing and inventory problems. Compile the results and report your findings to the class.

Competitive Events Prep

18. **Situation** You are the owner of a family clothing store located in the upper Midwest. One of the store's best selling items is cotton turtlenecks. The cotton turtlenecks sell well in all departments—men's, women's, and children's. For many seasons, you have used one vendor. Unfortunately, the vendor can no longer supply seasonal fashion colors, but can still supply the basic colors. Your buyer has asked for your advice in finding a vendor to supply the fashion color turtlenecks in a comparable quality and price.

Activity Explain to the buyer some of the factors to consider when selecting a new vendor for the turtlenecks.

Evaluation You will be evaluated on how well you meet these performance indicators:

- Conduct vendor searches.
- Describe the nature of buyer reputation and vendor relationships.
- Explain company buying/purchasing policies.
- Negotiate contracts with vendors.
- Explain the buying process.

 Go to connectED.mcgraw-hill.com for more information about this activity and other competitive events.

Standardized Test Practice

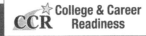 CCR ★ College & Career Readiness

Directions Choose the letter of the best answer. Write the letter for the answer on a separate piece of paper. For question #2, if the answer is False, rewrite the statement to make it true.

1. What kind of costs are associated with giving up the use of money tied up in inventory?
   A. Obsolescence costs
   B. Shrinkage costs
   C. Insurance costs
   D. Opportunity costs

2. A trade discount is a discount that a vendor gives to a buyer who places large orders.
   T
   F

> **Test-Taking Tip**
> Test anxiety can lower your test score. Talk with your family, teachers, and counselors about ways to manage and reduce test stress.

Production Management and Distribution

Chapter Objectives

SECTION 16.1
From Idea to Product

Discuss how entrepreneurs develop new products.

Explain the product development process.

SECTION 16.2
Production and Distribution

Explain what is involved in production management.

Describe the activities that are part of distribution management.

Discovery Project
Ensuring Quality Products

Key Question *How do business owners ensure the quality of their products?*

Project Goal
Choose a product with which you are familiar. It can be an electronic device, a clothing item, a type of food, or other type of product. Imagine that you are in charge of quality control for this product. Determine how you would ensure quality and produce a plan that describes your quality control strategies.

Think About...
➤ What product will you choose?
➤ What will you check to ensure the quality of the product?
➤ How will you present your quality control plan?

21st Century Skills
Business Literacy *How do quality standards reflect a business's target market?*

Evaluate
 Go to connectED.mcgraw-hill.com to download a rubric that you can use to evaluate your final project.

Q: *I am evaluating all of my assets to find sources for capital to start a production company. What are examples of liquid assets and fixed assets? Is one easier to sell than the other?*

A: Liquid assets are accounts or securities that can easily be converted to cash at little or no loss of value. These include money in bank accounts, money market mutual funds, and U.S. Treasury bills. Actively traded stocks and bonds are liquid assets in the sense that they are easy to sell, but the price is not guaranteed. Selling fixed assets, such as real estate or equipment, requires more time and negotiation.

Connect the Photo

Your Order Has Been Shipped Production and distribution are two ways entrepreneurs introduce their products to the market. By the time the product is ready for shipping, it's been through a long and rigorous cycle of product development and quality control based on customer feedback. *Why are transportation, shipping, and delivery planning so important to businesses?*

Comstock Images / Alamy

From Idea to Product

Reading Guide

Before You Read ▪▪▪▪▪▪▪▪▪▪▪▪▪▪▪

Connect In what ways do entrepreneurs develop products differently from large companies?

The Main Idea

Entrepreneurs work with limited resources, so they must find creative ways to develop and manufacture their products. Product development is a long process based on feedback from customers who test the product.

Objectives

Discuss how entrepreneurs develop new products.

Explain the product development process.

Content Vocabulary

◇ product development
◇ prototype

Academic Vocabulary

You will see these words in your reading and on your tests. Use the academic vocabulary glossary to look up their meanings.

■ automate
■ complex

Graphic Organizer

Draw a chart like the one shown. As you read, write the four steps of product development.

 Go to connectED.mcgraw-hill.com to download this graphic organizer.

The Four Steps of Product Development

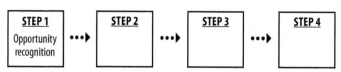

| STEP 1 Opportunity recognition | ••▶ | STEP 2 | ••▶ | STEP 3 | ••▶ | STEP 4 |

Product Development for Entrepreneurs

The transformation from idea to marketable product is a lengthy process. In this section, you will learn how entrepreneurs develop new products with limited resources.

What Is Product Development?

Product development is the process of creating new or improved products. It involves taking an idea for a product, designing it, building a model, and testing it. Most large companies with big budgets have research and development departments that develop new products. They can afford to make mistakes and still succeed. The same cannot be said for small business owners with limited resources.

Some consider the product development phase to be the riskiest part of start-up. Consequently, an entrepreneur may have difficulty raising money to develop a new product. However, through creative thinking, many entrepreneurs find the funds they need.

Outsourcing Product Development

To reduce the costs of product development, you can use outsourcing. In other words, you can hire people or companies to handle tasks that you cannot do or choose not to do. Outsourcing can provide your new venture with a network of for-hire experts.

Gregg Levin, for example, developed the PerfectCurve®, a product that prevents baseball caps from losing the curve on the brim after washing. However, Levin did not have the knowledge, ability, or money to set up a complete manufacturing facility. So he outsourced it. He hired a plastics manufacturer to make the product. Then he had the finished product sent to a Boston rehabilitation program site. There, people with disabilities assembled and packaged it.

When outsourcing product development tasks, draw up contracts with all companies with which you do business. This will prevent misunderstandings about schedules, expectations, and tasks. Some of the areas of product development that can be outsourced include:

- component design
- materials specifications
- machinery to process
- ergonomic design
- packaging design
- assembly drawings and specifications
- user guides and owner manuals

When your company begins to earn a healthy profit, you can bring certain product development tasks in-house. You can even make some tasks **automated**. Doing so allows you to better control quality and speed of production.

 Reading Check **Inference** Why do some people say product development is risky?

Developing Green Products

Eco-Products started out as a distributor of earth-friendly products. In 2005, the Boulder, Colorado-based company began manufacturing its own products. Using a technology that replaced petroleum-based plastic with "corn plastic" and styrofoam with sugarcane, the company now creates products such as cups, food containers, cutlery, and plates and bowls that are compostable and made from renewable resources.

◈ **Critical Thinking**
Do you have an idea for a green product that would replace something that is not environmentally friendly? Write a paragraph identifying the product and how it would improve upon the current product.

Design for the Masses
method outsourced the packaging design for one of its first products to Karim Rashid, a famous product designer. *What are some other aspects of product development that can be outsourced?*

The Product Development Process

Product development for entrepreneurs is not a linear process. Although it appears to move forward in a step-by-step manner, it is actually a very **complex** process. An entrepreneur may start developing a product, but along the way, he or she may discover something new that changes the direction of development.

For example, suppose you are developing a new video game for children aged 6 to 10. Once you have a prototype, you decide to hold a focus group to see how children respond. Their comments and your observations send you back to the drawing board to do some redesign work. This process may repeat itself several times before you achieve the final product.

The four steps of product development are:

1. **Opportunity recognition** Entrepreneurs are opportunity seekers. For example, the inventor of Nerf® foam toys knew parents wanted toys that children could throw indoors without damaging furniture.
2. **Concept investigation** Study the market to make certain there is sufficient demand.
3. **Product design** Design the product on paper or on a computer. Make sure the needs and wants of potential customers are incorporated. Also include input from the people involved in marketing, producing, and financing the product.
4. **Prototype building and testing** A **prototype** is a working model of a product. Often you cannot gauge a product until you actually see, use, and handle it. Test the prototype or working model with actual customers.

● As You Read ▪▪▪

Interpret Once you build a prototype, with whom should you test it?

William Andrew/Getty Images

Designing It Right the First Time

You should design your product right the first time. Three good reasons for doing so are:

1. **The cost of design** Starting over or redesigning costs more than the original work. In addition, delays caused by redesigning could cause you to miss a window of opportunity in a dynamic market.

2. **The quality and marketability of the product** How carefully you design your product determines quality, reliability, and success in the market. Getting customer input at the early stages of design helps ensure a successful launch.

3. **The time to launch** If you design your product properly, you will not have to go back and make changes. Besides adding to production costs, making changes increases the time needed to release the final product. In that lost time, customer needs may have changed.

Building a Prototype

The first prototype you build may not look like the final product. However, it should work like the final product. Gregg Levin built several prototypes of the PerfectCurve. He used clay, wood, and other materials before making a final decision. Throughout the process, he fine-tuned the product. With the working prototype, he received better customer input because they could actually see and use the product.

SECTION 16.1 | Review

After You Read ■■■■■■■■■■■■■

Self-Check

1. **Identify** product development tasks that entrepreneurs can outsource.
2. **List** the basic steps in the product development process.
3. **Explain** why product design is so important.

Think

4. **Determine** the steps an entrepreneur took to move from idea to physical product by interviewing a local business owner.

English Language Arts/Writing

5. **Compound Words** A compound word is one that contains two words put together to create a new word with a meaning that is different from either of the smaller words that make it up. Look at the following words and identify the three words that are compounds; use each in a sentence: *outsourcing, prototype, warehouse, design, baseball,* and *budget*.

 Go to **connectED.mcgraw-hill.com** to check your answers.

Production and Distribution

Reading Guide

Before You Read ■■■■■■■■■■■■■■■

Connect What do you need to know about managing the production of your product?

The Main Idea

Coming up with an idea for a product or service is only a small part of creating a successful business—you have to turn that idea into reality. Production and distribution are two ways entrepreneurs bring new products to market.

Objectives

Explain what is involved in production management.

Describe the activities that are part of distribution management.

Content Vocabulary

◇ Gantt chart
◇ PERT diagram
◇ quality control
◇ quality circle
◇ productivity
◇ automation

◇ logistics
◇ common carrier
◇ contract carrier
◇ private carrier
◇ freight on board
  (FOB)

Academic Vocabulary

You will see these words in your reading and on your tests. Use the academic vocabulary glossary to look up their meanings.

■ vehicle   ■ component

Graphic Organizer

Draw a chart like the one shown. As you read, write the four steps of product development.

 Go to connectED.mcgraw-hill.com to download this graphic organizer

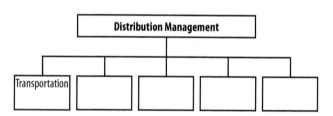

In Production Both small and major auto companies have electric cars, plug-in hybrids, and other innovative new cars in production. *What is a disadvantage of outsourcing the production of your product?*

Idealink Photography/Alamy

Production Management

Once you have developed a prototype, you are ready to plan production. Outsourcing enables a new company to manufacture a product without having to invest in workplace costs. However, you have less control over the quality of the product and the speed of the process.

The principles of production management are the same for all types of businesses. Production management has three functions: acquiring the resources needed to create a product, planning how to convert those resources into products, and making sure the products meet the standards set for them.

Scheduling

Businesses plan their production by making schedules. These schedules describe each activity that must be completed to produce goods or services. Schedules include estimates of the amount of time each activity will take to complete, including activities that are critical to the completion of the project. There are two widely used graphic scheduling techniques: Gantt charts and PERT diagrams.

As You Read ■■■

List What are the basic principles of production management that apply to all types of businesses?

Gantt Charts

A **Gantt chart** is a graphic schedule of a project's phases, activities, and tasks plotted against a timeline. A Gantt chart is an effective way to depict basic information about a project. Using a Gantt chart can help you to keep track of tasks and manage the dependencies among tasks. Tasks are listed on the vertical axis. The time required for each task is shown on the horizontal axis. In **Figure 16. 1**, individual orders (tasks) are listed vertically. Solid bars span the period over which each order is scheduled to be produced. Broken bars indicate actual production activity.

Gantt charts are simple and helpful. They force you to think through the steps of a job. You must estimate the time needed for each part of production. They also let you track actual progress against planned activities once the project is under way. You can immediately see what should have been achieved at a point in time. They enable you to see how remedial action may bring the project back on course. They are also used to show the beginning and ending dates of several projects going on simultaneously. Gantt charts may be simple versions created on graph paper or more complex automated versions created using project management software applications.

● **Figure 16.1** Gantt Chart

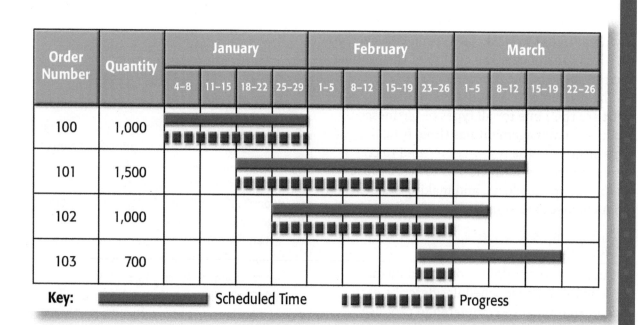

Order Number	Quantity	January				February				March			
		4–8	11–15	18–22	25–29	1–5	8–12	15–19	23–26	1–5	8–12	15–19	22–26
100	1,000												
101	1,500												
102	1,000												
103	700												

Key: ▬▬▬▬▬ Scheduled Time   ▪▪▪▪▪▪▪▪▪ Progress

● **Project Tracking Tool** Gantt charts make it easy to compare planned work (solid lines) with actual progress (broken lines). For example, if you were looking at this chart on February 26, Order 100 would be completed, and Order 102 would be 5/6 completed and on schedule. *Where would Orders 101 and 103 be?*

PERT Diagram

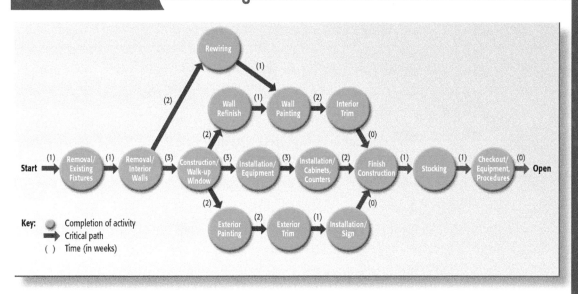

Key:
- ● Completion of activity
- ➤ Critical path
- ( ) Time (in weeks)

Scheduling Tool This PERT diagram lays out the process of remodeling a building for use as a food carry-out business. *What is the least amount of time required for completion of the project?*

PERT Diagrams

PERT stands for Program Evaluation and Review Technique. A **PERT diagram** is a project schedule that is arranged in a diagram. PERT diagrams are useful for scheduling more complex projects.

To use the PERT technique, identify the project's major activities. Then arrange the activities on the diagram in order. Connect with arrows those activities that must occur in a fixed sequence. Finally, estimate and indicate how much time is needed to complete each activity. An example of PERT scheduling is illustrated in **Figure 16.2**.

The longest path through the diagram is called the critical path. Activities on this path dictate the length of time needed to complete the project. By completing these activities on schedule, you can control the length of the project.

Controlling Quality

Quality control is the process of making sure the goods or services you produce meet certain standards. Standards can be set for appearance, performance, and consistency. In a frozen yogurt shop, customers expect the same quality and quantity every time they buy a cup or a cone.

The standards you set for your business reflect the market segment you are targeting. Customers who want high quality will pay more for it. Customers who want low prices will expect reasonable, but not particularly high, quality.

Quality control takes time and costs money, but it is a way to ensure customer satisfaction. How do you achieve quality control? Two common ways are quality circles and inspection.

Quality Circles

A **quality circle** is a small group of employees who do similar jobs and meet regularly to identify ways to improve the quality of what they do. They ultimately improve quality. This approach has been used successfully by large manufacturers such as Ford. However, the concept also works for small operations. Quality circles improve quality because they require employees to be responsible for their work. They give employees the power to make decisions about quality. For example, employees can stop production to correct defects before a product is completed. Quality circles are also a way to motivate employees. They give employees a vested interest in the success of the company.

Inspection

Inspection is one way to control quality. If you use inspections, you must decide whether to perform them during or after the job. When you inspect your product depends on what you are selling.

If you manufacture complex equipment, you will probably inspect your product at several stages during production. That way, defects are caught and corrected before they end up in the final product. This approach saves time and money. If you provide a service such as dry cleaning, however, a final inspection is more appropriate. There are no points in the process where you could inspect the work.

You must also decide whether to inspect every product or just a sample of the product. When making this decision, cost is the determining factor. Any product that is used up when it is tested is normally sampled randomly for quality.

Managing Other Areas of Production

Productivity, automation, and preventive maintenance are additional areas of production that should be managed effectively. These areas are important to all types of businesses.

ETHICS and BUSINESS

Keeping High Standards

Situation You have been in quality control for your entire career and have worked for many high-profile businesses, helping to assure that their products are of the highest quality. You currently work as quality control manager at a toy manufacturing plant.

Reporting a Problem You have become aware of a design flaw in a toy for children ages 6 months to 1 year. One of the small parts will easily come loose creating a potential choking hazard. You immediately notify the manager of production and request that production be stopped.

English Language Arts/Writing

Doing What Is Right The production manager refuses to stop production because of the loss of business from orders that would not be filled and the cost of stopping his workers. Is his response ethical?

1. Why is the production manager's response both unethical and illogical?
2. Write a one-page report explaining your reasoning.

GLOBAL WORKPLACE

Polish: Language of Consonance

Apart from Russian, Polish has the largest number of speakers of any Slavic language. Polish is the official language of Poland and a minority language in countries such as the Czech Republic, Belarus, Lithuania, Russia, and France. The United States, with its history of immigration, also hosts large pockets of Polish speakers in Illinois, New York, and New Jersey. Though Polish uses the same Latin alphabet as English, non-speakers will notice the use of diacritical marks (accents) and the high ratio of consonants to vowels, as in *trzy*, Polish for "three."

Eye Contact The Polish appreciate direct eye contact. Looking people in the eye, they believe, reflects the speaker's integrity and honesty.

Science Since antiquity, Poland has been famous for its amber. Large deposits were mined and sold along the Amber Route from the Baltic Sea to the Adriatic Ocean. Research the origins of amber and some of the products that make use of its materials. Summarize your research in a one-page report.

Common Polish Words and Phrases	
Hello	witaj
Goodbye	do widzenia
Yes/ No	tak/nie
Please	proszę
Thank you	dziękuję
You're welcome	nie ma za co

Productivity

Productivity is a measure of how much a business produces in a given time. It also can be expressed in terms of the output of each worker per unit of time. Productivity ensures a strong economy by slowing inflation and creating greater profits, greater product demand, higher wages, low interest rates, and more jobs.

Businesses can use productivity rates to measure and improve employee performance. Machinists at a tool factory might have an average productivity rate of 35 units per day. A worker who produces only 25 units a day is not very productive and may even hurt the business. Owners must find workers who contribute to increased sales by working productively.

Automation

Automation is the use of machines to do the work of people. Automation can cut production time, reduce errors, and simplify procedures. However, it also can be expensive. Manufacturing and clerical tasks often lend themselves to automation. New ventures that perform these tasks need to budget for technology to automate their systems. This ensures that they stay competitive by reducing time to market.

Transportation Instead of outsourcing distribution of your products, you can handle it yourself. *What is one advantage of moving and selling your products yourself?*

Maintenance

Maintenance of machinery is a key factor in production management. There are three basic ways to manage maintenance:

1. **Organize your production process.** Arrange it so that when one machine is down, the work can be shifted to other working machines.
2. **Build up inventories at each stage of the production process.** That way, other machines can continue to run while you are repairing a faulty machine.
3. **Conduct preventive maintenance.** Fix machines before they break down and check regularly for possible failure points.

> ✓ **Reading Check Recall** What is quality control?

Distribution Management

Distribution management includes transportation, shipping and receiving, storage and warehousing, materials handling, and specification of delivery terms. It controls the movement of a product from the manufacturer to customers.

Transportation

Part of distribution management is **logistics**, the planning, execution, and control of the movement and placement of people and/or goods. Logistics involves figuring out how to move a product from the producer to the customer. Shipping a product by plane, truck, railroad, pipeline, or waterway is regulated by federal and state agencies.

Transporters are classified into three categories. A **common carrier** is a firm that provides transportation services at uniform rates to the general public. FedEx and UPS are both examples of common carriers. A railroad is an example of a contract carrier. A **contract carrier** is a shipping company that transports freight under contract with one or more shippers. A **private carrier** is a business that operates its own **vehicles** for the purpose of transporting its own products and materials.

You can handle the logistics yourself or outsource it. To decide, ask yourself three questions:

1. Is your competition using transportation as a competitive advantage?
2. Are you seeking markets in other countries?
3. Are you having problems with shipments you are handling yourself?

If you answer "yes" to any of these questions, you may need assistance from a logistics firm.

Tech Savvy

Cinema George

In 1977, George Lucas barnstormed theaters with the groundbreaking movie *Star Wars*. In 2002, Lucas struck back with *Attack of the Clones*, the first big-budget, high-profile movie shot in digital. The next push for movies is digital distribution. Digital distribution could save money. A single film print costs over $1,000; multiply that by several thousand movie theaters and it equals a lot of money. Digital "prints" can be saved to affordable discs or beamed directly to digital cinemas by satellite. *Why might a film distributor prefer to send films digitally?*

© David Schaffer/age fotostock

Shipping and Receiving

Shipping and receiving require sound procedures. You should prepare shipping documents and mailing labels carefully, and check for errors that could cause delays. You also need to record what has been taken from inventory so that you can replenish stock when inventories begin to run low.

With receiving, you should determine whether orders have been filled correctly by verifying incoming shipments against the original order and the invoice. Many receiving clerks use handheld scanners to record bar codes on incoming products. Shipments are checked for discrepancies in quantity, price, and discounts.

Storage and Warehousing

Some manufacturers have warehouses for storing inventory for sale. Entrepreneurs with limited resources might not be able to afford their own storage facilities. Instead, they may have a wholesaler store and distribute their products. They may also store goods in a public warehouse.

Business Case Study

Map Your Way to Success

Use a PERT chart to see where you're going and how to get there

Successful entrepreneurs are organized. They know where they're going, and they use the right project-management tools to help them get there. One such tool is called a PERT chart, short for Program Evaluation Review Technique. It is a diagram that helps to map the sequence of tasks within a project.

To make a PERT chart, follow these steps:

1. Make a list of tasks that must be included to complete a project, with the estimated completion time of each.
2. Sort the tasks according to what needs to be done first, second, and so on.
3. Number your tasks, starting with "1."
4. Create a series of milestones, such as deadlines by which work must be done.
5. Draw your diagram, with the tasks as arrows leading to milestones as circles. Draw arrows between tasks that are prerequisites for other tasks.

A PERT chart helps you visualize a project at a glance. It helps you see how tasks relate to add up to your final goal.

Active Learning

PERT charts are one of many project-management tools useful for entrepreneurs. Use the Web to research PERT charts and other project-management tools (paper or electronic). Pick one tool and use it to plan out the tasks and milestones involved in organizing a plant-a-garden day. Share your tool, and its pros and cons, with the class.

Materials Handling

There is more to distribution than transportation and storage. You also need to handle the products without damaging them. Materials handling includes dealing with shipping containers and forklifts. It also includes other aids that help you move product within your facility and out to the customer.

Delivery Terms

All shipments have delivery terms. Delivery terms identify who is responsible for the various **components** of distribution.

Free On Board

The most favorable delivery term for a small business owner is "free on board," or FOB. **Free on board (FOB)** is a delivery term that designates a shipment as delivered free of charge to a buyer. This means that the seller pays all freight costs. In addition, the title to the goods passes to the buyer when the goods leave the manufacturer. Once the goods leave the warehouse, the responsibility for costs and loss go to the buyer.

SECTION 16.2 | Review

After You Read ∎∎∎∎∎∎∎∎∎∎∎∎∎

Self-Check
1. **Compare** and contrast Gantt charts and PERT diagrams.
2. **Name** two ways to approach quality control.
3. **Identify** two ways to increase productivity in a business.

Think
4. **Determine** the best mode of transportation for a video game company that ships software from Atlanta, Georgia, to Singapore.

Mathematics
5. **Shipping Goods** Kara Sagatelian works for a company that uses contract carriers to ship its product. Kara scheduled a shipment of goods from Chicago, Illinois, to Denver, Colorado using the railroads. The distance between the cities is 917 miles. If the trip lasted 19.10 hours, what was the average speed of the train? Round the answer to the nearest whole number.

   Math Concept **Numbers and Operations** Writing a formula can help you determine how to solve a problem.

   Step 1 Write a formula that will show how to solve for the average speed.

   Step 2 Solve for the average speed.

Go to connectED.mcgraw-hill.com to check your answers.

Entrepreneurs *in Action*

April Pride Allison
Principal
KaarsKoker

Q *What do you do?*

A I am a home accessories product designer. I started as an interior designer, but I needed a better solution for lighting accessories for my clients, so I designed candle sleeves and a business was born.

Q *What kind of training and education helped you get this job?*

A My education in architecture and decorative arts plays a role in my design approach, grasp of proportions, and knowledge of materials. A comfort with math is also key because designs and packing require specific measurements.

Q *What do you enjoy most about your job?*

A My job involves every aspect of getting a product to market: design, project management, order fulfillment, sales, inventory control, marketing. Marketing a product is fascinating because the rules have changed. Traditional print and TV are being complemented with Internet tools such as blogs, which gives me, as a designer and business owner, greater freedom to share information about my product.

Q *How did you become interested in your field?*

A I was always a good student and tended to be better in math than other subjects. Also, I have always been creative. These two strengths made architecture a natural choice for school, but interior design was a better fit. Ultimately, product design has been the most interesting, because it touches on many skills I have developed over the years.

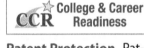

☆ **College & Career**
CCR **Readiness**

Patent Protection Patents do a lot to encourage innovation by providing legal protections to inventors.
1. Research the process of applying for a patent.
2. Should you get professional help to apply for a patent? How much does that cost?
3. Summarize your findings in a one-page report.

Career Facts

Real-World Skills	Academic Skills	Career Cluster
Creativity, Time Management, Communication	Mathematics, Fine Arts	Manufacturing

April Pride Allison

Review and Assessment

Visual Summary

Production Management and Distribution

Idea to Product Product development is considered the highest risk and the most costly part of start-up.

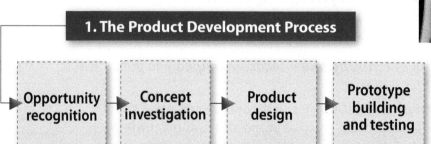

| 1. The Product Development Process |

Opportunity recognition → Concept investigation → Product design → Prototype building and testing

| 2. Production Management |

Step 1	**Acquire** the resources needed for production.
Step 2	**Plan** the steps to convert the resources into products.
Step 3	**Make** sure the products meet the standards set for them.

| 3. Distribution |

↓

| 4. The Customer |

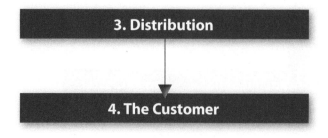

(t)William Andrew/Getty Images; (b)© David Schaffer/age fotostock

Review and Assessment

Vocabulary
1. On a sheet of paper, use each of these terms and words in a written sentence.

Content Vocabulary

◇ product development
◇ prototype
◇ Gantt chart
◇ PERT diagram
◇ quality control
◇ quality circle

◇ productivity
◇ automation
◇ logistics
◇ common carrier
◇ contract carrier
◇ private carrier
◇ freight on board (FOB)

Academic Vocabulary

■ automate
■ complex
■ vehicle
■ component

Key Concepts
2. **Discuss** how entrepreneurs develop new products.
3. **Explain** the product development process.
4. **Explain** what is involved in production management.
5. **Describe** the activities that are part of distribution management.
6. **Explain** why it is important to involve potential customers in the design prototype process.
7. **Compare and contrast** Gantt charts and PERT diagrams.
8. **Describe** how distribution can make or break a business.
9. **Explain** why quality control is important.

Academic Skills

Mathematics
10. **Product Design Costs** Vidski Athletics spent $123,500 developing a new style of baseball mitt. The design costs of the mitt were $89,750. What percent of the total development cost were the product design costs? Round the answer to nearest whole number percent.

   Math Concept **Rounding** For some problems, a rounded number makes more sense than a precise answer.
   Step 1 Divide the design cost by the total development cost.
   Step 2 Multiply the decimal by 100 to convert it to a percent.
   Step 3 Look at the digit in the place to the right of the place to which you are rounding. If it is 5 or greater, round up. If it is 4 or less, do not change it.

English Language Arts
11. **Gantt Charts** Your class is working in groups of four to produce research reports on the history of manufacturing. Each team member has a different job. One will research the 1800s; one will research the 20th century; one will combine the two reports and add an introduction and conclusion; one will edit and proofread. Create a Gantt chart to show how this report might be completed over a period of six weeks.

Academic Skills *(continued)*

Social Studies

12. Paradigm Shifts In the early 1800s, goods were transported across the U.S. chiefly by canals. The completion of the transcontinental railroad in 1869 marked a *paradigm shift* in which the canal system was in effect replaced by the railroads. Identify at least one such other paradigm shift or significant event in transportation and explain its impact in a paragraph.

Science

13. Quality Testing Maintaining quality takes knowledge and resources, and sometimes also science. Businesses responsible for providing our homes, factories, and farms with clean water rely on scientific methods to test their product for purity. Research water quality testing and write a paragraph or two about how science helps ensure that the water we use is safe.

Real-World Skills

Persuasion Skills

14. Difficult Decisions You work for the chamber of commerce in a city with many manufacturing jobs. An entrepreneur tells you he is going to have his product manufactured in China because labor is cheaper. Write the entrepreneur a letter that lists several advantages for manufacturing the product in your city.

21st Century Skills

Information Literacy

15. You're an Inventor Spend a few minutes thinking up an invention, then go to the U.S. Patent and Trademark home page and search for patents for products similar to your idea. Write a short report describing your invention and any similar patents you find.

Connect to Your Community

16. Interview a Product Designer Interview someone in your community who has created a new product or service. Find out how the product prototype was developed. Ask if the production process was outsourced. If not, why not? Determine what quality control methods were used during the production process. Find out how the product is distributed to customers.

17. Visit a Manufacturer Visit a manufacturing firm in your community. Identify activities associated with (1) transportation, (2) storage, (3) product handling, and (4) inventory control. During a class discussion, compare your findings with those of another group. How are the companies similar? How are they different?

Competitive Events Prep

18. Situation You are the owner of a lighting and lamp store and are in the process of adding a line of lamps from a new vendor. The lamps are of high quality and are sure to become good sellers. The vendor has agreed to ship lamps purchased from the line directly to the customer. However, the direct shipping means a delay of one day longer than your store delivery. This also means that the store can sell the lamps at somewhat lower prices since the store does not have to store the lamps or deliver them to the customers.

Activity You are to explain the agreement with the new vendor to your staff.

Evaluation You will be evaluated on how well you meet these performance indicators:
- Explain the relationship between customer service and distribution.
- Explain storing considerations.
- Explain channel-member relationships.
- Negotiate contracts with vendors.
- Conduct staff meetings.

 Go to connectED.mcgraw-hill.com for more information about this activity and other competitive events.

Standardized Test Practice

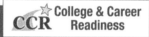
College & Career
Readiness

Directions Choose the letter of the best answer. Write the letter for the answer on a separate piece of paper. For question #2, if the answer is False, rewrite the statement to make it true.

1. Which of the following areas of product development cannot be outsourced?
   A. Opportunity recognition
   B. Component design
   C. Packaging design
   D. User guide and owner manuals

2. Productivity is a measure of how much a business produces in a given time.
   T
   F

Test-Taking Tip
Learn ahead of time the kind of test you will be taking, when and where the test will be, and what materials to bring.

CHAPTER

17

Managing Operations and Staffing

Chapter Objectives

SECTION 17.1

Managing Operations

Explain the significance of operational plans.

Describe the purpose of operating policies, rules, and regulations.

SECTION 17.2

Staffing and Company Policies

Explain the staffing process.

Determine the need for additional policies.

Discovery Project

Health Benefits

Key Question **?** *What is health insurance and why is it an important benefit?*

Project Goal

Compare and contrast the health care plans of different businesses in your community. Examine what these plans cost both the employees and the businesses. Interview an employee of one of these businesses about a presciption, procedure, or other health care service they have had covered by insurance. If possible, determine what the service would cost if the employee did not have health insurance.

Think About...

➤ *How will you obtain information about businesses' health care plans?*

➤ *How will you compare and contrast the plans?*

➤ *What will you do with your research?*

21st Century Skills

Health Literacy *How would health care considerations affect your decision about whether or not to accept a company's job offer?*

Evaluate

 Go to connectED.mcgraw-hill.com to download a rubric that you can use to evaluate your final project.

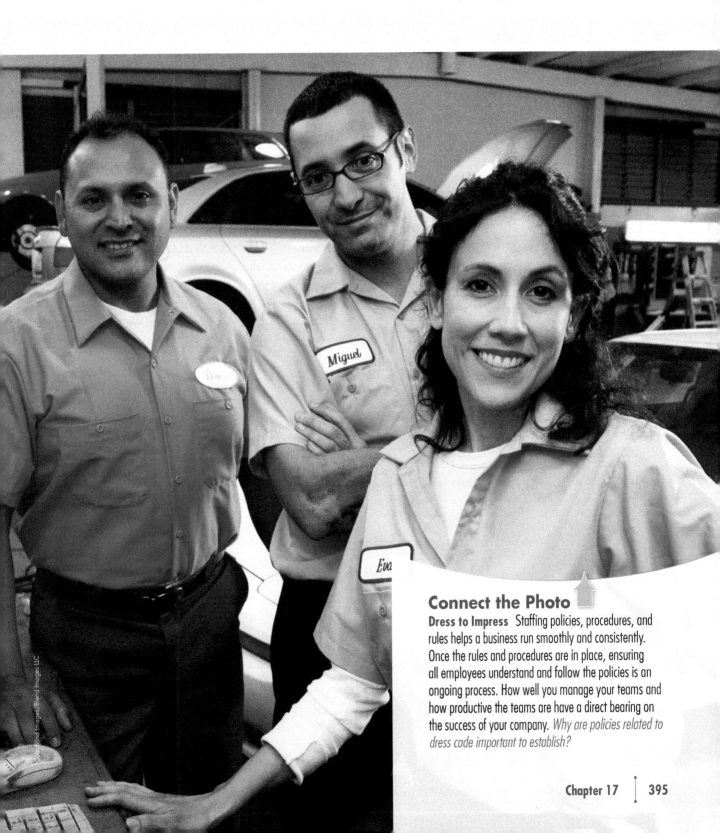

Ask AN EXPERT

Q: *I am working for a small start-up with only six employees. My employer cannot afford to offer health insurance through the company. I am a healthy person and have a very tight budget; do I really need to buy health insurance coverage?*

A: It may seem as if you are saving money by not paying a monthly insurance premium. However, this strategy may end up costing you more money in the long run. Accidents and illnesses happen, and emergency room visits and follow-up care can easily cost thousands of dollars. Without insurance, you are responsible for the entire payment. There are personal plans that serve different needs and budgets.

Connect the Photo

Dress to Impress Staffing policies, procedures, and rules helps a business run smoothly and consistently. Once the rules and procedures are in place, ensuring all employees understand and follow the policies is an ongoing process. How well you manage your teams and how productive the teams are have a direct bearing on the success of your company. *Why are policies related to dress code important to establish?*

Managing Operations

Reading Guide

Before You Read ▪▪▪▪▪▪▪▪▪▪▪▪▪

Connect What would be the most important policies for the business you are planning?

The Main Idea

For your operation to run smoothly, there has to be consistency in the way things are done and how people are treated. This is achieved by implementing policies and rules.

Objectives

Explain the significance of operational plans.

Describe the purpose of operating policies, rules, and regulations.

Content Vocabulary

◇ policy
◇ rule
◇ credit
◇ return policy
◇ rework policy

Academic Vocabulary

You will see these words in your reading and on your tests. Use the academic vocabulary glossary to look up their meanings.

▪ obtain
▪ indicate

Graphic Organizer

Draw a chart like the one shown. As you read about the three Cs of credit, label each point of the triangle one of the Cs.

 Go to connectED.mcgraw-hill.com to download this graphic organizer.

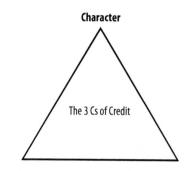

Character

The 3 Cs of Credit

Implementing Operational Plans

Managers put operational plans into action. These plans govern the day-to-day business operations, which include the policies, rules, and staffing concerns that keep a business going. When you start a business, you might manage the operation alone. However, as your business grows, you may have to delegate your responsibilities to some of your employees.

Policies

Policies simplify day-to-day management so you do not have to make the same decisions again and again. A **policy** is a statement of guiding principles and procedures that serves as a guideline for daily business operations. Policies should always support the company's goals and objectives.

A business may have a policy about working hours or overtime pay. Policies are meant to handle recurring situations, but they are flexible. They leave room for interpretation. Permitting an employee to come in late when he or she has a doctor's appointment is an example of policy flexibility.

Rules

In contrast, rules tell employees exactly what they should and should not do. A **rule** is a standard that is set forth to guide behavior or actions. Rules leave no room for interpretation. "Employees shall wear hard hats in all construction areas" and "All employees shall get two weeks of vacation after one year of service" are rules. At times, rules also impose restrictions on customers to regulate their actions, such as rules that restrict the use of cell phones.

> ✔ Reading Check **Compare and Contrast** What is the difference between a policy and a rule?

Business Casual Businesses have different policies about what kind of attire employees are allowed to wear. *Would you allow your employees to dress casually or would you require them to dress in business clothes? Why?*

(l)Sam Edwards/OJO Images/age fotostock; (r)James Hardy/PhotoAlto/SuperStock

● As You Read ▪▪▪

Explain What kind of business should consider implementing a no-credit policy?

Operating Policies, Rules, and Regulations

Not all rules or policies apply to all types of businesses. However, most policy statements include hours of operation, credit policies, return and rework policies, delivery policies, customer service policies, and employee and customer safety policies.

Hours of Operation

Hours of operation are an important part of a business's place strategy. When can your customers come to your location? Are you able to deliver your product to customers when they want it? Hours should be set to suit customers. For example, a movie theater might be open later on Fridays and weekends when most people want to see movies. In contrast, a wholesaler might be open 9 to 5 on weekdays, when customers, typically businesses, could phone in orders.

Credit Policies

Pricing entails more than what you charge for your goods or services. It also addresses how much your customers can pay for them. One important part of your pricing strategy is credit. **Credit** is an arrangement for deferred payment for goods and services. Credit allows a business or an individual to **obtain** products in exchange for a promise to pay later.

Your first decision will be whether to offer credit and/or outside financing. Credit may encourage sales and give you a competitive edge, but it also ties up your money. You can also lose money if a customer defaults. A no-credit policy suits businesses that sell low-priced items and consumable goods. That is why some convenience stores and restaurants do not offer credit. However, businesses that sell big-ticket items and companies who want to encourage customers to buy in large quantities should make their products easy to buy.

If you offer credit, you need to develop a credit policy. You must select the form(s) of credit you will extend. You also have to decide to whom you will offer credit and in what amounts.

Always Open Many retailers operate Websites that allow customers to shop around the clock. *What is one disadvantage of selling merchandise online?*

Ingram Publishing/SuperStock

Several types of credit plans are available. Four major types are described below:

- **Bank Credit Cards** Many businesses accept bank credit cards sponsored by Visa and MasterCard. Since the bank that issues the card (not the customer) pays the bill, there is less risk. However, bank card issuers take a percentage of each charged purchase as a collection fee.
- **Charge Accounts** With charge accounts, the business gets the full purchase price plus a finance charge (a form of interest) if the balance is not paid within the established time limit. However, the business pays all costs associated with collecting on these accounts and assumes the risk of nonpayment.
- **Installment Plans** Businesses that sell costly goods or services might offer installment plans. Some furniture stores let customers make a down payment and then make regular payments. The costs and risks are similar to those of charge accounts.
- **Financing** Financing sales through a bank is usually reserved for expensive goods, such as new cars. With this form of credit, the business gets its money quickly. Since the customer's credit history must be checked and approved, they may be inconvenienced by delays at the time of purchase.

Other specialized credit plans include cards offered by stores just for their customers. There are also debit cards, which allow funds to be withdrawn directly from a customer's checking account, and revolving accounts, to which purchases can be added on an ongoing basis. Revolving accounts usually require a minimum payment, have a balance limit, and charge interest on the balance. Some businesses, such as car dealers, may have arrangements with lenders.

Most businesses that offer credit have standards to determine who is eligible. These standards are often based on a customer's character, capacity, and capital, concepts that Chapter 19 discusses. Because of these standards, it is important for consumers to maintain a good credit rating.

Return and Rework Policies

You may choose to have a **return policy**, which establishes the conditions under which items that have been ordered, shipped, or delivered may be returned, and a **rework policy**, which establishes the conditions under which items will be reworked. Reworking is the act of doing something again because it was not done right the first time. A fair policy for replacements, refunds, or repairs helps maintain customer goodwill.

Web Savvy

Save the Date

Instead of using a paper calendar or whiteboard on a hallway wall, 21st century workers use online calendars. Online calendars allow workers to collaborate; share what they are working on; and post deadlines, meetings, interviews, and other time-sensitive items. Managers can use shared calendars to give employees assignments due on certain dates and times. Co-workers can also see where their colleagues will be at any given time. *What are some shared calendar tools that you have seen or used?*

Business Case Study

Fair Play in the Workplace

Make your workplace respectful *and* productive by setting ground rules for behavior

Policies and rules for employees are essential. Every small business owner needs to decide—and communicate—what is acceptable. An employee manual is the ideal place to do this.

Employee manuals cover a range of topics, from working hours and benefits to standards of conduct. For example, they often describe the dress code, business ethics, discipline policies, and grievance procedures.

Here is some advice on setting workplace policies:

- Explain dress codes in terms of safety and respect for customers and clients, not fashion.
- Make all employees aware of anti-discrimination and anti-sexual harassment laws.

- Ensure that discipline and grievance procedures are handled uniformly and confidentially.
- Convey that you want your place of business to demonstrate fairness and mutual respect.

Employee policies must be applied and enforced impartially and consistently. This ensures fairness to all employees and protects the company from charges of discrimination. The Small Business Administration (SBA) and Equal Employment Opportunity Commission (EEOC) provide information on company policies that entrepreneurs need to consider.

Active Learning

Make a sample Code of Conduct for a small business. Cover subjects such as appearance, ethics, family members working together, and so on. Be specific. For example, rather than saying, "Be financially responsible," say, "Employees are not permitted to use office funds or equipment for personal benefit." Discuss with two or three other students how the policies can be applied and enforced fairly.

Delivery Policies

Whether to deliver is another part of your place strategy. For some service businesses, a delivery policy can be the key to success. Domino's Pizza built a national reputation with its original delivery policy. It promised "Delivery in 30 minutes, or it's free."

Customer Service Policies

Good customer service is essential. In the long run, it is more costly to have an unhappy customer than it is to provide good service. Research **indicates** that 91 percent of dissatisfied customers will not return. In addition, they will usually tell other people not to frequent the business either.

You should consider having a customer service policy that addresses complaints. Most businesses use the policy "The customer is always right." Your policies can also cover courtesy to customers. Some businesses require their clerks to ask departing customers, "Did you find everything you were looking for?"

There are several other factors to consider. Will you have a service policy? In other words, if something you sell stops working within a certain time limit, will you fix it? Will restrooms be open to the public or locked and usable only by customers? Will you maintain a certain shopping climate by having particular lighting or housekeeping standards? Will you guarantee a certain response time or offer warranties to guarantee materials and workmanship?

Employee and Customer Safety

The financial costs of an on-site accident can ruin a small business. However, you can take basic precautions to reduce your liability. Train your employees in safety and emergency procedures. Reinforce training with signs posted throughout the workplace.

You also need to protect your customers. A sign can keep customers away from potentially damaging equipment: "Authorized personnel only." A restaurant can let guests know when a section of the floor has been mopped. You should make it clear to customers not to use certain facilities, such as elevators, during emergencies.

Go Green

Green Policies

Businesses are switching out incandescent light bulbs and replacing them with compact fluorescent lights. Though a CFL bulb comes with a higher price tag initially, it can save over $30 in electricity costs over its lifetime and save 2,000 times its weight in greenhouse gases. CFLs also fit into most standard household light sockets.

◈ **Critical Thinking**
Why would businesses make conserving energy a company policy? Summarize your answer in a paragraph.

SECTION 17.1 Review

After You Read ■■■■■■■■■■■■■

Self-Check
1. **Identify** the purpose of policies in managing operations.
2. **Compare and Contrast** policies and rules.
3. **Identify** the most critical factor in setting hours of operation for a business.

Think
4. **Describe** how students who have jobs can employ the principles of safety in their work-based experiences.

English Language Arts/Writing
5. **Paragraph Organization** Well-written paragraphs are often organized in three ways: (1) they present a cause-and-effect relationship; (2) they explain a concept by making a statement and following it with examples; or, (3) they pose a question and follow it with an answer. Examine each paragraph in Section 17.1. Decide if the paragraph is written in one of these ways, and write a sentence for each that explains your choice.

🚀 Go to connectED.mcgraw-hill.com to check your answers.

Staffing and Company Policies

Reading Guide

Before You Read ···············
Connect What kinds of personnel decisions will you have to make in your planned business?

The Main Idea
Staffing determines who carries out the work of your company and how your company is perceived. Consequently, staffing policies and decisions have a direct bearing on the success of your company.

Objectives
Explain the staffing process.
Determine the need for additional policies.

Content Vocabulary
◇ line organization
◇ staff
◇ line-and-staff organization
◇ project organizations
◇ job description
◇ job specification
◇ résumé
◇ recruit
◇ benefits
◇ wages
◇ piece rate

Academic Vocabulary
You will see these words in your reading and on your tests. Use the academic vocabulary glossary to look up their meanings.
■ process
■ structure

Graphic Organizer
Draw a chart like the one shown. As you read, write notes about job descriptions on the left and notes about job specifications on the right.

 Go to connectED.mcgraw-hill.com to download this graphic organizer.

Job Description	Job Specification
	describe skills

Staffing Your Operation

If you intend to run a one-person operation, your staffing plan will be simple. For most businesses, however, you probably will not be able to do all of the work yourself. Even when hiring only one or two employees, you should familiarize yourself with the staffing **process**.

Organizational Structures

Your first staffing task is to design an organizational **structure**. The easiest way to do this is to develop an organization chart. This diagram includes all of the jobs in your business and shows how they are related. Your organization chart should help you delegate responsibility, authority, and work. Each job may not require a full-time employee. Stay open to other possibilities, such as consultants and part-time employees.

Line Organizations

Many new businesses use a **line organization**. Here managers are responsible for accomplishing the main objectives of the business. They are also in the direct chain of command. Top management, such as an owner/manager, makes the decisions that affect the whole company. Middle management implements the decisions. Supervisory, or first-line, management supervises the activities of employees. Employees then carry out the plans made by top and middle management.

At start-up, you may have a line organization with only two levels of management. An example is shown in **Figure 17.1**. As the business grows, you may need to hire first-line managers for buying, warehousing, and sales. In the meantime, those responsibilities fall to your assistant manager.

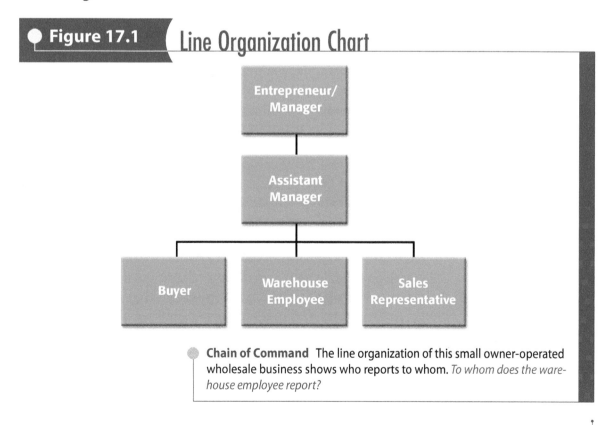

Figure 17.1 Line Organization Chart

Chain of Command The line organization of this small owner-operated wholesale business shows who reports to whom. *To whom does the warehouse employee report?*

ETHICS and BUSINESS

Accepting Gifts

Situation A year ago you opened a landscape design company. Your company is doing well, but, as of now, you do not have all of the staff you need. You must outsource much of the work until you can afford to hire more staff.

Outsourcing Work DirtyWork is one of the businesses you have hired to help with your projects. They are a local company that operates heavy equipment. You have hired them to move dirt for your landscaping designs. Lately, you have not been happy with their work and are considering hiring another company.

English Language Arts/Writing

Gift or Bribe DirtyWork has sent you an expensive portfolio engraved with your initials as a thank you for the work you gave them. They know you will be outsourcing work for a new project.

1. Should you accept the gift from Dirty-Work? Should you continue to hire them?
2. Write a one-page company policy for your employees on accepting gifts from vendors.

Line-and-Staff Organizations

Besides adding a layer of line managers as your organization grows, you must hire staff personnel. The term *staff* often refers to employees in general. Technically, however, **staff** refers to managers and others who provide support and advice for line managers. Examples of staff activities include accounting, legal services, and training. When you add staff to your line organization, it becomes a **line-and-staff organization**.

Project Organizations

Project organizations supplement the line and line-and-staff structures. **Project organizations** are usually temporary organizations brought together from different parts of the business for special projects. For example, you might assemble experts from sales, purchasing, production, and shipping departments. Their goal may be to design a system for cutting delivery time by 50 percent. The project is carried out by teams or committees. The group may have responsibility to both a line manager and a staff manager.

Employees assigned to these groups work on an as-needed basis or until the project is done. Then they return to their assignment in the formal organization. Matrix, task-team, and interdisciplinary setups are examples of project organizations.

Job Descriptions and Job Specifications

For each position in your organization chart, you need to write a job description. A **job description** is a statement that describes the objectives of a job and its duties and responsibilities. You should then write a second statement—a job specification. A **job specification** is a document that details the abilities, skills, educational level, and experience needed by an employee to perform the job. Think of it as a kind of want ad.

Identifying Staffing Gaps

Examine the résumés of everyone involved in the start-up business to identify staffing needs. A **résumé** is a summary of work and academic history, skills, and experience. Compare the résumés with your job descriptions and specifications. You will be able to recognize gaps in your organization's staffing. These gaps highlight the areas where you will need to look for outside assistance.

Personnel Policies

Businesses must establish personnel policies that oversee the "people" aspect of the business. A business should set employee standards before recruiting, screening, and hiring employees. Pay and benefits policies must be in place, and procedures for maintaining employee files should be established. Personnel policies also encompass employee training and development.

Employee Standards

The people you hire affect what customers and clients think of your company. Your employees make up the company's face, voice, and reputation. That is why entrepreneurs establish hiring policies. All personnel decisions that you make will reflect this policy.

The type of people you hire depends on the type of business. For a retail operation, you may want social individuals. For a bookkeeping service, you probably want people who are detail-oriented. Under any circumstances, you want people who project a positive, professional image. You should set out these kinds of traits in your policy statement. Other personnel decisions you make will also reflect this policy.

Recruiting and Screening Employees

You can use classified ads and state-run and private employment agencies to **recruit**, or bring in, prospective employees. School and college placement offices, union hiring halls, and word of mouth are other sources. Each recruitment method reaches a different type of applicant. Listing a job opening on an Internet job board attracts computer-literate applicants. Use the recruiting method that best suits the position you want to fill.

When you begin to attract applicants, you must screen them. This usually involves having applicants submit an application form or a résumé. Either one helps you see how well an applicant matches up to your job specification. You can immediately eliminate those applicants who do not fit your requirements.

If you are impressed by someone's application or résumé, you should schedule an interview. It is illegal to ask the interviewee certain types of questions (age, religion, ethnicity, etc.). By meeting the applicant, you find out more about his or her qualifications. You can also learn about the person's interpersonal and communication skills. You may also want to test the applicant to evaluate intelligence, aptitude, achievement, interest, personality, and honesty. Be sure your tests relate to the job.

● **As You Read** ....
Identify What kind of employees would you want to hire for a bookkeeping service?

India has the second largest population in the world, and is the most populated democracy, with more than 1.2 billion people. While it also has the greatest number of people in poverty, that percentage is dropping, having decreased from 60% in 1981 to 42% in the early 2000s. Unfortunately, that percentage is still high when compared to the global poverty rate of 26%.

Bollywood India's film industry produces about twice as many films annually as the United States. Many of these films come out of Mumbai, where the term *Bollywood* emerged, a meshing of Bombay (the former name of Mumbai) and Hollywood.

Social Studies The outsourcing of work from Western countries to India has become a big industry and continues to grow. India's National Association of Software and Service Companies estimates that it could be a $225 billion industry by the year 2020. At the same time, outsourcing can bring into question the ability to properly staff and manage people on another continent. Research how Western companies handle staffing and management of employees in India and summarize your findings in a one-page report.

Common Hindi Words and Phrases	
Hello/Hi	namaste
Goodbye	namaste
Yes/No	ji ha/ji nahi
Please	kripaya
Thank you	dhanyavad
You're welcome	koi bat nahi

Conducting Interviews

To conduct effective interviews, follow these guidelines:

1. Define what you are looking for before the interview.
2. Conduct interviews in private. Do not use panel interviews.
3. Put interviewees at ease. Treat them with respect.
4. Ask general background questions first, more specific questions later.
5. Encourage the interviewees to talk. Be a good listener.
6. Confirm key observations several times during the interview.
7. Provide an opportunity for interviewees to ask questions.
8. Look for how interviewees conduct themselves.
9. Look for what the person will bring to the job.
10. Obtain enough information to make a sound decision.

Finally, you can request character references. Former employers can tell you about a person's previous job performance. Teachers, coaches, and other references can tell you about an applicant's reliability and work ethic.

> **Reading Check Explain** What is an example of an optional benefit for employees?

Pay, Benefits, and Training

To attract and retain the kind of employees you want, you must do two things. First, you must pay a competitive wage or salary. Second, you need to offer competitive employee benefits. **Benefits** are extras that workers receive on a job.

Pay

Wages are an amount of money an employee receives for every hour the employee works. A salary is a fixed amount of pay an employee receives for each week, month, or year the employee works. Paying a competitive wage or salary means paying a rate similar to rates offered by other businesses with similar employee needs.

Another way to pay is based on productivity. Productivity pay can be a **piece rate** (so much per unit produced) or a commission. Sometimes employees receive a combination of productivity pay and salary. You will probably choose your pay plan based on the standard for your industry.

Benefits

Some employee benefits are required by law. These include the employer's contribution to Social Security, unemployment compensation, and workers' compensation. Optional benefits include paid vacation days, paid sick days, health and life insurance, flextime, pensions, and child care. Companies offer benefits together with pay as a way to attract and keep good employees. Most full-time workers receive benefits. Most temporary and part-time workers do not receive benefits.

Keep cost in mind as you consider the benefits to offer your employees. Compensating your employees is a major business expense. Typically, benefits for an employee run between 20 and 40 percent of salary.

Training and Development

New employees work better and are more efficient when they receive immediate training. Unless your business is highly technical, you will provide this early on-the-job training.

As your operation grows, you may need to hire a specialist to handle employee training and long-term development. You can also contract with outside consultants to provide these services.

Health Benefits To compete with other employers, companies offer many forms of health care. *How does this benefit the employee and employer?*

Personnel Records

Staffing responsibilities include making decisions about establishing and maintaining personnel files. For your own use, you need contact information and training and performance records. For government agencies, you must keep certain documents for a specified period. An employee's records can all be kept in the same file or in separate file categories. Maintaining separate categories facilitates auditing and also ensures privacy where necessary.

Developing Additional Policies

You have many different policies and rules to consider for your operation. To make sure that you will not miss any that are essential, make a list of the operational rules and policies that apply. Then, check competitors' operations. Observe and ask questions to determine your competitor's policies. If possible, review their policy statements and find out which ones you are missing. Set up focus groups or survey potential customers to get feedback about policies they want. Once your business is under way, check to see that your policies are working through periodic monitoring.

SECTION 17.2 Review

After You Read ▬▬▬▬▬▬▬▬▬

Self-Check
1. **Compare and Contrast** line managers and staff managers.
2. **Write** a sample job description and job specification for a position in your business.
3. **Describe** the recruitment methods you would use to reach prospective employees for your proposed business and why you would them.

Think
4. **Produce** a complete set of policy statements for your proposed business.

Mathematics
5. **Operating Costs** The warehouse manager at a paper company earns a salary of $29,400 per year. The benefits package he receives is 32% of his base salary. How much will the manager's compensation add to the company's monthly operating costs?

(**Math Concept**) **Multi-Step Problems** Multi-step problems require that more than one calculation be performed.

Step 1 Determine the annual cost of the benefit package by multiplying.

Step 2 Calculate the cost per month by dividing.

🚀 Go to connectED.mcgraw-hill.com to check your answers.

Entrepreneurs *in Action*

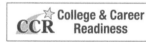

Andre Guererro
Owner and Chef
The Oinkster

Q *What do you do?*

A When I open a new restaurant, I spend most of my time there until it gets rolling. I'll develop the concept and the menu. Then I hire all the kitchen staff and train them. I spread out the cooks I have good relationships with to help me with training. Cooks come and go; it's difficult to put together a crew. We have a pizza guy at BoHo who has years of experience. Because I know him well, I know I can trust him.

Q *What kind of training and education did you need to get this job?*

A I don't have any formal education in cooking. I did go to UCLA and took restaurant management courses. I grew up in a family that nourished a love and passion for food. It's hard to teach someone to appreciate good food. How do you teach somebody how a sauce is supposed to taste?

Q *What do you enjoy most about your job?*

A I love the people. I love the atmosphere. I've worked in jobs where you had to put a tie on, an uptight rigid environment in an office. There's just no way I can do that. If my crew puts out food that's perfectly cooked, with the plating very clean and precise, they can goof off at the end of the night.

Q *How did you become interested in your field?*

A I've always loved bridging creativity with business. The whole process of taking an idea and bringing it to life is really fulfilling and challenging. Business is just a way to bring cool ideas into the world to share with other people.

Improving Service You are a consultant who helps restaurants manage their operations. You really want your favorite restaurant to become your customer.

1. Think of the restaurant as a business that must provide services while containing costs.
2. Write a letter to the manager of the restaurant explaining the importance of carefully managing operations.
3. In your letter, include specific proposals for how the restaurant could change the management of its operations to save money while maintaining or improving services.

Career Facts

Real-World Skills	Academic Skills	Career Cluster
Speaking, Listening, Problem-Solving	English Language Arts, Family & Consumer Sciences	Hospitality & Tourism

Andre Guerrero

Visual Summary

Managing Operations and Staffing

Day-to-Day Operations Establishing policies and rules allows your business to run smoothly.

- Credit
- Hours of Operation
- Return
- Safety
- **Operating Policies**
- Rework
- Customer Service
- Delivery

Types of Organizations To determine your specific staffing needs, you should design an organization chart and write job descriptions and job specifications.

Line Organizations	Line-and-Staff Organizations	Project Organizations
• Owner/manager makes decisions • Middle management implements the decisions • First-line managers supervise employees • Employees carry out plans	• Includes staff personnel • Staff provide support and advice to line managers • Staff activities include accounting, legal services, and training and development	• Supplement line-and-staff structures • Usually temporary • Brought together from different parts of the business for special projects

Ingram Publishing/SuperStock

Vocabulary

1. On a sheet of paper, use each of these terms and words in a written sentence.

Content Vocabulary

◇ policy
◇ rule
◇ credit
◇ return policy
◇ rework policy
◇ line organization
◇ staff

◇ line-and-staff organization
◇ project organizations
◇ job description
◇ job specification
◇ résumé
◇ recruit
◇ benefits

◇ wages
◇ piece rate

Academic Vocabulary

■ obtain
■ indicate
■ process
■ structure

Key Concepts

2. **Explain** what operational plans include.
3. **List** five common operating policies that apply to most businesses.
4. **Explain** how credit policies are related to marketing strategies.
5. **Define** return and rework policies.
6. **Summarize** the staffing process.
7. **Identify** techniques for effective interviewing.
8. **Examine** circumstances that might cause you to revise your policies.
9. **Explain** how you can be sure your policies are working.

Academic Skills

Mathematics

10. **Installment Plans** Relosa's Furniture Emporium offers customers zero interest installment plans on purchases of more than $5,000. If a customer purchases $8,350 of furniture on a 36-month installment plan, what is the monthly payment? The sales tax rate is 5.2%.

Math Concept **Percents** Percents have decimal equivalents that we use when calculating. 100% = 1; 5.2% = 0.052

Step 1 Determine the total price (selling price plus sales tax) by adding 1 + 0.052 and multiplying the sum by the selling price.

Step 2 Divide the total cost of the furniture by the number of months in 3 years to determine the monthly payment.

English Language Arts

11. **Word Origins** The terms *entrepreneur* and *résumé* both came into the English language from French. In fact, about 30% of English words are derived from French. Research the influence of the French language on the development of English. Write a paragraph or two explaining why the influence of French on English is so great.

Academic Skills *(continued)*

Social Studies

12. Rules Worth Following Conduct a survey that asks people from different age groups about their work lives. Ask them to identify workplace rules they think make the business better and those they think should be changed or eliminated. Compile your results in a graph or pie chart.

Science

13. Help Wanted Imagine that you are the personnel director of a large high-tech firm that invests heavily in scientific research. Your job is to hire all the employees for a new department that will develop products for the future. What personality traits and characteristics will you look for? Prepare a brief talk describing your ideal managers, scientists, and lab assistants. Be ready to explain why these traits and characteristics are important.

 Real-World Skills

Interview Skills

14. People Mean Money Interview the owner of a local business about staffing costs. Find out what it costs the business to employ the average worker for one year, beyond wages or salaries. Summarize your findings in a one-page report.

21st Century Skills

Communication and Collaboration

15. Service and a Smile Form a small discussion group of three to four students. Pick a local restaurant that you all know and discuss ways to improve its operations. Select a member of your group to share your findings with the class.

 Connect to Your Community

16. Organizational Charts Working in small groups, collect several examples of organization charts from local businesses. Compare and contrast their structures. Draw an organization chart for your school's administration and compare it with those you collected. Share your findings with the class.

17. Paying Employees Choose a business you would like to own. Determine what the pay and benefits for employees would cost your business.

- Use newspapers, occupational forecasting reports, and employment services to determine salaries/wage rates for the positions you need to fill.
- Contact the IRS, state tax office, and other appropriate agencies to obtain information about employer costs and withholding requirements.

Competitive Events Prep

18. Situation You own an appliance store. The store's return policy allows customers returning items with a sales receipt to either exchange the merchandise or receive a refund for the purchase price by the method of payment. Customers returning merchandise without a receipt will receive an exchange or refund for the amount of the item's current price. A customer returns a coffee pot and has no receipt. The original price was $59.99. It is now on sale for $34.99. The customer insists the coffee pot was purchased at full price and demands a refund in that amount.

Activity Explain the store's exchange/refund policy to the customer and why a receipt is necessary for a full price refund.

Evaluation You will be evaluated on how well you meet these performance indicators:

- Interpret business policies to customers/clients.
- Handle customer/client complaints.
- Show empathy and respect for others.
- Use appropriate assertiveness.

 Go to **connectED.mcgraw-hill.com** for more information about this activity and other competitive events.

Standardized Test Practice

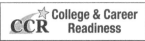

College & Career Readiness

Directions Choose the letter of the best answer. Write the letter for the answer on a separate piece of paper. For question #2, if the answer is False, rewrite the statement to make it true.

1. All of the following are part of the three Cs of Credit, except:
   A. Capacity
   B. Capital
   C. Charisma
   D. Character

2. A commission is a fixed amount of pay an employee receives for each week, month, or year worked.
   T
   F

> **Test-Taking Tip**
> When taking a test, do not worry about how quickly other test-takers finish; take your time and concentrate.

CHAPTER 18

Managing Human Resources

Chapter Objectives

SECTION 18.1
Developing and Keeping Human Resources

Identify the components of human resource management.

SECTION 18.2
Motivating Employees

Explain how managers influence motivation.

Describe ways to maximize employee performance.

Explain the importance of delegation.

Explain how to assess motivational techniques used to increase performance levels.

Discovery Project

Conflict Resolution

Key Question *How do managers resolve problems, conflicts, and other disputes?*

Project Goal

Ask a local business owner, teacher, school administrator, or other manager to let you observe them as they resolve a conflict or issue between co-workers or students. Take note of the techniques the manager uses to mediate the discussion and reach a compromise. Share what you learn about conflict resolution with your class.

Think About...

➤ *What questions do you want to ask the manager about resolving disputes?*
➤ *How does the manager approach the disputing parties and the problem?*
➤ *Do you think the manager effectively resolved the conflict? Why or why not?*

21st Century Skills

Social and Cross-Cultural Skills *How is creativity an important part of resolving conflicts?*

Evaluate

 Go to connectED.mcgraw-hill.com to download a rubric that you can use to evaluate your final project.

Q: *My grandmother gave me a savings bond for my birthday. I am thinking about cashing in the bond to purchase stock in a new entertainment company. How are bonds different than stocks?*

A: Bonds are loans you make to corporations or governments. Unlike buying stocks (or equity securities), which make you a part-owner in a company, buying bonds (or debt securities) makes you a creditor. There are several different types of bonds: corporate bonds, municipal bonds, U.S. Treasury bonds, U.S. Treasury bills, and agency bonds. Each type of bond has different minimums and terms.

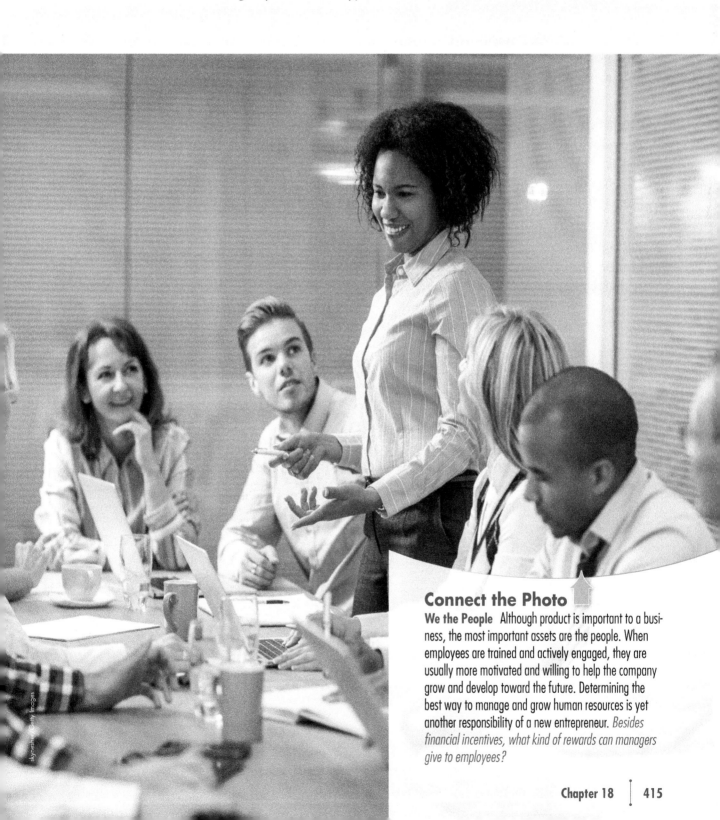

skynesher/Getty Images

Connect the Photo

We the People   Although product is important to a business, the most important assets are the people. When employees are trained and actively engaged, they are usually more motivated and willing to help the company grow and develop toward the future. Determining the best way to manage and grow human resources is yet another responsibility of a new entrepreneur. *Besides financial incentives, what kind of rewards can managers give to employees?*

Developing and Keeping Human Resources

Reading Guide

Before You Read ■■■■■■■■■■■■■
Connect What training would you need to provide to employees in your business?

The Main Idea
People are the most important resource of a small business. The employees that are recruited, hired, trained, and kept have a major impact on the company's performance.

Objectives
Identify the components of human resource management.

Content Vocabulary
◇ human resources
◇ human resource management
◇ labor union
◇ educational activities
◇ developmental activities
◇ cost effective
◇ employee complaint procedure
◇ Pregnancy Discrimination Act

Academic Vocabulary
You will see these words in your reading and on your tests. Use the academic vocabulary glossary to look up their meanings.
■ labor   ■ achieve

Graphic Organizer
Draw a chart like the one shown. As you read, write down the seven components of human resource management.

 Go to connectED.mcgraw-hill.com to download this graphic organizer.

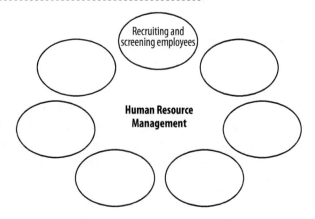

Recruiting and screening employees

Human Resource Management

Developing Human Resources

The human resources of a business represent one of its largest investments. **Human resources** are the people employed in a business, commonly referred to as *personnel*. People offer more than just **labor** to a business. They contribute character, ethics, creativity, intellectual energy, and social and business connections.

Human Resource Management

Human resource management is the part of business concerned with recruiting and managing employees. Its main goals are to facilitate performance and improve productivity. Several components make up human resource management:

- Recruiting and screening employees
- Managing dealings with unions
- Overseeing employee training and development
- Overseeing pay and benefits
- Resolving day-to-day problems
- Ensuring equal opportunity
- Handling employee termination

Recruiting and Screening Employees

As your business grows, you must add new employees. You must also replace employees.

As Chapter 17 explains, you can use Internet job boards, classified ads, employment agencies, school and college job placement offices, union hiring halls, and word of mouth to recruit employees. Established businesses can also recruit by asking for referrals from current and former employees and customers. They can also recruit walk-ins by hanging a help wanted sign at the place of business. Other sources are recruiting from within and recruiting from competitors.

Recruiting from Within

Promoting someone who works for you has several advantages. You already know the employee's work habits. Recruiting and training costs are kept low. Disruption of your operation is minimized. Finally, other employees become motivated to work harder for promotions. One disadvantage is that employees who are not promoted sometimes feel resentful. Another is that hiring only from within limits opportunities for bringing "new thinking" into the company.

Recruiting from Competitors

Hiring employees away from the competition also has advantages. The principal advantage is that the new hires already have the skills to do the job. They also can offer insight into competitors' operations. On the downside, recruiting from competitors can start a costly cycle of raiding each other's personnel. In some instances, it may cost less to train someone with no experience. An experienced worker may have to be untrained before being trained in your procedures.

Tech Savvy

The Progressive Workplace

A manager's job is to motivate employees. Motivated employees are more creative and productive, and, hopefully, invest more time in the current job than searching for the next one. Google and Microsoft, technology companies that rely on creative workforces, are going the extra mile to keep employees. These technology giants have constructed buildings that are not so much offices as workplace wonders. Google's headquarters offer organic food, a gym, and massages to employees, who are encouraged to spend 20 percent of work time on personal growth. Microsoft's research building, Building 99, has bookshelves in the hallways, an anechoic chamber for super-quiet brainstorming, and movable walls and air vents. *Why would Google and Microsoft invest millions of dollars creating a creative workplace environment?*

Screening

An established business owner uses the same screening methods that a new entrepreneur employs. Both review applications, conduct interviews, and check references. However, more people are included in the hiring process of an established business. For example, the prospective employee's immediate supervisor might be involved.

Dealings with Unions

As the manager of a small business, you may not like the idea of labor unions. They do represent some loss of control and their demands can cause a strain on financial resources. Nonetheless, if you understand why unions exist, you will be better able to make decisions about them.

A **labor union** is an organization that represents workers in their dealings with employers. Workers join unions to strengthen their ability to bargain for wages, benefits, job security, working conditions, and other concerns.

How you deal with unions will depend on your own unique circumstances. Many small businesses are not affected by union activity. However, some industries, such as construction and textile manufacturing, are unionized. Your dealings with unions will also be affected by the status of right-to-work laws in the state where your business is located. One approach is to head off employee concerns by establishing practices of fair treatment and open communication.

Overseeing Training and Development

Training and developing employees becomes more complex as a business grows. You must provide initial training for new hires. In addition, you must offer ongoing training to improve the job performance of current employees.

ETHICS and BUSINESS

Human Resources

Situation You have just graduated with a master's degree in business communication and have received PHR (Professional in Human Resources) certification. A small software development company has hired you to head their human resources department.

New Hire You have been asked to hire a software engineer. The woman in mind would have to leave a good job and relocate to work at the company. You have become aware that the company is having financial problems and likely will not be able to meet payroll.

English Language Arts/Writing

Deciding the Right Action The software engineer you would like to hire would stand to lose a lot if she left her current position, moved, took the job, and then did not get paid. As the head of human resources, what do you think you should do?

1. What is your responsibility to the company you work for? What is your responsibility to current and future employees?
2. Write a one-page report explaining your reasoning.

Fair Wages American Apparel®, a fast-growing retail clothing company, promotes fair wages and work environments for its textile workers. Often, textile labor is outsourced to countries with lower wages and worse work environments. *How do companies like American Apparel use their progressive human resource management for marketing purposes?*

Along with training, you should add education and development to your plans. **Educational activities** are actions that prepare employees for advancing in the organization. An example is a human relations workshop. **Developmental activities** are actions that prepare managers to lead the company into the future. An example is an industry conference. Here are the four steps in planning a training and development program:

1. **Determine Your Needs.**   Figure out your immediate, intermediate, and long-range training and development needs. Do you and other managers lack strategic planning skills? You may need developmental activities. Do you want key employees to be ready to move into management as you expand? They would need educational activities. Do too many customers leave without buying? Your employees may need training.

2. **Design Your Program.**   After you determine your needs, you must decide how to meet them. Will you create a program yourself? Will you designate someone else to do it? With the latter, you might need a full-time employee, a consultant, or a combination of the two. The local chapter of the American Society for Training and Development (ASTD) can help you find a consultant. **Figure 18.1** on page 420 describes some of the training and development techniques you can use if you decide to do the training and development yourself.

3. **Implement Your Program.**   If you want your program to make a difference, two things must occur. First you have to provide time and money for the program. Then you must follow up, making sure employees use what they learn on the job.

4. **Evaluate Your Program.**   After your program is up and running, you should evaluate it. You want to know how effective it is. This means determining whether the program's objectives were **achieved**. For example, did sales improve?

You should also determine how cost effective the program was. **Cost effective** means economically worthwhile in terms of what is achieved for the amount of money spent.

Figure 18.1 — Training and Development Techniques

On-the-job training	Employees learn the job on the job site under the direction of their manager or an experienced employee.
Vestibule training	Training takes place at a location away from the job that is equipped to simulate the actual work site.
Classroom teaching	Lecture, discussion, case studies, role playing, and other traditional classroom techniques are used to provide knowledge and problem-solving skills needed to perform the work.
Web-based instruction	Programs delivered through the Internet or the company's Intranet ensure that the information presented is the same for each trainee. It is often used in connection with other techniques.
Coaching	Employees receive ongoing instruction and feedback regarding job performance from their manager or designated coach.
Mentoring	Employees receive one-on-one assistance from an established employee to help them get oriented within the organization and develop their potential.
Job rotation	Employees are moved from one job situation to another to provide them with a variety of job experiences and/or an understanding of the total operation.
Conferences and seminars	Several trainees or employees meet with experts off the job to learn how to deal with specific concerns or to exchange ideas.

Training and Developing Employees Many types of training and development techniques are available for managers. *Which techniques count as learning by experience?*

Overseeing Pay and Benefits

You should review your employees' compensation packages regularly. Make sure they include the latest benefits required by law. Also consider adding benefits you could not afford at start-up. For instance, you might offer pensions, profit sharing, or bonuses to be more competitive.

Expanding benefits costs more than money. It also adds to your responsibilities. For example, businesses that offer pensions are subject to the Employee Retirement Income Security Act. This act regulates pension plans. It makes sure eligible employees receive their pensions. This means you must manage the investment of pension fund moneys to meet the standards of the act. This, in turn, means more paperwork.

 Reading Check Compare and Contrast What are some advantages and disadvantages of hiring employees away from competitors?

Resolving Day-to-Day Problems

You should encourage employees to resolve disputes using problem-solving techniques and human relations skills. However, some employee conflicts are more difficult than others.

Handling Employee Complaints

An **employee complaint procedure** is a formal procedure for handling employee complaints. It should be put in writing and distributed to employees. This is an effective form of staff communication. The first step may be the employee informing the supervisor of the concern. The second step may be an appeal to the next-level supervisor or an impartial committee. Although many problems have no clear-cut solutions, the manager or business owner must make a decision regarding every employee complaint.

Ensuring Equal Opportunity

As an employer and manager, you must ensure that employees are not discriminated against. It is illegal to discriminate on the basis of race, color, gender, religion, national origin, age, or physical impairment. You must set standards for your employees' behavior. You must inform them that discrimination is not acceptable.

Laws and regulations are designed to protect employees. They are enforced by the Equal Employment Opportunity Commission (EEOC). One law you may deal with is the **Pregnancy Discrimination Act**. The Pregnancy Discrimination Act is a federal law that requires that employers treat their pregnant employees like all other employees when determining benefits. The EEOC's sexual harassment guidelines are also important. Sexual harassment is any unwelcome behavior of a sexual nature. The EEOC forbids sexual harassment. Other laws affecting employees are discussed in Chapter 8.

Handling Problem Employees and Terminations

You might make every effort to hire the right people and give them the best possible training. Unfortunately, some employees still may not work out. They may perform below expectations. Their actions may be contrary to the company's goals.

When this happens, you can try to help them work out their problems. You may be able to guide them through finding a solution. Perhaps you come up with a mutually acceptable way to change their thinking or actions. In some cases, the solution may be professional counseling or assistance.

Against Discrimination A business cannot discriminate against people who are differently abled. *What are some aids that a business can provide to employees who are differently abled?*

Realistic Reflections

Disciplinary Action

In the end, the only realistic way to deal with a problem may be through disciplinary action. This may include docking an employee's pay or termination (firing). Neither situation is easy for anyone involved, and both should be handled tactfully.

Terminations, in particular, require special handling. It is important to have a document trail that proves that you have cause before firing. If possible, schedule a meeting for the end of the day. Give the employee exact reasons for the action. Explain severance pay and unemployment compensation. You may want to suggest other job options more suited to the person's skills. Keep in mind that the way you handle the situation can impact your relationship with other employees.

Other Causes for Termination

Not all of the problems you deal with are brought on by employees. Things sometimes occur both in or out of the job setting that are beyond anyone's control. For example, you may have to terminate an employee because of a drop in business, rather than something they have done. Those situations call for special sensitivity on your part.

SECTION 18.1 Review

After You Read

Self-Check

1. **Compare and Contrast** the advantages and disadvantages of recruiting from within.
2. **Identify** the advantages and disadvantages of adding employee benefits.
3. **Summarize** a manager's responsibility for making sure employees are not discriminated against.

Think

4. **Produce** an employee handbook on dispute resolution techniques. Include a written procedure for handling employee complaints.

English Language Arts

5. **Keeping Good Employees** Sandra Han owns a real estate marketing firm. She pays her employees a salary that is slightly under the industry standard. Consequently, employees often work for her to get experience but then leave to earn more money. What can Sandra do to retain employees besides raising salaries? Write a two-paragraph essay that suggests alternative methods to improve employee retention.

Go to connectED.mcgraw-hill.com to check your answers.

Motivating Employees

Reading Guide

Before You Read ■■■■■■■■■■■■■■■
Connect What motivates employees?

The Main Idea
One of an entrepreneur's tasks is to motivate employees. Employees who are motivated produce more and better work.

Objectives
Explain how managers influence motivation.
Describe ways to maximize employee performance.
Explain the importance of delegation.
Explain how to assess motivational techniques used to increase performance levels.

Content Vocabulary
◇ Theory X
◇ Theory Y
◇ hygiene factors
◇ motivating factors
◇ telecommuting
◇ family leave
◇ flextime
◇ performance evaluation

Academic Vocabulary
You will see these words on your reading and in your tests. Use the academic vocabulary glossary to look up their meaning.
■ theory
■ significant

Graphic Organizer
Draw a chart like the one shown. As you read, write down the six motivational techniques.

 Go to connectED.mcgraw-hill.com to download this graphic organizer.

Motivational Techniques
✔ Provide meaningful work.
✔ _____
✔ _____
✔ _____
✔ _____
✔ _____
✔ _____

As You Read ...

Describe What kinds of assumptions do managers make about employees?

How Managers Influence Motivation

Communication is a key factor that affects employee motivation. You must communicate goals and objectives clearly if employees are to meet them. How employees are regarded and treated also affects their motivation. There are many **theories** about how this works.

Assumptions Managers Make

In *The Human Side of Enterprise*, Douglas McGregor identifies two sets of assumptions, which he calls Theory X and Theory Y, that managers make about employees. **Theory X** is the belief that employees are basically lazy and need constant supervision. **Theory Y** is the belief that employees are responsible, like to work, and want intrinsic rewards.

Business Case Study

Bullying Has No Place on the Job

Demanding top performance is okay, but when does it cross the line to bullying?

Small business owners are passionate about their businesses and motivating their employees. You want—and deserve—to get the best from your employees. Be aware, however, of the line between pushing and bullying.

Always:
- show respect for every employee.
- keep your own negative opinions about employees to yourself.
- offer guidance and assistance to others.
- walk away if you feel yourself getting angry; make an appointment with the person to talk about the subject later.
- stop any workplace bullying.
- listen to any employee who reports being bullied.
- make it known your company has a no-bullying policy.
- put up posters with positive quotations that promote respect among employees.

- create a team atmosphere rather than a rigid hierarchy.

Never:
- threaten, humiliate, or intimidate another person, especially if that person is an employee and you are the boss.
- abuse anyone verbally, electronically, or physically.
- sabotage another employee's work.
- engage in any form of bullying behavior.

Active Learning

Using your computer skills or skills with poster board and art materials, create a poster that promotes respect among people. Choose from a school-based theme, a world theme, or a workplace theme. Display all the posters in the hallway. Choose two students to create and decorate a voting box, and then invite students from other classes to vote for the poster they think best represents respect for others.

GLOBAL WORKPLACE — Employment Prospects, New and Old

Egypt, a country in North Africa that borders both the Mediterranean and the Red Sea, has one of the most developed economies of the Middle East, with well-developed tourism, agriculture, and service industries.

Zero Unemployment The city of Damietta, with a population of more than one million, claims that no one in the city is unemployed. That is because nearly everyone works in one of the approximately 60,000 carpentry shops, which make handcrafted furniture for export, a skill that has been passed from one generation to the next. The governor estimates that Damietta exports $100 million worth of furniture annually.

Turning Dreams into Reality Samsung, the electronics company based in Korea, has launched a "Real Dreams" program in Egypt, partnering with Egyptian young professional group Nahdet El Mahrousa, in the hopes of fostering a culture of youth entrepreneurship. It will target students and out-of-school youth, to improve their employment prospects. Research the "Real Dreams" program in Egypt and summarize your findings in a one-page report.

Common Arabic Words and Phrases		
Hello	سلام	salam
Goodbye	مع السلامة	maasalaamah
Yes/ No	نعم / لا	naam/la
Thank you	شكرًا	shokran
You're welcome	عفوًا	Aafwaan

As you might imagine, managers who make Theory X assumptions do not motivate employees very well. In most small businesses, Theory Y assumptions are most effective. Some managers combine elements of both theories. They allow employees freedom in some aspects of their professional lives and control their actions in others.

Hygiene Factors Versus Motivating Factors

According to Frederick Herzberg, people are influenced by two types of factors. Herzberg calls factors such as money, working conditions, and fair company policies hygiene factors. **Hygiene factors** do not improve situations, but keep them from getting worse. Herzberg says that hygiene factors work only in the short run. However, they do ensure that employees are not dissatisfied.

In contrast, Herzberg defined **motivating factors** as factors that motivate employees, such as achievement, recognition, responsibility, advancement, growth, and the reward from doing the work itself. Many of these are part of Theory Y's assumptions. Both McGregor and Herzberg emphasize the value of work, the importance of achievement, and the assumption of responsibility.

 Reading Check Connect What are the benefits of having motivated employees?

Maximizing Employee Performance

There are several motivational techniques that can help you maximize employee performance. They include providing meaningful work; allowing scheduling flexibility; involving employees in decision making; giving recognition; providing performance evaluations; and rewarding performance.

Provide Meaningful Work

Employees who are motivated by their work relate to it in a special way. They take pride in it. To prompt such feelings, a job must be meaningful. It must offer a range of duties and responsibilities.

If your employees' jobs do not fit this description, consider redesigning them. You can do this by increasing the tasks, responsibilities, and scope of a job. Alternatively, you could make a job more rewarding and less monotonous by adding elements at a higher skill level.

Allow Scheduling Flexibility

Allowing employees to plan and manage their own work schedule sends a clear message of trust. Flexible scheduling takes a variety of forms:

- **Telecommuting** involves performing some or all of the job away from the business. The key is technology. Computers, smart phones, tablets, and overnight delivery services allow employees to work at home, on the road, or during business trips.
- **Family leave** allows employees to take time off work to attend to **significant** personal events, such as births, deaths, and family illnesses, without fear of job loss. The Family Medical Leave Act, which requires large companies to offer family leave, is discussed in Chapter 8.
- **Flextime** allows employees to choose the work hours and days that are most effective for their personal lives. For example, an employee might work four 10-hour days instead of five 8-hour days.

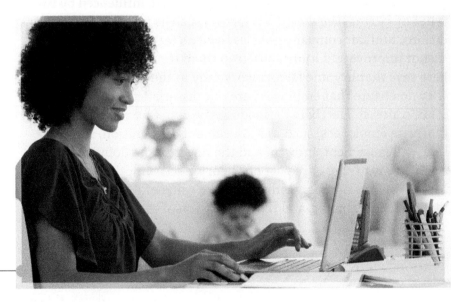

Workplace Flexibility Technology is key to telecommuting, which involves performing some or all of the job away from the business. *Would you be willing to offer telecommuting in your business? Why or why not?*

JGI/Jamie Grill/Blend Images LLC

These techniques can lead to increased productivity, but they do not lend themselves to every work situation. An auto mechanic cannot work at home; neither can an electrician.

Involve Employees in Decision Making

Let employees make suggestions. Suggestions may be about where the organization is going and what their roles will be. This management approach has two positive outcomes. First, it gives employees a sense of purpose. Second, it allows employees to see their own ideas put to work. Both lead to extra motivation and a sense of ownership.

You can also involve employees by using quality circles, which are described in Chapter 16, or by having managers and employees jointly set objectives and periodically assess progress.

Give Recognition

Public acknowledgment of an employee's contributions is important. Every day you may have many opportunities to give recognition informally. It may be a simple matter of praising employees when you see them doing a good job. It could involve giving credit to an employee for a useful idea or suggestion.

You can also give employees formal recognition. A letter of appreciation is one example. Presenting plaques or awards at meetings or banquets is another.

When you recognize an employee's contributions, they are more likely to continue to perform well. You also increase the morale and motivation of your other employees.

Provide Performance Evaluations

A **performance evaluation** is the process of judging how well an employee has performed the duties and responsibilities associated with a job. Formal evaluations are usually done once a year and can be very motivational. In a private meeting with the employee, you evaluate the person's strengths and weaknesses. You can also give tips to help the employee become more productive. Informal evaluations may be given more often.

Reward Performance

Systems for rewarding performance are used to acknowledge employee achievement. Usually, they rely on financial rewards. Many employees measure personal value and success with their salary and bonuses. However, reward systems can include things besides money. Other options are special assignments, job titles, and promotions. These, too, can represent acknowledgment and achievement.

Web Savvy

Instant Messaging and Employees
Not long ago, instant messaging—or "IMing"—was viewed as a nuisance or even a passing fad. But IM has become a powerful business tool. As more and more companies use telecommuting and distance workers, IM is a great—and free—way for colleagues to have immediate access to one another. And with IM available on most smart phones, it has truly become a simple and effective way for teams to always stay in touch with one another. *What are some different instant messaging services and how are they different?*

Delegating Responsibility

Delegating responsibility is a useful management tool. When you delegate, you give an employee the authority to and responsibility for carrying out some of your work. This allows you to work on other things, while at the same time motivating and showing confidence in the employee. It also prepares employees for more responsibility.

Before you decide to delegate responsibility, you must be sure the employee is both capable and willing. You also have to trust that the employee can handle the job; the final responsibility still rests with you.

Evaluating Employee Motivational Techniques

Motivational techniques used daily will usually yield quick feedback. You might have to make some adjustments, but you probably will not have to formally evaluate their effectiveness. In contrast, you need to formally evaluate techniques that require a large commitment of company time and resources, such as flextime, quality circles, and awards banquets.

SECTION 18.2　Review

After You Read ▪▪▪▪▪▪▪▪▪▪▪▪▪

Self-Check

1. **Explain** the difference between McGregor's Theory X and Theory Y.
2. **List** three ways to maximize employee performance.
3. **Name** four questions to ask when reviewing an employee motivation program.

Think

4. **Explain** how money can be used as both a hygiene factor and a motivating factor.

Mathematics

5. **Unpaid Leave** Dmitri was going to take 14 weeks of unpaid leave from a small music production company to take care of a sick family member. Dmitri earns $28,420 per year. How much money will Dmitri give up during his leave?

    Math Concept **Number and Operations** Writing a number sentence can help you determine what operations to use to solve a problem.

    Step 1 Write a number sentence to determine how much Dmitri earns each week.

    Step 2 Multiply the weekly salary by the number of weeks he will be on leave to determine the total amount Dmitri will give up.

Go to connectED.mcgraw-hill.com to check your answers.

Entrepreneurs *in Action*

Alex Payson
Co-Owner
Blue State Coffee

Q *What do you do?*

A I'm responsible for almost all operations. I was the first employee and I opened the first store, so I was responsible for finding vendors and contractors and then running the store. We now have two more stores; I am still the primary manager for one of them. I'm also in charge of all Web site operations.

Q *What kind of training and education did you need to get this job?*

A I had no formal business training. I received a bachelor's degree from Brown University, but I was studying biology. But I was also working in the food industry, in cafes and restaurants. That taught me the basics of the food industry.

Q *What do you enjoy most about your job?*

A The diversity of roles I get to play, and having the chance to be innovative. Every day brings new challenges. The hardest part for me is the human resources angle: interpersonal skills. Brewing a cup of coffee isn't easy, but its very predictable, and after a while you find a formula for doing it just right. I haven't found that formula yet for being a good manager. Being easygoing and patient is a gift.

Q *How did you become interested in your field?*

A Blue State let me combine my two backgrounds: my training in biology and my work experience with food. Being sustainable, eco-friendly, and "green" is very important to me. My scientific background helps me make that happen in this industry, and coffee was the first opportunity that presented itself.

Building a Work Force

You run a restaurant and catering business. Your employees sometimes work on site in peoples' homes.

1. Write a help-wanted ad describing the type of employees you want to hire.
2. In a paragraph, tell new employees how they should behave with customers.
3. Motivate your employees with a short written description of your bonus program.

Career Facts

Real-World Skills	Academic Skills	Career Cluster
Interpersonal Skills, Time Management	Science, English Language Arts	Agriculture, Food & Natural Resources

Alex Payson

Visual Summary

Managing Human Resources

Hiring Staffing a business, whether ongoing or start-up, requires the same steps.

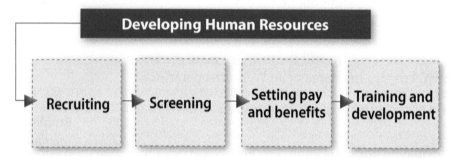

Developing Human Resources

Recruiting → Screening → Setting pay and benefits → Training and development

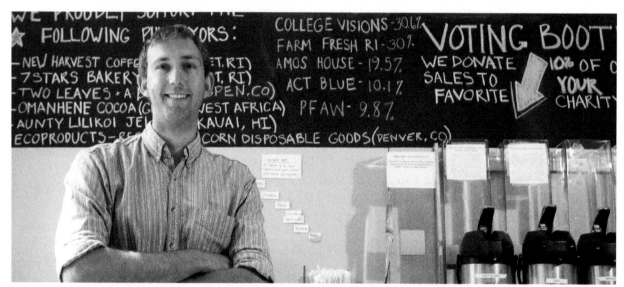

Influence There are several ways to get the most from employees.

Motivating Employees

Provide meaningful work → Allow for schedule flexibility → Involve employees in decision making → Give recognition → Provide performance evaluations → Reward performance

Alex Payson

Review and Assessment

Vocabulary

1. On a sheet of paper, use each of these terms and words in a written sentence.

Content Vocabulary

◇ human resources
◇ human resource management
◇ labor union
◇ educational activities
◇ developmental activities
◇ cost effective
◇ employee complaint procedure

◇ Pregnancy Discrimination Act
◇ Theory X
◇ Theory Y
◇ hygiene factors
◇ motivating factors
◇ telecommuting
◇ family leave
◇ flextime

◇ performance evaluation

Academic Vocabulary

■ labor
■ achieve
■ theory
■ significant

Key Concepts

2. **Identify** the components of human resource management.
3. **Describe** the advantages and disadvantages of recruiting from competitors.
4. **List** the techniques available for training and developing employees.
5. **Rank** the options available when an employee does not work out.
6. **Explain** how managers influence motivation.
7. **Describe** ways to maximize employee performance.
8. **Explain** the importance of delegation.
9. **Explain** how to assess motivational techniques used to increase performance levels.

Academic Skills

Mathematics

10. **Training Costs** An accounting firm determined it was losing an average of $9,300 per employee because employees were not proficient with new software. Three employees are being sent for two days of training. The costs of the training are: Registration: $550 per employee; Travel and Lodging: $625 per employee; Salary and Benefits: $175 per employee for each day out of the office; and Temporary Replacements: $1,200. Assuming the training fixes the problem, will it be cost effective?

Math Concept **Making Inferences** You can infer that, to be cost effective, the cost of the training must be less than the average loss.

Step 1 Write an equation that will determine the total cost of the training.
Step 2 Compare the cost of the training to the amount the firm was losing to determine whether the training is cost effective.

English Language Arts

11. **Synonyms** The suffixes –tion and –ment are often used to turn verbs into nouns. Find words in this chapter ending in –tion or –ment that have meanings similar to the following words: *pay, firing, hiring, pension.*

Academic Skills *(continued)*

Social Studies

12. Labor Unions In recent years, the influence of labor unions in the United States has been declining. However, the opposite was the case at the beginning of the twentieth century, when unions were gaining membership and strength. Identify reasons for the rise of unions one hundred years ago and for their decreasing role in society today.

Science

13. The Scientific Method Scientists solve problems using the scientific method. Find out more about how and why scientists use the scientific method. Write a few paragraphs explaining how a variation on the scientific method could be useful to managers and employees in an entrepreneurial business setting.

Real-World Skills

Learning Skills

14. Training Methods Have you had a job or helped as a volunteer? How did you learn what to do—by asking co-workers, through formal training, or by other methods? If you have not had a job, how would you expect your employees to learn how to do their jobs? In a few paragraphs, describe your experiences or plans and explain which would work best and why.

21st Century Skills

Creativity and Innovation

15. Motivate Classmates Recall the information in this chapter about motivating employees and apply those lessons creatively to motivating students. If you were in charge of running your school, how would you motivate students to improve their attendance, homework, and grades? Give your answers in the form of a motivational speech.

Connect to Your Community

16. Plan for Training Imagine you own a local business with which you are familiar. Consider the training and development of your employees and prepare a plan that includes immediate, intermediate, and long-range training and development needs; types of programs offered; implementation procedures; and evaluation procedures.

17. Tips from Local Managers Interview an entrepreneur or small business manager in your community about the techniques used to motivate employees. As a class, compile your results. Are there similarities among companies? Which techniques would motivate you?

Review and Assessment

CHAPTER
18

Competitive Events Prep

18. Situation You own a sporting goods store that has 15 employees. You have agreed to have your staff work with the local chapter of the Special Olympics to assist with coaching children. The store will provide all necessary equipment. You are hoping for 100% staff participation in the program, but participation is voluntary. With one exception, the staff is enthusiastic and eager to begin.

Activity Approach the reluctant employee about the reason for not participating. You are to attempt to discover the reason(s) the employee is reluctant to participate, and gently try to persuade the employee to join in the program.

Evaluation You will be evaluated on how well you meet these performance indicators:

- Enlist others in working toward a shared vision.
- Explain the role of business in society.
- Participate as a team member.
- Foster positive working relationships.
- Demonstrate honesty and integrity.

 Go to connected.mcgraw-hill.com for more information about this activity and other competitive events.

Standardized Test Practice

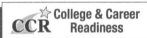

Directions Choose the letter of the best answer. Write the letter for the answer on a separate piece of paper. For question #2, if the answer is False, rewrite the statement to make it true.

1. All of the following are components of human resource management, *except*:
   A. Handling employee termination
   B. Ensuring equal opportunity
   C. Overseeing employee training and development
   D. Overseeing purchasing and distribution

2. Theory X is the belief that employees are responsible, like to work, and want intrinsic rewards.
   T
   F

> **Test-Taking Tip**
> Pay attention to key words in the question and in each answer choice.

Business Plan Project

Getting Organized

To succeed with your marketing efforts, you need to research and plan. *Who are your competitors? How will you reach your customers?*

Objectives

In this project, you will complete these parts of your business plan:

- Determine what equipment and technology your company will need.
- Select a method for ensuring quality control.
- Describe your company's organizational structure.

The Skills You'll Use

- **Academic Skills** English Language Arts, Mathematics, Economics
- **Real World Skills** Organization, Productivity, and Accountability
- **21st Century Skills** Productivity and Accountability; Business Literacy

▶ Operational Plan

The Operational Plan section of the business plan includes information about the business's location and zoning, property ownership or lease terms, equipment needed, manufacturing processes, channels of distribution, key suppliers, purchasing processes, storage needs, inventory control procedures, and quality control measures.

Step 1 **Plan Your Equipment Needs** Every new business needs equipment and machinery. Create a chart like the one below to document the equipment your proposed business will need.

Type of Equipment	Purpose	Technology Requirements	Purchase or Lease	Cost

Step 2 **Describe How You Will Control Quality**
Write a brief description of your proposed business's quality assurance policies. Include an explanation of the quality control measures that will be taken. Describe how you will evaluate the effectiveness of your quality control program.

▶ Organizational Plan

The Organizational Plan offers information about the business's legal structure, methods of and responsibilities for record keeping, and legal and insurance issues. It also covers the people aspects of the business, including staffing and training of personnel and the organizational structure of the planned business.

Step 1 **Plan Your Human Resources** Diagram and describe the organizational structure of the business. Develop a job description for each position on the organizational flowchart, including skill sets needed and salaries offered. Develop charts or graphs that classify employees by function, skill set, hourly pay, and part-time or full-time status.

Issue	Description	Implications
Type of Legal Business Form		
Advantages of Legal Type		
Legal Agreements		
Legal Liability Issues		
Government Regulations		
Environmental Regulations		
Zoning Matters		
Licensing Requirements		

Step 2 **Consider Legal Issues** Create a chart like the one above to organize information about legal issues that may affect your proposed business.

Use the **Business Plan Project Appendix** on pages **572-583** to explore the content requirements of a business plan in more detail.

Business Plan Project Template Go to connectED.mcgraw-hill.com for a business plan template that you can use to write your own business plan.

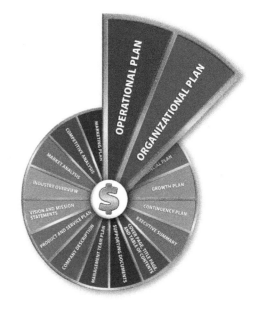

My Business Plan
When you have completed your Project, put your statements, charts, and other research in your Business Plan Portfolio.

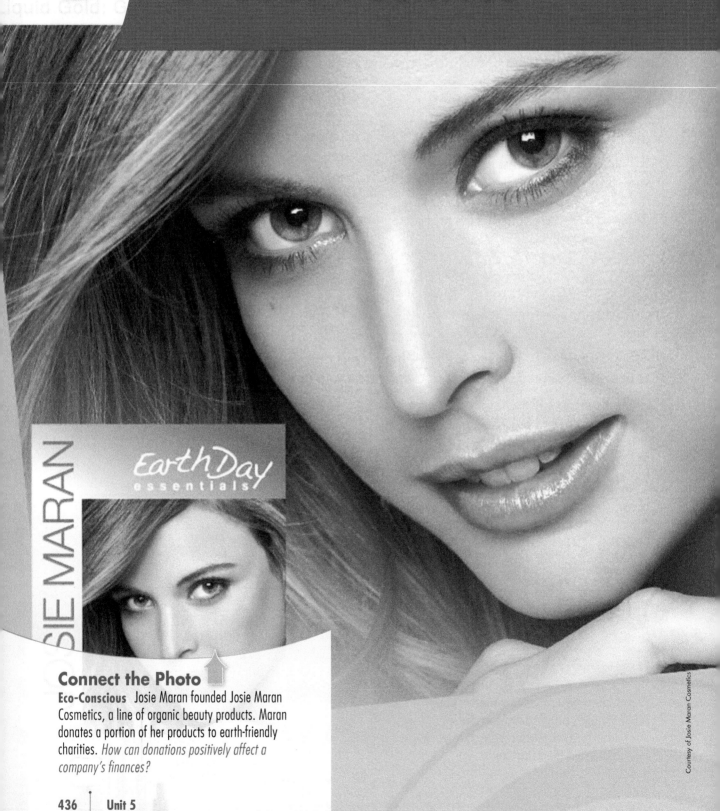

UNIT

5

Managing the Finances of Your Business

Connect the Photo

Eco-Conscious Josie Maran founded Josie Maran Cosmetics, a line of organic beauty products. Maran donates a portion of her products to earth-friendly charities. *How can donations positively affect a company's finances?*

Courtesy of Josie Maran Cosmetics

Business Plan Project

Preview

Planning Your Finances

As an entrepreneur, you will need to create budgets, keep accurate records, and analyze finances. Will you borrow money to start up your new company? Will you purchase accounting software and balance your own books? Will you seek tax credits for using energy efficient products?

The **Business Plan Project** will help you address and organize some of these concerns by focusing on these sections of the business plan:

▶ The **Financial Plan** section of a business plan presents past and current finances and financial forecasts and explains the assumptions made when calculating forecast figures.

▶ The **Growth Plan** looks at how the business will expand in the future.

Prepare for the Business Plan Project

As you read this unit, use this checklist to prepare for the Business Plan Project:

- Brainstorm a list of possible start-up costs that might be necessary to get your new business going.
- Research different types of online personal accounting software, including their strengths and weaknesses.
- Interview a school administrator or local business owner about controlling costs.

Chapter Objectives

SECTION 19.1
Financing the Small Business Start-Up

Describe the resources available to entrepreneurs for starting a business.

Compare and contrast sources of financing for start-up ventures.

Describe the importance of financial planning.

SECTION 19.2
Obtaining Financing and Growth Capital

Describe the information needed to obtain financing.

Explain the types of growth financing available to entrepreneurs.

Describe how to calculate start-up capital requirements.

Discovery Project
Funding a Business

Key Question *How are privately owned businesses in your community funded?*

Project Goal
Work with a partner to conduct a survey of privately owned businesses in your community. Find out the method used to finance the company. Did they use funds from personal savings, friends and family, private investors, partners, venture capitalists, or state-sponsored venture capital?

Think About...
➤ *How will you identify privately owned local businesses?*
➤ *What questions will you ask the business owners?*
➤ *How will you present the results of your survey?*

 21st Century Skills
Innovation *What other resources might be available to fund a small business?*

Evaluate
 Go to connectED.mcgraw-hill.com to download a rubric that you can use to evaluate your final project.

Q: *I am the sole proprietor of an independent record label that has grown rapidly over the last six months. Now that my business and staff have grown, I am considering incorporating my business. What are the advantages of incorporating?*

A: The main advantage to incorporating is the limited liability of the incorporated company. There are also many potential tax benefits, such as the small business deduction or tax deferral. Corporations can also sell shares and raise equity capital, a big advantage because equity capital generally does not have to be repaid and incurs no interest.

Purestock/SuperStock

Connect the Photo

Money Makes Businesses Go 'Round There are many common sources of money for start-up businesses: personal savings, friends and family, private investors, partners, and venture capitalists. However, before determining where the money is going to come from, entrepreneurs need to figure out how much they need. *Which source of money do you think is the most risky? Why?*

Financing the Small Business Start-Up

Reading Guide

Before You Read ▪▪▪▪▪▪▪▪▪▪▪▪▪▪

Connect Why is financial planning so important?

The Main Idea

Most start-up funds come from an entrepreneur's personal resources such as savings; however, there are other common sources of funding.

Objectives

Describe the resources available to entrepreneurs to start a business.

Compare and contrast sources of financing for start-up ventures.

Describe the importance of financial planning.

Content Vocabulary

◇ bootstrapping
◇ factor
◇ equity capital
◇ equity
◇ risk capital
◇ angel
◇ venture capital
◇ venture capitalist
◇ dept capital
◇ operating capital
◇ line of credit
◇ trade credit

Academic Vocabulary

You will see these words in your reading and on your tests. Use the academic vocabulary glossary to look up their meanings.

■ resource   ■ associate

Graphic Organizer

Draw a Venn diagram like the one shown. As you read, write notes about debt financing in the left circle and notes about equity financing in the right. In the overlapping portion, write notes that apply to both.

 Go to **connectED.mcgraw-hill.com** to download this graphic organizer.

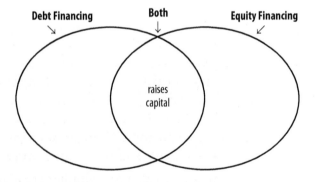

Debt Financing   Both   Equity Financing

raises capital

Entrepreneurial Resources

Finding the **resources** to launch a business is a creative process. It is one of the unique talents of entrepreneurs. It requires understanding the differences between short-term and long-term capital needs.

Short-Term and Long-Term Needs

Short-term needs are **associated** with activities that are not part of normal operations, such as the costs of start-up, or a seasonal increase in sales that requires purchasing more inventory than normal. Long-term needs generally relate to preparation for future growth and often involve the purchase of capital assets, such as equipment and facilities.

Bootstrapping

Most entrepreneurs get their businesses launched by bootstrapping. **Bootstrapping** involves operating as frugally as possible and cutting all unnecessary expenses. Entrepreneurs accomplish this by borrowing, leasing, and partnering to acquire resources. Bootstrapping consists of:

- **Hiring as few employees as possible** Employees generally are the greatest single business expense. Entrepreneurs often get by as long as they can without hiring employees. They do this by hiring independent contractors who have their own businesses and offer specialized services. The independent contractor handles his own taxes and insurance.
- **Leasing anything you can** Do not tie up your money in equipment or a building. If you lease, you usually have no down payment, and costs are spread out over a long period of time enabling you to hang onto your cash.
- **Being creative** When Marianne Szymanski started a toy research company in Milwaukee, she knew she could not afford a research and test center. Instead, she used crowdfunding to seek contributions. Crowdfunding is raising money for a business through monetary contributions from people who believe in the produce or service.

Entrepreneurs can also ask suppliers to allow longer payment terms. They can require customers to pay in advance or pay half up front and half upon delivery. They can also sell their accounts receivable to a factor. A **factor** is an agent who handles an entrepreneur's accounts receivable for a fee.

The factor pays the entrepreneur cash for the receivables. He or she charges a fee of 1 or 2 percent on each account, plus interest on the cash advance. The factor then assumes the responsibility of collecting the accounts receivable from the customer. Using a factor gives a business immediate cash from credit transactions.

Go Green

Microcredits: Helping People and the Environment

Thailand's Khao Yai National Park was continually being exploited by poor villagers who needed its natural resources, which include thousands of species of plants, birds, and animals. Illegal logging and hunting caused extensive damage to the park. The Community-Based Integrated Rural Development Center (CBIRD Center) stepped in, offering the villagers microcredits. Microcredits are small, low-interest loans designed to spur entrepreneurship. These microcredits helped the villagers build businesses such as mini-farms that help them make money without harming the environment.

◈ **Critical Thinking**
How would the use of microcredits help the global economy as a whole? Explain your answer in a paragraph.

As You Read
Recall What is bootstrapping?

Business Case Study

What Hatches Small Businesses? An Incubator!

Mentoring, money, and more await at small business incubators

A business incubator is a support system that provides resources and services to entrepreneurs with fledgling businesses. Incubator programs are sponsored by private companies, municipalities, and colleges and universities.

Cash incubators typically provide from $6,000 to $18,000, but they offer more than just money. Entrepreneurs may receive office space, mentoring and coaching, consultations from lawyers and accountants, product-showcase opportunities, and valuable networking connections. Capital is usually provided in exchange for equity in the business, but the other services are free.

Many incubators favor technology businesses, while others prefer to help start-ups such as minority-owned businesses, sustainable and renewable resource companies, or nonprofit arts organizations.

You can find incubators in all parts of the country, as well as virtual incubators online. How do you locate an incubator for your new business? A good place to start is the National Business Incubation Association (NBIA), which has both a search engine and a directory of about 1,400 incubators in the United States.

Active Learning

Write a one-page letter to interest a small business incubator in helping you with a start-up business. Describe the proposed product or service and request the funding you'll need, as well as other resources and services such as office space, a mentor or lawyer, and so on. Explain why the incubator should select your business.

Start-Up Money

A new business has no track record to prove that it will survive. For that reason, it may have a hard time attracting investors. Because of this, the main source of start-up money for entrepreneurs is personal resources—friends, family, and others who believe in the entrepreneur.

These resources come in several forms: savings, credit cards, loans, and investments. If you plan to start a business, you should begin saving now. You should also identify people and other resources you can approach in the future when you need them.

 Reading Check Compare and Contrast What is the difference between equity financing and debt financing?

Financing the Start-Up

To finance a new business, entrepreneurs can use banks, finance companies, investment companies, and government grants. Two broad types of financing for new ventures are equity and debt financing.

Sources of Equity Financing

Equity capital is cash raised for a business in exchange for an ownership stake in the business. **Equity** is an ownership in a business. For example, an investor might invest $50,000 in your business in exchange for a 25 percent ownership stake.

Equity funding is sometimes called risk capital. **Risk capital** is money invested in companies where there is financial risk. Individuals who invests in a business risk their own money. If the business is successful, the investors make a return on the investment. However, if the business does poorly, the investors may lose money. If the business fails altogether, the entire investment might be lost.

Personal Savings

The number one source of start-up capital is the entrepreneur's personal savings. The U.S. Department of Commerce reports that 67 percent of new businesses started without borrowing any money. When a business does borrow money, entrepreneurs should contribute more than half of the start-up capital so that they maintain control of the business.

Friends and Family

In order to start up their own businesses, entrepreneurs often borrow money from their friends and relatives. Before you do this, you need to weigh the advantages and disadvantages of this option. Consider what will happen to the relationship if the business fails and the investment is lost.

Private Investors

An **angel** is a private investor who funds start-up companies. Angels are nonprofessional financing sources. They are often friends, relatives, and business associates who invest because of their belief in a business concept and founding team.

The most common way to find an angel is through networking. Many angels have banded together so that they can jointly invest larger amounts of capital.

Partners

By finding a partner or partners with similar goals, you can share the costs of a business. You can also divide up the responsibilities. Your business can also form a strategic alliance with another business that has special skills you need.

When entering a partnership, put the partnership agreement in writing and have it reviewed by an attorney. Chapter 7 discusses partnerships in greater detail.

Tech Savvy

Wraparound Television

In technology, innovations are conceived every day, yet not every innovation leads to profitability. General Electric has developed a process that prints Organic Light Emitting Diodes (OLEDs), for use in television screens and mobile phone displays, in a process similar to printing newspapers off rolls of paper. Sony researchers have used OLEDs to create full-color television screens so thin they bend. Imagine a television display worn as wraparound sunglasses or hung like wallpaper. Sony has invested research money; now they hope consumers will catch on. *Why would General Electric or Sony invest money in cutting-edge technologies like Organic Light Emitting Diodes?*

Venture Capitalists

Venture capital is a source of equity financing for small businesses with exceptional growth potential and experienced senior management. It is a pool of investor capital that is managed by the fund's managers, often called "venture capitalists." The primary goal of the **venture capitalist** is to make money for investors. Because they rarely fund start-up ventures, venture capital firms fund less than 1 percent of all ventures, and those ventures are typically in high-tech, high-growth areas.

State-Sponsored Venture Capital Funds

State funds are sometimes used to encourage the creation of new businesses and jobs. Because they are not as profit-focused, these funds are more likely to support a small business. To locate such funds, check with your local economic development corporation.

Sources of Debt Financing

Sources of debt capital are far more numerous than sources of equity capital. **Debt capital** is the money raised by taking out loans. With debt financing, an entrepreneur borrows money and must repay it with interest. When an entrepreneur raises capital by borrowing, he or she retains full ownership of the business. However, the loan must be carried as a liability on the business's balance sheet and you must be certain that your business can generate enough cash flow to repay the loan.

Many companies have found themselves in trouble by taking on more debt than they could repay. Therefore, you must consider the impact of interest rates (the cost of borrowing) on short- and long-term financing. Short-term rates are typically higher, but in either case, you need to calculate the total cost of using debt sources. This includes the principal amount borrowed and the total interest you must pay on the loan.

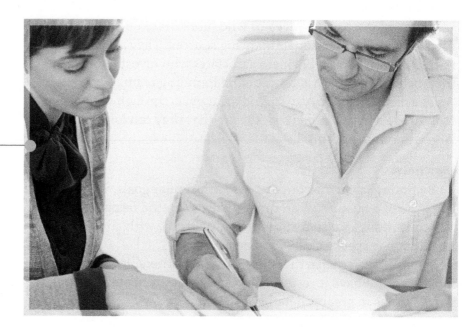

Giving Credit Entrepreneurs often meet with financial planners to determine the best way to fund their new business. *What is the number one source of start-up money for new entrepreneurs?*

Rob Daly/OJO Images/age fotostock

Banks

Banks were once the primary source of operating capital. **Operating capital**, or working capital, is the money a business uses to support its operations in the short term. Today, however, banks are conservative in their lending practices. They are likely to lend only to well-established businesses.

An established business can usually get a line of credit (a loan) from a bank. A **line of credit** is an arrangement whereby a lender agrees to lend up to a specific amount of money at a certain interest rate for a definite period of time. The company can then borrow against that credit line and pay back the money on a regular basis. You might be able to borrow money using your business assets as security. If you do not pay back the loan, the bank can take those pledged assets.

Web Savvy

Venture Capital and the Internet
Start-up companies often seek out venture capital. Getting venture capital is not easy, but the Internet has made it easier for entrepreneurs to locate angel investors and make contact with them. Recent years have seen a very high number of Internet start-ups seeking venture capital. This, coupled with the dot-com crash of the early 2000s, has made investors choosier than ever. *What are the pros and cons of using venture capital to start a business?*

Trade Credit

Businesses grant **trade credit** to other businesses for the purchase of goods or services. It is a source of short-term financing provided by companies within your industry or trade. Suppose you purchase goods from a supplier on 60 days of credit, interest free. This means you must pay the supplier within 60 days of receiving the goods.

Minority Enterprise Development Programs

Funded by the private sector and the Small Business Administration, MESBICs (Minority Enterprise Small Business Investment Companies) provide funding to businesses whose owners are at least 51 percent ethnic minority, female, or disabled. The SBA also helps such businesses secure contracts and find strategic partners.

Commercial Finance Companies

Commercial finance companies provide a more expensive alternative to commercial banks. Finance companies are less conservative than banks, and they typically are willing to take more risks. Consequently, they also charge more. Some form of security is usually required for a loan.

SBA Loan

If the Small Business Administration approves your request for a loan, it will use a commercial bank to process and release the money. It will also guarantee repayment to the lender of up to a maximum of 90 percent of the loan should your business fail. The SBA assures the bank that it can lose only the portion of the loan that is not guaranteed. You and anyone with more than 20 percent ownership also must guarantee the loan with your personal assets. The SBA lends public funds to qualified veterans and people with disabilities.

Small Business Investment Companies (SBICs)

SBICs are privately managed venture capital companies. The SBA licenses them to provide equity and debt financing to young businesses. The government provides funding at favorable rates to the SBIC. The SBIC then matches the funding with its own capital. SBICs invest in start-up ventures about twice as often as venture capitalists.

Financial Planning for Your Business

Financial planning means finding the right financial resources at the right time in the right amount. It provides you with a better chance of securing the money you need when you need it.

Financial planning starts with identifying your business's stages of growth. Then you must identify critical milestones that require more resources. One milestone may be hiring your first employee. Another may be moving to a larger facility.

Another financial planning consideration is identifying business advisers who can introduce you to funding sources. Experienced advisers will help you locate "smart" money, that is, investors and others who bring money, expertise, guidance, and contacts to your business.

Financial planning includes hiring the best management expertise you can. The founding team may have worked without pay for an equity stake in the business. However, you must pay the management personnel you hire at market rates.

SECTION 19.1 Review

After You Read ■■■■■■■■■■■■■■■

Self-Check
1. **Describe** bootstrapping and how can it help entrepreneurs start a business.
2. **Explain** the difference between debt and equity financing.
3. **Identify** the most common source of start-up capital for entrepreneurs.

Think
4. **Determine** the best source of financing to use if you would like to retain as much control of your business as possible.

English Language Arts
5. **Acronyms** An acronym is a word formed from the initial letters of a phrase. For example, MESBIC stands for Minority Enterprise Small Business Investment Companies. Some acronyms become familiar words with frequent use. Research the following words and identify the phrases from which they were formed: *laser, radar, scuba, sonar*.

Go to connectED.mcgraw-hill.com to check your answers.

Obtaining Financing and Growth Capital

Reading Guide

Before You Read ■■■■■■■■■■■■■■■
Connect Why are more funding sources available for growth than for start-up?

The Main Idea
Additional sources of funding become available when entrepreneurs are ready to grow their businesses. Entrepreneurs must calculate business milestones and financial needs so they can communicate this information to potential funders.

Objectives
Describe the information needed to obtain financing.
Explain the types of growth financing available to entrepreneurs.
Describe how to calculate start-up capital requirements.

Content Vocabulary
◇ pro forma
◇ character
◇ capacity
◇ capital
◇ collateral
◇ conditions
◇ due diligence
◇ private placement
◇ initial public offering (IPO)
◇ stock
◇ working capital
◇ contingency fund

Academic Vocabulary
You will see these words in your reading and on your tests. Use the academic vocabulary glossary to look up their meanings.
■ invest
■ emphasis

Graphic Organizer
Draw a chart like the one shown. As you read, list the five Cs that bankers rely on to determine the acceptability of a loan applicant.

 Go to connectED.mcgraw-hill.com to download this graphic organizer.

The 5 Cs
C haracter _____
C _____
C _____
C _____
C _____

Synced Up Venture capitalists look for tech firms with huge growth potential, like companies who produce smart wristbands that can be synchronized with smart phones. *Why are venture capitalizes willing to tolerate a great deal of risk?*

How to Obtain Financing

Once you have identified potential sources of financing, you must create pro forma financial statements to include in your business plan to support the financing request. **Pro forma** refers to proposed or estimated financial statements based on predictions of how the actual operations of the business will turn out. Your plan must include income statements, cash flow statements, and balance sheets. All of these statements provide a financial road map for the business. They give potential investors and other sources of funding a sense of confidence that you know what you are doing.

Chapter 21 discusses these financial statements in more detail. In this section, you will discover what investors and others look for in a new business.

What Venture Capitalists Expect

As an entrepreneur, your primary goal is to build a business that survives and grows. The goal of the venture capitalist is to achieve a large capital gain, or return on investment, in a short period of time. At the outset, you and the venture capitalist do not have the same goals.

Venture capitalists rarely **invest** in start-up companies. When they do, however, they typically look for high-growth technology firms with huge market potential. A "high growth" firm is growing at least 20% every year. Because of the high level of risk in these ventures, venture capitalists want at least a 10 times return on their investment in about five to seven years. If your business is in the growth stage, venture capitalists may want only five to seven times their investment because the risk has gone down.

Management Teams

When looking at investment opportunities, venture capitalists look for businesses with good management teams. They believe a good team is the key to success. They also look for businesses with large, growing markets.

The process of obtaining funding from venture capitalists is slow, often taking months. Therefore, you should seek venture capitalists long before you actually need money.

● **As You Read** ■■■■■■■■
Identify What do bankers look for when screening an application for a business loan?

What Private Investors Expect

Private investors, often called angels, are often former entrepreneurs who want to take a different role in venture start-up. Unlike many venture capital firms, angels enjoy getting involved in the business. They typically invest in businesses they understand or in businesses where they know the entrepreneur. Today many angel investors network with like-minded investors, pooling their funds to invest in larger opportunities.

These investors typically find opportunities in their local metropolitan area through friends and business associates. On average, these investors, like venture capitalists, aim to get ten times their investment at the end of five years. Similar to bankers and venture capitalists, private investors want to see a strong management team.

What Bankers Expect

Bankers have different needs than venture capitalists. They must invest conservatively and follow strict rules about how to invest the bank's money. Therefore, they are most interested in a company's ability to repay a loan. That means they will examine a company's cash flow to determine whether the company has enough cash flow to pay monthly expenses and the loan payment.

ETHICS and BUSINESS

Social Responsibility

Situation You are working hard to open your own coffee store. Everything is set except for some of the financing. However, you have identified an elderly couple who are very interested in investing in your business.

Asking Tough Questions The couple wants to interview you before committing to help with your financing. They ask if you have a policy for social responsibility in your company. They wonder whether your coffee will come from sellers who destroy rain forests for farming or companies that treat their workers unfairly.

English Language Arts/Writing

Global Awareness Many business owners do not know or pay attention to where their product comes from or how it is produced. Their concern is only with profitability. Is this a socially responsible attitude?

1. How could you ensure that your company does not do business with companies that are not socially responsible?
2. Write a one-page policy that addresses your business's plans for social responsibility.

The Five Cs

While businesses make credit decisions based on an applicant's character, capacity, and capital, as Chapter 17 discusses, bankers rely on five Cs to determine the acceptability of a loan applicant. The bankers' five Cs are:

- **Character** A bank must believe in the character of the entrepreneur. **Character** is a borrower's reputation for fair and ethical business practices. Banks will consider your business experience, as well as your dealings with other local businesses. Your reputation in the community and among creditors is important. Like venture capitalists, bankers recognize the value of a good management team.
- **Capacity** **Capacity** refers to the ability of a business to pay a loan in view of its income and obligations. Banks look for businesses with sufficient cash flow to repay the loan.
- **Capital** Banks place a strong **emphasis** on whether a business has a financially stable capital structure. **Capital** is the net worth of a business, the amount by which its assets exceed its liabilities. Capital is used to operate a business. Banks prefer businesses that do not have too much debt.
- **Collateral** Banks are more likely to lend to businesses with valuable assets, or collateral. **Collateral** is security in the form of assets that a company pledges to a lender. If a business is unable to repay its loan, the bank then has the right to claim these assets.
- **Conditions** Banks consider all of the conditions of the environment in which the business will operate. **Conditions** are the circumstances at the time of the loan request. Business conditions include potential for growth, amount of competition, location, and type of ownership. It is not uncommon for banks to check insurance coverage. They may even demand that the entrepreneur obtain certain types of insurance, depending on the risk involved in the business.

To be considered for a commercial bank loan, you and your business must score high on all five Cs. Therefore, it is important for you and your business to maintain a favorable credit rating.

It is also important to establish a relationship with your banker before you ask for money. Let the banker see your business plan. Keep the banker up to date on major happenings with your business. If you take the time to build a strong relationship, the banker will already know the business and you when it comes time to ask for a loan.

Types of Growth Financing

When your business is ready to grow, you may find more financing options than you had at start-up. If your company has established a successful track record, some of the risk for investors is reduced. You have proven your concept, so more people are interested. In this section, you will learn about some of the types of financing available to grow your business.

Venture Capital (VC) Companies

Venture capital (VC) companies are unlikely sources of funding for most start-ups. With a proven concept and huge potential for growth, however, your business may attract venture capital.

Ownership Interest

Besides expecting very high rates of return, VC companies may also require a significant ownership interest. However, if your business is more established and less risky, the VC will want less in return for its investment. VCs also look for intellectual property and a strong market.

Finding a VC

The best way to find a VC company is through an introduction by someone close to it. You will probably be asked to supply a business plan and present it to the partners in the VC firm. If the firm decides that your company has a sound plan, it will begin due diligence. **Due diligence** is the investigation and analysis a prudent investor does before making business decisions. This means that the VC will run background checks on you, your team, and your business. If the experts like what they see, the terms of the agreement will be negotiated and an agreement made.

GLOBAL WORKPLACE — Tanzania: Great Vistas

Tanzania abounds in natural beauty and is home to the Serengeti Plain, Ngorongoro Crater, and the tallest mountain in Africa, Mount Kilimanjaro. Elephants, lions, rhinoceros, giraffes, and cheetahs populate the lowlands, and attract millions of tourists every year. Approximately 120 ethnic groups co-exist within Tanzania's borders, united by Swahili, Tanzania's common language, but speaking languages from all four major African language groups. Yet, despite Tanzania's natural and cultural wealth, it ranks as the third poorest nation in the world.

Hand Etiquette Tanzanians consider it improper to eat with the left hand. The taboo against the left hand extends to touching, shaking hands, and handing someone an object.

Social Studies The development of Tanzanian entrepreneurship has been encouraged  by what are called *microloans* or *microcredit*. Research microfinance and in a one-page essay decide whether or not microloans might be useful to entrepreneurs in your hometown.

Common Swahili Words and Phrases	
Hello	hujambo
Goodbye	kwaheri
Yes/ No	ndio/hapana
Please	tafadhali
Thank you	asante sana
You're welcome	asante kushukuru

Private Placements

Private placement is a way to raise capital by selling ownership interests in your private corporation or partnership. **Private placement** is a private offering or sale of securities directly to a limited number of investors who meet certain suitability standards. These ownership interests are called securities.

If you raise capital this way, follow Securities and Exchange Commission Regulation D. Regulation D states that your investors must meet certain requirements, such as they must be "sophisticated." Use a qualified attorney to set up the private placement memorandum. If your business fails, this memorandum details what investors can and cannot expect from you.

Initial Public Offerings (IPOs)

The **initial public offering (IPO)** is the sale of stock in a company on a public stock exchange. **Stock** is a type of security that signifies ownership in a corporation and represents a claim on part of the corporation's assets and earnings. An IPO is a popular way to raise money for growth. All proceeds of the IPO go to the company. However, once you have undertaken an IPO, your company is no longer private. It is public.

Public companies are regulated heavily by the SEC and the federal government. All of the company's information must be made available to the public. In effect, the entrepreneur no longer owns the company. The CEO is responsible primarily to the the shareholders, of which the entrepreneur is one, who now own the company. The IPO process is expensive and lengthy, with entrepreneurs spending up to a year preparing for the date of a public offering.

There are five steps to becoming a public company with stock for sale on a public stock exchange:

1. **Choose an underwriter or investment banker.** These professionals sell securities and help you through the initial public offering process, much like a tour guide.
2. **Draw up a letter of intent.** This letter outlines the terms and conditions between you and the underwriter and gives the initial price range for the stock.
3. **File a registration statement with the SEC.** This document is called a "red herring" or prospectus. It spells out the potential risks of investing in the initial public offering. You also need to choose the stock exchange where your stock will sell.
4. **Announce the offering in the financial press.** The advertisement you place in the financial paper is called a "tombstone."
5. **Do a road show.** This is a tour of all major institutional investors to market the offering. This is done so the offering can be sold in one day, the "coming out" day.

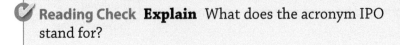 **Reading Check Explain** What does the acronym IPO stand for?

Start-Up Costs

Lease and security deposit	Most leases require the advance payment of a security deposit to the landlord.
Furniture, fixtures, and equipment	Your business may need computer hardware, software, and peripherals like fax machines and scanners.
Promotion expenses and office supplies	Initial advertising and promotion expenses include signs, business cards, and brochures.
Fees and licenses	Start-up businesses need funds to pay for accounting and legal fees, which may include permits and licenses.

● **Start-up Costs** Before you start your business, you must purchase capital expenditures such as furniture. *What are some more examples of capital expenditure?*

Calculating Your Start-Up Capital Needs

You already know you can acquire money to start or grow your business. Now you need to calculate exactly how much money your business requires. To do this, you will have to estimate start-up costs, which include capital expenditures, working capital (operating costs), and contingency funds.

Start-Up Costs

Start-up costs are those costs you incur before you start the business. To figure start-up costs, you need to talk to suppliers, vendors, manufacturers, distributors, and others in your industry. They can help you determine what you need and how much it will cost.

Suppose you are starting a simple retail business that offers computer classes and technical support. Your list of start-up costs might look like those found in **Figure 19.1**.

You need to calculate what it will cost to purchase or lease equipment and facilities. These are called capital expenditures and are usually one-time expenses. Equipment, furniture, and fixtures are included as capital expenditures. They should be included in your start-up costs. You can reduce the amount of start-up capital by cutting capital expenditures.

Operating Costs

Operating costs, often referred to as **working capital**, is the amount of cash needed to carry out daily business operations. It ensures that the business has a positive cash flow after covering all of its expenses. Working capital covers the time between selling your product or service and receiving payment from the customer.

Contingency Funds

No one can predict the future. That is why you should include extra funds, called contingency funds, when you calculate start-up needs. A **contingency fund** is an extra amount of money that is saved and used only when absolutely necessary. These funds are used if customers do not pay on time or to cover unforeseen business expenses.

SECTION 19.2 Review

After You Read ■■■■■■■■■■■■■

Self-Check

1. **Summarize** what private investors look for when investing in a new business.
2. **Explain** why venture capital is not a good source of start-up capital.
3. **Name** the three categories of funds you need to estimate to determine your start-up needs.

Think

4. **Describe** a start-up business that would attract venture capital.

Mathematics

5. **Start-Up Costs** You are creating a summary of your start-up costs to present to your investors. The start-up costs are as follows:
   - **Office furniture** $1,250
   - **Lease deposit** $850
   - **Equipment** $950
   - **Supplies** $175
   - **Fees and licenses** $100

   Choose the type of graph that will best represent how your investors' money is being spent—a line graph, a bar graph, or a pie chart—and explain how you will make it.

   Math Concept **Displaying Data** Data can be represented in many ways. Line graphs show change over time; bar graphs show relationships; and pie charts show how various parts relate to the whole.

   Step 1 Determine the purpose of the graph you want to create.
   Step 2 Choose the best type of graph for the task.

 Go to connectED.mcgraw-hill.com to check your answers.

Entrepreneurs *in Action*

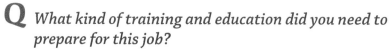

Doug Juanarena
Founder and President
GenTek Ventures

Q *What do you do?*

A My company helps young technology companies grow by assisting in raising growth capital and forming strategic partnerships. We also assist young entrepreneurs with the development of their strategy and business planning. From time to time, we take on operating roles until the company is in the position to recruit a qualified full-time staff.

Q *What kind of training and education did you need to prepare for this job?*

A I have an electrical engineering degree. I worked as a research engineer for NASA upon graduation and have been founder and CEO of three technology businesses over the past 30 years. Most of my training in business has come from on-the-job training. Along the way I received much help from advisors and mentors.

Q *What do you enjoy most about your job?*

A I enjoy helping young, smart people build and grow their businesses. It is challenging and rewarding to develop a strategy and business plan, raise capital, and then watch the company grow and compete.

Q *How did you become interested in your field?*

A I have always been interested in technology. I grew up watching the Mercury/Gemini and Apollo space programs and was fascinated by the science and engineering that put people on the moon.

CCR ☆ **College & Career Readiness**

Start Me Up Your friend is opening a business that will develop smart phone apps. Advise your friend on the best ways to finance his business.

1. Use the Internet and this chapter to research different forms of start-up financing.

2. List and briefly describe these sources—everything from personal savings to venture capital firms.

3. Pick the type of financing you think would be best for your friend's smart phone apps business. Write a one-page report explaining your choice.

Career Facts

Real-World Skills	Academic Skills	Career Cluster
Interpersonal Skills, Long-Range Planning, Organization	Mathematics, Economics, Science	Finance; Science, Technology, Engineering & Mathematics

Doug Juanarena

Visual Summary

Financing Your Business

Financing Options Equity and debt sources are two options for financing the business.

Financing the Start-Up	
Equity Financing	**Debt Financing**
Personal savings	Banks
Friends and family	Trade credit
Private investors	MESBICs
Partners	Finance companies
Venture capitalists	SBA loans
State-sponsored funds	SBICs

Good Credit Banks look for evidence of the five Cs when determining the acceptability of a loan applicant.

The Five Cs	
Character	A borrower's reputation for fair and ethical business practices
Capacity	The ability of a business to pay back a loan
Capital	The net worth of the business
Collateral	Security in the form of assets pledged to the lender
Conditions	Circumstances at the time of the request

Martin Barraud/Caia Image/Glow Images

Review and Assessment

CHAPTER 19

Vocabulary

1. On a sheet of paper, use each of these terms and words in a written sentence.

Content Vocabulary
◇ bootstrapping
◇ factor
◇ equity capital
◇ equity
◇ risk capital
◇ angel
◇ venture capital
◇ venture capitalist
◇ debt capital
◇ operating capital

◇ line of credit
◇ trade credit
◇ pro forma
◇ character
◇ capacity
◇ capital
◇ collateral
◇ conditions
◇ due diligence
◇ private placement

◇ initial public offering (IPO)
◇ stock
◇ working capital
◇ contingency fund

Academic Vocabulary
■ resource
■ associate
■ invest
■ emphasis

Key Concepts

2. **Describe** the resources available to entrepreneurs to start their business.
3. **Compare and Contrast** sources of financing for start-up ventures.
4. **Describe** the importance of financial planning.
5. **Describe** the information needed to obtain financing.
6. **Explain** the types of growth financing available to entrepreneurs.
7. **Describe** how to calculate start-up capital requirements.
8. **Determine** how you might use bootstrapping to help get your new business off the ground.
9. **Identify** the difference between private placements and initial public offerings.

Academic Skills

Mathematics

10. **Start-Up Costs** Chuck Dixon wants to start a country music Website. He estimated the start-up costs to be $7,300, the operating costs for the first six months to be $5,200, and personal expenses to be $8,750. Chuck has saved $10,750. How much money will he need to borrow?

Math Concept **Numbers and Operations** Writing a number sentence can help you think through what operations to use to solve the problem.
Step 1 Write a number sentence that helps you determine the difference between total cost of the new business and how much Chuck has saved.
Step 2 Subtract the savings from the total to determine how much to borrow.

English Language Arts

11. **Financial Planning** How would you go about developing a financial plan for the first ten years of your business? Write a one-page report that summarizes the concepts you have learned in this chapter, including types of funding, growth milestones, and contingency plans.

Academic Skills *(continued)*

Social Studies

12. The Bank of the United States Alexander Hamilton, the first Secretary of the Treasury of the United States, established the First Bank of the United States in 1791. Find out more about this episode in the early years of our country. Write a paragraph explaining why Hamilton believed the United States needed a central bank and why some people opposed his plan.

Science

13. Alternative Energy Venture capitalists are looking to invest in clean energy start-up companies. Research the various forms of clean energy, including solar, wind, tides, and thermal. Identify the pros and cons of each and tell which you think will become more important in the future.

Real-World Skills

Research Skills

14. Start-Up Fuel Many entrepreneurs finance their businesses with loans, including loans from the Federal Government's Small Business Administration (SBA). Go to the SBA's Website and research how to qualify and apply for an SBA loan. Summarize your findings in a short report.

21st Century Skills

Entrepreneurial Literacy

15. Pick the Winner Hold your own business-plan competition. Find three business plans on the Internet, choose the one you think is the best and explain the reasons for your choice in a one-page report.

Connect to Your Community

16. Loan Applications Go to a local bank and obtain a loan application. Fill it out to the best of your ability. Make a list of questions about the things you do not understand. Go back to the bank and get the answers. If possible, invite a banker to your class to answer questions about loans to small business owners.

17. IPOs Use a search engine or Web directory to research three companies that have recently sold stock on a public stock exchange for the first time. Identify the Securities and Exchange Commission rules and regulations for IPOs. Describe the ways the companies managed and marketed their offering. Use a spreadsheet application to present the results of your research in a table.

Competitive Events Prep

18. **Situation** You are the manager of an independent bookstore. You have studied entrepreneurship and worked hard to learn this business. You are beginning the process of starting your own bookstore. You are also investigating sources of financing for your proposed business. Now you plan to meet with a friend who works for a financial services firm to discuss your business plans in general, but specifically sources of financing for your business including both equity and debt financing.

Activity You are to prepare for the meeting by listing the difference between equity and debt financing and possible sources of each financing type.

Evaluation You will be evaluated on how well you meet these performance indicators:

- Distinguish between debt and equity financing for venture creation.
- Describe considerations in selecting capital resources.
- Explain sources of financial assistance.
- Demonstrate responsible behavior.
- Prepare simple written reports.

 Go to connectED.mgraw-hill.com for more information about this activity and other competitive events.

Standardized Test Practice

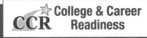 **College & Career Readiness**

Directions Choose the letter of the best answer. Write the letter for the answer on a separate piece of paper. For question #2, if the answer is False, rewrite the statement to make it true.

1. Which of the following is a source of equity capital?
   A. Commercial banks
   B. MESBICs
   C. Venture capitalists
   D. Commercial finance companies
2. Capacity refers to the ability of a business to pay a loan in view of its income and obligations.
   T
   F

Test-Taking Tip
To control the stress of test-taking, view the test as an opportunity to show how much you have studied and receive a reward for the studying you have done.

Accounting and Financial Reporting

Chapter Objectives

SECTION 20.1
Financial Record Keeping

Explain the important role accounting plays in business.

Explain the accounting system for a small business.

Describe the importance of daily sales and cash receipts reports.

SECTION 20.2
Preparing Financial Statements

Describe the items of information included on each financial statement.

Identify ongoing accounting activities.

Explain how technology helps business owners with all the accounting functions.

Discovery Project
Tracking Finances

Key Question *How can technology help me keep track of my financial information?*

Project Goal

Choose a minimum of five bookkeeping software products to compare and contrast. Determine the criteria you will use to compare and contrast the software products. Then, using your criteria, rank the products from 1 to 5, with 1 being the best product.

Think About...

➤ How will you find and research the software products?
➤ What criteria will you use to evaluate the software?
➤ How will you present your findings?

21st Century Skills

Productivity and Accountability *Why is it important for a business to keep accurate financial records?*

Evaluate

 Go to connectED.mcgraw-hill.com to download a rubric that you can use to evaluate your final project.

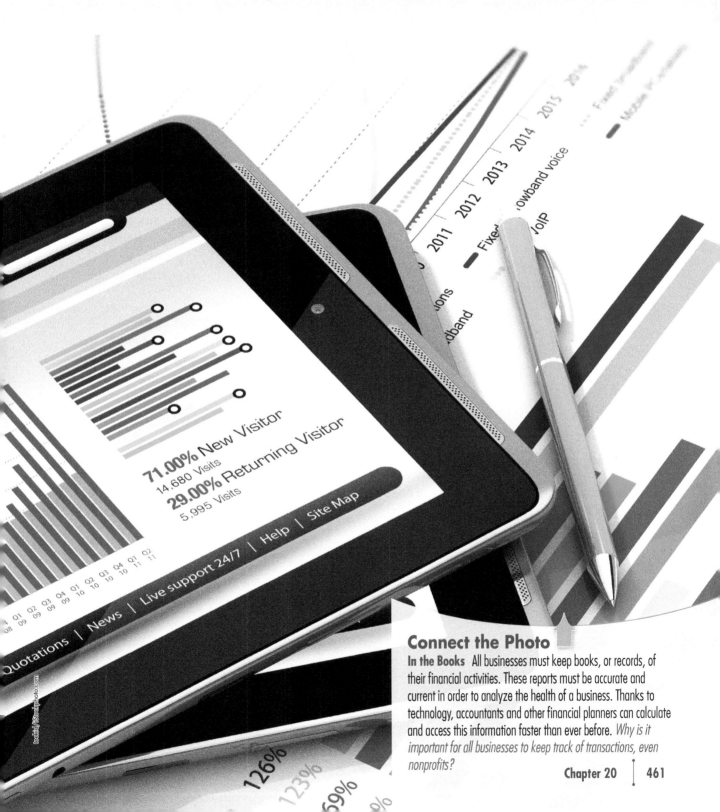

Ask AN EXPERT

Q: *Now that my business and staff have grown, I am considering incorporating my business. How will I know if my donations will be tax deducible?*

A: A gift of cash or property must meet certain criteria in order to be tax-deductible. You must actually donate cash or property. A pledge to donate is not deductible until you actually pay. You must contribute to a qualified organization with 501(c)(3) tax-exempt status. You must be able to itemize. Giving to charity is a great tax planning strategy, but it only works for people who are eligible to itemize their deductions. You must meet record keeping requirements, which includes saving canceled checks, acknowledgment letters from the charity, and appraisals for donated property.

Connect the Photo

In the Books All businesses must keep books, or records, of their financial activities. These reports must be accurate and current in order to analyze the health of a business. Thanks to technology, accountants and other financial planners can calculate and access this information faster than ever before. *Why is it important for all businesses to keep track of transactions, even nonprofits?*

Financial Record Keeping

Before You Read ▪▪▪▪▪▪▪▪▪▪▪▪▪▪

Connect Why do businesses use the same accounting system?

The Main Idea
All businesses must record and report all financial activities using established concepts and procedures.

Objectives
Explain the important role accounting plays in business.

Explain the accounting system for a small business.

Describe the importance of daily sales and cash receipts reports.

Content Vocabulary
◇ GAAP
◇ financial reports
◇ accounting period
◇ calendar year
◇ fiscal year
◇ assets
◇ current assets
◇ accounts receivable
◇ fixed assets
◇ liabilities
◇ accounts payable
◇ owner's equity
◇ chart of accounts
◇ debits
◇ credits
◇ cash basis
◇ accrual basis
◇ journal
◇ journalizing
◇ general journal
◇ posting

Academic Vocabulary
You will see these words in your reading and on your tests. Use the academic vocabulary glossary to look up their meanings.
▪ convert
▪ transfer

Graphic Organizer
Draw a chart like the one shown. As you read, write the numbers 1 to 5 on the lines to list the accounting procedures in the proper order.

⬆ Go to connectED.mcgraw-hill.com to download this graphic organizer.

Accounting Procedures

_____ Post amounts to the general ledger

_____ Analyze business transactions

_____ Prepare the balance sheet

_____ Enter amounts in a general journal

_____ Prepare an income statement

Accounting for Business

Accounting plays a vital role in the day-to-day activities of every business. Accounting records and reports encourage efficiency and profitability by keeping track of how much is earned and how much is spent.

Accounting principles and procedures are universal. All U.S. businesses, large and small, use the same system, which follows established accounting guidelines called "generally accepted accounting principles," or **GAAP**. If all businesses use the same system of recording and reporting financial information, anyone interested in examining a business's records will be able to understand its financial reports.

The accounting system is designed to collect, record, and report financial transactions that affect your business. **Financial reports** or statements are documents that summarize the results of your business operation and provide a picture of its financial position. These reports indicate to banks, financial institutions, and potential investors or buyers how well your business is doing. They also provide you with the financial information needed to make sound business decisions.

Accounting Assumptions

When creating accounting books, you will make two assumptions about your business. First, assume that your business will operate as a separate entity. This means that the records and reports of your business must be kept completely separate from your personal finances. Second, assume that your financial reports always cover a specific period of time. A block of time covered by an accounting report is called an **accounting period**. The accounting period can be a month or a quarter (three months), but the most common period is one year.

● As You Read ....
Compare and Contrast How do methods differ for hand-kept and computerized accounts ?

ETHICS and BUSINESS

Accounting for Your Business

Situation Your athletic shoe company is doing well. You have had a great third quarter and you are considering expanding and creating a new line of products. You have asked your accountant to gather the paperwork necessary to apply for a loan.

Questionable Accounting While he is preparing the loan paperwork, your accountant suggests altering the way some transactions are recorded so it will look better to the loan review committee and improve your chances of getting a loan. What he is suggesting is not illegal, but it is questionable.

English Language Arts/Writing

Right or Wrong Some business owners would appreciate the accountant's suggestion and would use it to help get the loan. Others would consider the suggestion unethical. How would you respond to the accountant's suggestion?

1. Would you allow the accountant to alter the way transactions are recorded? Would you keep your accountant?
2. Write a one-page memo to your accountant explaining your reasoning.

Web Savvy

Software as a Service

For a long time, software was a product that came in a box—you bought it, installed it, and it was yours. But recent years have seen a shift to a new model called "software as a service," usually abbreviated SaaS. In this model, you do not buy software but subscribe to it. CODA, QuickBooks Online, Freshbooks, and Xero are all Web-based accounting programs that do not cost anything to start using, but charge a monthly fee. One of the main benefits of SaaS, aside from lower upfront cost, is that there is never a need to upgrade, as the software provider does that for you. *What are some possible drawbacks to using SaaS for business?*

Calendar and Fiscal Years

If your one-year period begins on January 1 and ends on December 31, it is called a **calendar year**. However, you can choose to have your year begin and end in months other than the calendar year. This is referred to as a **fiscal year**. If you run your business on a fiscal year, it must be the same 12-month period year after year. For example, a snowboarding shop would not want to end its year on December 31—its busiest time. Instead, it might operate on a fiscal year from July 1 to June 30. However, a convenience store probably does not have a busiest time period and might choose to use a calendar year instead. With either a calendar year or fiscal year, taxes will be paid on that period of time.

The Accounting Equation

The accounting equation is the basis for keeping financial records. The equation is as follows:

$$\text{ASSETS} = \text{LIABILITIES} + \text{OWNER'S EQUITY}$$

Assets are anything of value that the business owns. They include items such as cash, equipment, or buildings. Assets are further broken down to include current assets and fixed assets. **Current assets** are cash or other items that can be **converted** to cash fairly quickly and are used by the business within a year. Cash, supplies, merchandise, and accounts receivable are all examples of current assets. **Accounts receivable** is the amount customers owe your business. **Fixed assets** are items that will be held for more than one year. These could include equipment, trucks, and buildings.

Liabilities are the debts of the business. The most common account used in this classification is **accounts payable**. This is the amount your business owes to creditors. The total amount of assets minus total liabilities will give you the worth of the business or the **owner's equity**.

As an example, if Jenny had a fabric store that had total assets of $64,000 and total liabilities of $21,000, Jenny's equity in the business is $43,000. Jenny could say that the worth of her business is $43,000.

ASSETS	=	LIABILITIES	+	OWNER'S EQUITY
$64,000	=	$21,000	+	$43,000

Notice that the value or worth of a business is not the amount of assets it owns.

The Accounting System

All businesses use the same accounting system. Each business has different accounts, but the procedures for recording, summarizing, and reporting the financial information are the same.

Creating Accounts

When you create the books of your business, you create accounts for each of the three categories in the accounting equation. An account shows the balance for a specific category such as cash or equipment. The accounts for a small delivery business could be as follows:

ASSETS	=	LIABILITIES	+	OWNER'S EQUITY
CASH IN BANK		ACCOUNTS PAYABLE		MATT HOYT, CAPITAL
ACCOUNTS RECEIVABLE				
OFFICE EQUIPMENT				
DELIVERY EQUIPMENT				

The list of accounts a business uses in its operation is called the **chart of accounts**. The chart of accounts for one business will be somewhat different from the chart of accounts for another.

GL⬤BAL W⬤RKPLACE — Two Countries for the Price of One

Canada is one of the wealthiest nations in the world, with a high per-capita income, and its government has a very low debt. In fact, among G8 members (which includes Canada, France, Germany, Italy, Japan, Russia, the United Kingdom, and the United States), Canada recently had the lowest government debt burden.

Nation within a Nation Quebec, the only of Canada's 10 provinces where French is the principal language, has repeatedly sought independence. Following referendums in Quebec aiming to achieve that goal in 1980 and 1995, the Canadian House of Commons decided to symbolically recognize Quebec as a "nation within a united Canada" in 2006.

Economics The IFRS (International Financial Reporting Standards), effective January 1, 2011, requires all publicly accountable, profit-oriented companies in Canada to use the same financial reporting standards. That also means there will be opportunities relating to IFRS preparation. Research what type of entrepreneurial opportunities could emerge in Canada to help companies prepare for IFRS and summarize your findings in a one-page report.

Common French Words and Phrases	
Hello	bonjour
Goodbye	au revoir
Yes/ No	oui/non
Please	s'il vous plait
Thank you	merci
You're welcome	de rien

Double-Entry Accounting

Most businesses use a double-entry accounting system. This means that when a business transaction occurs, it affects two or more accounts. The accounts may increase or decrease, and these changes are identified by entering debits or credits. **Debits** are the left side of an account. **Credits** are the right side of an account. The rules of accounting regarding debits and credits are as follows:

FOR ALL ASSETS AND EXPENSES ACCOUNTS
Debits *increase* the balance.
Credits *decrease* the balance.

FOR ALL LIABILITY AND REVENUE ACCOUNTS
Debits *decrease* the balance.
Credits *increase* the balance.

For example, a debit increases the balance in the Cash in Bank (an asset) account, and a credit decreases the balance. A credit increases the balance in Accounts Payable (a liability), and a debit decreases the balance.

Cash or Accrual Basis

Income and payments may be recorded in two ways. If you use a **cash basis**, you record your income when it is received and your expenses when they are paid. If you use the **accrual basis**, you record income when it is earned and expenses when they are incurred. Most businesses operate under the accrual basis. This means they record unpaid bills and expenses as Accounts Payable and money owed to the business from sales as Accounts Receivable.

● **Figure 20.1** General Journal Entries

	DATE		DESCRIPTION	DEBIT	CREDIT	
			GENERAL JOURNAL		PAGE 36	
1	May	4	Office Equipment	3 000 00		1
2			Cash in Bank		3 000 00	2
3						3
4		6	Delivery Equipment	9 000 00		4
5			Accounts Payable/Wilton Auto		9 000 00	5
6						6

● **Daily Record Keeping** Suppose you sold $500 in office equipment for cash. *What account would be debited?*

Keep Your Cold Cash Out of Hot Water

Who cares about mixing personal and business money? The IRS!

One of the first things to do when starting a business is to open a bank account that is separate from your personal accounts. You may not care if your personal and business money merge, but the Internal Revenue Services does, and so do your customers. Separating your accounts helps with financial records and helps you establish a professional image.

Having dedicated business accounts provides you with proper records that help you manage your taxes, bills, and other payments. Although the IRS does not require you to keep separate records, you are required to provide accurate recordkeeping for your business. Keeping separate accounts makes that easier, saving you time. If you use an accountant, it also saves you money. Mistakes on your taxes could lead to an expensive, time-consuming audit.

When you make payments, using a check or card from your business also makes you look professional and helps promote your brand.

Active Learning

Identify a business owner, accountant, or bookkeeper with whom you could chat. Set an appointment by phone to ask that person for his or her advice about the importance of keeping personal and business records separate. Write a summary. Exchange your summary with another student. Proofread each other's work, and then discuss the contents.

Journalizing Business Transactions

A **journal** is like a financial diary of the business. If you keep a diary or a personal journal, each day you write down important events that may occur. A business does the same thing with a journal. The process of recording business transactions in a journal is called **journalizing**. In journalizing you record the business transactions as they occur, usually on a daily basis. The most common journal is the **general journal**. This is an all-purpose journal that records any business transaction. **Figure 20.1** on page 466 shows how two business transactions are entered in a general journal.

In the first journal entry, the business paid cash for some office equipment. Office Equipment is an asset account. The Office Equipment account is increasing and is debited. Cash in Bank is an asset account and is decreasing and therefore credited. In the second entry, delivery equipment was purchased on account (on credit). The account Delivery Equipment is an asset and is debited, and Accounts Payable is a liability and is credited.

Figure 20.2 — Posting to the General Ledger

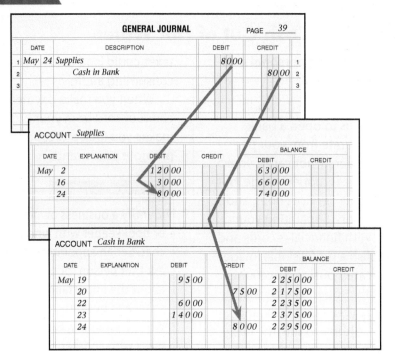

Managing Errors Suppose the entry on the 16th for Supplies was credited in error. *Would the incorrect balance be higher or lower than the one that is shown?*

Special Journals

If a business gets larger, it may find that using one journal is not sufficient to keep track of all its transactions. The business can then set up separate journals, called special journals, which record specific types of transactions. Commonly used special journals include the following:

- A cash receipts journal is a special journal in which cash and checks received are posted.
- A cash disbursements journal is a special journal in which payments made in cash or check form are posted.
- A sales journal is a special journal in which sales on account are posted.
- A purchases journal is a special journal in which purchases on account are posted.

Posting to the General Ledger

A general ledger is a collection of all accounts created for your business. Examples of general ledger accounts are Cash in Bank, Supplies, Accounts Payable, and Sales.

By looking at the general journal, you cannot easily determine the balance in each of your accounts. You may want to know how much cash you have, how much your business owes in Accounts Payable, or what your sales have been for the fiscal period.

In order to find the balance of each account, you must **transfer** the amounts recorded in the general journal to the general ledger accounts. The process of transferring amounts from the general journal to accounts in the general ledger is called **posting**. After you have posted all the journal entries, the final balance in each account will appear in the balance column. **Figure 20.2** on page 468 illustrates a business transaction that has been recorded in the general journal and posted to the two accounts in the general ledger. Notice both of the general ledger accounts, Supplies and Cash in Bank, have current balances. The balance in Supplies is $740 and the balance in Cash in Bank is $2,295.

Cash in Bank is an asset account. On the general ledger, debits increase the balance, and credits decrease the balance. However, because it is an asset account, the balance is always in the debit balance column.Post your journal entries to the general ledger as often as necessary to keep your accounts current. However, posting weekly is probably sufficient to give you a good idea of how well your business is doing.

☑ **Reading Check Recall** What is a general ledger?

 Figure 20.3

Summary of Sales and Cash Receipts

January 26, 2016

Cash Receipts

Cash sales	$2,160.85
Collections on account	160.35
Miscellaneous receipts	69.77
Total Cash Receipts	$2,390.97

Cash on Hand

Cash in the register

Coins	$75.31
Bills	780.00
Checks	1,635.66
Total Cash on Hand	$2,490.97

Less opening cash/petty cash fund

Petty cash slips	$20.55
Coins and bills	79.45
Petty Cash Fund	100.00
Total Cash Deposit	$2,390.97

Sales

Cash sales	$2,160.85
Credit sales	465.39
Total Sales	$2,626.24

Total Daily Sales A summary tells the total daily sales. *Where on the summary are the daily sales totalled?*

Using Sales and Cash Receipts Report

Businesses that have regular daily sales should prepare a daily report of sales and cash receipts. An example of a daily sales and cash receipts report is given in **Figure 20.3** on page 469.

The Cash Receipts section lists cash sales, collections on account, and miscellaneous receipts. The Cash on Hand section of the report shows the amount in the register broken down into bills, coins, and checks. It also includes the opening cash balance, which must remain in the register.

At the end of the Cash on Hand section, calculate how much cash to deposit in the bank for the day. To do this, subtract the opening cash balance from the amount in the register. The amount for Total Cash Deposit must agree with the amount for Total Cash Receipts. If the amounts are not equal, you should check to make sure you recorded all cash transactions in the correct amounts. You should also check to make sure you gave all customers the correct amount of change.

The final section of the report tells you the total daily sales. This includes the cash sales and the sales on account. This information is vital to analyze sales trends and to maintain a positive cash flow.

SECTION 20.1 | Review

After You Read

Self-Check

1. **Explain** why businesses must follow a set of standards and procedures in keeping accounting information.
2. **Compare and Contrast** a cash basis and an accrual basis.
3. **Define** double-entry accounting systems.

Think

4. **Describe** the difference between accounts receivable and accounts payable.

English Language Arts

5. **Critical Review** Obtain an annual report from a company you are familiar with or one you would like to know more about. Review the report critically in small groups. Have each group member read the report, looking carefully at such features as the executive summary and the use of visuals. Discuss how well the report communicates the strengths of the company, the challenges it faces, and the strategies they will employ to achieve success. Create a brief group presentation about the annual report.

Go to connectED.mcgraw-hill.com to check your answers.

Preparing Financial Statements

Reading Guide

Before You Read ■■■■■■■■■■■■■

Connect Why would you need financial statements for your business?

The Main Idea
The ability to identify financial statements for a business, to understand what is reported by each, and to realize the importance of having accurate, up-to-date information is key to the financial health of your business.

Objectives
Describe the items of information included on each financial statement.
Identify ongoing accounting activities.

Explain how technology helps business owners with all the accounting functions.

Content Vocabulary
◇ income statement
◇ balance sheet
◇ cash flow
◇ statement of cash flows

Academic Vocabulary
You will see these words in your reading and on your tests. Use the academic vocabulary glossary to look up their meanings.
■ consist
■ fund

Graphic Organizer
Draw a chart like the one shown. As you read, write the three types of financial statements.

 Go to connectED.mcgraw-hill.com to download this graphic organizer.

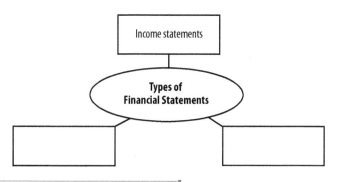

Types of Financial Statements

To operate a business profitably, you will need to have up-to-date financial information. You cannot make sound business decisions if you do not have current figures. Financial statements provide this vital information.

The primary financial statements are the income statement, also called a Profit and Loss (or "P&L") statement, and the balance sheet. A third statement, called the statement of cash flows, is also often used.

Income Statement

At the end of an accounting period, you want to know how much money your business made or lost. You will want to know how much was made in sales and where the money went. This information is reported on the income statement. An **income statement** is a report of the revenue, expenses, and net income or loss for the accounting period. Remember, the revenue coming in minus the expenses going out results in the net income or net loss for the period.

The income statement for different types of business operations varies in content. A service business would have sales, expenses, and net income as illustrated in **Figure 20.4**. A merchandising business would also include the cost of merchandise purchased for resale. This is illustrated in **Figure 20.5** on page 473.

Figure 20.4 Service Business Income Statement

Akita Dog Walking Service Income Statement
Year Ended December 31, 2016

Revenue

Sales	$74,400

Operating Expenses

Advertising Expense	6,000
Interest Expense	2,400
Insurance Expense	4,300
Miscellaneous Expense	800
Rent Expense	12,000
Utilities Expense	3,800
Total Expenses	29,300
Net Income	45,100

Revenue Accounts An income statement for a service business often has one account under revenue. *Why does this business need only one revenue account?*

Merchandising Business Income Statement

Dean's Bait and Tackle Income Statement

Year Ended December 31, 2016

Revenue

Sales		$450,000
Costs of Merchandise Sold		250,000
Gross Profit on Sales		200,000

Operating Expenses

Advertising Expense	35,000	
Interest Expense	3,200	
Insurance Expense	2,300	
Miscellaneous Expense	2,700	
Rent Expense	41,000	
Salary Expense	16,400	
Utilities Expense	3,900	
Total Expenses	104,500	
Net Income	95,500	

Gross Profit A merchandising business has goods to buy, markup, and sell. *What is another term for gross profit?*

Balance Sheet

The other primary financial statement is a balance sheet. A **balance sheet** is a report of the final balances of all asset, liability, and owner's equity accounts at the end of an accounting period. The main purpose of the balance sheet is to present your business's financial position on a specific date. It reports what a business owns, owes, and is worth. This is your present financial situation. It is like taking a financial photo of your business on the last day of the period. An example of a balance sheet is illustrated in **Figure 20.6** on page 474.

Balance sheets **consist** of three sections: assets, liabilities, and owner's equity. The balance sheet represents the basic accounting equation.

ASSETS = LIABILITIES + OWNER'S EQUITY

Both the income statement and balance sheets provide vital financial information for your business. However, neither document shows how the cash position of the business changed during the period. For a business, **cash flow** is the amount of cash that is available at any given time.

Balance Sheet

Balance Sheet December 31, 2016		
Assets		
Cash in Bank	$6,800	
Accounts Receivable	2,700	
Computer Equipment	7,300	
Office Equipment	8,100	
Supplies	1,100	
Total Assets		26,000
Liabilities		
Accounts Payable	3,400	
Notes Payable	7,200	
Total Liabilities		10,600
Owner's Equity		
Marigrace El Hage, Capital		15,400
Total Liabilities & Owner's Equity		26,000

● **Net Worth** A balance sheet shows how much a business is worth. *How much equity does the owner have in this business?*

Statement of Cash Flows

The **statement of cash flows** reports how much cash your business took in and where the cash went. **Figure 20.7** on page 475 is an example of a cash flow statement. Your statement of cash flows is often a major consideration when you want to borrow money for your business. Potential investors and lenders want to see cash flowing into your business in a constant, positive manner.

☑ **Reading Check Summarize** What are the consequences of having a negative cash flow?

Ongoing Accounting Activities

In order to have accurate, up-to-date financial information, accounting procedures and activities must be done on a continuing basis.

Weekly Accounting Activities

In order to properly have financial information when it is needed, some accounting activities should be done each week.

Posting to the General Ledger

Posting on a weekly basis will help keep your account balances accurate. Vital financial information is available if business decisions need to be made.

Keeping Track of Payments and Receivables

Keeping track of your business bills is important so that you are not late on payments. By reviewing which bills are due on a weekly basis, you can pay your bills on time.

Accounts Receivable should be categorized to determine those that are current and those that are over 30, 60, and 90 days past due. This enables you to make decisions regarding extending further credit and the need for collection follow-up.

Keeping Payroll Records

If your business has employees, you need to keep accurate and complete payroll records. These include amounts earned by employees, deductions for taxes and other items, and the amount paid to employees each week. This information must be up to date in order to pay your payroll taxes to local, state, and federal governments.

Keeping Tax Records

In addition to payroll taxes, businesses also owe taxes for sales tax, state and federal unemployment tax, and other local, state, and federal business taxes. Examine these on a weekly basis to ensure that you meet your tax obligations on time.

● **Figure 20.7**   **Cash Flow Statement**

Cash Flow Statement
March 31, 2016

Cash Receipts		$23,000
Disbursements		
Equipment	$12,000	
Cost of Goods	2,500	
Selling Expense	200	
Salaries	700	
Advertising	130	
Office Supplies	20	
Rent	200	
Utilities	90	
Insurance	170	
Taxes	70	
Loan Principal and Interest	240	
Total Disbursements		16,320
Net Cash Flow		$6,680

● **Receipts and Expenditures** If a business has more money coming in than going out, it has a positive cash flow. If more money goes out than comes in, it has a negative cash flow. *Which situation does this statement illustrate?*

Filing of Records

Properly filing all business documents ensures easy reference. These include purchase orders, invoices received with purchases, bills, receipts, contracts, and any business correspondence.

Monthly Accounting Activities

Some accounting activities should be done on a monthly basis.

Preparing Financial Statements

Financial statements report the financial position of your business. In order to make sound business decisions, this information must be available.

Paying Payroll Tax Deposits

You must be sure all payroll taxes are paid in a timely manner. These include all local, state, and federal tax deposits for payroll withholding. Records of the payments of all taxes and bills and cancelled checks should be filed for proof of payment.

Reconciling the Bank Statement

You will receive a monthly bank statement that includes all banking activity for the month. When you receive this statement, you should reconcile, or balance your checking account, immediately and verify the accuracy of your banking activities.

Balancing the Checkbook

Balancing a checkbook is not difficult if you have entered all transactions. The steps for balancing a checkbook are as follows:

1. Write the bank statement balance on the first line of the reconciliation form.
2. List any outstanding deposits on the appropriate line and add them to the balance. Outstanding deposits are those that have not yet been added to your account.
3. Compare the canceled checks or those checks listed on your statement with your check register or check stubs. Check off all items that have been returned to you or listed as paid. These represent amounts that have been subtracted from your account.
4. List service charges and outstanding checks on the appropriate lines and subtract them from the balance. Outstanding checks are checks you have written that do not yet show on your statement. They represent money you have paid that has not yet been removed from your account. The result of these calculations is the adjusted bank balance.
5. Compare the balance from your checkbook to the adjusted bank balance. The two figures should be the same.
6. If there is a difference, go back and check your work. Be sure that all your calculations are correct. Verify that all checks, deposits, and service charges have been accounted for in the reconciliation.

Saving Time Computers help small-business owners generate annual reports quickly and accurately. *Which accounting activities should be done on a monthly basis?*

Balancing and Replenishing the Petty Cash Fund

If your business uses a petty cash **fund**, this should be verified and replenished on a monthly basis. A petty cash fund is used to purchase items that are too inexpensive to pay by check. Every time money is withdrawn from the petty cash fund, a receipt or voucher should be prepared. Once a month, the amount left in cash plus the total receipts should equal the fund's fixed balance. A check should be written for the total receipts and the cash brought back up to its fixed amount.

Technology and Other Options

Recording, summarizing, and reporting financial information can be an extremely time-consuming activity. This can be a major concern when you are trying to start a new business. How can you keep records and still find time to manage everything else that needs to get done? Fortunately, there are many options.

Hiring Professionals

One option to meet your accounting needs is for you to hire professional help. For example, you may want to consider adding a bookkeeper to your staff. A bookkeeper can handle all the forms, journal entries, and payroll for your busines. You can also hire a CPA (certified public accountant) to audit your books and prepare your tax returns.

Go Green

Tax Credits for Helping the Environment

The Tax Incentives Assistance Program (TIAP) provides information for businesses and consumers about how they can benefit from federal income tax incentives for using energy efficient products and technologies. For businesses, these include using qualified solar water heating, combined heat and power systems, and hybrid vehicles.

❖ **Critical Thinking**
Do you think the federal government should encourage consumers to be more energy efficient by giving tax incentives? Write a paragraph explaining why you think TIAP incentives are a good or bad use of government resources.

Balancing the Checkbook

Technology offers entrepreneurs the ability to automate the accounting functions. Daily, weekly, monthly, and annual reports can be generated quickly and accurately. With software and hardware being very affordable, most small businesses use some form of automated accounting. Even if you use automated accounting—unless you are in that business—it may be to your advantage to also utilize professional or technical assistance.

SECTION 20.2 · Review

After You Read

Self-Check

1. **Identify** another frequently used name for an income statement.
2. **Explain** why a balance sheet is sometimes referred to as a financial photo of a business.
3. **Describe** what could happen if a business fails to pay its bills on time.

Think

4. **Determine** if it is possible to keep too many financial records; explain why or why not.

Mathematics

5. **Cash Flow** Eliza Blanca was determining the cash flow for her business. She had cash receipts that totaled $24,420. The list of disbursements is as follows:

Equipment	$13,000
Cost of Goods	$3,400
Selling Expenses	$450
Salaries	$875
Advertising	$110
Office Supplies	$95
Rent	$350
Utilities	$95
Insurance	$220
Taxes	$85

What is the net cash flow of Eliza's business?

Math Concept · **Math Terminology** The term *receipts* means cash in, or revenue. The term *disbursements* means cash out, or payments. Receipts less disbursements is net cash flow.

Step 1 Add together the values of all the disbursements to determine the total.

Step 2 Subtract the total disbursements from the cash receipt total to determine the net cash flow.

 Go to connectED.mcgraw-hill.com to check your answers.

Entrepreneurs *in Action*

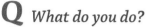

Alice Dickerson
Owner
Necessity Breeds Invention

Q *What do you do?*

A I create and manage niche Web sites, including *A Guide to the Private School Admissions Process* (privateschooladmissions.com), and *Positive Vocabulary* (positivevocabulary.com). I also developed a customized database to track all of my income and expenses. I use a checking account for direct deposits and a PayPal™ account for online transactions.

Q *What kind of training and education did you need to get this job?*

A My professional expertise is in advertising and marketing. My passion for the Internet grew out of that. I love the process, being involved with an idea from concept to fruition.

Q *What do you enjoy most about your job?*

A I don't consider what I do as a "job." It's more of a hobby or a passion with the benefit of a very modest income.

Q *How did you get interested in your field?*

A My first Website came about when I was developing a workbook for my son, who was applying to a private high school. I wanted him to take ownership of the process. He enjoyed using it and I was encouraged by others to self-publish it. That was such a great experience—hits on the Web site and my book selling online—that when I get an idea now, I research it and create it. My motto is "think, create, disseminate."

College & Career Readiness

Financial Reporting
Two of the most common financial statements for small businesses are balance sheets and income statements.
1. Explain what a balance sheet is and how it is used.
2. Explain what an income statement is and how it is used.
3. Contrast the two types of statements.

Career Facts

Real-World Skills	Academic Skills	Career Cluster
Creativity, Research, Internet Skills	English Language Arts, Fine Arts	Marketing

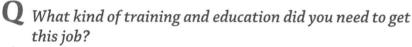

Alice Dickerson

Review and Assessment

Visual Summary

Accounting and Financial Reporting

Record Keeping
The accounting equation is the basis for keeping financial records. Use this equation.

ASSETS = LIABILITIES + OWNER'S EQUITY

The Accounting Equation	
Assets	Anything of value that the business owns (current assets, accounts receivable, and fixed assets).
Liabilities	The debts of the business (accounts payable).
Owner's equity	The worth of the business; the total amount of assets minus total liabilities.

Financial Information Financial statements provide vital information to help you make sound business decisions.

Financial Statements	
Income statement	Reports revenue, expenses, and net income
Balance sheet	Gives the financial position of the business on a specific date
Statement of cash flows	Reports how much cash your business took in and where the cash went

Purestock/SuperStock

Review and Assessment

20

Vocabulary

1. On a sheet of paper, use each of these terms and words in a written sentence.

Content Vocabulary

◇ GAAP
◇ financial reports
◇ accounting period
◇ calendar year
◇ fiscal year
◇ assets
◇ current assets
◇ accounts receivable
◇ fixed assets
◇ liabilities

◇ accounts payable
◇ owner's equity
◇ chart of accounts
◇ debits
◇ credits
◇ cash basis
◇ accrual basis
◇ journal
◇ journalizing
◇ general journal

◇ posting
◇ income statement
◇ balance sheet
◇ cash flow
◇ statement of cash flows

Academic Vocabulary

■ convert
■ transfer
■ consist
■ fund

Key Concepts

2. **Explain** the important role accounting plays in every business.
3. **Identify** five general ledger accounts that might be found in a small business.
4. **Explain** the accounting system for a small business.
5. **Describe** the importance of daily sales and cash receipts reports.
6. **Describe** the items of information included on each financial statement.
7. **Identify** ongoing accounting activities.
8. **Explain** the purpose of a petty cash fund.
9. **Describe** how technology helps business owners with all the accounting.

Academic Skills

Mathematics

10. **Bookkeeping** Your bookstore has been open for six months. The net cash flow for the first month was $110. Business improved, and the net cash flow for the next five months was as follows: $3,850, $2,700, $1,980, $4,200, $3,500. What are the mean and median of cash flow? Which provides a better forecast for the coming months?

   Math Concept **Measures of Central Tendency** In a given sequence of numbers, the mean is the average and the median is the number in the middle.
   Step 1 List the numbers in sequence from least to greatest.
   Step 2 Calculate the mean (average) and identify the median. If there is an even number of elements in the sequence, average the middle two to find the median.

English Language Arts

11. **Detail-Oriented** Your aunt just opened an insurance agency. She has asked you to help her choose a good bookkeeper. Write a paragraph detailing the skills and characteristics the new employee should have.

Chapter 20 · Accounting and Financial Reporting   481

Academic Skills *(continued)*

Social Studies

12. International Relations A favorable currency exchange rate means that a business in the United States can produce goods more cheaply in a foreign country. What are the positive benefits to the economy of the United States in such a case? Are there any negative effects? Explain.

Science

13. Liquid Crystals Many entrepreneurial businesses have sprung up in recent years that build on advances in liquid crystal technology. Liquid crystals are unusual because they exhibit properties of a liquid and a solid at the same time. Explain how liquid crystals resemble liquids and how they resemble solids. Identify how they are used and why entrepreneurs are interested in them.

Real-World Skills

Research Skills

14. Who Makes Bank? Pick three U.S. public companies and locate their most recent financial quarterly reports online. Write down each company's net profit, and show where you found the quarterly reports. Track down the actual reports, not just news stories about the companies.

21st Century Skills

Technology Literacy

15. What's Your P&L? While people and businesses are very different, the same principles of financial management can apply. Use a spreadsheet program to create an income statement for your business.

Connect to Your Community

16. Assets and Liabilities As a class, select a local business. Working in teams, make a list of the assets and of the debts or liabilities you believe the business might have. Compare your lists as a class.

17. Preparing Statements Form teams that contain at least one classmate who has a job. Ask the job supervisor or manager about the financial statements that have proven to be most helpful in running the business. How often are these statements prepared? How are they helpful? If possible, collect samples. Share your findings with the class.

Review and Assessment

CHAPTER 20

Competitive Events Prep

18. Situation You are planning to open a cleaning business that specializes in antique rugs and carpets. Your partner is an expert in this field, while your expertise is in financial management. You have secured the necessary financing and are ready to open. Your partner has little knowledge of the financial statements necessary to operate a business, so you are planning a conversation with your partner about financial statements.

Activity Prepare for your conversation by listing each of the primary financial statements and a brief description of the information each provides.

Evaluation You will be evaluated on how well you meet these performance indicators:

- Prepare estimated/projected income statement.
- Estimate cash flow needs.
- Prepare estimated/projected balance sheet.
- Interpret financial statements.
- Address people properly.

 Go to connectED.mcgraw-hill.com for more information about this activity and other competitive events.

Standardized Test Practice

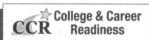
College & Career
Readiness

Directions Choose the letter of the best answer. Write the letter for the answer on a separate piece of paper. For question #2, if the answer is False, rewrite the statement to make it true.

1. What is another name for an income statement?
   A. Balance sheet
   B. Profit and Loss statement
   C. Statement of cash flows
   D. General ledger
2. If you record income when it is earned and expenses when they are incurred, you are operating under an accrual basis.
   T
   F

Test-Taking Tip
If you have time at the end of a test, check your answers and solutions. Make sure you answered each part of every question and that your answers all seem reasonable.

CHAPTER 21

Financial Management

Chapter Objectives

SECTION 21.1
Analyzing Your Finances

Describe the purpose of comparative financial statements.

Describe how different ratios are calculated.

Explain why financial statements are essential for decision making.

SECTION 21.2
Managing Your Finances

Describe ways to help manage your cash flow.

Explain the importance of controlling capital expenditures.

Describe ways to control your taxes.

Describe how you can manage credit offered to customers.

Discovery Project

Keeping Accurate Records

Key Question *How do different business records relate to each other?*

Project Goal
Working in small groups, brainstorm a list of questions about how businesses handle financial records. For example, how do missing or inaccurate records affect other business records? Contact a local business's accountant or bookkeeper and conduct an interview using the list questions you have prepared. Present your findings to your class.

Think About...
➤ *How will you locate an accountant or bookkeeper?*
➤ *What questions will you ask during the interview?*
➤ *How will you present the results of your interview?*

21ˢᵗ Century Skills
Communication *How would you explain the importance of keeping accurate business records to a friend?*

Evaluate
 Go to connectED.mcgraw-hill.com to download a rubric that you can use to evaluate your final project.

Ask AN EXPERT

Q: *I need to hire someone to keep track of the finances for my new go-cart track. Will I need to hire a separate bookkeeper and accountant?*

A: Bookkeeping is simply the recording of financial transactions. Transactions include sales, purchases, income, and payments by a company. Bookkeeping is usually performed by a bookkeeper and should not be confused with accounting. The accounting process is usually performed by an accountant. The accountant creates reports that are based on the recorded financial transactions recorded by the bookkeeper.

Rob Daly/OJO Images/age fotostock

Connect the Photo

Let's Talk About Money Important decisions cannot be made without the valuable information that financial records and reports provide. *Why should entrepreneurs use the services of accountants and financial advisors?*

SECTION 21.1

Analyzing Your Finances

Reading Guide

Before You Read ▪▪▪▪▪▪▪▪▪▪▪▪▪

Connect What is the purpose of an income statement?

The Main Idea

By maintaining and analyzing financial records and reports, business owners and other interested parties have the information necessary to make sound business decisions.

Objectives

Describe the purpose of comparative financial statements.

Describe how different ratios are calculated.

Explain why financial statements are essential for decision making.

Content Vocabulary

◇ comparative financial statement
◇ ratio analysis
◇ current ratio
◇ working capital
◇ debt ratio
◇ net profit on sales ratio
◇ operating ratio
◇ quick ratio

Academic Vocabulary

You will see these words in your reading and on your tests. Use the academic vocabulary glossary to look up their meanings.

▪ ratio
▪ statistics

Graphic Organizer

Draw a chart like the one shown. As you read, list each type of ratio under the financial statement in which it is reported.

 Go to **connectED.mcgraw-hill.com** to download this graphic organizer.

Income Statement	Balance Sheet
	current ratio

Using Financial Statements

Every business prepares two primary financial statements. The first is the income statement, also called a Profit and Loss (or "P&L") statement, which reports the revenue, expenses, and net income or loss for the period. The second is the balance sheet, which reports the assets, liabilities, and owner's equity accounts.

As You Read ━━━━━━━

Illustrate Why do business owners compare financial statements from more than one time period?

Comparative Financial Statements

When a financial statement is prepared at the end of the month or fiscal period, it reflects the success or failure of the business over that period of time. However, business owners also examine the income statement and balance sheet for two different accounting periods to learn even more about the health of their business. A financial statement with data from two accounting periods is called a **comparative financial statement**.

Comparative Income Statement

An example of a comparative income statement is shown in **Figure 21.1** on page 488. Notice that the amounts for each category are given for a two-year period. The amounts are then compared, and the differences are expressed in both dollars and percentages. This lets the owner compare the present amounts in important categories to the previous year's amounts in order to identify any significant changes.

Comparative Balance Sheet

A comparative balance sheet is illustrated in **Figure 21.2** on page 489. The amounts in each category should be analyzed to determine why they increased or decreased during the last period

ETHICS and BUSINESS

Start-Up Money

Situation You want to start a gardening center in an inner city neighborhood. The neighborhood has a rough reputation, but you are interested in helping to create new jobs and opportunities to help improve the area. First, however, you must find the money to get started.

Shopping for a Loan You begin researching financial institutions that offer loans to entrepreneurs. Because of full disclosure laws, you are able to find out which institutions are most likely to give loans to businesses in the inner city. You decide to focus your search on these institutions.

English Language Arts/Writing

Full Disclosure Some financial institutions decline to make loans or make fewer loans to businesses in less-developed neighborhoods. Some people consider this to be good business; others feel it is unethical. What do you think?

1. How might full disclosure cause financial institutions to be more ethical in their dealings?
2. Write a one-page newspaper editorial explaining your reasoning.

Comparative Income Statement

Austen's Poetry, Books, and Music
Comparative Income Statement
For the Year Ended December 31, 2016

	Previous Year	Current Year	Dollar Change	Percent Change
Revenue:				
Sales	284,180	291,203	+7,023	+ 2.5%
Cost of Merchandise Sold:	182,734	190,721	+7,987	+ 4.4%
Gross Profit on Sales:	101,446	100,482	-964	-1.0%
Operating Expenses:				
Advertising	5,830	5,318	-512	-8.8%
Insurance	2,617	2,695	+78	+3.0%
Maintenance	2,811	3,416	+605	+21.5%
Miscellaneous	1,862	1,907	+45	+2.4%
Salaries	17,902	18,523	+ 621	+3.5%
Rent	14,200	15,800	+1,600	+11.3%
Utilities	4,192	3,784	-408	-9.7%
Total Operating Expenses	49,414	51,443	+2,029	+ 4.1%
Net Income	52,032	49,039	-2,993	-5.8%

● **Tracking Income** A comparative income statement lets you compare this year with last year. *Which expense had the greatest percent increase?*

Ratio Analysis

Ratio analysis involves the comparison of two or more amounts on a financial statement and the evaluation of the relationship between these two amounts. Owners, lenders, and creditors use ratio analysis to determine the financial strength, activity, or bill-paying ability of the business. The amounts for the different ratios are taken from the "current year" columns of the comparative income statement and balance sheet.

Current Ratio

The **current ratio** compares current assets (cash or items that can be converted to cash quickly) and current liabilities (debts due within a year). These amounts are found on the balance sheet. The current ratio indicates the ability of a business to pay its bills. The **ratio** is calculated as follows:

$$\frac{\text{CURRENT ASSETS}}{\text{CURRENT LIABILITIES}} = \text{CURRENT RATIO}$$

Based on the balance sheet presented in Figure 21.2, the current assets and current liabilities for Austen's Poetry, Books, and Music for the current period are:

CURRENT ASSETS:	
CASH IN BANK	$24,937
ACCOUNTS RECEIVABLE	4,626
MERCHANDISE	79,271
SUPPLIES	3,522
TOTAL	112,356
CURRENT LIABILITIES:	
ACCOUNTS PAYABLE	$28,725

The current ratio is calculated using information from the "current year" balance sheet.

$$\frac{\text{CURRENT ASSETS } 112,356}{\text{CURRENT LIABILITIES } 28,725} = 3.91 \text{ TO } 1$$

Austen's Poetry, Books, and Music has about $3.91 of current assets for every $1 in current liabilities. A ratio of 2:1 or higher is considered favorable by creditors and lenders.

Figure 21.2	**Comparative Balance Sheet**

Austen's Poetry, Books, and Music
Comparative Balance Sheet
December 31, 2016

	Previous Year	Current Year	Dollar Change	Percent Change
Assets				
Cash in Bank	22,743	24,937	+2,194	+9.6%
Accounts Receivable	4,390	4,626	+236	+5.4%
Merchandise	82,297	79,271	-3,026	-3.7%
Supplies	3,028	3,522	+494	+16.3%
Display Equipment	31,821	39,035	+7,214	+22.7%
Office Equipment	6,339	5,602	-737	+11.6%
Total Assets	150,618	156,993	+6,375	+4.2%
Liabilities				
Accounts Payable	27,734	28,725	+ 991	+3.6%
Notes Payable	33,937	31,204	-2,733	-8.1%
Total Liabilities	61,671	59,929	-1,742	-2.8%
Owner's Equity				
Austen St. James, Capital	88,947	97,064	+8,117	9.1%
Total Liabilities				
& Owner's Equity	150,618	156,993	+6,375	+4.2%

Tracking Worth Comparing changes in the worth of a business is very important. *Did this business increase or decrease in value?*

GLOBAL WORKPLACE
Ireland: After the Celtic Tiger

Despite having a population of less than five million people, Ireland has produced an impressive body of literature. Four Irish authors have won the Nobel Prize for Literature: George Bernard Shaw, William Butler Yeats, Samuel Beckett, and Seamus Heaney. In addition, James Joyce is considered by many to be one of the most important authors of the 20th century.

Knowledge Economy In the 1990s and early 2000s, Ireland experienced a dramatic economic boom that transformed it from one of Europe's poorest countries to one of its wealthiest. Growth was so rapid that the country was called the "Celtic Tiger." The government agency Science Foundation Ireland was founded in 2003 to invest in research that would lead to entrepreneurship in biotechnology and information, communication, sustainability, and energy-efficient technologies. The world's largest offshore wind farm is located at Arklow Bank off the coast of Wicklow.

Social Studies The Global Recession, combined with a series of Irish financial scandals involving falsified balance sheets, not only ended the boom but plunged Ireland into an economic crisis. Research how the growth in Ireland's economy may have influenced its current troubles and summarize your findings in a one-page report.

Common Irish Words and Phrases	
Hello	Dia dhuit
Goodbye	Slán leat/Slán agat
Yes/ No	Sea /Ní hea
Please	Le do thoil
Thank you	Go raibh maith agat
You're welcome	Tá failte romhat

Working Capital

Businesses use information from the "current year" balance sheet to determine **working capital**, or the capital available to carry out daily operations. To do this, use the amounts from the current ratio calculation but subtract current liabilities from current assets.

$$\text{CURRENT ASSETS} - \text{CURRENT LIABILITIES} = \text{WORKING CAPITAL}$$
$$112{,}356 \quad - \quad 28{,}725 \quad = \quad 83{,}631$$

Austen's Poetry, Books, and Music has a working capital of $83,631.

Debt Ratio

The **debt ratio** measures the percentage of total dollars in the business provided by creditors. The debt ratio is calculated using information from the "current year" income statement.

$$\frac{\text{TOTAL LIABILITIES}}{\text{TOTAL ASSETS}} = \text{DEBT RATIO}$$
$$\frac{59{,}929}{156{,}993} = 38.2\%$$

The debt ratio for Austen's Poetry, Books, and Music is 38.2%. This means that 38.2% of Austen's assets are burdened by debt. If the debt ratio is high, it means that creditors are supplying a large portion of the operating capital.

Net Profit on Sales Ratio

Net profit on sales ratio shows the number of cents left from each dollar of sales after expenses and income taxes are paid. The net profit on sales is calculated using amounts from the "current year" income statement.

$$\text{NET INCOME} \div \text{SALES} = \text{NET PROFIT ON SALES RATIO}$$
$$49{,}039 \div 291{,}203 = 16.8\%$$

It is best to compare the net profit on sales ratio to other similar businesses. If you find your net profit is below other similar businesses, your prices may be too low or your expenses too high.

Operating Ratio

The **operating ratio** shows the relationship between each expense and total sales as reported on the income statement. The formula is as follows:

$$\frac{\text{EXPENSES}}{\text{SALES}} = \text{OPERATING RATIO}$$

If sales for the year for Austen's Poetry, Books, and Music were $291,203 and rent expense was $15,800, the operating ratio would be 5.4%. This means that the rent represents 5.4% of sales.

$$\frac{\$15{,}800}{\$291{,}203} = 5.4\%$$

This analysis will also give you a sense of whether or not your expenses are in line with other similar businesses. The ratio should be calculated for each expense account. If an expense appears to be much higher than industry averages, which are often published in trade publications, it should be examined for better, more efficient operation. This type of analysis enables owners to identify possible problem areas quickly.

Quick Ratio

A **quick ratio** is a measure of the relationship between short-term liquid assets and current liabilities. Short-term liquid assets include cash and accounts receivable. The quick ratio is calculated using amounts found on the balance sheet.

$$\frac{\text{CASH} + \text{ACCOUNTS RECEIVABLE}}{\text{CURRENT LIABILITIES}} = \text{QUICK RATIO}$$

$$\frac{29{,}563}{28{,}725} = 1.02$$

Management Decision Making

The financial statements and reports provide you with vital financial **statistics**. You must analyze this information, identify problem areas, and make decisions. At times, risks must be taken. With accurate financial data, you can make decisions with greater confidence. Constant examination and analysis of the financial information about your business operations are essential to success.

Many entrepreneurs think of themselves as bookkeepers—the people who "keep the books." They believe they do not have the skills and knowledge to interpret and analyze accounting documents. As your business grows, you should consider using software and a financial advisor. Software can organize payroll, manage invoicing, and prepare income tax returns. Working with an accountant or financial advisor also has advantages.

An accountant or other financial advisor will make sure your records are in order. Accountants are trained professionals whose job is to optimize profits and minimize risks. They assure that your financial records are kept according to accounting standards, that all reports are completed and analyzed, and that your taxes are calculated and paid. They can also help you set realistic goals and evaluate your progress.

SECTION 21.1 — Review

After You Read

Self-Check

1. **Explain** why it is good to compare financial information from two different periods.
2. **Identify** two different types of ratios and how they are used to assess the strength of a business.
3. **Explain** why past and present financial information is used to plan for the future.

Think

4. **Describe** how your financial statements would be affected if some merchandise purchased for your store was not recorded.

English Language Arts

5. **Money Spent** In the poem, "The Hardship of Accounting," Robert Frost writes: "Nobody was ever meant/To remember or invent/What he did with every cent." What do you think Frost meant with these lines? Was he being serious or ironic? Do you agree with his sentiment? Find the full poem at the library or on the Internet and respond to it in a one-paragraph essay.

Go to connectED.mcgraw-hill.com to check your answers.

SECTION 21.2

Managing Your Finances

Reading Guide

Before You Read ■■■■■■■■■■■■■■

Connect Why do business owners need to make sales projections?

The Main Idea
Careful management of your business finances is an essential element for running a successful business.

Objectives
Describe ways to help manage your cash flow.

Explain the importance of controlling capital expenditures.

Describe ways to control your taxes.

Describe how you can manage credit offered to customers.

Content Vocabulary
◇ variable expenses   ◇ capital expenditures
◇ fixed expenses   ◇ credit bureaus
◇ budget

Academic Vocabulary
You will see these words in your reading and on your tests. Use the academic vocabulary glossary to look up their meanings.
■ volume   ■ monitor

Graphic Organizer
Draw a chart like the one shown. As you read, list variable expenses on the left and fixed expenses on the right.

 Go to connectED.mcgraw-hill.com to download this graphic organizer.

Variable Expenses	Fixed Expenses
	Rent

Planning for Profits

Profits do not just happen. Business owners have to plan for them. Planning for profits includes forecasting sales, evaluating profit potential, controlling costs, and budgeting.

Forecasting Sales

Profit planning begins with forecasting sales. As an ongoing business, you can base your projections on sales records of previous periods. You can also include in those projections consideration for the rate of sales growth in your industry and geographic area as well as the rate of growth of the gross national product. In addition, you should adjust your forecast based on economic factors such as inflation or recession.

Suppose that in the car accessory industry, sales have been up 5 percent per year for the last three years and inflation rates have been stable at 2 percent. If you sold $300,000 of iPod docking stations last year, this is how you could forecast sales:

$$5\% + 2\% = 7\%$$
$$.07 \times \$300{,}000 = \$21{,}000$$
$$\$300{,}000 + 21{,}000 = \$321{,}000$$

In order to keep up with inflation (2 percent) and the industry increase in sales (5 percent), you need a 7 percent increase over this year's sales. If this year's sales are $300,000, you would forecast a $21,000 increase in sales ($321,000) for the next year.

Evaluating Profit Potential

If you are satisfied with your forecast, you do not need to adjust your profit planning. However, most business owners want to improve their company's profit picture. One way to increase sales revenue is by selling more to your current customers and going into new markets. For example, you might add new products to your product line, such as sun visors. Or, you might sell products to businesses, such as accessories for corporate fleet vehicles. Increasing revenues costs money in advertising, sales people, and so forth. The fastest way to increase profits is to reduce costs.

Before you decide to invest in a change, you have to evaluate its profit potential. One way to evaluate profit potential is with break-even analysis. This shows how many units of product must be sold to make a profit based on the change. The break-even formula looks like this:

$$\frac{\text{FIXED COST}}{(\text{SELLING PRICE} - \text{VARIABLE COST})} = \text{BREAK-EVEN POINT}$$

● **As You Read ▪ ▪ ▪**
Describe How do business owners plan for profits?

Fixed and Variable Expenses

Variable expenses are business expenses that change with the **volume** of product produced such as supplies, wages, and production materials. **Fixed expenses** are expenses that do not change with the number of units produced. Examples include insurance and rent.

Suppose you read about a potential market in making portable backboards for basketball tournaments. The article predicts sales of 100 units in your region this year. You can sell each backboard for $250. The materials, labor, and other variable expenses will be about $150. Because you have to buy equipment to run your business, your fixed expenses will be $5,000. How many units would you have to sell to break even?

$$\frac{\$5,000}{\$250 - \$150} = \frac{\$5,000}{\$100} = 50 \text{ UNITS}$$

The break-even point is 50 units. For every unit over 50, you will have $100 ($250 − $150) going toward profit. However, if sales are fewer than 50, there would be no profit. If you had to spend more than $10,000 for fixed expenses, for example, there would be no profit.

Business Case Study

Financial Help, A Good Investment

You can do your own accounting. But should you?

Should you hire a bookkeeper or accountant to keep your financial records? It depends on how complex your business is—and how much time you have to devote to keeping your finances in order.

Business owners can hire a bookkeeper, an accountant, or both to help manage the finances. **Bookkeepers** keep track of income and expenses. They pay bills, create and send invoices, and handle payroll. **Accountants** have more training than bookkeepers, and are usually paid more. They look at the big picture and advise businesses on financial decisions. They also prepare complex documents such as profit-and-loss statements and tax returns. **Certified Public Accountants** (CPAs) are accountants who have passed a licensing exam.

Hiring a financial professional costs money. However, it saves valuable time and ensures that your records are accurate. It can save you money on your taxes, and even help make sure your business follows the law.

Active Learning

Use the Web to research bookkeepers, accountants, and CPAs. Make a chart listing the typical work tasks, skills, education, and average annual income of each. Write a description of the pros and cons of hiring each of these professionals for a small business, part-time or full-time.

Profits and Market Research

Just because there is a potential market demand for 100 units, it does not mean that your company will capture all 100 units in sales. Your forecasts need to be realistic and based on thorough market research. You can use this analysis to evaluate changes in your marketing mix.

Controlling Costs

If there is a big difference between your costs and the industry average, you should investigate and identify possible problems. Suppose your shipping costs have doubled over last year. You may want to find an alternative way to deliver your products to save money. **Figure 21.3** on page 497 identifies additional ways to control costs.

Budgeting

A **budget** is a formal, written statement of expected revenue and expenses for a future period. It is one of the most important financial tools for a business. Using data from previous periods, a projected income statement, also called a *pro forma income statement*, is prepared for the next fiscal period. This offers a glimpse into the future and provides a basis for business decisions.

A budget should be compared periodically with actual income and expenses. If the actual amounts are not reasonably close to the budgeted figures, you will need to make adjustments.

 Reading Check **Compare and Contrast** What is the difference between fixed expenses and variable expenses?

Managing Cash Flow

A goal of efficient financial management is to assure a constant flow of cash through the business. This is not always easy to do. Economic and financial conditions change. Expenses are sometimes under control and then rapidly increase, often due to growth. A business can be growing and profitable and still run into serious problems. If sufficient cash is not available, merchandise cannot be replaced, bills cannot be paid, and funds for future growth cannot be invested.

Using a Cash Budget

In order to help **monitor** your business's cash flow and control operations, you can create a cash budget such as the one shown in **Figure 21.4** on page 498. It records estimated cash flow, actual cash flow, and the difference between the two amounts.

Businesses often prepare cash budgets for a three-month period. By recording and analyzing the line items each month, any significant changes from the budgeted amounts can be quickly identified and addressed.

Improving Your Cash Flow

Certain areas in a business operation have more room for improving cash flow than others. Some are described below:

- **Closely monitor your credit and collections.** If a customer is past due with a payment, take immediate action.
- **Take advantage of credit terms.** Pay all bills on time but take all discounts and the time available to you.
- **Manage inventory carefully.** Excess inventory or the wrong items can tie up cash. If items do not sell, cut prices, sell them, and generate additional cash. Hold only the amount of inventory you need to safely cover projected sales.
- **Offer cash discounts.** Offer discounts to customers for early payment.
- **Set up a cash reserve for uncollectible accounts.** Create a cash fund to offset the effect of unpaid receivables.
- **Monitor payroll expenses.** Examine the number of hours employees need to work to run your business efficiently.
- **Put cash surpluses to work.** If you have excess cash on hand, invest it.
- **Reduce expenses.** Reduce expenses if they are not in line with the amount of business you are doing.

Remember, cash flowing through a business is like blood flowing through your body. A steady cash flow is essential for good business health. You cannot pay your bills with profit. A healthy business must have a healthy cash flow.

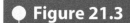

● Figure 21.3 Ways to Control Costs

Lease the Business Location	Instead of buying a building, lease one. If costs are too high, consider relocating to an area where costs are lower.
Lease the Equipment	You keep more of your cash by leasing equipment instead of buying it. If you want to buy equipment, depending on the type of business, you could consider purchasing used equipment.
Hire Part-Time Help	If you hire part-time workers, your labor costs will be lower.
Monitor and Control Utility Costs	Conservation is an excellent way to save money. Energy can be a big business expense, so do not use energy if you do not need to.

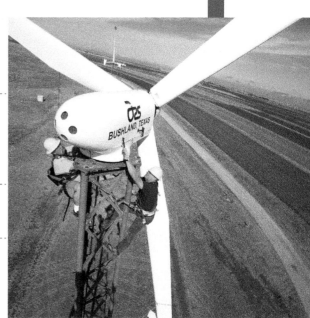

Cost Control Employing energy saving devices and practices is an excellent way to cut down on business expenses. *What are some things you can do to conserve energy?*

Stephen Ausmus/USDA-ARS

Long-Range Planning

Capital expenditures are long-term commitments of large sums of money to buy or replace physical assets such as property, buildings, or equipment. To plan for capital expenditures, determine if you can pay for the asset. Then consider the amount of revenue it will generate and how long it will take to pay for itself.

Managing Taxes

Chapter 8 discusses legal obligations to pay taxes. However, there are some additional tax considerations:

- **Time income to control when it is taxed.** Scheduling fourth quarter sales for the beginning of the upcoming year will defer taxes to that tax year.
- **Time deductions.** During high-income years, identify expenses that can be deducted during that year.
- **Choose the most beneficial depreciation method.** New businesses often have more to write off than they have in income. It is better for them to spread write-offs over time.

Figure 21.4 **Cash Budget**

For Quarter Ending _____	MONTH 1			MONTH 2			MONTH 3		
	EST.	ACT.	DIF.	EST.	ACT.	DIF.	EST.	ACT.	DIF.
Projected Cash Receipts									
Cash sales									
Collections on accounts receivable									
Other income									
Total Receipts									
Projected Cash Disbursements									
Purchases (raw materials, merchandise)									
Advertising									
Dues, subscriptions, licenses									
Insurance									
Travel and entertainment									
Utilities									
Notes payable									
Other _____									
_____									
_____									
_____									
_____									
Total Disbursements									
Net Cash Increase (Decrease)									

Cash Budget The cash budget form has three columns for each month. *What is the purpose of such a layout?*

- **Write off uncollectible accounts.** If you are extending credit, you can write off accounts deemed uncollectible.
- **Claim research and development expenses.** You may not have many of these, but be aware that they are deductible.
- **Keep records of all expenses.** Any honest expense is deductible, but it is up to you to keep the records.

Managing Credit

Offering credit to customers offers several advantages. The main advantage is that it tends to increase sales volume because most customers like to use credit. In addition, credit allows you to build closer relationships with customers by making purchasing easier and by making it easier to sell by telephone, Internet, or mail. Credit account records also provide a useful marketing tool.

The main disadvantage of offering credit to customers is the difficulty of collecting money owed in a timely manner. Other disadvantages include slow-paying customers who affect cash flow, interest added to the cost of money borrowed in order to extend credit, and the additional costs of credit checking, bookkeeping, billing, and collections.

Granting Credit

Credit management begins before credit is given to a customer. The process of granting credit to customers consists of five steps.

1. **Obtaining information.** Have the customer submit information on employment, income, assets, liabilities, and credit references.
2. **Checking credit and background.** Credit bureaus are agencies that collect information on how promptly people and businesses pay their bills. These bureaus charge a fee to provide information to businesses that are considering loan or credit applications.
3. **Evaluating credit applications.** When a business extends credit to consumers, it assumes that some people will be unable or unwilling to pay their debts. Therefore, lenders establish policies for determining who will receive credit. Above all, a credit applicant must have a good credit history. Businesses that extend consumer credit consider the credit applicant's character, capacity, and capital. Bankers making large commercial loans also consider collateral and the conditions under which the loan is granted, as Chapter 19 discusses.
4. **Making your decision.** You can extend a certain amount of credit to a customer or you may require a cosigner, collateral, a down payment, or other credit terms.
5. **Informing the customer.** Under the Truth in Lending Act, businesses must inform customers how finance charges are calculated, when the charges begin, when payment is due, and what the penalities are for late payment.

Tech Savvy

Day Traders

Day trippers undertake day-long trips to scenic destinations. Day traders, on the other hand, buy and sell stocks, currencies, and commodities from the convenience of a home office, a bedroom, or a laptop in a busy airport. Computers store and communicate information. But when they're hooked into networks, as when a day trader's home computer is linked to computers that run electronic stock exchanges—through online stock brokerage firm E*TRADE, for example—you've got a home-based business on your hands. Day traders are the computer age's answer to the New York Stock Exchange's floor traders; only rather than shouting buy-sell orders across a noisy exchange floor, day traders click a mouse. *How has E*TRADE facilitated the development of a brand of home-based business?*

Collecting Accounts

A business can collect accounts internally or externally. The most effective internal collection procedures involve progressively forceful steps:

1. Start with timely notification before the bill is due.
2. Once an account is past due, send a reminder notice to the customer.
3. If there is no response to numerous mailings, contact the customer by telephone.

If you cannot collect an account yourself, you have to get help externally. One option is to hire a collection agency. The agency will charge a fee—usually 33 to 50 percent of the amount collected.

SECTION 21.2 — Review

After You Read ▪▪▪▪▪▪▪▪▪▪▪▪▪▪

Self-Check

1. **Explain** why forecasting data for a future period provides a basis to make decisions regarding your business operation.
2. **Explain** why cash flow is a critical part of financial planning.
3. **Explain** why you should carefully examine your finances before entering long-term financial commitments.

Think

4. **Determine** some of the disadvantages a business would have if it did not prepare a budget.

Mathematics

5. **Break-Even Point** Paley Enik is determining the profit potential of producing a new inflatable raft for his sporting goods company. The fixed costs of producing a raft total $4,750. Variable costs total $290 for each raft. Paley sets the selling price at $350. What is the minimum number of rafts that must be sold in order to break even?

Math Concept **Equations** Remembering equations will help you solve problems.

$$\frac{\text{Fixed Costs}}{\text{Selling Price} - \text{Variable Costs}} = \text{Break-even Point}$$

Step 1 Subtract the variable costs of each raft from the selling price

Step 2 Divide the fixed costs by the difference between the variable costs and the selling price.

Go to connectED.mcgraw-hill.com to check your answers.

Entrepreneurs *in Action*

Mel R. Hertz
Owner/Founder
Derand Capital Management Group

Q *What do you do?*

A I am a financial planner at Derand Capital Management Group, a boutique financial services advisory firm. I advise clients on all their financial affairs—including investing, retirement, estate planning, and insurance—or design a plan to address a single aspect of their finances.

Q *What kind of training and education did you need to get this job?*

A A financial background is really helpful. I also recommend becoming a Certified Financial Planner and being up to speed on current insurance trends, even if you don't plan on selling or marketing insurance.

Q *What do you enjoy most about your job?*

A I love having clients meet their financial goals or, when they first start, just setting those goals. Most people don't plan to fail. They just fail to plan. Most will spend more time planning a weekend party than they do for their financial futures.

Q *How did you become interested in your field?*

A I got my MBA with a major in finance back in 1968. There wasn't even one course on personal finance. It was all corporate finance. At that time I tried to go to work for a major brokerage firm but they wouldn't hire me since I was too young. Eleven years later, I was unhappy with how my stockbroker was handling my account and I decided now is the time to become a financial planner.

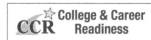

CCR ☆ **College & Career Readiness**

Balancing the Books
Find out what is hardest for small businesses in terms of financial management.

1. Interview a finance professional at a local accounting firm.
2. Ask what type of help small businesses request most. What is the most common mistake small businesses make? What is most rewarding and most challenging about working with small businesses? What advice would you offer to someone starting a business?
3. Explain what you learned in a one-page report.

Career Facts

Real-World Skills	Academic Skills	Career Cluster
Interpersonal, Organization, Planning	Mathematics, Economics	Finance

Mel Hertz

Review and Assessment

Visual Summary

Financial Management

- **Sizing Up** Owners, lenders, and creditors use ratio analysis to determine the financial strength, activity, or bill-paying ability of a business.

Ratio Analysis	
Current ratio	Compares current assets and current liabilities.
Debt ratio	Measures the percentage of total dollars in the business provided by creditors.
Net profit on sales ratio	Shows the number of cents left from each dollar on sales after expenses and income taxes are paid.
Operating ratio	Shows the relationship between each expense and total sales.
Quick ratio	A measure of the relationship between short-term liquid assets and current liabilities.

- **Planning Ahead** Entrepreneurs have to plan for profits by forecasting sales, evaluating profit potential, controlling costs, and budgeting.

Planning for Profits	
Sales Forecasts	Base projections on sales records of previous periods.
Profit Potential	Use break-even analysis to evaluate profit potential before investing.
Control Costs	Investigate costs and identify possible problems.
Budget	Write a formal written statement of expected revenue and expenses for a future time period.

Nonwarit/Shutterstock

Vocabulary

1. On a sheet of paper, use each of these terms and words in a written sentence.

Content Vocabulary

◇ comparative financial statements
◇ ratio analysis
◇ current ratio
◇ working capital
◇ debt ratio
◇ net profit on sales ratio

◇ operating ratio
◇ quick ratio
◇ variable expenses
◇ fixed expenses
◇ budget
◇ capital expenditures
◇ credit bureaus

Academic Vocabulary

■ ratio
■ statistics
■ volume
■ monitor

Key Concepts

2. **Describe** the purpose of comparative financial statements.
3. **Describe** how the operating ratio is calculated.
4. **Explain** why financial statements are essential for decision making.
5. **Describe** why evaluating profit potential is a useful technique to plan for profits.
6. **Describe** ways to help manage your cash flow.
7. **Explain** the importance of controlling capital expenditures.
8. **Describe** ways to control your taxes.
9. **Describe** how you can manage credit offered to customers.

Academic Skills

Mathematics

10. **Total Sales** Sonoma Cassidy's jewelry store had a net income of $67,032 last year. The net profit on sales ratio for the same time period was 21.68%. What were the total sales during that time period? How would the ratio change with an increase in sales?

Math Concept **Using Symbols** Letters and other symbols can be used to stand for unknown quantities.

Step 1 Chose a symbol to represent the unknown, the total sales.
Step 2 Write and solve an equation using the symbol as the unknown quantity.
Step 3 Solve the equation with a larger quantity of total sales to see how the ratio changes.

English Language Arts

11. **Expanding Horizons** Research a small business in your area that has recently expanded. Write a report on all the reasons you can think of that motivated the business owner to expand, as well as the challenges the owner must have faced.

Academic Skills (continued)

Social Studies

12. **Paying Taxes** Business are responsible for collecting and paying payroll taxes for each of its employees. In a recession, when fewer people work and pay taxes, the government may find that it cannot pay for all of the services it wants to provide. Find out what steps the government has taken during past recessions. Explain the effects of their actions.

Science

13. **Negative Flows** When water is removed from underground aquifers for industrial, agricultural, and personal use, the aquifers are usually recharged as part of the Water Cycle (evaporation, condensation, precipitation, and runoff and absorption). Explain what might cause an aquifer to be used up. Compare this to a negative cash flow for a business.

 ## Real-World Skills

Spreadsheet Skills

14. **Analysis** What financial statements and other information does a small business need to thoroughly analyze its finances? Compose a paragraph to explain your answer.

21st Century Skills

Communication and Collaboration

15. **Managing Money** Practice active listening during an interview with a classmate, friend, or family member. Ask how your subject manages his or her money. Pay attention to your subject's words and how, including body language, those words are said. Write a paragraph describing what you learn about the person's relationship with money.

 ## Connect to Your Community

16. **Locate a business in your area.** Ask the owner if he or she could name the fixed expenses incurred by the business. Give an oral report to the class on the expenses named by the owner.

17. **Interview a small business owner in your town.** Ask the owner to describe some of the business activities that take place on a daily, weekly, monthly, quarterly, and yearly basis. Write a report detailing the business activities mentioned. In the report, categorize business activities as production, marketing, management, or finance. Describe the interdependence each business activity has with marketing.

Review and Assessment

Competitive Events Prep

18. Situation You own a shoe store in a strip mall in a suburban area with many families and young children. Your sales have been growing. You currently accept payment in the forms of cash, debit card, and major credit cards. You are considering offering customers a store credit card but are not sure and would like to get your lead sales person's opinion.

Activity You are to discuss the advantages and disadvantages of extending credit to your customers. Prepare for your discussion with the lead sales person by making notes about the advantages and disadvantages of extending credit.

Evaluation You will be evaluated on how well you meet these performance indicators:
- Establish credit policies.
- Describe use of credit bureaus.
- Develop billing and collection policies.
- Manage cash flow.
- Prepare simple written reports.

 Go to **connectED.mcgraw-hill.com** for more information about this activity and other competitive events.

Standardized Test Practice

Directions Choose the letter of the best answer. Write the letter for the answer on a separate piece of paper. For question #2, if the answer is False, rewrite the statement to make it true.

1. Which kind of ratio compares current assets to current liabilities?
   A. Current ratio
   B. Debt ratio
   C. Net profit on sales ratio
   D. Operating ratio
2. Profit planning begins with evaluating profit potential.
   T
   F

> **Test-Taking Tip**
> Work on a problem until you get stuck. Think about it for a minute or two, and if nothing comes to mind, drop it and go on to another problem.

Business Plan Project

Planning Your Finances

How well you manage your finances helps determine whether or not your venture opens its doors, stays in business, and grows. *How will you make the best use of your resources and maximize profits?*

Objectives

In this project, you will complete these parts of your business plan:

- Determine start-up costs and expenses.
- Write a proposal that describes all of your funding needs.
- Explain what kind of effect growth will have on your business.

The Skills You'll Use

- **Academic Skills** Mathematics, English Language Arts
- **Real World Skills** Financial Literacy, Problem Solving
- **21st Century Skills** Financial and Economic Literacy; Productivity and Accountability

▶ Financial Plan

The Financial Plan section of a business plan presents past and current finances. It also presents financial forecasts and explains the assumptions made when calculating these forecast figures. The Financial Plan also includes the investment proposal and three key financial statements: a cash flow statement, income statement, and balance sheet.

Step 1 **Evaluate Start-Up Costs and Expenses** When starting a new business, there are many start-up and one-time expenses. Create a chart to document the amounts of money required for each of the start-up costs and expenses listed. Include items such as lease, deposits, furniture, equipment, inventory, and licenses.

Step 2 Write an Investment Proposal Write an investment proposal that describes why you are applying for financing, how much money you need, how you plan to raise the money, and the specific uses for the funding. Project when investors can expect to earn a profit.

▶ Growth Plan

The Growth Plan looks at how the business will expand in the future. Investors and lenders like to know that a business has plans to deal with growth in a controlled way.

Step 1 Describe Your Growth Strategies Write a description of your proposed business's growth strategies. Address all of these issues in your description:
- How and when the business will grow
- Products or services the business will develop to achieve growth
- How growth strategies focus on the business's areas of expertise
- How market research will be used to support and justify growth
- What critical skills are needed to effectively manage growth
- How you will evaluate and initiate revisions to growth strategies

Effects of Growth	
Business Location	Manufacturing Process & Costs
Warehousing & Storage Needs	Financial Control Procedures
Human Resource Expenses	Record Keeping Policies
Management & Staffing Needs	Legal & Insurance Issues
Company Goals & Objectives	Sales Team & Sales Process
The Business's Target Market	Promotional Goals & Messages
Technology & Equipment Needs	Marketing Mix Strategies

Step 2 Consider the Effects of Growth Before growing a business, you must consider the effects of the growth. Write an explanation of how your planned growth will affect the areas listed in the chart above.

Use the **Business Plan Project Appendix** on pages **572–583** to explore the content requirements of a business plan in more detail.

 Business Plan Project Template Go to connectED.mcgraw-hill.com for a business plan template that you can use to write your own business plan.

My Business Plan
When you have completed your Project, put your statements, charts, and other research in your Business Plan Portfolio.

Growing Your Business

Connect the Photo

A Breath of Fresh Air Wind energy is a fast-growing market in the United States, especially in Texas. Texas produces more wind energy than any other state at wind farms like Horse Hollow Wind Energy Center, which is the world's largest wind farm. *What are some challenges of expanding your business?*

Business Plan Project

● *Preview*

Finishing Touches

How can going green help your company grow faster? Will you donate profits or products to charities? Being responsible to employees, customers, and the community enhances your venture's reputation. Protecting your business, planning for growth, and practicing ethics will help your business prosper.

The **Business Plan Project** will help you address some of these concerns and put the finishing touches on your business plan by focusing on these sections:

▶ The **Contingency Plan** examines the the greatest risks to the business, and suggests plans to minimize the risk.

▶ The **Executive Summary** explains a business plan's key points.

▶ The **Cover Page, Title Page, and Table of Contents** offer basic information about the company and the plan's structure and contents.

▶ The **Supporting Documents** section of the business plan includes items, exhibits, and documentation relevant to the business.

● Prepare for the Business Plan Project

As you read this unit, use this checklist to prepare for the Business Plan Project:

- Determine how local businesses reduce the risk of shoplifting and other kinds of crime.
- Discuss emergency situations with your teachers and administrators, and how to plan for them.
- Identify local businesses that give back to the community.

Risk Management

Chapter Objectives

Discovery Project
Insuring Your Business

Key Question *What types of insurance are available to business owners?*

Project Goal
All businesses face risks of one sort or another. Many of the risks can be managed through the purchase of the right type of business insurance. Research the different types of insurance that are available to businesses. Include a brief description of what the insurance covers.

Think About...
➤ How will you conduct your research?
➤ How many types of insurance will you investigate?
➤ How will you present your research once it has been completed?

21st Century Skills
Business Literacy *What types of business insurance are most often purchased in your community?*

Evaluate
 Go to connectED.mcgraw-hill.com to download a rubric that you can use to evaluate your final project.

Q: *I recently purchased my first car and started getting quotes for auto insurance. I was surprised to learn how much insurance costs. What can I do to lower my insurance rates?*

A: Statistically, young drivers fall into a high risk category for auto insurance and generally have to pay higher premiums. However, there are ways young drivers can lower their insurance costs: driving used vehicles, getting good grades, taking defensive driving courses, and simply shopping around for the best deal.

Connect the Photo

Under Lock and Key Although risk is just part of the entrepreneurial life, there are ways to reduce the amount of risk and run a successful profitable business. Through risk planning and management, business owners can decrease risk. *What kinds of risks do you think high-tech companies might face?*

GodfriedEdelman/iStockphoto.com

Identifying Business Risks

Reading Guide

Before You Read ━━━━━━━━━━━━━

Connect Which type of pure risk is most likely to affect your business?

The Main Idea

Risk is a fact of life for entrepreneurs. To build a successful business and maximize profits, they must understand risk and make decisions to deal with it.

Objectives

Explain why risk is inevitable.
Describe speculative risk.
Describe three categories of pure risk.

Content Vocabulary

◇ speculative risk
◇ pure risk
◇ burglary
◇ robbery
◇ electronic credit card authorizer
◇ negligence

Academic Vocabulary

You will see these words in your reading and on your tests. Use the academic vocabulary glossary to look up their meanings.

▪ commit
▪ distinct

Graphic Organizer

Draw a chart like the one shown. As you read, fill in the chart with the three areas of pure risk.

Go to connectED.mcgraw-hill.com to download this graphic organizer.

Pure Risk

Crime

Risk Is Inevitable

In its daily operations, every business faces risk—the possibility of loss or injury. For example, if you decide to extend credit, you run the risk that some customers will not pay. If you construct a building, you run the risk that it will be destroyed by fire. If you rely on a partner for sales, you risk sudden loss should something happen to the person.

These and other business risks fall into two general categories: speculative risk and pure risk.

Speculative Risk

Speculative risk involves taking a chance for profit or loss. Speculative risks are inherent to the business. When you buy machinery, obtain new inventory, or construct a building, you are taking a speculative risk. Most business decisions involve speculative risks. If the product succeeds in the market, you realize a profit. If it does not, you have losses. Chapter 23 discusses speculative risks.

Pure Risk

Pure risk is the threat of a loss to your business without any possibility of gain. The threat of employee theft, burglary, and robbery are pure risks to your business. So are natural disasters, such as floods, earthquakes, and tornadoes, as well as accidents involving customers and employees. In this chapter, we will identify the pure risks that new businesses face as well as some ways that entrepreneurs can deal with those risks.

Crime

Small businesses are 35 times more likely than large businesses (those with sales in excess of $5 million) to be victims of crime. Retail stores are most likely to experience crime because so many people pass through them in the course of a business day. As a result, the cost of crime is also highest for retail operations.

Consider an example. Suppose a music store loses a $15 CD due to shoplifting every day for a year. In that case, the store loses $5,475 a year ($15 × 365 = $5,475). If the store operates at a 10 percent profit margin, it must sell $54,750 worth of merchandise to make up the loss ($5,475 ÷ 0.10 = $54,750)!

Shoplifting

Shoplifting is the most common retail crime. It accounts for the loss of more than $13 billion worth of goods per year—or about 3 percent of the price of any item.

A shoplifter is anyone who takes an item from a store without paying for it. Shoplifting often takes place when stores are understaffed.

As You Read

Classify What is one example of a pure risk for a business?

Prevention

To reduce the risk of shoplifting, use the following techniques:

- Train employees to recognize shoplifters. Shoplifters may act nervous, browse a long time, carry large bags, or wear bulky clothing. When in groups, one or two may create a disturbance while others shoplift.
- Keep the store well lit and display cases low so you can see your entire operation at a glance.
- Employ two-way mirrors, peepholes, or closed-circuit TV.
- Use tamper-proof price tickets or electronic tags.
- Hire a uniformed security guard.

Catching Shoplifters

If you spot a shoplifter, the safest approach is to alert a police officer. Let the police officer confront the person. Usually, this is done outside the store to make the legal case against the shoplifter stronger. The laws for apprehending shoplifters vary from state to state, but in general, store owners must also see the person take the merchandise, identify the merchandise as belonging to the store, and prove that the merchandise was not paid for.

Once a shoplifter is caught, you must decide whether to prosecute. By pressing charges, you are telling other would-be shoplifters that crime will not be tolerated in your store. As a result, you reduce your risk of becoming a shoplifting victim again.

Employee Theft

The U.S. Chamber of Commerce estimates the cost of employee theft at over $20 billion a year. In addition, they indicate that employees are 15 times more likely to steal from employers than non-employees. And, they believe that employee theft contributes to 30 percent of all business failures.

Business owners are sometimes careless about the way they handle cash. Money constantly coming in and going out can tempt workers. A large number of voided or no-sale transactions may signal that an employee is covering up theft. A good rule is not to let only one person control a transaction from beginning to end. Instead, have one person handle the funds and another record or account for them.

To prevent employee theft, hire honest people. Use a thorough application process. Ask for and check character references. Aptitude and psychological tests can also be helpful. Certain types of businesses can require applicants to take a polygraph, or lie-detector test. (Check with your attorney to see if your business can conduct preemployment polygraph testing.)

Employee theft can also be reduced by establishing policies, controls, security procedures, and penalties that send a message. Specifically:

- Let employees know—verbally and in writing—that employee theft is not tolerated.
- Lock all doors that do not need to be used for entry or exit.

- Watch your trash. Dishonest employees sometimes hide stolen items in the trash to get them out of the building undetected.
- Control the distribution of keys and other security devices.
- These measures tell employees that people who steal are likely to get caught.

Burglary

The act of breaking into and entering a building with the intent to **commit** a felony is called **burglary**. (A felony is a serious crime, such as stealing.) The problem and cost of burglary is growing, but there are ways to minimize your risk.

- **Site selection** Select your business site carefully. Consider the level of crime in the area and select a secure building for your enterprise.
- **High-quality locks** Install high-quality locks and control access to the keys.
- **Alarm systems** With a supervised alarm system, all points of entry are constantly monitored from a central location. An alarm alerts police to trouble. A nonsupervised alarm is active only when the owner arms it. These alarms may also be set to alert the police.
- **Security guards** Some businesses employ a security guard to patrol the premises when the business is closed.
- **Proper lighting** The use of lighting deters burglars. Many owners leave lights on in the building at night. Floodlights in parking lots and at rear entrances also make it difficult for someone to break in unnoticed.

Reduce Your Risk To reduce the risk of burglary, many business owners leave lights on in the building at night. *Will you be concerned about crime in your business? Why or why not?*

ETHICS and BUSINESS

Getting Credit

Situation You have known your business partner, Josh, for several years and have always thought he was very honest. Your working relationship with him has been positive. In addition, you have seen your business grow because of his innovative ideas.

Using Credit Wisely Because your business is thriving, the local bank has authorized a rather high line of credit for you to make some upgrades that you have been putting off. The upgrades are going well and it looks like you will not need to use your entire line of credit.

English Language Arts/Writing

Misuse of Credit Josh decides to use the unused credit for some personal purchases. You are concerned that this is unethical and could eventually end up hurting your business. What should you do?

1. How would you explain to Josh your concerns about him using business credit for personal purchases?
2. Write a one-page letter explaining your concerns.

Robbery

Robbery involves the taking of property by force or threat. Most robberies involve a weapon. It is the business owner's responsibility to protect employees and customers. This means doing what the robbers ask, so they will take what they want and leave without harming anyone.

If you are robbed, try to get a description of the person(s) committing the crime. Note a robber's height, hair color, and **distinct** features or mannerisms. These details can help police identify the thief.

One security measure you can use is a safe. Using a safe minimizes the amount of cash you keep in the register (a robber's likely target). Surveillance cameras are another valuable measure. When placed where potential robbers can see them, they, too, serve as a deterrent.

Stolen Credit Cards

Using credit cards or checks to pay for purchases is a major convenience for consumers. To businesses, they can be a source of financial loss. Stolen credit cards are used to run up huge bills. Customers may write checks against insufficient funds or closed accounts.

There are ways to identify an invalid or stolen credit card. Many businesses use **electronic credit card authorizer** machines that verify whether a credit card is good. They are linked to a central credit bureau that identifies stolen or invalid cards. Other companies call a central authorization phone number to check credit cards. This allows them to find out if a card is good before they complete a sale.

Bad Checks

Bad checks represent another problem for businesses. As a deterrent, companies charge a service fee if a customer's check is returned from the bank. In addition, many states have passed laws making the writing of bad checks a crime, imposing stiff fees. Many businesses place signs by their cash registers announcing these penalties.

Business owners can also reduce the number of bad checks with a check reader, which enables you to accept checks from customers while having the check guaranteed and electronically deposited. It also identifies accounts with a history of bad checks.

If you do not have a check reader, you should insist on more than one piece of identification, including a driver's license. Compare the photo to the person; also, write the customer's driver's license number on the check.

Counterfeit Money

Counterfeit money is an ongoing concern for businesses. To determine if a bill is genuine, check to see if the bill looks and feels like money. Also, bills larger than $5 use color shifting ink in the lower-right-hand corner. All bills larger than $2 now have a watermark matching the portrait. Finally, all bills larger than $2 have a security thread that matches the denomination.

Cyber Crime

Because companies are increasingly relying on technology and the Internet, the threat of cyber crime, or computer-related crime, is growing. Cyber criminals have developed a variety of ways to access computers and steal or damage information. These illegal acts are not limited to outsiders. They are often committed by employees.

Hackers

Hackers sometimes break into computers just to show off. At other times, they have more sinister motives, such as business espionage, fraud, or embezzlement. By taking a few precautions, business owners can reduce their chances of becoming victims. These measures include securing important data by using passwords, installing firewalls, and using encryption software.

Viruses, Worms, and Trojan Horses

Other hackers have malicious damage as their goal. They may create viruses, worms, or Trojan horses to infect computers at random. Attacks by these programs can destroy data, erase hard drives, or damage networks. Some Trojan horses as well as spyware can obtain user information without their knowledge.

Web Savvy

Digital Evidence

Crime scene investigators are a familiar sight in film and television, dusting for fingerprints and looking for other kinds of forensic evidence. *Forensics* is the application of science in legal questions. One of the fastest growing branches of forensics is digital forensics. Digital forensic techniques are used to analyze and repel hacker attacks, to gather evidence against dishonest employees, and to prosecute pirates who illegally share files. Digital evidence can be gathered from many sources, including hard drives, mobile/smart phones, and RFID tags. Companies like VoomTech™ provide law enforcement with high-tech products to conduct investigations. Other entrepreneurs, like Erin Nealy Cox of Stroz Friedberg, provide digital forensic services to businesses and government agencies. *What are some other potential sources of digital evidence?*

Disaster 101 Unfortunately, the only way to prevent some natural disasters is to move to a different state or region. *What kinds of natural disasters occur in your state? What could you do to protect your business from them?*

Antivirus Software

The simplest way to protect against computer viruses is to install an antivirus program. These programs also protect against worms and viral Trojan horses. In addition, antispyware programs should be installed to defend against spyware and similar Trojan horses.

Other Security Precautions

There are other steps you can take to guard against computer, or cyber, crime. One is to physically secure equipment and disks to reduce the possibility of theft. Another is to organize tasks so no one employee has access to every file. You can also train your employees to be security conscious.

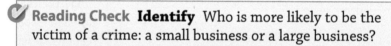

Reading Check **Identify** Who is more likely to be the victim of a crime: a small business or a large business?

Other Types of Pure Risk

Crime is not the only risk a business faces. Business owners need to be aware of the dangers posed by natural disasters. In addition, they need to be prepared for the possibility of accidents or injuries.

Natural Disasters

Many owners have lost everything due to natural disasters such as fires, earthquakes, hurricanes, tornadoes, and floods. Protecting your business from these risks can be difficult. The surest way to prevent flood or tornado damage, for example, is to choose a location that does not have a history of such disasters. That may mean moving to higher ground or another geographic area. If you are planning to locate your business in a hurricane-prone area or active earthquake zone, you can have your building inspected by a structural engineer. Then, if necessary, have it reinforced to withstand the winds or tremors.

Fires

Protecting your business against fire is simpler. You can install smoke detectors and sprinkler systems to help protect you and your staff. They can also extinguish fires before they grow too big. When choosing a safe for cash and important documents, you can buy one that is fireproof.

Accidents and Injury

Another risk that concerns businesses is accidents. Workers can hurt themselves and others on the job. Customers can slip and fall on the premises. Accidents like these can be financially devastating to a small business. For example, a company can be held responsible for an act of negligence. **Negligence** is the failure to exercise reasonable care. At the very least, a business would be required to pay the medical expenses of the person injured. The company might also have to pay amounts awarded by a jury in a lawsuit. Unfortunately for business owners, in recent years, the number of such lawsuits has been increasing, and so has the size of the awards.

SECTION 22.1 Review

After You Read ▪▪▪▪▪▪▪▪▪▪▪▪▪▪

Self-Check
1. **Explain** the difference between speculative risk and pure risk.
2. **Identify** the business owner's primary responsibility in the event of a robbery.
3. **Describe** how a natural disaster that occurs in your community affects businesses.

Think
4. **Produce** a three-column chart. Label it "Crime, Natural Disaster, and Accidents and Injury." Identify risks your proposed business would face in each category.

English Language Arts/Writing
5. **Preventing Theft** Unfortunately, employee theft is a major risk for many types of businesses. Business owners come up with many creative solutions to preventing employee theft, such as posting signs that encourage customers to ask for receipts. Research other creative ways to prevent employee theft in a retail business by visiting a bookstore, using the Internet, and conducting interviews with local business owners. Try to identify methods that are different from those mentioned in the text.

Go to connectED.mcgraw-hill.com to check your answers.

SECTION 22.2

Dealing with Risk

Reading Guide

Before You Read ■■■■■■■■■■■■■

Connect What are some kinds of insurance with which you are familiar?

The Main Idea

It is impossible to completely protect your business from pure risks, but you can lessen their impact through risk management and planning.

Objectives

List the four risk management strategies.
Describe the steps involved in selecting an insurance agent.
Discuss the procedures for deciding on security measures.
Develop emergency response plans for potential crises.

Content Vocabulary

◇ premium
◇ business interruption insurance
◇ casualty insurance
◇ errors-and-omissions insurance
◇ product liability insurance
◇ fidelity bonds
◇ performance bonds
◇ workers' compensation insurance

Academic Vocabulary

You will see these words in your reading and on your tests. Use the academic vocabulary glossary to look up their meanings.

■ error
■ factor

Graphic Organizer

Draw a chart like the one shown. As you read, fill in the chart with the four risk management strategies.

 Go to connectED.mcgraw-hill.com to download this graphic organizer.

Risk Management Strategies

Risk avoidance	

Risk Management Strategies

Risk management is preventing or reducing business loss. It involves a three-stage process.

1. In the first stage of the process, the company identifies the risks to which it is exposed.
2. The second stage involves estimating potential losses from those risks.
3. Finally, the best way to deal with each risk is determined in the third stage.

Many people assume that insurance is the only way to deal with risk. While it is important, there are other options. In fact, in some situations, they may be less costly or more practical than insurance.

This section will examine all four risk management strategies—avoidance, reduction, transfer, and retention. It will also provide examples of business risks that can be addressed with each strategy. In addition, this section will discuss decisions to consider when completing your risk management plans.

Business Case Study

Before Flying Too High, Calculate the Risks

What's the difference between a constructive risk-taker and a destructive showoff?

Entrepreneurs by nature are risk-takers. Calculated risks are healthy for a business, but foolish risks are not. How can you, as a young entrepreneur, know the difference? Try these four suggestions:

- Balance risk and reward. You may not have a crystal ball to see into the future, but to the best of your ability look ahead and honestly predict the results.
- Seek the input of others. Every successful person has help. Put together the best team and truly listen to their opinions.
- Find a good compromise. Look for a healthy balance between risk and safety. For example, is there a way to reduce risk by committing less money, time, or effort to a chancy project?
- Stay the course but adjust. Along the way to success, it's easy to get discouraged. Remind yourself of the reasons for your original plan and make course corrections that are needed to stay on track.

> **Active Learning**
>
> Use the Web to learn about risk management. Read a short article from a reputable newspaper or business magazine about managing business risks. Find at least three risk-management tips in the article and write them as bullet points. Share what you learned with the class.

● **As You Read** ▪▪▪

Identify What strategies can be used to reduce the risk of fire?

Risk Avoidance

When you locate your business in a safe area, you are using a risk avoidance strategy. You are attempting to avoid crime by shunning environments in which it is more likely to occur. Does your decision guarantee that you will not be the victim of burglary, robbery, or shoplifting? No, but it does reduce your chances.

Risk Reduction

For risks that cannot be avoided, businesses adopt a risk reduction strategy. Many of the procedures mentioned in Section 22.1 are examples of this strategy. Suppose you own a retail store and are installing a sprinkler system. You are trying to prevent damage to your inventory or loss of your building. You may not be able to avoid a fire, but you can reduce the damage it does. When you place electronic tags on expensive merchandise, you are attempting to discourage theft. You may not be able to eliminate shoplifting, but you can reduce it.

Business owners should take these steps to reduce risk:

- **Design work areas to lower the chances of accident or fire.** This includes offices, retail spaces, and manufacturing floors.
- **Educate employees about the safe use of equipment.** Make sure employees know how to handle emergency situations.
- **Check and service safety equipment.** Test fire extinguishers and smoke detectors regularly. Do the same for security equipment, such as burglar alarms.
- **Test company products under the most extreme conditions in which they will be used.** Inform consumers about how to use your products safely. Provide instructions for correct use of products as well as warnings about possible hazards.

Risk Transfer

Suppose you have located your business in a relatively crime-free part of town (risk avoidance). You have also installed locks, burglar alarms, and sufficient lighting (risk reduction). Still, you may experience losses.

What else can you do to protect your business against possible losses? Most likely you will use the third strategy—risk transfer. Usually, that means buying insurance to cover any losses. You pay a fee, called a premium, to transfer some of your risk to an insurance company. A **premium** is the price of insurance an insured person or business pays for a specified risk for a specified period of time.

If you want to purchase insurance, you must be able to demonstrate an insurable interest in property or life. That means you could suffer a loss, financial or otherwise, from a fire, an accident, a death, or a lawsuit.

Extreme Testing Company products should be tested under the most extreme conditions in which they will be used. *Why should this be done?*

fStop/SuperStock

The following steps will help you plan for insurance coverage:
- Identify those risks you may want to insure against.
- Prioritize your list in terms of importance.
- Research insurance costs and coverages.
- Compare those costs to the probability and cost of loss.
- Make your decisions regarding the risks you want to insure against.

The four types of business insurance that may be needed are: property insurance, casualty insurance, life insurance, and workers' compensation insurance.

Property Insurance

Your business may own a wide range of physical property. This property is usually classified as real property or personal property. Real property includes buildings and things attached to them. Personal property is anything that is unattached, such as a vehicle. These distinctions are made for legal purposes and, consequently, carry over to insurance coverages. Each type of property must be insured separately. In addition, certain risks, such as floods and earthquakes, require separate policies.

A business's standard insurance policy might protect the premises against burglary, robbery, fire, and water damage. Coverage for the last risk, however, would be limited to damage from storms or broken water mains. It would not include flood damage. It may also have high deductibles on certain natural disasters.

Businesses can also take advantage of insurance that deals with the consequences of property damage. **Business interruption insurance** is insurance coverage against potential losses that result from having to close a business for insurable reasons.

Casualty Insurance

Suppose an accident occurs on your business premises. The result could be a lawsuit blaming your business for the accident. The lawsuit may demand payment for medical expenses, lost wages, legal fees, and pain and suffering.

To protect your business, you would need casualty insurance. **Casualty insurance** is insurance coverage for loss or liability arising from a sudden, unexpected event such as an accident. Casualty insurance also covers the cost of defending your business in court against claims of property damage.

There are many different types of casualty insurance. **Errors and omissions insurance** is insurance coverage for any loss sustained because of an **error** or oversight on the business's part. **Product liability insurance** is insurance coverage that protects a business from injury claims that result from use of the business's products. **Fidelity bonds** are a form of insurance that protects a company in case of employee theft. **Performance bonds** are insurance coverage that protects a business if work or a contract is not finished on time or as agreed.

Go Green

The "New" New Orleans

In 2005, Hurricane Katrina devastated New Orleans, flooding almost 80 percent of the city. Katrina is considered to be the worst natural disaster in American history. Many social entrepreneurs and non-profit organizations such as the Make It Right Foundation worked together to rebuild New Orleans as a sustainable community, with safe and healthy homes built quickly from earth-friendly materials that preserve the spirit of New Orleans.

◈ **Critical Thinking**
Use an Internet search engine to research the advantages and disadvantages of sustainable design. Summarize your findings in a short report.

Workers' Compensation
The amount of compensation an injured employee receives is partially based on how serious the injury is. *How does an employee file for workers' compensation?*

Life Insurance

Imagine the loss a new business would incur if its owner died unexpectedly. Financial loss would only be part of the tragedy. In the event of an insured person's death, the insurance company pays the face value of the policy. This money allows the business time to make a decision about replacing the key person. It offsets some of the losses that may occur during the transition.

Selecting an Insurance Agent

Just like your attorney and your accountant, your insurance agent will be a key component of your team. Before talking to an agent, define the risks your business faces and find out about the types of insurance required in your state.

Workers' Compensation

Business owners are required by law to make contributions to the state workers' compensation plan. **Workers' compensation insurance** is insurance that is required by the government and paid for by employers to provide medical and income benefits to employees injured on the job. Job-related, such as carpal tunnel syndrome, covered.

The amount of compensation a worker receives is based on a number of **factors**. It depends on the wages or salary of the employee. It also depends on how serious the injury is and whether the injury is permanent. To file for compensation, an injured or ill employee must submit a claim with the compensation board. The board decides how much money to pay out.

The program is designed to free businesses from the threat of employee lawsuits. Workers who accept benefits under the program are barred from suing their employers over their injuries. However, in some states, workers' compensation premiums are a major financial burden for businesses. Therefore, many people consider workers' compensation costs to be a key indicator of a state's attitude toward business.

Risk Retention

In some instances, a company can not transfer a business risk. Either the firm can not get insurance or it can not afford the policies that are offered. In these circumstances, the business must self-insure. In other words, the owner puts aside a certain amount of money every month to help cover the costs of a loss. The owner is keeping, or retaining, the risk.

 Reading Check **Recall** What is a premium?

aabejon/Getty Images

Choosing Safety and Security Precautions

Some of the safety and security options available to small businesses were discussed in Section 22.1. Many other options are available to small businesses. You can install secured doors and windows, burglar alarm systems, and panic buttons. Fire alarms, smoke detectors, and sprinkler systems provide protection from fires. Other options include guards, guard dogs, and patrol services.

Assessing Security

How do you decide which options are right for your company? First, assess your needs. Consider your type of business, its location, and the number of employees. Then list specific problem areas. Do you have exposed outdoor equipment? Is vandalism common in your neighborhood?

When you have completed your assessment, ask a professional security company to conduct a review. The company should be able to spot weaknesses and areas of concern. It should also help you prioritize your security needs. Before contracting with a security company, research its background and check its references.

Greece: Land of Heroes

Greece was the birthplace of Western civilization. The Ancient Greeks gave the world democracy, epic poetry, myths, theater, geometry, and the Olympics. Studies have shown that Greeks' pride in their nation and culture is the highest of all European nations. As with ancient times, shipping and maritime industries are very important. Tourism and the service industry are also crucial, as are agriculture and the growing IT and telecommunications industry.

Island Hopping Greece is a nation of sunny islands and breathtaking views. Not surprisingly, Greeks are warm and hospitable. When meeting someone for the first time, most Greeks shake hands, smile, and make eye contact. To succeed in business, it is important to develop personal relationships.

Social Studies The last decade has been unstable for Greek business owners, due to

political riots that damaged businesses in Athens, major wildfires that swept the countryside, and rampant criminal use of prepaid cell phones. Research some of the other risks that international businesses expanding into Greece might face. Summarize your findings in a one-page report.

Common Greek Words and Phrases

Good afternoon	καλημέρα	kalispera
Goodbye	αντίο	andio
Yes/ No	ναι / όχι	ne/ochi
Please	παρακαλώ	parakalo
Thank you	ευχαριστώ	ef kharisto
You're welcome	παρακαλώ	parakalo

Planning for Emergencies

No matter how many preventive measures you take or how much insurance you buy, disasters do happen. When they occur, they can overwhelm a small business.

Your risk management objective should be to have procedures in place before a crisis occurs. Emergency response planning will minimize your losses and get you back in business quickly. Although there will be similarities, you should draw up plans for each possibility. Each plan should include a list of priorities and actions to take. These actions may include assessing the damage, calling 911 to report the disaster or emergency, calling for evacuation, and having evacuated employees report to a central location.

To prepare for emergencies, you should compile emergency phone numbers and floor plans for rescue teams. You should have important records tagged for quick removal. Your employees should be familiar with your emergency plans. Provide and post copies. Carry out practice emergency drills on a regular basis.

SECTION 22.2 | Review

After You Read ▪▪▪▪▪▪▪▪▪▪▪▪▪

Self-Check

1. **List** specific steps you can take to reduce risk.
2. **Explain** the value of property insurance.
3. **Describe** how to determine the proper amount of insurance coverage for your business.

Think

4. **Construct** a set of circumstances that would call for a risk retention strategy.

Mathematics

5. **Calculating Losses** Jaclyn Boswell estimated that her business will earn profits of $38,000 this year. In previous years her business lost one-twentieth of the profits to shoplifting and 2 percent to employee theft. Given the losses in past years, what is a more accurate profit total?

Math Concept **Operations with Percents** Percents can be expressed as fractions or decimals, which are easier to work with when performing calculations.

Step 1 Convert the percent and fraction to decimals.

Step 2 Multiply the estimated profits by the sum of the decimals to calculate the losses.

Step 3 Subtract the losses from the profits to better estimate the profits.

🚀 Go to connectED.mcgraw-hill.com to check your answers.

Entrepreneurs *in Action*

Melisssa Goodballet
Owner/Founder
My Thrive Pilates

Q *What do you do?*

A I am the founder and owner of My Thrive Pilates and Yoga, located in the Washington, DC Metro Area.

Q *What kind of training and education did you need to get this job?*

A I went to the University of Nevada, Las Vegas, where I became a fully certified Pilates instructor through their dance program.

Q *What do you enjoy most about your job?*

A I feel best when I am teaching and showing people how to stay fit and healthy. I enjoy the challenge of owning and running my own studio. I like the personal relationships you build when working with the individual clients who have specific needs.

Q *How did you become interested in your field?*

A I have always been a very athletic and active person. I fell in love with Pilates and how it transformed my body. My very first Pilates instructor came up to me one day after class and asked, "Would you be interested in teaching Pilates?" and I answered, "Yes!" We had lunch and she explained all the details, costs, and benefits. I later applied and was accepted into the program. I never thought I would be a 20-something who owns my own business and who gets paid to work out! I am so grateful to have taken a chance.

CCR College & Career Readiness

Write a Proposal You are a risk management consultant. Write a proposal to the owner of a fitness studio explaining how you can help the business better manage risk.

1. Using a word processor, describe your services.
2. On paper, or with a presentation program, create a diagram that illustrates how you help businesses. This can be as simple as before and after descriptions in boxes connected by an arrow.
3. Using a spreadsheet program, create a table listing your services and their prices.

Career Facts

Real-World Skills	Academic Skills	Career Cluster
Fitness, Speaking, Listening	Health, Physical Education	Health Science

Review and Assessment

Visual Summary

Risk Management

Pure Risk
Pure risk is the threat of a loss to your business without any possibility of gain.

Dealing with Risk Businesses can use four strategies to deal with risks. Entrepreneurs may obtain property, casualty, life, and workers' compensation insurance. They should also put security and emergency measures in place as well as preventive measures to minimize risks.

Dealing with Risk	
Risk avoidance	Locate your business in a safe area.
Risk reduction	Design work areas to lower the chances of accident or fire. Educate employees about the safe use of equipment. Check and service safety equipment. Test company products under the most extreme conditions in which they will be used.
Risk transfer	Obtain property, casualty, life and workers' compensation insurance.
Risk retention	Put aside a certain amount of money every month to help cover the costs of a potential loss.

Review and Assessment

Vocabulary
1. On a sheet of paper, use each of these terms and words in a written sentence.

Content Vocabulary
◇ speculative risk
◇ pure risk
◇ burglary
◇ robbery
◇ electronic credit card authorizer
◇ negligence

◇ premium
◇ business interruption insurance
◇ casualty insurance
◇ errors-and-omissions insurance

◇ product liability insurance
◇ fidelity bonds
◇ performance bonds
◇ workers' compensation insurance

Academic Vocabulary
■ commit   ■ error   ■ distinct   ■ factor

Key Concepts
2. **Explain** why risk is inevitable.
3. **Describe** speculative risk.
4. **Describe** three categories of pure risk.
5. **List** the four risk management strategies.
6. **Describe** the steps involved in selecting an insurance agent.
7. **Explain** why insurance can or cannot eliminate risk.
8. **Discuss** the procedures for deciding on security measures.
9. **Develop** emergency response plans for potential crises.

Academic Skills

Mathematics
10. **Check One, Check Two** Prasad Bodas, a retail business owner, charges customers a three percent penalty for writing a bad check. Prasad increases the penalty by adding an additional $15.00 fee. Write an equation you could use to determine the penalty for writing any bad check. What is the penalty for writing a bad check in the amount of $286?

    Math Concept **Problem Solving** You can think of equations as number sentences that explain a situation using numbers and operations.
    Step 1 Write an equation using a variable, x, to represent the unknown, in this case the dollar amount of the bad check.
    Step 2 Substitute $286 for the unknown and solve the equation.

English Language Arts
11. **Risk Reduction** You have decided to install an alarm system in your retail business. Call several companies in your community and ask them to send you information about their systems. In a one-page essay, evaluate the products and choose the one that best serves your needs.

Academic Skills *(continued)*

Social Studies

12. **Reduce, Transfer, Retain** Work with a partner to research ten local businesses. Group them according to the type of business, such as retail, manufacturing, or service. Identify any similarities or differences among the groups in terms of how they might approach risk management. Estimate how much the businesses would spend to reduce, transfer, or retain risk.

Science

13. **Hurricane Zones** Hurricanes are natural disasters that can be devastating to homes, businesses, and infrastructure. They represent a significant risk for people living in areas commonly affected by them. Explain how a hurricane forms and identify the areas where they are likely to pose a significant risk.

 Real-World Skills

Research Skills

14. **Risky Business** Risk management does not always work as advertised. Research how risk-management strategies at financial firms may have caused the recent recession. Summarize your findings in your own words in one or two paragraphs.

21st Century Skills

Critical Thinking & Problem Solving

15. **Risk to the News** The business of selling newspapers is under threat, partly due to the availability of free online news. There are no easy answers for the newspaper industry, but maybe you can come up with one. Write a one-page strategy document advising the owner of a newspaper on how to be more successful in today's environment.

 Connect to Your Community

16. **Analyze Risk** Working in small groups, select a local business and consider the risks the business likely faces. Create a chart or spreadsheet with the following headings: Potential Risks; Ways to Avoid Risk; Ways to Reduce Risk; Types of Insurance Necessary; Other Ways to Transfer Risk; and Risks That Must Be Retained. Compare your findings with the rest of the class.

17. **Compare Insurance** Interview two insurance agents who specialize in business insurance. Ask them about the insurance needs of your business, the type of insurance they recommend, and the approximate cost of the policies. How do their recommendations differ?

Review and Assessment

CHAPTER

22

Competitive Events Prep

18. **Situation** You own a dry cleaning shop with an excellent location. The business has an outstanding reputation. In addition to clothing, the business also handles specialty items such as bridal gowns. While training a new salesperson, you mention the insurance, which covers the building, equipment, and items that you clean. The new employee wants to know why you carry so much insurance.

Activity Explain why you carry insurance and some of the risks that the business can be protected against by purchasing insurance.

Evaluation You will be evaluated on how well you meet these performance indicators:

- Describe the concept of insurance.
- Describe types of business risk.
- Explain ways to transfer risk.
- Demonstrate responsible behavior.

 Go to **connectED.mcgraw-hill.com** for more information about this activity and other competitive events.

Standardized Test Practice

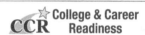 ☆ **College & Career Readiness**

Directions Choose the letter of the best answer. Write the letter for the answer on a separate piece of paper. For question #2, if the answer is False, rewrite the statement to make it true.

1. _____ is the threat of a loss to your business without any possibility of gain.
   A. Speculative risk
   B. Risk reduction
   C. Pure risk
   D. Risk avoidance
2. Product liability insurance is coverage that protects a business from injury claims that result from use of the business's products.
   T
   F

> **Test-Taking Tip**
> In a multiple-choice test, be sure to read the questions first, then read all the answer choices before you choose.

Chapter 22 · Risk Management | **531**

CHAPTER

23

Making Your Business Grow

Chapter Objectives

SECTION 23.1
Making Your Business Grow

Evaluate the three primary methods for growing your business.

Describe intensive growth strategies that can be used to take advantage of opportunities within a current market.

Discuss integrative growth strategies that can be used to expand a business within its industry.

Explain diversification growth strategies that can be used to take advantage of business opportunities outside a business's market or industry.

SECTION 23.2
Challenges of Expansion

Describe the challenges that come with growth.

Explain what it takes to acquire growth capital.

Discuss the types of growth funding.

Discovery Project

Expanding Your Business

Key Question *What information is needed to apply for a loan to expand a business?*

Project Goal
Contact local financial institutions that offer loans for business expansion. Ask for a copy of the application a business owner would have to fill out to apply for a loan. Compare and contrast the loan applications and determine the common components as well as the differences.

Think About...
➤ How will you go about selecting and contacting financial institutions?
➤ What criteria will you use to compare the application forms?
➤ How will you present your findings?

 21st Century Skills
Financial Literacy What back-up plan might you have in place in case a loan request was refused?

Evaluate
⊘ Go to connectED.mcgraw-hill.com to download a rubric that you can use to evaluate your final project.

Ask
AN
EXPERT

Q: *I plan to take business and accounting classes at my local community college before starting my new business. Are there any tax credits that I can use to help pay for my education?*

A: You may qualify to claim a lifetime learning tax credit of up to $2000 each year for qualified higher educational expenses for yourself, your spouse, or a dependant if your modified adjusted gross income falls within the limits set by Congress. The education must be one or more courses but does not have to be part of a degree program.

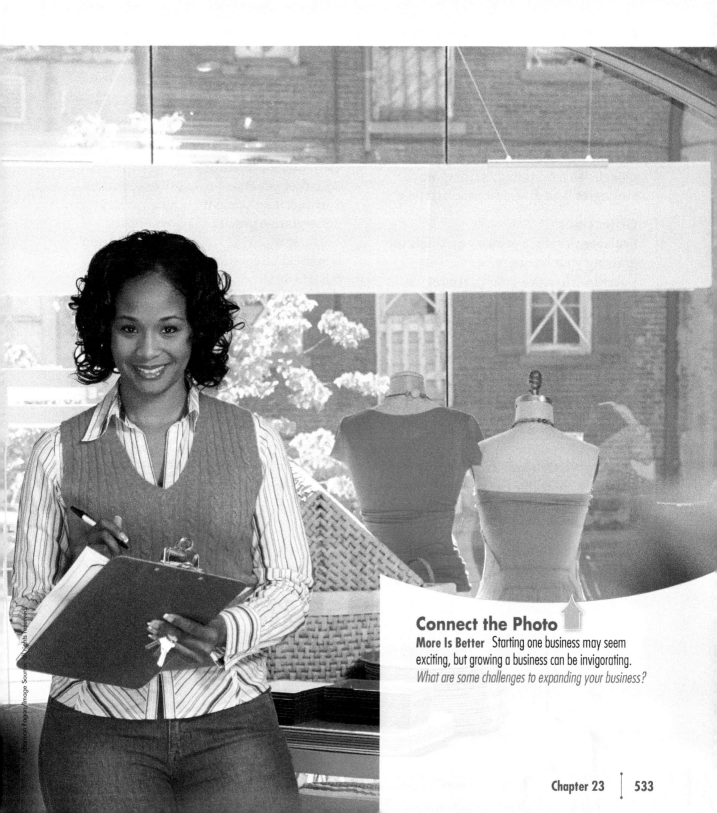

Connect the Photo
More Is Better   Starting one business may seem exciting, but growing a business can be invigorating. *What are some challenges to expanding your business?*

Making Your Business Grow

Reading Guide

Before You Read ▪▪▪▪▪▪▪▪▪▪▪▪▪▪

Connect How do you grow a business?

The Main Idea
Growing a business requires research and planning. Three broad categories of strategies can be used to grow a business: intensive strategies, integrative strategies, and diversification strategies.

Objectives
Evaluate the three primary methods for growing your business.
Describe intensive growth strategies that can be used to take advantage of opportunities within a current market.
Discuss integrative growth strategies that can be used to expand a business within its industry.
Explain diversification growth strategies that can be used to take advantage of business opportunities outside a business's market or industry.

Content Vocabulary
◇ market penetration
◇ market development
◇ integrative growth strategies
◇ vertical integration
◇ horizontal integration
◇ diversification growth strategies
◇ synergistic diversification
◇ horizontal diversification
◇ conglomerate diversification

Academic Vocabulary
You will see these words in your reading and on your tests. Use the academic vocabulary glossary to look up their meanings.
▪ enhance
▪ alternative

Graphic Organizer
Draw a chart like the one shown. As you read, categorize the different types of growth strategies.

 Go to **connectED.mcgraw-hill.com** to download this graphic organizer.

Intensive	Integrative	Diversification

Planning the Growth of Your Business

If an entrepreneur puts together a great team and develops a compelling business concept, the new business probably will not stay small for very long. Growth is the natural by-product of a successful start-up. It helps a business maintain its competitive advantage by staying ahead of the competition. Some entrepreneurs fear growth because they do not want to lose control of the business. Their fear is understandable because the growth period of a new venture is both an exciting and a risky time.

Growth Within the Current Market

For a business that wants to take advantage of opportunities within a current market and increase sales to its target customers, there are several possible intensive growth strategies. These growth strategies include market penetration, market development, and product development.

Market Penetration

Market penetration is an attempt to increase sales in your current market. You can do this in a variety of ways:

- **Find ways to get your customers to use your product more often.** For example, the makers of Arm & Hammer® Baking Soda increased sales by suggesting new ways to use it. Customers once purchased baking soda only for cooking purposes. Now baking soda is used as an ingredient in toothpaste. Customers also use it to keep their refrigerators smelling fresh.
- **Attract your competitors' customers.** A retail store owner might locate near a competitor to encourage comparison shopping.
- **Go after people in your present market who are not using products like yours.** Marcel Ford found new customers for his silk plant cleaner by demonstrating the product in Costco® outlets. People who would not have picked his product off the shelf readily saw and experienced its benefits.

Web Savvy

Avatars and Gravatars

In many online and virtual communities, participants are able to post a picture or control an animated character that appears along with their comments. The generic term for this is an *avatar*, meaning that it is representative of that particular person. But with so many people active on so many different communities, the *gravatar* has become particularly useful. Short for "globally recognized avatar," a gravatar is associated with a single email address. Once you have a gravatar assigned to your email, it will automatically appear on all online communities that recognize gravatars. *How can entrepreneurs use avatars and online communities to grow their businesses?*

Growth Strategies Intensive growth strategies exploit opportunities within a current market. *How can you decide which strategies to use to achieve growth?*

Steady Growth, Not Overgrowth, Brings Success

Growth is great—when you're ready for it

In business, overnight success is the exception, not the rule. Unexpected success sounds great, but it can bring headaches such as neglected customers, lowered-quality product, too much loan debt, and stress for you and your employees

Businesspeople advise following these tactics to grow at just the right speed:

- **Put quality first.** This helps you keep the clients you already have.
- **Have discipline.** Jump on a new idea only when you have the time and resources to make it work.
- **Test new ideas before committing.** Start small. For example, introduce a new product in a limited market or focus groups. Then roll out a finished product you know is up to your standards.

- **Plan your resources.** Make sure you have the right resources, such as well-trained employees, raw materials, and solid market research, before you aim to expand.

If you aim for steady growth, you're more likely to make it big in the long run.

Active Learning

Set a timer for 15 seconds and build a pyramid of paper cups as quickly as you can. If it collapses, start over and keep going while the clock is still running. Then repeat the exercise without a timer. Which method resulted in an attractive, stable product? Did the timed method actually take less time? Write a paragraph explaining how this exercise applies to business growth.

Market Development

With **market development**, a business expands its product to reach new locations. A business can open a branch in another community. It can also go nationwide or expand internationally.

Franchising

Franchising is one way to grow a business geographically. California Pizza Kitchen®, Beard Papa's®, and most automobile dealerships are examples of franchises. Franchisers sell the right to do business under the company's name. For a fee, the franchiser also provides training, promotion, and other assistance.

Advantages of Franchising

One of the biggest advantages of franchising is that you can expand the business with someone else's money. Franchising also makes it easy for you to manage your growing organization.

● **As You Read** ▪▪▪

Integrate What is the relationship between growth and competitive advantage?

With franchising, you personally train your franchisees. They, in turn, hire and are responsible for the employees who work for them. You do not have to oversee the workers.

Disadvantages of Franchising

However, franchising has its challenges. It is like starting your business all over again. You must prepare training manuals, write operating instructions, and prepare market and competitor analyses. In addition, the costs of setting up the franchise structure add up. There may be legal, accounting, consulting, and training costs. It may be a long time before a franchise turns a profit. One company in Memphis sold more than 70 franchises. However, it did not show a profit for a year. Waiting three to five years for a profit is not uncommon.

Going Global

Do not limit your growth to the United States. United States franchises can be found throughout the Pacific Rim, Europe, and many other parts of the world. You can find a Hard Rock Cafe® in Beijing and a Timberland® shoe store in London. Businesses other than franchises form partnerships and enjoy tremendous success in global markets. Foreign businesspeople come to the United States looking for franchisers and partners. They want to take successful business concepts back to their countries.

Product Development

Product development is another way to increase sales to existing customers. This is the introduction of brand new or improved products to the marketplace. In most industries, companies must continually develop new products to keep customers interested. New products are those that did not exist previously while improved products simply **enhance** existing products. You have probably noticed companies advertising "new and improved" versions of existing products.

Integrative Growth Strategies

Integrative growth strategies are growth strategies that enable your company to expand within the industry by growing vertically or horizontally within the value chain. The value chain consists of all the businesses in the industry from producers to retailers that a product must go through until it reaches the market.

Grow Green

What color is one of the energy sector's fastest growing industries? If you said "green," you guessed right. Because wind power has almost zero fuel costs and relatively low maintenance costs, more entrepreneurs are becoming interested. As larger, multi-megawatt wind turbines become mass-produced, startup costs will come down, encouraging more growth. Many states provide property tax exemption to wind businesses. The wind power industry expects the industry to continue growing quickly, despite the recent recession.

◈ **Critical Thinking**
Why would some manufacturing companies prefer to purchase their power from wind farms? Write a one paragraph response.

Globalization When considering franchising, do not limit your growth to the United States. *What brings foreign businesspeople to the United States?*

Vertical Integration

Vertical integration is the merging of companies that are in the same value chain of a product. With vertical integration, a company expands in two ways. It acquires suppliers upstream in the value chain. It also acquires distribution outlets downstream in the chain.

When you integrate forward or downstream in the value chain, you attempt to gain control of the distribution systems for your product. Generally, you can do this in two ways. First, you can eliminate intermediaries by selling directly to end users. This allows you to reduce the price and save your company money. Second, you can acquire the distributors, retailers, or dealers of your products. In addition, many manufacturers, such as Nike® and Mikas®, have opened retail stores, selling at a discount to consumers.

Horizontal Integration

Horizontal integration involves increasing your market share and expanding your business by buying up competitors. For example, you may decide to purchase a company that has a product and market compatible with yours. An example is a gas station that purchases an auto parts store. Both businesses serve the same general customer base but in different ways.

Diversification Growth Strategies

Diversification growth strategies are growth strategies that involve investing in products or businesses that are different from yours. Businesses often diversify when they have exhausted opportunities within their present industry or market. Unlike growth strategies within the current market or integrative strategies within the industry, this strategy takes advantage of opportunities outside a current market or industry by synergistic, horizontal, or conglomerate diversification.

Synergistic Diversification

Trying to find new products, processes, or businesses that are technologically compatible with yours is called **synergistic diversification**. This type of diversification is often used to gain economies of scale. For example, you may buy a business that is technologically similar to yours but which produces different products. In this way, you can use your current processes to expand your product line without having to develop new products yourself.

Horizontal Diversification

To seek products that are technologically unrelated to yours is **horizontal diversification**. When you diversify in this manner, you are attempting to sell the new product or service to your current customers. For example, Nike, which manufactures athletic shoes, began selling sports clothing and accessories to its customers.

Conglomerate Diversification

Use **conglomerate diversification** to look for products or businesses that are totally unrelated to yours. In this way, you might find an enterprise that fills a gap in your business. For example, suppose your primary business requires employees to travel a great deal. You may purchase a travel agency to cut costs and provide convenience for your employees. Another **alternative** would be to buy the building in which your company is located. You could then lease the extra space to another business as a new source of revenue.

Questions to Ask

Diversification can be profitable, but it also can be distracting, particularly at start-up or in the early years of a company. Before you choose to diversify, make sure your primary business is under control and healthy. It should be showing a profit and generating a positive cash flow.

Ask yourself if you are knowledgeable about the new product or service, and if you think you can manage the extra paperwork, finances, and decisions. Determine if the new business will require additional staff or materials or a new work space. If so, how much will this cost?

SECTION 23.1 Review

After You Read ==============

Self-Check

1. **Compare** and contrast market development and product development.
2. **List** drawbacks to franchising your business.
3. **Identify** strategies for expanding your business to another country.

Think

4. **Describe** how a restaurant could use diversification strategies to grow its business.

English Language Arts/Writing

5. **Design an Ad** A well-written ad for a newspaper or magazine includes a strong headline with a selling message, one or two subheads that clarify or extend the selling message, and body copy that explains the benefits of the product offered in the headline. A well-designed ad incorporates color, interesting imagery, white space, and a logotype identifying the business. Design an ad for a business or franchise you would someday like to start. Ask your classmates to critique your work.

Go to connectED.mcgraw-hill.com to check your answers.

Challenges of Expansion

Reading Guide

Before You Read ▪▪▪▪▪▪▪▪▪▪▪▪▪▪
Predict What are some factors that affect growth?

The Main Idea
It costs money to make money. You need to understand the type of funding you are looking for as well as your costs in time and money to get it.

Objectives
Describe the challenges that come with growth.
Explain what it takes to acquire growth capital.
Discuss the types of growth funding.

Content Vocabulary
◇ private placement
◇ prospectus
◇ public stock offering
◇ employee stock option plan (ESOP)

Academic Vocabulary
You will see these words in your reading and on your tests. Use the academic vocabulary glossary to look up their meanings.
■ expand
■ impact

Graphic Organizer
Draw a chart like the one shown. As you read, write the factors that affect the ability of a business to grow.

 Go to connectED.mcgraw-hill.com to download this graphic organizer.

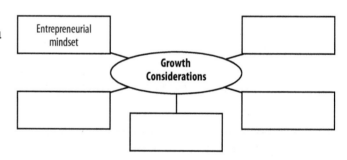

ETHICS and BUSINESS

Expanding Your Business

Situation Your business partner has finally convinced you that it is time to expand your screen printing business and open a new store across town. You were hesitant at first because of the money it will take, but now you are excited.

Searching for a Loan Since your partner is in charge of the company's finances, he has offered to take on the task of finding funding for the expansion. He begins by checking local financial institutions and fills out a loan application request for the bank where you have your company's accounts.

English Language Arts/Writing

Misleading Information As you review the application, you notice that he has used some creative bookkeeping to make your business look more profitable than it might actually be. While not illegal, the practice might be questionable.

1. How do you feel about what your partner has done? Do you feel that this is ethical behavior?
2. Write a one-page dialogue between you and your partner in which you share your feelings about the misleading information.

Challenges that Come with Growth

Expansion is a natural outgrowth of a successful business. A business that expands and diversifies has the advantage. However, you must consider whether your business is suited for growth. Several factors affect the ability of a business to grow:

- **Target market characteristics** If the niche you created is small, your ability to grow will be limited. To grow further, you must **expand** outside the initial market to new markets.
- **Innovativeness** If your industry thrives on innovation, you must learn to innovate better and faster than others.
- **Ability to delegate** Many entrepreneurs are successful at recognizing opportunity and starting a business. However, they may not have management skills. You may need to hire a professional manager to run the business.
- **Shared vision** To grow successfully, everyone in your company needs to share the same vision and work to achieve it.
- **Systems and controls** The appropriate systems and controls need to be in place. These involve such diverse areas as management, marketing, finances, and record keeping. Systems and controls ensure that your business can deal effectively with the demands of growth.

The Challenge of Multiple Sites

When you move from an owner-operated business to additional sites, you can become distanced from customers and employees. Consequently, it may not be easy to keep up with their needs. This is particularly true when your other locations are overseas. You may have to modify your marketing plan and organizational strategy to suit the culture of the country in which you are doing business.

> ● **As You Read** ▪▪▪▪▪▪▪
> **Determine** What is one of the biggest challenges of having multiple business sites?

Thriving Tech Rosetta Stone, Ltd., makers of the Rosetta Stone® language learning software, enjoyed a successful initial public offering even during a major recession. *Why must technology businesses be prepared to grow quickly?*

Management Questions

You must decide whether your new business location will operate independently, or be controlled by the main business location. Sometimes the main location controls common functions that are easily centralized. Another arrangement has the branch concentrate on day-to-day operations and send detailed records to the main location on a regular basis.

Additional Staff

Expansion requires additional managers. It can be an expensive and difficult undertaking to find people who have the necessary skills and who can be trusted. One of the best ways to hire is to look to hire people referred to you by current employees.

The Effect on Record Keeping

With expansion, record-keeping requirements become more complicated. You need an accounting system that tracks key data at all locations. Fortunately, technology makes record keeping easier to accomplish. Plan for the purchase of a networked computer system and the appropriate software before you grow the business.

The Problem with Success

Entrepreneurs should watch the industry and the market for new trends and changes that can have a significant **impact** on their business. Many business owners, flushed with success, take money out of the business or invest in expensive overhead. If the market changes and business slows, they may be saddled with payments they cannot make.

Finding Growth Capital

When financing expansion, try the same sources you used to start the business. These include personal savings, friends, family, and banks. Chapter 19 discusses some of these options. However, the amount required for expansion is often more than you needed at start-up and may require additional types of funding.

Growth is costly. It takes money to raise money and you pay all of the costs of raising the money before you receive it. Consequently, it can put a strain on the limited resources of your business. However, by demonstrating that your business is successful, you can easily raise growth capital.

> **Reading Check** **Connect** Would you invest your profits back into the business? Why or why not?

Types of Growth Funding

As more cash comes into your business and less cash leaves, you can use the excess to fund expansion. This is known as funding growth internally. Internal funding is the best source of expansion capital because it is inexpensive, and you control it. You also do not have to give up any equity in your business or take on any debt. Unfortunately, most fast-growing businesses require more cash than they can generate and still maintain operations.

Private Placement

Private placement is a way to raise money by selling investment interests in your business to private investors or venture capitalists. You need to develop a type of business plan called a prospectus. A **prospectus** is a formal document that details the risks involved in the private offering. Its purpose is to give investors the information they need to make informed decisions. Get help from an attorney to do this correctly because you may have to register the private placement with the SEC.

GLOBAL WORKPLACE — Argentina: Two to Tango

Argentina, the second largest country in South America, is rich with natural resources. Agriculture is an important part of the economy: Argentina is one of the world's largest producers of honey, soybeans, corn, and wheat.

However, less than one-tenth of Argentina's 40 million people live in rural areas. The majority live in Argentina's modern, sophisticated cities, such as the capital, Buenos Aires.

Most Argentines are also well-educated. Like other Latin American cultures, individualism is less important to Argentines than strong group relations.

Spanish with a Twist Eighty-five percent of Argentina's population is of European descent, mostly Italian or Spanish. As a consequence, Argentine Spanish is heavily influenced by Italian and sounds different than most other Spanish in Latin America.

Social Studies The World Bank considers Argentina to be a secondary emerging market. Telecommunications has been a fast

growing industry, with 75 percent of the population using mobile phones and more than 16 million Argentineans online. In a small group, brainstorm a list of possible entrepreneurial opportunities that may exist because of this growth and present your list of ideas to the rest of the class.

Common Argentine Spanish Words and Phrases	
Hello	¡hola!
Goodbye	Adiós
Yes / No	Sí/No
Please	Por favor
Thank you	Gracias
You're welcome	De nada

Public Stock Offering

Only corporations can raise money by selling shares of stock, or making a **public stock offering** on a public stock exchange, such as the New York Stock Exchange or the NASDAQ. To make a public stock offering, your corporation should show increasing revenues for several years. It should also have revenues of at least $50 million annually. The public offering process is regulated by the SEC to protect the public from illegal or poorly prepared offerings that could endanger investors' money.

Employee Stock Option Plan

An **employee stock option plan (ESOP)** is a source of financing in which a company gives its employees the opportunity to buy a portion of the business. To raise money with an ESOP, you must have at least 25 employees and revenues of $5 million. An attorney can tell you whether you meet additional requirements.

SECTION 23.2 | Review

After You Read ■■■■■■■■■■■■■■■

Self-Check

1. **Identify** some challenges of operating multiple sites.
2. **Name** two types of growth funding available to growing businesses.
3. **Describe** employee stock option plans.

Think

4. **Explain** why high tech businesses may grow faster than others.

Mathematics

5. **Making More Money** Your start-up business had increasing revenues over its first six months. Your records show the revenues as $3,400; $3,910; $4,301; $4,946.15; $5,440.76; $6,256.88. By what percentage did your monthly revenue grow from month to month? If the pattern of increasing revenues continues what will be the next month's revenues?

   Math Concept **Patterns** A sequence of numbers that changes in a consistent way forms a pattern. Patterns can be determined by analyzing how each number is different from the one that comes before and after.

   Step 1 Divide each number by the number that precedes it to determine the increase.

   Step 2 Extend the pattern to determine the value of the next month's increase.

   Step 3 Multiply the last month's revenue by the percent increase to determine the next month's revenues.

⊘ Go to connectED.mcgraw-hill.com to check your answers.

Entrepreneurs *in Action*

Joanna Meiseles
Founder and Former CEO
Snip-its

Q *What do you do?*

A I established Snip-its™ hair care salon for kids and built it into a successful franchise business. I no longer work on the day-to-day operations. These days I source partnership organizations that will help the brand expand into new markets. I'm creating an educational video with a non-profit and training new franchisees that enter our system.

Q *What kind of training and education did you need to get this job?*

A I graduated from Duke University, and I learned a lot through the school of hard knocks. My learning came from on-the-job training and a determination to make my dream come true. Most people told me I couldn't do it, but I'm from a family of entrepreneurs and entertainers.

Q *What do you enjoy most about your job?*

A I love seeing families leaving Snip-its with a smile and saying that they will tell their friends. It is especially rewarding making kids feel great about how they look.

Q *How did you become interested in your field?*

A In 1993, I took my first son Ben, then 3 years old, to get a haircut. I assumed there would be a place for kids, but there wasn't. We went to a family walk-in salon. It wasn't horrible, but it wasn't everything I hoped it would be. When I got home, I said to my husband, "I should open a children's hair salon," and he said, "You should, and you should call it Snip-its." Immediately, I had an idea and a name. I knew I was on to something great!

College & Career Readiness

Growth History
Research a business in your community. Find out how the business grew to its present size.

1. Select a company in your state or city. Local chains are a great choice.
2. Find out what strategies the company used to grow. For example, the business may have expanded by franchising.
3. Convey your findings in a one-page report.

Career Facts

Real-World Skills	Academic Skills	Career Cluster
Interpersonal Skills; Presentation Skills	English Language; Mathematics	Education & Training

Review and Assessment

Visual Summary

Making Your Business Grow

New and Improved Several strategies provide opportunities for growth within a current market.

Intensive Growth Strategies	
Market Penetration	Attempt to increase sales in your current market.
Market Development	Expand product to reach new locations.
Product Development	Introduce brand-new or improved products to existing customers.

Mergers & Acquisitions Integrative growth strategies give you the opportunity to grow within your industry either vertically or horizontally.

Integrative Growth Strategies	
Vertical Integration	The merging of companies that are in the same distribution chain of a product.
Horizontal Integration	Increasing market share and expanding business by buying up competitors.

Now Selling Diversification growth strategies provide opportunities outside the market or industry in which your business normally operates.

Diversification Growth Strategies	
Synergistic	Finding new products or businesses that are technologically compatible.
Horizontal	Seeking products that are technologically unrelated.
Conglomerate	Looking for products or businesses that are totally unrelated.

Vocabulary

1. On a sheet of paper, use each of these terms and words in a written sentence.

Content Vocabulary

◇ market penetration
◇ market development
◇ integrative growth strategies
◇ vertical integration
◇ horizontal integration
◇ diversification growth
  strategies

◇ synergistic diversification
◇ horizontal diversification
◇ conglomerate
  diversification
◇ private placement
◇ prospectus
◇ public stock offering

◇ employee stock option plan
  (ESOP)

Academic Vocabulary

■ enhance
■ alternative
■ expand
■ impact

Key Concepts

2. **Evaluate** the three primary methods for growing a business.
3. **Describe** intensive growth strategies.
4. **Discuss** integrative growth strategies used to expand a business within its industry.
5. **List** several types of diversification growth strategies.
6. **Identify** the challenges that come with growth.
7. **Explain** what it takes to acquire growth capital.
8. **Name** the types of growth funding.
9. **List** the steps you would take to expand a business internationally.

Academic Skills

Mathematics

10. **Payback Time** Halena is a restaurant owner. As part of her franchise agreement, she must pay 7.5 percent of first-year profits to the parent company, and 4.8 percent of second-year profits. If Halena's franchise made $87,650 and $94,850 in the first and second years respectively, how much does she owe the parent company?

Math Concept **Percents** Percents can be thought of as parts of a whole, which is represented by the number 100.
Step 1 Divide the percents by 100 to convert them to decimals.
Step 2 Multiply the profits by the decimal to calculate the amount to be paid.

English Language Arts

11. **Editing** Rewrite the following paragraph, correcting the errors in spelling, punctuation, and usage: "Managing the growth of a start up company requires intensive, integration, or diversification strategies. Financing expansion is also a chalenge. First round financing includes money from personal-savings friends and family and banks. Second round financing is used to make a venture more stable."

Academic Skills (continued)

Social Studies

12. **Going Green** More and more entrepreneurs recognize the importance of environmentally-friendly practices and products to the growth of their businesses. Choose a company with which you are familiar or would like to know more about. Look at annual reports, Web sites, advertisements, and news releases for information about how the company is addressing the growing demand for green technology. Write a paragraph or two describing the company's green strategy.

Science

13. **Batteries** The demand for better batteries is growing, given the explosion of portable electronic devices and electric vehicles in our world. Green investors are currently interested in funding research that will lead to a new generation of more-powerful, longer-lasting batteries. Research how a battery works and write a brief explanation.

Real-World Skills

Research Skills

14. **Rich Uncle Sam** Who is the largest buyer of goods and services in the world? Signing the U.S. government as a customer is a fantastic way to grow a business. Research the steps involved in competing for a government contract. Summarize your findings in a one-page report.

21st Century Skills

Media Literacy

15. **Hot Stocks** Use the Internet to discover which companies are growing fastest this year. Continue your research until you learn some of the challenges these companies are facing because of their growth. Summarize your findings in a one-page report.

Connect to Your Community

16. **Planned Growth** Interview an entrepreneur about plans to grow the business. Identify the type of strategy being used. Is it appropriate for this business?

17. **Going Global** Imagine that your business has been very successful over the last five years. You have been thinking about expanding internationally. Prepare a written document justifying your expansion plans. Include the following:

- The international market(s) where you think expansion is appropriate for your type of business
- Growth strategy options given the type of business and the fact that it is new
- Method(s) for raising expansion capital

Review and Assessment

Competitive Events Prep

18. Situation You own a successful business and work with a community program that advises potential entrepreneurs. Currently, you are working with a woman who makes and sells purses and tote bags. The woman has been very successful selling her bags to family and friends. She does all of the design, sewing, and selling and would like to expand her business by selling her bags to select specialty stores. In order to do this, she will need to hire a seamstress and invest in equipment and supplies.

Activity You are to offer the purse and tote bag maker general information about business expansion. Prepare an outline of the information you will discuss with the purse and tote bag maker.

Evaluation You will be evaluated on how well you meet these performance indicators:
- Describe entrepreneurial planning considerations.
- Select target markets.
- Determine product/service to fill customer need.
- Describe the use of operating procedures.
- Delegate responsibility for job tasks.

 Go to connectEDmcgraw-hill.com for more information about this activity and other competitive events.

Standardized Test Practice

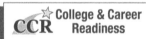

Directions Choose the letter of the best answer. Write the letter for the answer on a separate piece of paper. For question #2, if the answer is False, rewrite the statement to make it true.

1. _____ involves increasing your market share and expanding your business by buying up your competitors.
   A. Vertical integration
   B. Market penetration
   C. Horizontal integration
   D. Synergistic diversification

2. Any company can raise money by selling shares of stock.
   T
   F

Test-Taking Tip
When taking handwritten tests, write as neatly as possible. Double-check your grammar, spelling, and punctuation.

CHAPTER

24

Social and Ethical Responsibility

Chapter Objectives

SECTION 24.1

Social Responsibility

Explain the relationship between entrepreneurs and social responsibility.

Discuss how entrepreneurs can contribute to their communities.

SECTION 24.2

Ethical Responsibility

Define ethics and ethical behavior.

Explain how to develop a code of ethics.

List special ethical problems that entrepreneurs face.

Discovery Project

Responsibility and Profitability

Key Question *How can being socially responsible help a business succeed?*

Project Goal

Working with a partner, create a survey to identify businesses that people in your community think are *not* socially responsible. Have them explain why. Ask more questions that will help you determine how this perception affects the business, such as: Do you still shop at the business? Do you shop at a competitor?

Think About...

➤ *How will you select people to take your survey?*

➤ *What are some more questions you could ask about the perception of socially responsibility?*

➤ *How will you present your survey results?*

21ˢᵗ Century Skills

Leadership and Responsibility *Why do groups that promote social responsibility pay special attention to large corporations?*

Evaluate

 Go to connectED.mcgraw-hill.com to download a rubric that you can use to evaluate your final project.

Q: *I want to start investing and also do my part for the environment. How can I avoid investing in companies that pollute?*

A: Green mutual funds have become popular with eco-minded investors. Green fund managers use investor money to buy stock in companies that meet environmental requirements and standards. You can also research companies with progressive environmental practices on the Internet.

Blend Images/Ariel Skelley/Getty Images

Connect the Photo

We're in This Together Entrepreneurs who run their businesses with social responsibility gain more than just profit; they gain loyalty from customers and personal satisfaction. When entrepreneurs establish ethics and moral codes by which they run their business, employees, community members, and customers will respond positively. *How can companies use their social practices as part of their marketing plans?*

Social Responsibility

Reading Guide

Before You Read ■■■■■■■■■■■■■

Connect What does it mean to be socially responsible?

The Main Idea
Businesses must do more than provide jobs and make a profit. They also are expected to run their business responsibly.

Objectives
Explain the relationship between entrepreneurs and social responsibility.
Discuss how entrepreneurs can contribute to their communities.

Content Vocabulary
◇ philanthropy
◇ social responsibility
◇ Environmental Protection Agency (EPA)

Academic Vocabulary
You will see these words in your reading and on your tests. Use the academic vocabulary glossary to look up their meanings.
■ require
■ demonstrate

Graphic Organizer
Draw a chart like the one shown. As you read, write notes about how businesses can protect customers and the environment.

 Go to connectED.mcgraw-hill.com to download this graphic organizer.

Protecting Customers	Protecting Environment
make safe products	

Entrepreneurs and Social Responsibility

As You Read ▪▪▪▪▪▪▪
Compare and Contrast What is the difference between social responsibility and philanthropy?

History is filled with entrepreneurs who made generous contributions to society. John D. Rockefeller, who revolutionized the petroleum industry, gave more than a half-billion dollars to charity in the late 1800s. His money still fights hunger and disease. More recently, Microsoft founder Bill Gates set up the largest charitable foundation in history, with a gift of $27 billion. The Bill and Melinda Gates Foundation provides funds to improve schools and promote health care around the world.

What Social Responsibility Means

Social responsibility, however, involves more than **philanthropy**, or making charitable donations to improve human welfare. It means running your enterprise responsibly every day. **Social responsibility** is the principle that companies should contribute to the welfare of society and not be devoted solely to profits. Social responsibility **requires** a business to acknowledge that it has a contract with society that includes many duties. It must make safe products. It must treat customers well and employees fairly. It should be run honestly.

Being socially responsible can inspire loyalty in employees and customers. That is why many socially responsible businesses experience great success. In fact, there is much evidence that social responsibility is associated with improved business performance. Studies have found a direct relationship between social responsibility and profitability. Customers associate a socially responsible business with trust and integrity, so they are more comfortable dealing with such a business. Similarly, they typically will not purchase from a company that has been linked with disreputable conduct. Companies such as Chipotle® and Burt's Bees® are able to attract a loyal customer base that is willing to pay a little more for socially responsible products.

ETHICS and BUSINESS

Running Eco-Friendly Businesses

Situation Your home remodeling company does reconstruction, painting, and other jobs for homeowners. Your business is doing well. Most of your business comes from word-of-mouth from satisfied customers.

Going Green A new customer tells you that she and her neighbors are considering remodeling their homes, but are concerned about pollution. She asks whether the products you use are environmentally friendly. Do you use low- or no-VOC paint, for example?

English Language Arts/Writing

Green Products You currently do not use environmentally friendly products because they cost more and would cut into your profit. If you raise prices, you could lose business.

1. Would you switch to environmentally friendly products and risk making less money? Or would you continue to use your current products?
2. Write a one-page report explaining your reasoning.

Youth + Drive = Success

For a new generation of entrepreneurs, success comes from following your dream

Being kids didn't stop Jason Li or Adora Svitak from doing what they love and achieving success. In fact, their age helped them find new opportunities others had missed.

Jason Li always had a passion for the environment. When he learned that electronics were poisoning landfills, he wanted to make a change. As a sophomore in high school he founded electronics recycling company iReTron, which buys used electronics and safely recycles them for parts. This benefits customers and the environment.

Adora Svitak noticed that few adults really listened to what children had to say. At age 12, she rocketed to fame as a speaker at the TED conference with her talk "What Adults Can Learn from Kids."

The author of multiple books, Svitak has engaged millions of readers and viewers with her passion for youth empowerment and the power of language.

Creative entrepreneurs like Jason and Adora use innovation to solve a real need, enabling them to do what they love and also make money.

Active Learning

What need do you see going unmet in your world? How could you turn that insight into a business that enables you to do what you love? Sketch out a webpage that depicts and describes your dream business and the need it fills. Use either computer software or pen and paper to create the sketch.

Your Responsibility to Customers

Businesses must act responsibly toward their customers. Companies must not mislead customers about a product's quality, performance, or safety. Information must be given about proper use, and unsafe products must be labeled as such. The free market is the consumer's best protector. Because businesses are free to compete with one another in satisfying consumer wants, they are more motivated to offer the best quality products at the lowest prices.

Two other forces that protect customers are consumers' rights organizations and government regulation. Institutions such as the Consumers' Union have provided consumers with information about the quality, safety, and costs of competing products.

Laws also affect how businesses are run. The Truth-in-Lending Act requires businesses to fully inform their customers about purchases. The Fair Credit Billing Act requires businesses to respond quickly to consumer complaints. Businesses that break such laws can face stiff fines and punishment.

Government regulations have led businesses to improve their service to customers. However, most successful businesses see customer service as a competitive advantage on its own. Some state and local governments also require businesses to post government ratings on how well they follow health and safety regulations.

Your Responsibility to the Environment

Have you noticed how many ads are environmentally oriented? Oil companies try to show how they save rare birds from harm. Chemical companies describe how they protect crops without poisoning the soil. Soap companies advertise recyclable boxes.

Companies want to **demonstrate** to customers that they are environmentally responsible. To create and enforce environmental standards, in 1970, the U.S. government formed the Environmental Protection Agency (EPA). The **Environmental Protection Agency (EPA)** is an independent federal agency established to coordinate programs and enforce regulations aimed at reducing pollution and protecting the environment. For example, The EPA joined with the U.S. Department of Energy to create the Energy Star program to protect the environment through energy efficient products and practices. Businesses and consumers can save a lot of money by making choices that use less energy.

Aquaculture Many companies provide top-quality seafood that is sustainably wild caught or farmed in fisheries. By doing so, they hope to make oceans healthier. *Which federal agency regulates pollutants?*

Mark Dierker/Bear Dancer Studios

Business and the Environment

In response to federal laws and consumer concerns, more businesses are taking responsibility for protecting the environment. Large companies even employ environmental affairs executives to help them achieve their goals in an environmentally responsible manner. These efforts may increase the company's costs in the short term, but they also may enable a company to charge higher prices, to increase market share, or both.

For example, Ciba®, a Swiss dye manufacturer, developed textile dyes that require less salt than traditional dyes. The result was cleaner waterways and lower water treatment costs for businesses that use their dyes. Ciba gained market share and charges more for the low-salt dyes because of their value.

Many firms are working to eliminate wasteful practices and the emissions of pollutants and chemicals from their manufacturing processes. Other companies are seeking ways to improve products so that they perform more efficiently. For example, car makers who have moved to producing cars that achieve higher miles per gallon are creating more efficient products.

 Reading Check Explain What does "EPA" stand for?

● Figure 24.1 **Making a Contribution**

Donate Your Products and Services

Donating a portion of what you produce can mean a lot to those who receive it. Starbucks Foundation makes sizable donations to community groups across the country and the globe.

Get Your Employees Involved in Philanthropy

Partners (employees) at Starbucks spend almost 1 million hours contributing to community service each year. You can encourage your employees to give back to the community by providing time each month for them to volunteer.

Join with Other Companies to Promote Social Responsibility

Starbucks Foundation partnered with (RED)™ to help fund HIV/AIDS treatment programs, education, and prevention in communities around the world. You can organize a group of local or global businesses and organizations to work on a community project.

● **Giving Back** Founded in Seattle, Washington, Starbucks's mission statement states "To inspire and nurture the human spirit—one person, one cup, and one neighborhood at a time." *How else can a company contribute to a community?*

Contributing to the Community

You do not need to be a big corporation to contribute to society. Many small businesses have found creative ways to be generous with their products, services, expertise, and people. Examples of ways to contribute are shown in **Figure 24.1** on page 556.

As a small business owner, you have a responsibility to treat your employees fairly. Additional benefits are up to you. The government encourages businesses to offer flextime, health care, and assistance to the physically challenged. Some businesses offer other perks, such as on-site child care. These benefits may cost you money; however, happy, productive, and loyal workers usually are the result.

Personal responsibility goes hand in hand with being a socially responsible employee. An employee who is socially responsible is honest, trustworthy, and has integrity. Taking supplies from your employer or giving friends unauthorized discounts are not acceptable practices. Responsible employees should maintain high ethical standards when dealing with coworkers, management, and customers.

SECTION 24.1 Review

After You Read

Self-Check

1. **Explain** what it means to be socially responsible.
2. **Name** two areas in which your business could become socially responsible.
3. **List** two examples of things a business can do to be socially responsible.

Think

4. **Select** a local business that you believe is socially responsible and summarize the contributions it makes to the community.

English Language Arts

5. **Word Roots** Use a dictionary to match each of the following words with its original meaning. Determine which root means "love of" and which means "mankind" or "humans."

Word	Original Meaning
1. philology	a. love of, or search for, wisdom and knowledge
2. philosophy	b. love of learning and the study of literature
3. philanthropy	c. love of harmonic music
4. philharmonic	d. love of mankind
5. anthropology	e. the study of humans

Go to connectED.mcgraw-hill.com to check your answers.

Ethical Responsibility

Reading Guide

● **Before You Read** ▪▪▪▪▪▪▪▪▪▪▪▪▪
Connect What is character?

The Main Idea
Ethics are guidelines for human behavior and form the basis for a person's character. They are the moral code by which people live and conduct business. Ethics help people decide how to act in situations where moral issues are involved by setting standards for moral behavior.

Objectives
Define ethics and ethical behavior.
Explain how to develop a code of ethics.
List special ethical problems that entrepreneurs face.

Content Vocabulary
◇ ethics
◇ ethical behavior
◇ business ethic
◇ code of ethics
◇ conflict of interest
◇ bribe

Academic Vocabulary
You will see these words in your reading and on your tests. Use the academic vocabulary glossary to look up their meaning.
■ conflict
■ perceive

Graphic Organizer
Draw a chart like the one shown. As you read, list five ethical dilemmas entrepreneurs might face.

 Go to connectED.mcgraw-hill.com to download this graphic organizer.

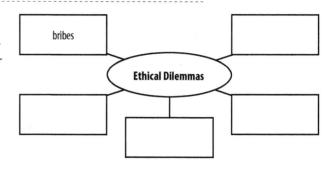

What Does It Mean to Be Ethical?

Ethics are guidelines for human behavior. They are the moral code by which people live and conduct business. **Ethical behavior** is conduct that adheres to this moral code. Ethics help people decide how to act in situations where moral issues are involved. They set the standards for moral, or ethical, behavior.

● **As You Read** ▪▪▪▪▪
Determine What is the role of values in determining your ethics?

Understanding Your Values

Your values govern your actions in dealing with others. Your values are reflected in your character and in your reputation in the community. The six basic values that make up a person's character include trustworthiness, respect, responsibility, fairness, caring, and citizenship. Your business will be shaped by your values in these six areas. Understanding your value system will help you make better decisions and resist actions that go against your values.

What Are Business Ethics?

Business ethics is the study of behavior and morals in business situations. Business ethics begin at the top. A business owner who does not act ethically cannot expect employees to act ethically. The standards of ethical behavior within a business are determined in large part by the business owner's principles and values. Many problems and ethical **conflicts** can be avoided if business owners clearly communicate their ethical expectations to their employees.

Are Everyone's Ethics the Same?

People do not share the same ethical values. For example, most employees understand that workplace equipment is provided for them to use on the job, not for their personal use. Others believe it is acceptable to take things from their employers because the employer "will never miss it." They may take pens and reams of paper or use company e-mail or mail services for personal use.

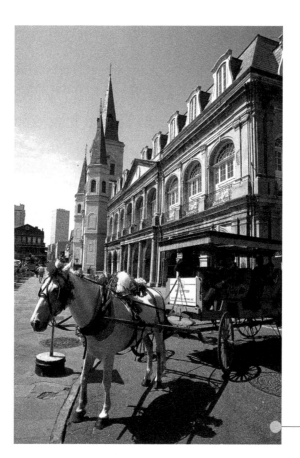

The Big Easy Many entrepreneurs rooted their companies in New Orleans because they believed it was up to entrepreneurs — not the government or big business — to rebuild the city after Hurricane Katrina. *What kinds of principles and values do you think these entrepreneurs might have?*

TongRo Image Stock/Alamy

Fair Trade Kantara Crafts, founded by Oberlin College graduate Alia Kate (right), promotes "Fair Trade," which means that it seeks to pay good living wages to the women who manufacture its products. *Why do some businesspeople avoid international markets?*

Employers and Ethics

Employers can be dishonest, too. They may try to avoid paying taxes by not reporting employee earnings. They may fail to report or remedy unsafe working conditions.

Because not everyone has high ethical standards, entrepreneurs need to create clear policies that communicate what is and what is not acceptable conduct in the workplace. That way, the ethical standards become the rules that employees must follow to maintain their jobs.

At Special Risk — Small Businesses

Because large businesses are usually in the public eye, their leaders must be very careful about how they conduct business. Unethical practices quickly will be aired in the media and on the Internet, possibly leading to the loss of customers or sales opportunities.

Small businesses, however, are not watched as carefully as large businesses. For this reason, they are often more vulnerable to unethical practices. In addition, small businesses are generally less structured. Because small companies have fewer systems and controls in place, and because they are more informal in nature, they are often prone to conduct that might be **perceived** as unethical.

Web Savvy

Green Computing

Smart companies are working to reduce their *carbon footprint,* or the amount of greenhouse gas they produce. The Internet itself has a big carbon footprint, and many companies are switching to "green servers," which use less energy than traditional servers. But most consumers are not aware of what goes on at a company's Web server. If these businesses educated their customers about their green efforts, they might improve their public image and increase customer loyalty. *What businesses can you think of that publicize their efforts to protect the environment?*

Alia Kate

Developing a Code of Ethics

A **code of ethics** is a group of ethical behavior guidelines that govern the day-to-day activities of a profession or organization. Many entrepreneurs develop an explicit code of ethics that spells out appropriate conduct for their business so employees will understand what is expected of them. There is, however, a practical reason why entrepreneurs should have a code of ethics. It can be used to help defend the company against a criminal action should an employee violate federal law. The code will show that the company did not condone such actions.

Written or Unwritten Codes

Codes of ethics can be written or unwritten. Unwritten codes are simply norms, or ways of doing things that have come about over time. For example, in your business, it may be understood from discussions during staff meetings that salespeople do not accept gifts, including meals, from clients or customers. This rule would not be written down but rather it might be passed on verbally.

Formal, or written, codes usually grow out of unwritten ones. As a company's business and number of employees grow, so does the potential for misunderstandings. A written set of guidelines reduces the chance of unethical behavior.

Follow these steps to create a code of ethics:

1. **Brainstorm ethical dilemmas.** Do this with your employees. Come up with potential ethical problems the company might face because of the type of business it conducts.

2. **Discuss potential solutions.** Have employees offer suggestions on how to handle these situations. This will give you a sense of employees' values and help everyone reach an agreement. This is particularly important when you have employees from many different cultures and value systems.

3. **Write a set of general guidelines.** Base them on your discussions. The guidelines should offer a range of acceptable ways to deal with different situations to recognize the differences in value among your employees.

4. **Improve your code.** When a new situation or solution occurs, discuss it. Then add it to your guidelines.

As part of its code of ethics, Cray Research, Inc., asks its employees to use the following question as a standard of conduct. How would I feel if my actions appeared on the front page of the newspaper for my family and friends to see? You may want to incorporate this standard into your personal ethical values—and into your business. It is an easy way to think about the impact of the decisions you make.

 Reading Check **Paraphrase** Why should business owners develop written ethics policies?

Go Green

The Green Building Makeover

Buildings cost a lot of money to heat and maintain. No wonder businesses are outfitting their old buildings with "green" technology, such as energy-efficient LED lights, HVAC systems, and insulation to reduce operating costs. Cheaper than a new "green" building or extensive renovations, green retrofits allow businesses to shave costs and improve energy efficiency without stretching the budget.

◈ **Critical Thinking** Businesses often hire consultants to make recommendations for improving efficiency. Imagine your school has hired you to recommend ways to improve energy use and recycling efforts to save costs. Write a one-page proposal listing your recommendations.

Special Problems for Entrepreneurs

Entrepreneurs operate in dynamic environments under a great deal of pressure. In such situations, people may decide to put aside ethics for short-term gains. Below are some typical ethical problems an entrepreneur might face.

Conflict of Interest

A **conflict of interest** is a clash between a person's private interests and his or her responsibilities in a position of trust. Suppose a newly opened resort offered free stays to journalists with many other benefits during their stay. The resort would benefit from the free publicity. However, the gesture would also create a conflict of interest for the journalists. Why? They are supposed to be objective. How can they report anything negative about the resort after being treated so well? Their gratitude toward the resort and their responsibility to their readers would be in conflict.

What should the journalists do? Many would say that they should turn down the trips. That would be a sacrifice to many of them, but it would be the right thing to do.

GLOBAL WORKPLACE · Vietnam: Moving Forward

The Vietnam War had a devastating effect on the country, including its economy. In 1986, more than a decade after the war ended, economic reforms that included elements of a market economy were introduced. Success came quickly: From 1990 to 1997, gross domestic product grew annually at an eight percent clip, continuing at around a seven percent rate from 2000 to 2005.

Two Wheels Are Better than Four According to the World Bank, as of 2006, automobiles accounted for less than five percent of the vehicular trips in the major cities of Ha Noi and Ho Chi Minh City. Motorcycles, on the other hand, accounted for between 60 to 65 percent, and bicycles another 25 percent.

Social Studies While Vietnam signed an agreement with the United States in December 2001 that increased its exports to the U.S.,

there remain trade barriers, some because of Vietnam's human rights record, which has been categorized as "poor," according to the U.S. Department of State. Research Vietnam's human rights record, describing how its ethical responsibilities are tied into its economic future, and summarize your findings in a one-page report.

Common Vietnamese Words and Phrases	
Hello/Hi	xin chao
Goodbye	tam biet
Yes/No	co/ khong
Please	lam on
Thank you	cam on
You're welcome	khong co chi

Desperate Measures

There is a saying that "you do what you have to do to survive." A store owner in debt may be tempted to circulate negative advertisements about a competitor to bring in more business. Those actions would be unethical even if the allegations were true. It is important to live by one's code of ethics in all situations, no matter how difficult that may be. Your actions affect your business's reputation and once tarnished, that reputation often cannot be regained.

Cultural Differences

Dealing in international business presents challenging ethical dilemmas for Americans. In fact, some businesspeople avoid international markets because of such difficulties. That, however, is a mistake. We live in a global world and every business is affected in some way by international markets. When doing business with other countries, it is important to understand the ethical expectations of that country's culture. It is also critical to know what is permitted under U.S. laws.

Bribes

Bribes are payments made to secure special services for a company or special consideration for its products. In the United States, bribes are illegal. In many other parts of the world, however, they are an accepted part of doing business. They are seen as courtesies or gifts. Therefore, before doing business abroad, you must clearly state your company's policy on giving or accepting bribes. In general, it is best to follow U.S. law regarding bribes even when doing business in another country.

© William Ryall 2007

Digital Piracy Some international communities are less respectful of copyrights held by people in other countries. *Why is it important to remain ethical and ignore short-term profits?*

Patent or Copyright Infringement

Some governments are not respectful of patents and copyrights held by people in other countries. They infringe on the rights of a foreigner, forcing the person to go to court to enforce the law. Other countries have a long patenting or copyrighting process that foreigners must go through. As a consequence of the delay, local businesses have more time to familiarize themselves with the protected items. If they so choose, they can then submit similar patents or copyrights and receive approval before the foreign patent or copyright seeker.

Long Term Versus Short Term

It may seem that businesses that ignore ethical considerations gain substantial profits. In the short term, they may. However, you are in business for the long run. Your integrity and reputation will keep customers coming back. Following an ethical code of behavior is the best way to grow a thriving business.

SECTION 24.2　Review

After You Read ━━━━━━━━━━━━━

Self-Check

1. **Explain** why it is important to understand your value system.
2. **Identify** reasons why small businesses are at special risk for ethics violations.
3. **List** some examples of ethical problems an entrepreneur might face.

Think

4. **Describe** how a socially responsible firm improves quality of life.

Mathematics

5. **Donations** You own a small chain of 12 grocery stores. You want to donate food baskets to 300 families. Each basket will contain 15 items of food. How many items of food are needed to meet your goal? If each store donates an equal number of items, how many items would each store need to donate?

Math Concept **Problem Solving** Solving some problems requires you to sort out needed information from unneeded information.

Step 1 Write and solve an equation that will calculate the number of food items needed to meet the goal.

Step 2 Divide the total number of items by the total number of stores to determine the number of items each store will contribute.

Go to connectED.mcgraw-hill.com to check your answers.

Entrepreneurs *in Action*

Maxine Clark
Founder, Chairman, and Chief Executive Bear
Build-A-Bear Workshop, Inc.

Q *What do you do?*

A My job is to ensure that our company is staying true to our core values. Our values are the compass that guides us through the good times and the challenging times.

Q *What kind of training and education did you need to get this job?*

A I have over 30 years of experience in retail and a bachelor's degree from the University of Georgia. I strongly encourage furthering your education whenever and wherever possible. All levels of education will help you discover how you can contribute to making the world a better place.

Q *What do you enjoy most about your job?*

A I truly enjoy the opportunity to make a difference. Build-A-Bear Workshop® has always had a principle mission of giving back to the community. The company has donated over $20 million to organizations that support children's health and wellness, animal welfare, literacy, and education causes.

Q *How did you become interested in your field?*

A My parents told me that I could be anything that I wanted to be. I loved to pretend and loved to shop with my mom. We shared many Saturday afternoons at the department store window-shopping. I loved the displays and seeing what was new and exciting. I took this experience with me when I began to develop ideas for Build-A-Bear Workshop.

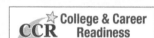
College & Career Readiness

Determine Meaning
Many businesses talk about social responsibility. What does this actually mean?

1. Investigate the definition of social responsibility for businesses.
2. Research a business that claims to be socially responsible.
3. Weigh the truth of this claim. Are the business's claims of socially responsibility justified, or are they just talk? Detail what you learn in a one-page report.

Career Facts

Real-World Skills	Academic Skills	Career Cluster
Leadership, Social Responsibility, Creativity	English Language Arts, Social Studies	Business Management & Administration

Courtesy of Maxine Clark

Review and Assessment

Visual Summary

Social and Ethical Responsibility

In Good Company Social responsibility is a business's contract with society to make safe products, treat customers and employees fairly, and conduct business honestly.

Entrepreneurs and Social Responsibility	
Responsibility to Customers	• Do not mislead customers about quality, performance, or safety. • Give information about proper use. • Label unsafe products appropriately. • Obey laws such as the Truth-in-Lending Act and the Fair Credit Billing Act.
Responsibility to the Environment	• Follow standards set by the Environmental Protection Agency (EPA). • Design environmentally safe products, packaging, and processes. • Dispose of hazardous waste properly. • As much as possible, reduce, reuse, or recycle waste.
Responsibility to Employees	• Treat employees fairly. • Offer benefits to make employees happy, productive, and loyal. • Have employees help develop ethical standards.

Make a Contribution Entrepreneurs can contribute to the community in several ways.

Contribute to the Community		
Donate Donate products or services to the community.	**Community Service** Encourage employees to participate in community service.	**Collaborate** Join other companies to work on community projects.

Digital Vision Ltd./SuperStock

Review and Assessment

Vocabulary

1. On a sheet of paper, use each of these terms and words in a written sentence.

Content Vocabulary

◇ philanthropy
◇ social responsibility
◇ Environmental Protection Agency (EPA)
◇ ethics

◇ ethical behavior
◇ business ethics
◇ code of ethics
◇ conflict of interest
◇ bribe

Academic Vocabulary

■ require
■ demonstrate
■ conflict
■ perceive

Key Concepts

2. **Summarize** the relationship between entrepreneurs and social responsibility.
3. **Discuss** how entrepreneurs can contribute to their community.
4. **Define** ethics and ethical behavior.
5. **Explain** how to develop a code of ethics.
6. **List** special ethical problems that entrepreneurs face.
7. **Compare and Contrast** social responsibility and ethical responsibility.
8. **Describe** how socially responsible firms improve quality of life.
9. **Explain** why everyone's code of ethics is not the same.

Academic Skills

Mathematics

10. **Reduce, Reuse, Recycle** In an effort to protect the environment, dozens of local businesses are starting a recycling program. The program will cost each of the 33 businesses $42 a month. What is the total cost of the program for a full year?

Math Concept **Logical Reasoning** Real-life problems involving math require logical step-by-step reasoning.
Step 1 Multiply the monthly rate for the service by the number of businesses to determine the monthly cost.
Step 2 Multiply the monthly fee by the number of months the service is being used.

English Language Arts

11. **Social Responsibility and the Novel** Many British and American novels describe the impact of businesses that are not socially responsible. Upton Sinclair's portrayal of early 20th-century corporate greed in *The Jungle* was so powerful that it helped spur passage of the 1906 Pure Food and Drug Act. In *David Copperfield*, Charles Dickens described his own childhood experiences working in a gloomy boot-blacking factory during the Industrial Revolution. Find *David Copperfield* at a local library or on the Internet and read Chapter 11. Summarize the chapter in a one-page report.

Academic Skills *(continued)*

Social Studies

12. **Sustainable Enterprises** Many of today's entrepreneurs are creating socially responsible businesses that provide products manufactured or grown in a way that preserves the environment and brings prosperity to people in developing countries. Work with a partner to research such a business and write a profile of the people who created it.

Science

13. **Ethics and Energy** Entrepreneurs in the energy industry are developing substitutes for gasoline and other nonrenewable energy sources. This has led to a high demand for ethanol, which can be made from corn. However, this has also caused corn prices to rise, which has raised food prices for many of the world's poorest communities. Work with a partner to research this problem and recommend a socially responsible policy for the use of corn in ethanol.

Real-World Skills

Creating a Vision

14. **Business Angels** You are starting a business and would like it to be as socially and ethically responsible as possible while remaining profitable. Write a one-page company policy for social and ethical responsibility.

21st Century Skills

Leadership and Responsibility

15. **Whistle Blower** In the course of your work at a manufacturing company, you discover that the products the company makes are unsafe. If you do not report this you believe people will be hurt or killed. If you do, you think you will lose your job. Explain what you do and why in a short essay.

Connect to Your Community

16. **Code of Ethics** With your classmates, create a formal class code of ethics. Compare and contrast it to a business's code. Include the following:

   - Purpose of the code
   - Social principles (general guidelines)
   - Ethical principles (general guidelines)
   - Potential ethical dilemmas and solutions

17. **Local Responsibility** As a class, develop and implement a service project to promote the idea of social responsibility in your community. Organize into teams to select projects, coordinate students, and promote and implement the event.

Review and Assessment

CHAPTER
24

Competitive Events Prep

18. **Situation** You own a restaurant and catering business. You like to be involved in the community and to be socially responsible. Your community is interested in "going green." You are planning to discuss some ideas about how to make your business more environmentally friendly.

Activity Prepare a presentation for a staff meeting that includes your suggestions and ideas for making your business better for the environment. Begin the meeting by explaining the importance of being socially responsible while maintaining high standards.

Evaluation You will be evaluated on how well you meet the following performance indicators:

- Explain the nature of environmental regulations.
- Explain the role of business in society.
- Describe the relationship between government and business.
- Participate as a team member.
- Coach employees.

 Go to connectED.mcgraw-hill.com for more information about this activity and other competitive events.

Standardized Test Practice

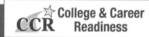

Directions Choose the letter of the best answer. Write the letter for the answer on a separate piece of paper. For question #2, if the answer is False, rewrite the statement to make it true.

1. Large businesses must be more careful than small businesses about how they conduct business because they are _____

    A. in the public eye.

    B. less structured.

    C. not watched as carefully.

    D. less formal.

2. Only large corporations can contribute to the community.

    T

    F

> **Test-Taking Tip**
> Concentrate when taking a test. Do not worry about how good a student you are or whether you should have studied more. Pay attention to one question at a time.

Business Plan Project

Finishing Touches

The research, planning, and management skills it takes to start and protect your business will also allow it to survive, grow, and profit. *How will you tie all of your projects together to present a finished product?*

Objectives

In this project, you will complete these parts of your business plan:

- Identify potential risks to your business and how to minimize for them.
- Summarize the key points in your business plan.
- Organize your research and documentation.

The Skills You'll Use

- **Academic Skills** English Language Arts, Social Studies
- **Real World Skills** Communication, Presentation
- **21st Century Skills** Flexibility and Adaptability; Communications Literacy

▶ Contingency Plan

The Contingency Plan examines the assumptions in the business plan and the greatest risks to the business and suggests plans to minimize the risk.

Step 1 **Brainstorm Potential Problems** Brainstorm a list of potential problems that could cause your business to fail. Describe how to deal with any of the situations should they arise.

Step 2 **Plan Solutions for Potential Problems** Describe how the company will respond to these changes:

Situation	
Demographic Shifts	Product Liability Lawsuits
Socioeconomic Trends	Lower-than-Projected Sales
Economic Events	Lower-than-Projected Revenue

Caiaimage/Glow Images

▶ Executive Summary

The Executive Summary recounts the key points in the business plan. It is written last because it summarizes the most important information from the business plan. Investors rely on it to decide if the business concept interests them.

Step 1 **Recap Key Issues** In six paragraphs, describe your company's mission, goals, objectives, current stage of development, owners, and key management team members.

Step 2 **Explain the Essentials** Describe the company, business model, legal structure, industry, product or service, target market, and the unique opportunity.

▶ Cover Page, Title Page, Table of Contents, and Supporting Documents

Every business plan should have a cover page, title page, and table of contents. A good business plan also includes documentation that is relevant to the business.

Step 1 **Gather Basic Information** Gather this basic information: company name; names, titles, and addresses of the owners; business address; phone number; Web site address; and e-mail address.

Step 2 **Collect Supporting Documents** The Supporting Documents section of the business plan includes items, exhibits, and documentation relevant to the business. Gather as many of these items as you can:

the owners' resume	specifications of machinery
the owners' tax returns	business location map
financial statements	copy of lease or purchase agreement
franchise contract	contracts and licenses
partnership agreement	other legal documents

Use the **Business Plan Project Appendix** on pages **572-583** to explore the content requirements of a business plan in more detail.

Business Plan Project Template Go to connectED.mcgraw-hill.com for a business plan template that you can use to write your own business plan.

My Business Plan
When you have completed your Project, put your statements, charts, and other research in your Business Plan Portfolio.

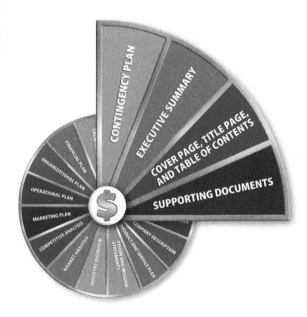

The Business Plan
An Entrepreneur's Road Map to Success

Developing a good business plan can put you and your business on the path to success. The Business Plan Project Appendix explains the content requirements for the essential elements of a business plan.

A business plan summarizes an entrepreneur's proposed venture. It provides an organized report of a company's goals and how management intends to achieve those goals. It is a work-in-progress that should evolve as your business evolves. Developing a business plan is like outlining a strategy for turning your business concept into a reality.

For detailed instructions and worksheets to help you prepare your business plan, refer to the *Business Plan Project Workbook*.

What Is a Business Plan?

A good business plan will help you:

- **Guide** your company's operations.
- **Present** your company's strategic vision.
- **Persuade** lenders and investors to finance your business.
- **Measure** performance and identify areas for improvement.
- **Make** sound business decisions.

Assignment

Select a business that you are interested in starting. Then develop a business plan for the venture. When you are finished writing the business plan, package the business plan using the guidelines on pages 121–122. Then present it and defend it in an oral presentation.

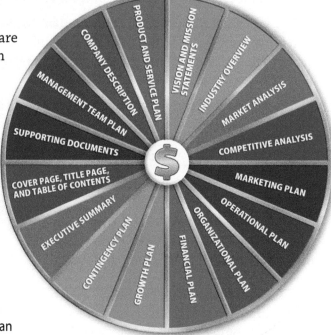

 Business Plan Project Template
Go to **connectED.mcgraw-hill.com** for a business plan template that you can use to write your own business plan.

My Business Plan
When you have completed all the parts of your business plan, put them in your personal portfolio along with all your statements, charts, and other research.

Business Plan Project Appendix

▶ Management Team Plan

The Management Team section of the business plan presents your management team's qualifications for making the venture a success.

Key Management
- Describe each management team member, including title, abilities, duties, education, previous industry and related work experience, and past successes.
- Describe the benefits that team members will provide to the company.
- Provide copies of the owners' tax returns, personal financial statements, and résumés.

Advisors and Professional Service Providers
- Describe the role, responsibilities, and members of the advisory board, if you have one.
- List the outside consultants the company will use, such as accountants, attorneys, Web designers, and insurance agents.

▶ Company Description

The Company Description outlines the company's basic background information, business concept, and goals and objectives.

Business History and Description
- Explain your reasons for starting a new business or expanding an existing one.
- Describe the entrepreneurial opportunity.
- Provide a history of the business with development milestones that have been completed to date and the current status of the business.
- Describe the legal structure of the business and tell why you chose it.
- Include details about prior funding, royalty, partnership, and joint venture agreements.

Goals and Objectives
- Establish the business's goals and objectives and relate them to the investment you seek.
- Explain why you think the venture will succeed.

▶ Product and Service Plan

The Product and Service Plan describes the features and benefits of the business's products and services.

Overview of Products and Services
- Describe the product or service, including purpose, size, shape, colors, features, benefits, cost, functionality, design, quality, capabilities, technology, protections, and unique selling points.
- Describe competing and similar technology.
- Describe the need the product or service addresses in the market and how it benefits customers.
- Explain briefly how the product or service will be produced, the materials required, and the type of labor needed.

Product Development Status
- Discuss the history and current status of product development.
- Provide projected dates for achieving other stages of development.

Business Plan Project Appendix

▶ Vision and Mission Statements

The Vision and Mission Statements section of the business plan sets forth the guiding principles by which a company functions. These statements should be clear and concise. They communicate what the business stands for, what its founders believe in, and what the company intends to achieve.

Vision Statement

- Write a vision statement that establishes the scope and purpose of your company and reflects its values and beliefs.
- Express the company's vision in broad terms so that it will stand the test of time.
- Convey the future of the company as its founders see it.
- Develop strategies for achieving the vision of the business.
- Establish criteria for monitoring achievement of the vision.

Mission Statement

- Write a mission statement that expresses the specific aspirations of the company, the major goals for which it will strive.
- Define the direction in which the company will move.
- Convey a challenging yet achievable mission that the organization will be dedicated to accomplishing.
- Develop strategies for achieving the mission of the business.
- Establish criteria for monitoring achievement of the mission.

▶ Industry Overview

Your business plan must address basic trends and growth within the industry. Think of your industry as those companies providing similar, complementary, or supplementary products and services.

Industry Trends and Growth

- Describe the industry, including size, by both revenue and number of firms.
- Describe how the industry functions, including a general explanation of the industry's distribution system.
- Describe the barriers of entry to the industry.
- Describe the past and future trends in the industry, including growth trends.
- Explain the factors that are influencing growth or decline in the industry.
- Include the failure rate in the industry.
- Describe the typical profitability in the industry.
- Describe the government regulations that affect the industry.
- Describe the local, national, or international industry standards.
- Include current and historical industry employment data.
- Provide visualizations of industry data (charts, tables, graphs).

▶ Market Analysis

The Market Analysis section of the business plan presents your market research and features a customer demographic profile that defines the traits of the company's target market. Information about potential target markets should originate from primary and secondary research resources.

Business Plan Project Appendix

Target Market Demographic Profile
- Write a demographic profile of the company's target market.
- Identify and explain market segments.
- Describe the market niche served.
- Describe the size of the target market.
- Explain whether your market is domestic or international and describe the cultures and ethnicities within it.
- Describe the geographic statistics of your target market.
- Describe what members of the target market do for a living, their level of income, their social and economic status, and their level of education.
- Describe the ages, genders, family structures, lifestyle, and leisure activities of the target market.
- Explain what motivates the target market.
- Answer specific questions about your target market that are directly related to your products or services.
- If your product or service is marketed to businesses, describe the target market in terms of industry, product and/or service, geographic location, years in business, revenue, number of employees, and buying motivations.
- Describe how you analyzed your target market.
- Provide visualizations of demographic, geographic, and psychographic data (charts, graphs, tables).

Target Market Projections
- Describe the proportion of the target market that has used a product or service like the company's product or service before.
- Project how much of the product or service the target market will buy (gross sales and/or unit sales).

Market Trends and Growth
- Describe current trends and trends that have been forecast to occur within the target market.
- Describe the market's historical growth, current market size, and growth potential.
- Provide visualizations of market trend statistics (charts, graphs, tables).

Customer Needs Analysis
- Conduct market research to uncover customers' wants and needs and to survey their impressions of the business and its promotions.
- Use the market research results to write a customer needs analysis that interprets and prioritizes the needs of the business's current and future customers.
- Prepare a visualization that presents highlights from your research.
- Explain how the company will meet the target market's needs.

▶ Competitive Analysis

The Competitive Analysis section of the business plan should demonstrate that the proposed business has an advantage over its competitors. You can gather information on competitors by viewing their Web sites; by talking to their customers, vendors, suppliers, and employees; by attending trade shows; and by searching newspaper and magazine databases.

Business Plan Project Appendix

Competitive Overview
- Identify, investigate, and analyze your top direct competitors, businesses that are offering identical or similar products or services as your business.
- Identify, investigate, and analyze your top indirect competitors, businesses that are offering products and services that are close substitutes.
- Identify, investigate, and analyze your top future competitors, existing companies that are not yet in the marketplace but could enter the marketplace at any time.
- Explain whether the business will have nonlocal competitors.
- State the locations of your top competitors.
- Describe how long your competitors have been in business.
- Describe the products and services your competitors sell and how much they sell (in units and sales dollars).
- Evaluate your competitors' product selection, quality, and availability.
- Describe the markets or market segments your competitors serve.
- Describe the benefits offered by the competition.
- Describe your competitors' images and their level of growth and success.
- Describe your competitors' advertising and promotion strategies.
- Describe your competitors' pricing policies and pricing structures.
- Explain competitors' customer service and after-sale service policies.
- Assess your competitors' financial condition and level of debt.
- Evaluate your competitors' equipment and production capacity.
- Outline the strengths and weaknesses of each of your competitors.
- Include charts or pie graphs showing the market share among your competitors.
- Prepare a grid or table that presents highlights from your research.

Competitive Advantage
- Describe the competitive advantage of your venture.
- Explain the key assets that your business has and its competitors do not have.
- Differentiate your company's products and services from your competitors'.
- Describe how your business strategies and marketing mix strategies will help you attract and defend market share.
- Explain the percentage of the market the business intends to capture and how this will be achieved.

▶ Marketing Plan
A Marketing Plan describes a company's marketing mix strategies or how it plans to market, promote, and sell its products or services.

Marketing Mix Strategies
- Write a marketing plan with product, place, price, promotion, and people strategies.
- Describe the marketing mix strategies and explain the message they are meant to convey.
- Describe the company's plan for finding the best market.
- Explain how the marketing mix strategies will be implemented and evaluated for effectiveness.

Business Plan Project Appendix

Product Strategy
- Describe your product, including how it functions, its design, image, appearance, packaging, labeling, warranties, service, and support.
- Describe the product's branding, including brand name(s), brand marks, trade names, trade characters, trademarks, logos, and corporate symbols.

Place Strategy
- Explain how your product will be made available to customers and where it will be sold.
- Describe channels of distribution and how they will help to foster market penetration.

Price Strategy
- State your company's pricing objectives and pricing strategy goals.
- Develop a pricing structure that takes into account fixed and variable costs, the competition, company objectives, proposed positioning strategies, the target market, and the consumer's willingness to pay.
- Describe the typical prices in the industry and how your business's prices compare.
- Determine what forms of payment you will accept.

Promotion Strategy
- Explain the company's promotional goals and promotional messages and how they will appeal to the target market.
- Develop a pre-opening promotional plan to establish a positive image.
- Detail the promotions to be used, such as advertising and publicity.
- Describe the specific marketing mediums the company will use to deliver the promotional message to the target market. Include how often each will be used, what they will cost, why you chose them, and why they will appeal to the target market.
- Describe the marketing materials you will you need, who will design them, how much they will cost, and how they will be designed to appeal to the target market.
- Describe the sales team, the sales process, and the sales incentives the company will offer.
- Provide your media budget and detail the cost of marketing materials per prospect.
- Provide examples of marketing materials.
- Describe how you will evaluate the effectiveness of promotional strategies.

People Strategy
- Explain how you will recruit, hire, and train the people and employees who will help you to achieve business success.

▶ Operational Plan
The Operational Plan section of the business plan includes information about all the processes that take place in the business.

Location
- Describe where your business will be located, the number of locations, the zoning, the square footage needed, the layout and type of space, and renovations needed.

Appendix · Business Plan Project   577

Business Plan Project Appendix

- Explain why you chose the location.
- State the average traffic count in front of the outlet.
- Describe any factors that hinder or help accessibility to the business and visibility of the site.
- Describe the businesses near your business's site, including target markets.
- Describe any community sign laws and local parking laws.
- Identify tax rates and state how they compare to other sites you considered.
- Project costs associated with the location.
- Describe how much the business can expand before it will need to relocate.
- Provide a map of the business location and facility layout blueprints.

Property Ownership or Lease Terms
- Detail the terms of the lease or purchase of the property.
- Provide a copy of the proposed lease or building space purchase agreement.

Equipment Needs
- Describe and provide blueprints and specifications for the machinery and equipment needed.
- Explain whether you will purchase or lease the equipment.

Manufacturing Processes and Costs
- Describe the manufacturing process and the technology requirements.
- Assess the manufacturing process in terms of direct and indirect costs.

Suppliers and Purchasing
- Outline your key suppliers and the purchasing process.
- Provide copies of purchase orders and letters of intent from suppliers.

Storage and Inventory
- Analyze the inventory needed to open and operate the business.
- Describe storage needs, space required, and costs involved.
- Explain inventory control procedures, equipment, and technology.

Channels of Distribution
- Describe the channels of distribution and the associated costs.
- Explain the degree of difficulty in gaining industry distribution access.

Quality Measures and Safety
- Describe how quality will be measured, controlled, and improved.
- Explain security precautions and health and safety regulations.

▶ Organizational Plan

The Organizational Plan offers information about the business's legal structure, methods of and responsibilities for record keeping, and legal and insurance issues. It also covers the people aspects of the business, including staffing and training of personnel, and the organizational structure.

Legal Structure
- Describe your legal structure and why it is advantageous for your company.
- Describe any legal agreements governing how owners can exit the company, how the company can be dissolved, how profits will be distributed, and who will have financial responsibility for losses.
- Project future changes in the company's legal structure and how such changes would benefit the company.

- Provide a copy of your partnership agreement if you have formed a partnership.
- Provide a copy of the Articles of Incorporation if the company is formed as a corporation.
- Provide a copy of the franchise contract and supporting materials if the company is a franchise.

Record Keeping
- Describe the accounting system that will be used and why it was chosen.
- Describe what record keeping will be done internally and who will be responsible for keeping internal records.
- Explain when the business will use an outside accountant, such as to finalize monthly/year-end statements.
- Describe who within the company has the expertise to read and analyze the financial statements provided by outside accountants.
- Describe how you will use your financial statements to implement changes to make your company more profitable.

Legal and Insurance Issues
- Describe any legal considerations that will impact your business, such as legal liability issues, government regulations, environmental regulations, zoning matters, or licensing requirements.
- Identify the insurance company the business will use, the types of insurance the business will need, and the costs involved.

Labor, Staffing, and Training
- Outline human resource policies, including staffing and personnel management procedures.
- Diagram and describe the organizational structure of the business.
- Provide an organizational flowchart.
- Develop a job description for each position on the organizational flowchart, including skill sets needed and salaries offered.
- Describe how many employees the business will have and in what types of positions.
- Outline hours of operation, scheduling policies, and types of shifts worked by employees.
- Complete a work schedule for a typical work week.
- Develop charts or graphs that classify employees by function, skill set, hourly pay, and part-time or full-time status.
- Identify situations where outsourcing should be used for hiring needs.

▶ Financial Plan
The Financial Plan presents past and current finances and financial forecasts and explains the assumptions made when calculating forecast figures. It includes the investment proposal and three key financial statements: a cash flow statement, income statement, and balance sheet.

Investment Proposal
- Describe why you are applying for financing and how you plan to raise and use the money.
- Describe various investment structures and project when investors can expect to earn a profit.

Business Plan Project Appendix

- Identify, categorize, and analyze the start-up costs and fixed and variable operating expenses.
- Project the total cash needed to start the business.
- Include details about revenue streams and prior funding agreements.

Exit Strategy
- Outline the business life cycle and explain your long-term plans for the business.
- Explain how your investors can expect to recoup their investment and earn a sufficient return.
- Define how investors can cash out their investment and achieve liquidity.

Cash Flow Projection
- Plan a cash budget that forecasts cash inflow (cash revenue from sales) and outflow (cash disbursements) projections for the first year and quarterly or yearly projections for the second and third years.

Projected Three-Year Income Statement (Profit And Loss Statements)
- Prepare a three-year income projection that includes monthly projections for revenues, expenses, and profits for the first year and quarterly or yearly projections for the second and third years.

Projected Balance Sheet
- Prepare a projected balance sheet (assets, liabilities, and net worth) with quarterly projections for the first year and yearly projections for the second and third years.

Break-Even Analysis
- Prepare a break-even analysis detailing when the company's expenses will match the income.
- Present the data in a graph format with sales on the X-axis and units sold on the Y-axis.

Historical Financials
- Provide cash flow statements, income statements, and balance sheets from the last three years if the company is an existing business.

Financial Assumptions
- State the assumptions on which the financial projections are based.
- Explain how you derived forecasts for sales, costs of goods sold, operating expenses, accounts receivable, collections, accounts payable, inventory, taxes, and other items.
- Disclose whether the financial statements have been audited by a certified public accountant.

Financial Ratios
- Calculate liquidity ratios to measure creditworthiness.
- Calculate profitability ratios to show operational performance.
- Calculate turnover ratios to measure changes in certain assets and to expose nonincome-producing assets.

▶ Growth Plan

Planned growth can be very rewarding, and unplanned growth can be chaotic. The Growth Plan looks at how the business will expand in the future. Investors and lenders like to know that a business has plans to deal with growth in a controlled way.

Growth Strategies

* Describe how and when the business owners would like the business to grow.
* Describe the products or services the business will develop to achieve growth.
* Describe the planned growth cycle.
* Describe how the business's growth strategies focus on the business's areas of expertise.
* Describe whether market research will be used to support and justify growth strategy decisions.
* Identify the critical skills that are needed to effectively manage growth.
* Explain how you will evaluate and initiate revisions to growth strategies.

Business Location Issues

* Assess the current business location and how it can accommodate growth.
* Explain if growing the business will mean having to relocate the business to a larger facility.
* Analyze the costs involved in expanding or upgrading current facilities and/or moving to new facilities.
* Evaluate whether the business's lease agreement allows for modifications to the building and facilities.
* Describe alternative affordable premises.
* Explain if and when warehousing and storage facilities will be expanded to accommodate growth.

Effects of Growth

* Explain how planned growth will affect human resource expenses and management and staffing needs.
* Describe how planned growth will affect company goals and objectives.
* Assess if the business's target market will be affected by the growth plan.
* Describe how planned growth will affect technology and equipment needs.
* Describe how planned growth will affect the manufacturing process and costs.
* Explain how planned growth will affect financial control procedures, record keeping policies, and legal and insurance issues.
* Evaluate how planned growth will affect the sales team and sales process.
* Describe how planned growth will affect promotional goals and messages and marketing mix strategies (product, place, price, promotion, and people decisions).

Growth Financing

* Examine how growth costs will affect the overall financial health of the business in the short term and the long term.
* Evaluate growth financing options and describe the best plan to finance growth.
* Provide visualizations of growth projections (charts, tables, graphs).

▶ Contingency Plan

The Contingency Plan examines the assumptions in the business plan and the greatest risks to the business and suggests plans to minimize the risk.

* List and examine the assumptions in the business plan.

Business Plan Project Appendix

- Examine risks that could cause the business to fail.
- Categorize business risks as human, natural, or economic; as speculative, controllable or uncontrollable; and as insurable or uninsurable.
- Identify the most significant risks that the new venture faces and describe plans the business owners have developed to deal with any of the situations should they arise.
- Describe how the company will respond to changes in market conditions caused by demographic shifts, socioeconomic trends, economic events, energy costs, and changes in government policies.
- Explain how the company will anticipate and respond to competitive threats from expected and unexpected sources, price cutting by competitors, and the introduction of new products by competitors.
- Explain how the company will handle cost overruns.
- Outline contingencies to meet staffing challenges and limit problems due to a dependence on key people.
- Describe how the company will respond if projected sales and revenue targets are not achieved.
- Describe the company's contingency plan in case of a major accident, event, or disaster that interrupts cash flow.
- Explain how the company will respond to product liability lawsuits.

▶ Executive Summary

The Executive Summary recounts the key points in the business plan. It is written last because it summarizes the most important information from the business plan. Investors rely on it to decide if the business concept interests them. The executive summary should be just two pages long, and it should answer who, what, where, why, when, and how.

- Describe the company's mission, goals, objectives, current stage of development, owners, and key management team members.
- Describe the company, business model, legal structure, industry, product or service, target market, and the unique opportunity.
- Include evidence that justifies the soundness and future success of the opportunity.
- Describe the strategies the company will use to beat the competition.
- Include financial highlights such as:
  - The investment you are seeking
  - How much equity you would be willing to transfer
  - Collateral offered
  - How the funds will be used
  - How and when any loans will be repaid
  - Three-year projections of sales
  - Estimated annual after-tax profits

▶ Cover Page

Every business plan should have a Cover Page. It is the first page the investor sees when he or she reads the business plan. Include this information:

- The company name, address, phone number, Web site address, e-mail address, and company logo

Business Plan Project Appendix

▶ Title Page

The page following the cover page is the Title Page. It includes this basic information about the business and the business plan:
- The company name
- The names, titles, and addresses of the owners
- The date the business plan was issued
- The name of the person who prepared the business plan

▶ Table of Contents

The Table of Contents details the components of the business plan and the page numbers where they can be found within the business plan. Include this information in the Table of Contents:
- The titles of the major sections and subsections of the business plan
- The page number where each section and subsection is located

▶ Supporting Documents

The Supporting Documents section of the business plan includes items, exhibits, and documentation relevant to the business. Include these items:
- Copies of the owners' résumés, personal financial statements, and tax returns
- For franchised businesses, a copy of the franchise contract
- For franchised businesses, all supporting documents provided by the franchisor
- For partnerships, a copy of the partnership agreement
- For corporations, a copy of the Articles of Incorporation
- Photos, blueprints, and detailed specifications of products
- An organizational blueprint
- Photos and blueprints of the layout of the business's facilities
- Photos, blueprints, and detailed specifications for all equipment and machinery
- A map of the business location
- Copy of proposed lease or purchase agreement for building space
- Copy of contracts, licenses, and other legal documents
- Copies of purchase orders and letters of intent from suppliers
- Business cards
- Market research highlights
- Marketing materials
- Press releases
- Visualizations of industry data, demographic data, and market trend statistics

Math Handbook

Number and Operations

▶ *Understand numbers, ways of representing numbers, relationships among numbers, and number systems*

Fraction, Decimal, and Percent

A percent is a ratio of a number to 100. To write a percent as a fraction, drop the percent sign, and use the number as the numerator in a fraction with a denominator of 100. Simplify, if possible. For example, $76\% = \frac{76}{100}$, or $\frac{19}{25}$. To write a fraction as a percent, convert it to an equivalent fraction with a denominator of 100. For example, $\frac{3}{4} = \frac{75}{100}$, or 75%. A fraction can be expressed as a percent by first converting the fraction to a decimal (divide the numerator by the denominator) and then converting the decimal to a percent by moving the decimal point two places to the right.

Comparing Numbers on a Number Line

In order to compare and understand the relationship between real numbers in various forms, it is helpful to use a number line. The zero point on a number line is called the origin. The points to the left of the origin are negative, and those to the right are positive. The number line below shows how numbers in fraction, decimal, percent, and integer form can be compared.

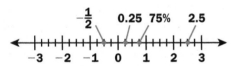

Percents Greater Than 100 and Less Than 1

Percents greater than 100% represent values greater than 1. For example, if the weight of an object is 250% of another, it is 2.5, or $2\frac{1}{2}$, times the weight.

Percents less than 1 represent values less than $\frac{1}{100}$. In other words, 0.1% is one tenth of one percent, which can also be represented in decimal form as 0.001, or in fraction form as $\frac{1}{1,000}$. Similarly, 0.01% is one hundredth of one percent or 0.0001 or $\frac{1}{10,000}$.

Ratio, Rate, and Proportion

A ratio is a comparison of two numbers using division. If a basketball player makes 8 out of 10 free throws, the ratio is written as 8 to 10,

8:10, or $\frac{8}{10}$. Ratios are usually written in simplest form. In simplest form, the ratio 8 out of 10 is 4 to 5, 4:5, or $\frac{4}{5}$. A rate is a ratio of two measurements having different kinds of units—cups per gallon, or miles per hour, for example. When a rate is simplified so that it has a denominator of 1, it is called a unit rate. An example of a unit rate is 9 miles per hour. A proportion is an equation stating that two ratios are equal. $\frac{3}{18} = \frac{13}{78}$ is an example of a proportion. The cross products of a proportion are also equal. $\frac{3}{18} = \frac{13}{78}$ and $3 \times 78 = 18 \times 13$.

Representing Large and Small Numbers

In order to represent large and small numbers, it is important to understand the number system. Our number system is based on 10, and the value of each place is 10 times the value of the place to its right. The value of a digit is the product of a digit and its place value. For instance, in the number 6,400, the 6 has a value of six thousands and the 4 has a value of four hundreds. A place value chart can help you read numbers. In the chart, each group of three digits is called a period. Commas separate the periods: the ones period, the thousands period, the millions period, and so on. Values to the right of the ones period are decimals. By understanding place value you can write very large numbers like 5 billion and more, and very small numbers that are less than 1, like one-tenth.

Scientific Notation

When dealing with very large numbers like 1,500,000, or very small numbers like 0.000015, it is helpful to keep track of their value by writing the numbers in scientific notation. Powers of 10 with positive exponents are used with a decimal between 1 and 10 to express large numbers. The exponent represents the number of places the decimal point is moved to the right. So, 528,000 is written in scientific notation as 5.28×10^5. Powers of 10 with negative exponents are used with a decimal between 1 and 10 to express small numbers. The exponent represents the number of places the decimal point is moved to the left. The number 0.00047 is expressed as 4.7×10^{-4}.

Factor, Multiple, and Prime Factorization

Two or more numbers that are multiplied to form a product are called factors. Divisibility rules can be used to determine whether 2, 3, 4, 5, 6, 8, 9, or 10 are factors of a given number.

Multiples are the products of a given number and various integers.

For example, 8 is a multiple of 4 because $4 \times 2 = 8$. A prime number is a whole number that has exactly two factors: 1 and itself. A composite number is a whole number that has more than two factors. Zero and 1 are neither prime nor composite. A composite number can be expressed as the product of its prime factors. The prime factorization of 40 is $2 \times 2 \times 2 \times 5$, or $2^3 \times 5$. The numbers 2 and 5 are prime numbers.

Integers

A negative number is a number less than zero. Negative numbers like −8, positive numbers like +6, and zero are members of the set of integers. Integers can be represented as points on a number line. A set of integers can be written {..., −3, −2, −1, 0, 1, 2, 3, ...} where ... means continues indefinitely.

Real, Rational, and Irrational Numbers

The real number system is made up of the sets of rational and irrational numbers. Rational numbers are numbers that can be written in the form $\frac{a}{b}$ where a and b are integers and $b \neq 0$. Examples are 0.45, $\frac{1}{2}$, and $\sqrt{36}$. Irrational numbers are non-repeating, non-terminating decimals. Examples are $\sqrt{71}$, π, and 0.020020002....

Complex and Imaginary Numbers

A complex number is a mathematical expression with a real number element and an imaginary number element. Imaginary numbers are multiples of i, the imaginary square root of −1. Complex numbers are represented by $a + bi$, where a and b are real numbers and i represents the imaginary element. When a quadratic equation does not have a real number solution, the solution can be represented by a complex number. Like real numbers, complex numbers can be added, subtracted, multiplied, and divided.

Vectors and Matrices

A matrix is a set of numbers or elements arranged in rows and columns to form a rectangle. The number of rows is represented by m and the number of columns is represented by n. To describe the number of rows and columns in a matrix, list the number of rows first using the format $m \times n$. Matrix A is a 3×3 matrix because it has 3 rows and 3 columns. To name an element of a matrix, the letter i is used to denote the row and j is used to denote the column, and the element is labeled in the form $a_{i,j}$. In matrix A below, $a_{3,2}$ is 4.

$$\text{Matrix A} = \begin{pmatrix} 1 & 3 & 5 \\ 0 & 6 & 8 \\ 3 & 4 & 5 \end{pmatrix}$$

A vector is a matrix with only one column or row of elements. A transposed column vector, or a column vector turned on its side, is a row vector. In the example below, row vector b' is the transpose of column vector b.

$$b = \begin{pmatrix} 1 \\ 2 \\ 3 \\ 4 \end{pmatrix}$$

$$b = \begin{pmatrix} 1 & 2 & 3 & 4 \end{pmatrix}$$

▶ Understand meanings of operations and how they relate to one another

Properties of Addition and Multiplication

Properties are statements that are true for any numbers. For example, $3 + 8$ is the same as $8 + 3$ because each expression equals 11. This illustrates the Commutative Property of Addition. Likewise, $3 \times 8 = 8 \times 3$ illustrates the Commutative Property of Multiplication.

When evaluating expressions, it is often helpful to group or associate the numbers. The Associative Property says that the way in which numbers are grouped when added or multiplied does not change the sum or product. The following properties are also true:

- **Additive Identity Property:** When 0 is added to any number, the sum is the number.

- **Multiplicative Identity Property:** When any number is multiplied by 1, the product is the number.

- **Multiplicative Property of Zero:** When any number is multiplied by 0, the product is 0.

Rational Numbers

A number that can be written as a fraction is called a rational number. Terminating and repeating decimals are rational numbers because both can be written as fractions. Decimals that are neither terminating nor repeating are called irrational numbers because they cannot be written as fractions.

Math Handbook

Terminating decimals can be converted to fractions by placing the number (without the decimal point) in the numerator. Count the number of places to the right of the decimal point, and in the denominator, place a 1 followed by a number of zeros equal to the number of places that you counted. The fraction can then be reduced to its simplest form.

Writing a Fraction as a Decimal

Any fraction $\frac{a}{b}$, where $b \neq 0$, can be written as a decimal by dividing the numerator by the denominator. So, $\frac{a}{b} = a \div b$. If the division ends, or terminates, when the remainder is zero, the decimal is a terminating decimal. Not all fractions can be written as terminating decimals. Some have a repeating decimal. A bar indicates that the decimal repeats forever. For example, the fraction $\frac{4}{9}$ can be converted to a repeating decimal, 0.4

Adding and Subtracting Like Fractions

Fractions with the same denominator are called like fractions. To add like fractions, add the numerators and write the sum over the denominator. To add mixed numbers with like fractions, add the whole numbers and fractions separately, adding the numerators of the fractions, then simplifying if necessary. The rule for subtracting fractions with like denominators is similar to the rule for adding. The numerators can be subtracted and the difference written over the denominator. Mixed numbers are written as improper fractions before subtracting. These same rules apply to adding or subtracting like algebraic fractions. An algebraic fraction is a fraction that contains one or more variables in the numerator or denominator.

Adding and Subtracting Unlike Fractions

Fractions with different denominators are called unlike fractions. The least common multiple of the denominators is used to rename the fractions with a common denominator. After a common denominator is found, the numerators can then be added or subtracted. To add mixed numbers with unlike fractions, rename the mixed numbers as improper fractions. Then find a common denominator, add the numerators, and simplify the answer.

Multiplying Rational Numbers

To multiply fractions, multiply the numerators and multiply the denominators. If the numerators and denominators have common factors, they can be simplified before multiplication. If the fractions have different signs, then the product will be negative. Mixed numbers can be multiplied in the same manner, after first renaming them as improper fractions. Algebraic fractions may be multiplied using the same method described above.

Dividing Rational Numbers

To divide a number by a rational number (a fraction, for example), multiply the first number by the multiplicative inverse of the second. Two numbers whose product is 1 are called multiplicative inverses, or reciprocals. $\frac{7}{4} \times \frac{4}{7}$ = 1. When dividing by a mixed number, first rename it as an improper fraction, and then multiply by its multiplicative inverse. This process of multiplying by a number's reciprocal can also be used when dividing algebraic fractions.

Adding Integers

To add integers with the same sign, add their absolute values. The sum takes the same sign as the addends. An addend is a number that is added to another number (the augend). The equation $-5 + (-2) = -7$ is an example of adding two integers with the same sign. To add integers with different signs, subtract their absolute values. The sum takes the same sign as the addend with the greater absolute value.

Subtracting Integers

The rules for adding integers are extended to the subtraction of integers. To subtract an integer, add its additive inverse. For example, to find the difference $2 - 5$, add the additive inverse of 5 to 2: $2 + (-5) = -3$. The rule for subtracting integers can be used to solve real-world problems and to evaluate algebraic expressions.

Additive Inverse Property

Two numbers with the same absolute value but different signs are called opposites. For example, -4 and 4 are opposites. An integer and its opposite are also called additive inverses. The Additive Inverse Property says that the sum of any number and its additive inverse is zero. The Commutative, Associative, and Identity Properties also apply to integers. These properties help when adding more than two integers.

Absolute Value

In mathematics, when two integers on a number line are on opposite sides of zero, and they are the same distance from zero, they have the same absolute value. The symbol for absolute value is two vertical bars on either side of the number. For example, $|-5| = 5$.

Multiplying Integers

Since multiplication is repeated addition, $3(-7)$ means that -7 is used as an addend 3 times. By the Commutative Property of Multiplication, $3(-7) = -7(3)$. The product of two integers with different signs is always negative. The product of two integers with the same sign is always positive.

Dividing Integers

The quotient of two integers can be found by dividing the numbers using their absolute values. The quotient of two integers with the same sign is positive, and the quotient of two integers with a different sign is negative. $-12 \div (-4) = 3$ and $12 \div (-4) = -3$. The division of integers is used in statistics to find the average, or mean, of a set of data. When finding the mean of a set of numbers, find the sum of the numbers, and then divide by the number in the set.

Adding and Multiplying Vectors and Matrices

In order to add two matrices together, they must have the same number of rows and columns. In matrix addition, the corresponding elements are added to each other. In other words $(a + b)_{ij} = a_{ij} + b_{ij}$. For example,

$$\begin{pmatrix} 1 & 2 \\ 2 & 1 \end{pmatrix} + \begin{pmatrix} 3 & 6 \\ 0 & 1 \end{pmatrix} = \begin{pmatrix} 1+3 & 2+6 \\ 2+0 & 1+1 \end{pmatrix} = \begin{pmatrix} 4 & 8 \\ 2 & 2 \end{pmatrix}$$

Matrix multiplication requires that the number of elements in each row in the first matrix is equal to the number of elements in each column in the second. The elements of the first row of the first matrix are multiplied by the corresponding elements of the first column of the second matrix and then added together to get the first element of the product matrix. To get the second element, the elements in the first row of the first matrix are multiplied by the corresponding elements in the second column of the second matrix then added, and so on, until every row of the first matrix is multiplied by every column of the second. See the example below.

$$\begin{pmatrix} 1 & 2 \\ 3 & 4 \end{pmatrix} \times \begin{pmatrix} 3 & 6 \\ 0 & 1 \end{pmatrix} = \begin{pmatrix} (1\times3)+(2\times0) & (1\times6)+(2\times1) \\ (3\times3)+(4\times0) & (3\times6)+(4\times1) \end{pmatrix} = \begin{pmatrix} 3 & 8 \\ 9 & 22 \end{pmatrix}$$

Vector addition and multiplication are performed in the same way, but there is only one column and one row.

Permutations and Combinations

Permutations and combinations are used to determine the number of possible outcomes in different situations. An arrangement, listing, or pattern in which order is important is called a permutation. The symbol P(6, 3) represents the number of permutations of 6 things taken 3 at a time. For P(6, 3), there are $6 \times 5 \times 4$ or 120 possible outcomes. An arrangement or listing where order is not important is called a combination. The symbol C(10, 5) represents the number of combinations of 10 things taken 5 at a time. For C(10, 5), there are $(10 \times 9 \times 8 \times 7 \times 6) \div (5 \times 4 \times 3 \times 2 \times 1)$ or 252 possible outcomes.

Powers and Exponents

An expression such as $3 \times 3 \times 3 \times 3$ can be written as a power. A power has two parts, a base and an exponent. $3 \times 3 \times 3 \times 3 = 3^4$. The base is the number that is multiplied (3). The exponent tells how many times the base is used as a factor (4 times). Numbers and variables can be written using exponents. For example, $8 \times 8 \times 8 \times m \times m \times m \times m \times m$ can be expressed $8^3 m^5$. Exponents also can be used with place value to express numbers in expanded form. Using this method, 1,462 can be written as $(1 \times 10^3) + (4 \times 10^2) + (6 \times 10^1) + (2 \times 10^0)$.

Squares and Square Roots

The square root of a number is one of two equal factors of a number. Every positive number has both a positive and a negative square root. For example, since $8 \times 8 = 64$, 8 is a square root of 64. Since $(-8) \times (-8) = 64$, -8 is also a square root of 64. The notation $\sqrt{}$ indicates the positive square root, $-\sqrt{}$ indicates the negative square root, and $\pm\sqrt{}$ indicates both square roots. For example, $\sqrt{81} = 9$, $-\sqrt{49} = -7$, and $\pm\sqrt{4} = \pm2$. The square root of a negative number is an imaginary number because any two factors of a negative number must have different signs, and are therefore not equivalent.

Logarithm

A logarithm is the inverse of exponentiation. The logarithm of a number x in base b is equal to the number n. Therefore, $b^n = x$ and $\log_b x = n$. For example, $\log_4(64) = 3$ because $4^3 = 64$. The most commonly used bases for logarithms are 10, the common logarithm; 2, the binary logarithm; and the constant e, the natural logarithm (also called $ln(x)$ instead of $\log_e(x)$). On page 588 is a list of some of the rules of logarithms that are important to understand if you are going to use them.

Math Handbook

$$\log_b(xy) = \log_b(x) + \log_b(y)$$
$$\log_b\frac{x}{y} = \log_b(x) - \log_b(y)$$
$$\log_b\frac{1}{x} = -\log_b(x)$$
$$\log_b(x)y = y\log_b(x)$$

▶ Compute fluently and make reasonable estimates

Estimation by Rounding

When rounding numbers, look at the digit to the right of the place to which you are rounding. If the digit is 5 or greater, round up. If it is less than 5, round down. For example, to round 65,137 to the nearest hundred, look at the number in the tens place. Since 3 is less than 5, round down to 65,100. To round the same number to the nearest ten thousandth, look at the number in the thousandths place. Since it is 5, round up to 70,000.

Finding Equivalent Ratios

Equivalent ratios have the same meaning. Just like finding equivalent fractions, to find an equivalent ratio, multiply or divide both sides by the same number. For example, you can multiply 7 by both sides of the ratio 6:8 to get 42:56. Instead, you can also divide both sides of the same ratio by 2 to get 3:4. Find the simplest form of a ratio by dividing to find equivalent ratios until you can't go any further without going into decimals. So, 160:240 in simplest form is 2:3. To write a ratio in the form *1:n*, divide both sides by the left-hand number. In other words, to change 8:20 to *1:n*, divide both sides by 8 to get 1:2.5.

Front-End Estimation

Front-end estimation can be used to quickly estimate sums and differences before adding or subtracting. To use this technique, add or subtract just the digits of the two highest place values, and replace the other place values with zero. This will give you an estimation of the solution of a problem. For example, 93,471 − 22,825 can be changed to 93,000 − 22,000 or 71,000. This estimate can be compared to your final answer to judge its correctness.

Judging Reasonableness

When solving an equation, it is important to check your work by considering how reasonable your answer is. For example, consider the equation $9\frac{3}{4} \times 4\frac{1}{3}$. Since $9\frac{3}{4}$ is between 9 and 10 and $4\frac{1}{3}$ is between 4 and 5, only values that are between 9×4 or 36 and 10×5 or 50 will be reasonable. You can also use front-end estimation,

or you can round and estimate a reasonable answer. In the equation 73×25, you can round and solve to estimate a reasonable answer to be near 70×30 or 2,100.

Algebra

▶ Understand patterns, relations, and functions

Relation

A relation is a generalization comparing sets of ordered pairs for an equation or inequality such as $x = y + 1$ or $x > y$. The first element in each pair, the x values, forms the domain. The second element in each pair, the y values, forms the range.

Function

A function is a special relation in which each member of the domain is paired with exactly one member in the range. Functions may be represented using ordered pairs, tables, or graphs. One way to determine whether a relation is a function is to use the vertical line test. Using an object to represent a vertical line, move the object from left to right across the graph. If, for each value of x in the domain, the object passes through no more than one point on the graph, then the graph represents a function.

Linear and Nonlinear Functions

Linear functions have graphs that are straight lines. These graphs represent constant rates of change. In other words, the slope between any two pairs of points on the graph is the same. Nonlinear functions do not have constant rates of change. The slope changes along these graphs. Therefore, the graphs of nonlinear functions are *not* straight lines. Graphs of curves represent nonlinear functions. The equation for a linear function can be written in the form $y = mx + b$, where m represents the constant rate of change, or the slope. Therefore, you can determine whether a function is linear by looking at the equation. For example, the equation $y = \frac{3}{x}$ is nonlinear because x is in the denominator and the equation cannot be written in the form $y = mx + b$. A nonlinear function does not increase or decrease at a constant rate. You can check this by using a table and finding the increase or decrease in y for each regular increase in x. For example, if for each increase in x by 2, y does not increase or decrease the same amount each time, the function is nonlinear.

Linear Equations in Two Variables

In a linear equation with two variables, such as $y = x - 3$, the variables appear in separate terms and neither variable contains an exponent other than 1. The graphs of all linear equations are straight lines. All points on a line are solutions of the equation that is graphed.

Quadratic and Cubic Functions

A quadratic function is a polynomial equation of the second degree, generally expressed as $ax^2 + bx + c = 0$, where a, b, and c are real numbers and a is not equal to zero. Similarly, a cubic function is a polynomial equation of the third degree, usually expressed as $ax^3 + bx^2 + cx + d = 0$. Quadratic functions can be graphed using an equation or a table of values. For example, to graph $y = 3x^2 + 1$, substitute the values -1, -0.5, 0, 0.5, and 1 for x to yield the point coordinates $(-1, 4)$, $(-0.5, 1.75)$, $(0, 1)$, $(0.5, 1.75)$, and $(1, 4)$. Plot these points on a coordinate grid and connect the points in the form of a parabola. Cubic functions also can be graphed by making a table of values. The points of a cubic function form a curve. There is one point at which the curve changes from opening upward to opening downward, or vice versa, called the point of inflection.

Slope

Slope is the ratio of the rise, or vertical change, to the run, or horizontal change of a line: slope = rise/run. Slope (m) is the same for any two points on a straight line and can be found by using the coordinates of any two points on the line:

$$m = \frac{y_2 - y_1}{x_2 - x_1}, \text{ where } x_2 \neq x_1$$

Asymptotes

An asymptote is a straight line that a curve approaches but never actually meets or crosses. Theoretically, the asymptote meets the curve at infinity. For example, in the function $f(x) = \frac{1}{x}$, two asymptotes are being approached: the line $y = 0$ and $x = 0$. See the graph of the function below.

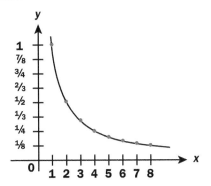

▶ *Represent and analyze mathematical situations and structures using algebraic symbols*

Variables and Expressions

Algebra is a language of symbols. A variable is a placeholder for a changing value. Any letter, such as x, can be used as a variable. Expressions such as $x + 2$ and $4x$ are algebraic expressions because they represent sums and/or products of variables and numbers. Usually, mathematicians avoid the use of i and e for variables because they have other mathematical meanings ($i = \sqrt{-1}$ and e is used with natural logarithms). To evaluate an algebraic expression, replace the variable or variables with known values, and then solve using order of operations. Translate verbal phrases into algebraic expressions by first defining a variable: Choose a variable and a quantity for the variable to represent. In this way, algebraic expressions can be used to represent real-world situations.

Constant and Coefficient

A constant is a fixed value unlike a variable, which can change. Constants are usually represented by numbers, but they can also be represented by symbols. For example, π is a symbolic representation of the value $3.1415\ldots$. A coefficient is a constant by which a variable or other object is multiplied. For example, in the expression $7x^2 + 5x + 9$, the coefficient of x^2 is 7 and the coefficient of x is 5. The number 9 is a constant and not a coefficient.

Monomial and Polynomial

A monomial is a number, a variable, or a product of numbers and/or variables such as 3×4. An algebraic expression that contains one or more monomials is called a polynomial. In a polynomial, there are no terms with variables in the denominator and no terms with variables under a radical sign. Polynomials can be classified by the number of terms contained in the expression. Therefore, a polynomial with two terms is called a binomial ($z^2 - 1$), and a polynomial with three terms is called a trinomial ($2y^3 + 4y^2 - y$). Polynomials also can be classified by their degrees. The degree of a monomial is the sum of the exponents of its variables. The degree of a nonzero constant such as 6 or 10 is 0. The constant 0 has no degree. For example, the monomial $4b^5c^2$ had a degree of 7. The degree of a polynomial is the same as that of

Math Handbook

the term with the greatest degree. For example, the polynomial $3x^4 - 2y^3 + 4y^2 - y$ has a degree of 4.

Equation

An equation is a mathematical sentence that states that two expressions are equal. The two expressions in an equation are always separated by an equal sign. When solving for a variable in an equation, you must perform the same operations on both sides of the equation in order for the mathematical sentence to remain true.

Solving Equations with Variables

To solve equations with variables on both sides, use the Addition or Subtraction Property of Equality to write an equivalent equation with the variables on the same side. For example, to solve $5x - 8 = 3x$, subtract $3x$ from each side to get $2x - 8 = 0$. Then add 8 to each side to get $2x = 8$. Finally, divide each side by 2 to find that $x = 4$.

Solving Equations with Grouping Symbols

Equations often contain grouping symbols such as parentheses or brackets. The first step in solving these equations is to use the Distributive Property to remove the grouping symbols. For example $5(x + 2) = 25$ can be changed to $5x + 10 = 25$, and then solved to find that $x = 3$.

Some equations have no solution. That is, there is no value of the variable that results in a true sentence. For such an equation, the solution set is called the null or empty set, and is represented by the symbol $\emptyset$ or {}. Other equations may have every number as the solution. An equation that is true for every value of the variable is called the identity.

Inequality

A mathematical sentence that contains the symbols < (less than), > (greater than), ≤ (less than or equal to), or ≥ (greater than or equal to) is called an inequality. For example, the statement that it is legal to drive 55 miles per hour or slower on a stretch of the highway can be shown by the sentence $s \le 55$. Inequalities with variables are called open sentences. When a variable is replaced with a number, the inequality may be true or false.

Solving Inequalities

Solving an inequality means finding values for the variable that make the inequality true. Just as with equations, when you add or subtract the same number from each side of an inequality, the inequality remains true. For example, if you add 5 to each side of the inequality $3x < 6$, the resulting inequality $3x + 5 < 11$ is also true. Adding or subtracting the same number from each side of an inequality does not affect the inequality sign. When multiplying or dividing each side of an inequality by the same positive number, the inequality remains true. In such cases, the inequality symbol does not change. When multiplying or dividing each side of an inequality by a negative number, the inequality symbol must be reversed. For example, when dividing each side of the inequality $-4x \ge -8$ by -2, the inequality sign must be changed to ≤ for the resulting inequality, $2x \le 4$, to be true. Since the solutions to an inequality include all rational numbers satisfying it, inequalities have an infinite number of solutions.

Representing Inequalities on a Number Line

The solutions of inequalities can be graphed on a number line. For example, if the solution of an inequality is $x < 5$, start an arrow at 5 on the number line, and continue the arrow to the left to show all values less than 5 as the solution. Put an open circle at 5 to show that the point 5 is *not* included in the graph. Use a closed circle when graphing solutions that are greater than or equal to, or less than or equal to, a number.

Order of Operations

Solving a problem may involve using more than one operation. The answer can depend on the order in which you do the operations. To make sure that there is just one answer to a series of computations, mathematicians have agreed upon an order in which to do the operations. First simplify within the parentheses, often called graphing symbols, and then evaluate any exponents. Then multiply and divide from left to right, and finally add and subtract from left to right.

Parametric Equations

Given an equation with more than one unknown, a statistician can draw conclusions about those unknown quantities through the use of parameters, independent variables that the statistician already knows something about. For example, you can find the velocity of an object if you make some assumptions about distance and time parameters.

Recursive Equations

In recursive equations, every value is determined by the previous value. You must first plug an initial value into the equation to get the first value, and then you can use the first value to determine the next one, and so on. For example, in order to determine what the population of pigeons will be in New York City in three years, you can use an equation with the birth, death, immigration, and emigration rates of the birds. Input the current population size into the equation to determine next year's population size, then repeat until you have calculated the value for which you are looking.

▶ Use mathematical models to represent and understand quantitative relationships

Solving Systems of Equations

Two or more equations together are called a system of equations. A system of equations can have one solution, no solution, or infinitely many solutions. One method for solving a system of equations is to graph the equations on the same coordinate plane. The coordinates of the point where the graphs intersect is the solution. In other words, the solution of a system is the ordered pair that is a solution of all equations. A more accurate way to solve a system of two equations is by using a method called substitution. Write both equations in terms of y. Replace y in the first equation with the right side of the second equation. Check the solution by graphing. You can solve a system of three equations using matrix algebra.

Graphing Inequalities

To graph an inequality, first graph the related equation, which is the boundary. All points in the shaded region are solutions of the inequality. If an inequality contains the symbol $\leq$ or $\geq$, then use a solid line to indicate that the boundary is included in the graph. If an inequality contains the symbol $<$ or $>$, then use a dashed line to indicate that the boundary is not included in the graph.

▶ Analyze change in various contexts

Rate of Change

A change in one quantity with respect to another quantity is called the rate of change. Rates of change can be described using slope:

$$\text{slope} = \frac{change\ in\ y}{change\ in\ x}$$

You can find rates of change from an equation, a table, or a graph. A special type of linear equation that describes rate of change is called a direct variation. The graph of a direct variation always passes through the origin and represents a proportional situation. In the equation $y = kx$, k is called the constant of variation. It is the slope, or rate of change. As x increases in value, y increases or decreases at a constant rate k, or y varies directly with x. Another way to say this is that y is directly proportional to x. The direct variation $y = kx$ also can be written as $k = \frac{y}{x}$. In this form, you can see that the ratio of y to x is the same for any corresponding values of y and x.

Slope-Intercept Form

Equations written as $y = mx + b$, where m is the slope and b is the y-intercept, are linear equations in slope-intercept form. For example, the graph of $y = 5x - 6$ is a line that has a slope of 5 and crosses the y-axis at $(0, -6)$. Sometimes you must first write an equation in slope-intercept form before finding the slope and y-intercept. For example, the equation $2x + 3y = 15$ can be expressed in slope-intercept form by subtracting $2x$ from each side and then dividing by 3: $y = -\frac{2}{3}x + 5$, revealing a slope of $-\frac{2}{3}$ and a y-intercept of 5. You can use the slope-intercept form of an equation to graph a line easily. Graph the y-intercept and use the slope to find another point on the line, then connect the two points with a line. Analyze characteristics and properties of two- and three-dimensional geometric shapes and develop mathematical arguments about geometric relationships

Geometry

▶ Analyze characteristics and properties of two- and three-dimensional geometric shapes and develop mathematical arguments about geometric relationships

Angles

Two rays that have the same endpoint form an angle. The common endpoint is called the vertex, and the two rays that make up the angle are called the sides of the angle. The most common unit of measure for angles is the degree. Protractors can be used to measure angles or to draw an angle of a given measure. Angles can be classified by their degree measure. Acute angles have measures less than 90° but greater

Math Handbook

than 0°. Obtuse angles have measures greater than 90° but less than 180°. Right angles have measures of 90°.

Triangles

A triangle is a figure formed by three line segments that intersect only at their endpoints. The sum of the measures of the angles of a triangle is 180°. Triangles can be classified by their angles. An acute triangle contains all acute angles. An obtuse triangle has one obtuse angle. A right triangle has one right angle. Triangles can also be classified by their sides. A scalene triangle has no congruent sides. An isosceles triangle has at least two congruent sides. In an equilateral triangle all sides are congruent.

Quadrilaterals

A quadrilateral is a closed figure with four sides and four vertices. The segments of a quadrilateral intersect only at their endpoints. Quadrilaterals can be separated into two triangles. Since the sum of the interior angles of all triangles totals 180°, the measures of the interior angles of a quadrilateral equal 360°. Quadrilaterals are classified according to their characteristics, and include trapezoids, parallelograms, rectangles, squares, and rhombuses.

Two-Dimensional Figures

A two-dimensional figure exists within a plane and has only the dimensions of length and width. Examples of two-dimensional figures include circles and polygons. Polygons are figures that have three or more angles, including triangles, quadrilaterals, pentagons, hexagons, and many more. The sum of the angles of any polygon totals at least 180° (triangle), and each additional side adds 180° to the measure of the first three angles. The sum of the angles of a quadrilateral, for example, is 360°. The sum of the angles of a pentagon is 540°.

Three-Dimensional Figures

A plane is a two-dimensional flat surface that extends in all directions. Intersecting planes can form the edges and vertices of three-dimensional figures or solids. A polyhedron is a solid with flat surfaces that are polygons. Polyhedrons are composed of faces, edges, and vertices and are differentiated by their shape and by their number of bases. Skew lines are lines that lie in different planes. They are neither intersecting nor parallel.

Congruence

Figures that have the same size and shape are congruent. The parts of congruent triangles that match are called corresponding parts. Congruence statements are used to identify corresponding parts of congruent triangles. When writing a congruence statement, the letters must be written so that corresponding vertices appear in the same order. Corresponding parts can be used to find the measures of angles and sides in a figure that is congruent to a figure with known measures.

Similarity

If two figures have the same shape but not the same size they are called similar figures. For example, the triangles below are similar, so angles A, B, and C have the same measurements as angles D, E, and F, respectively. However, segments AB, BC, and CA do not have the same measurements as segments DE, EF, and FD, but the measures of the sides are proportional.

For example, $\dfrac{\overline{AB}}{\overline{DE}} = \dfrac{\overline{BC}}{\overline{EF}} = \dfrac{\overline{CA}}{\overline{FD}}$.

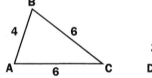

Solid figures are considered to be similar if they have the same shape and their corresponding linear measures are proportional. As with two-dimensional figures, they can be tested for similarity by comparing corresponding measures. If the compared ratios are proportional, then the figures are similar solids. Missing measures of similar solids can also be determined by using proportions.

The Pythagorean Theorem

The sides that are adjacent to a right angle are called legs. The side opposite the right angle is the hypotenuse.

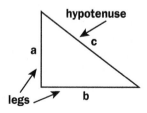

Math Handbook

The Pythagorean Theorem describes the relationship between the lengths of the legs *a* and *b* and the hypotenuse *c*. It states that if a triangle is a right triangle, then the square of the length of the hypotenuse is equal to the sum of the squares of the lengths of the legs. In symbols, $c^2 = a^2 + b^2$.

Sine, Cosine, and Tangent Ratios

Trigonometry is the study of the properties of triangles. A trigonometric ratio is a ratio of the lengths of two sides of a right triangle. The most common trigonometric ratios are the sine, cosine, and tangent ratios. These ratios are abbreviated as *sin*, *cos*, and *tan*, respectively.

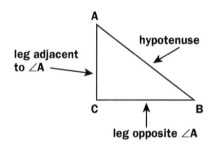

If $\angle A$ is an acute angle of a right triangle, then

$$sin \angle A = \frac{\text{measure of leg opposite } \angle A}{\text{measure of hypotenuse}},$$

$$cos \angle A = \frac{\text{measure of leg adjacent to } \angle A}{\text{measure of hypotenuse}}, \text{ and}$$

$$tan \angle A = \frac{\text{measure of leg opposite } \angle A}{\text{measure of leg adjacent to } \angle A}.$$

▶ Specify locations and describe spatial relationships using coordinate geometry and other representational systems

Polygons

A polygon is a simple, closed figure formed by three or more line segments. The line segments meet only at their endpoints. The points of intersection are called vertices, and the line segments are called sides. Polygons are classified by the number of sides they have. The diagonals of a polygon divide the polygon into triangles. The number of triangles formed is two less than the number of sides. To find the sum of the mea-

sures of the interior angles of any polygon, multiply the number of triangles within the polygon by 180. That is, if *n* equals the number of sides, then $(n - 2)\,180$ gives the sum of the measures of the polygon's interior angles.

Cartesian Coordinates

In the Cartesian coordinate system, the *y*-axis extends above and below the origin and the *x*-axis extends to the right and left of the origin, which is the point at which the *x*- and *y*-axes intersect. Numbers below and to the left of the origin are negative. A point graphed on the coordinate grid is said to have an *x*-coordinate and a *y*-coordinate. For example, the point (1,–2) has as its *x*-coordinate the number 1, and has as its *y*-coordinate the number –2. This point is graphed by locating the position on the grid that is 1 unit to the right of the origin and 2 units below the origin.

The *x*-axis and the *y*-axis separate the coordinate plane into four regions, called quadrants. The axes and points located on the axes themselves are not located in any of the quadrants. The quadrants are labeled I to IV, starting in the upper right and proceeding counterclockwise. In quadrant I, both coordinates are positive. In quadrant II, the *x*-coordinate is negative and the *y*-coordinate is positive. In quadrant III, both coordinates are negative. In quadrant IV, the *x*-coordinate is positive and the *y*-coordinate is negative. A coordinate graph can be used to show algebraic relationships among numbers.

▶ Apply transformations and use symmetry to analyze mathematical situations

Similar Triangles and Indirect Measurement

Triangles that have the same shape but not necessarily the same dimensions are called similar triangles. Similar triangles have corresponding angles and corresponding sides. Arcs are used to show congruent angles. If two triangles are similar, then the corresponding angles have the same measure, and the corresponding sides are proportional. Therefore, to determine the measures of the sides of similar triangles when some measures are known, proportions can be used.

Transformations

A transformation is a movement of a geometric figure. There are several types of transformations. In a translation, also called a slide,

Math Handbook

a figure is slid from one position to another without turning it. Every point of the original figure is moved the same distance and in the same direction. In a reflection, also called a flip, a figure is flipped over a line to form a mirror image. Every point of the original figure has a corresponding point on the other side of the line of symmetry. In a rotation, also called a turn, a figure is turned around a fixed point. A figure can be rotated 0°–360° clockwise or counterclockwise. A dilation transforms each line to a parallel line whose length is a fixed multiple of the length of the original line to create a similar figure that will be either larger or smaller.

▶ *Use visualizations, spatial reasoning, and geometric modeling to solve problems*

Two-Dimensional Representations of Three-Dimensional Objects

Three-dimensional objects can be represented in a two-dimensional drawing in order to more easily determine properties such as surface area and volume. When you look at the triangular prism, you can see the orientation of its three dimensions, length, width, and height. Using the drawing and the formulas for surface area and volume, you can easily calculate these properties.

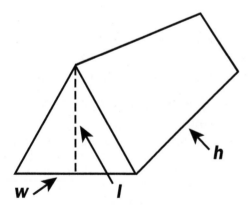

Another way to represent a three-dimensional object in a two-dimensional plane is by using a net, which is the unfolded representation. Imagine cutting the vertices of a box until it is flat then drawing an outline of it. That's a net. Most objects have more than one net, but any one can be measured to determine surface area. Below is a cube and one of its nets.

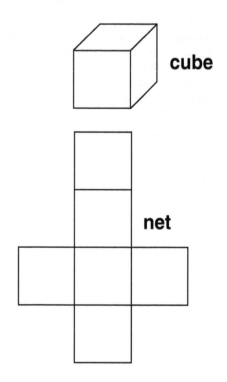

cube

net

Measurement

▶ *Understand measurable attributes of objects and the units, systems, and processes of measurement*

Customary System

The customary system is the system of weights and measures used in the United States. The main units of weight are ounces, pounds (1 equal to 16 ounces), and tons (1 equal to 2,000 pounds). Length is typically measured in inches, feet (1 equal to 12 inches), yards (1 equal to 3 feet), and miles (1 equal to 5,280 feet), while area is measured in square feet and acres (1 equal to 43,560 square feet). Liquid is measured in cups, pints (1 equal to 2 cups), quarts (1 equal to 2 pints), and gallons (1 equal to 4 quarts). Finally, temperature is measured in degrees Fahrenheit.

Metric System

The metric system is a decimal system of weights and measurements in which the prefixes of the words for the units of measure indicate the relationships between the different measurements. In this system, the main units of weight, or mass, are grams and kilograms. Length is measured in millimeters, centimeters, meters, and kilometers, and the units of area are square millimeters, centimeters, meters, and kilometers. Liquid is typically measured in milliliters and liters, while temperature is in degrees Celsius.

Selecting Units of Measure

When measuring something, it is important to select the appropriate type and size of unit. For example, in the United States it would be appropriate when describing someone's height to use feet and inches. These units of height or length are good to use because they are in the customary system, and they are of appropriate size. In the customary system, use inches, feet, and miles for lengths and perimeters; square inches, feet, and miles for area and surface area; and cups, pints, quarts, gallons or cubic inches and feet (and, less commonly, miles) for volume. In the metric system use millimeters, centimeters, meters, and kilometers for lengths and perimeters; square units millimeters, centimeters, meters, and kilometers for area and surface area; and milliliters and liters for volume. Finally, always use degrees to measure angles.

▶ *Apply appropriate techniques, tools, and formulas to determine measurements*

Precision and Significant Digits

The precision of measurement is the exactness to which a measurement is made. Precision depends on the smallest unit of measure being used, or the precision unit. One way to record a measure is to estimate to the nearest precision unit. A more precise method is to include all of the digits that are actually measured, plus one estimated digit. The digits recorded, called significant digits, indicate the precision of the measurement. There are special rules for determining significant digits. If a number contains a decimal point, the number of significant digits is found by counting from left to right, starting with the first nonzero digit. If the number does not contain a decimal point, the number of significant digits is found by counting the digits from left to right, starting with the first digit and ending with the last nonzero digit.

Surface Area

The amount of material needed to cover the surface of a figure is called the surface area. It can be calculated by finding the area of each face and adding them together. To find the surface area of a rectangular prism, for example, the formula $S = 2lw + 2lh + 2wh$ applies. A cylinder, on the other hand, may be unrolled to reveal two circles and a rectangle. Its surface area can be determined by finding the area of the two circles, $2\pi r^2$, and adding it to the area of the rectangle, $2\pi rh$ (the length of the rectangle is the circumference of one of the circles), or $S = 2\pi r^2 + 2\pi rh$. The surface area of a pyramid is measured in a slightly different way because the sides of a pyramid are triangles that intersect at the vertex. These sides are called lateral faces and the height of each is called the slant height. The sum of their areas is the lateral area of a pyramid. The surface area of a square pyramid is the lateral area $\frac{1}{2}bh$ (area of a lateral face) times 4 (number of lateral faces), plus the area of the base. The surface area of a cone is the area of its circular base (πr^2) plus its lateral area (πrl, where l is the slant height).

Volume

Volume is the measure of space occupied by a solid region. To find the volume of a prism, the area of the base is multiplied by the measure of the height, $V = bh$. A solid containing several prisms can be broken down into its component prisms. Then the volume of each component can be found and the volumes added. The volume of a cylinder can be determined by finding the area of its circular base, πr^2, and then multiplying by the height of the cylinder. A pyramid has one-third the volume of a prism with the same base and height. To find the volume of a pyramid, multiply the area of the base by the pyramid's height, and then divide by 3. Simply stated, the formula for the volume of a pyramid is $V = \frac{1}{3}bh$. A cone is a three-dimensional figure with one circular base and a curved surface connecting the base and the vertex. The volume of a cone is one-third the volume of a cylinder with the same base area and height. Like a pyramid, the formula for the volume of a cone is $V = \frac{1}{3}bh$. More specifically, the formula is $V = \frac{1}{3}\pi r^2 h$.

Upper and Lower Bounds

Upper and lower bounds have to do with the accuracy of a measurement. When a measurement is given, the degree of accuracy is also stated to tell you what the upper and lower bounds of the measurement are. The upper bound is the largest possible value that a measurement could have had before being rounded down, and the lower bound is the lowest possible value it could have had before being rounded up.

Data Analysis and Probablity

▶ *Formulate questions that can be addressed with data and collect, organize, and display relevant data to answer them*

Histograms

A histogram displays numerical data that have been organized into equal intervals using bars that have the same width and no space between them. While a histogram does not give exact data points, its shape shows the distribution of the data. Histograms also can be used to compare data.

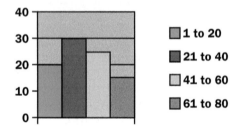

Box-and-Whisker Plot

A box-and-whisker plot displays the measures of central tendency and variation. A box is drawn around the quartile values, and whiskers extend from each quartile to the extreme data points. To make a box plot for a set of data, draw a number line that covers the range of data. Find the median, the extremes, and the upper and lower quartiles. Mark these points on the number line with bullets, then draw a box and the whiskers. The length of a whisker or box shows whether the values of the data in that part are concentrated or spread out.

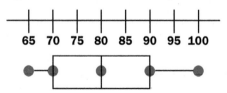

Scatter Plots

A scatter plot is a graph that shows the relationship between two sets of data. In a scatter plot, two sets of data are graphed as ordered pairs on a coordinate system. Two sets of data can have a positive correlation (as x increases, y increases), a negative correlation (as x increases, y decreases), or no correlation (no obvious pattern is shown). Scatter plots can be used to spot trends, draw conclusions, and make predictions about data.

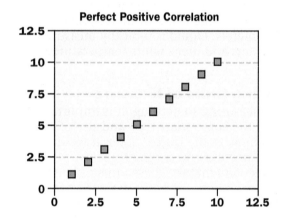

Randomization

The idea of randomization is a very important principle of statistics and the design of experiments. Data must be selected randomly to prevent bias from influencing the results. For example, you want to know the average income of people in your town but you can only use a sample of 100 individuals to make determinations about everyone. If you select 100 individuals who are all doctors, you will have a biased sample. However, if you chose a random sample of 100 people out of the phone book, you are much more likely to accurately represent average income in the town.

Statistics and Parameters

Statistics is a science that involves collecting, analyzing, and presenting data. The data can be collected in various ways—for example through a census or by making physical measurements. The data can then be analyzed by creating summary statistics, which have to do with the distribution of the data sample, including the mean, range, and standard error. They can also be illustrated in tables and graphs, like box-plots, scatter plots, and histograms. The presentation of the data typically involves describing the strength or validity of the data and what they show. For example, an analysis of ancestry of people in a city might tell you something about immigration patterns, unless the data set is very small or biased in some way, in which case it is not likely to be very accurate or useful.

Categorical and Measurement Data

When analyzing data, it is important to understand if the data is qualitative or quantitative. Categorical data is qualitative and measurement, or numerical, data is quantitative. Categorical data describes a quality of something and can be placed into different categories. For example, if you are analyzing the number of students in different grades in a school, each grade is a category. On the other hand, measurement data is continuous, like height, weight, or any other measurable variable. Measurement data can be converted into categorical data if you decide to group the data. Using height as an example, you can group the continuous data set into categories like under 5 feet, 5 feet to 5 feet 5 inches, over 5 feet five inches to 6 feet, and so on.

Univariate and Bivariate Data

In data analysis, a researcher can analyze one variable at a time or look at how multiple variables behave together. Univariate data involves only one variable, for example height in humans. You can measure the height in a population of people then plot the results in a histogram to look at how height is distributed in humans. To summarize univariate data, you can use statistics like the mean, mode, median, range, and standard deviation, which is a measure of variation. When looking at more than one variable at once, you use multivariate data. Bivariate data involves two variables. For example, you can look at height and age in humans together by gathering information on both variables from individuals in a population. You can then plot both variables in a scatter plot, look at how the variables behave in relation to each other, and create an equation that represents the relationship, also called a regression. These equations could help answer questions such as, for example, does height increase with age in humans?

▶ Select and use appropriate statistical methods to analyze data

Measures of Central Tendency

When you have a list of numerical data, it is often helpful to use one or more numbers to represent the whole set. These numbers are called measures of central tendency. Three measures of central tendency are mean, median, and mode. The mean is the sum of the data divided by the number of items in the data set. The median is the middle number of the ordered data (or the mean of the two middle numbers). The mode is the number or numbers that occur most often. These measures of central tendency allow data to be analyzed and better understood.

Measures of Spread

In statistics, measures of spread or variation are used to describe how data are distributed. The range of a set of data is the difference between the greatest and the least values of the data set. The quartiles are the values that divide the data into four equal parts. The median of data separates the set in half. Similarly, the median of the lower half of a set of data is the lower quartile. The median of the upper half of a set of data is the upper quartile. The interquartile range is the difference between the upper quartile and the lower quartile.

Line of Best Fit

When real-life data are collected, the points graphed usually do not form a straight line, but they may approximate a linear relationship. A line of best fit is a line that lies very close to most of the data points. It can be used to predict data. You also can use the equation of the best-fit line to make predictions.

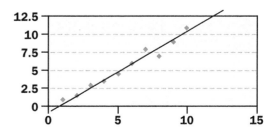

Stem and Leaf Plots

In a stem and leaf plot, numerical data are listed in ascending or descending order. The greatest place value of the data is used for the stems. The next greatest place value forms the leaves. For example, if the least number in a set of data is 8 and the greatest number is 95, draw a vertical line and write the stems from 0 to 9 to the left of the line. Write the leaves from 10 to 95 to the right of the line, with the corresponding stem. Next, rearrange the leaves so they are ordered from least to greatest. Then include a key or explanation, such as $1|3 = 13$. Notice that the stem-and-leaf plot on page 598 is like a histogram turned on its side.

Math Handbook

```
0|8
1|3 6
2|5 6 9
3|0 2 7 8
4|0 1 4 7 9
5|1 4 5 8
6|1 3 7
7|5 8
8|2 6
9|5
```

Key: **1|3 = 13**

▶ Develop and evaluate inferences and predictions that are based on data

Sampling Distribution

The sampling distribution of a population is the distribution that would result if you could take an infinite number of samples from the population, average each, and then average the averages. The more normal the distribution of the population, that is, how closely the distribution follows a bell curve, the more likely the sampling distribution will also follow a normal distribution. Furthermore, the larger the sample, the more likely it will accurately represent the entire population. For instance, you are more likely to gain more representative results from a population of 1,000 with a sample of 100 than with a sample of 2.

Validity

In statistics, validity refers to acquiring results that accurately reflect that which is being measured. In other words, it is important when performing statistical analyses, to ensure that the data are valid in that the sample being analyzed represents the population to the best extent possible. Randomization of data and using appropriate sample sizes are two important aspects of making valid inferences about a population.

▶ Understand and apply basic concepts of probability

Complementary, Mutually Exclusive Events

To understand probability theory, it is important to know if two events are mutually exclusive, or complementary: the occurrence of one event automatically implies the non-occurrence of the other. That is, two complementary events cannot both occur. If you roll a pair of dice, the event of rolling 6 and rolling doubles have an outcome in common (3, 3), so they are not mutually exclusive. If you roll (3, 3), you also roll doubles. However, the events of rolling a 9 and rolling doubles are mutually exclusive because they have no outcomes in common. If you roll a 9, you will not also roll doubles.

Independent and Dependent Events

Determining the probability of a series of events requires that you know whether the events are independent or dependent. An independent event has no influence on the occurrence of subsequent events, whereas, a dependent event does influence subsequent events. The chances that a woman's first child will be a girl are $\frac{1}{2}$, and the chances that her second child will be a girl are also $\frac{1}{2}$ because the two events are independent of each other. However, if there are 7 red marbles in a bag of 15 marbles, the chances that the first marble you pick will be red are $\frac{7}{15}$ and if you indeed pick a red marble and remove it, you have reduced the chances of picking another red marble to $\frac{6}{14}$.

Sample Space

The sample space is the group of all possible outcomes for an event. For example, if you are tossing a single six-sided die, the sample space is {1, 2, 3, 4, 5, 6}. Similarly, you can determine the sample space for the possible outcomes of two events. If you are going to toss a coin twice, the sample space is {(heads, heads), (heads, tails), (tails, heads), (tails, tails)}.

Computing the Probability of a Compound Event

If two events are independent, the outcome of one event does not influence the outcome of the second. For example, if a bag contains 2 blue and 3 red marbles, then the probability of selecting a blue marble, replacing it, and then selecting a red marble is $P(A) \times P(B) = \frac{2}{5} \times \frac{3}{5}$ or $\frac{6}{25}$.

If two events are dependent, the outcome of one event affects the outcome of the second. For example, if a bag contains 2 blue and 3 red marbles, then the probability of selecting a blue and then a red marble without replacing the first marble is $P(A) \times P(B \text{ following } A) = \frac{2}{5} \times \frac{3}{4}$ or $\frac{3}{10}$. Two events that cannot happen at the same time are mutually exclusive. For example, when you roll two number cubes, you cannot roll a sum that is both 5 and even. So, $P(A \text{ or } B) = \frac{4}{36} + \frac{18}{36}$ or $\frac{11}{18}$.

Career Skills

MAKING CAREER CHOICES

A career differs from a job in that it is a series of progressively more responsible jobs in one field or a related field. You will need to learn some special skills to choose a career and to help you in your job search. Choosing a career and identifying career opportunities require careful thought and preparation.

STEPS TO MAKING A CAREER DECISION

The *Career Plan Project Workbook* is available at this book's Online Learning Center at **connectED.mcgraw-hill.com**. It provides information and worksheets that can help you develop the essential elements of a career plan. You can use this workbook to explore the three core areas of career decision making: self-assessment, career exploration, and goal setting. Then you can follow step-by-step directions to create your own career plan. These are the five basic steps to making a career decision:

1. Create a self-profile with these headings: lifestyle goals, values, interests, aptitudes, skills and abilities, personality traits, learning styles. Fill in information about yourself.

2. Identify possible career choices based on your self-assessment.

3. Gather information on each choice, including future trends.

4. Evaluate your choices based on your self-assessment.

5. Make your decision.

After you make your decision, create a career plan that explains how you will reach your goal. Include short-term, medium-term, and long-term goals. In making your choices, explore the future opportunities in this field or fields over the next several years. What impact will new technology and automation have on job opportunities in a rapidly evolving workplace environment? Remember, if you plan, you make your own career opportunities.

COLLEGE AND CAREER PORTFOLIO

A college and career portfolio is a collection of information about a person, including documents, projects, and work samples that show a person's skills, talents, and qualifications. It includes information needed for a job search or to apply for college. Turn to the end of this Career Skills Handbook for more information and instructions for creating your own college and career portfolio.

CAREER RESEARCH RESOURCES

In order to gather information on various career opportunities, there are a variety of sources to research:

- **Libraries** Your school or public library offers books, magazines, pamphlets, videos, and other print, online, and multimedia reference materials on careers. The U.S. Department of Labor publishes the *Dictionary of Occupational Titles (DOT),* which describes about 20,000 jobs and their relationships with data, people, and things; the *Occupational Outlook Handbook (OOH),* with information on more than 200 occupations; and the *Guide for Occupational Exploration (GOE),* a reference that organizes the world of work into interest areas that are subdivided into work groups and subgroups.

- **The Internet** The Internet is a primary source of research on any topic. It is especially helpful in researching careers.

- **Career Consultations** Career consultation, an informational interview with a professional who works in a career that interests you, provides an opportunity to learn about the realities of a career.

- **On-the-Job Experience** On-the-job experience can be valuable in learning firsthand about a job or career. You can find out if your school has a work-experience program, or look into a company or organization's internship opportunities. Interning gives you direct work experience and often allows you to make valuable contacts.

Career Skills

 **THE JOB SEARCH**

To aid you in your actual job search, there are various sources to explore. You should contact and research all the sources that might produce a job lead, or information about a job. Keep a contact list as you proceed with your search. Some job search resources include:

- **Networking with family, friends, and acquaintances.** This means contacting people you know personally, including school counselors, former employers, and professional people.

- **Cooperative education and work-experience programs.** Many schools have programs in which students work part-time on a job related to one of their classes. Many also offer work-experience programs that are not limited to just one career area, such as marketing.

- **Newspaper ads.** Reading the Help Wanted advertisements in your local papers will provide a source of job leads, as well as teach you about the local job market.

- **Employment agencies.** Most cities have two types of employment agencies, public and private. These employment agencies match workers with jobs. Some private agencies may charge a fee, so be sure to know who is expected to pay the fee and what the fee is.

- **Company personnel offices.** Large and medium-sized companies have personnel offices to handle employment matters, including the hiring of new workers. You can check on job openings by contacting the office by telephone or by scheduling a personal visit.

- **Searching the Internet.** Cyberspace offers multiple opportunities for your job search. Many Web sites provide lists of companies offering employment. There are thousands of career-related Web sites, so find those that have jobs that interest you. Companies that interest you may have a Web site, which may provide information on their benefits and opportunities for employment.

 APPLYING FOR A JOB

When you have contacted the sources of job leads and found some jobs that interest you, the next step is to apply for them. You will need to complete application forms, write letters of application, and prepare your own résumé. Before you apply for a job, you will need to have a work permit if you are under the age of 18 in most states. Some state and federal labor laws designate certain jobs as too dangerous for young workers. Laws also limit the number of hours of work allowed during a day, a week, or the school year. You will also need to have proper documentation, such as a green card if you are not a U.S. citizen.

JOB APPLICATION

You can obtain the job application form directly at the place of business, by requesting it in writing, or over the Internet. It is best if you can fill the form out at home, but some businesses require that you fill it out at the place of work.

Fill out the job application forms neatly and accurately, using standard English, the formal style of speaking and writing you learned in school. You must be truthful and pay attention to detail in filling out the form.

PERSONAL FACT SHEET

To be sure that the answers you write on a job or college application form are accurate, make a personal fact sheet before filling out the application:

- Your name, home address, and phone number
- Your Social Security number
- The job you are applying for
- The date you can begin work
- The days and hours you can work
- The pay you want
- Whether or not you have been convicted of a crime
- Your education
- Your previous work experience
- Your birth date

- Your driver's license number if you have one
- Your interests and hobbies, and awards you have won
- Your previous work experience, including dates
- Schools you have attended
- Places you have lived
- Accommodations you may need from the employer
- A list of references—people who will tell an employer that you will do a good job, such as relatives, students, former employers.

LETTERS OF RECOMMENDATION

Letters of recommendation are helpful. You can request teachers, counselors, relatives, and other acquaintances who know you well to write these letters. They should be short, to the point, and give a brief overview of your important accomplishments or projects. The letter should describe your character and work ethic.

LETTER OF APPLICATION

Some employees prefer a letter of application, rather than an application form. This letter is like writing a sales pitch about yourself. You need to tell why you are the best person for the job, what special qualifications you have, and include all the information usually found on an application form. Write the letter in standard English, making certain that it is neat, accurate, and correct.

RÉSUMÉ

The purpose of a résumé is to make an employer want to interview you. A résumé tells prospective employers what you are like and what you can do for them. A good résumé summarizes you at your best in a one- or two-page outline. It should include the following information:

1. **Identification** Include your name, address, telephone number, and e-mail address.
2. **Objective** Indicate the type of job you are looking for.
3. **Experience** List experience related to the specific job for which you are applying. List other work if you have not worked in a related field.

4. **Education** Include schools attended from high school on, the dates of attendance, and diplomas, degrees, licenses, or certifications earned. A professional certification is a designation earned by a person to assure qualification to perform a job or task. You may also include courses you are taking or have taken that are related to the job you are applying for.
5. **References** Include up to three references or indicate that they are available. Always ask people ahead of time if they are willing to be listed as references for you.

A résumé that you put online or send by e-mail is called an electronic résumé. Some Web sites allow you to post them on their sites without charge. Employers access these sites to find new employees. Your electronic résumé should follow the guidelines for a print résumé. It needs to be accurate. Stress your skills and sell yourself to prospective employers.

COVER LETTER

If you are going to get the job you want, you need to write a great cover letter to accompany your résumé. Think of a cover letter as an introduction: a piece of paper that conveys a smile, a confident hello, and a nice, firm handshake. The cover letter is the first thing a potential employer sees, and it can make a powerful impression. The following are some tips for creating a cover letter that is professional and gets the attention you want:

- **Keep it short.** Your cover letter should be one page, no more.
- **Make it look professional.** Key your letter on a computer and print it on a laser printer. Use white or buff-colored paper. Key your name, address, phone number, and e-mail address at the top of the page.
- **Explain why you are writing.** Start your letter with one sentence describing where you heard of the opening. "Joan Wright suggested I contact you regarding a position in your marketing department," or "I am writing to apply for the position you advertised in the Sun City Journal."

Career Skills

- **Introduce yourself.** Give a short description of your professional abilities and background. Refer to your attached résumé: "As you will see in the attached résumé, I am an experienced editor with a background in newspapers, magazines, and textbooks." Then highlight one or two specific accomplishments.

- **Sell yourself.** Your cover letter should leave the reader thinking, "This person is exactly who we are looking for." Focus on what you can do for the company. Relate your skills to the skills and responsibilities mentioned in the job listing. If the ad mentions solving problems, relate a problem you solved at school or work. If the ad mentions specific skills or knowledge required, mention your mastery of these in your letter. (Also be sure these skills are included on your résumé.)

- **Provide all requested information.** If the Help Wanted ad asked for "salary requirements" or "salary history," include this information in your cover letter. However, you do not have to give specific numbers. It is okay to say, "My wage is in the range of $10 to $15 per hour." If the employer does not ask for salary information, do not offer any.

- **Ask for an interview.** You have sold yourself, now wrap it up. Be confident, but not pushy. "If I would be an asset to your company, please call me at [insert your phone number]. I am available for an interview at your convenience." Finally, thank the person. "Thank you for your consideration. I look forward to hearing from you soon." Always close with a "Sincerely," followed by your full name and signature.

- **Check for errors.** Read and re-read your letter to make sure each sentence is correctly worded and there are no errors in spelling, punctuation, or grammar. Do not rely on your computer's spell checker or grammar checker. A spell check will not detect if you keyed "tot he" instead of "to the." It is a good idea to have someone else read your letter, too. He or she might notice an error you overlooked.

 **INTERVIEW**

Understanding how to prepare for and follow up on interviews is critical to your career success. At different times in your life, you may interview with a teacher or professor, a prospective employer, a supervisor, or a promotion or tenure committee. Just as having an excellent résumé is vital for opening the door, interview skills are critical for putting your best foot forward and seizing the opportunity to articulate why you are the best person for the job.

RESEARCH THE COMPANY

Your ability to convince an employer that you understand and are interested in the field you are interviewing to enter is important. Show that you have knowledge about the company and the industry. What products or services does the company offer? How is it doing? What is the competition? Use your research to demonstrate your understanding of the company.

PREPARE QUESTIONS FOR THE INTERVIEWER

Prepare interview questions to ask the interviewer. Some examples include:

- "What would my responsibilities be?"
- "Could you describe my work environment?"
- "What are the chances to move up in the company?"
- "Do you offer training?"
- "What can you tell me about the people who work here?"

DRESS APPROPRIATELY

Nonverbal communication is 90 percent of communication, so dressing appropriately is of the utmost importance. Wear clothing that is appropriate for the job for which you are applying. In most situations, you will be safe if you wear clean, pressed, conservative business clothes in neutral colors. Pay special attention to grooming. Keep makeup light and wear very little jewelry. Make certain your nails and hair are clean, trimmed, and neat. Do not carry a large purse, backpack, books, or coat. Simply carry a pad of paper, a pen, and extra copies of your résumé and letters of reference.

EXHIBIT GOOD BEHAVIOR

Conduct yourself properly during an interview. Go alone; be courteous and polite to everyone you meet. Relax and focus on your purpose: to make the best possible impression.

- Be on time.
- Be poised and relaxed.
- Avoid nervous habits.
- Avoid littering your speech with verbal clutter such as "you know," "um," and "like."
- Look your interviewer in the eye and speak with confidence.
- Use nonverbal techniques to reinforce your confidence, such as a firm handshake and poised demeanor.
- Convey maturity by exhibiting the ability to tolerate differences of opinion.
- Never call anyone by a first name unless you are asked to do so.
- Know the name, title, and the pronunciation of the interviewer's name.
- Do not sit down until the interviewer does.
- Do not talk too much about your personal life.
- Never bad-mouth your former employers.

BE PREPARED FOR COMMON INTERVIEW QUESTIONS

You can never be sure exactly what will happen at an interview, but you can be prepared for common interview questions. There are some interview questions that are illegal. Interviewers should not ask you about your age, gender, color, race, or religion. Employers should not ask whether you are a parent, married or pregnant, or question your health or disabilities.

Take time to think about your answers now. You might even write them down to clarify your thinking. The key to all interview questions is to be honest, and to be positive. Focus your answers on skills and abilities that apply to the job you are seeking. Practice answering the following questions with a friend:

- "Tell me about yourself."
- "Why do you want to work at this company?"

- "What did you like/dislike about your last job?"
- "What is your biggest accomplishment?"
- "What is your greatest strength?"
- "What is your greatest weakness?"
- "Do you prefer to work with others or on your own?"
- "What are your career goals?" or "Where do you see yourself in five years?"
- "Tell me about a time that you had a lot of work to do in a short time. How did you manage the situation?"
- "Have you ever had to work closely with a person you didn't get along with? How did you handle the situation?"

AFTER THE INTERVIEW

Be sure to thank the interviewer after the interview for his or her time and effort. Do not forget to follow up after the interview. Ask, "What is the next step?" If you are told to call in a few days, wait two or three days before calling back.

If the interview went well, the employer may call you to offer you the job. Find out the terms of the job offer, including job title and pay. Decide whether you want the job. If you decide not to accept the job, write a letter of rejection. Be courteous and thank the person for the opportunity and the offer. You may wish to give a brief general reason for not accepting the job. Leave the door open for possible employment in the future.

FOLLOW UP WITH A LETTER

Write a thank-you letter as soon as the interview is over. This shows your good manners, interest, and enthusiasm for the job. It also shows that you are organized. Make the letter neat and courteous. Thank the interviewer. Sell yourself again.

ACCEPTING A NEW JOB

If you decide to take the job, write a letter of acceptance. The letter should include some words of appreciation for the opportunity, written acceptance of the job offer, the terms of employment (salary, hours, benefits), and the starting date. Make sure the letter is neat and correct.

Career Skills

STARTING A NEW JOB

Your first day of work will be busy. Determine what the dress code is and dress appropriately. Learn to do each task assigned properly. Ask for help when you need it. Learn the rules and regulations of the workplace.

You will do some paperwork on your first day. Bring your personal fact sheet with you. You will need to fill out some forms. Form W-4 tells your employer how much money to withhold for taxes. You may also need to fill out Form I-9. This shows that you are allowed to work in the United States. You will need your Social Security number and proof that you are allowed to work in the United States. You can bring your U.S. passport, your Certificate of Naturalization, or your Certificate of U.S. Citizenship. If you are not a permanent resident of the United States, bring your green card. If you are a resident of the United States, you will need to bring your work permit on your first day. If you are under the age of 16 in some states, you need a different kind of work permit.

You might be requested to take a drug test as a requirement for employment in some states. This could be for the safety of you and your coworkers, especially when working with machinery or other equipment.

EMPLOYABILITY SKILLS

You will need employability skills to succeed in a rapidly evolving workplace environment. These skills include personal and interpersonal skills, such as functioning effectively as part of a team and demonstrating leadership skills, no matter what position you are in. There are also certain qualities and behaviors that are needed to be a good employee:

- Attend work regularly.
- Be prompt.
- Make the most productive use of your time.
- Be cooperative, responsible, and honest.
- Obey company rules.
- Have a positive attitude.
- Show enthusiasm and pride.
- Tolerate differences.
- Be open-minded.

- Show respect.
- Be flexible.
- Take initiative.
- Be willing to learn new skills.
- Listen attentively.
- Use an appropriate voice.
- Demonstrate planning and time-management skills.
- Keep your workplace clean and safe.
- Understand the legal and ethical responsibilities related to your job.
- Understand the relationship between health and achievement.
- Understand and avoid the implications of substance abuse.

LEAVING A JOB

If you are considering leaving your job or are being laid off, you are facing one of the most difficult aspects in your career. The first step in resigning is to prepare a short resignation letter to offer your supervisor at the conclusion of the meeting you set up with him or her. Keep the letter short and to the point. Express your appreciation for the opportunity you had with the company. Do not try to list all that was wrong with the job.

You want to leave on good terms. Do not forget to ask for a reference. Do not talk about your employer or any of your coworkers. Do not talk negatively about your employer when you apply for a new job.

If you are being laid off or face downsizing, it can make you feel angry or depressed. Try to view it as a career-change opportunity. If possible, negotiate a good severance package. Find out about any benefits to which you may be entitled. Perhaps the company will offer services for finding new employment.

TAKE ACTION!

It is time for action. Remember the networking and contact lists you created when you searched for this job. Reach out for support from friends, family, and other acquaintances. Consider joining a job-search club. Assess your skills. Upgrade them if necessary. Examine your attitude and your career choices. Decide the direction you wish to take and move on!

BUILD YOUR COLLEGE AND CAREER PORTFOLIO

A college and career portfolio is a collection of information about a person, including documents, projects, and work samples that showcase a person's academic and professional skills, talents, accomplishments, and qualifications. It includes the information needed for a job search or for applying for college. Your portfolio can be a paper portfolio in a folder, a digital portfolio with electronic files, or a combination of both. You can use your college and career portfolio throughout your life to keep track of your academic and career goals and accomplishments.

- **Personal Fact Sheet** When you apply for a job, you will probably fill out an application that asks for information that may not be on your résumé. For that reason you should include a personal fact sheet in your college and career portfolio. Include all of the items listed on pages 600–601.

- **Evaluate Yourself** The information you know about yourself can help you choose a career that is right for you. Update your self-evaluation periodically to make sure you are on the right path.

- **Conduct Career Research** Create a section for your portfolio called Career Research. Include information about career clusters and careers that interest you and sources of information you find helpful. Also include notes from career interviews and career evaluations. Update the Career Research section of your portfolio as you continue to explore your career options.

- **Prepare a Career Plan** After you have made a career decision, you can make a career plan. Create a section for your portfolio called career plan. Your first step in making your career plan is setting a career goal. Then you can set the short-term goals, medium-term goals, and long-term goals that will lead you to your career goal. Include goals related to education or training and other experiential learning. Review, update, or create new career plans as you continue to explore your career options.

- **Résumé and Cover Letter** Your college and career portfolio should include your résumé and a sample cover letter that you can use when following up job leads. When you find a job that interests you, note the qualifications required. Then customize your cover letter and résumé so that they are tailored to the job. Relate the skills you have to the skills required for the job.

- **Develop References** You should supply references when you apply for a job. You may also need them when applying for college. Include a list of your references in your college and career portfolio. Include each person's name, title and company, address, phone number, and e-mail address. If your references will provide written letters of reference, include copies in your portfolio. People to ask include former managers, teachers, counselors, or other trusted adults in the community who can comment on your reliability and attitude.

- **Showcase Your Technology Skills** The best way to show an employer what you know about technology is by demonstrating your technology skills! As you research the career that interests you, take note of the hardware, software, and other technology tools that are current in the field. Then, learn to use the technologies and include examples that show your mastery of these tools in your college and career portfolio. Include a list of hardware and software that you know how to use.

- **Awards, Honors, and Certifications** If you have received awards or honors, include any relevant information about them in your college and career portfolio. Also, if you have any licenses or certifications related to your continuing education or job search, also include these in your portfolio.

Career Skills

REVIEW KEY CONCEPTS

1. What are the five steps to making a career decision?

2. What three types of goals should a career plan include?

3. Why is a personal fact sheet useful?

4. What are employability skills?

5. What is the role of professional certifications in a career search?

6. What is the role of a career and college portfolio?

7. What are the functions of résumés and portfolios?

8. Why is it important to demonstrate leadership skills?

9. What are five positive work qualities?

10. What are three questions you should be prepared to answer in a job interview?

CRITICAL THINKING

11. Compare and contrast the role of a résumé and a cover letter.

12. Analyze why your career choice might change as you get older.

13. Predict the consequences of choosing a career that conflicts with your personal values.

14. Evaluate how tracking employment trends and technology trends can help you manage your own career.

15. Explain why it is important to think critically, demonstrate strong communication skills, and function effectively as part of a team in order to be successful in the workplace.

16. Analyze the importance of time management and project management skills in your chosen career field. Explain your answer.

CHALLENGE YOURSELF!

17. Imagine that you have been asked to work on a project team either at school or where you work.

    - Think about the leadership and teamwork skills that you would need to be a successful member of the project team.

    - Demonstrate your knowledge of leadership and teamwork skills by creating a checklist that outlines what these skills are.

    - Work with a partner to identify how you would demonstrate these skills and behaviors in a work or school environment. Relate the skills to the "Employability Skills" section elsewhere in this handbook. For example, offering to perform a task that another team member cannot complete may demonstrate initiative and support for a fellow team member.

18. Research careers of personal interest to you. Look at career Web sites to find job opportunities and accompanying duties.

    - Find out what type of education, certification, job training, and experience are required to meet your career goals.

    - Create a five-year plan that breaks down your goals.

    - What do you need to do now in order to meet your goals? What will you need to do next year? How will you assess your progress?

Glossary

accounting period A block of time, such as a month, a quarter, or a year, covered by an accounting report. (p. 463)

accounts payable The amount a business owes to creditors. (p. 464)

accounts receivable The amount customers owe a business. (p. 464)

accrual basis An accounting system in which income is recorded when it is earned, and expenses are recorded when they are paid. (p. 466)

achiever A person with a record of success. (p. 42)

advertising The paid nonpersonal presentation of ideas, goods, or services directed at a mass audience by an identified sponsor by means of print and broadcast. (p. 278)

advertising agency A company that acts as intermediary between a business and the media to communicate a message to the target market. (p. 290)

angel A private, nonprofessional investor, such as a friend, a relative, or a business associate, who funds start-up companies. (p. 443)

appointments The furniture, equipment, and accessories contained in a building. (p. 212)

approach A salesperson's first contact with a customer. (p. 307)

asset Anything of value that a business owns, such as cash, equipment, or building. (p. 464)

automation The use of machines to do the work of people. (p. 385)

bait-and-switch advertising A deceptive and illegal method of selling in which a customer, attracted to a store by an advertised sale, is told either that the advertised item is unavailable or is inferior to a higher-priced item that is available. (p. 186)

balance sheet A report of the final balances of all asset, liability, and owner's equity accounts at the end of an accounting period. (p. 473)

barriers to entry A condition or circumstance that makes it difficult or costly for outside firms to enter a market to compete with established firm or firms. (p. 140)

beneficiary A person who receives value in terms of monetary or other value by circumstances represented in a legal document, i.e., will, insurance policy, etc. (p. 107)

benefit Something that promotes or enhances the value of a product or a service to the customer. (p. 106)

benefits Any extra compensation that workers receive on a job, such as paid vacation and sick days, flextime, and child care. (p. 407)

"best prospect" list A list compiled by the government of products that other countries are looking to purchase. (p. 87)

bootstrapping Operating a business as frugally as possible and cutting all unnecessary expenses, such as borrowing, leasing, and partnering to acquire resources. (p. 441)

brainstorm To think freely in order to generate ideas. (p. 58)

brand The name, symbol, or design used to identify a product. (p. 227)

brand loyalty The tendency to buy a particular brand of a product. (p. 140)

break-even point The point at which the gain from an economic activity equals the costs involved in pursuing it. (p. 262)

bribe A payment made to secure special services for a business or special consideration for its products; illegal in the United States, it is accepted in some other parts of the world as a part of doing business. (p. 563)

budget A formal, written statement of expected revenue and expenses for a future period. (p. 496)

Glossary

bundle pricing A pricing technique in which several complementary products are sold at a single price, which is lower than the price would be if each item was purchased separately. (p. 259)

burglary The act of breaking into and entering a building with the intent to commit a felony (a serious crime). (p. 515)

business broker Someone whose job it is to bring buyers and sellers of businesses together for a fee. (p. 69)

business concept A clear and concise description of a business opportunity. It contains four elements: the product or service, the customer, the benefit, and the distribution. (p. 105)

business cycle The general pattern of expansion and contraction that the economy goes through. (p. 16)

business ethics The study of behavior and morals in a business situation. (p. 559)

business failure A business that has stopped operating, with a loss to creditors, and one that no longer appears on the tax rolls. (p. 24)

business interruption insurance Insurance coverage against potential losses that result from having to close a business for insurable reasons; insurance pays net profits and expenses while a business is shut down for repairs or rebuilding. (p. 523)

business model A description of how entrepreneurs plan to make money with their business concepts. (p. 111)

business plan A document that describes a new business and a strategy to launch that business. (p. 113)

buying process A series of steps a customer goes through when making a purchase. (p. 306)

calendar year The accounting period of time from January 1 to December 31. (p. 464)

campaign A series of related promotional activities with a similar theme. (p. 276)

capacity The legal ability to enter into a binding agreement. (p. 178) A borrower's ability to repay a debt as judged by lenders. (p. 450)

capital The buildings, equipment, tools, and other goods needed to produce a product or the money used to buy these items. (p. 36) The net worth of a business, the amount by which its assets exceed its liabilities. (p. 450)

capital expenditure A long-term commitment of a large sum of money to buy new equipment or replace old equipment. (p. 498)

carrying capacity The ability of industry to support new growth. (p. 131)

cash basis An accounting system in which income is recorded when it is received, and expenses are recorded when they are paid. (p. 466)

cash discount An amount deducted from the selling price for payment within a specified time period. (p. 358)

cash flow The amount of cash available to a business at any given time. (p. 473)

casualty insurance Insurance coverage for loss or liability arising from a sudden, unexpected event such as an accident and for the cost of defending a business in court against claims of property damage. (p. 523)

C-corporation An entity that pays taxes on earnings; its shareholders pay taxes as well. (p. 159)

census tract A small geographic area into which a state or country is divided for the purpose of gathering and reporting census data (p. 198)

channel of distribution The path a product takes from producer or manufacturer to final user or consumer. (p. 229)

character A borrower's reputation for fair and ethical practices, including business experience, dealings with other businesses, and reputation in the community. (p. 450)

chart of accounts The list of accounts a business uses in its operation. (p. 465)

climate A prevailing atmosphere or attitude in a business. (p. 338)

Glossary

code of ethics A group of ethical behavior guidelines that govern the day-to-day activities of a profession or organization. (p. 561)

collateral Security in the form of assets that a company pledges to a lender. (p. 450)

commission A fee for services rendered based on a percentage of an amount sold; payment is based on sales alone. (p. 316)

common carrier A firm that provides transportation services at uniform rates to the general public. (p. 386)

communication The process of exchanging information. (p. 339)

comparative financial statement A financial statement with financial data from two accounting periods used as an analysis tool by a business owner. (p. 487)

competition The rivalry among businesses for consumer dollars. (p. 34)

competitive advantage A feature that makes a product more desirable than its competitors'. (p. 142)

competitive matrix A tool for organizing important information about a business venture's competition. (p. 109)

complexity The number and diversity of contacts with which you must deal. In business, firms that operate in complex industries have more suppliers, customers, and competitors than firms in other industries. (p. 132)

conceptual skill A skill that enables a manager to understand concepts, ideas, and principles. (p. 345)

conditions The circumstances at the time of the loan request, including potential for growth, amount of competition, location, form of ownership, and insurance. (p. 450)

conflict of interest A clash between a person's private interests and his or her responsibilities in a position of trust. (p. 562)

conglomerate diversification A diversification growth strategy in which a business seeks products or businesses that are totally unrelated to its own products or business. (p. 539)

consideration What is exchanged for the promise to do something or refrain from doing something and causes a contract to be binding. (p. 178)

consumer pretest A procedure in which a panel of consumers evaluate an ad before its release. (p. 292)

contingency fund An extra amount of money that is saved and used only when absolutely necessary, such as for unforeseen business expenses. (p. 454)

contract A binding legal agreement between two or more persons or parties. (p. 177)

contract carrier A shipping company that transports freight under contract with one or more shippers. (p. 386)

controlling The process of comparing expected results (objectives) with actual performance. (p. 336)

cooperative advertising An arrangement in which advertising costs are divided between two or more parties. (p. 290)

copyright A legal device that protects original works of authors, including books, movies, musical compositions, and computer software, for the life of the author plus 70 years. (p. 176)

corporate venture A new venture started inside a larger corporation. (p. 56)

corporation A business that is registered by a state and operates apart from its owners. It issues shares of stock and lives on after the owners have sold their interest or passed away. Corporations can purchase goods and services, sue and be sued, and conduct all types of business transactions. (p. 159)

cost effective Economically worthwhile in terms of what is achieved for the amount of money spent. (p. 419)

credit An arrangement for deferred payment for goods and services; credit allows a business or individual to obtain products in exchange for a promise to pay later. (p. 398) An addition to the right side of an account that decreases the balance for all assets and expense accounts and increases the balance for all liability and revenue accounts. (p. 466)

Glossary 609

Glossary

credit bureau An agency that collects information for a fee on how promptly people and businesses pay their bills. (p. 499)

current asset Cash or any other item that can be converted to cash quickly and used by a business within a year. (p. 464)

current ratio The comparison of current assets (cash or other items that can be converted to cash quickly) and current liabilities (debts due within a year), used to indicate the ability of a business to pay its bills. (p. 488)

customer benefit An advantage of personal satisfaction that a customer will get from a product. (p. 304)

customer needs analysis A study that pinpoints the features and benefits of goods or services that customers value. (p. 143)

customer profile A complete picture of a venture's prospective customers, including geographic, demographic, and psychographic data. (p. 142)

debit An addition to the left side of an account that increases the balance of all assets and expense accounts and decreases the balance of all liability and revenue accounts. (p. 466)

debt capital Money raised by taking out loans, which must be repaid with interest. (p. 444)

debt ratio The measurement of the percentage of total dollars in a business that is provided by creditors. (p. 490)

demand The quantity of goods or services that consumers are willing and able to buy at various prices. (p. 12)

demographics Personal characteristics that describe a population by age, gender, income, ethnic background, education, and occupation, among others. (p. 60)

descriptive research The collection of information to determine the status of something, such as in developing a customer profile. The information may include age, gender, occupation, income, and buying habits and can be collected through questionnaires, interviews, or observations. (p. 135)

development activity An action, such as an industry conference, that prepares managers to lead the company into the future. (p. 419)

diminishing marginal utility The effect or law that establishes that price alone does not determine demand, and other factors, such as income, taste, and the amount of product already owned, play a role as well. (p. 13)

direct channel The means of delivering a service or product directly to the customer, such as via a Web site. (p. 117)

directing The process of guiding and supervising employees, often one-on-one, while they work. (p. 336)

discontinuance A business that disappears from the tax rolls because it may be operating under a new name or because the owner has purposely discontinued in order to start a new business. (p. 24)

discount pricing A pricing technique that offers customers reductions from the regular price; some reductions are basic percentage-off discounts and others are specialized discounts. (p. 259)

disposable income Money people have to spend after paying for necessary expenses. (p. 88)

distribution channel The means by which a product or service is delivered to the customer. (p. 117)

diversification The process of investing in products or businesses with which an existing business is not currently involved. (p. 242)

diversification growth strategy A growth strategy that involves investing in products or businesses that are different from a company's own products, using synergistic, horizontal, or conglomerate diversification. (p. 538)

due diligence The investigation and analysis a prudent investor does before making business decisions. (p. 451)

 E

economic base A major source of income usually characterized as "primarily industrial," "primarily service-oriented," or by another category that indicates the main source of income. (p. 197)

economics The study of how people allocate scarce resources to fulfill their unlimited wants. (p. 7)

economy of scale A situation where the cost of producing one unit of a good or service decreases as the volume of production increases; the decrease of production costs relative to the price of goods and services. (p. 140)

educational activity An action, such as a human relations workshop, that prepares employees for advancing in the organization. (p. 419)

elastic demand Situations in which a change in price creates a change in demand. (p. 13)

electronic credit card authorizer A machine that verifies whether a credit card is good, that is, not stolen or invalid. (p. 516)

emotional buying motive A feeling a buyer associates with a product, such as recognition or prestige. (p. 305)

employee complaint procedure A formal procedure for handling employee complaints, usually in writing and distributed to employees. (p. 421)

employee stock option plan (ESOP) A source of financing in which a company gives its employees the opportunity to buy a portion of the business; to raise money with an ESOP, a business must have at least 25 employees and revenues of $5 million. (p. 544)

enterprise zones Specially designated areas of a community that provide tax benefits to new businesses locating there; communities may also provide grants for new product development. (p. 22)

entrepreneur An individual who undertakes the creation, organization, and ownership of a business. (p. 7)

entrepreneurship The process of recognizing an opportunity, testing it in the market, and gathering resources necessary to go into business. (p. 7)

Environmental Protection Agency (EPA) An independent federal agency established to coordinate programs and enforce regulations aimed at reducing pollution and protecting the environment. (p. 555)

Equal Employment Opportunity Commission (EEOC) The government agency charged with protecting the rights of employees; it ensures that employers do not discriminate against employees because of age, race, color or natural origin, religion, gender, or physical challenge. (p. 181)

equilibrium The point at which consumers buy all of a product that is supplied. At this point, there is neither a surplus nor a shortage. (p. 14)

equity An ownership in a business. (p. 443)

equity capital Cash raised for a business in exchange for an ownership stake in the business. (p. 443)

errors and omissions insurance Insurance coverage for any loss sustained because of an error or oversight on a business's part, such as a mistake in advertising. (p. 523)

ethical behavior Conduct that adheres to the moral code by which people live and conduct business. (p. 559)

ethics Guidelines for human behavior; the moral code by which people live and conduct business. (p. 559)

exclusive distribution Placement of a product where its number of sales outlets are limited to one per area. (p. 230)

executive summary A brief recounting of the key points contained in a business plan. (p. 114)

Glossary

exploratory research The initial collection and analysis of information used when very little is known about a subject; it forms a foundation for later research. (p. 135)

export management company An organization that handles all the tasks related to exporting for a manufacturer. (p. 90)

exporting The selling and shipping of goods to other countries. (p. 79)

F

façade The face or front of a building. (p. 212)

factor An agent who handles an entrepreneur's accounts receivable for a fee. (p. 441)

factors of production The resources businesses use to produce the goods and services that people want. (p. 11)

family leave A policy that allows employees to take time off work to attend to significant personal events, such a births, deaths, and family illness, without fear of job loss. (p. 426)

feasibility analysis The process that tests a business concept; it allows the entrepreneur to decide whether a new business concept has potential. (p. 107)

feature A distinctive aspect, quality, or characteristic of a product or service. (p. 106)

FICA (Federal Insurance Contributions Act) A Social Security payroll tax, figured as a percentage of an employee's income; an employer is required to contribute an amount equal to the amount deducted from each employee's paycheck. (p. 186)

fidelity bond A form of insurance that protects a company in case of employee theft. (p. 523)

financial report A statement or document that summarizes the results of a business operation and provides a picture of its financial position. (p. 463)

financing cost The cost of interest paid to borrow money. (p. 362)

fiscal year The accounting period of time that begins and ends in months other than the calendar year. (p. 464)

fixed Costs and expenses that are not subject to change depending on the number of units sold. (p. 251)

fixed asset Any item that will be held by a business for more than one year, such as equipment, a truck, or a building. (p. 464)

fixed expense A business expense that does not change with number of units produced, such as insurance and rent. (p. 495)

flextime A policy that allows employees to choose the work hours and days that are most effective for their personal lives. (p. 426)

focus group A group of people whose opinions are studied to determine the opinions that can be expected from a larger population. (p. 135)

foreign joint venture An alliance between an American small business and a company in another nation. (p. 90)

foundation skills The skills used in all jobs and when setting up and running a business. (p. 39)

franchise A legal agreement to begin a new business in the name of a recognized company. (p. 67)

franchisee The buyer of a franchise who is given the right to its product, process, or service. The buyer receives the way of operating a business and a product with name recognition. (p. 67)

franchisor The seller of a franchise who is giving the buyer its planning and management expertise. (p. 67)

free enterprise system An economic system in which people have important rights: to make economic choices of what products to buy, to own private property, and to choose to start a business and compete with other businesses. (p. 9)

Free on board (FOB) A delivery term that designates a shipment as delivered free of charge to a buyer. (p. 388)

freight forwarder A company that arranges shipments and prepares necessary exporting paperwork. (p. 90)

Glossary

GAAP Generally accepted accounting principles established to allow all businesses to use the same system of recording and reporting financial information. (p. 463)

Gantt chart A graphic schedule of a project's phases, activities, and tasks plotted against a time line. (p. 382)

general journal An all-purpose journal that records any business transaction. (p. 467)

general partner A participant in a partnership who has unlimited personal liability and takes full responsibility for managing the business; all partnerships must have at least one general partner. (p. 155)

geographics The study of the market based on where customers live, including region, state, country, city, and/or area. (p. 133)

global economy The interconnected economies of the nations of the world. (p. 79)

goods Tangible (or physical) products of our economic system that satisfy consumers' wants and needs. (p. 11)

goodwill The favor and loyalty a business acquires by its good reputation. (p. 67)

Gross Domestic Product (GDP) The total market value of all goods and services produced by workers and capital within a nation during a given period. (pp. 15, 81)

guarantee An assurance of the quality of a product. (p. 240)

historical research The study of the past to explain present circumstances and predict future trends. (p. 136)

horizontal diversification A diversification growth strategy that involves seeking products that are technologically unrelated to a company's own products or business. (p. 538)

horizontal integration Increasing a business's market share and expanding by buying up competitors. (p. 538)

human relations The study of how people relate to each other. (p. 342)

human resource management The part of business concerned with recruiting and managing employees; the main goals are to facilitate performance and improve productivity. (p. 417)

human resources The people employed in a business, commonly referred to as personnel. (p. 417)

hygiene factor A factor that does not improve a situation, but keeps situations from getting worse. (p. 425)

image The impression people have of a company; a company's personality. (p. 275) The mental picture and feelings people have when thinking about a business or its products or services. (p. 338)

importing The buying or bringing in goods from other countries to sell. (p. 79)

incentive A reward or advantage that helps businesses, including lower taxes, cheaper land, and employee training programs. (p. 198)

income statement A report of the revenue, expenses, and net income or loss for the accounting period. (p. 472)

incubator An enterprise that is set up to provide flexible and affordable leases, office space, equipment, management assistance, mentoring assistance, and access to financing for new businesses. (p. 204)

indirect channel The means of delivering a service or product indirectly to the customer, such as through a wholesaler. (p. 117)

industrial market A group of customers who buy goods or services for business use. (p. 133)

industrial park An area set aside in a community for industrial use. (p. 201)

industry A collection of businesses with a common line of products or services. (pp. 107, 131)

Glossary

industry average The standard used to compare costs among companies; usually expressed as a percentage. (p. 288)

inelastic demand Situations in which a change in price has little or no effect on demand for products. (p. 13)

initial public offering (IPO) The sale of stock in a company on a public stock exchange. (p. 452)

innovation A new way of doing things; a new idea, method, or device. (p. 57)

insurance cost The cost associated with insuring inventory. (p. 362)

integrative growth strategy A growth strategy that allows a company to expand within the industry by growing vertically or horizontally. (p. 537)

intellectual property law The group of laws that regulate the ownership and use of creative works. (p. 173)

intensive distribution Placement of a product in all suitable sales outlets. (p. 230)

intermediary A person or business that is involved in the process of moving a product from the manufacturer or producers to the final users, including wholesalers, retailers, distributors, and agents. (p. 229)

International Business Exchange (IBEX) The electronic commerce system that allows businesses to sell products and services online anywhere in the world. (p. 87)

interpreter A person who translates one language into or from another. (p. 86)

investment The amount of money a person puts into his or her business as capital. (p. 36)

invoice An itemized statement of money owed for goods shipped or services rendered. (p. 360)

J

job description A statement that describes the objectives of a job and its duties and responsibilities (p. 404)

job specification A document that details the abilities, skills, educational level, and experience needed by an employee to perform a job. (p. 404)

journal A financial diary of a business. (p. 467)

journalizing The process of recording business transactions, usually on a daily basis as they occur. (p. 467)

L

label The part of the package used to present information about the product. (p. 227)

labor union An organization that represents workers in their dealings with employers. (p. 418)

layout A floor plan or map that shows the interior and exterior arrangement of a business, including such items as display cases, lighting fixtures, traffic patterns, landscaping, and parking spaces. (p. 206)

lead time The gap in time between placing an order and receiving delivery. (p. 368)

liability A debt of a business. (p. 464)

liability protection Insurance against debt and actions of a business. (p. 153)

license A certificate that shows that the holder of the document has the necessary education and training to perform a job. (p. 177)

limited liability Partial responsibility of a corporate shareholder; he or she is responsible only up to the amount of the individual investment. (p. 161)

limited liability company (LLC) A company whose owners and managers have limited liability and some tax benefits, but avoids some restrictions associated with Subchapter S corporations. (p. 162)

Glossary

limited partner A partner in a business whose liability is limited to his or her investment; a limited partner cannot be actively involved in managing the business. (p. 156)

line of credit An arrangement whereby a lender agrees to lend up to a specific amount of money at a certain interest rate for a specific period of time. (p. 445)

line organization A form of business organization where managers are responsible for accomplishing the main objectives of the business and are in the direct chain of command. Top management makes the decisions that affect the entire company; middle management implements the decisions; supervisory, or first-line, management supervises the activities of employees; and employees carry out the plans made by top and middle management. (p. 403)

line-and-staff organization A form of business organization that incorporates staff into line organization. (p. 404)

logistics The planning, execution, and control of the movement and placement of people and/or goods, part of distribution management. (p. 386)

M

manager A person who is responsible for directing and controlling the work and personnel of a business, or a particular department within a business. (p. 333)

markdown The amount of money taken off an original price. (p. 264)

market A group of people or companies who have a demand for a product or service and are willing and able to buy it. (p. 132)

market development An attempt by a business to reach new locations for its products. (p. 536)

market penetration An attempt to increase sales in a business's current market. (p. 535)

market positioning The act of identifying a specific market niche for a product. (p. 142)

market research The collection and analysis of information aimed at understanding the behavior of consumers in a certain market. (p. 135)

market segment Subgroup of buyers with similar characteristics, segmented by geographics, demographics, psychographics, and buying characteristics. (p. 132)

market segmentation The process of grouping a market into smaller subgroups defined by specific characteristics. (p. 132)

market share A portion of the total sales generated by all competing companies in a given market. (p. 142)

market structure The nature and degree of competition among businesses operating in the same industry; market structure affects market price. (p. 10)

marketing mix The five marketing strategies used to reach a market: product, place, price, promotion, and people. (p. 226)

marketing objective What a business wants to accomplish through its marketing efforts, such as market share, projected profitability, and pricing. (p. 225)

marketing plan A plan used by a business to guide its marketing process to a desired conclusion based on information obtained through market research and target market decisions. (p. 225)

marketing tactic An activity that needs to be taken to carry out a marketing plan; part of an action plan. (p. 235)

markup The amount added to the cost of an item to cover expenses and ensure a profit. (p. 263)

mission statement A declaration of the specific aspirations of a company, the major goals for which it will strive. (p. 115)

model inventory A target inventory of what a business thinks it will need to keep in stock. (p. 355)

monopoly A market structure in which a particular commodity has only one seller. (p. 10)

morale A state of an individual psychological well-being based on a sense of confidence, usefulness, and purpose. (p. 319)

Glossary

motivating factor A factor that motivates employees, such as achievement, recognition, responsibility, advancement, growth, and the reward from doing the work itself. (p. 425)

multiple-unit pricing A pricing technique in which items are priced in multiples, such as 3 items for 99 cents. (p. 258)

need A basic requirement for survival. (p. 11)

negligence The failure to exercise reasonable care. (p. 519)

net profit on sales ratio The number of cents left from each dollar of sales after expenses and income taxes are paid. (p. 491)

networking The process of building and maintaining informal relationships with people whose acquaintance could bring about business opportunities. (p. 343)

new venture organization The infrastructure or foundation that supports all the products, processes, and services of a new business. (p. 23)

news release A brief newsworthy story that is sent to the media. (p. 280)

niche A small, specialized segment of the market based on customer needs discovered in market research. (p. 57, 142)

nonprofit corporation A legal entity that makes money for reasons other than the owner's profit. It can make a profit, but the profit must remain within the company and not be distributed to shareholders. (p. 162)

nonverbal communication Communication not involving words, transmitted through actions and behaviors, such as facial expressions, gestures, posture, and eye contact. (p. 342)

objection Any concern, hesitation, doubt, or other reason a customer has for not making a purchase. (p. 307)

obsolescence cost The cost associated with products or materials that become obsolete while in inventory. (p. 362)

odd/even pricing A pricing technique in which odd-numbered prices are used to suggest bargains, such as $19.99. (p. 258)

oligopoly A market structure in which there are just a few competing firms. (p. 11)

online business A company that conducts business by means of the Internet. (p. 53)

operating capital Money a business uses to support its operations in the short term. (p. 445)

operating ratio The relationship between each expense and total sales as reported on the income statement. (p. 491)

operational plan A short-term objective that helps achieve a tactical plan, including policies, rules and regulations, and budgets for day-to-day operations. (p. 334)

opportunity An idea that has commercial value when consumers are ready and willing to buy that product. (p. 22)

opportunity cost The cost associated with giving up the use of money tied up in inventory. (p. 362)

order getting Seeking out buyers and giving them a well-organized presentation; sometimes referred to as "creative selling." (p. 303)

order taking The completion of a sale to a customer who has sought out a product. (p. 303)

organizing The grouping of resources in combinations that will help you reach your objectives. (p. 335)

outsourcing Hiring people and other companies to handle tasks a business can not do or chooses not to do itself. (p. 55)

owner's equity The total amount of assets minus total liabilities; the worth of a business. (p. 464)

package The physical container or wrapper used to present information. (p. 227)

partnership An unincorporated business with two or more owners who share the decisions, assets, liabilities, and profits. (p. 155)

patent A document that grants to an inventor the right to exclude others from making, using, or selling an invention or other intellectual property during the term of the patent. (p. 174)

patent pending The status of an invention between the time a patent application has been filed and when it is issued or rejected. (p. 175)

penetration pricing A method used to build sales by charging a low initial price to keep unit costs to customers as low as possible. (p. 257)

performance bond Insurance coverage that protects a business if work or a contract is not finished on time or as agreed. (p. 523)

performance evaluation The process of judging how well an employee has performed the duties and responsibilities associated with a job. (p. 427)

permit A legal document giving official permission to run a business. (p. 177)

personal selling Selling conducted by direct communication with a prospective customer. (p. 303)

PERT diagram A project schedule that is arranged in a diagram used for scheduling more-complex projects. (p. 383)

philanthropy The act of making charitable donations to improve the welfare of society. (p. 553)

piece rate A means of compensation based on an amount per unit produced. (p. 407)

planning The act of setting goals, developing strategies, and outlining tasks and timelines to meet those goals. (p. 334)

policy A statement of guiding principles and procedures that serves as a guideline for daily business operations and supports the company's goals and objectives. (p. 397)

posting The process of transferring amounts from the general journal to accounts in the general ledger. (p. 469)

preapproach The marketing activities that precede a salesperson's approach to a prospective customer that are intended to help achieve a successful sale. (p. 306)

Pregnancy Discrimination Act A federal law that requires that employers treat their pregnant employees like all other employees when determining benefits. (p. 421)

premium Any item of value that a customer receives in addition to the good or service purchased; designed to attract new customers or build loyalty among existing customers, they may include coupons and gifts. (p. 281) The price of insurance a person or business pays for a specified risk for a specified time. (p. 522)

preselling The act of influencing potential customers to buy before contact is actually made. (p. 276)

prestige pricing A pricing technique in which higher-than-average prices are used to suggest status and prestige to the customer. (p. 258)

price discrimination The charging of different prices for the same product or service in different markets or to different customers. (p. 183)

price fixing An illegal practice in which competing companies agree, formally or informally, to restrict prices within a specified range. (p. 252)

price gouging Pricing above the market when no other retailer is available. (p. 252)

price lining A pricing technique in which items in a certain category are priced the same. (p. 258)

price skimming The practice of charging a high price on a new product or service in order to recover costs and maximize profits as quickly as possible; the price is then dropped when the product or service is no longer unique. (p. 257)

primary data Information that is collected for the first time, is current, and relates directly to the collector's study. (p. 137)

private brand A brand that is owned and initiated by a wholesaler or retailer. (p. 240)

private carrier A business that operates vehicles primarily for the purpose of transporting its own products and materials. (p. 386)

Glossary

private placement A private offering or sale of securities directly to a limited number of institutional investors who meet certain suitability standards; ownership interests are called securities. (pp. 452, 543)

pro forma Proposed or estimated financial statements based on predictions of how the actual operations of the business will turn out. (p. 448)

product development The process of creating new or improved products, involving taking an idea for a product, designing it, building a model, and testing it. (p. 377)

product liability insurance Insurance coverage that protects a business from injury claims that result from use of the business's products. (p. 523)

product mix All the products a company makes or sells. (p. 228)

product positioning How consumers see a product in comparison to another product, achieved through quality, availability, pricing, and uses. (p. 228)

productivity A measure of how much a business produces in a given time, or the output of each worker per unit of time. (p. 385)

profile A set of characteristics or qualities that identifies a type or category of person. (p. 41)

profit Money that is left over after all expenses of running a business have been deducted from the income. (p. 9)

project organization A temporary organization brought together from different parts of a business for a special project. (p. 404)

promotional mix The combination of different promotional elements that a company uses to reach and influence potential customers. (p. 276)

promotional pricing A pricing technique in which lower prices are offered for a limited period of time to stimulate sales. (p. 258)

prospect A potential customer. (p. 303)

prospecting A systematic approach to developing new sales leads or customers, who are identified through referrals, public records, or surveys. (p. 306)

prospectus A formal document that details risks involving in the private offering; its purpose is to give investors the information they need to make informed decisions. (p. 543)

prototype A working model used by entrepreneurs to determine what it takes to develop their products or services. (pp. 107, 378)

psychographics The study of consumers based on social and psychological characteristics, including personality, values, opinions, beliefs, motivations, attitudes, and lifestyle elements. (p. 133)

psychological pricing A pricing technique, most often used by retail businesses, that is based on the belief that customers' perceptions of a product are strongly influenced by price; it includes prestige pricing, odd/even pricing, price lining, promotional pricing, multiple-unit pricing, and bundle pricing. (p. 258)

public domain Intellectual property whose protection has expired; it belongs to the community at large and people can use any aspect of the property free of charge. (p. 174)

public relations Activities designed to create goodwill toward a business or control damage done by negative publicity. (p. 281)

public stock offering The sale of shares of stock on a public stock exchange. (p. 544)

publicity Placement in the media of newsworthy items about a company, product, or person. (p. 280)

purchasing Also known as procurement, the buying of all the materials needed by the organization. (p. 355)

pure risk The threat of a loss to a business without any possibility of gain, such as robbery or employee theft. (p. 513)

quality circle A small group of employees who do similar jobs and meet regularly to identify ways to improve the quality of what they do. (p. 384)

quality control The process of making sure the goods or services a business produces meet certain standards, such as appearance, performance, and consistency. (p. 383)

quality control program A set of measures built into the production process to make sure that products or services meet certain standards and performance requirements. (p. 337)

quantity discount A discount that a vendor gives to a buyer who places large orders. (p. 358)

quick ratio A measure of the relationship between short-term liquid assets, which include cash and accounts receivable, and current liabilities. (p. 491)

ratio analysis The comparison of two or more amounts on a financial statement and the evaluation of the relationship between these two amounts, used to determine the financial strength, activity, or bill-paying ability of a business. (p. 488)

rational buying motive A conscious, logical reason to make a purchase, such as convenience or comfort. (p. 305)

rebate A return of part of the purchase price of a product used as an incentive for customers to purchase the product. (p. 281)

recruit To bring in prospective employees; businesses use classified ads, employment agencies, and other placement offices to find potential employees. (p. 405)

resale price maintenance Price fixing imposed by a manufacturer on wholesale or retail resellers of its products to deter price-based competition. (p. 252)

résumé A summary of academic and work history, skills, and experience of a prospective employee. (p. 405)

return on investment (ROI) The amount earned as a result of an investment. (p. 254)

return policy A policy that establishes the conditions under which items that have been ordered, shipped, or delivered may be returned. (p. 399)

rework policy A policy that establishes conditions under which items will be reworked, that is doing something again because it was not done right the first time. (p. 399)

risk capital Money invested in companies where there is financial risk. (p. 443)

robbery The taking of property by force or threat, usually by means of a weapon. (p. 516)

role model A person with attitudes and achievements that others wish to emulate. (p. 38)

rule A standard set forth to guide behavior and actions; a rule tells employees exactly what they should and should not do. (p. 397)

safety stock A cushion of products or materials that prevents a business from running out of inventory while waiting for an order. (p. 368)

salary A fixed amount of pay an employee receives for each week, month, or year the employee works. (p. 316)

sales call report An account of sales activities, including such items as number of calls made, orders obtained, and miles traveled. (p. 317)

sales check A written record of a sales transaction. (p. 311)

sales force A group of employees involved in the selling process. (p. 303)

sales forecast An estimate of sales for a given period, such as the next quarter. (p. 313)

sales planning The process that involves determining the goals and timing of sales efforts. (p. 313)

Glossary

sales quota A performance goal assigned to a salesperson for a specific period. (p. 315)

sales territory A geographical area in which existing and potential customers are grouped. (p. 314)

scarcity The difference between demand and supply; limited resources. (p. 11)

secondary data Information that been collected by someone else. (p. 137)

secured fund A form of guaranteed payment, such as a credit card, a cashier's check, a wire transfer, or cash. (p. 359)

selective distribution Placement of a product where its number of sales outlets are limited in an area. (p. 230)

selling price The actual or projected price per unit. (p. 262)

service mark A word, symbol, sign, or color that describes a service business. (p. 176)

services Intangible (nonphysical) products that satisfy consumers' wants and needs. (p. 11, 54)

shareholder An owner of shares of stock in a corporation. (p. 159)

shrinkage cost The cost associated with the loss of inventory items that are broken, damaged, spoiled, or stolen. (p. 362)

situational management The style of adapting the management approach to particular circumstances. (p. 341)

Small Business Administration (SBA) The federal agency that provides services to small businesses and new entrepreneurs, including counseling, publications, and financial aid. (p. 120)

social responsibility The principle that companies should contribute to the welfare of society and not be solely devoted to maximizing profits. (p. 553)

social entrepreneurs A type of entrepreneur who recognizes a social problem and uses entrepreneurial methods to create, organize, and manage a venture to address it. (p. 55)

sole proprietorship A business that is owned and operated by one person. (p. 153)

specialty item An advertising device that includes giveaways, such as pens, T-shirts, and caps, printed with a business name or logo that serve as a reminder of a business. (p. 279)

specialty magazine A periodical published for people with special interests, such as sports, camping, fashion, and a variety of other areas. (p. 62)

speculative risk Risk that is inherent to a business, involving the chance of either profit or loss. (p. 513)

staff The managers and others who provide support and advice to line managers, such as accounting, legal, and training activities. (p. 404)

Standard Industrial Trade Classification (SITC) codes A system that details the kinds of products that are traded in specific countries and how well certain products do in different marketplaces. (p. 87)

start-up resources The capital, skilled labor, management expertise, legal and financial advice, facility, equipment, and customers needed to start a business. (p. 22)

statement of cash flows A report of how much cash a business took in and where the cash went. (p. 474)

stock A type of security that signifies ownership in a corporation and represents a claim on part of the corporation's assets and earnings. (p. 452)

storage cost The cost associated with renting or buying space needed to store inventory. (p. 362)

strategic alliance A partnership formed among two or more companies. (p. 56)

strategic plan A long-range objective based on long-term goals used to map out a business for three to five years. (p. 334)

Subchapter S corporation A corporation that is taxed like a partnership; profits are taxed only once at the shareholder's personal tax rate. These corporations can have only one class of stock. (p. 162)

suggestion selling Selling additional goods to a customer to go along with a product or products the customer purchases. (p. 307)

supply The amount of goods or services that producers are willing to provide. (p. 14)

sustainability The ability to achieve economic, social, and environmental goals without compromising the ability of future generations to meet their own needs. (p. 55)

sweepstakes A simple game of chance used by a business to get customers interested in what the company has to offer. (p. 281)

SWOT analysis A strategic planning technique that analyzes a company's strengths, weaknesses, opportunities and threats in the external sales environment. (p. 318)

synergistic diversification A diversification growth strategy that involves finding new products or businesses that are technologically compatible with a company's products or business. (p. 538)

T

tactical plan A midrange objective that focuses on a period of one year or less, built on specific objectives with target dates. (p. 334)

target customer One most likely to buy a business's products and services. (p. 107)

target market A specific group of customers whom a business wishes to reach. (p. 132)

tariff A type of trade barrier imposed by a government as a tax on imported or exported goods. (p. 80)

team building The act of encouraging teamwork through activities designed to foster respect, trust, cooperation, camaraderie, and communication among employees. (p. 338)

telecommuting The act of performing some or all of a job away from the business. (p. 426)

Theory X An assumption that states the belief that employees are basically lazy and need constant supervision. (p. 424)

Theory Y An assumption that states the belief that employees are responsible, like to work, and want intrinsic rewards. (p. 424)

time management The process of allocating time effectively. (p. 344)

trade area The region or section of the community from which a business draws customers. (p. 199)

trade association An organization made up of individuals and businesses in a specific industry that works to promote that industry. (p. 121)

trade barrier A restriction on goods entering or leaving a country. (p. 80)

trade credit Credit one business grants to another business for the purchase of goods or services; a source of short-term financing provided by one business within another business's industry or trade. (p. 445)

trade discount A discount from the list price of an item allowed by a manufacturer or wholesaler to a merchant. (p. 358)

trade intermediary An agency that serves as a distributor in a foreign country. (p. 90)

trade magazine A periodical published for a specific type of business or industry. (p. 62)

trade mission An opportunity offered by the U. S. government and private agencies to small businesses to travel to other countries in order to meet and talk with foreign agents, distributors, or potential business partners. (p. 87)

trade show A gathering or exhibition where vendors and manufacturers introduce new items and promote established products and services. (p. 62)

trademark A word, symbol, design, or color that a business uses to identify itself or something it sells; it is followed by the registered trademark symbol ™. (p. 176)

Glossary

Uniform Commercial Code (UCC) A group of laws that regulates commercial business transactions. (p. 184)

Uniform Trade Secrets Act (USTA) A law that protects intellectual property, such as a formula, device, idea, process, pattern, or compilation of information that is not general knowledge to or accessible by other people. (p. 173)

unit pricing The pricing of goods on the basis of cost per unit of measure, such as a pound or an ounce, in addition to the price per item. (p. 252)

unlimited liability Full responsibility for all debts and actions of a business. (p. 153)

usage rate How quickly inventory will be used in a given period of time. (p. 368)

value chain The distribution channel through which a product or service flows from the producer to the customer. (pp. 111, 131)

values The beliefs and principles by which you choose to live that define who you are, shape your attitudes and choices, and help you identify your priorities. (p. 65)

variable Costs and expenses that are subject to change depending on the number of units sold. (p. 251)

variable expense A business expense that changes with each unit of product produced, such as supplies, wages, and production materials. (p. 495)

vendor A business that sells inventory to a merchant. (p. 355)

venture A new business undertaking that involves risk. (p. 7)

venture capital A source of equity financing for small businesses with exceptional growth potential and experienced senior management. (p. 444)

venture capitalist An individual investor or investment firm that invests venture capital professionally. (p. 444)

vertical integration The merging of companies that are in the same distribution chain of a product, either by acquiring suppliers upstream in the distribution channel or acquiring distribution outlets downstream in the channel. (p. 538)

vision statement A declaration of the scope and purpose of a company. (p. 115)

wages An amount of money an employee receives for every hour he or she works. (p. 407)

want Something that you do not have to have for survival, but would like to have. (p. 11)

warehousing The act of holding and handling goods in a warehouse. (p. 366)

warranty of merchantability A guarantee on the quality of goods or services purchased that is not written down or explicitly spoken. (p. 185)

workers' compensation insurance Insurance that is required by the government and paid for by employers to provide medical and income benefits to employees injured on the job, or for job-related illnesses. (p. 524)

working capital The amount of cash needed to carry out the daily operations of a business that ensures a positive cash flow after covering all operating expenses. (pp. 454, 490)

workstation An area in a business with equipment for a single worker. (p. 208)

wrongful termination The right of an employee to sue his or her employer for damages if he or she is terminated for an unacceptable reason. (p. 182)

Academic Glossary

A

accurate Free from error, especially as the result of care. (p. 39)

achieve To attain a desired end or aim. (p. 419)

acquire To come into possession or control of something. (p. 67)

alternative One of two or more choices or courses of action. (p. 539)

analyze Distinguishing the parts of something in order to discover its true nature. (p. 113)

approach The taking of preliminary steps toward a particular purpose. (p. 341)

assess To determine the importance, size, or value of someone or something. (p. 131)

associate To connect one thing with another in the mind. (p. 441)

authority Power to influence or command thought, opinion, or behavior. (p. 153)

automate To operate by use of a self-acting or self-regulating mechanism. (p. 377)

automatic Done by machine. (p. 197)

C

commit To obligate or pledge oneself. (p. 515)

community A body of persons of common and especially professional interests scattered through a larger society. (p. 333)

compare Examine and note the similarities or differences of. (p. 336)

complex A whole structure (such as a building) made up of interconnected or related structures. (p. 378)

component A constituent part; ingredient. (p. 388)

concept An idea generalized from particular instances. (p. 225)

conduct To direct or take part in an operation or management. (p. 53)

conflict Competitive or opposing action of incompatibles. (p. 559)

consist To be composed or made up of. (p. 473)

constant Something invariable or unchanging. (p. 237)

contact To get in communication with. (p. 87)

control To exercise power or influence over something. (p. 33)

convert To change from one form or function to another. (p. 464)

create To make or bring into existence something new. (p. 55)

crucial Of extreme importance. (p. 303)

D

demonstrate To prove or make clear by reasoning or evidence. (p. 555)

determine To settle or decide by choice of alternatives or possibilities. (p. 38)

distinct Distinguishable to the eye or mind as discrete; separate. (p. 516)

domestic Of, relating to, or originating within a country. (p. 80)

E

emphasis Special importance or significance. (p. 450)

enable To make possible, practical, or easy. (p. 7)

enhance To increase or improve in value, quality, desirability, or attractiveness. (p. 537)

ensure To make sure, certain, or safe. (p. 255)

environment The aggregate of social and cultural conditions that influence the life of an individual or community. (p. 20)

error Something produced by mistake. (p. 523)

establish To put on a firm basis; set up. (p. 198)

estimate To judge tentatively or approximately something's value, worth, or significance. (p. 288)

evaluate To determine the significance, worth, or condition of, usually by careful appraisal and study. (p. 16)

expand To increase the extent, number, volume, or scope of. (p. 541)

Academic Glossary

F

factor An active contributor to the production of a result. (p. 524)

focus A center of activity, attraction, or attention. (p. 105)

formula A general fact, rule, or principle expressed in mathematical symbols. (p. 263)

function The action for which a person or thing is specially fitted or used or for which a thing exists. (p. 208)

fund A sum of money or other resources set apart for a specific purpose. (p. 477)

G

generate To bring into existence (p. 162)

goal the end toward which effort is directed. (p. 254)

guarantee An assurance for the fulfillment of a condition. (p. 33)

I

impact A significant or major effect. (p. 542)

income A gain or recurrent benefit, usually measured in money, that derives from capital or labor. (p. 133)

indicate To point out or point to. (p. 400)

interactive Involving the actions or input of a user. (p. 284)

invest To commit money in order to earn a financial return. (p. 448)

L

labor Human activity that provides the goods or services in an economy; or workers available for employment. (p. 417)

legal Of or relating to law. (p. 176)

M

maintain Keep in an existing state. (p. 275)

method A way, technique, or process of or for doing something. (p. 363)

minimum The least quantity assignable, admissible, or possible. (p. 356)

monitor To watch, keep track of, or check. (p. 496)

O

objective Something toward which effort is directed. (p. 65)

obtain Gain or attain, usually by planned action or effort. (p. 398)

overseas Of or relating to movement, transport, or communication over the sea. (p. 90)

P

perceive To attain awareness or understanding of something or someone. (p. 560)

percent A value determined on the basis of a whole divided into 100 equal parts. (p. 263)

period A portion of time determined by some recurring phenomenon. (p. 313)

potential Possibility for development. (p. 107)

predict To foretell on the basis of observation, experience, or scientific reason. (p. 237)

principle A comprehensive and fundamental law, doctrine, or assumption. (p. 345)

process A continuous operation. (p. 403)

project To plan, figure, or estimate for the future. (p. 144)

purchase To obtain by paying money or its equivalent. (p. 362)

purpose The goal or intended outcome of something. (p. 185)

R

ratio The relationship in quantity, amount, or size between two or more things. (p. 488)

region A broad geographic area distinguished by similar features. (p. 81)

register To secure official entry in a system of public records. (p. 159)

regulate To bring under the control of law or constituted authority. (p. 183)

Academic Glossary

relationship The state of being related or interrelated. (p. 357)

require To call for as suitable or appropriate. (p. 553)

resource A source of supply or support. (p. 441)

sequence A continuous or connected series. (p. 208)

series A number of things or events of the same class coming one after another in spatial or temporal succession. (p. 306)

significant Of a noticeably or measurably large amount. (p. 426)

source One that provides information. (p. 117)

statistic Part of or a whole collection of quantitative data. (p. 492)

structure Something arranged in a definite pattern of organization. (p. 403)

target To set as a goal or mark. (p. 225)

technical Of or relating to proficiency in a practical skill. (p. 156)

technique A method of accomplishing a desired aim. (p. 315)

technology A manner of accomplishing a task using technical processes, methods, or knowledge. (p. 21)

theory A belief, policy, or procedure proposed or followed as the basis of action. (p. 424)

transfer To convey from one person, place, or situation to another. (p. 469)

trend Prevailing tendency or inclination. (p. 140)

unique Distinctively characteristic. (p. 288)

vary To make differences between items. (p. 177)

vehicle A means of carrying or transporting something. (p. 386)

volume Mass or the representation of mass. (p. 495)

Index

Index

Index

Index

Line-and–staff organization type, 404
Line of credit, 445
Listening skills, 39, 58
Logistics, distribution, 386
Loyalty, of customers, 227

M

Magazines, 62, 282–283
Maintenance, 386
Management, 332–347
    automation in, 385
    function of, 332–339
    leadership and, 333
    maintenance in, 386
    open-book financial, 467
    positive climate by, 338
    principles of, 346
    productivity in, 385
    of purchasing, 355–360
    quality control in, 383
    scheduling, 383
    skills of, 333, 340–347
    styles of, 337, 340–347
    teamwork and, 333
    See also Distribution;
      Employees, motivating;
      Financial management;
      Human resources; Opera-
      tions; Production; Risks
Management-by-objectives, 427
Management team plan, in business plans, 115
Manufacturing business, 201, 206–208
Markdowns, 264
Market
    analysis of, 108
    development of, 536–537
    penetration of, 535
    segmentation of, 132–134
    share of, 142, 265
    structures of, 10
    target, 107, 132–134, 142–144
Marketing
    cost analysis of, 323
    objectives of, 225
    test, 144

Marketing plans, 224–243
    in business plans, 114–122
    marketing mix in, 226–234
    people strategy in, 226, 241
    place strategy in, 229, 240–241
    price strategy in, 224, 241–242
    product strategy in, 227–228, 238–240
    promotion strategy in, 234, 241–242
    objectives in, 225
    research and, 225, 226, 237
    tactics in, 235
Market research, 130–138
    conducting, 135–138
    industry analysis in, 131–132
    in marketing plans, 224–235
    on price, 265
    target customer analysis in, 132–134
Markup, 263–264
Materials handling, 388
Math skills, 39, 343
McGregor, Douglas, 424–425
Media, advertising, 282
Mexico, NAFTA and, 84
Minority Enterprise Small Busi-ness Investment Companies (MESBICs), 445
Misleading advertising, 186
Mission statement, in business plans, 115
Model inventory, 355
Money, 9, 11, 12, 16, 17. *See also* Financing
Monopolistic competition, 10
Monopoly, 10–11
Morale, in sales force, 323
Motivating employees. *See* Employees, motivating
Multiple sites, of business, 541–542
Multiple-unit pricing, 259
Multitasking, 119, 336
Mutual benefit corporations, 163

N

National Resource Center for Consumers Legal Services, 188
Natural disasters, risk of, 518
Needs and wants, 11, 143, 310–313
Negligence, 519
Negotiation, 90
Net profit on sales ratio, in financial management, 491
Networking skills, 343
Newspapers, 60, 62, 282
New venture organization, 22–23
Nonperiodic reordering of inventories, 368
Nonprice competition, 19
Nonprofit businesses, 55
Nonprofit corporations, 162
Nonverbal communication, 342
North American Free Trade Agreement (NAFTA), 84

O

Objections, overcoming, in sales, 311
Objectives, 225, 424, 427
Obsolescence costs, of inventories, 361
Occupational Safety and Health Act of 1970, 63, 183
Odd/even pricing, 258
Office space, 208, 212, 453
Official Gazette, U.S. Patent Office, 63
Oligopoly, 10–11
One-price policy, 256
Open-book financial manage-ment, 467
Open layout, in retail business, 209
Operating capital, 445
Operating ratio, in financial management, 491
Operational analysis, 317
Operational planning, 334–335
Operations, 396–401
    credit policies in, 398–399
    customer service policies in, 398
    delivery policies in, 400
    hours of, 398

Index

Index